T3-BOD-419

ARTS AND CULTURES OF MAN

ELTON M. DAVIES

INTEXT EDUCATIONAL PUBLISHERS

College Division of Intext

Scranton San Francisco Toronto London

Library of Congress Catalog Card Number: 70-111938

ISBN 0-7002-2193-X

PREFACE

Art, man's speech in visual form, freed from the tyranny of words, gives birth to two opposing kinds of human action. One, a force from within outward, is the action of artists speaking *with* or *through* art forms. The other, responding to a force from without inward, is the action of aestheticians speaking *about* art forms, and of art historians speaking about the origin and fate of those forms. That both forces may interact positively and equally in a single life experience has been illustrated in the life and work of some creative men. But more often we tend to gravitate toward one pole or the other, with the view that for us, personally, the opposite pole is unimportant or perhaps out of reach.

Arts and Cultures of Man with its accompanying project manual is designed to fuse the creative act with the pursuit of human knowledge for their mutual enlivenment rather than to isolate or oppose them. Successive chapters of the book describe different forms of human society, drawing on history, sociology, and economics as the author has judged valuable. But their chief purpose is to show the visual arts as emerging from those cultures in response to human needs, drives, and aspirations (an appendix gives a corresponding summary of music history, with illustrative recordings). The successive projects in the manual, on the other hand, embody experiences with techniques relevant to the cultures under study. Each of the sixty projects contains a nucleus of information as a starting point for some form of open-ended creative action. The nucleus sheds light on some point in the past; the outcome belongs to the living present.

The book is planned to cover either one academic year or two. Within either time period it is intended to be flexible. Each chapter is so constructed that it can be used in collaboration with the project manual to support the launching of certain studio activities. Or emphasis can be shifted, with possible omission of the manual, in the direction of art history and social history. Here the book relies on paradigms or outstanding examples, rather than attempting a general and therefore necessarily more superficial coverage. Extensive reading lists at the chapter ends are present to fill in otherwise neglected areas. Different students can go to different depths in one chapter and its accompanying projects, depending on their bent and abilities. Perhaps only a few will use all of any one. If so, that is a valuable few.

The contents of this book have been enriched through the efforts of a number of persons who have my lasting gratitude. The following have read large portions and made extensive important comments: Albert B. Elsasser, graduate research archeologist, Lowie Museum of Anthropology, University of California, Berkeley; Sheila MacArthur Johannson, Department of History, U.C. Berkeley; the Reverend William M. Weber, St. John's-by-the-Sea, West Haven, Connecticut; and Haridas Chaudhuri, director, the Cultural Integration Fellowship Ashram, San Francisco. Dean Snyder, Associate Professor of Design, California College of Arts and Crafts, Oakland, was invaluable in exploring problems connected with the plan of the Parthenon and of Piero della Francesca's Brera Madonna. Ann Basart, Department of Music, U.C. Berkeley, was indispensable in preparing the list of recordings in Appendix A. Charles E. Hamilton, acting head, the East Asiatic Library, U.C. Berkeley, provided sensitive translations of calligraphy by the emperors NanSung Li-Tsung and Sung Hui-Tsung. The whole manuscript was reviewed at least once by my wife. Others who have contributed valuable comments to particular areas are Carl Chiarenza, editor of *Contemporary Photographer;* Vera Greenlaw of Flagstaff, Arizona, and Palo Alto, California; Professors Lawrence W. Levine and Saul Silverman of the University of California, Berkeley; Professor Herbert Diamante of the University of Nevada, Las Vegas; and Sophie de Vries, the Lincoln Center, Oakland. I nevertheless assume full responsibility for the contents of this book, which is everywhere an expression of my own final judgment.

In a sense the book owes its existence in print to the late Italo L. de Francesco, president of Kutztown College, Pennsylvania, who strongly recommended the manuscript to the publishers and encouraged its broad scope. The publishers in turn have given me complete freedom, at no point attempting to limit or modify any of the book's contents. For this act of confidence I am especially grateful to Kenneth Gromlich and Gerald Stashak, publication managers of International Textbook Company. John Wargo, the company's production manager, has been equally generous in the difficult task of giving the book the physical format envisioned while it was being written.

Berkeley, California
December, 1971

ELTON M. DAVIES

CONTENTS

Two ancient images of the god Janus, guardian of doorways. Above, a silver coin of refined workmanship, from the Greek island of Tenedos, minted about the third century B.C. Below, a roughly cast bronze coin from Rome, minted about the same time.

Lowie Museum of Anthropology, University of California, Berkeley. Photos John Bridgman

PROLOGUE

Janus, the Roman god who protected house entrances, could look in opposite directions at once, and with different faces. His friendly face looked inward upon the Roman home. His forbidding one looked outward on the street and the world. Like Janus, every work of art has two faces, two aspects. One is familiar, understandable, and inviting. And then there is the other, the strange, mysterious, even threatening aspect that can sometimes fascinate us, sometimes repel us. But, unlike Janus, the two sides are seldom in balance, half one and half the other.

Some works of art seem to be just about all friendly familiarity. They invite us in with hardly a trace of cool remoteness or mystery. This may mean an extremely pleasant experience for the viewer, or a tame, boring one. It depends on the work of art. It also depends on the viewer. Some people prefer comfort and security; others like challenge.

Other works of art are real strangers. They present an alien face which defies the viewer to enjoy them, much less understand them. Anything in the work that suggests the friendly, the familiar, or the inviting is hard to find. To some people such works can be fascinating, to others frightening, and to still others merely irritating. Again it depends on the work of art, and it depends on who is doing the viewing.

Spend some time looking at the pictures on the next several pages. The ten works of art shown there come from a wide variety of places and times. They were created for different purposes. But notice that the only description given of each is to tell how large the original is and the material from which it is made. Otherwise they are identified only by numbers. This is not to keep you permanently in the dark as to who made them, or when, or where. That will be cleared up later. The aim now is to illustrate a point. So please do the following three things.

1. After examining all ten pictures, select one with which, more than any other, you feel on terms of understanding: you think you know what it is all about more completely than any of the others. Then select another which, more than any other, makes you feel the opposite, shut out and confused by its refusal to explain itself.

2. Next, on paper, write why the work of art in the first picture makes you feel on familiar terms with it, and why the second makes you feel the opposite. The statements do not have to be long, but make them complete. That is, if you have more than one reason for your feelings, give them.

3. Now look at the two pictures of your choice again. Examine the familiar looking one for something you find unfamiliar or hard to explain (you may have to look hard). Write a brief description of what it is. Then examine the other picture for something in it that you find familiar or understandable. Whatever it is, describe that briefly too.

I Tempera on cardboard, 40 × 30 in.

II Tempera on wood panel, 45 × 36 in.

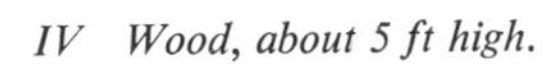

IV Wood, about 5 ft high.

III Limestone, 2 ft high.

V Bronze, about 5 ft high.

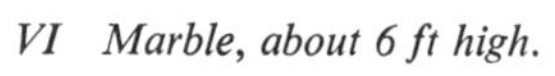

VI Marble, about 6 ft high.

VII Pastels on paper, 12 × 15¼ in.

VIII Oils on canvas, 23 × 70 in.

IX Limestone, about natural size.

X Bronze, about natural size.

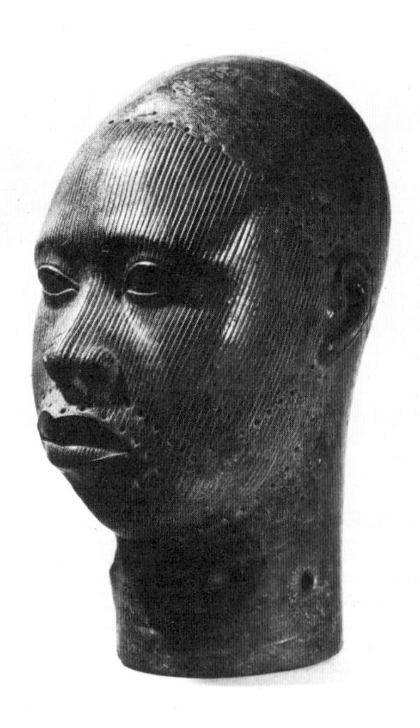

When everyone in your group has completed his or her study, get together and compare results. There is a good deal to compare. Start by putting a chart on the chalk board such as the one which follows.

Picture number	I	II	III	IV	V	VI	VII	VIII	IX	X
A										
B										

In row A, tally the votes that each work of art received for being the most easy to understand. In row B, tally votes, in the same way, for the works of art found least easy to understand.

Next try this: select the picture (or, it may be, pictures) which received the most votes as understandable. Find out in group discussion the different reasons people gave as to why it seemed so. Was there a good deal of agreement on this, or were there marked differences in view? Before you leave this, find out the different reasons for finding it *hard* to understand. Again, was there general agreement here or the opposite?

Now turn to the picture (or pictures) which led in votes as most difficult to understand. Find out what the reasons were. Did they concur or diverge? And last of all, find out what people could understand even in this picture. Was there agreement or disagreement?

What do you now conclude about the artistic tastes of the members of your group? Do you tend to agree? Or are you an assortment of strong minded individualists? Or, perhaps, do you find yourselves somewhere in between?

Australian native's pendant of shell with incised abstract pattern and cord of braided human hair.

Chicago Natural History Museum

Bushman painting on a cave wall, Basutoland, South Africa. It shows a successful raid by Bushmen on the cattle of Zulu invaders. Three Bushmen drive off 14 head of cattle while other Bushmen hold off a superior force of spear-wielding Zulus. The unknown artist has shown accurately the markings on the Zulu cattle. Actual size about 3×4½ ft.

Copied by George Stow about 1867

1

HUNTING SOCIETIES

The Bushmen of South Africa

In the spring of 1797 a young Englishman named John Barrow landed in Cape Town, South Africa on an unusual mission. He had been sent by the British government to explore a colony on the Cape of Good Hope which Great Britain had just captured from the Netherlands. Barrow spent almost a year traveling over the southern tip of Africa. On his return to London in 1798 he wrote a fascinating report of his findings.

The Dutch had founded their colony at Cape Town in 1652. For over a hundred years before Barrow arrived, Dutch colonists, armed with muskets, had been pushing northward from that center in their heavy ox-drawn wagons into the great open country beyond. Their ambition was to cover the newly found land with grazing sheep and cattle. But the natives, or Bushmen as the Dutch called them, willed otherwise. For in spite of their small size (averaging less than five feet), they had a determination of iron and great resourcefulness in defending the land that had been theirs since time began.

To make their life still more bitter, the heroic little Bushmen, besides fighting their Dutch invaders from the south, had for a long time been fighting another crushing invasion, this one from the north. Tribes of tall Africans, the Basutos, the Bechuanas, and the Zulus, who for centuries had been living a highly organized life in middle Africa, came spreading southward armed with long-bladed spears, cowhide shields, and iron battle axes. They too were cattle breeders and herdsmen, and like all cattlemen, they too were land hungry. The Bushmen, in little wandering hunting groups, fought back, north and south. Their chief weapons were slender reed hunting arrows, whose ostrich bone tips were spotted with poison. The dismal fight began around 1700 and dragged on for over two hundred years.[1]

John Barrow saw what was going on and included a shocked account of it in his reports. His sympathies were clearly with the Bushmen, who, unlike Barrow, left no written description of their stubborn, tragic, two-way defense. They had no writing and, in their way of life, needed none. But they left their story in pictures painted on their native rocks. And today whoever is patient enough to travel over the South African hills and valleys, looking at cave walls, cliff walls, and boulders as he goes, can see it all painted there.

Bushman Painting

Colonel Laurens Van der Post, whose ancestors generations ago were among the Dutch colonists who settled South Africa, grew up on a South African farm where Bushmen had lived and hunted only a few years before he was born. In 1958 Colonel Van der Post wrote of the Bushman:

> Much of his painting has been thoughtlessly destroyed or has crumbled away from weather and time. Yet there is so much left . . . It is astonishing . . . what power they still possess to provoke an almost unbearable nostalgia for the vanished painter and for the spirit that possessed him.

Copied by Schultz

Bushman rock painting of African antelopes (called eland*) in flight. Original about 3 ft long. Orange Free State, South Africa.*

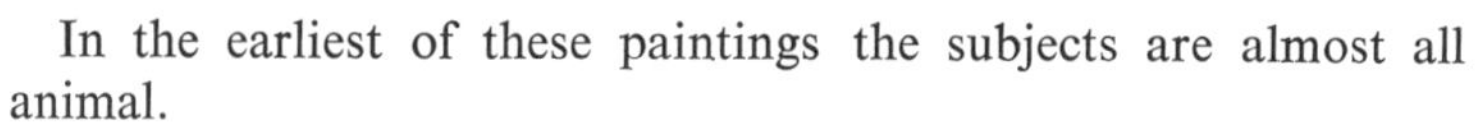

> In the earliest of these paintings the subjects are almost all animal.
>
> I know one painting where a frightened herd of running eland is shown with such a gift of movement that when I first experienced its impact I had the illusion, with all the vividness of reality, of seeing them suddenly charging across the rock and away over the side of the hill.
>
> However, gradually the Bushman himself came to figure in the animal scene. Subjects become more complex . . . . He is there as child, husband, hunter, and fighter, his women always in close support . . . . Suddenly tall black men are splashed, like giant exclamation marks of printer's ink, all over . . . . The Bushman raises himself to gianthood to meet them. The struggle becomes desperate. Raid and counter-raid and massacre multiply; the security . . . that for so long sanctified the stone vanishes. The pools of blood on the rocks steadily grow bigger. A new invader with a gun intrudes . . . Paintings of an enemy in red coats and riflemen on horses are briefly seen. Then abruptly the antique art vanishes from the ancient land.
>
> The last of the Bushman painters was shot down in a raid in the Basuto Hills and picked up dead with a zebra thong round his middle to which were attached ten little horns, each filled with a different-coloured paint.
>
> We other races went through Africa like locusts devouring and stripping the land for what we could get out of it. The Bushman was there solely because he belonged to it.[2]

The Bushman did indeed belong to South Africa. We now know that he or ancestors much like him lived in the same place, at peace and undisturbed, longer than any other of us on this earth. The oldest remains he left perhaps go back nearly 12,000 years. Not 1,200 years, but 12,000. While Egypt was still an untamed, beast-ridden swamp, the little Bushmen were perhaps living their simple, wise, ingenious lives much as they were when John Barrow saw them.

Now the bravest of those who are still alive have retreated to parts of Africa where pursuers cannot follow, or if following, cannot survive. In the swamps of the Okavango River and in the heart of the Kalahari Desert a few Bushmen are at last left alone to live their lives as they choose, amid the risk of malaria in the swamps and death by thirst in the desert.

What manner of person is this Bushman, in stature so small, but in courage so great? Here are some of John Barrow's comments, made over a hundred and sixty years ago, and still valid:

> The Bushmen are certainly a most extraordinary race of people. In their persons they are extremely diminutive. The tallest of the men measured only four feet nine inches . . . Their activity is incredibly great . . . On rough ground, or up the sides of mountains, horsemen have no chance of keeping pace with them.
>
> They assured me that there was no such person [as a chief among them]; that everyone was master of his own family, and acted entirely without control, being at liberty to remain with, or quit, any society he might incidentally have joined, according as it might suit his convenience.
>
> Universal equality prevails . . . When one feasts they all partake, and when one hungers they all equally starve.[3]

Bushmen among trees and grass, enjoying their native land before its invasion. Size of the original about 6×4 ft. Orange Free State.

Copied by Lutz

A Bushman family, standing before their temporary grass shelter in the Kalahari Desert. Four generations are present, since the Bushman family usually includes a larger group of relatives than does ours.

Photo N. R. Farbman. Copyright Time, Inc.

The Bushman Personality

> In disposition he is lively and cheerful . . . His cheerfulness is the most extraordinary, as the morsel he procures to support existence is earned with danger and fatigue. He neither cultivates the ground nor breeds cattle . . . The bulbs of the iris, and a few roots, . . . are all that the vegetable kingdom affords him.
>
> The marks of their industry appeared in every part of the country, in their different plans for taking game: one was by making deep holes in the ground and by covering them over with sticks and earth; another by piling stones on each other in rows, with openings . . . in such places as it was intended the game should pass . . . In this manner were lines continued across the plains . . . for several miles.[4]

Such large-scale works clearly required the cooperative labor of many Bushmen.

> Their mechanical skill appeared in their arrows, which are finished with great neatness; in the baskets placed in the rivers for the purpose of taking fish, ingeniously contrived and well executed; in the mats of grass, of which their huts are composed; and in their imitations of different animals, designed on the smooth faces of the rocks.[5]

In 1956, when Colonel Van der Post showed copies of such animal paintings from South Africa to some Bushman friends he had made in the Kalahari Desert:

> the two old people, man and woman, began crying as if their hearts would break and hid their heads in their arms. But the younger men instantly crowded around and exploded with sounds of astonishment as if suddenly they saw something that, until then, had been only rumor.[6]

How It Was Done

How did the Bushman make his rock pictures? It seems that he worked in two ways. Wherever he could, he painted. But where the rock surface was not suited to paint, because it was too smooth to hold pigment or too much exposed to the weather, he chipped out his picture, just enough to expose the pale unweathered rock beneath the darker surface.

From out of the past, like faded snapshots found in an old box in the attic, come two recorded descriptions of Bushman artists at work. The first of the two was made about fifty years ago.

A BUSHMAN PAINTER AT WORK.

> The colors used by the Bushman artists are brown, red, yellow, blue, and sometimes white. Haematite was used . . . and blue and white clay . . . These were ground up fine with stones and mixed with boiling fat. They were allowed to cool. This produced a crayon . . . But liquid paint applied warm to the surface was also employed. One method of painting witnessed by the writer was as follows: the artist, a half-bred Bushman, first took a pebble and rubbed the surface of the granite boulder on which he was going to paint as smooth as he could, and wiped away all the dust carefully. Then he took a burnt stick and drew the outline of the figure, in this case a zebra . . . Next he took a lump of dry paint, his crayon in fact, and rubbed it over the figure, roughly filling in the outline. Then he brushed away all the dust, and then he took a small feather brush, some liquid paint which he heated in a small hollow pebble, and laid this carefully on the figure, and the painting was complete.

Copied by M. H. Tongue. Copyright Clarendon Press, Oxford

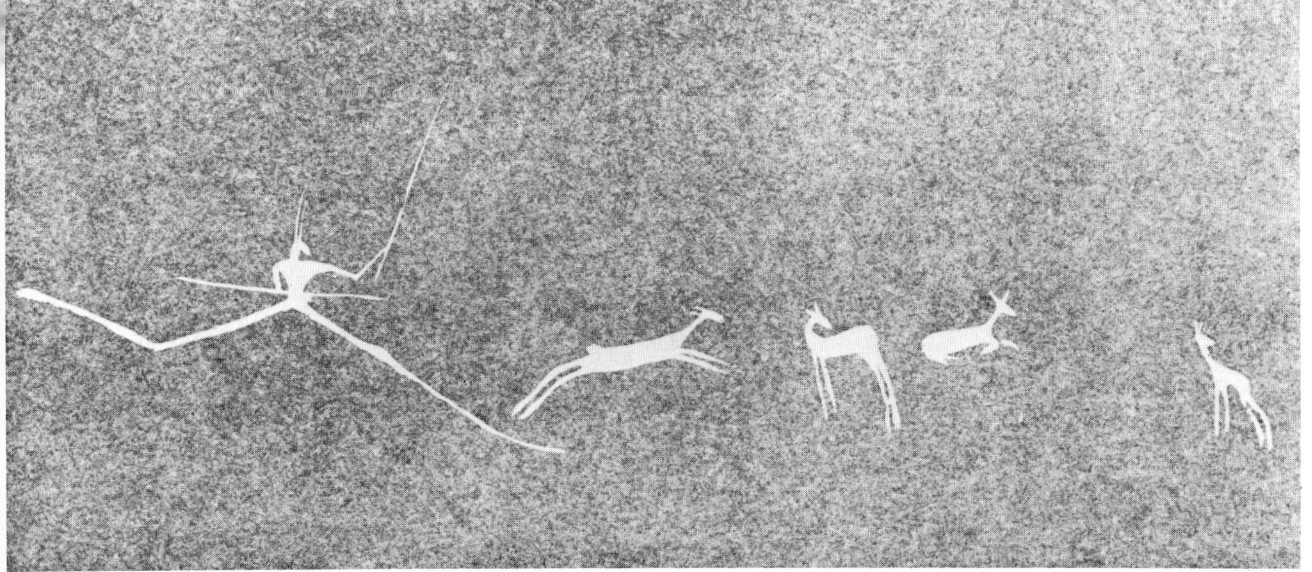

The Bushman hunter as he saw himself.

Copied by Mannsfel

Bushmen on a hunt or raid. Length of original rock painting about 20 in. George Barrow wrote: "Their bows of tough wood, strung with twisted sinew, are remarkably small; and in the hands of anyone but a Bushman would be entirely useless... A complete leather or aloe-bark quiver contains about seventy or eighty arrows . . . and, in addition to these, a few small brushes to lay on the poison."

> He painted a zebra, a tortoise, a porcupine and some guinea-fowl, and it took him the best part of three hours . . . The figures were quite small, only about three inches high, and he did not work hard, as he stopped to smoke more than once.[7]

A BUSHMAN STONE ENGRAVER AT WORK. The other glimpse seems to be more recent. The warden of a game preserve bordering the Kalahari Desert persuaded a bushman to hammer out a stone engraving for him.

> With the aid of a sharp stone tool, using his right and left hands alternately, the Bushman pecked out an episode involving a lion, an ostrich and a human being, adding on top of them, in the form of a circle, a number of antelopes. Whilst doing this he hummed and sang to himself, giving expression to his pleasure in what he was creating by exclamations and peals of laughter.[8]

The Women's Art

Rock painting and chipping seems to have been strictly a man's occupation for the Bushmen. Both art-forms came to an end when the people were driven into the swamps and deserts, where suitable rocks cannot be found. But the Bushman women had, and still have, their own art-forms. These center around the business of making themselves beautiful.

BEADS. Every Bushman woman has a collection of necklaces and at least one elegant bead headband for special ceremonies and dances. All these she makes in her spare time by patiently chipping and grinding each bead from the thick white shell of ostrich eggs. Colonel Van der Post watched them:

> Hour after hour they would sit chipping nimbly and delicately with the sharp end of a springbuck ram's bone at a fragment of shell in order to produce one little round disk from the brittle and fragile raw material. Sometimes, too, they carved greater beads out of a crimson root and amber wood . . .[9]

COSMETICS. Bushman women and girls often dust themselves with sweet-smelling powder, which they make from aromatic shrubs. They carry this in the shell of a baby tortoise, and apply the powder with a puff of jackal's tail fur. Before dances and other festive occasions some girls paint red spots on their forehead, cheeks, and chin. The paint is a mixture of fat and powdered red stone (haematite or red ochre).

TATTOOING. Bushman women feel that certain kinds of tattooing increase their charm. Miss Elizabeth Thomas, who knows the Kalahari Desert well, describes a young Bushman mother named Twechwe, who became a friend of hers:

> She had her row of scars . . . delicate and arching over her brow, making her eyes seem wider; as well as a row of striped scars along her thighs. These, say Bushmen, are made to imitate the beauty of zebras, and many women wear them, having been decorated when they were still young. It is a painful procedure. The cuts are made on the thighs and forehead with a knife or ax blade, then charcoal is rubbed in, but the woman told us later that in her case it had been worth the pain and trouble because, she said, she was extremely ugly and had been made more beautiful.[10]

A good many Bushman women seem to be sure of their beauty and feel no need for tattooing. They carry merely a vertical scar on the forehead, showing that they have been through the long, solemn, tribal initiation into womanhood.

Bushman girls in their homemade beads of ostrich shell.

Courtesy Mrs. Lawrence K. Marshall and Alfred Knopf

Art-Forms for Both Men and Women

MUSIC. Bushmen are wonderfully musical. They have a rich store of songs for every occasion and have invented at least a half-dozen musical instruments, played by men and women for pleasure. Their idea of a tune is different from ours. They repeat one musical phrase endlessly, enjoying its rhythm, and, as it were, soaking themselves in its mood, whether gay or sad. (For a recording of Bushman music, see Appendix A.)

DANCING. They combine this music with their wonderful sense of drama and mimicry to create a wealth of dances which every Bushman knows by heart. At night, when the men's hunting and the women's search for roots and wild melons is over, part of a group will form a singing and clapping orchestra while the rest dance. Usually a dance is devoted to the life and habits of one kind of animal and reveals how keenly the Bushmen have observed and how deeply they respect wild creatures. Sometimes the play ceases to be a dance and becomes a sort of dramatic game without music. Here is just one of the many that have been described.

DRAMATIC GAMES. Springbok and lion play:

> The girls act as springboks with little children as the kids. Two or three men act as lions. The girls . . . imitate in cries and actions the graceful springboks with wonderful skill. They prance along plucking at the grass and pretending to feed; every now and then, uttering whistles of alarm, they bunch together with the kids between them; then run off again bounding over imaginary tracks and obstacles. The lions stalk with consummate skill and crouch at strategic spots. Every now and then one of them makes a rush and a bound, catching a kid and pretending to rend and devour it. Soon all the kids are lying about "dead," and the real fun commences when the lions catch the plump springboks, which they do with much tantalizing on the part of the girls, and much enjoyment on their own part. [On one occasion] one springbok had long evaded two lions till eventually both sprang at once from opposite sides,

Bushman rock painting illustrating a legend in which a man changes into a frog. Another man seems to be attacked by a swarm of bees.

Bushmen enjoying a dramatic dance. The audience claps and sings while dancers perform, impersonating some animal, or perhaps their favorite insect, the mantis.

but instead of catching the girl, they caught one another and then was depicted a wonderful imitation of a lion fight, with roaring, snarling and contortion of faces. One lion eventually emerged with nose bleeding furiously.[11]

STORY TELLING. Bushmen are highly gifted as story tellers. One of their favorite evening pastimes is to sit around a fire while someone with a special gift dramatically pours out one tale after another. The stories are of several kinds. Some are intended for children. Others, such as "The Young Man Who Was Carried Off by a Lion," are for a more sophisticated audience.

Besides such tales, there is a group of stories of a very different kind: sacred myths describing the creation of the world and of man. These are secrets, which the older Bushmen solemnly pass on to Bushman boys while they go through the long, hard ceremonies, spread over a year or more, of initiation into manhood. Such myths are not for entertainment around a campfire. No Bushman will reveal them to any man outside his own people unless he feels for the outsider a secure and confident friendship. Needless to say, such occasions have been rare.

Bushman wisdom has its own character, but it is based on a way of life so different, on the surface, from our own that we are in danger of missing what lies beneath that surface. A white man, in a rather cruelly joking mood, once asked an old Bushman his age, knowing that Bushmen have developed no system for counting above ten. The old man quietly replied, "I am as old as my bitterest disappointments; I am as young as my boldest dreams."[12]

Art, Artist, Craftsman, and Design: Some Tentative Definitions

Before we go further we may well ask, what do we mean by the word *art?*

It is of greater importance that you arrive at your own concept of this word than that you learn one from some place such as this book. The tentative definition advanced here is therefore intended to give you something to challenge, to test repeatedly, and perhaps to modify and alter past recognition. It is presented as a starting point.

In this book a work of art is suggested to be any device which men bring into being in order to reveal to themselves or to their fellow men their concept of themselves, their world in its many aspects, or the universe. This revealing must not be a mere accident. It must be to some degree intentional. For a work of art must have a creator who knows that he is creating, even though he may not be aware of *all* that he is creating. A Bushman who painted his concept of a herd of antelope knew in one sense exactly what he was making. But he was also unaware that other men such as ourselves would later see his work as charged with dynamic rhythm.

Revealing something is vital to a work of art, but that alone is not enough. A laugh, or a scream of pain, reveal much about someone, but we do not consider them as art. A work of art has to be organized, must have related parts, and that organization must contribute to what the work of art tells us, and must be in a way responsible for making it speak. Organization that is dull smothers speech; it is not art. In the words of Henri Matisse, one of the great founders of twentieth-century painting, "The whole arrangement of my picture is expressive. The placement of figures or objects, the empty spaces around them, the proportions, everything plays a part." It is to this arrangement or organization of a work of art that we apply the words *design* and *composition*. Design may be at least partly unconscious, as in the art of children. Again it may be calculated with extreme precision, as in ancient Egypt, and in some aspects of art today.

Skill or efficiency in making something is important, but for a work of art it is not enough and sometimes can even be irrelevant. A steel-bladed adze bought in a hardware store is an effective tool. A stone-bladed adze made by a New Zealand Maori is much less effective, but it has been given a shape which expresses the maker's belief that the tool is the dwelling place of a spirit and is worthy, like a person, of a proper name. To the degree that a maker's energies are focused on skillful production for effective use he is a *craftsman*. To the degree that his effort is focused on revelation he is an *artist*.

In brief, *a work of art is suggested to be any thing man-made which (to some degree) consciously reveals man or his world to himself, and which has been given a structure contributing to that revelation.*

In our discussion of Bushman society we have considered all aspects of their life as creative artists, whether in painting, stone chipping, music, dance, drama, narrative, or personal adornment. The complexity of larger societies will prevent us from considering the many forms of their arts so broadly. We shall have to be selective and shall therefore favor a few of the arts above the rest. We shall favor the visual arts, especially those of painting, sculpture, architecture, and design.

What Does Bushman Art Mean to Us? Definitions of Style, Rhythm

A work of art "lives" simply by making something come alive in the people who see it. Just as no two of us are exactly alike as persons, so will that "something" that comes alive differ from one of us to another. But the more one looks at the world's art, and the more one becomes familiar with the lives and outlooks of the people creating it, the larger and more responsive does this "something" in each of us tend to grow. Such growth is a gradual process. It takes patience and time. It takes an open mind.

What Bushman art means to you or me can be found only indirectly.[13] It can be discovered when each of us as individuals looks at reproductions such as those in this book or elsewhere, and then gives depth to this viewing by reading about the Bushmen as thinking, feeling persons caught up in a certain way of life. When looking at one of these reproductions, try to visualize the way the original looked on its rock wall; also, consider why the Bushman created it, and the conditions under which he worked. Here are some suggestions as to where, in observing Bushman art, our various interests are likely to overlap.

BUSHMAN STYLE. Bushman art is strong in *style.* Before going further, let us take a beginning look at the complex meaning of this word. Let us look at just one side of that meaning, and say that *the style of a work of art is the effective influence of the artist's personality upon it.* A camera creates no style by itself. When its shutter is released, it merely records on film what is in front of the lens. If a photograph exhibits style, that is either because of a happy accident or because the creative photographer has dominated the machine and made it do his will.

Eland cows and Bushmen. Length of original rock painting over 8 ft. Southern Rhodesia.

Copied by Lutz

RHYTHM. One sign of a Bushman artist's style is that his work is full of rhythm. We all know what rhythm is in music; it is the regular repetition of sound. Rhythm in art is the repetition of form.[14] If a form is repeated regularly and monotonously, over and over, it does not hold our attention long. Such uniform repetition is good as decoration, when one wishes to create a pleasing effect but also when one wishes the observer's attention to move on to something else. For this reason, regular repetition of form is often used on clothing. Candy stripes or polka dots on a dress or blouse can create a most refreshing impression, but they quickly pass our attention on to the girl wearing them. Hereafter, we shall call this kind of rhythm *decorative rhythm.*

Rhythm in a *work of art* must hold the viewer's attention steadily and firmly, not point somewhere else. To do this, one brings in *variation.* Instead of lulling the viewer's mind with monotony, one jolts it by continually making it readjust. One alters the distance, or interval, between the repeated forms. One moves them out of a straight line or rotates them. One changes their size or their color. One can even somewhat change the form itself. But *you must keep the likeness from form to form dramatically strong; that is where the rhythm lies.* Henceforth, we shall call this kind of rhythm *dynamic rhythm.*

So far in this book there are nine examples of Bushman painting. Notice how often in one picture the same form is repeated—almost, but not quite. The form itself keeps slightly changing. So, sometimes, does its size, its position, or its color.

Two Bushman shamans *or medicine men "possessing a water bull," that is,, controlling the source of rain. Fish surrounding the bull symbolize water. Original rock painting about 22 in. long.*

Copied by Stow. Copyright Methuen & Co., London

Australian Museum, Sidney

Australian native painting on bark. A hunter chases kangaroos. People of different cultures sometimes appear to do the same thing but for widely different reasons. The markings on the bull on the opposite page are the Bushman way of showing that it is a spirit bull or force of nature, not an ordinary one. The markings on the kangaroos serve a different purpose, an X-ray sketch of the animals' insides, showing viscera and the location of meat.

Bushman Materials

Apart from style, there is something else worth studying about the art of the Bushman. This is the painting materials that he developed. They are easy to acquire and prepare, so easy that we risk overlooking their ingenuity and their beautiful fitness for their purpose.

The Bushman: The Hunter Still Among Us

The Bushman way of life, which we glimpsed in the first part of this chapter, is in a way not unique. It belongs to a larger group, which anthropologists call *the hunting-fishing-foodgathering societies.* On page 30 you will find a list of the characteristics of these societies. There was once a time, thousands of years ago, when all mankind on this planet, all our ancestors, lived in this way. Then within the past 8,000 years, in just a few places, men slowly developed other ways of providing a living. Once man had really mastered them, these methods spread, as profitable inventions will, from one people to another. Today the hunting-fishing man and his teammate, the vegetable-foraging woman, linger on only in remote corners of the earth. Under the fierce, driving pressure of our modern civilization, with its mushrooming population, the chance of even these poor remnants to survive another fifty years is slight.

Let us now look briefly at five other hunting-foraging peoples, and at some of the visual art which they have created. Of these peoples, two have long since vanished from the Earth; only traces of their art remain. A third became extinct within this century. The fourth and fifth still manage to survive, in remote parts of the planet.

Two natives of Melville Island, off Australia's north coast, painting grave posts. Brushes are pieces of cane chewed to a pulp at one end

Courtesy Qantas Australian Airlines

Some Other Hunting Societies in Today's World

There are some other hunting-fishing-foodgathering societies which still survive as ghosts of their former selves, or at least did until recently. Each has created its own expressive art-forms.

The Natives of Australia

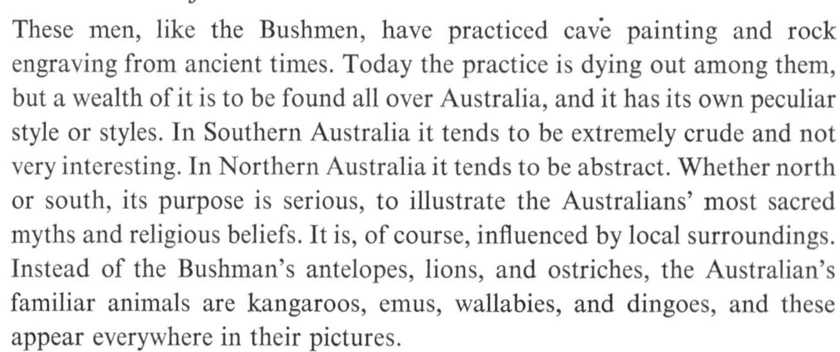

These men, like the Bushmen, have practiced cave painting and rock engraving from ancient times. Today the practice is dying out among them, but a wealth of it is to be found all over Australia, and it has its own peculiar style or styles. In Southern Australia it tends to be extremely crude and not very interesting. In Northern Australia it tends to be abstract. Whether north or south, its purpose is serious, to illustrate the Australians' most sacred myths and religious beliefs. It is, of course, influenced by local surroundings. Instead of the Bushman's antelopes, lions, and ostriches, the Australian's familiar animals are kangaroos, emus, wallabies, and dingoes, and these appear everywhere in their pictures.

The Australians are much more interested in what we would call "decoration" than are the Bushmen. They ornament their spears, spear-throwers, boomerangs, and shields, often in a rich, striking manner. Their body adornment for dances and other ceremonies is highly inventive (and takes hours to apply).

The California Aborigines

When the Spanish colonized California in the late eighteenth century, they found hunting-fishing-foodgathering tribes, the Yokuts, Yanas, and others, all along the Pacific coast up to San Francisco Bay and beyond.[15] The rock and cave paintings of these tribes, although largely ignored, can still be found in remote spots throughout the state. This was probably the men's art. The women's art, basket making, was carried to such a high degree of perfection that it is sometimes spoken of as the California Indians' only important art-form. See illustrations on pages 32 and 72 and the map on page 49.

The last survivor of these Indians still following his prehistoric mode of living was seized in a starving condition for what was assumed to be cattle stealing in 1911. He was a member of the Yahi subgroup of the Yana tribe. A kindly anthropologist, Alfred Kroeber, arranged his release and took him to Berkeley, California. There "Ishi" spent the last five years of his life in comparative comfort and dignity. Ishi was what he called himself. But *Ishi* is simply the Yahi word for *man*. From even the kindest of white men he kept his true name an eternal secret.

Costanoan Indian hunters, as interpreted by M. L. Choris from studies he made while visiting California in 1816. By that date the Indian way of life had begun to change under the influence of the Spanish Franciscan missions. Choris has probably tried here to envision the Indians in their original state.

urtesy Bancroft Library, University of California, Berkeley

The Eskimos: Alaska, Northern Canada, and Greenland

The ingenious technique by which the Eskimos have kept themselves alive in a desolation of snow and ice is one of the great heroic achievements of the human race. Surrounded by unbelievable hardship, they have cheerfully developed their own way of life. This includes more than one kind of art, created from the few materials at hand. See the map on page 49.

The men are sculptors, in ivory, stone, and wood. When they wish to draw, they etch their drawing on a walrus tusk or some other handy piece of ivory, then blacken the scratches with soot. They have been known to prefer this method to the seemingly easier one of pencil and paper.

The women's art-form consists of preparing and sewing sealskin and other skins and furs into beautiful, functional garments. (An Eskimo bride must prove her worth by making the groom a pair of boots. These are then filled with water. If they do not leak a drop over night, she has made the grade.)

Lowie Museum of Anthropology, University of California, Berkeley

Eskimo bladder festival, celebrated each December in a karigi, *or men's social house. Its purpose is to entertain the spirits of animals killed by hunters during the year, so that these spirits, contained in the bladders hung from the ceiling, will return to the sea, there to be born again. This ivory and wood model, made about 75 years ago, omits the hide covering of the house, whose interior could become very warm.*

Courtesy Canadian Film Board

Above, stencil print by the Eskimo artist Kenouiak. She cuts through layers of sealskin until only a thin membrane is left, through which she then forces ink onto paper. Below, Kenouiak herself.

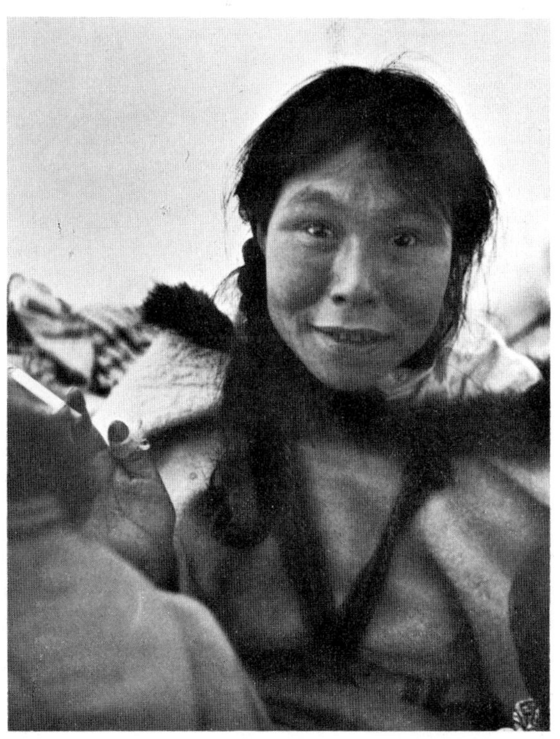

Prehistoric engraving on reddish sandstone, on a rock face in the Fezzan region of the Sahara Desert. No elephant has been able to live in this part of North Africa for thousands of years. The unknown artist visualized the animal as walking on the shadowline caused by the sharp change in angle of the rock surface. Actual engraving over 4½ ft long. The engraved line has been whitened with chalk for photographing.

Prehistoric North Africa

There was a time, several thousand years ago, when the greatest desert in the world, the Sahara, did not exist. Where now there is nothing but a sea of sand and rock, great grassy plains and forests once spread. Buffalo, elephants, ostriches, antelope, and giraffes roamed over it. Rivers wound through it, and hippopotami wallowed in their running water. Men and women lived there too, hunting the animals and probably fishing the streams and foraging the ground. We know this from the stone tools they left scattered about and from the engravings they left on the rocks. But of what they were like physically we have only a scant idea. So far just one skeleton of a primitive man has been found in the Sahara region.

The change from this garden of Eden for men and animals to the present sandy desolation was extremely gradual and is probably still going on. A primitive man between his birth and his death would perhaps have noticed no change. But over several generations changes did begin to be serious. From their abandoned camping grounds we can see how ancient men at one time lived high up on river banks to avoid floods, then as the rivers dwindled moved stage by stage down into the stream beds, then retreated to lakes and oases, and finally altogether vanished. Even in Roman times, less than two thousand years ago, the Sahara seems to have been easier to cross than it is today, and in some places probably supported inhabitants.

The Sahara Desert contains the greatest natural storehouse of rock painting in the world. But most of it is by peoples of other cultures than the hunting-fishing-foraging ones which we are considering in this chapter.

Prehistoric Europe

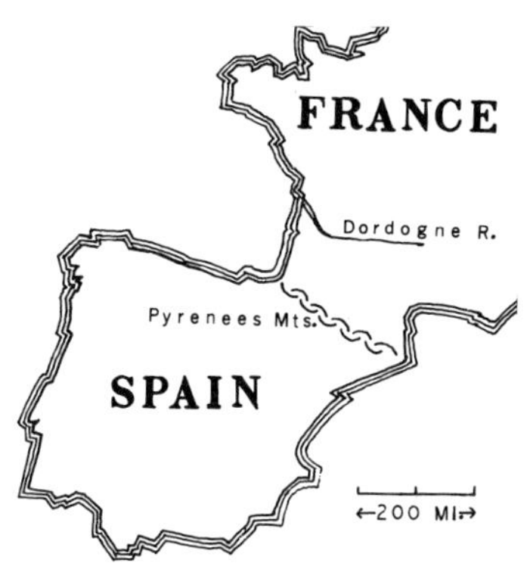

Since about 1880, archeologists working in France and northern Spain have been discovering, one by one, deep caves that had lain sometimes forgotten and unentered for thousands of years.

On their walls, over and over again, one can see drawings and paintings made by a primitive race of men, now long vanished. Over a hundred sites of such primitive art have so far been found.

The first of these caves to be discovered was at Altamira, in northern Spain; a series of beautifully painted bulls runs along its ceiling. The last so far found, and perhaps the most marvelous, was discovered in 1940 at Lascaux in southern France by some boys chasing a rabbit. On the light-colored walls and ceilings of this long tunnel-like cave, unknown primitive artists created wild horses, deer, bison, and some magnificent black and white bulls, some of them twenty feet long—the largest rock paintings known anywhere.

As a group these Spanish and French paintings resemble Bushman art in their materials (earth colors, charcoal, etc.) and in the truth of their animal drawing. But in other ways they are markedly different. They are often larger. Human beings rarely appear, and the pictures seldom if ever seem to tell a story. All we see is a mysterious succession of animals, mostly of a subarctic type. Europe was going through an ice age when they were painted. There is another difference too. The paintings are buried deep in almost inaccessible caverns and natural tunnels, suggesting that their purpose may have been secret, perhaps for tribal initiations. Bushman art is much more exposed.

The age of the European paintings is also much greater than any African art yet found. It is the oldest known in the world, created from 32,000 to 12,000 years ago, a time so remote that to our imaginations it is practically meaningless.

Mural painting of wild bulls, horses and reindeer, one of many found in the now-famous cave at Lascaux, southern France. It is believed the mural was created perhaps 16,000 years ago, as the stone age art of Western Europe was approaching its mature level of development.

Photo courtesy Jean Vertut

Photo courtesy Jean Vertut

Stone age sculpture, found in a cave of the Roc de Sers, southern France.

But painting was only one of the ways in which these remote artists worked. The oldest images seem to have been carved or hammered out on rock surfaces in low relief. Deep in one cave, forms of bison were found sculptured in clay. And in many places, lying about on cave floors, little figures of animals and women, carved from bone, horn, or chipped pebbles, have turned up. These seem usually to belong to the early part of this immense period of 20,000 years. On cave walls and ceilings, animal outlines were often engraved by deep scratching, then filled in with color, sometimes by blowing powdered pigment onto a prepared surface.

Since the same caves seem to have been in use sometimes for thousands of years, we find animal drawings and paintings often placed one on top of another, as older ones were outmoded, or re-created for reasons lost to us. The changes in style as the centuries and millenia passed seem to us to have been unbearably gradual. And throughout that time the chief subjects remained constant: the same wild horses, bison, reindeer, wild bulls and cows, mammoths, and a few wild bears, lions, and imaginary beasts. When men drew themselves, it was as lesser beings and with a stiffness contrasting unfavorably with the naturalness and vitality of the animal pictures. Women usually appear in little sculptured forms, fat and voluptuous.

Photo courtesy Jean Vertut and Count Begouen

Clay images of bison, found deep in the cave called Tuc d'Audoubert, French Pyrenees.

Courtesy Superintendent of Antiquities, Palermo

Stone age hunters dancing. A rock drawing recently found in the cave of Addaura, Monte Pellegrino, Sicily. Carved perhaps 15,000 years ago, the figures are shown in vigorous motion. They have the free, living quality which marks the best (to us) of hunting society art the world over. Height about 3 ft.

Until recently the art of Europe's prehistoric caves was thought to be a mere hodgepodge of pictures, drawn without concern for relationships. But the French archeologist Annette Laming-Emperaire, after a painstaking study of all the sites, has shown that there are familiar groupings which appear repeatedly, that in places, especially at Lascaux, the ancient artists worked with the large-scale composition of animal groups in mind, and that certain animals are often related to definite parts of caves (for example, the most dangerous kinds were often placed deepest). The unraveling of the mystery of their meaning will challenge us for years to come, perhaps forever.

Skeletal remains of "cave men" who lived sometime during this ancient period have been found near the French village of Cro-Magnon. They were tall, well proportioned, and (judging by their skull shape) possessed a brain very much like that of modern man. They appear to have lived by hunting.

One mark of this remote European culture, which at one time seemed important to archeologists, is that its people had not yet learned to give stone a smooth, polished surface with abrasives. For this reason they are said to have lived in the *Paleolithic period* (Greek origin: *paleo* = old; *lithos* = stone). The term has been extended to all hunting societies, past or present, as described in this chapter. Each is said to be living in a *Paleolithic culture*. (See page 46 for the contrasting meaning of *Neolithic culture*.)

Some Characteristics of Hunting Societies

Most important social unit: the family.

Largest social group: a few families (sometimes called a *horde*) living together in one large hunting area and roaming over that area according to need, but keeping strictly within it (except when on formal visits to other hordes or when on feuding raids against them).

Leadership and government: none, or of a highly informal nature. The man with the greatest talent for leadership in one horde simply gravitates to that position. The real governing force is the desperate need for food. This compels harmony and cooperation among all members.

Means of getting food: there is division of labor. (The men hunt and fish; the women forage for roots, seeds, fruit, and vegetables.) There is also a high degree of cooperation, especially among the men when running down large game or landing large fish.

Greenland Eskimo ivory image of Tupilaka, the spirit of cannibalism, who, they believe, takes possession of people at times of extreme starvation. The figure forcefully conveys the horror with which Eskimos regard the dehumanizing experience which starvation forces upon them.

Private Collection. Photo Lloyd Ullberg

Attitude toward food: since all cooperate in getting it, all share in it. This is one of the most remarkable characteristics of hunting societies. There is no such thing as stinginess or secretly holding back food from others, even from the lazy (though these are scorned).

Attitude toward human life: at times of starvation the least self-reliant are the first to suffer. Infants, especially if sickly, may be killed soon after birth. Old people often volunteer to separate themselves from the group and thus die.

Attitude toward children: if they survive infancy, they are greatly loved and seldom if ever disciplined. When adolescence is reached, all this suddenly changes. In a series of puberty initiations the young people are grimly taught the traditions of the horde and the responsibilities of living in it. They are thus transformed in a year or less from children to adults.

Knowledge: hunting people show an amazing practical knowledge of the animals, plants, and materials of their local area. They know the usefulness not only of each plant or animal, but of each part—each plant fibre and each animal sinew and bone. They show high technical and artistic skill in making things from these materials. Outside of this local knowledge, their ideas are often inaccurate. They tend to regard themselves as the most important people in the world (tribal names are often simply the local word for *man*). And they may think their dwelling place is the center of the universe.

Superstition: because hunting men are surrounded by so much that they do not know or cannot control (like the coming and going of food-animals, of good and bad weather, and of disease), they tend to be extremely superstitious and rely on medicine men (or *shamans*) to help them control these unknown forces through spells and incantations.

Religion: all hunting people respect the human soul as immortal. They each have a group of sacred legends describing the creation of the world, of animals, and of themselves. And they respect and revere animals as part of this creation, even when killing them for food.

From Australian Aboriginal Decorative Art, F. D. McCarthy

Abstract design carved by Australian natives in a tree trunk, New South Wales. Such designs are created sometimes for initiation ceremonies, sometimes as grave markers. Each design has a meaning, either as a symbol for a local group, or as a representation of some myth.

The Art of Hunting Societies

Although the life of hunting societies is simple and their social units are small, we can see already in their art certain kinds which are present also in more complex societies.

When we speak of the kinds of art we probably think first, *is it painting? sculpture? drama? dance?* or *some other kind?* But art can also be looked at in another way: we can ask, *what source inspired it?* Then we can look at it in still a third way: we can ask, *for what purpose was this art created?*

When we consider the *kinds* of hunting-society art, we find already many of those with which we also are familiar: painting, drawing, sculpture, dance, games, and the beginnings of drama, poetry, fiction, and myth, sometimes merging one into another.

Photo courtesy Campbell Grant

Chumash Indian rock painting, Ventura County, California. Length about 12 ft.

When we consider their art as to its *sources*, we recognize that much of it springs directly from the creator's intense daily experience, in this case hunting. Repeatedly we see the image of the hunted animal portrayed in painting, drawing and sculpture, sometimes crudely, sometimes with complex fidelity, but always vividly. Animal behavior is mimicked or dramatized in dances and dramatic games. Animals often become the chief characters in stories and myths. But in hunting-society art we also see much that springs from within the artist. We discover imaginary creatures never seen on land or sea. And forms which we would call *abstract* (a word discussed in the next chapter) appear repeatedly. Sometimes these abstract forms appear sprawled over rock walls or, as in Australia, scratched deeply into the ground. Sometimes they are carved or painted on weapons, apparel, or ceremonial objects. Sometimes they are painted or tattooed directly on the human body.

When we consider the *purposes* of hunting-society art we find that these are many sided, just as with us. Some of it seems to spring from sheer enjoyment and the spirit of play. Some, on the other hand, is intensely focused on utility, especially when the intent is the practice of magic. At such times images of animals, and patterns of dance or chanting, become parts of spells cast with the intent of ensuring success in hunting or the healing of sickness. Again the purpose may be to convey meaning through *symbolism* (a word discussed in Chapter 3). A fish, for example, may be a symbol for water, hence rain or a rainy season. Abstract forms seem often to have such symbolic meanings. Sometimes their meaning can be simple, a certain pattern standing for some animal or bird, and hence denoting a particular human group or horde. Patterns on weapons and other objects seem usually to have this purpose, rather than that of mere decoration in our sense of the word (filling an otherwise empty space). Sometimes the meaning can be much deeper and more complex: abstract or semi-abstract forms drawn or carved on rock walls, tree trunks, or the ground during initiation ceremonies seem intended to illustrate myths of the creation of the world or of mankind.

NOTES

1 The Bushmen were different from the Hottentots, another primitive people who fiercely opposed the Dutch at this time.

2 L. Van der Post, *The Lost World of the Kalahari* (Morrow, New York 1958), pp. 24–29. Perhaps the order in which Van der Post suggests the paintings were made is not entirely accurate, but he seems to have caught their spirit with remarkable sympathy.

3 From Chapter III, *An Account of Travels into the Interior of Southern Africa*, J. Barrow (Cadell and Davies, London, 2nd ed., 1806).

4 J. Barrow, *ibid.*

5 J. Barrow, *ibid.*

6 L. Van der Post, *The Lost World of the Kalahari*, p. 242.

[7] Dornan, *Pygmies and Bushmen of the Kalahari* (Seeley, Service & Co, London, 1925), pp. 188–189. Observation made prior to 1914.

[8] Erik Holm, *The Art of the Stone Age*, Crown, New York, p. 156.

[9] L. Van der Post, *The Lost World of the Kalahari*, p. 241.

[10] *The Harmless People*, Elizabeth Marshall Thomas (Knopf, New York, 1959), pp. 42–43.

[11] Jones and Doke (ed.), *Bushmen of the Southern Kalahari* (University of Witwatersrand Press, Johannesburg, 1937), pp. 95–96.

[12] Students may wish to begin using the Projects Manual available as a campanion to this book.

[13] Unless you are one of the fortunate few who can search out the originals on the South African rocks.

[14] The word *rhythm* has also a second meaning in the field of art. It may mean a gradation of colors or values.

[15] See page 49 for the distinction between these and most other North American Indians.

BOOKS ON HUNTING SOCIETIES

BUSHMEN

The Harmless People, E. M. Thomas (Knopf, New York, 1959).
Kalahari, Jens Bjerre (Michael Joseph, London, 1960).
The Lost World of the Kalahari, L. Van der Post (Morrow, New York, 1958).
National Geographic Magazine, June, 1963.

FOLK TALES

African Folk Tales and Sculpture, Bollingen Series XXXII (Pantheon, 1952), contains three Bushman tales.
The Mantis and his Friends, D. Bleek (Miller, Capetown, South Africa).

ROCK PAINTINGS

Rock Paintings of the Drakensberg, A. R. Willcox (Max Parrish, London, 1960).
Rock Paintings in South Africa, Stow and Bleek (Methuen, London, 1930).
Cave Artists of South Africa, E. Rosenthal (A. A. Balkema, Capetown, South Africa, 1953).

MUSIC, MUSICAL INSTRUMENTS, DANCES AND DRAMATIC GAMES

Bushmen of the Southern Kalahari, Jones and Doke (ed.) (University of Witwatersrand Press, Johannesburg, South Africa, 1937).

PREHISTORIC NORTH AFRICA

The Search for the Tassili Frescoes, P. Lhote (Du Hon, New York, 1959).

PREHISTORIC EUROPE

The Stone Age Hunters, G. Clark (McGraw-Hill, New York, 1968).
The Art of the Stone Age (Crown, New York, 1961), pp. 15–17.
Prehistoric Man, J. Augusta (Hamlyn, London, 1960), plates 23–51, with text.
Lascaux Paintings and Engravings, A. Laming (Pelican paperback, 1959).
The Evolution of Paleolithic Art, A. Leroi-Gourhan (Scientific American, February, 1968, pp. 59–70).

FILM

Lascaux, Cradle of Man's Art, sound, color, 17 minutes, International Film Bureau.

PRIMITIVE AUSTRALIA

The Australian Aborigines, How to Understand Them, A. P. Elkin (Angus & Robertson, Sidney, Australia, 1964).
Desert Peoples: The Walbiri Aborigines of Central Australia, N. J. Meggitt (Angus & Robertson, Sidney, Australia, 1962).
Yulengor, W. S. Chaseling (Epworth Press, London, 1957, *and* Essential Books, Inc., Fair Lawn, New Jersey).
Australia—Aboriginal Art—Arnhem Land, Graphic Society for UNESCO, New York, 1954).
Dawn of Art: Painting and Sculpture of Australian Aborigines, K. Kupke (Viking Press, New York, 1965).

FILMS

Primitive People—Australian Aborigines, sound, black and white, 33 minutes, British narration, United World Films.
For background, *Bushland Color Studies*, sound, color, 11 minutes, Australian News and Information Bureau.

ESKIMOS

Eskimo Masks: Art and Ceremony, D. J. Ray (University of Washington Press, Seattle, 1968).
Eskimo Sculpture, Jorgen Meldgaard (Potter, New York, 1960), 48 pages, 75 illustrations.
Eskimo Prints, J. H. Houston (Barre Publishers, Barre, Massachusetts, 1967).
Across Arctic America, Narrative of the Fifth Thule Expedition, Knud Rasmussen (Putnam, New York, 1927), 388 pages, 64 illustrations.
Land of the Long Day, D. Wilkinson (George Harrap, Ltd., London, 1956).
The Eskimos, S. Bleeker (Morrow, New York, 1959).

FILMS

The Eskimo Hunters, color, sound, 20 minutes, United World Films.
Eskimo Arts and Crafts, color, sound, 22 minutes, International Film Bureau, Inc.
Nanook of the North, silent black and white, 54 minutes, Athena Films. This is Robert Flaherty's epic. Two years after the film was completed the Eskimo who had taken the lead in it died of starvation. Such is the harsh life of the Eskimo.

CALIFORNIA ABORIGINES

Ishi in Two Worlds, A Biography of the Last Wild Indian in North America, T. Kroeber (University of California Press, Berkeley, 1961).
Ishi, Last of His Tribe, T. Kroeber (Parnassus Press, Berkeley, 1964).
The Conflict Between the California Indian and White Civilization, S. F. Cook (University of California Press, 1943).
The Mission Indians, S. Bleeker (Morrow, New York, 1956).
The Rock Paintings of the Chumash, C. Grant (University of California Press, 1965).

GENERAL

The Epic of Man, by the editors of Life, pp. 11–53 and 242–255.
For recordings of hunting society music see Appendix A.

Dominion Museum. Wellington, N. Z.

Ancestor image from a tribal house of the Maori people, New Zealand. He is believed to have been a leader of the pioneers who made the long voyage to New Zealand from Tahiti by double canoe about 600 years ago. He is represented in this form to show that he is now in the spirit world, from which he can wield power over tribal affairs.

Maori tribal houses are rich store houses of tradition, each piece of carved wood illustrating some person or event in the tribe's past.

2

THE FIRST FARMING SOCIETIES

People Who Have Begun to Raise Crops and Tame Animals, But Who Still Must Rely Somewhat on Hunting, on Fishing, or on Food Gathering from Wild Plants

Preview

The life of the hunter-fisherman and of his root-digging, seed-collecting, berry-picking wife is probably one of the riskiest known to man. How do we know? Because there have always been so few of them. As we saw in Chapter 1, it usually takes an enormous piece of land, sometimes as big as a large county, to support one of their little hordes composed of just a few families. To stay alive, such a horde must keep restlessly on the move over its own vast hunting area, the men always alert for game, the women hopefully eyeing every plant. To such people, death by starvation is always near. To live they depend heavily on luck and on the wear and tear of endless search.

Men and women began to free themselves from such a harsh life when they began to learn how to conquer luck—how to make a food supply grow when and where they wanted it. They did this, of course, by finding out how to raise their own food plants and how to tame and raise animals. They became farmers and herdsmen instead of hunters. After their discovery of how to make fire, this was men's first major step forward in the conquest of luck.

But the change-over has been neither simple nor fast. It began perhaps ten thousand years ago, and in some parts of the world it is still going on. Even two centuries ago, that in-between kind of man, the hunting-farmer, could still be found on this planet in millions. Most American Indians, before the arrival of Europeans, were hunter-farmers. So were the natives of much of central Africa, of most of Polynesia, of Fiji, of New Guinea, of Borneo, and many other places.

These people have made an enormous, many-sided contribution to the art of the world. No art museum is complete without a collection or an occasional exhibition of their work. Some museums are devoted to it entirely. Our own art has not only been deeply influenced by it, but originally grew out of it. Therefore, let us try to understand and appreciate this art in all its rich variety. But if we are to do so, we must also try to understand what the life of the hunter-farmer was like, and in some places still is like.

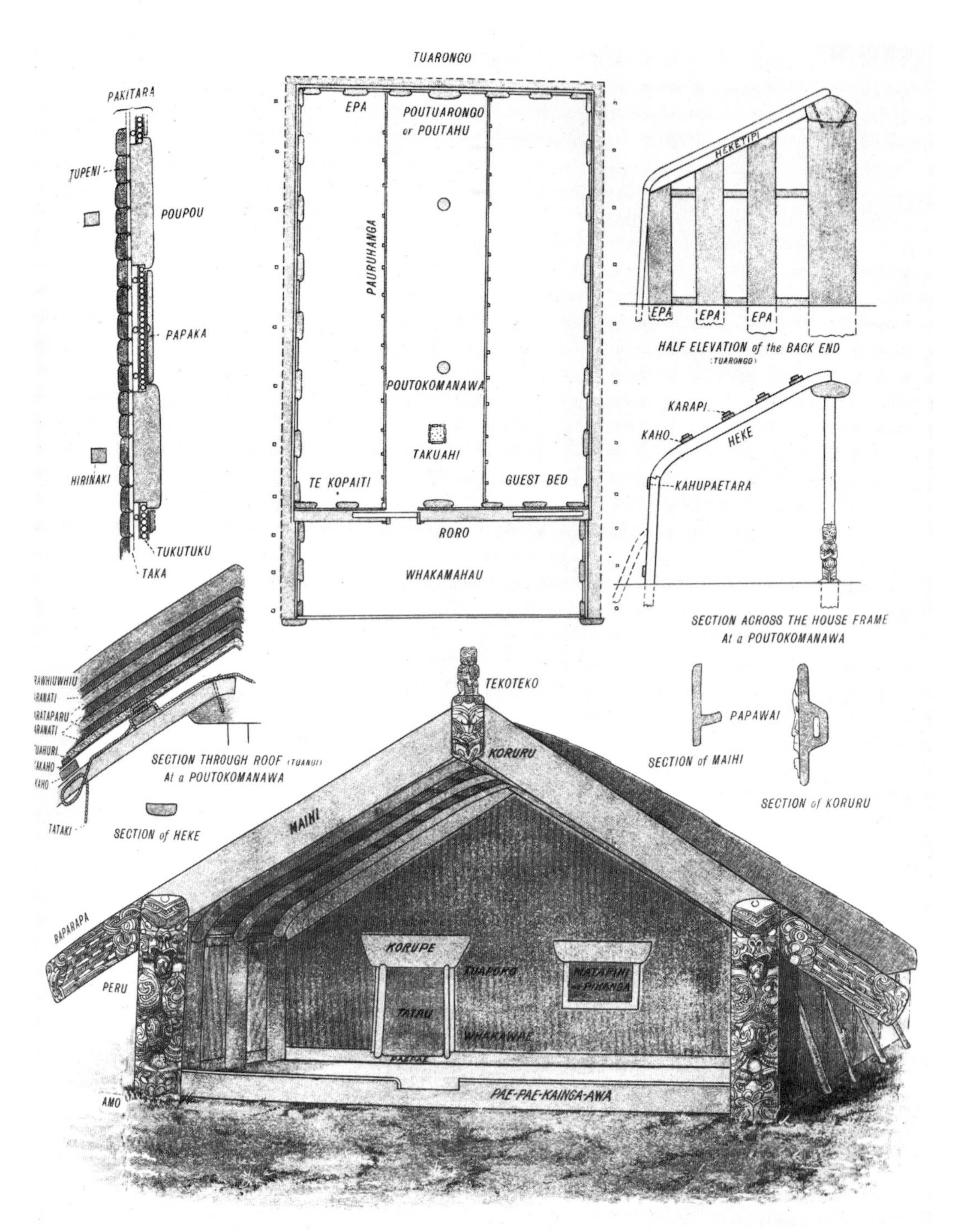

Courtesy Royal Society of N. Z.

With the invention of farming, human life became settled instead of roving. Architecture, an entirely new art form, appeared. The Maori, long before European explorers discovered New Zealand, had developed their own method of constructing massive tribal houses, whose great beams and interior wall panels were carved with the imaginary likenesses of former chiefs and heroes.

Such a house took years to complete and required cooperation among many men of different abilities: medicine men or shamans *to "bless" the building site with the correct spells; architects to plan the building; unskilled labor to hew and haul the timber; carpenters using stone tools to construct the frame and sew the parts together with rope; matting weavers; wood carvers; shell cutters to make inlay for the carving; painters who made their own red and black paint and created designs for the rafters; and a chief to organize the whole project.*

The workmen were often from more than one tribe. They were not hired but invited, were supplied with food while on the job, and were presented with gifts on its completion. To build such a house therefore required years of planning beforehand, for extra land had to be cultivated to provide the additional food.

Another new art form, the decorated vessel, a symbol of tribal power. A Maori war canoe as seen by the first European voyagers to New Zealand. Such a canoe was made from a single enormous tree trunk, felled and shaped with stone tools. Strakes, or side boards, were then added, as were the carved prow and stern pieces. Through all these parts holes were bored with stone drills, and the whole was sewn together with stout cord. The tall stern piece, draped with black feathers, had a special purpose. It was the dwelling place of the vessel's mana, *or soul, whose presence governed its success and good luck.*

Primitive Farming

First let us look at a typical primitive farm as it still exists in some places today, such as the Pacific Islands and New Guinea, unchanged after thousands of years. It is usually extremely small, less like a farm than a neatly kept vegetable garden. Poor tools and the grinding toil that they require are one cause for this. But primitive farming is also wasteful of land. Hunter-farmers do not yet understand how to keep soil enriched through such devices as crop rotation. Consequently, they are forever deserting one exhausted plot and clearing off a new one nearby, which they must then cultivate for the first time.

These little gardens, maintained by such labor, will seldom fully support people. Not only do they produce too little, but they also tend to produce only the starchy part of a well-balanced diet. To sustain life the men must therefore go hunting or fishing while the women stay home to work the farms. In other words, *a hunter-farmer has developed enough farming skill to raise only a part of his food supply*. But even this modest achievement has made some profound changes in his life.

The Effects of Primitive Farming

Permanent Dwelling Place

Just as the hunting family must always be on the move to look for new game, so the farming family must stay in one place to look after its crops. Life becomes pinned down. Even if the hunter has to spend days away from home, he must always come back to where his farm is and where his hardworking wife is. So life becomes centered in one small place. And men begin to have a good reason for building strong, permanent shelters. The complicated art of house construction, therefore, comes slowly into being.

Measurement of Time Becomes Important

The life of the farmer has to be systematic. There are only certain limited times of the year that are right for planting, and these come regularly. Other limited times are right for harvesting. What is more, the farmer must *plan ahead* for these times. Before planting there is a long period of breaking up the ground, often with a period of clearing and burning-off before that. Harvesting takes its own careful preparations; baskets or jars must be made to hold farm produce, and granaries must be built to store them. Therefore, the farmer must think about time in a more exact, far-sighted way than the hunter does.

The hunter-farmer keeps track of the time of year partly by watching the world of nature around him, partly by watching for big seasonal changes in the weather, and partly by watching the stars, moon, and sun. The calendar, which gives the number of days in a year and assigns to each day a distinguishing name and number, is usually still unknown to him.

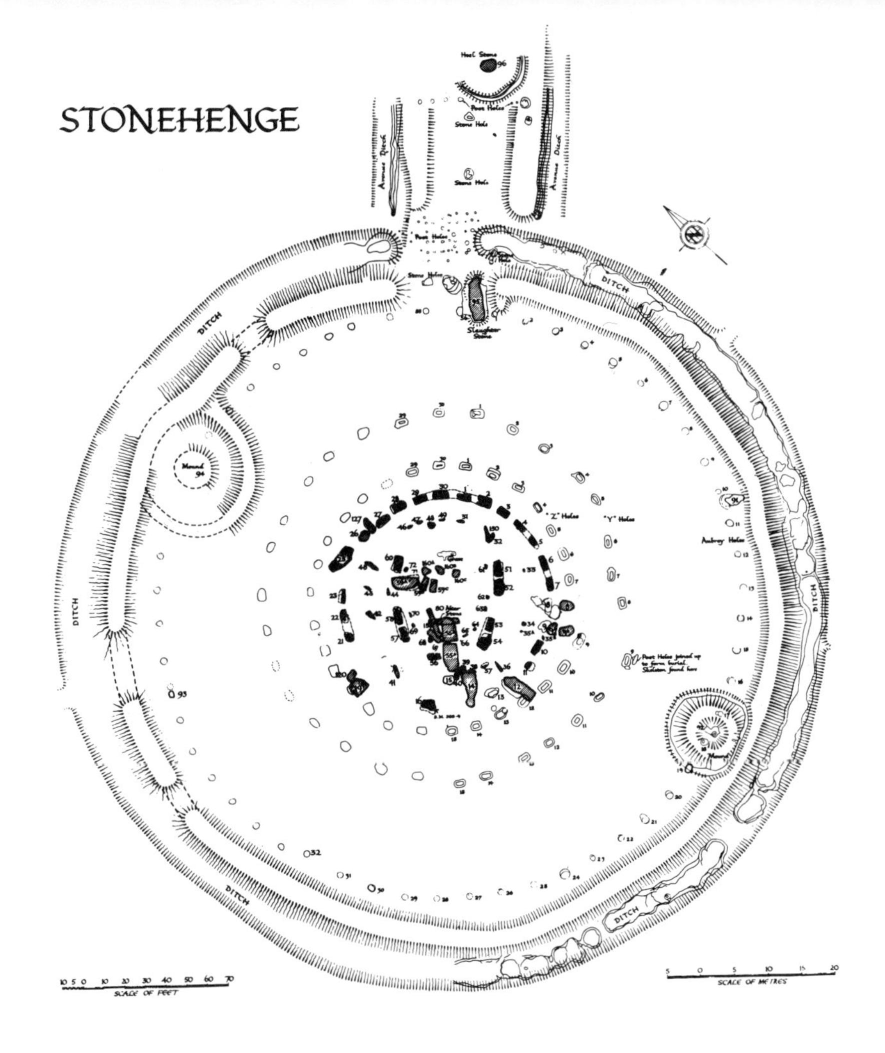

The plan of Stonehenge, a circle of huge stones on Salisbury Plain in southern England, whose origin and purpose have long been a puzzle. The astronomer Gerald Hawkins has recently shown with the help of a computer that it was probably erected between 1900 and 1600 B.C., and that it was a practical device for foretelling eclipses of the sun and moon. It also marks important divisions of the year: midsummer, midwinter, and the spring and fall equinoxes.

Stonehenge as seen from a helicopter in 1963.

Courtesy British Ministry of Public Buildings and Works (Crown Copyright)
Courtesy British Ministry of Public Buildings and Works (Crown Copyright)

A Maori instrument of peace. An adze with stone blade lashed with cord to a carved handle. It was looked on as having mana, or a soul of its own.

Leisure Time

The hard work of primitive farming comes only at certain times of year. After planting, the crops must have time to grow. After harvesting, no crops will grow at all for some months. The hunter-farmer spends this time in various ways, such as preparing for the next season, hunting and fishing, or making raids on other tribes. *But beyond these he finds time for that precious thing called leisure, when men and women can use their time creatively.* Because he has more leisure, the hunter-farmer is freer to develop skills and freer to use his imagination in creating beautiful works of art than is the hunter. Hunter-farmer art, therefore, is generally on a more highly organized level, as one can observe simply by comparing the illustrations of Chapters 1 and 2. But leisure time alone will not fully account for the differences, as we shall see later.

More People

Perhaps the most revolutionary effect which the invention of even the crudest kind of farming has had upon human living has been to cause the population to increase. More people could live on less land. It has been estimated that when farming as a way of life first spread across Europe several thousand years ago in what is called the Neolithic period, a prehistoric population explosion resulted, and the number of people increased thirty or forty fold. This increase in numbers, in turn, had its own effects on people's lives.

The Effects of Larger Population

Group Organization: Clan, Tribe

When a population grows, obviously more people must live together in one place than before, and this creates new problems. How are the people to organize so that community work gets done and so that friction is kept down? Primitive farmer-hunters solved this problem by enlarging the only social organization they already knew—the family. They grouped themselves into *extended families*, composed not merely of parents and children, but of uncles, aunts, cousins, and even more distant relatives, until each family had swelled to fifty or even a hundred. We call such a group of kinfolk a *clan*. Its leader was usually the eldest or most able male (or, in some societies, female) member.

The members of a clan, in order to have a feeling of belonging, must trace their relationship back to one common ancestor, or to a line of common ancestors. Therefore, ancestors could become enormously important. Anything that helped to keep ancestors vividly, dramatically alive in the imagination helped to unite the clan. Artists spent endless skill and patience creating startling, impressive ancestor-images. Sometimes these images were set in special houses like those the ancestors had once lived in. Here offerings of food were taken regularly, to keep ancestral influence strong. Some of the images were of enormous size, placed in shrines, and worshiped as gods. Everyone in the clan could then take pleasure in believing himself to be of divine origin. Sometimes we find the ancestor of a clan represented by some animal or bird whose strength or cunning the clan especially respected. Such an animal or bird is called a *totem*. (For examples, see page 56.) All these beliefs seem to have had a common purpose: to supply something vivid and dramatic around which primitive people could unite.

But even a clan could be too small to meet the risks of hunting-farming life. Therefore, we find clans joining to form a still larger group, sometimes with thousands of members. Such a group we call a *tribe*. *A tribe is a group of two or more clans which have joined to act as one social unit under the leadership of a chief, and which generally believe themselves to be interrelated.*

Sometimes a tribe hung together loosely. The clans of the Maori, for example, would meet once or twice a year for community ceremonies, or would assemble quickly when some danger threatened. For the rest of the time each clan would live independently. Other tribes, such as those of the American Indians, were tightly united, and the clans out of which they were originally built were hard to recognize. But so long as they were there, and *people were loyal to family ties before all else*, the social group was a tribe and a tribe only. The tribe is so characteristic of hunting-farming peoples that we shall henceforth usually refer to them as *tribal societies*.

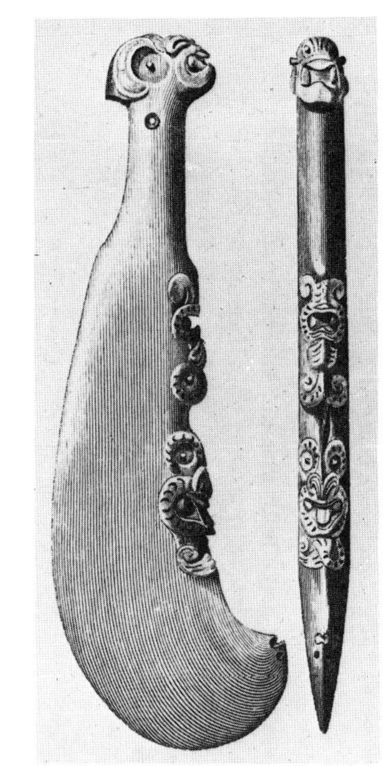

Maori instruments of war. Two war clubs, the one above of whalebone, that below of stone.

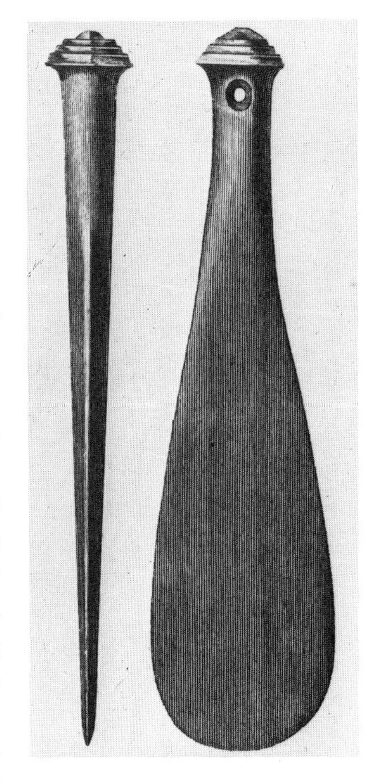

Relations Between Tribes—War and Diplomacy

Among the works of art produced by hunter-farmers, one often finds beautifully designed and decorated weapons, intended not for the slaying of animals, but of men. They are proof that a terrible new institution, organized warfare, had appeared, as a result of the crowding of people against people after the greater food supply increased their numbers. How did such warfare start? Since there was never quite enough food to satisfy the needs of most primitive people, the neatly tilled garden-farms of a neighboring tribe easily became tempting cause for a raid, especially at harvest time. A war chief in one tribe might therefore organize such a raid, leading a picked band of fighters to make an attack. If the attack was successful, the other tribe might bide its time and then make a counter-raid, but solely with revenge in mind. An endless seesaw of revenge raids could start. Neighbors ceased to be neighbors and became relentless enemies.

On such raids, enemy warriors were killed and captives were taken. The heads of the slain were often carefully preserved as trophies. Captives were put to grimly practical use of some sort. They might be killed for food or made to work, perhaps at tilling garden-farms. The practices of cannibalism and of slavery came into being. But slavery has never been important among primitive people. Every slave has to eat, and food was usually too hard to obtain thus to be wasted.

But, shocked by the horrors of war, tribal societies, like us, have repeatedly sought ways to reduce friction and relax tensions between crowding

Photo Royal Society of New Zealand

Carved wooden food bowl with lid, for a distinguished guest at a feast between Maori tribes. The left-hand supporting figure wears the traditional expression of war, the right-hand one that of peace.

An observer of the Maori 100 years ago, while they were still following their native customs, said of them: "They excelled in order and regularity, which they carried into almost everything they did, as shown in the symmetry of their carved designs of almost mathematically true scrolls and patterns; in the planting of their crops; in their measured paddling to 'time and stroke'; and, above all, in their war dance."

groups. In New Zealand, for example, one entire tribe of Maori would occasionally invite another to a feast. The invitation, delivered by an expert speech-maker, would be made a year or more in advance, and planning would have started well before that. For the enormous store of food consumed and gifts bestowed during such a feast took more work and cooperation to collect than would the building of a great tribal canoe.

On the appointed day, when the guests came flocking in, they often found the feast, with its accompanying gifts, mounted on an enormous wooden structure, adorned with flags of tapa cloth. Lengthy speeches were exchanged, and food was at last distributed with a careful regard for everyone's rank. Guests and hosts then enjoyed themselves together for a week or so. During such a feast public affairs and problems could be discussed under the friendliest circumstances. Over a hundred years ago, when the custom of intertribal feasts was dying out, a Maori chief was quoted as saying, "These feasts have many times been the means of keeping the peace between us, and may be of service again."[1]

Partial Specialization

As the number of people in one group increases *there is a greater chance for a variety of talents to be found in that group*. This, of course, means that a large community has a chance to benefit from a wider range of skills among its members than does a small one.

Because of the two factors, *predictable leisure time* and *greater range of talents in one group*, we find that the extended families and tribes of hunter-farmers often contain a good many *part-time specialists*—people who can spare *some* time, but not *all* of it, from hunting or farming to handle some other task or develop some other single skill. Some important kinds of primitive part-time specialists are the following.

POLITICAL LEADERS OR CHIEFS. A little horde of hunter-food-gatherers often has no leadership at all. But a tribe, containing hundreds or even thousands, cannot operate in this manner. We therefore find tribes developing a carefully worked-out organization. Often the heads of the clans in the tribe act as a governing counsel. They often choose from the tribe a leader to be the chief. Since the family is so important in tribal societies, we often find chiefs being selected over and over again from just one family, perhaps one with an unusually famous ancestor. We also find that one tribe may have several chiefs, each with a different duty: a war chief or general, a *talking chief* to handle peaceful relations with other tribes, and perhaps still another to act as judge in disputes between tribe members.

MEDICINE MEN, SHAMANS, PRIEST-MAGICIANS. Although farmer-hunters have more control over their surroundings, especially the food supply, than do hunters, the unknown forces in their lives are still at times overwhelming. Hunter-farmers are so much more at the mercy of the unknown than we are that it is hard for us to imagine how constantly fear influences their lives. To deal with these forces which they do not understand, they have developed their own methods. These methods the human race is outgrowing. Their replacement by others, such as scientific study and technical invention, is still gradual and so far only partial.

The farmer-hunter sees every event in his life as the action of invisible spirits, either friendly or hostile. The means he uses in trying to control them are called *magic*. When he attempts to cure disease, change the weather, attract game animals, protect crops from blight, achieve success in love or creation, or destroy enemies, he believes that his own efforts may be useless unless helpful spirits aid him, or unless harmful ones are rendered powerless.

Each tribe or other language-group has its own names for these spirit beings, for the *mana* or power which they can give, and for the *taboos* or incorrect human acts which can bring ruin by angering them. But the customary way all have of dealing with them is magical.

Just as a chief's duty is to deal with what everybody can see, the world of food-getting, warfare and diplomacy, so the other world that no one can see, the world of friendly or dangerous spirits, is the business of the *medicine man* or *shaman*. Chiefs and shamans tend to be the most respected and powerful members of a tribe.

The practices of shamans differ from culture to culture almost beyond recognition, but certain characteristics unite them. Perhaps their most familiar practice is the casting of spells, the saying of just the right words or performing the correct acts, which will supposedly bind a spirit to human will and compel it to do as commanded. Any error in reciting or acting out the spell may render it useless, or, worse, loose the spirit to terrible destructive action. The memorizing of such spells often requires years of practice; the shaman must be a specialist indeed.

Another way in which shamans have attempted to connect the human and spirit worlds is by allowing themselves to become the connecting link, permitting invisible spirits to take possession of them and act through them. Possession by a power other than one's self is one way of accounting for many forms of unnatural or abnormal behavior. Thus persons who are insane, epileptic or subject to trances are in tribal societies often regarded

A Maori chief, as drawn by an artist with the British explorer Captain Cook, about 1770. Tattooing was a respected art form among the Maori. Note resemblance between its pattern and that of the wood carvings, pages 36, 46.

Dominion Museum, Wellington, N. Z.

Maori ancestor image, carved wood, height about 5 ft.

with awe and respect as having been chosen by other-worldly beings for their temporary home. And thus tribal men often have a profound respect for dreams, believing them to be gifts from the spirit world. They treat with reverence the different techniques for producing trances or visions in normal people, for instance, prolonged fasting, narcotics and hypnotic dance rituals. Among many peoples it has been the shaman's duty to use one or another of these techniques to force himself into a trance-like state, so that a healing spirit may act through him to cure a patient, a prophesying spirit may speak through him to foretell the future, and so on. Such beliefs have been carried over into other, more complex societies.

Among all the shamans or medicine men who have walked this earth, many have doubtless been simple plodding practioners of a trade, fully believing their spell-casting power. Others have been charlatans, cynically using the superstitions of their fellow tribesmen as a tool for their own prestige. Still others seem to have been, for their time and place, profound thinkers, sometimes poets, who tried to see past the jumble of spells they had memorized to a deep, unified interpretation of life and the universe. From men such as these probably have come the beginnings of what we know today as philosophy and religion. Outstanding examples of this higher type of medicine man are still to be found, for example, among the Navaho Indians. For a fuller description see page 53.

CRAFTSMEN, CRAFTSWOMEN, ARTIST-CRAFTSMEN. The farmer-hunter craftsman usually carries his craft to a much higher level of excellence than a hunter ever can. He works with better tools; his techniques or skills are superior; and an older craftsman has often carefully trained him (the beginnings of apprenticeship).

If he carves in wood the results sometimes astonish us, both for size and complexity.

If he works in stone or bone he not only grinds or chips out the shape he wants, but often gives it a fine polish. This single skill, that of polishing stone with an abrasive (usually a piece of rough sandstone) has been over-emphasized. It has been used to name the entire farmer-hunter stage of human development. Anthropologists call it the Neolithic period (Greek origin: *neo* = new, *lithos* = stone). Any people, past or present, with a way of life like that so far described in this chapter is said to be living in a *neolithic culture*.

He has developed pottery from the making of crude, small containers to the forming of elegantly shaped bowls, dishes and large jars, but without using a potter's wheel.

He (more often she) has advanced weaving from the making of fish traps, small baskets, and simple mats to the weaving of true cloth. The women have discovered how to spin thread from plant fiber or from animal wool or hair. And step by step they have invented the *loom*, on which they convert this thread into hammocks, blankets, loin cloths, sashes, belts, and head-bands. In farmer-hunter societies cloth garments begin to replace leather ones. As for farmer-hunter basket weaving, it is often a highly advanced art.

All this can be called *technical improvement*. But something else is re-markable about farmer-hunter craftsmen. They go to enormous labor to make objects, as we would say, beautiful. They often create tools or weapons which are sculptured, and pottery, baskets, or woven cloth which are patterned, sometimes simply, sometimes richly. They are more than merely workmen who do a thorough job. We should therefore call them *artist-craftsmen.*

But their motives for this sculpturing and patterning are likely to be far removed from ours. We tend to think of "ornament" or "decoration" merely as something one puts on a plain object to make it, supposedly, more pleasing. In tribal societies the purpose seems generally to be deeper. A tool or weapon may be given a shape which will suggest that it has a life of its own; it may then be given a name as if it were a person. The Maori adze often bears a proper name, as if alive. Patterns on baskets and blankets often have a magical purpose, or a mythical meaning. Sometimes these are so old that they have been half forgotten. Even so, they tend to have greater significance than "decoration" as we usually think of it.

THE ARTIST-CRAFTSMEN'S ATTITUDE TOWARD THEIR WORK. Two forces have tended to bind almost every move made by a primitive artist-craftsman or craftswoman (we are of course speaking here of those still uninfluenced by alien cultures, such as our own). These two forces are custom and superstition.

If, for example, a man is a woodworker, his master has taught him how to use his tools, not necessarily in the best way, but in the way they have (supposedly) always been used. The technique is a part of tribal custom which nobody questions. He is in many cases taught that the knowledge of his craft was first given to the tribe by some famous ancestor, now living in the spirit world, and that the power to practice his craft depends on that being's good will. To the woodworker everything about his craft thus becomes sacred, or frought with magic. He may be in constant fear lest he violate any of its rules of practice. For in so doing he may anger the unseen being in the other world, who may then punish him by bad luck, accident, sickness, or loss of skill.

The forms he gives his work are often, he believes, part of this sacred tradition. He will be fearful, therefore, of changing these forms. The shapes and patterns of objects created in tribal societies which strike us as being so vivid, dramatically strange, or elegant have many times actually been evolved gradually, almost imperceptibly, as a part of tribal custom. If, on the other hand, a craftsman does create new forms, he is likely to believe that it is not he, but some being from the spirit world, acting through him, who is making the innovation. For example, Northwest Coast Indians, when creating masks for certain rituals, would do so only after a period of solitary fasting, during which, they believed, a spirit being would appear and show the creator the form the mask must take.

It is not only the techniques and forms of his craft which the wood carver holds in awe, but the materials also. When he has to cut down a tree, he takes care to appease its guardian spirit, lest it take revenge.

What is true of woodworkers is true of the other crafts, whether pottery, weaving, stoneworking, farming, or the business of successful hunting. Each is watched over by some spirit guardian. Each involves practices and materials which are looked on as sacred. Among some people these beliefs are more intensely followed than among others. But they tend to be present in some form everywhere.

Lowie Museum of Anthropology, University of California, Berkeley. Photo Eugene Prince

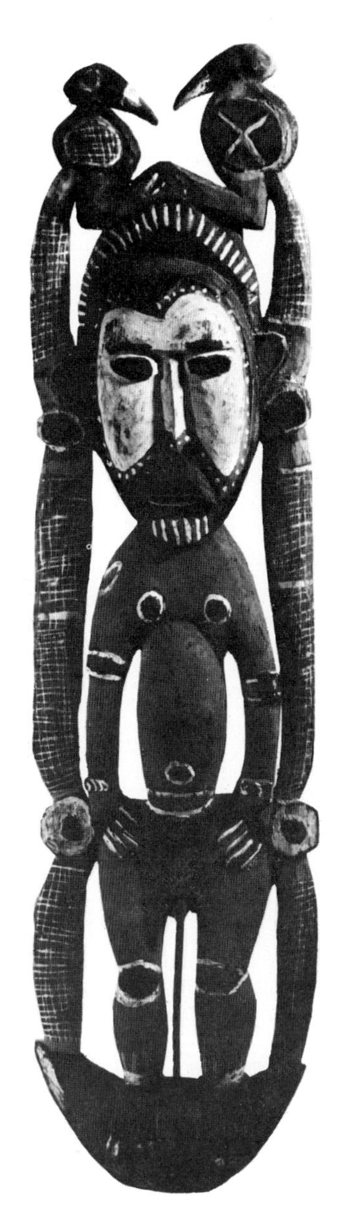

Ancestor image with two totem birds, from the Maprik Hills area, New Guinea. It was used in ceremonies at the annual yam harvest. Carved wood, height about 4 ft.

For a further consideration of the art of hunting-farming societies, especially the use of space and of abstract forms, see pages 69–73.

A Further Meaning for Style

Let us come back to that word of complex meaning, *style*. On page 19 we saw that style can mean the character that an artist's personality gives to what he creates. But what if the artist has been so strongly dominated by his tribe or his entire culture that it has shaped him through and through? *Style then becomes an expression, not just of himself, but of an entire people, and of the customs and conventions that bind them together.*

This kind of style becomes vividly clear when we look at the works of art produced by hunting-farming societies. With experience one can often recognize not only the part of the world from which each object comes, but even the particular tribe whose craftsmen made it. The craftsmen themselves have been forgotten; in each locality custom dominated them all.

Let us now look at some of the world's tribal cultures which have become famous for the art they produced, or are still producing.

Maori pataka *or granary, carved wood inlaid with shell. In the right foreground is the stern post of a canoe.*

Dominion Museum, Wellington, N. Z.

American Indian Art: Three Examples

The shock of collision with pioneering white men originally from Europe has all but totally destroyed the native culture of the American Indians. Now that most of it has vanished, we have difficulty realizing how enormously varied it was.

The American Indian was usually a typical hunter-farmer, relying largely on the cultivation of maize, a crop originally developed in ancient Mexico which gradually spread from tribe to tribe northward over the continent. Where maize would not grow, the Indian usually relied entirely on hunting, fishing, and gathering. These regions were Canada (where the summer season was too short for maize growing), California (with no summer rains), and the prairies (where the sod was resistant to the digging stick). Here we shall briefly consider just three Indian groups. Two are distinguished for their strongly developed artistic style. The third is remarkable for *adaptive and cultural* creation.

The Indians of the Southwest

The Pueblo Indians are a small cluster of extremely conservative tribes,[2] who have stubbornly preserved their way of life longer, perhaps, than any other North American Indian group, that is, for a period of a thousand years. Slow changes in climate have forced them to shift their place of abode, as the ruins of houses in places now desert mutely prove. Today the Pueblos live on reservations in the near-deserts of New Mexico and Arizona. The Spaniards introduced them to two imported domestic animals, the horse and the sheep, and taught them the craft of silver-smithing. We shall consider Pueblo art outside these areas of influence.

White House ruin, Canyon de Chelle, Arizona.

Photo Ansell Adams

ARCHITECTURE. The most imposing achievement of the Pueblos, the one first to strike the eye, is their stone-walled, wood-raftered architecture, now abandoned—the great cliff dwellings in shallow canyon wall caves, high above the river beds where once the Indians farmed. A study of these castlelike ruins shows two types of buildings: rectangular dwellings still containing the remains of family living, and circular "temples" with the remains of altars. Today's Pueblo Indians continue to build villages somewhat as their ancestors did, but now the building material is adobe mud and the location is level ground. A Pueblo village is like an apartment house, usually more than one story high. Connected to each village are one or more roofed, underground *kivas* or sacred rooms used for magical practices.

POTTERY. The Pueblos extensively practiced the craft of pottery. Pottery, at least broken pieces of it, lasts indefinitely. We can therefore study that of the Pueblo Indians backward for centuries, simply by searching for fragments in their abandoned villages. Today a few Pueblo potters continue to keep alive this ancient tradition. Both the shape of their bowls, jars, and dishes and the decorations they apply to them are developments from those of the distant past.

Left, a Zuni Indian woman, New Mexico, building up a large jar from field clay. Below, a completed jar.

CEREMONIAL COSTUME. The spectacular ceremonies which still center around kivas present a bizarre spectacle to visitors. The kiva is a symbol of the underworld, from which, the Pueblos believe, they as a race once came, and to which their souls depart at death to join their ancestors. They believe that spirits (called *kachinas*) from this other world possess certain powers, some to cure diseases, others to bring rain, to produce fertile crops, or to win intertribal wars (now no longer waged). They believe that the right ceremonies bring one kind of kachina up into this world, where they act effectively for a short time by inhabiting or "possessing" the bodies of men masked and costumed to impersonate them.

Calling up kachinas is the privilege of secret societies, one society for each kind of kachina. Thus one *kachina society* is concerned with rain making, another with healing, another with ensuring a fertile maize crop, and so on. Each society has its own secret kachina-raising rituals and its own strange and distinctive costume and mask, all carefully determined by tradition. These costumes are exactly copied on small images used to instruct Pueblo children in kachina lore and to prepare them for the societies into which they will later be initiated. Such "kachina dolls," made gaudy with commercial paint, are now produced for the tourist trade. The whole culture is slowly disappearing.

Three images of kachinas *or spirits, each governing a different aspect of Hopi Indian life.*

Lowie Museum of Anthropology, University of California, Berkeley. Photo John Bridgman

Navaho sand painting.

SAND PAINTING. Part of the ritual performed in a kiva to bring kachinas from the underworld includes the creating of sacred designs in sand on the kiva floor in front of the altar. The Navajos, an invading tribe who settled beside the Pueblos centuries ago and learned their ways, took this part of the ceremony and developed it to fit their particular beliefs. They brought it above ground, entrusted sand painting to their priest-magicians or medicine men, and made it the chief ritual for commanding the healing spirits of the other world to act in this one. In Navajo hands, sand painting became one of the most remarkable art-forms developed in North America. Medicine men developed a large "vocabulary" of beautifully clear images, each with its own definite meaning. Combining these in elegant, symmetrical designs of soft colored, skillfully poured sand had various magic purposes. And the chants and ceremonies that attended their making would draw large audiences from miles around to watch and participate throughout an entire night or day. Not only are sand paintings impossible to preserve, but ritual always requires their destruction during a ceremony. Our knowledge of them therefore depends largely on the memory or copying of spectators, or on drawings volunteered by the medicine men themselves.

Museum of Navaho Ceremonial Art, Santa Fe, New Mexico

Lowie Museum of Anthropology, University of California, Berkeley

Kwakiutl Indians costumed for ceremonial dances, photographed in front of a communal house about 1914. The lower parts of three totem poles appear in the background.

The Indians of the Northwest Pacific Coast

The west coast of Canada, all the way from Washington to Alaska, is guarded by clusters of beautiful, heavily forested islands. And here for centuries has lived perhaps the only people in the world who developed a settled life and a large population organized into clans and tribes *without* relying on farming at all. How was this achieved? Thanks to the bounty of nature. There is probably no spot on earth where wild food—fish, game, and berries—is so plentiful. The enormous runs of salmon, crowding in from the Pacific each spring to their freshwater spawning grounds, could supply whole tribes with enough fish (fresh or preserved by drying) to last an entire year. And this was only one of several rich food resources. Therefore, the Indians of this region[3] lived in permanent villages near their fishing grounds and had leisure for other things besides the harsh business of supplying food. They were free to become *part-time specialists*. That is, although every man had to be a hunter-fisherman, and every woman a berry picker, still there was also time for the men to be chiefs, medicine men, or craftsmen-artists, and for the women to be weavers of beautiful garments. The culture today is rapidly vanishing.

MATERIALS. Their great source of creative material was the cedar tree. Not only did the men hew it, hollow it for canoes, split it into planks for houses, and carve sculpture from it in their tribal style, all with stone tools, but they had also developed the art of *shaping it by steaming*. And the women twisted the tough, stringy, cedar bark into cord for weaving.

Another source of materials was the wild mountain sheep, whose wool the women spun and wove, and whose horns the men carved into spoons and ladles. The only metal known was copper, which could be used when collected or mined in a pure state, and was therefore scarce and precious. The American Indians had not discovered ways to extract metal from ore.

ART AS A "WEAPON." There may well have been a time when fighting between these tribes was savagely destructive. Probably that is why they learned to avoid it by developing the art of intertribal feasting in a peculiarly personal manner. Such feasts, called *potlatches*, were an actual substitute for warfare. There is a distinction worth noting here: whereas the intertribal feasts of the Maori described earlier served to relax tensions, potlatches kept such tensions steadily mounting. When one chief invited another to a potlatch it was no carefree, happy occasion, but a challenge between chiefs and between tribes. The host's hospitality—the rich food served, the gifts bestowed on the guests, the works of art destroyed in their presence by fire or breakage, and the slaves occasionally murdered before their eyes—were all grim demonstrations of wealth and power. In their way they said, "I and my tribe can afford this extravagance. Can you?" The challenge could only be met, in perhaps a year or two, by a return feast, which had to outdo the first one or bring disgrace to the givers. Much Northwest Indian art was created with an eye to its possible use in such contests, either to heighten the impressive display of the potlatch or to supply works of value and beauty whose destruction would be difficult for another tribe to match.

Deep food tray of cedar wood, 20 inches long, Tsimshian Tribe. The four sides were carved from a single cedar plank, the design on one side and three deep grooves on the other. The grooves were then steamed and the plank bent into a rectangle.

Originally such trays were carved to represent an animal, with head at one end, flanks on the sides and tail at the other. Gradually Indian artists changed the body parts into conventional forms whose interesting arrangement became more important than the realism they replaced.

Museum of Anthropology, University of British Columbia

Lowie Museum of Anthropology, University of California. Photo John Bridgman

Northwest Indian potlatch bowl supported by an eagle totem-image. Kwakiutl Tribe.

THE TOTEM OR TRIBAL SYMBOL. The Canadian Indians, like other primitive people, relied on family ties to hold them together in clans and tribes and to decide who among them should be chiefs. But they made clan and tribe individuality more fiercely dramatic by choosing as a symbol for each a powerful animal or bird. The bear, shark, killer whale, eagle, hawk, and raven thus became images standing for great clans or families. Each group arrogantly displayed carved or painted images of its *totem animal or bird* on its houses, on its *totem poles*, on its tools, weapons, and canoes, and on the blankets and hats worn by its chiefs. No one outside the group might safely wear it.

A totem may be described as an animal or bird which a group claims as its distinguishing symbol. The group often treats living specimens of its totem with respect or awe.

Lowie Museum of Anthropology, University of California, Berkeley

Kwakiutl woman painting totem-image on a chief's hat. Photographed about 1914.

CEREMONIAL COSTUME. Perhaps the most remarkable creations of the Canadian Coast Indians were their astonishingly expressive masks, made with a magic purpose. Medicine men, chiefs, and members of secret societies, when masked and costumed, danced the dances and acted out the sacred dramas in which for a time they *became* the beings from the other world which they were impersonating. To form an impression of the appearance of these masks when in use, we must imagine them being worn by a costumed dancer in violent motion to the accompaniment of chanting or beats on a box drum and seen by flickering firelight.

Ceremonial triple mask. The wearer appears first as a fish. As his dance continues he pulls a cord transforming him into a hawk. At the climax he pulls another cord revealing a human face. Kwakiutl Tribe.

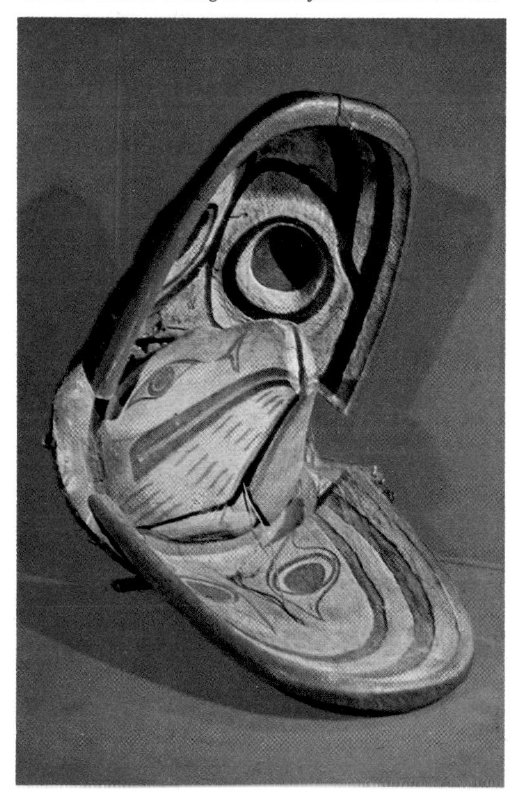

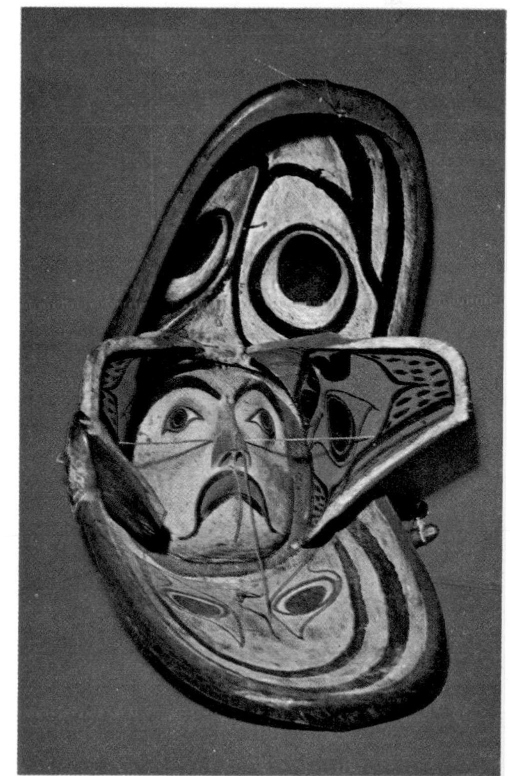

Museum of Natural History, New York. Photos John Bridgman

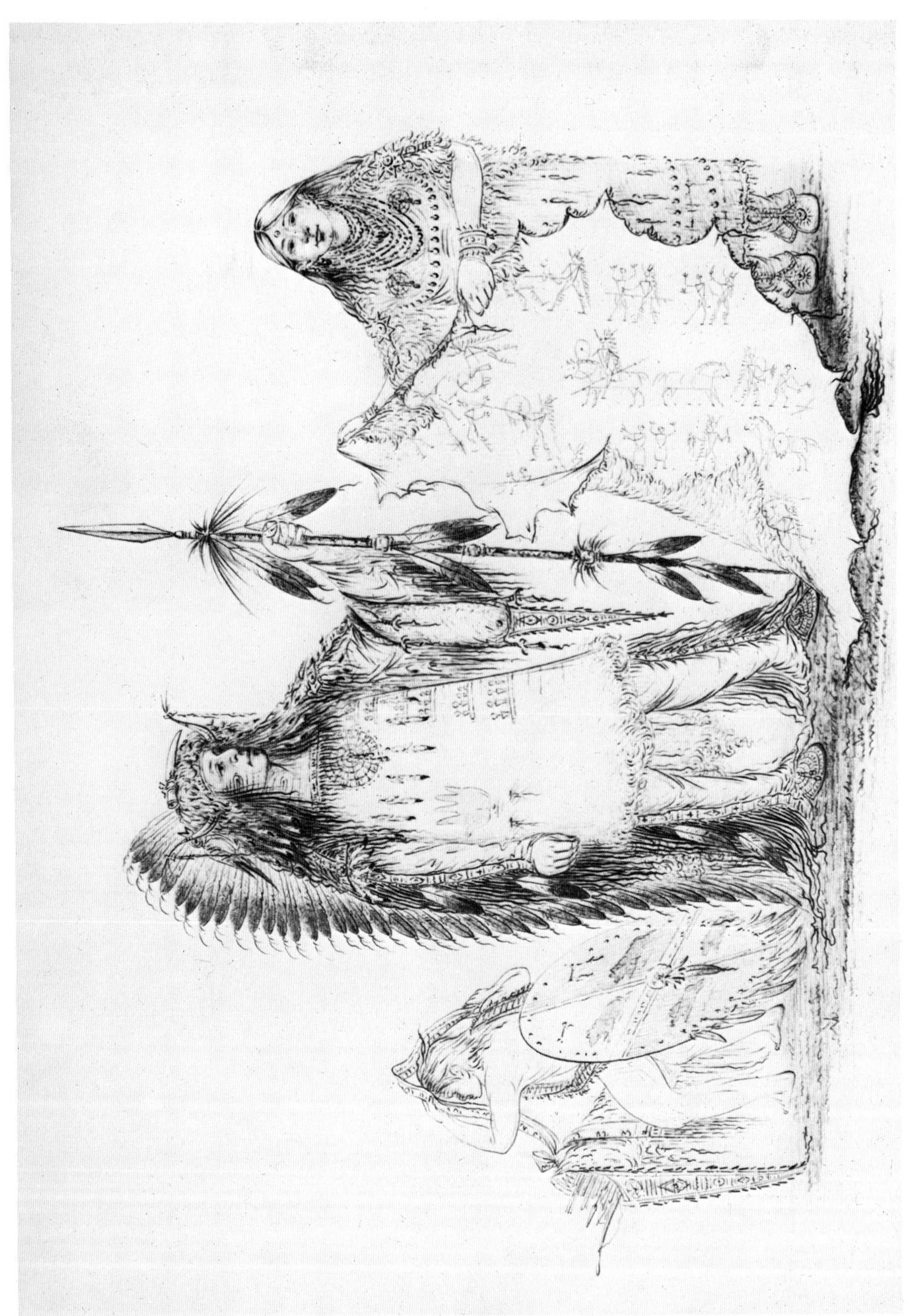

Plains Indian Chief Four Bears, with his squaw, who holds a buffalo hide recording the chief's exploits. Drawing by George Catlin from sketches made in 1832.

New York Public Library

The Indians of the Plains

When Columbus made Europe's first contact with the West Indies in 1492, the Indians of the great Mississippi basin of the American mainland were leading an unspectacular and precarious life as roving hunters and gatherers. When the men hunted, they stalked rabbits, deer, and the formidable buffalo by stealth, patience, and trickery. When they traveled, they trudged on foot, the women carrying the burdens or loading them on poles dragged by their one domesticated animal, the dog.

But when the Spaniards began to colonize northern Mexico, New Mexico, and Arizona at the end of the sixteenth century, introducing horses and cattle, they occasionally used Indians as stable boys and grooms. Little did they realize what they were bringing upon themselves. The Indians, after recovering from their terror at the first sight of horses, and after thinking of them next as animals to be slaughtered for food, quickly learned the art of horse breeding, horse breaking, and riding. Horses and the knowledge of how to use them fanned out northward through the whole prairie west of the Mississippi, spreading from tribe to tribe.

Once he possessed horses, the Plains Indian's life was transformed. He was now the master of the buffalo and could kill in a few days enough to feed himself for a year. We have no records to rely on, but the additional food supply must have made the Plains Indian population mushroom. Eighteenth and early nineteenth century explorers from the East and North found on the plains a people highly conscious of tribal organization under the leadership of chiefs, a probable sign of a large population.

Thus freed, the Plains Indian could use his mount to roam far and wide in search of adventure and the excitement and glory of intertribal warfare. His apparel of hides, adorned with paint, porcupine quillwork, and feathers, assumed a showiness suited to the new life of freedom and adventure. And it was not long before the Indians were striking back at the Spanish colonists, carrying out sweeping raids even into Mexico to plunder and drive off hundreds, perhaps thousands, of horses and cattle. The Spanish advance northward toward the heart of the continent was stopped dead in its tracks, never to be resumed.

It is the dashing Indian of the prairies, with his warbonnet of eagle feathers, his lance, shield, and bow, and his horse of Spanish origin, who has created the image of the "Indian" in the minds of most of the civilized world. And it was in the course of the terrible conflict between Plains Indians and American pioneers, in which the Indians were annihilated or herded onto reservations, a beaten remnant, that the image became widespread. But it fails to convey the Plains Indians' other creative achievements in what might be called cultural expression. These were the development of the great annual ceremonials of the sun dance, and, at their history's end, of the tragic, self-destructive ghost-dance cult.

Smithsonian Institution, George Catlin Collection

A Sioux encampment on the upper Missouri River. In the foreground women are drying buffalo meat and stretching buffalo hides. Painting by George Catlin, 1832. Catlin did for the Indians of the North American continent what John James Audubon did for the birds and mammals of its eastern half. He spent years traveling from one tribe to another, recording a way of life which the march of another civilization has since completely destroyed.

America Needs Its Indians

The American Indians, who once possessed the total breadth of this land, find themselves today crowded onto 2.9 per cent of it, much of that fraction so poor in quality that no white man wants it. Their poverty is extreme, and death at all ages from preventable diseases is enormously higher than for non-Indians. Worse perhaps than material wretchedness are the attitudes of the powerful alien civilization which surrounds them, attitudes of hostility, contempt, or indifference, as expressed from time to time by the breaking of time-honored treaties and, even in the recent past, by acts of annihilation. Particularly insulting is the patronizing view that American Indians must be "brought into the mainstream of American life" on the assumption that their own culture is of no comparative importance.

In the face of such overwhelming odds a younger generation of Indians is emerging who have assessed white American culture and found it in certain respects seriously wanting. They are organizing themselves across tribal lines and are fighting, by all lawful means possible, for the preservation of their own ancient culture. They have found in traditional Indian values a possible cure for the malfunctioning of a society which constantly destroys or pollutes the natural world, even at the risk of its own survival, in order to achieve short-range goals of immediate profit or temporary enjoyment. The thoughtful Indian recognizes that such a society desperately needs to seek an active harmony with nature, rather than new ways to exploit it, and that it needs to discover a sense of reverence for all forms of life rather than merely to dismiss those other than human as "lower." Is it any wonder that Indians should fight for the preservation of a culture in which such values of harmony and reverence are central?

Horsemen of the Hidatsa Tribe surround part of buffalo herd. Painting by George Catlin, 1832.

Smithsonian Institution, George Catlin Collection

TERREEOBOO, KING of OWHYHEE, bringing PRESENTS to CAPT.N COOK.

Cook's Voyages, London, 1785

Hawaiian king on an official voyage, as seen in about 1780 by an English artist accompanying the explorer Captain Cook.

The Peoples of Polynesia

The islands of Polynesia in the Pacific Ocean are thinly scattered across an enormous triangle, each side over 4000 miles long. The southwest corner is New Zealand, the southeast is Easter Island. The Hawaiian Islands, our own fiftieth state, lie at the apex. About 200 years ago the British explorer Captain Cook was the first European to notice that the natives of this enormous spread of islands could understand each other in conversation. And it is now clear that they were and are united in other significant ways: by the foods they cultivate,[4] by their customs, by their myths, and above all by their physical appearance. They are descended from some of the world's greatest sailors and explorers, and they still keep alive the memory of the daring voyages these heroes made centuries ago in double canoes from island to island, across vast stretches of ocean. The starting point seems to have been Tahiti, roughly in the triangle's center. Whence the Polynesians came before that no one can be sure, but it was probably Indonesia, 2000 years ago or more.

Through long separation the people of each Polynesian island group developed a local culture or way of life somewhat of its own. The New Zealand Maori were by far the greatest wood carvers and architects. The Easter Islanders were the most impressive stone cutters, even though their statues were monotonously alike. The Hawaiians were the most highly developed in farming and in the art of government.

The Art of Ancient Hawaii

CEREMONIAL COSTUME: FEATHERWORK. When first discovered by explorers in the late eighteenth century, the Hawaiians were passing beyond a stage of government by chiefs into one of rule by kings, a political distinction to be discussed in Chapter 3. The power of a king is greater than that of a chief. He is consequently surrounded by more symbols of this power—more pomp and decoration. The Hawaiians relied on the feathers of rare birds to provide the brilliant materials for this kingly display. The creation of feather cloaks, feather-covered wicker helmets, and the great feather plumes which were borne in a king's presence, was an art in itself.

TAPA CLOTH MAKING AND DECORATION. When the original colonists from Tahiti reached Hawaii by double canoe, perhaps around the year 1350 A.D., they brought with them several domestic plants, among them the paper mulberry. The warm, mild climate of Hawaii was right for the cultivation of this tree and for the light clothing made from its bark. The Hawaiians gradually developed the making of *tapa cloth* to a higher level than any other Polynesian group.

Tapa cloth, made by soaking and beating the inner bark of young mulberry saplings into a thin, tough, flexible paper, was an art practised by women, in special houses sacred to Lauhuki, the spirit-being who gave tapa cloth makers their special power. Beating was done with blocks marked with a fine design, giving the cloth a patterned texture, visible only when held up to the light. The cloth was then bleached in a nearby drying yard until "clearer than the light of the moon, whiter than the snow upon the mountains."

The cloth was then ready for decoration. It could easily be dyed, and Hawaiian women developed a greater variety of dye colors than any other Polynesian group. Red, pink, yellow, green, pale blue, violet, gray, and black were available, often in several shades and varieties. Sometimes a tapa cloth would be dyed and then laid on another undyed sheet, and the two pounded till they became one piece, colored on one surface, white on the other.

But the most beautiful method of decoration was achieved by block printing, a craft watched over, so the Hawaiian women believed, by Laahana, the spirit who gave them this art. The final touch of elegance was given to the finest printed tapa cloths by mixing native perfume with the dye. Thus, to quote a Hawaiian of another generation, "It becomes a fragrant thing with a soft pleasant odour like a cool morning."

Although tapa cloth making, dyeing, and printing were all women's arts, that of making the tools was work for men. They shaped the wooden beaters, anvils, and dye-blocks, and chipped out the stone dye-bowls which the women then put to use. This beautiful craft is now dead, in Hawaii at least, and has been for years.

Initiation mask of carved wood. Tschokue Tribe, Kasai Province of the Congo. Just as the favorite visual art form of the Bushmen seems to have been drawing and painting, so that of the more complex societies of central and western Africa tends to be sculpture.

Royal Belgian Museum of Central Africa, Tervuren

On facing page, collection of embroidered pile cloth from the Congo, Central Africa.

The Arts of Western and Central Africa

The people of Western and Central Africa, south of the Sahara Desert and near the Equator, live under conditions which vary vastly from one region to another: in one place dense rain forests, in another immense parched prairies, sun-scorched by day and freezing by night, in still others land inviting to farmers. In consequence the people have adapted themselves over the centuries to a wide variety of living patterns, each suited to its own locality. In the rain forests hunting hordes can still be found. In more open country, crop planting, the raising of native cattle, or a combination of both, supplement or largely replace hunting. Here the people live in tribes or in more complex groupings which show an evolution beyond the tribal state. In still other regions an *agrarian economy* is possible, depending entirely on crop raising[5] and domesticated animals. This kind of economy, and a form of society (the *kingdom*) which it tends to make possible, are discussed in Chapter 3. The ancient kingdoms of Africa bore names such as Ashanti, Benin, Dahomey, Ghana, and Mali, some of which are still associated, closely or loosely, with certain parts of the land.

Throughout this vast complex region the people have long practiced all the crafts which we have so far described: house building, carving in wood, stone, bone and horn, bark-cloth making, weaving, pottery. In the more complex societies still other kinds of craftsmen have been well known for centuries: skillful ironsmiths, casters of the alloys brass and bronze, workers in gold. And in the heart of each kingdom was its capital town where dwelt the king, a living sacred symbol of the kingdom's power, surrounded by pomp and display involving not one but many arts: costume creation, pageantry, dancing, music.

One of these kingdoms, with a tradition continuing unbroken to the present, had its capital at Ife (EE-feh); see the map. The wealth pouring in to kings of ancient Ife as tribute from surrounding conquered tribes flowed out again as pay for artists whose task it was to preserve the likeness of these rulers, generation after generation, in enduring images of brass and fired clay. Today many of these remarkable portraits are preserved in a museum founded by His Highness Adesoji Aderemi, the last king (or *Oni*) of Ife, who is now a citizen of Nigeria. Through his permission two of these noble heads are shown on page 6. Their age is believed to be about 700 years. On the page facing them are shown two royal heads of sculptured stone from Chartres Cathedral in northern France, created at about the same time.

The African kingdoms, like the other social and political organizations of Africa, have suffered either mutilation or destruction at the hands of European colonizers, especially during the nineteenth century. Out of the resulting chaos the new self-governing nations of Africa, their boundaries often cutting arbitrarily across old social and political lines, are now emerging in a mixed atmosphere of suffering and hope. This great surge into a more modern but not necessarily better civilization is leading to the creation of a new African art. But this art in its turn is developing from what is already there, Africa's many-sided traditional art, remarkable for its combination

Ceremonial stool belonging to a chief of the Baluba Tribe in the Congo.

Smithsonian Institution

Linden Museum, Stuttgart

of bold simplicity and subtlety. The inspiration for this traditional art has sprung from belief in magic, from reverence for ancestors and sacred rulers, and from membership in secret societies. That of the new will stem from other sources, created by life in increasingly industrialized states each governed by some modern form of democracy or dictatorship.

Lowie Museum of Anthropology, University of California, Berkeley

Fertility doll from the ancient kingdom of Ashanti, West Africa. Resemblance to the human figure becomes symbolic only. Height 1 ft.

The traditional arts of Africa are also inspiring some developments thousands of miles away, as Americans of African descent are rediscovering their rich heritage after centuries of believing they had none. They no longer feel compelled to lean on the European-American culture which surrounds them, but are free to combine it as their taste directs with the best that Africa has to offer, knowing that over the centuries their ancestors there created the forms of art, music, and dress which were best suited to themselves, physically, emotionally, and spiritually. Nor is this a mere copying process on the part of Afro-Americans, but an adaptive, inventive one, from which new forms of art, and perhaps entire new arts, promise to grow.

Some Characteristics of Farming-Hunting Societies

Most important social unit: the family. This is not only the first refuge of every man, woman, and child, but kinship also becomes the force holding together the much larger *extended family or clan,* which is a cluster of relatives.

Largest social group: the *tribe,* or group of two or more clans, usually held together by blood relationship (real or imagined). The tribe is customarily located in permanent farming-villages, scattered over the tribe's clearly defined territory.

Leadership and government: usually centered in a *chief,* who organizes tribal working teams, settles disputes, plans large enterprises, and sets policies of war or peace with other tribes. He is more a leader than a ruler, usually relying for advice on a council of older men or heads of families, and on popular opinion. Sometimes two or more chiefs share the burden of government (for example, the "war" chiefs and the "talking" chiefs of Samoa).

Means of getting food: laborious farming with crude tools supplements hunting, fishing, and gathering, but does not replace them completely. Nobody is entirely free from the burden of getting food. But the effects of farming are many and great: (a) a larger population is supported; (b) life ceases to be wandering, haphazard, and based on the need of the moment; it becomes settled, organized, and based on planning; (c) some gifted or privileged persons, such as chiefs, priest-magicians, or artist-craftsmen, are free to become part-time specialists.

Attitude toward food: same as for hunting societies. (See page 30.)

Attitude toward human life: (a) *within one's own tribe,* life is respected somewhat as in hunting societies, with one exception. Respect for life often increases with increase in rank. Ceremonies attending the birth, marriage, and death of chiefs are often more elaborate than those for lesser persons. (b) *Outside one's own tribe,* persons easily become the object of ridicule, contempt, capture, or murder.

Attitude toward children: in many tribes, children lead a carefree, indulged life until the training time for initiation into the tribal societies begins. (See page 30.) Examples of this are found in many African and American Indian tribes. In others, preparation for adulthood somewhat resembles our own, that is, a long process of education without initiation into societies, for example, the Maori.

Knowledge: see page 30 for full description. Since tribal societies are much larger and more stable than hunting hordes, more knowledge is transmitted more reliably from one generation to the next. For example, tribal history is sometimes carefully preserved for long periods. But all such transmission has to be from memory and by word of mouth.

In *technical knowledge*, tribal societies are far advanced. Simple farming, food preservation, weaving, pottery, carpentry, architecture, and the creation of objects from polished stone are all largely or totally unknown to hunter-fishermen. Such an advance requires *part-time specialists,* who can devote a large part of their time to just one occupation. Perhaps most important of all is the tribal man's advanced knowledge of how to use planning and organization, both in his life and in the things he creates.

Rites of passage: in the tribal stage of human culture we find highly developed ceremonies which celebrate the most crucial moments in human life—birth, recognition of puberty, marriage, and death. Each of these moments marks a transition or *passage* from one state of existence to another: from lifelessness to life; from childhood to manhood or womanhood; from the single state to family responsibility; and from life back again to the lifeless state. They are therefore commonly known as rituals or *rites* of passage. As practiced in today's urban world, rites of passage (weddings and funerals, for instance) still contain traces of customs whose origins go back to tribal times. Thus there exists a thread of continuity with our ancient past, making, in a sense, all men, whether past or present, one.

Superstition: for a description of the role played in primitive living by a belief in magic, especially as it applies to medicine men or shamans, who specialize in magic, and to artist-craftsmen, whose lives are dominated by it, see pages 45–47.

Religion: the worship of gods, which tends to involve the emotion of reverence, appears in tribal societies, but is crowded into the background by the practice of magic, which involves to a more intense degree the emotion of fear. The distinction between religion and magic will be described more clearly in the next chapter.

Carved wood drum from the ancient African kingdom of Benin, now part of Nigeria. Height about 32 in.

University of Pennsylvania Museum

Collection of David Ames, Mill Valley, California

A ruler of the kingdom of Fon on an official journey. Cast brass piece from Dahomey. Length 22 in.

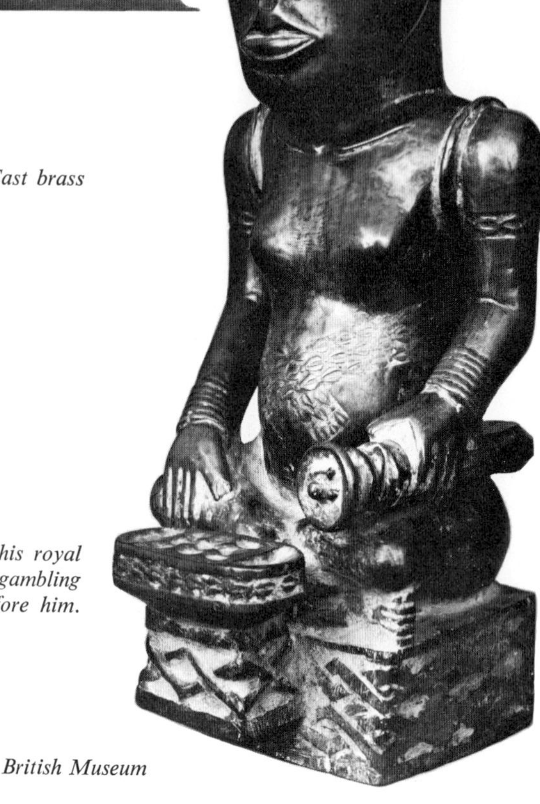

Shamba Bololongo, seated and wearing the insignia of his royal rank. He ruled from 1600 to 1620. In order to discourage gambling in his kingdom he invented a game of skill, shown before him. Carved and polished wood, Central Congo.

British Museum

PRIMITIVE WAYS OF KEEPING LARGE SOCIAL GROUPS UNITED

Family ties, close or remote: this is the basis of tribal unity everywhere.

Need for cooperation in obtaining food: this is a "must" in a complex process like farming, and is also needed in hunting, fishing, and gathering.

Initiation ceremonies into tribal societies: the severe training and awe-inspiring initiations through which young persons must pass to become members can "shape" them for life as loyal and obedient tribe members.

Dramatic, easily visible symbols, standing for the whole tribe: for these each tribe member can easily feel loyalty, devotion, and even worship. Such symbols take different forms, such as: (a) a famous (or imaginary) ancestor who founded the tribe and to whom every tribe member is supposedly related; images of such ancestors are often placed in a community house, meeting place, or shrine (for example, among the Maori); (b) a totem animal or bird, often prominently displayed on houses, clothing, weapons, etc. (for example, the Canadian Indians); (c) a ruling chief, whose personal life and health are sometimes treated as sacred symbols of the life and health of the whole tribe (for example, in Central Africa).

What Does the Art of Tribal Societies Mean to Us?

The Hunter-Farmer's Use of Space

The Bushman paintings of Chapter 1 suggest that the men who made them gave no thought to filling a limited space. They had plenty of cave wall. They started drawing wherever the surface was flat and easy to reach, and they stopped whenever they had come to the end of what they had in mind. The dynamic rhythm which is so strong in their work was probably caused by the muscular action of a well-coordinated man happily putting down pictures as they came to him, making things up as he went along.

But a glance at the illustrations of the present chapter shows something entirely different. Here we find that the space is not, like a cave wall, limitless, as if generously provided by nature. Instead, space has become valuable, something to think about carefully before a work of art is even started. Every object, whether house, canoe, statue, ceremonial mask, tool, or area for a sand painting, owes its shape and size to frugal human thinking.

This thoughtfulness for the use of limited space is perhaps one cause for a certain rigidity in the art of tribal societies, especially sculpture. Figures are seldom in motion, but stand or sit with tense limbs and staring or squinting eyes, almost as if bound to one spot.

Human figure reduced to severe geometric symplicity. Height 33 in. From the Caroline Islands.

Non-Recognition of Personal Differences

Besides the thoughtful use of space and the rigidity of human forms, there is often still another peculiarity—a sameness between figures intended for the same purpose, even though the figures represent persons who must have looked unlike. Consider, for instance, the image of Shamba Bololongo. This is a historical personage, one of a succession of rulers, each of whom, according to traditional practice, was commemorated with an image carved by a distinguished craftsman. A number of these images survive, and all, to the casual observer, look practically the same. When one looks closer the only real difference turns out to be some object the image is holding or (as in the example shown) is placed before him. It was this object which interested the sculptor as distinguishing one chief from another. Differences in features or body build were unimportant to him. In the same way, the ancestor images of central African tribes look practically identical until we learn to look for differences in tattooing pattern on the body or face. This, not personal distinctiveness, seems to have been the important thing to remember in one's ancestor. Otherwise the traditional tribal style dominates the image.

Tentative Explanations

How can we explain these strange practices? The careful use of space, the thoughtful choice of over-all form, suggests perhaps that space is something of which the farmer-hunter has been compelled to become conscious. The back-breaking labor of tilling the soil for a patch of yams, taro, or other food plant drives the shape of that patch, as it were, into the tiller's brain through his body. And once his crop is planted he may not wander from it for long, as a hunter can. Space, while freeing him from some of his hunger, exacts a penalty by holding him prisoner. Perhaps that is why primitive figures practically never run, walk or dance, but stand motionless.

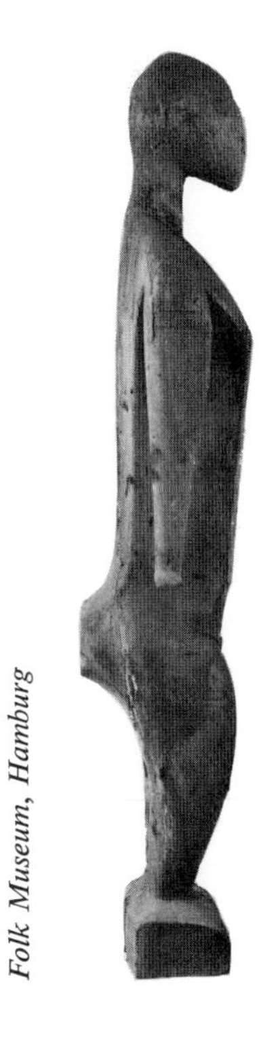

Folk Museum, Hamburg

But surely there is still another reason for this rigidity. The complex living-pattern by which a tribe survives rests upon common practices and beliefs which unite the members in cooperation and mutual understanding. These practices and beliefs are often drilled into each member from childhood with such dramatic intensity (through initiation rites and the training that goes before them) that individual differences become submerged, or never even have a chance to become important. So it is not just reliance on limited space, but the nature of tribal life itself, which probably explains the rigid pose, and the usually complete absence of distinct individuality, noticeable in works of tribal art representing persons. Differences that do exist (such as tattooing marks) are those placed on the person by the tribe. The highly individual portrait busts from thirteenth-century Ife already mentioned, suggest that they come from another level of culture, which will be considered in Chapter 3.

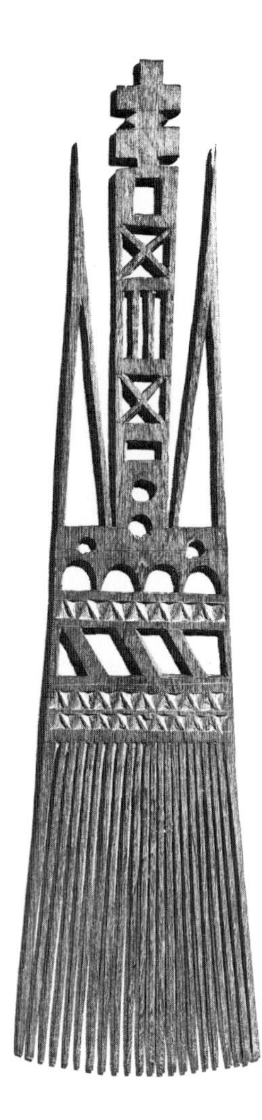

Royal Museum, Edinburgh

Comb from Polynesia.

Object Design in Tribal Societies

Let us next notice how the hunter-farmer *designed* objects, once he had carefully chosen their over-all size and shape. He knew nothing of geometry as a science. It had not yet been conceived. But in his work we can see him groping his way toward it. Even if he did not know what geometry was; *he clearly had a feeling for geometrical shapes.* He was forever using the circle, cylinder, square, rectangle, and other geometric forms as the basis for designing and decorating objects.

But the design which he used even more commonly than shapes like these was *the plan of his own body.* Man and most other familiar living creatures are built on the principle of *bilateral symmetry. Any object which can be divided into two identical but opposite, mirror-image parts by one intersecting plane, and by one only, is defined as bilaterally symmetrical.*

Language such as this would be lost on a farmer-hunter. It is our own way of talking, not his. But his work shows that he was just as capable of thinking of these things as we are. He probably thought, however, in terms of actions and flat or solid shapes, not words. And instead of using an imaginary plane as a dividing instrument, he would probably have preferred to think of a knife.

Man as a bilaterally symmetrical structure. One intersecting plane, and only one, can divide him into mirror-image parts.

Leonardo da Vinci

Lowie Museum of Anthropology, University of California, Berkeley

Navaho blanket, woven of natural-colored wools.

Why are we sure that he could recognize bilateral symmetry as a plan? Because, over and over again, he separates it from the place he found it, namely himself and animals, and uses it as a plan when making totally unlifelike things. That is, he *abstracts* it from one setting and applies it elsewhere. (See the accompanying illustrations for examples of this.)

Abstract (Latin origin: *abs* = from, *tractus* = drawn or taken) is a word much used in the art world, and with more than one meaning. So in this book it will appear in different places, and with different usages. Here we use it in its most literal sense, *to take from*. When we look at the five shapes in the illustrations, we find that there is just one thing they have in common: there is one idea we can *take from* or *abstract from* all of them. This is that each is identical on both sides of an imaginary center line, called an *axis*.

These five objects have just two things in common: all are bilaterally symmetrical and none is lifelike. Primitive man could have discovered bilateral symmetry as a basis for designing such objects only by observing it in his own body or in that of other living creatures.

A great many primitive bilaterally symmetrical objects are not so severely unlifelike as these. By being at least partially lifelike they betray the origin of their inspiration.

Breast ornament, carved wood inlaid with shell, from the Solomon Islands, Melanesia.

Australian Museum, Sydney

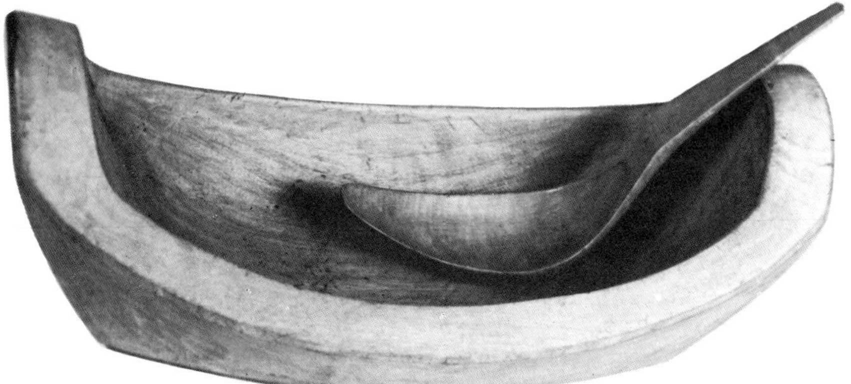

Northwest Indian food dish of cedar wood, and spoon of bighorn sheep horn.

Museum of Anthropology, University of British Columbia

De Young Memorial Museum, San Francisco

Yokuts Indian coiled basket, from Tulare County, California.

Advances in Decorative Rhythm: Weaving, Pottery, and Tapa Cloth

The invention of weaving led naturally to experimenting in decorative rhythms. Why? Because weaving is a mechanical process which depends upon the same act being steadily repeated. Therefore, it is fairly easy for the weaver to vary the act at regular intervals, by introducing thread of a different color, by skipping warp threads, and so on. And it thus became easy for primitive weavers to convert a plain blanket, mat, or basket into something more attractive.

Allover decorative rhythm obviously covers the whole woven surface. But *linear decorative rhythm* does not, and to apply it is therefore a challenge to one's imagination. Where will it be placed? Which part or parts of the object deserve the emphasis which a linear rhythm gives? How will the total surface of the object be divided between plainness and decoration? Note how these problems are solved in the basket shown.

Pottery making also leads naturally to the use of decorative rhythm. The easiest way to decorate a pot (and one of the most effective) is to place it in front of you, slowly turn it, and, as you do, make some kind of regular scratch or impress in the soft clay. The same can be done by painting with *slip*, or colored clay. This automatically produces a linear rhythm circling the pot. But the *selection* of where on the pot the rhythm shall be placed is not automatic. It is a matter for discrimination.

The most complex primitive method of applying decorative rhythm was perhaps that invented by the Hawaiians: block printing on tapa cloth. Before the work of decoration could even begin, dyes had to be invented and printing blocks had to be designed and carved.

Note: From this point on we shall call decorative rhythm by a shorter name, *pattern*.

Texture Becomes Important

Texture is another decorative effect which is developed automatically from primitive technical methods. The word comes from the Latin verb *texere*, to weave, and was once entirely associated with that craft and referred to the meshed quality of a woven surface. It has since been extended, so that at present *texture denotes the distinctive quality of any surface.*

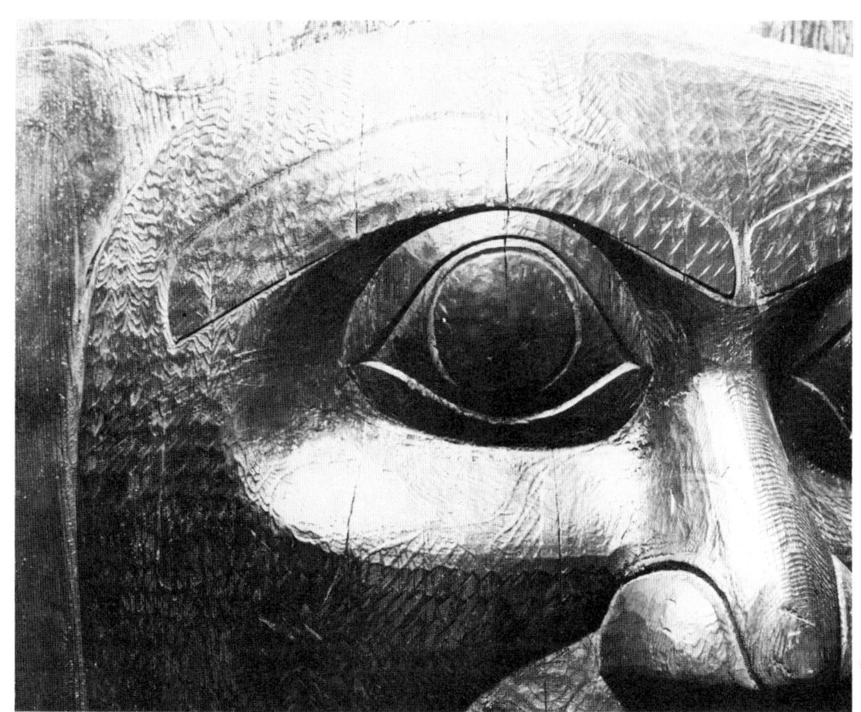

Museum of Anthropology, University of British Columbia

Northwest Indian carving, showing texture created by rhythmic adze marks.

NOTES

[1] Raymond Firth, *The Economics of the New Zealand Maori* (Wellington, New Zealand, 1959), p. 334.

[2] The most important of these tribes are the Zuni and the Hopi. The Navajos are of very different origin, but live in the neighboring territory and have been strongly influenced by Pueblo culture.

[3] The important tribes are the Tlingit, Haida, Tsimshian, Kwakiutl, Bella Coola, Nootka, and Salish.

[4] The coconut palm and the starchy taroroot (from which poi is made) were apparently spread throughout the Pacific Islands by early explorers and colonists traveling by double canoe.

[5] Centuries ago the farmers of West Africa developed several food sources which have more lately benefited the world at large. Of these the most familiar are sorghum grain and the watermelon.

BOOKS ON HUNTING-FARMING SOCIETIES, AND THEIR ART

GENERAL

Primitive Man, D. Fraser (Doubleday, New York, 1962). One of the Doubleday *Arts of Man Series.*

Primitive Art, L. Adam (Pelican paperback, 1949).

Primitive Art, Erwin O. Christensen (Viking Press, New York, 1955), covers Africa, the American continents, and Paleolithic Europe only.

Primitive Art, P. S. Wingert (Oxford University Press, New York, 1962).

History of Mankind, Vol. I, J. Hawks and Sir L. Woolley (Harper and Row, New York, 1963).

Folk Art of Primitive People, H. T. Bossert (Praeger, New York, 1955), survey of the applied arts of Africa, Asia, Australia, Oceania, North, and Central, and South America.

Larousse Encyclopedia of Prehistoric and Ancient Art (Prometheus Press, New York, 1957).

Shamanism: The Beginnings of Art, A. Lommel (McGraw-Hill, New York, 1967).

The Epic of Man, by the editors of *Life*, pages 54–65 and 256–269.

BOOKS ON THE AMERICAN INDIAN

For information on the different Indian tribes of North America, see the University of Oklahoma Series on the American Indian, begun in 1932 and still growing.

For further information on the art of the American Indians (with material on Mexico and Central and South America often included), see the following material.

Indian Art of the Americas, LeRoy H. Appleton (Scribners, New York, 1950).

The Eagle, The Jaguar and The Serpent: Indian Art of the Americas I. North America: Alaska, Canada, the United States, M. Covarrubias (Knopf, New York, 1954).

Indian Art in America: the Arts and Crafts of the North American Indian, F. J. Dockstader (N.Y. Graphic Society, Greenwich, Connecticut, 1961).

Indian Art of the United States, F. H. Douglas and R. D'Harnoncourt (Museum of Modern Art, New York, 1941).

NORTHWEST COAST INDIANS

Indians of the Northwest Coast, E. Gunther (Taylor Museum, Colorado Springs, 1951).

Art of the Northwest Coast Indians, B. Inverarity (University of California Press, Berkeley, California, 1950).

Native Arts of the Pacific Northwest from the Rasmussen Collection of the Portland Art Museum (Stanford University Press, California, 1949).

To Make My Name Good: A Reexamination of the Southern Kwakiutl Potlatch, P. Drucker and R. Heizer (University of California Press, 1967).

Patterns of Culture: A Study of the Civilizations of the Zuni Indians, the Natives of Dobu, and the Kwakiutl Indians, R. Benedict (Houghton Mifflin, Boston and New York, 1934), obtainable as paperback. This book contains no illustrations but gives a dramatic description of the cultures of both the Pueblo and Northwest Coast Indians.

PUEBLO INDIANS

American Indian Painting of the Southwest and Plains Area, D. Dutton (University of New Mexico Press, Albuquerque, 1968).

The Pottery of Santo Domingo Pueblo, K. M. Chapman (Laboratory of Anthropology, Santa Fe, New Mexico, 1936).

Pottery of the Southwestern Indians, P. E. Goddard, Science Guide No. 73 (American Museum of Natural History, New York, 1945).
Navajo Weaving, its Technique and History, C. A. Amsden (University of New Mexico Press, Albuquerque, 1949).
The Cultivation and Weaving of Cotton in the Prehistoric Southwestern United State, K. P. Kent (American Philosophical Society, Philadelphia, November, 1957).
Pueblo Gods & Myths, H. Tyler (Oklahoma University Press, 1964).
Ceremonial Costumes of the Pueblo Indians, Their Evolution, Fabrication, and Significance in the Prayer Drama, V. M. Roediger (University of California Press, Berkeley, California, 1961).
Dancing Gods: Indian Ceremonials of New Mexico and Arizona, E. Ferguson (University of New Mexico Press, Albuquerque, New Mexico, 1957). This book not only describes a great variety of dances, but also the condition of life under which the Indians somehow continue to keep them alive.
Navaho Witchcraft, C. Kluckhohn (Beacon BP243).
Beautiful on the Earth, M. E. Schevill (Hazel Dreis Editions, Santa Fe, 1947).

PLAINS INDIANS

America's Western Frontiers, J. A. Hawgood (Knopf, New York, 1967). A summary of the history of the trans-Mississippi west from pre-Columbian times to the present.
The Indian and the Horse, F. G. Roe (University of Oklahoma Press, 1955).
Plains Indians Painting, J. C. Ewers (Stanford University Press, 1939).
Black Elk Speaks, Being the Life Story of a Holy Man of the Oglala Sioux, as told to J. G. Neihardt, illustrated by Standing Bear (Morrow, New York, 1932).
The Treaty of Medicine Lodge, D. C. Jones (University of Oklahoma Press, 1967).
The Ghost Dance Religion and the Sioux Outbreak of 1890, J. Mooney (Phoenix paperback, p. 176).

INDIANS TODAY

The Indian, America's Unfinished Business, W. A. Brophy & S. D. Aberle (University of Oklahoma Press, 1967).
The New Indians, S. Steiner (Harper & Row, New York, 1968).

FILMS

Painting with Sand, sound, color, 10 minutes (Encyclopedia Britannica Films). Follows the creation of a Navajo sand painting from grinding of the colors to final destruction of the painting at the end of the healing ceremony.
The Loon's Necklace, sound, color, 10 minutes (Encyclopedia Britannica Films). Northwcst Coast Indian legend told entirely through the medium of authentic ceremonial masks and costumes.
Pueblo Arts, sound, color, 11 minutes (International Film Bureau, Inc.).

BOOKS ON PACIFIC AND AFRICAN PEOPLES, AND THEIR ART

POLYNESIA

The Art of the South Islands, Including Australia and New Zealand, A. Buehler and others (Art of the World Series, Crown, New York, 1960). This book gives some impression, among other things, of the startlingly fantastic art of New Guinea, omitted from this chapter.
The Maori as He Was, E. Best (Wellington, New Zealand, 1952).

The New Zealand Maori in Color, H. Dansy (A. H. & A. W. Reed, Wellington, New Zealand, 1963).
Aku Aku, The Secret of Easter Island, T. Heyerdahl (Allen & Urwin, London, 1958).
Arts and Crafts of Hawaii, P. H. Buck (Bishop Museum, Honolulu, 1957).
The Island Civilizations of Polynesia, R. C. Suggs (New American Library, New York, 1960), paperback.
Vikings of the Pacific, P. H. Buck (paperback, University of Chicago, Phoenix Book).
Arts of the South Seas, R. Linton and P. S. Wingert (Museum of Modern Art, New York, 1946).

FILMS

American Samoa, sound, color, 17 minutes (Paul Hoeffler Productions).
Polynesian Culture (*Samoa*), sound, color, 21 minutes (Arthur Barr Productions).

AFRICA, WEST AND CENTRAL

African Design, M. Trowell (Praeger, New York, 1960); 75 plates cover every aspect of African artistic production, grouped by medium and technique.
Africa, the Art of the Negro Peoples, E. Leuzinger (Art of the World Series, McGraw-Hill, New York, 1960).
African Sculpture, L. Segy (Dover, New York, 1958), paperback.
African Folk Tales and Sculpture (Bollingen Series No. XXXII, Pantheon, New York, 1952).
Traditional Art of the African Nations (Museum of Primitive Art, New York, 1961), paperback.
African Art, W. Schmalenbach (Macmillan, New York, 1954).
Ife in the History of West African Sculpture, F. Willett (McGraw-Hill, New York, 1967).
The Art of Benin, P. J. C. Dark (Chicago Natural History Museum, 1962), paperback.
Religion and Art in Ashanti, R. S. Rattray (Oxford, 1937). Chapters 23–28 describe traditional West African weaving, wood carving, pottery making, and lost-wax casting in bronze. Another chapter is entitled "The Aesthetic of Ashanti."
Traditional Nigerian art: *Nigerian Images: The Splendor of African Sculpture*, W. Fagg (Praeger, New York, 1963), 144 illustrations.
Modern Nigerian art: *Art in Nigeria*, U. Beier (Cambridge, 1960), paperback.
African Mud Sculpture, U. Beier (Cambridge, 1962).
Panoply of Ghana: Ornamental Art in Ghanian Tradition and Culture, A. A. Y. Kyerematen (Praeger, New York, 1964).
Africa, Its People and Their Culture History, G. P. Murdock (McGraw-Hill, New York, 1959).
A History of Africa to the Nineteenth Century, B. Davidson (Doubleday paperback, 1966).
The Life of a South African Tribe, H. Junod (University Books, New Hyde Park, New York, 1962). 2 vols; vol. 2 recommended.
African Political Systems, M. Fortas and E. E. Evans-Pritchard, ed. (Oxford, 5th ed., 1955); African systems of government prior to colonization.
Women of Tropical Africa, D. Paume (University of California Press); their traditional stabilizing role.
A History of Ghana, W. E. Ward (Praeger, New York, 1963).
The Story of Nigeria, M. Crowder (Praeger, New York, 1962.
Between the Sunlight and the Thunder: The Wildlife of Kenya, N. Simon (Houghton-Mifflin, New York, 1964); the modern condition of animals and man; illustrated.

BOOKS ON OTHER PRIMITIVE PEOPLES

NEW GUINEA

Art and Life in New Guinea, R. Firth (New York Studio Publication, 1936).
The High Valley, K. E. Read (Scribners, New York, 1965); tribal life today in central New Guinea, illustrated.

FARMER-HUNTERS OF SOUTH AMERICA

Hombu: Indian Life in the Brazilian Jungle, H. Schultz (MacMillan, New York, 1962); chiefly photographs; gives a remarkably intimate impression of tribal life.

PREHISTORIC EUROPE

The Dawn of European Civilization, V. Gordon Childe (Kegan Paul, rev. ed., 1947).
The Megalith Builders of Western Europe, G. Daniel (Pelican paperback A533).
Stonehenge Decoded, G. S. Hawkins and J. B. White (Dell paperback 8287, 1965).
I Built a Stone Age House, H. O. Hansen (John Day, New York, 1964).
The Petroglyphs of Siberia, A. P. Okladnikov (Scientific American, August, 1969, pp. 75–82).

FILMS

Buma, sound, color, 11 minutes (Encyclopedia Britannica Films). Presents the overall function of sculpture in African life.
The Stone Age, Beginning of History Series, sound, black and white, 20 minutes (Bailey Films).

IDENTIFICATION OF ILLUSTRATIONS I–X IN THE PROLOGUE

I Ben Shahn (1890–1970): *Father and Child*, 1946. Museum of Modern Art, New York.

II Baldassare Estense (1440?–1502): *Ugo de Sacrati and Family*, about 1480. Alte Pinakothek, Munich.

III Egyptian, fourth dynasty: funerary statue of Senu, priest of Cheops, and his wife. Found at Giza, near site of the Pyramid of Cheops. Lowie Museum of Anthropology, University of California, Berkeley. Photo John Bridgman.

IV Northwest Indian, Salish tribe: mourning figures, nineteenth century. Museum of Anthropology, University of British Columbia.

V Henry Moore (1898–): *Family Group*, 1945–49. Museum of Modern Art, New York.

VI Athenian (from Rhamnos): gravestone, about 330 B.C. National Museum, Athens. Copyright German Archeological Institute, Athens.

VII Pablo Picasso (1881–): *In the Cafe*, 1902. Collection of Mr. and Mrs. Lee A. Ault, New York.

VIII Antoine Watteau (1684–1721): *The Love Lesson*. New Palace, Potsdam.

IX French, thirteenth century: heads of king and queen from west portal of Chartres Cathedral. Marburg Photoarchiv.

X Kingdom of Ife, Equatorial Africa, thirteenth century: heads of former rulers (or *onis*). Collection of Sir Adesoji Aderemi, present Oni of Ife.

Menkauré, a king of Egypt's fourth dynasty, builder of her second largest pyramid. "What is the King of Upper and Lower Egypt? He is a god by whose dealings one lives, the father and mother of all men, alone, by himself, without an equal." So wrote Rekhmire, an Egyptian high minister of state, in about 1500 B.C.*, when Egypt was already 1700 years old, and Menkauré himself (also called Mycerinus) had been dead 1500 years.*

Museum of Fine Arts, Boston

3 THE FIRST AGRARIAN CIVILIZATIONS

People Who Have Developed Farming and Animal Husbandry to Such a Level That They Can Abandon Hunting, Fishing, and Food Gathering.

Preview

Tribal societies have often developed remarkably satisfactory patterns of living. We find tribes in which every member has so vital a sense of membership that theft and even stinginess do not exist. More than this, life can be charged with an emotional and spiritual richness which that of people in a complex modern urban society lacks. From birth to death every important phase in tribal man's life is dramatically celebrated, woven into the surrounding natural world by a mythology in which the whole tribe believes.

Belief in such a mythology can breed a sense of harmony with and respect for nature and all its creatures. When violence must be done by such acts as killing game or felling a tree, those who must perform such acts also perform others, seeking to bring nature and man back into harmony. Narcotics of various kinds, including tobacco, are in tribal societies controlled by becoming part of infrequently performed rituals, and the tribal mythology gives their effects a sacred interpretation.

Since technical specialization is at a fairly low level, every individual is a person of many developed abilities and skills. Each one knows the satisfaction of carrying to completion whatever artefact he begins, whether tool, weapon, vessel or garment, giving to it at the same time, if so desired, the shape or pattern which best embodies the spirit residing in it. Every one is a craftsman; every one may to some degree become an artist. Or the constructive enterprise may be on a grand scale, such as a communal house, a great canoe or a fish net, creating the exhilarating social experience of cooperation among many persons.

Education of young people is in part an informal matter of learning by example from adults in real-life situations. In part it may consist of preparation for dramatic ordeals, tests of courage or strength, fasts or initiation experiences whose preparation involves instruction in mythological lore by the tribe's elders. In an intact tribal society both kinds of education seem to be respected without question. Skepticism, rebellion and delinquency appear irrelevant.

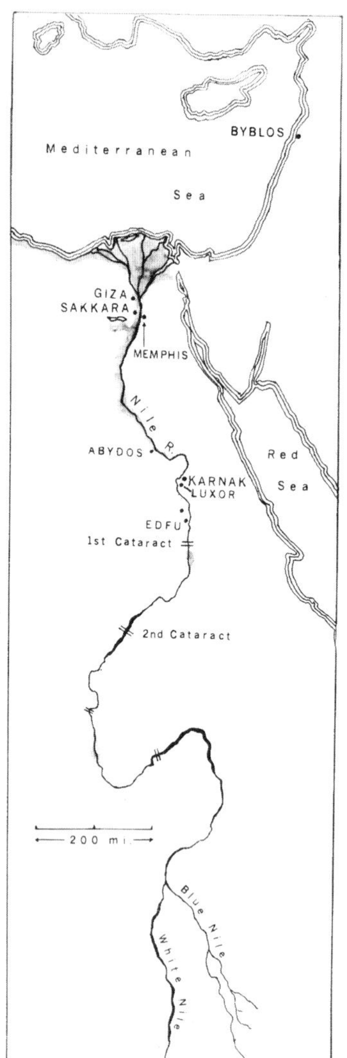

Tribal societies also have their severe limitations. The food problem is better solved than in hunting societies but is still far from satisfactory. Every one must work at producing or capturing it, and a local drought or a bitterly cold winter can cause widespread death by starvation. To a perilous degree tribal man is still vulnerable to nature's minor changes.

Another shortcoming is tribal society's insularity. While harmony and generosity may exist within one tribe, the attitude toward others can be violently the opposite; intense loyalty to one's own tribe springs in part from fear. The human population is split into a wide scattering of fairly small hostile camps, often seeking to annihilate one another. In each one the greatest hero is often the slayer of the most aliens, in battle or by treachery and stealth.

Still another shortcoming is the low level of technical development. When nobody can risk being a full-time specialist, invention and creation must remain simple. And in a society which is relatively small, chances for the presence of outstanding talent in any field is to that degree reduced. But a greater deterrent than these is the rigid thinking pattern common to tribes, where innovation is feared as a way of angering ancestors or other protective spirits who are believed to have taught the tribe its skills and mythology.

As men have struggled to surmount the limitations of inadequate food, capricious environment, social friction, ignorance and superstition, they have taken an irregular series of great innovative leaps. Each such leap has won them something. But at the same time they have often let something else get lost. For example, as we shall see, when men at length discovered sources of relatively cheaper food, they found they could afford to keep slaves. When societies grew until each contained millions, the frictions between them produced new horrors in warfare. As men have discovered new sources of power their desire to maintain harmony with nature has changed to a determination to plunder and exploit it. Men themselves can overcome or prevent these destructive results of constructive change. Men as free agents can make life on earth ever more fulfilling to every one, not merely a series of dazzling advances in one direction accompanied by tragic or disgraceful retreats in others.

The first limitation which men succeeded in surmounting was that of an inadequate food supply. In the span of time roughly between 8000 and 2000 B.C. communities in six or seven isolated areas on this planet succeeded in making hunting and foraging obsolete. Each discovered a group of local foods which men themselves could produce and which could completely satisfy the local population's dietary needs. As we shall see, conquest of this problem led to the conquest of others, leading to the creation of a new form of social organization, larger, more permanent, far more complex, and somewhat more innovative, than anything the world had yet seen. A few small tribal societies, released by such discoveries, were able to expand, spread and flower into the world's first *agrian civilizations*. In this chapter we shall consider one of these civilizations at some length and shall look with varying degress of brevity at five others. We shall see that the new form of society both demands and makes possible new directions in the arts. A larger, more complex, more powerful society requires a more imposing, more complex and permanent architecture. A new concept of men requires a new image of

Photo Lowie Museum of Anthropology, University of California, Berkeley

The Nile Valley, looking west, just after flood time. In the left foreground is the desert edge, and in the right foreground a mud-walled farming village. Beyond are fields, date palms, and pools of water left after the flood. Beyond these is the Nile itself, and then the green fields of its further bank. In the distance are the desert mountains of the valley's far side.

man, whether hewn in the round or painted on a flat surface. And mastery of new techniques, such as metal smelting, glass making and gem cutting, give the artist-craftsman new materials on which to work his form-giving will.

Egypt, Gift of the Nile

Egypt is perhaps the most strangely shaped land in the world. It is over 700 miles long,[1] but for most of that distance it is a mere meandering ribbon of a country, thirty miles wide or less throughout. It is the valley of one of the world's few northward flowing rivers, the Nile, a sunken strip of rich black soil[2] cutting through a brutally hostile red desert. Only at the northern end, where the Nile fans out into a delta 150 miles wide by 100 miles deep as it flows through seven mouths into the Mediterranean Sea, does Egypt broaden out. The contrast between the wide delta and the long narrow valley south of it has always given the impression of two distinct countries. In ancient times the Egyptians called their country the *Two Lands*. Today the enormous city of Cairo lies at their meeting point, close to the strategic spot where the first kings of Egypt, intent on keeping a firm hand on both regions at once, built their fortress-palaces over 5000 years ago.

The slow-flowing river is the secret of Egypt's enduring success as a country. For the Nile is no ordinary river. It has two sources. One, the White Nile, starts deep in central Africa. The other, the Blue Nile, springs from high in the Mountains of Ethiopia. The white source keeps steadily flowing all year. The blue source changes regularly from a spreading flood each summer when the mountain snows of Ethiopia melt, to a trickle the rest of the year. If the White Nile were the only water source, Egypt would have a steady water supply all year, but its soil would have been worn out long since. If the Blue Nile were the only source, Egypt's soil would be nourished with fresh muddy flood water every summer (the "milk of the Nile"), but for the rest of the year the river would be practically dry and the whole land would long since have died of thirst. It is the interacting of the two sources, one steadily flowing all year, the other rhythmically resurfacing the land with rich mountain mud, that makes the Nile the life-giving miracle that it is. The Egyptians thought of the year as divided into three seasons of about four months each: *coming forth*, or *flood time*, when the Nile flowed muddy red over the land; *cultivation*, when the fields were planted, crops sprouted, and the Nile, now subsided, ran clear blue; and *drought*, when the crops were harvested and the sluggish Nile, discolored with algae, flowed green. Herodotus, the great Greek traveler, who toured Egypt 2400 years ago, rightly described Egypt as "the gift of the Nile." But what the Nile gave, it could also withhold. When the winter snowfall in the Ethiopian mountains was heavy, the Nile floodwaters the following summer were generous, and Egypt reaped a fat harvest. When the mountain snowfall was light, Egypt suffered a lean year, and even, at times, a famine.

Metropolitan Museum of Art

Jars found in prehistoric Egyptian tombs. On them can be seen river boats with many oars, mountains, gazelles, cattle, ostriches, a few men and a woman.

Prehistoric Egypt

Twelve thousand years ago, when the Sahara Desert had not appeared and North Africa was still livable (see page 26), the Nile was a much broader river than today, and its valley was a swamp. Then, as the whole top of the African continent slowly dried out, century after century, the Nile gradually narrowed, and men kept moving downward, level by level, into the valley. We can follow this from the scattered tools and other objects which we still find along the valley today. The oldest objects, the crudely chipped stone weapons of hunters, are on the highest levels. Lower down we find signs of a later, more advanced culture: stone and bone weapons and tools which were polished or finely chipped and the signs of the beginning of farming. By the time the Nile had reached nearly its present size, perhaps 7000 years ago, human communities were strung for hundreds of miles along or near both banks, on rises of ground high enough to escape the annual floods.

We can surmise much about these prehistoric men. They were a farming-hunting people, small in stature. They cultivated little crop gardens, fished in the Nile with net and harpoon, hunted birds and small animals, and were at first overawed but later learned to conquer the powerful wild cattle with upward curved horns that lived in the Nile swamps, and the great hippopotami and crocodiles that swam in its waters. They lived in tribes, each led by its own chief, each protected by its own totem animal or bird. They fought fierce intertribal wars, but also carried on peaceful intertribal trade. Using the Nile as a highway, they sailed and rowed along it in boats whose hulls were probably great bundles of reeds, exchanging goods such as grain, pottery, and stone tools, over hundreds of miles. But the products of one region were so often like those of another that trading and commerce seem to have been simple, and were to remain so for thousands of years. For the next two thousand years Egyptian life changed and developed, slowly at first, then ever faster, until sometime well before the year 3200 B.C., in a burst of many-sided accomplishment, life in Egypt emerged on a new level; her prehistoric age came to an end and Egyptian history began.

Metropolitan Museum of Art

Three slate cosmetic palettes from prehistoric tombs. On these the Egyptians ground malachite, a green copper-bearing ore, and applied the powder as an outliner to their eyes, for dramatic effect.

Steps to the Agrarian Civilization

An Adequate Food Supply Is Developed

How did this change occur? No one knows the full answer, but we believe we know an important part of it. Before he can achieve anything great, man's first need is food. The primitive Egyptian first solved the food problem by making two discoveries: how to farm certain grasses for the seeds they would yield, and how to tame and live off certain animals. He created what is called an agrarian civilization, whose chief activity was farming.

EGYPTIAN GRAIN FARMING. The grasses which the Egyptians first learned to farm were the wild ancestors of the hard-kerneled wheat called *emmer*. Like most grains it is nourishing food, containing protein and some oil as well as much starch. Moreover, a small piece of land will produce heavily. It is a highly concentrated crop.[3] The early Egyptians also cultivated beans, lettuce, onions, melons, grapes, dates, and sources of oil such as sesame seed and the castor bean.

What made Egyptian crop-raising successful was the annual gift of the Nile, a freshly enriched soil. Planting a crop was a simple matter of breaking up the ground, scattering seed, and trampling it in with the feet. Nature did the rest. No farmer had to move because his land wore out. But successful crop raising also required several important human achievements, as seen in the following discussion.

Seed selection: at some unknown date the Egyptians learned to sort out for planting the quality of seeds they most wished to see reproduced. In this way they gradually developed a domestic grain superior to the wild.

Flood control and irrigation: the Egyptians learned to capture the Nile flood waters in huge shallow storage basins, and then to lead this off through a system of canals, so that great stretches of otherwise parched land were watered and nourished.

Improved methods of cultivation: the Egyptian hoe, with first a wooden blade and later sometimes a copper one, was a great improvement over the digging stick. But the greatest step forward was the invention of the *plow*. This was a crude wooden device—really a large hoe drawn by cattle—but it could do the work of four men in one day. Before this invention could be made use of, however, the Egyptians had to take another great step forward: developing animal husbandry.

Egyptian cattle being driven over harvested wheat to tread out the grain. A painting found on a tomb wall of the later or historic period, about 1500 B.C.

EGYPTIAN ANIMAL HUSBANDRY. Even after they had been civilized for centuries, the Egyptians were still experimenting with animal taming—finding out which species were suited to various human uses and which were not. Pictures exist in the tombs of nobles, for example, showing gazelles in corrals and hyenas being fattened in cages. However, the few animals they finally selected seem also to have been among those they first tamed: the dog for hunting; the donkey as a beast of burden; the goat and the long-horned Barbery sheep (covered with hair instead of wool) for meat and milk; the pig for meat; the goose for meat and eggs; and most important of all, the tall-horned native cattle for meat, milk, hide, bone, horn, and strength as a draught animal. These cattle had been a source of awe and reverence to the more primitive Egyptians. Some tribes had chosen the bull as their totem; others had chosen the cow. As Egypt cast off her tribal ways, these ancient totems became raised to the rank of gods and goddesses, as we shall see further on.

THE RESULTS OF EGYPTIAN FARMING. The Egyptians thus developed a *food complex* satisfying all their dietary needs. They could produce grain, vegetables, oils, meats, and milk products in great quantities and with only moderate labor. Since the land was also rich in wild game, hunting continued to be a part of Egyptian life, but it became a sport and lost its grim necessity. Several results followed logically upon the new food supply.

The population increased: since an acre of land could be made to produce more food than before, it could, therefore, support more people. Tribes grew in size and began pressing in upon each other.

The variety of talents multiplied: increase in the size of a group increased the number of different abilities likely to be found in that group.

The full-time specialist appeared: since men could now produce more food than before, and with less labor, part of the people (provided the year was favorable) could now produce food enough for all. Therefore, men were free to devote themselves to *full-time specialization*. Turn back to page 44 where part-time specialization is discussed. (a) The most necessary kind of specialist, on whom all others depended, was the full-time food producer, the farmer or peasant. He could raise enough to support not only himself, but other specialists on whom he in turn depended in various ways. These were: (b) the chief, who organized the tribe's manpower in peace and led it in war; (c) the medicine man or shaman, who attempted to control the unknown forces in tribal life by warding off bad luck, ensuring good crops, and ministering to disease; and (d) the artist-craftsman, who produced tools, weapons, clothing, and other equipment, including things of beauty, which men and women have always needed or valued. The fact that chiefs, shamans, and craftsmen were now free to devote their whole time to their callings began to change life profoundly.

Slavery became an institution: because of the better food supply, the practice of keeping slaves became more feasible than in hunting-farming societies.

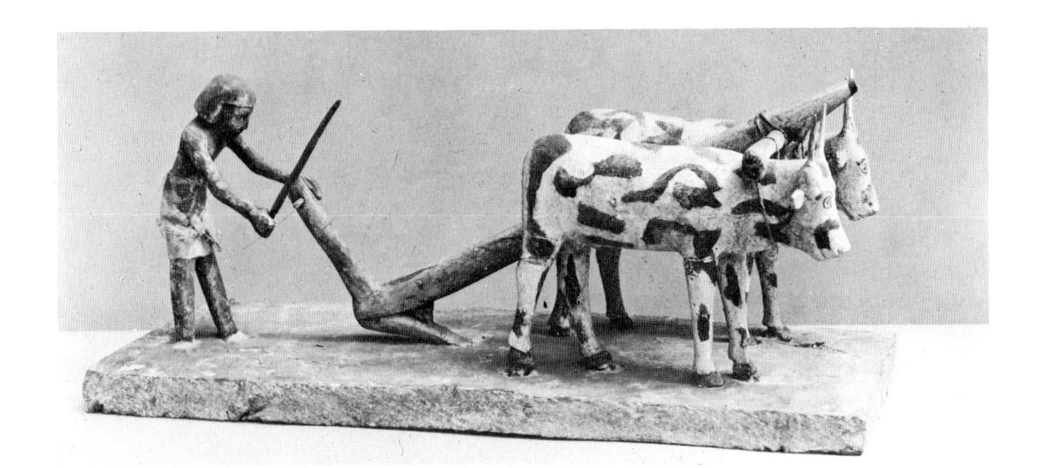

Metropolitan Museum of Art, gift of Valdemar Hammer, Jr.

An Egyptian technical breakthrough. One ox-drawn plow could do the work of four men, thus speeding up cultivation of the soil. More seed could be planted, more grain raised, and the food supply increased. This little model was found in a tomb dating from perhaps 2000 B.C.

Tribes Merge into Kingdoms

Tribal life, like any other, is full of temptations; and of these perhaps the greatest is the weakness or wealth, or both, of one's neighbor. We have seen that people in one tribe feel united because all are relatives sprung from a common ancestor, all respect the same totem, and all follow the same rigid customs. But what about one tribe's feeling toward another? Since each tribe often regards itself as the only important one in the world, others are, of course, considered inferior. Add to this, perhaps, the fact that the year has been a hard one, the crops have failed, the herds are starving, and hunting has been poor. In such a year it is easy for one tribe, headed by an aggressive, resourceful chief, to go forth to try to conquer another tribe and plunder it.

Suppose that such a raid is successful. Let us consider some ways in which the conquering tribe can treat the conquered. (a) They can put the entire tribe to death and take over their land, their animals, and their possessions. (b) They can put all the men to death, take the women as a valuable addition to their tribe and work-force without having to pay for them, and seize the other tribe's land and possessions as well. (c) They can merely exact from the conquered the payment of *tribute*, in grain, cattle, weapons, pottery, woven goods, or whatever the conquering tribe needs. A strong conquering tribe can then continue to demand the payment of tribute year after year.

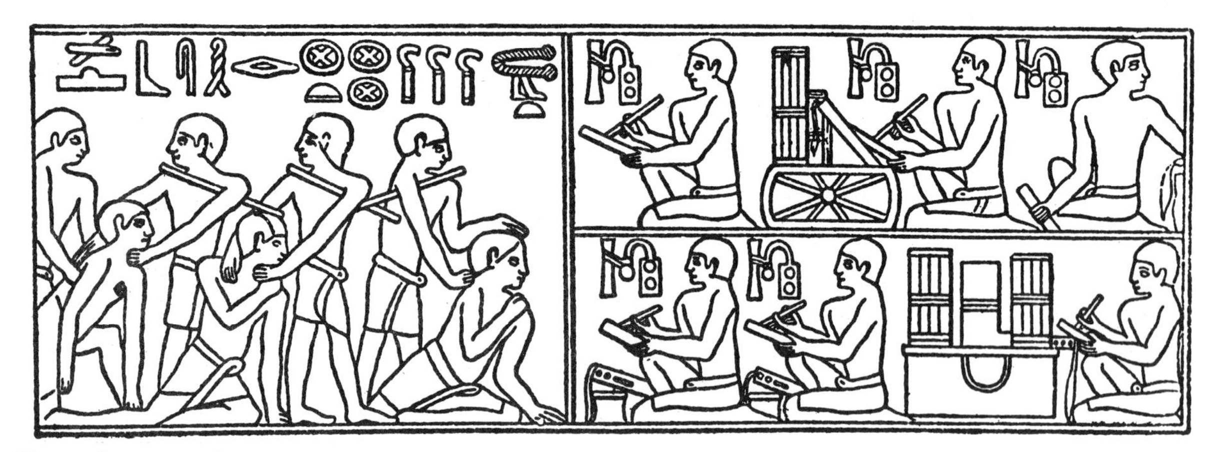

Tax gathering as the Egyptians experienced it. On the left the inscription reads: "Seizing the town rulers for a reckoning." On the right a team of scribes keep tax records.

Note that the third of these methods is useful only if a conquered tribe can produce an excess over and above its own needs. The rich Nile soil, and the food complex developed there, created such an excess. And it may be that the tribes along the Nile were merged into larger units through some such process of conquest and paying of tribute.

Once one tribe had conquered another and had put the conquered to work producing tribute, the conquerors became much more powerful. As a tribe they now controlled more people to till the soil, guard the cattle, and make clothing, tools, and weapons. The tribe could begin to support a group of men free to spend more of their time at feats of arms, that is, as an *army*. And a strong chief, no longer driven by need but by the sweet taste of former success, could then lead this army out to conquer new tribes.

Suppose now that a tribe has succeeded in making itself supreme over, not just one neighboring tribe, but all tribes for miles around. New problems immediately arise. Which peoples shall pay what tribute, and how much can each tribe bear to pay? How can revolts be recognized in time and crushed? Above all, how can something like order, law, and peace be brought to the alien and humiliated enemy? In solving these problems, everything depends on the alertness and wisdom of the conquering chief and the council of elders that surround him. If he fails to solve them successfully, he has his short day of conquering glory and then disappears into the oblivion of the past as just another robber chief. But if he solves them well enough to bind permanently a group of previously unrelated tribes into a single people under one ruler, he has ceased to be merely a chief. He has become a *king*. A successful king is a rare occurrence. For every king who has walked this earth, perhaps hundreds of chiefs have come and gone, leaving no trace.

THE UNITING OF EGYPT UNDER ONE KING. There was probably a time when a whole string of small kingdoms, each once a cluster of tribes, existed along the Nile. It is also probable that these kept merging, through war, into ever larger kingdoms. From the prehistoric evidence found in ancient burial places, we can conclude that one group gradually fought its way to control over all others. We can guess two things about this conquering group: their skeletons show that they were bigger than the other Nile dwellers, and they were a warlike people, for their totem, later their god, was a fierce bird of prey, the hawk. They seem to have conquered the people of the upper Nile first. The social pattern of a small ruling class dominating a population of working people probably started here, never again to disappear from Egypt.

All this is guesswork. Nothing becomes definite until actual historical records begin.[4] The oldest record to survive in Egypt is an oval slab of slate, about two feet tall, carved on both sides. It records, by pictures and a few word-symbols, that a king of upper Egypt named Hor-aha, or Fighting Hawk, conquered lower Egypt and united the two lands into a single kingdom.

From other historical evidence we have learned some things about Hor-aha (who was also known by the name *Men*, or *Menes*). He built a great fortress-palace of plastered mud-brick, known as the White Wall, close to where the Two Lands meet and where later the city of Memphis arose. In order to bind the Two Lands more firmly into one, he appears to have married a princess from lower Egypt.

He controlled the irrigation of all Egypt—an amazing achievement—and caused a *Nilometer*, or scale for measuring the height of the Nile, to be cut in rock near his palace. His engineers, of course, managed the operation. But his royal will directed them.

During his life he was revered as the dwelling place of Horus, the hawk god. It also appears that between his personal health and the prosperity of the land there was believed to be a connection. The vitality of the king, therefore, became of national concern. At intervals of years a great ceremony, the *Sed* festival, was held at which the king symbolically died and was reborn into renewed youth and strength, thus supposedly renewing the vitality of the land as well.

When he at length actually died, two tombs were built for him: a real one just across the Nile from his palace, and a symbolic one far up the river at Abydos, a spot which the Egyptians revered as sacred to Osiris, god of the dead. Both these tombs seem to have been model palaces, constructed of mud-brick coated with white and gaily colored plaster. But they were solid, not hollow, except for a chamber containing the king's body (at the tomb near Memphis) or an image of it (at Abydos). Other chambers in the otherwise solid mass of brick contained vast supplies of meat, bread, wine, oil, and cheese in jars, as well as tableware, furniture, and weapons. A long row of smaller tombs running around three sides of both royal tombs contained the bodies of servants who had been slain at his funeral. Near each tomb was also a long bricked-over mound containing a ship. A high wall surrounded the whole group of structures. The purpose was apparently to give the king's soul two places to dwell in, one near his old palace and the other near the

Egyptian battle axes with bronze blades. 2000 to 1800 B.C.

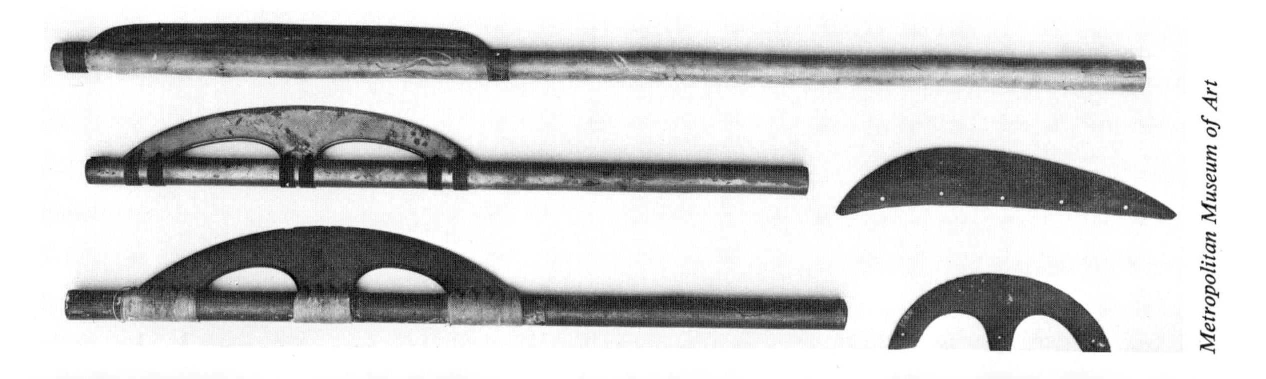

Metropolitan Museum of Art

A slate cosmetic palette fit for a goddess! Hor-aha's record of his conquest of lower Egypt, probably carved at his command as a thank offering to Hat-hor, the cow goddess. Hor-aha, wearing the tall crown of upper Egypt, and followed by his sandal bearer and foot washer, slays the king of lower Egypt with a blow of his mace. Horus, the hawk god, is also shown leading the conquered king of the papyrus marshes by the nose. Above, between two heads of the cow goddess, is the king's name sign.

Reverse side of Hor-aha's cosmetic palette. Here the king is shown wearing the crown of lower Egypt as he goes to inspect the bodies of his slain enemies. Before him goes his queen carrying lotus blossoms, and four standard bearers. Behind him comes his faithful sandal bearer. Below him two beasts, probably symbols of upper and lower Egypt, are being restrained from fighting. The circular hollow between their necks was intended for pigment grinding. At the bottom the king, symbolized by a strong bull, tramples on his enemy and breaks into his stronghold. Note: This object is usually called the Palette of Narmer, another Egyptian king. For a discussion of its probable real ownership see Archaic Egypt, *W. Emery (Penguin paperback), pages 32–57.*

Metropolitan Museum of Art, Dodge Fund. Cast of the original palette in the Cairo Museum

most sacred temples of the gods far up the Nile. In either place he would find everything waiting for him that he had enjoyed in life, including the presence of his servants. And in either of the two ships his soul could take its long journey on the River of Night to the Land of the Dead.

Hor-aha, the first king of the Two Lands, seems to have set the pattern for all who came after him for nearly 3000 years. During that time thirty royal families, or *dynasties*, succeeded each other on Egypt's throne. It is true that there were certain changes in the pattern. The practice of killing servants at the king's death was discarded. Brick gave place to stone as a building material for tombs, and a new era of architecture was launched. Objects left in the royal tombs became fewer and more elegant. As the written language developed, descriptions of the king's royal titles, and the glorious achievements of his reign, were carved on the tomb walls in long orderly rows of word-and-letter pictures. But the essentials were unchanged. The king while alive was a god, on whose active life the welfare of all Egypt depended. Without him the irrigation system could not be managed. The taxes could not be collected, nor could they be wisely spent to pay for administrators, public works, and great creations to the glory of the gods. And as the well-being of all Egypt dwelt, in a sense, in his body, so his health, "renewed" at intervals in the *Sed* festival, was believed to renew the health of the kingdom. When he died, the king's body, with his most precious possessions, was preserved for the after-life, a second tomb was built for him at Abydos, and a ship was at hand for his journey to the Dead.

Loyalty to Place Replaces Loyalty to Tribe

A kingdom, to become permanent, requires something more than force. The inhabitants must find an advantage in the new way of life which makes them prefer it to the old. Otherwise, revolts will be chronic. The Egyptians probably found one such advantage in *cooperative irrigation*. An intelligent and humane chief, after uniting several tribes under his rule, could coordinate the digging of canals and increase the number and size of basins for storing water so that more land could be cultivated and more crops produced. If he were farsighted he could build granaries for storage in case of a future famine. Blessed by advantages such as these, people could gradually forget their old tribal ties and could begin to think of themselves as loyal to a particular king who was giving them a new security. *The paying of tribute would cease to be a gift to the conqueror and would become taxes, or a payment made to keep a way of living in operation.*

By the time of Hor-aha, life in Egypt was already on a new level; *tribal life was vanishing*. The king laid his strong, organizing hand on the land and divided it into provinces called *nomes*. Over each nome was set a governor appointed by the king. Each governor saw that within his nome justice was upheld, irrigation maintained, taxes collected, troops raised for the king's army, and workmen assembled for the king's large-scale projects. Local color was replaced by methodical organization. Only one strong trace of local individuality remained: each region kept the local gods it had worshipped from prehistoric times. These had perhaps once been tribal totems, for most of them were animal gods or bird gods. Many came to be recognized as the official symbol of a particular nome.

Bibliotheque Nationale

Egyptian craftsmen at work as shown on a tomb wall painting from perhaps 2500 B.C. Top row center, rope makers are twisting fibres. Second row, boat builders shape river craft from bundles of papyrus stalks. Third through sixth rows, various kinds of carpentry are in progress, involving adze, chisel and mallet, axe, saw and drill.

Skills Develop and Trade Grows

As the load of producing food was taken over by a part of the people only, and as the rule of a single king brought internal peace to the land, craftsmen were free to develop new techniques and skills and to produce a great variety of goods, some of them necessities but many of them luxuries. Encouraged by the stable government, men found it easier and safer than before to trade these goods up and down the Nile valley. Thus, domestic commerce flourished, though it seems to have remained on a *barter* basis. That is, it involved a simple exchange of goods between traders, without the use of money. Egypt was first of all a land of farms and farmers, rather than of merchants. The goods produced throughout the land were also fairly uniform. This reduced the importance of trade.

Let us next look at ancient Egypt's outstanding technical achievements, other than farming. When doing so we must bear in mind that some of these were perhaps first discovered elsewhere. For Egypt was probably not the world's oldest *agrarian* civilization (one depending on farming). Sumeria, described later in this chapter, seems to have been older. And still older peoples, living in what are today southern Turkey and northern Iraq, discovered a few of the techniques (such as grain planting, copper smelting) at a still earlier time. Nevertheless, from whatever source the Egyptians drew the original inspiration for these skills, they certainly *developed* them in their own strongly Egyptian manner.

Not satisfied with the mere *production* of food, they advanced its *processing*, that is, the art of cookery. Bread, cheese, and wine, three of the world's oldest staples, are all prepared by complex processes, involving microorganisms, which were either invented or developed in Egypt. So was the skillful baking of cakes in shapes and colors pleasing to the eye. Paintings of their feasts show these elegant confections proudly displayed on tall stands, sometimes decorated with lotus blossoms.

Egyptian bronze dagger with ivory handle. Length, 9¼ in.

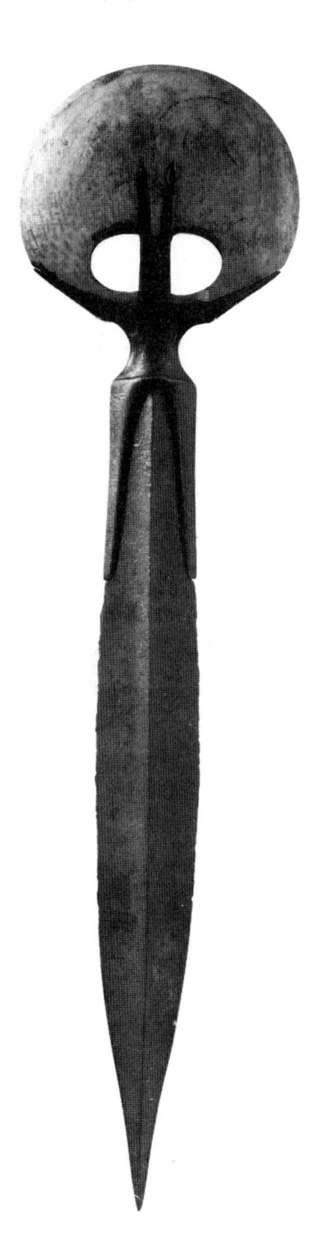

Lowie Museum of Anthropology, University of California, Berkeley

They discovered the flax plant growing wild in the Nile valley. From it they spun linen thread and developed to new refinements the art of weaving. Linen became the standard cloth for garments in Egypt and was woven in a variety of grades for different uses, from extremely coarse for sacking, to silken fine for the robe of a princess.

The Egyptians advanced the potter's craft by inventing or adopting the potter's wheel. But pottery in Egypt was for utility only. When it came to beauty the Egyptians preferred bowls and vases of alabaster and other attractive stones, ground by a technique that has been lost. These thin-walled vases can still be found in Egytian tombs. When a light is put in one of them, the translucent stone transmits a soft glow, possibly the world's first indirect lighting. See illustration, page 111.

Perhaps by accident at first, they discovered that if some kinds of rock are heated, a bright liquid trickles out of them which later hardens. Thus may have come into being the *smelting of metal.* Four metals were discovered: copper, tin, silver, and gold.

By melting copper and tin together they discovered the valuable alloy, *bronze*, which was harder than either of the metals that composed it. *Until the discovery of iron, bronze was the only hard metal available to the ancient world.* From it the Egyptians made not only weapons such as battle axes, spear heads, daggers, and swords, but carpenters' tools such as the saw, chisel, adze blade, and axe head, in fact, almost all the basic tools of the carpenter's trade.

By melting gold and silver together they discovered the alloy *electrum*, or white gold. Working chiefly in gold and electrum, they created the art of making jewelry and carried it to a high level of technique and design. Gold and silver were more plentiful in ancient times than today. They were displayed for their beauty in spectacular forms created by goldsmiths. Today we cast them in monotonous bricks and store them in vaults.

The Egyptians discovered how to make glass by heating sand, how to tint it, blow it, and cast it into small vessels. They also discovered *faience*, an opaque glasslike substance containing *natrun* and pulverized copper ore. After firing, this turned into a rich blue color. It was used as perhaps the world's first *pottery glaze.* Finally, they learned to make *enamels* from the ingredients of glass, and with this they decorated their metalwork and jewelry. See illustrations, pages 101 and 112.

Photo Ashmolean Museum, Oxford

Chest of wood, ivory and gold, found in the tomb of King Tutankhamen. The rhythmically repeated symbols on the sides represent plenty, kingly authority, and eternal life (neb, was, ankh).

Egyptian carpentry was of a high order. Native Egyptian trees, such as the *sycamore* and *acacia*, were twisted in shape. From their angular boughs Egyptian carpenters found it hard to make any large wooden construction. To meet this problem they invented just about all the joints known to modern cabinetmakers.

Woods imported from abroad were luxuries, fit for the use of kings and nobles only, and usually brought in by royal command in ships owned by the king. *Cedar*, from Syria, was straight timber of great length, suitable for seagoing ships, the rafters of palace halls, and flagstaffs to stand before palaces and temples. *Ebony*, from Nubia, south of Egypt, was a hard black wood suited to fine carving and furniture.

Egyptian paint, still to be seen on tomb and temple walls, has proved durable, since the *pigments* were chiefly mineral and the *binder* was well chosen to withstand aging. Egyptian taste is responsible for the vivid, clearly contrasting colors. Here, as in every other Egyptian achievement, we see their love of sharp definition.

Six geese, from an Egyptian tomb, about 2700 B.C.

Oriental Institute, University of Chicago

Equipped with metal tools and with other technical inventions, they were apparently the first people in the world to master the quarrying of stone, the precise working of it into geometric shapes, the transporting of it in large masses, and the erection from it of colossal buildings of planned design.

The basic Egyptian principle of construction was the *post and lintel*, that is, a horizontal crossbeam (lintel) resting on two vertical posts. Their great temples (which, besides tombs, were their only constructions in stone) were all built in this way. To assemble them required the Egyptian genius for organization, plus endless back-breaking labor, but only moderate ingenuity. It is thought that as each course of stones was laid, mud-brick was also laid to raise the level of the land enough to permit the dragging in of the next course of stones. When the building was finished, it was probably solid with earth. This had to be dug out from around the stone structure. Scaffolding was then erected for the polishing, carving, and painting of the stone walls, ceilings, and floors.

Above, the world's first major architectural construction in stone. Part of the great tomb complex created for Zoser, second king of Egypt's third dynasty, before 2700 B.C. *Shown here are the terraced pyramid which covers the king's tomb, and three columns of a temple. The name of the architect, Imhotep, is still preserved. Right, seated statue of Zoser himself.*

Metropolitan Museum of Art, Rogers Fund

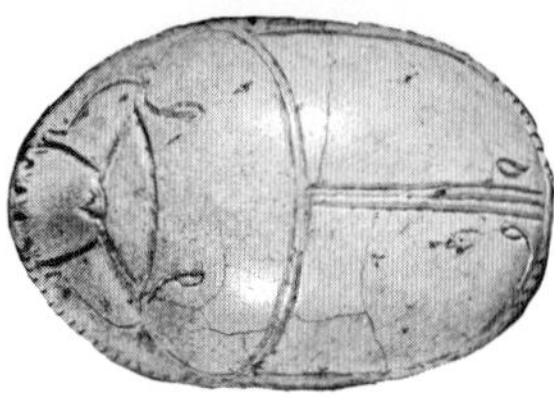

Lowie Museum of Anthropology, University of California, Berkeley

Left, tools of an Egyptian scribe: center, an example of informal writing (for the formal style see page 98, top); at sides, holders for reed pens; at bottom, containers for ink, and blocks for smoothing paper which was made from strips of papyrus stalk, glued together in layers. Above, an Egyptian stone seal, carved in shape of a scarab *or bettle. On the bottom appears the owner's name.*

Perhaps Egypt's crowning achievement was the invention of *writing*, and of cheap, efficient writing materials. The Egyptians also developed practical, uniformly standard units for the measurement of *time*, *distance* and *weight*. This required the invention of simple measuring devices: the sun dial and water clock, the measuring rod, and the scale. (Money, or the standard unit of *value*, was developed in another civilization, in Mesopotamia.)

Egyptian thinking, challenged by the demands of their large complex society, required *ideas*, often of a more complicated, abstract nature than those needed in smaller, tribal societies. Men forever seek to represent such abstract ideas visibly in order to convey them readily to their fellow men. Thus they come to create *symbols*—simple easily recognized forms intended to represent a deep or complex meaning. The two beasts with intertwined necks on Hor-aha's palette are such a symbol. They form a neat, balanced design, but beyond that they seem intended to convey the concept that two politically independent regions, after long struggle, have finally become united and restrained under one ruler. Later the standard symbol for this unity was a stalk of lotus (upper Egypt) and a stalk of papyrus (lower Egypt) knotted together. *Symbolism* is the practice of conveying such complex ideas through visually simple means.

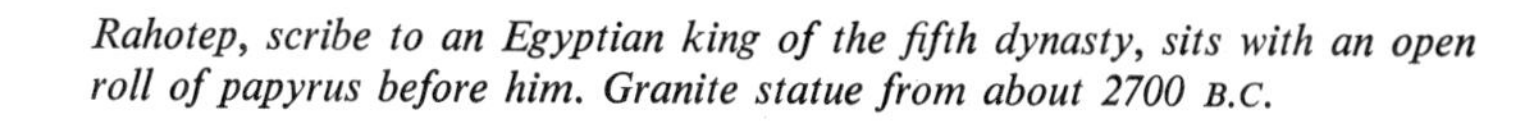

Rahotep, scribe to an Egyptian king of the fifth dynasty, sits with an open roll of papyrus before him. Granite statue from about 2700 B.C.

Metropolitan Museum of Art, gift of Edward S. Harkness

Metropolitan Museum of Art, Levi Hale Willard Bequest

Karnak, the mightiest of Egyptian temples, built in honor of the god Amon, "father of the gods, fashioner of men, creator of cattle, lord of all being." At its height this temple employed over 83,000 men, following 125 different trades, professions, and branches of responsibility. These ranged from the lowliest plowman of temple farmland to the chief priest of Amon, a person of immense power. As an example of complex cooperation, compare this with the description on page 36. This model reconstructs a cross section of the great central hall.

Magic Begins to Give Way to Religion

We have already seen that primitive people are intensely superstitious. They believe that unseen beings influence their lives at every turn and can be controlled only by casting the right spell, in the right manner, at the right time. We have also seen how primitive men have everywhere relied on shamans or medicine men to specialize in memorizing and casting these spells. This is discussed on pages 45–46.

But among primitive people there is another form of superstition which is very different from magic. This is the feeling and the manner in which they approach the being which in their minds is the living symbol of their tribe. This symbol, as we mentioned earlier, may be an ancestor, a totem animal, or the tribal chief himself. But whichever one of these the symbol is, belief concerning it can be intense. Primitive men sometimes appear to believe that the tribe has a soul[5] just like a single person, and that this soul inhabits the image of an ancestor, a totem, or their chief's living body. Their desire is to protect and nourish this tribal symbol, for they believe that in this way they are keeping the tribe itself alive and healthy. When we realize that primitive man without his tribe is in peril of starvation or murder, we can also realize how deep, how close to his heart, primitive man's devotion to a tribal symbol can be.

These emotions are distinct from those of magic, where the aim is to bind, bribe, or outwit the power of some spirit. They are, instead, emotions of awe, loyalty, and devotion which we call *religious.* When we find these emotions directed toward some being, visible or invisible, we say that he, she, or it is being worshiped as a *god.* And when we find that certain persons in a society have been given the special task of worshiping the god and caring for his house or temple, we call them *priests.*

Reconstruction by Hoelscher, Oriental Institute, University of Chicago

Entrance to the great temple of Amon, erected at Medinet Habu by Rameses III of the twentieth dynasty, about 1200 B.C., to adjoin his palace. The king is twice shown smiting his enemies with a mace, just as Hor-aha had done 2000 years before (page 88). On the left, aided by Amon, he wears the crown of upper Egypt. On the right, aided by the hawk god, Horus, he wears the crown of lower Egypt. The four flagstaffs were of cedar wood imported by sea from Lebanon.

We find the worship of gods becoming strong as tribes disappear and kingdoms emerge. And in early civilizations we find gods who betrey their tribal origins. There is the animal or bird god, who may once have been a tribal totem. And there is the god-king, descended from some conquering chief in whose body a tribal soul was believed to reside.

The priests of these early gods seemed also to have taken over the duties of the old shamans. They practised magic, since no distinction between magic and religion then existed. And as the art of healing slowly advanced, the temples of the gods were often the centers to which people went for relief.

The hold which the kings of Egypt had upon their millions of subjects was partly one of force, partly one of practical necessity, and partly one of superstition. The long rod of the police officer was always ready to smite whoever failed to follow orders, especially when it came to paying taxes. The life-giving efficiency of the irrigation system and the readiness of eaech nome's governor (appointed by the king) to hear complaints of injustice ware living proof that the king was the source of everybody's well-being. And above all was the belief that he was a god, whose health and vigor somehow influenced the land.

To maintain this belief among a million or more people, the king needed the support of the priesthood. For the people, in superstitious awe, worshiped whomever the priests worshiped. And this support was vital when a new king ascended the throne. Not until the priests had declared him to be a true successor to the former god-king, instead of a mere usurper, would the people believe in him. How did the kings of Egypt ensure this priestly support for themselves?

Like everything else in Egypt, the king controlled the appointment of the many different groups of priests along the Nile, each worshiping their local god. The kings could also finance the building and enlargement of temples

Reconstruction by Hoelscher, Oriental Institute, University of Chicago

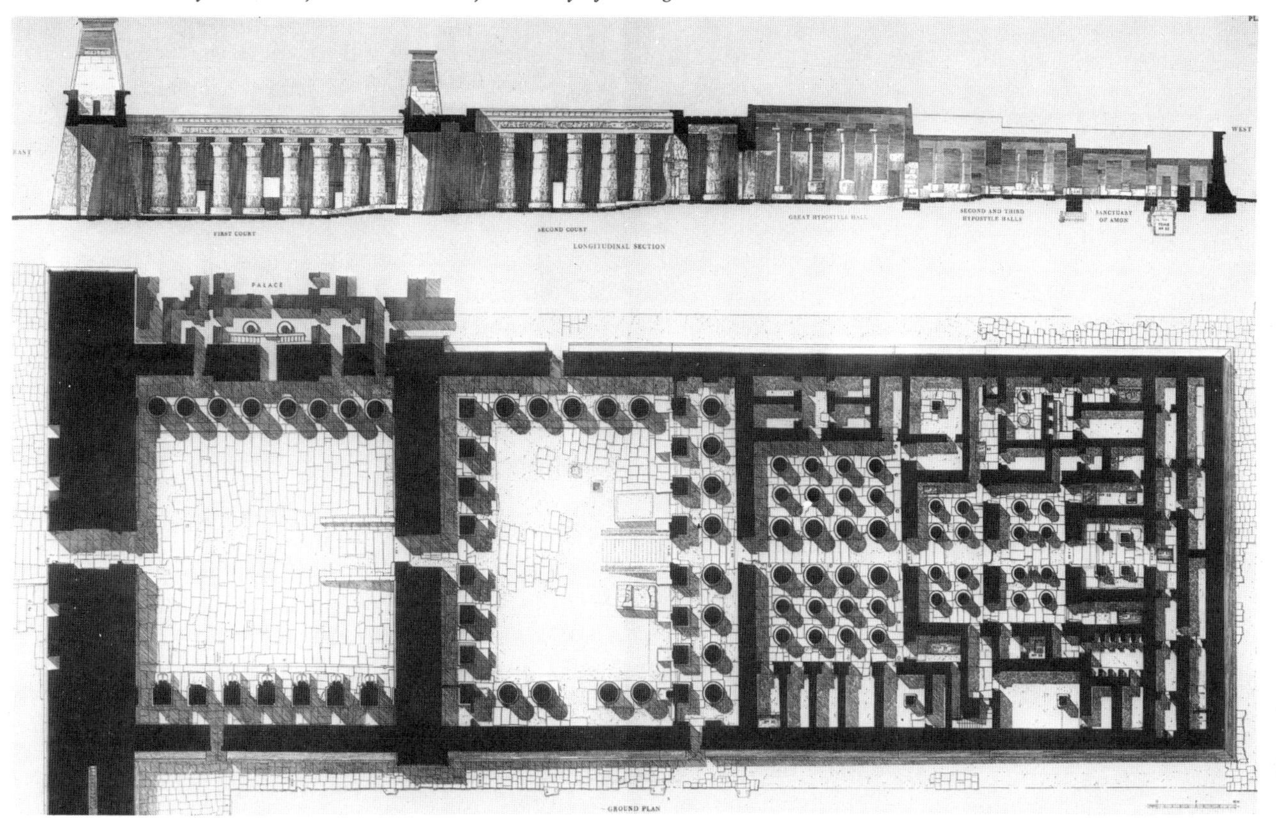

Section and plan of the temple shown on the opposite page. As one entered one passed through two open courtyards before stepping into the dark temple interior, lit only by high window slits like those at Karnak (page 95). One then passed through a forest of columns and four doorways before reaching the holy sanctuary of Amon. Beyond the sanctuary lay the king's own tomb, prepared during his lifetime. Temple length about 500 ft.

anyhwere they chose. The wealth pouring into the royal treasuries from the taxes on Egypt's annual harvests poured out again to support great building projects glorifying the gods. Since some regions and the priests of some gods were more influential than others, more wealth was lavished on them. Temples at such places as Edfu, Luxor, and especially Karnak kept growing and spreading as hundreds and even thousands of years came and went.

But even more important than the buildings themselves was the cost of their maintenance as sacred places. This the king provided by presenting to each temple, depending upon its needs, wide stretches of farmland complete with the laborers living upon it. The produce from the farms supported the temple's yearly operation, and wealth that would otherwise have flowed to the king was diverted to the temple.

EGYPTIAN RELIGION AS IT WAS PRACTICED. Let us consider how this wealth was used. The Egyptian concept of religion was enormously different from ours. For us it involves a whole congregation. We believe that it is important to enter a place of worship, preferably at least once a week, and there participate together in religious service, an experience intended to improve us personally. But no Egyptian, unless he was a king or other great personage, or, of course, a priest, ever saw the inside of a temple. A temple was the house of a god, maintained to keep him or her happy, well-nourished, and strong as the protector of the neighborhood or the country. Far within each temple was a sacred room, the Holy of Holies, in which a small shrine with doors was permanently sealed shut. Here lay the sacred object, whatever it might be, where dwelt the god. Before this was another shrine containing the god's statue. Here priests made daily offerings of food and drink to him. His image was washed, anointed with precious oils and perfumes, regularly reclothed in fresh linen, and his golden ornaments changed with the seasons. Costly incense was burned to delight his nostrils. Hymns were chanted in his praise to please his ears with sweet sound and his vanity with sweet words. In a really great temple the Holy of Holies would be surrounded with smaller ones, each containing the shrine of a lesser god. Each of these required similar, if simpler, services. Such ceremonies went on in an endless rhythm, three times daily, at sunrise, noon, and sunset.

Every few days the temple gates opened and there emerged a magnificent procession of chanting priests in white linen and white sandals. In their midst, carried on the shoulders of its bearers, came a great model of a ship on which rode the shrine of the god. He was being carried on a visit to the shrines of other neighboring gods, the journey sometimes lasting overnight. At such a time the common people, crowding along the route of travel, had their chance to come near him. Someone with a burning question requiring a yes or no answer might then cry out his question to the god in his shrine. If the bearers of the ship felt a supernatural force driving them forward, the answer was yes; if backward, no. But there were other ways to approach the god. Sick persons, and persons with more complicated questions to ask, were admitted to the temple's outer courtyards and were allowed to spend the night there. The god was expected to visit the sleeper in a dream and answer his question or prescribe a cure.

Statuette of an unknown Egyptian of the sixth dynasty, from his tomb at Giza. Limestone, height 15½ in.

Lowie Museum of Anthropology, University of California, Berkeley

At certain times of the year great crowds would gather before the temples to see the priests enact the dramatic lifestory of the local god. To simple people living dull lives such a display could be a thrilling event. It was also perhaps the only religious instruction they received. Though the scripts of a few of these great myth-dramas have come down to us, we can only guess at how they looked when performed.

The final connection between the people and the priesthood came at the time of death and burial. The corpse was given to the professional priest-embalmer, and when it had been preserved, supposedly for eternity (in salt if he was a poor man; in costly materials if he was rich), a priest from the local temple performed the magic ceremony of "opening the mouth." This, it was thought, would enable the dead person to breathe, speak, and enjoy all pleasures in the after-life.

If the Egyptians had not believed intensely in the future life, and if they had not believed that after death the *ba*, or soul, could return at will to enjoy whatever was left for it in the tomb, we would know little about them. For nearly all surviving Egyptian art is funeral art. The cemeteries are still yielding marvels and curiosities to the explorer. Many tombs contained images of the deceased, shown as they wished to look forever, at the height of their strength and health. The look in the eyes was always forward and the stride usually forward, full of confidence in an everlasting life under the kind rule of Osiris. To give them life, the eyes were usually inlaid, perhaps with alabaster or ivory, with irises and pupils of dark stone. The effect was vivid.

Naïvely assuming that life after death would resemble life before it, Egyptians were careful to place a *Ushabti* statue in a man's tomb. This little

Osiris, lord of the world after death. He was a god who embodied for the Egyptians the miracle of the ever-returning seasons. It was believed that he died each year during Egypt's drought and was reborn when the fields turned green again after the Nile floods. He was therefore believed also responsible for the miracle of man's rebirth into a future life after experiencing death in this one. Here he holds a shepherd's crook, as symbol of protection, and a flail, symbolizing the power to punish. Wood statuette, 43 in. high.

Lowie Museum of Anthropology, University of California, Berkeley

figure was properly blessed with the right spells so that it would come to life when needed and replace the soul of the man himself when commanded by the gods to work in the irrigation systems of heaven. For the Egyptians had no conception of the meaning of progress. This is a modern way of thinking that was unknown to the ancients. They were searching solely for *permanence*, a security against the terrible forces, known and unknown, to which primitive tribal life had been subject. So, although a great burst of creative achievement must have brought Egyptian civilization into existance, and although brilliant new steps were made at intervals later, the great *intellectual* drive of the thinking Egyptian was not toward invention but toward the maintenance of changeless order, it was hoped, forever.

TEMPLES AS CENTERS OF THOUGHT AND SCIENCE. One part of each of the greater temples seems to have been a building called the House of Life, and near it was another building or a room called the House of Books. Here the Egyptian priests probably developed the art of writing. And having done so (or, as they would have put it, received it from the god Thoth), they used it to record the ceremonies and rituals of their worship, the myths of their gods, their magic, and their store of knowledge.

The priests of the Houses of Life conducted schools to which were admitted boys ambitious to become scribes. *Scribe* was a broad term. These were the men who could read, write, draw, and do arithmetic, the bookkeepers and secretaries who were needed in thousands to keep records on farms and estates and to copy sacred texts in the temples. But scribes of ability could go on to be farm managers, government administrators, priests, engineers, and architects.[6] All such men, whether born of high or low rank, were a privileged class, freed from the wearing toil of farmers and artisans.

But the House of Life had still another function. Each was the intellectual center of its temple, and all of them together, spread along the Nile, probably formed the inquiring mind of Egypt. Here Egypt developed her science, her mathematics, and her philosophy, as far as these went.

Egyptian priest-astronomers determined the length of the year with practical accuracy, dividing it into twelve months of thirty days each, with five days' holiday (more on leap years) at each year's end. This is a more intelligent calendar than our own. Most of their other astronomical discoveries have been lost.

The regular, ever returning motion of stars and planets, and the regular rise and fall of the Nile, led them to the thoughtful conviction that the gods had created an orderly universe, moving according to an eternal design, and that if this were true of river and stars, it could also be true of everything else, even the affairs of daily life. From this they developed the concept of *maat*. He who orders his life so that it is in harmony with the eternal design of the gods possesses *maat*. His heart shall be at peace and he shall prosper. He who is at war with the world as the gods created it does not possess *maat* and shall eventually be destroyed, as it were, by friction. This concept, roughly stated here, seems to be vital to an understanding of Egyptian life and, as we shall see, of its art.

The priests believed that to possess *maat* was necessary not only in this life but also in the next. They taught that to enter the kingdom of Osiris, Lord of the Dead, a dead man's heart must be tested before the grim judges who sat at the gateway to Osiris' kingdom. The heart was placed on a great scale and weighed. If it was pure, it would be light as a feather, and its owner was free to enter the kingdom. Otherwise, the eternal crocodile was waiting to devour him.

In its way, this was a remarkable concept. *It placed the responsibility for the state of a man's soul on what he allowed himself to be and on how he governed his conduct.* But outside the temples, the belief of the people was still too primitive to accept it wholly. Magic was still the allpowerful force. There was no crime, most Egyptians believed, which could not be erased by casting the right spell. Even the eternal judges could be tricked and the heart be made to weigh lighter than it deserved! So the corpse was loaded with charms. Magic words were written on the strips of its linen winding sheet to forestall any possible mishap or past misdeed which might separate the soul from eternal life with Osiris.

Ani the scribe watches his heart being weighed against a feather (symbol of maat *or truth). If Anubis the jackal god decides that the scales balance, Ani will enter the afterlife. If not, the beast Amemit, far right, will devour his heart. Thoth the ibis god, scribe of the gods, who gave writing to mankind, records the weighing. Ani's* ba, *or soul, a human headed bird, anxiously watches. So does Ani's spirit of good luck, who stands under the scales. Above sit the ten serene gods who judge the afterlife. Part of a papyrus found in Ani's tomb.*

British Museum

Photo Forman. Copyright Paul Hamlyn, London

Gold funeral portrait of Tutankhamen, a young king of the eighteenth dynasty, who died about 1300 B.C. The eyebrows, eyelid linings, beard, and strips of the head covering are dark blue glass. The eyeballs are limestone, the irises obsidian. The green, blue, and red beads of the great necklace are semi-precious stones—green feldspar, lapis lazuli, and carnelian. The face is that of a youth who could command all Egypt and knew it.

Men Learn to Make Realistic Portraits

No one has yet explained the greatness of a work of art. Who can state the "formula" which might have shaped the statue of Menkauré (page 78)? There it stands, charged with serene power, an image of a god-king, austerely conceived so that no unnecessary form clutters it and no essential one is left out. Yet this masterpiece was executed in discouragingly resistant material, hard stone. More than being merely a curiosity, it has beauty. It has a power of its own to touch our emotions; it is in its way a revelation, a work of art, and therefore, like all works of art, a partial mystery. In certain ways it differs from the forms we have already studied.

The first thing we notice, in comparison with primitive art, is that the statue is *lifelike*. If we look at the illustration showing the funeral statue of an unknown fifth dynasty official and his wife (page 3), we see the same lifelike quality. It is outstanding in the portrait of Tutankhamen. This is so much our own way of looking at things that we take it for granted. But when we look at the primitive art that preceded it, we must ask what happened to make man start studying himself as he was, instead of inventing a strange conventional form which he *called* himself?

Since the king's health and vigor were believed to affect that of the whole country, it would be logical to create lifelike images of him in enduring materials, as an expression of the people's will to continued existence, or as an expression of the king's own will. The Egyptians also, like peoples in other times and places, appear to have believed in mysterious links between person and image. To embalm a man's body, to preserve it in rigid form so that the *ba* might return to it, and to create in stone or wood an image which would perpetuate a person's appearance, were two acts not clearly distinguished in their minds.

But the question still remains, why did the Egyptians believe that the image must be physically lifelike? As we have seen in the preceding chapter, West African images of ancestors and rulers were made identifiable simply by their tattooing patterns, or by symbols of the ruler's rank and reign. Why did the Egyptians go beyond this to bring their rulers to life in sculpture? And why did they go on to do the same thing for lesser officials in the country's government, in fact to any one, apparently, who could afford such an image and a tomb to house it?

Perhaps, when the rigid ties which had bound men into tribal groups were loosed, and when the old initiation rites became less savage, men could begin to look at themselves with greater freedom. The freedom may still have been incomplete. Conventions still stood partially between the viewer and the person he saw. But the step forward was definite, and its results are dramatically there for us to see. *Man had become aware of himself as a person and as an individual*, even if this awareness was at first limited to kings and other persons of power.

This awareness had another limitation. In the course of Egypt's 3000 year history, we see few signs that the awareness changed or deepened. It was as

Egyptian use of geometric planning. Left, Rameses III's temple at Medinet Habu (shown pages 96–7) within its precinct wall. Right, the geometric plan which seems to have determined the temple's proportions and its placement within the precinct. The temple fits between opposite sides of a decagon inscribed in a circle, and extensions of the decagon determine the precinct boundaries. For the probable Egyptian method of constructing a pentagon (and hence a decagon also) see page 110.

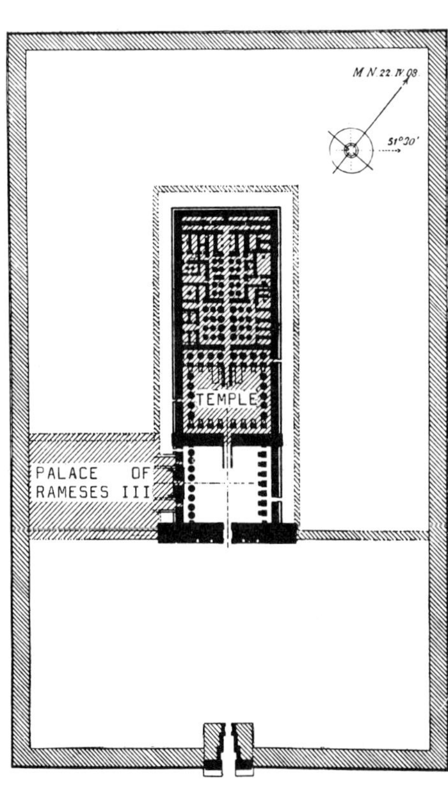

Plan by E. Moessel on reconstruction by Hoelscher

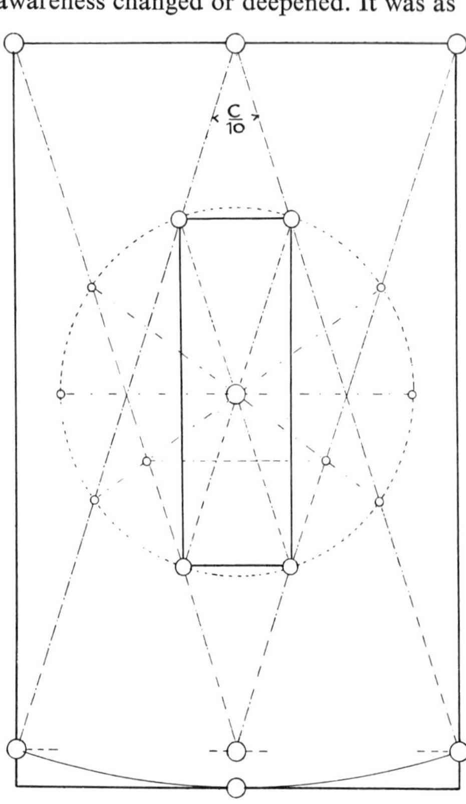

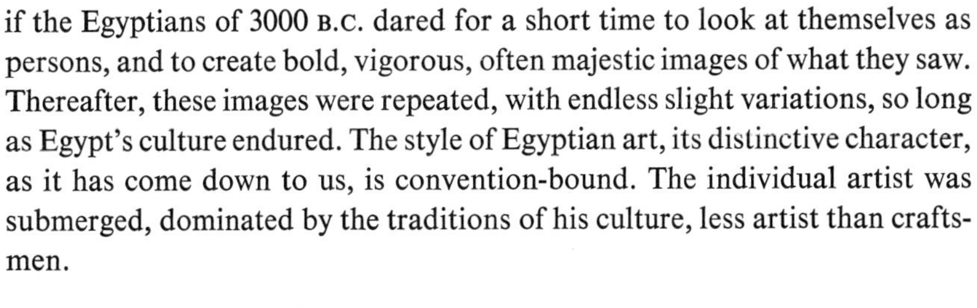

if the Egyptians of 3000 B.C. dared for a short time to look at themselves as persons, and to create bold, vigorous, often majestic images of what they saw. Thereafter, these images were repeated, with endless slight variations, so long as Egypt's culture endured. The style of Egyptian art, its distinctive character, as it has come down to us, is convention-bound. The individual artist was submerged, dominated by the traditions of his culture, less artist than craftsmen.

Oriental Institute, University of Chicago

Ptah, creator of the plan of the universe as the Egyptians imagined him. The granite statue was broken at the waist sometime in the distant past.

Design, or Planned Art, Appears

But Egyptian art possesses other qualities besides this. As one continues to study their architecture, sculpture, painting, or smaller works in precious materials, one becomes aware of the Egyptians' ability to place and proportion forms with taste. Egyptian art seldom seems cluttered. Forms are not only simple and distinct, but the space between them (the *negative space* as artists call it) has been thoughtfully planned. Even an Egyptian inscription places each picture-letter so that it can be enjoyed for itself and yet is part of something larger, namely, the whole inscription.

Whence came this quality? It seems to have had a connection with Egyptian religious beliefs. It may have been their manner of giving *maat* artistic form and of achieving it by a special means.

One of the few Egyptian gods who possessed a human rather than animal-headed form was Ptah, the chief god of Memphis. To the Egyptians, Ptah was the teacher and protector of all men who were makers or designers, from the greatest architect to the humblest craftsman. For Ptah, they believed, was the greatest maker of them all, the god who had created the universe itself. They naïvely believed that in forming it he had used the arts of surveying, architecture, and engineering. And, behind the outward appearance of the universe, Ptah, they believed, had hidden an invisible plan based on pure geometry. How else, they wondered, could the exactly recurring movements of the Sun, Moon, stars, and even the Nile be explained?

Thus, geometry was to the Egyptians a science to be treated with reverence, as a kind of glimpse into Ptah's own creatively planning mind. This belief, it appears, explains the care with which they guarded the secrets of elementary geometry within their House of Life, and why they seem to have believed that whoever practiced it was walking a path leading to *maat*, or oneness between the gods, the universe, and men.

Recent studies of a wide range of Egyptian works of art, both large and small, have shown that their design has a geometric basis. Examples from early and late periods make us think that the basic schemes changed little if at all over 3000 years. This would be in keeping with Egyptian conservatism. The actual making of such plans seems to have been the secret of a few privileged men, probably priests working in temples. Architects, perhaps, were among these few. Lesser men, who worked in stone, paint, wood, and precious metals, would sometimes perhaps be supplied with plans from the House of Life, already completed on papyrus, and squared off for enlargement without revealing the geometric scheme on which they were based.[7]

Whereas with us the purpose of planned design is to achieve a pleasing result, with the Egyptians the intent seems to have been deeply religious.

Three Examples of Egyptian Design

What were these basic designs? It seems likely that the Egyptians invented the straightedge and the compass, or instruments like them.[8] Using these, they appear to have discovered, among other things, how to construct one line perpendicular to another. And while experimenting with different right triangles, they discovered one whose properties touched them with wonder. As we shall see in later chapters, the relationships within this triangle have fascinated mathematicians and artists in other ages. The Egyptians seem to have been the first to appreciate it. It is interesting because its longer leg can be easily divided in extreme and mean proportion. It was this that must have moved the Egyptians with wonder (see diagram).

To divide line AC in mean and extreme proportion, that is so that $\frac{AC}{CE} = \frac{CE}{EA}$, *erect the perpendicular* $AB = \frac{1}{2}AC$, *and draw BC. With center B draw arc AD. Then with center C draw arc DE.*

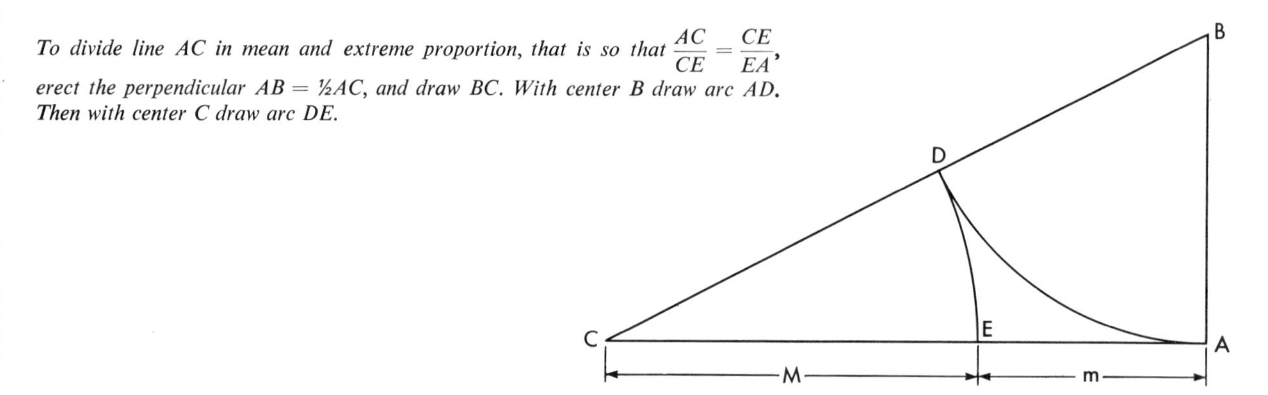

As a first example of the use of this construction, let us look at something small and of simple design: a little ivory and gold box found in the tomb of Tutankhamen, the Egyptian boy-king who died at the age of eighteen. The box was probably made about 1350 B.C., when Egypt's civilization, still at its height, had run far more than half its course.

Small ivory box with gold fittings, from the tomb of Tutankhamen. The fact that it was made for a god-king may explain why geometry, a sacred science to the Egyptians, seems to have determined its proportions. Or it may have been merely a matter of refined taste. No one, perhaps, will ever know. Dimensions of box: height, not including knob, 13.3 cm; width, 15.5 cm; breadth, 12.6 cm; height from ground to floor of box, 2.6 cm; width of legs and moldings, 1.6 cm; thickness of lid, 0.6 cm.

Cairo Museum, Object 80

One can find pleasure in this king's plaything from several points of view: its finished workmanship; the attractive color scheme of ivory against gold; and the pleasingly austere quality of its proportions. But in terms of geometry it is interesting because all its dimensions can be derived from a single $1:2:\sqrt{5}$ right triangle. A geometric construction of the box, based on that worked out by the Danish egyptologist Else C. Kielland, is shown.

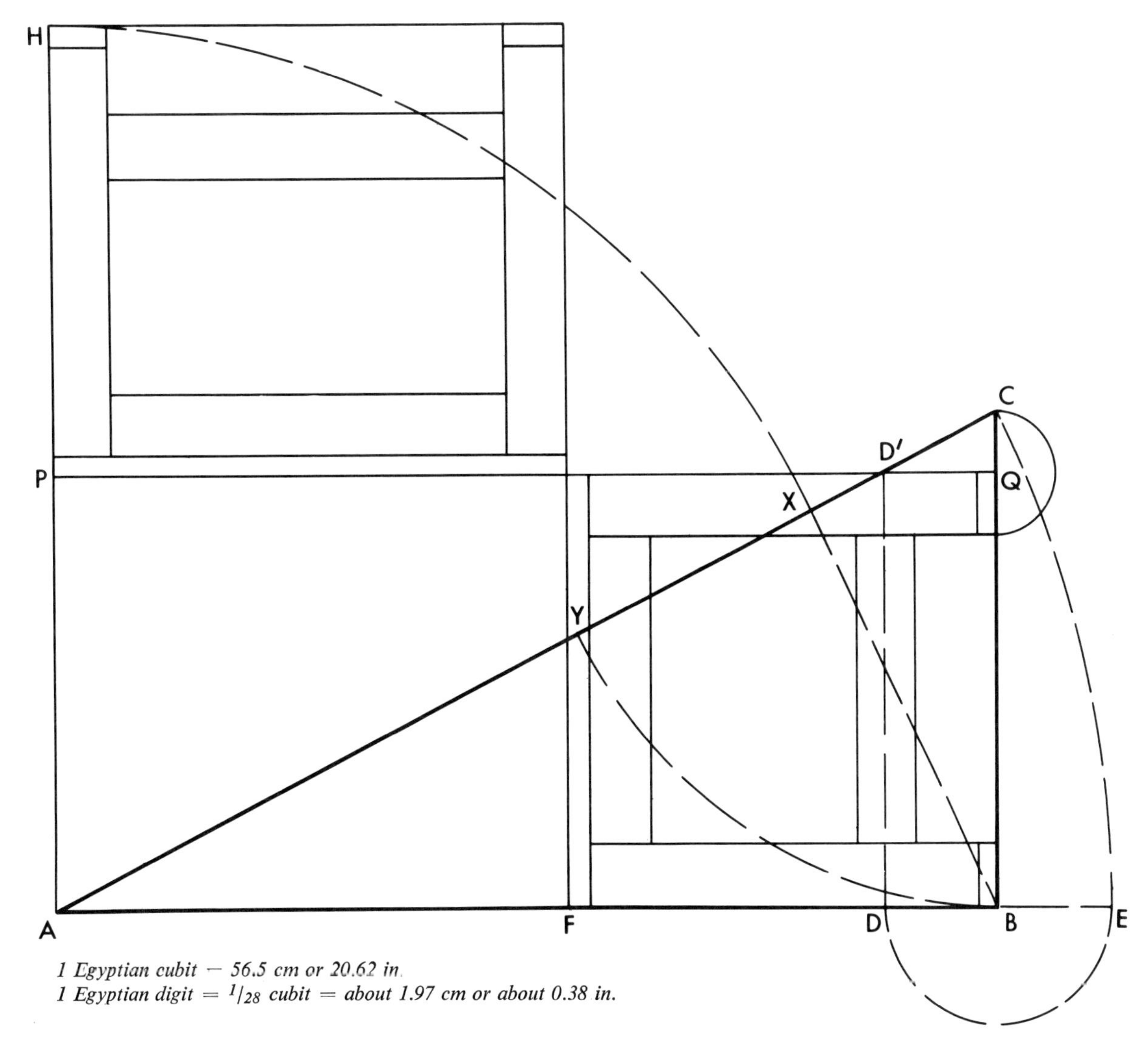

1 Egyptian cubit = 56.5 cm or 20.62 in.
1 Egyptian digit = 1/28 cubit = about 1.97 cm or about 0.38 in.

Top, front, and end of Tutankhamen's ivory box. The Egyptian designer seems to have started with the line AB, which is 15 Egyptian digits long (see table of values above). On AB he could have erected the $1:2:\sqrt{5}$ Triangle ABC, and then erected $BX \perp AC$. He could next draw the arcs HX and CE, and then the semi-circle DE, which determines DD′. These together determine the height, length and width of the box. CQ determines the width of legs and moldings. DD′ lies on the midline of the lower molding. The point Y lies on the midline of the lid.

Lowie Museum of Anthropology, University of California, Berkeley

A group of pyramids at Giza, near the Nile delta, each the tomb of an ancient Egyptian ruler. The nearest and largest is that of Cheops, a fourth dynasty king. Its construction required men in tens of thousands, working during the four months of flood time, when the Nile's high water permitted rafts carrying stone from distant quarries to float close to the pyramid site. Each stone, weighing 2½ tons, then required an 8-man team to drag it into position.

Now let us go to the opposite extreme in size, and to an earlier time in Egypt. Let us look at the measurements of the largest single monument in stone yet made by man, and surely the largest man-made object any one person has ever owned or perhaps ever will. This is the Great Pyramid of Cheops, constructed at his command almost 1200 years before Tutankhamen was born that is, somewhere near 2650 B.C. This astonishing mass, although multilated by man over the centuries, still shows clearly the simple but subtle geometric thinking which went into its construction.

The base of the pyramid is within a few inches of being 760 feet square (a distance about once and a half the height of the Washington Monument). The Egyptian unit of measure was the *cubit* (or forearm), standardized by them at what, to us, would be 20.62 inches. It seems, therefore, that the Egyptian architects planned a structure whose base would be 440 cubits on each side.

Their purpose, also, seems to have been to make the pyramid's four surfaces face exactly north, south, east and west, as determined by the rising and setting of the sun at the equinoxes. For they do so face with remarkable accuracy.

The sloping angle of the pyramid's faces is peculiar: 51°50′. What could have been the reason for this unusual slope? To guess at the reason we must compare it with the pyramid's other dimensions. Although men trying to use stone from the pyramid for their own buildings in the middle ages removed about 30 feet from the apex, it appears that the original height was close to 481 feet, or 280 cubits. The inclined distance up the side appears to have been slightly more than 356 cubits.

Let us now view the cross section of the pyramid as a pair of right triangles with a common altitude. We find that each right triangle has the following dimensions: legs, 220 cubits and 280 cubits, respectively; hypotenuse, slightly more than 356 cubits; angles, 90°, 51°50′, and 38°10′.

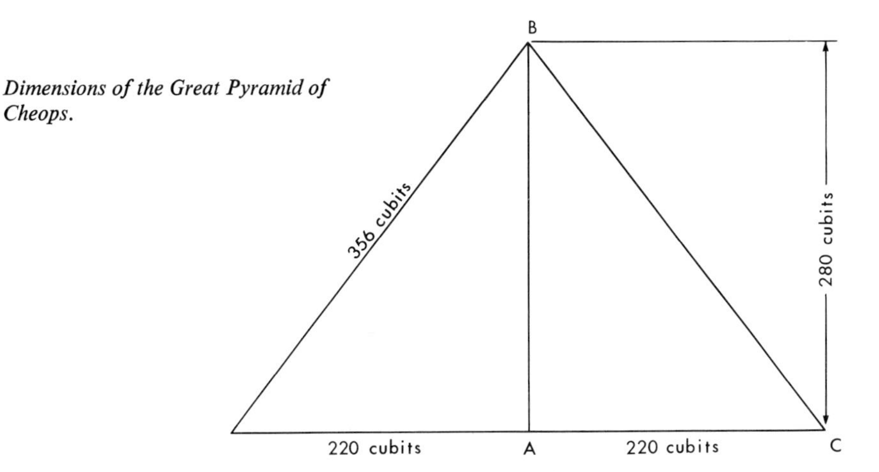

Dimensions of the Great Pyramid of Cheops.

These are the proportions of a unique triangle, the only one whose sides are in *geometric* progression. You can test this for yourself by dividing the length of the short leg into that of the long one, and the length of the long leg into that of the hypotenuse.[9] The quotients will be found to be equal to two decimal places.

How did the Egyptians arrive at the proportions of this pyramid? Here the $1:2:\sqrt{5}$ triangle comes into use again. The way to construct a right triangle whose sides are in geometric progression is as follows.

1. Divide the long leg of a $1:2:\sqrt{5}$ triangle in mean and extreme proportion (M and m).
2. Construct a rectangle whose length is M and width m.
3. With C as center, describe arc DB. Right triangle ABC will be the desired triangle.

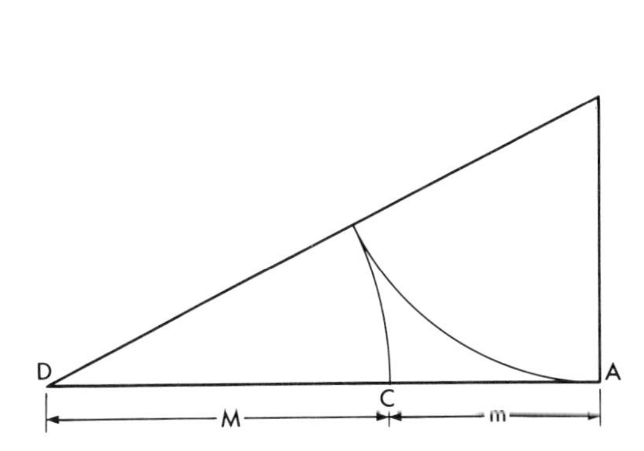

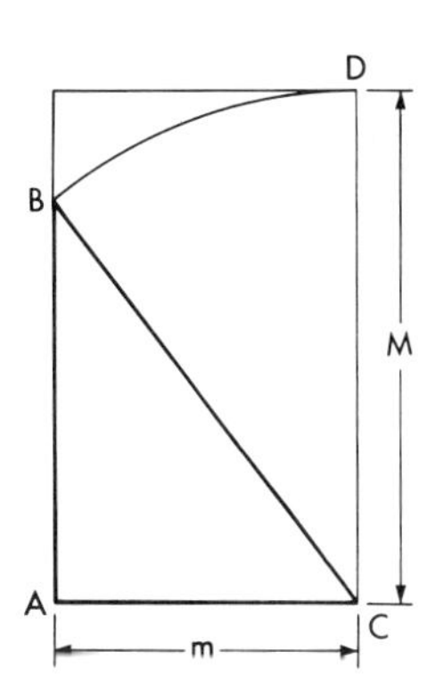

Notice that the resulting pyramid has a more commanding character than would have been the case if the cross section were two 45°, 45°, 90° triangles. As a form it is also more stable than would have been the case had the cross section been a pair of 30°, 60°, 90° triangles.

It is astonishing to realize that Egyptian engineers, using what must have been naïvely simple methods, were able to direct multitudes of men, working in quarries, on rafts, and at hauling ropes, so efficiently over a period of perhaps twenty years, that the original geometric concept was accurately embodied on this vast scale in stone.

Drawing by Snyder, after E. C. Kielland

Another Egyptian use of the 1:2:$\sqrt{5}$ triangle, this time bilaterally symmetrical. The isosceles right triangle is drawn within a square, with base DD′ and altitude BC. BC is then lengthened to A. N is the midpoint of AC, 0 the midpoint of BC. BC is divided in mean and extreme proportion at F. BG = CF. This construction, with or without the extension to A, seems to have been a favorite Egyptian basis for planning three-dimensional figures.

Before going on to a third example of Egyptian design-planning, let us look at an arrangement of the 1:2:$\sqrt{5}$ triangle which seems often to have been used as a foundation for planning their sculpture. This plan was discovered through the researches of E. C. Kielland, who studied a number of Egyptian antiquities in the Ny Carlsberg Museum (Copenhagen, Denmark) and elsewhere.

Statue of an unknown Egyptian king, carved toward the end of Egypt's long civilization, in about 200 B.C., after it had fallen before a foreign conquest and was ruled by Greek kings. But the king is still represented in the Egyptian manner, and its design plan is unchanged from former ages. The design plan as reconstructed by Kielland is shown opposite.

Ny Carlsberg Museum, Copenhagen

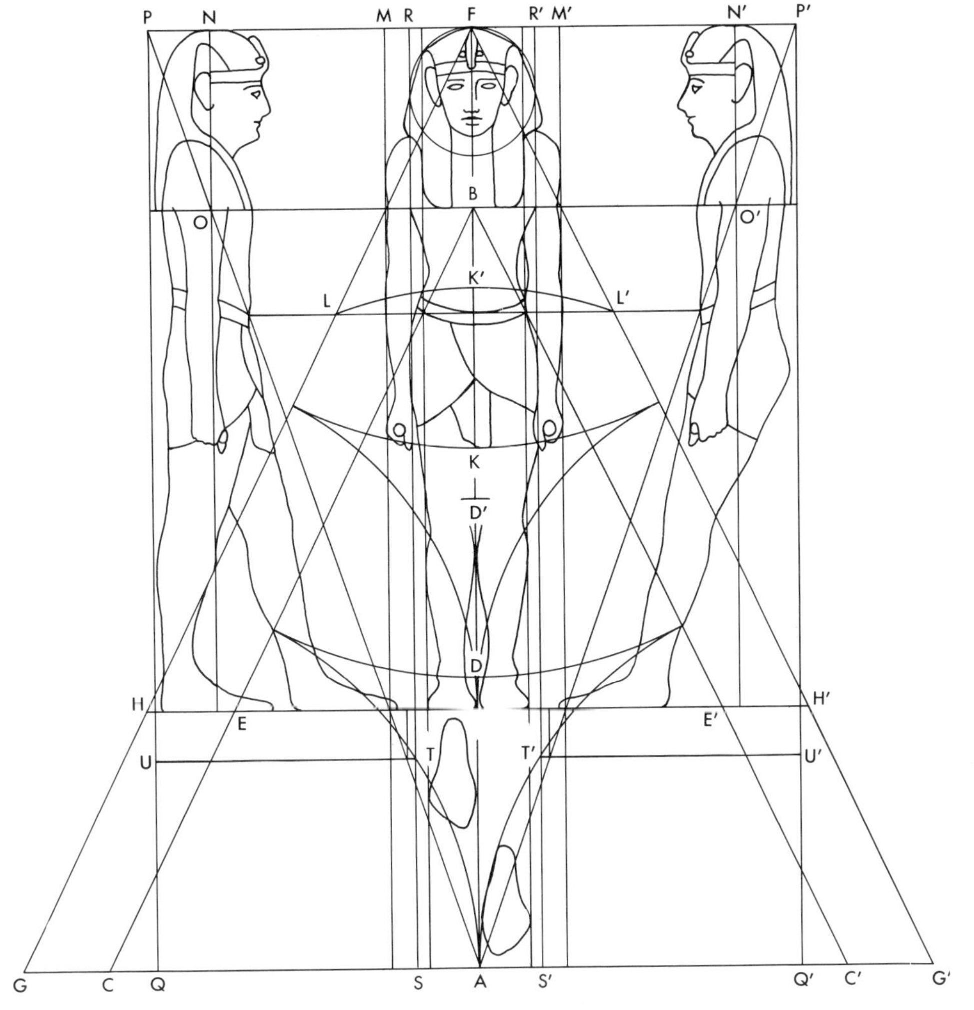

Drawing by Snyder, after Kielland

There are several ways to construct the design-plan shown here. The following is perhaps the simplest and clearest.

1. Draw CC' with midpoint A. Erect $AB \perp CC'$ so that $AB = CC'$. Draw $\triangle CBC'$.
2. Divide AB in extreme and mean proportion at D. Then mark the point D' so that $AD' = DB$.
3. Extend AB to F, so that $BF = DD'$. Mark off points G, G', so that $GG' = AF$, with A the midpoint of GG'. Draw $\triangle GFG'$.
4. Mark the points E and E' so that $AD = CE = C'E'$. Draw line EE' and extend it, creating $\triangle HFH'$, and cutting AF at J. Through B and F draw lines $\parallel$ the $\triangle$ base GG'.
5. Mark the points M, M', N, N', so that MM', NM, and $N'M'$ all $= BF$ (and BF is midpoint of MM'). Through N, M, M', N' rule lines $\parallel$ the vertical axis AF.
6. Draw lines AO and AO', extended to P and P'. Draw PQ and $P'Q' \parallel AF$. Draw RS and $R'S' \parallel AF$, so that QS and $Q'S' = AJ$.
7. Last of all draw UT and $U'T' \parallel GG'$.

The main dimensions of the statue are now determined: height of figure, length, breadth, and thickness of base. To obtain important measurements of the figure itself, divide JF in mean and extreme proportion at K. $JK' = KF$. Draw LL'.

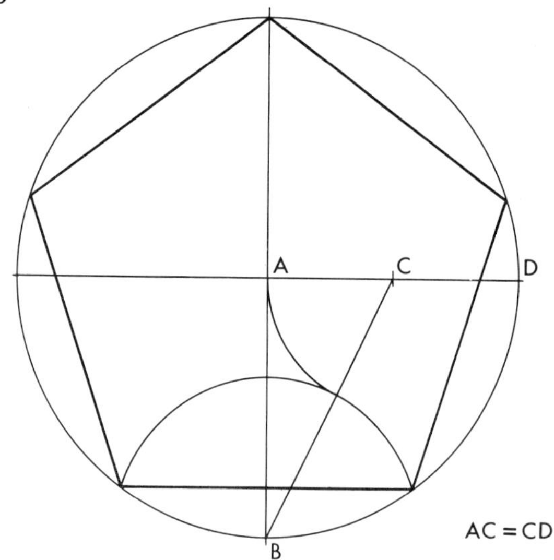

How to inscribe a pentagon within a circle by use of mean and extreme proportion. Divide the circle at right angles through its center A. Bisect radius AD at C, and draw BC. Divide BC in mean and extreme proportion, and continue the arc whose center is B until it cuts off an arc of the circle circumference. That arc will be 1/5 of the whole circumference. This was probably the Egyptian method for constructing a pentagon. From it they derived the pentagram, decagon, and decagram (see opposite page). These, they believed, possessed magic protective powers.

The Egyptians seem to have invented several other geometric constructions as bases for their design-plans. Which one was used probably depended in part on the shape of the object. It is possible, also, that each construction had its own magical purpose, of which we now have no idea, and which would make it suited to certain uses only.

One of these constructions, illustrated below, is a rectangle whose sides are to each other as 1 is to $\sqrt{2}$, and which is derived from a square.

An Egyptian landowner, backed by his farm overseer, inspects the produce of his lands. Limestone plaque from about 2900 B.C. The superimposed lines show its apparent design plan.

Rijksmuseum, Leyden. Design plan by D. Snyder after Moessel

An alabaster lamp in the form of lotus flowers and leaves, from the tomb of Tutankhamen. Lights placed within the cups shine through, shedding a soft light.

Cairo Museum

Three polygons used by the Egyptians in various ways. Top: pentagram. Middle: decagram. Bottom: decagon. Pentagrams were sometimes painted on wine jars, perhaps to keep the contents from spoiling!

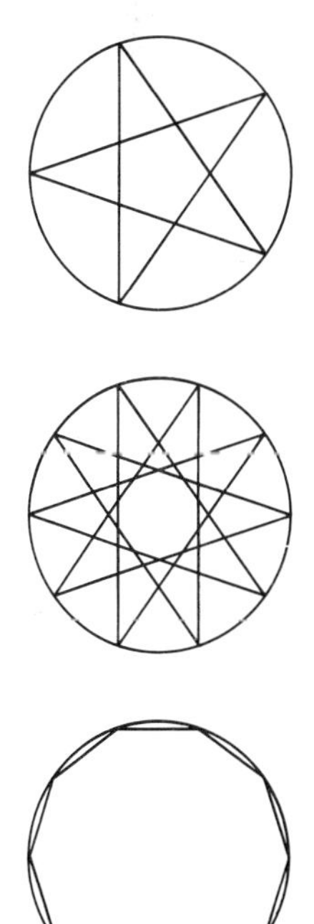

What Does Egyptian Art Mean to Us?

The Egyptians seem to have been acutely aware of the principles of artistic organization which we have already discussed in Chapters 1 and 2. Outstanding examples of all these principles can be found appearing repeatedly in what we have discovered of their art.

So much for the Egyptians on familiar ground. What new things can they show us? Let us discuss just two things, chosen because they are likely best to fit the interests and needs of persons reading this book. They are intended to arouse your interest in Egyptian accomplishment, not to exhaust it.

Egyptians as the World's First Conscious Designers

Earlier we saw geometrical plans which appear to have determined the design of three different Egyptian works of art, varying in age, scale, and form. In Projects 17 and 18 the reader can explore the geometric basis of two other examples. Let us now think about the value of such a design-basis.

The Egyptians seem to have been the first men to discover that *a geometric design-plan can heighten an object's beauty*. We have seen that their respect for such plans was probably chiefly religious. But if they planned even such trifles as jewelry and little ivory boxes, they must also have been keenly aware that such planning can transform the object as a work of art.

Necklace pendant belonging to a daughter of King Senusret II, of Egypt's twelfth dynasty. Gold, carnelian, lapis lazuli and green feldspar. The king's name is in the center oval between the hawk's heads. Height 1.8 in.

Metropolitan Museum of Art, Walters and Rogers Funds

The principles that were once the secret of priests, regarded with religious awe, are now the common knowledge of anyone attending a school of architecture or design. Let us recognize that in a sense the Egyptians were ahead of us in this field.

The Egyptian method of arriving at an object's design was markedly different from our own. Whereas we tend to consider the impression that the object will make upon the viewer from certain angles, one at a time, the Egyptian thought as if four different views of the object were seen at *once* (perhaps as Ptah saw it) and therefore interrelated them on one master plan before construction started. Egyptian wall painting seems to be in harmony with this way of thinking. Persons are represented by a scheme intended to give the viewer an immediate allover understanding of their form, rather than a photographic image from one fixed angle. This often results in an odd combination of front views and profiles, all in one figure.

Cedar wood statuette of King Senusret I. He wears the white crown of Lower Egypt (a twin statuette to this one shows him wearing the red crown of Upper Egypt). Twelfth dynasty. Height 28 in.

Metropolitan Museum of Art. Rogers Fund and E. S. Harkness

Egyptian Methods of Sculpture

Look at the three stone statues shown on pages 3, 78 and 108. You can see that the sculptor knew that he was working in a brittle substance, and that he was thinking about making the statues durable and permanent. He made the figures compact. The arms are close to the body, with no piercing of the stone between arms or legs. For additional strength each figure is backed by a stone support, all part of the same rock.

When an Egyptian sculptor worked in wood, he was just as aware of his material. Unlike stone, it is tough, springy, lighter, easier to work, and by its nature less durable. Accordingly, he took more liberties in carving it, making the arms and legs free from the body and from supporting masses. But he acknowledged something else about wood. He recognized it as having a fibrous structure with strength in only one direction, that in which the grain runs. He assembled his wood sculpture of several pieces, if necessary, so that the grain would run in the long direction of each part. Note the statue of a twelfth dynasty king. The joints at the shoulders, the bent elbow, and the feet, where the direction of the form changes, are visible (after about 4000 years of shrinkage inside a hot, dry, sealed tomb). See also the statuette, page 115.

Probably this statue was developed by a priest-designer on an over-all four-view plan. Front, side, and top views were then copied on a sheet of papyrus, without the geometric construction lines, but with a grid of cross lines on the figures, so that they could be copied by workmen and enlarged at will.

Egyptian Music and Dance

No papyrus on Egyptian music has ever been found. But we have ample evidence that they were, on all levels of society, a musical people, who enjoyed making harmonious sound and rhythm with voice, instruments, clapping hands, and, in the dance, with their feet. They also regarded singing, instrumental music, and the dance as forms of praise fit to please the gods in their temples. Pictures on temple and tomb walls, and the remains of the instruments themselves, amply prove this.

It seems probable that priests in the House of Life pursued research in music as keenly as in geometry, at least in the formative period of Egyptian civilization. They probably made elementary discoveries in the laws of sound, for example, that a taut, plucked string rises an octave in pitch if the weight holding it taut is doubled. They seem to have treated such discoveries with the same religious awe they did others, as a revelation of one more aspect of Ptah's plan for the universe. The power of music to bring joy and peace to the heart of performer and listener was probably looked on by them as one more sign that harmony could be found between the universal plan and man. They looked on music as another means to achieving *maat.*

This is conjecture. It is based on just one kind of indirect evidence, the presence of ideas like these in the works of Greek thinkers who spent years of study in Egypt and whose writings show other Egyptian influences. This will be discussed in Chapter 4.

Four Egyptian girls make music for a feast, while a fifth is about to dance. Part of a wall painting from a tomb of the eighteenth dynasty.

Oriental Institute, University of Chicago

Egyptian Literature

Egyptian writing has been preserved for us carved and painted on the stone walls of tombs. Such writing often makes delightful accompaniment to the pictures of Egyptian life so vividly portrayed there. Rather than merely saying what the picture is about, which is usually obvious, they quote what the people in the picture are saying. It is sad that all this freshness and bold wit was so clearly put down only to be sealed up from view. It was there, of course, to entertain the *ba*, or soul, of the deceased person, as he supposedly returned at will through his tomb's false door to enjoy the contents of his tomb.

The dry weather has also somehow preserved fragments of Egyptian writings on papyrus. Many of these, as found in the tombs, are endless magic spells to guard the soul after death. But parts of libraries have also been found, probably the valued possessions of priests. These fragments give a glimpse of Egyptian achievement in poetry and in prose fiction, practically the world's oldest.[10]

Rijksmuseum, Leyden

Egyptian use of dynamic rhythm. Egyptians leading Asiatic captives. From the tomb of the Egyptian general Horemheb.

Egypt: A Summary Appraisal

The outstanding trait of the Egyptians was perhaps their awareness of the value of order. In the early stages of their culture they learned to survive by cooperating with the rhythmic order of nature—the regular rise and fall of the Nile, the coming and going of the seasons, and the succession of day and night. From nature they learned to create order of their own, systems which determined the pattern of their society, their organization of labor, their architecture, and their art. Through the intelligent creation and maintenance of order their lives progressed from mere survival to that partial conquest of nature which we call civilization.

Aware of the source of their success, the Egyptians respected the ordering principle in themselves as a divine gift. A king, whose role was to impose outward order on the land was in their eyes the embodiment of a god. At the same time they looked with religious awe on each man's ability to achieve inner order (*maat*). This too they saw as a divine gift.

The Egyptians achieved a highly organized society, protected by an efficient army, adorned with splendid temples, timed by a calendar better planned than our own, and inspired by a philosophy which was the greatest of its time. But the natural state of the Nile valley, rhythmically changeless within, unusually isolated against influence from without, helped to make Egyptian systems for order static. Changelessness became an ideal; the country's creative forces were locked in rigid tradition for thousands of years. Egyptian society froze into a permanent pattern in which docile millions did the back-breaking work of producing the corps and other wealth, digging miles of irrigation canals, and dragging the stone for the erection of colossal pyramids and temples, all at the command of a small ruling class: kings, priests and government officials.

What seems rigid to us in our own fast-changing world was in its age a tremendous step forward. The permanence of Egyptian civilization, with its rewarding, even if unchanging, pattern of complex cooperation, was vastly preferable to tribal life, constantly at the mercy of weather, wild beasts and marauding neighbors. The achievement of permanence was in itself a cultural milestone, even though that permancence was only partial, and eventually gave way under the blows of violent, destructive change, inflicted from without.

The Egyptian ideal of changelessness speaks through their architecture, their sculpture and painting, even though what survives is partially wrecked, broken and defaced. The slight fortress-like slope of Egyptian temple pylons, the practice of giving stone sculpture as few protruding parts as possible, all express the will of a people deeply concerned with permanence. Next, their art is formally clear. Each form is as distinct to the viewer as the functions and duties of each Egyptian, from the Pharaoh or king, and the chief priest of Amon, down to the poorest peasant or slave, seem to have been in the Egyptian mind. And these forms, whether they be the columns of a temple or the figures on a tomb wall, are spaced out in a carefully controlled manner, proclaiming timeless, frictionless order as still another Egyptian ideal. The colossal images of their rulers bring this ideal serenely to life. They appear capable of maintaining such a state of order throughout all eternity.

Cairo Museum

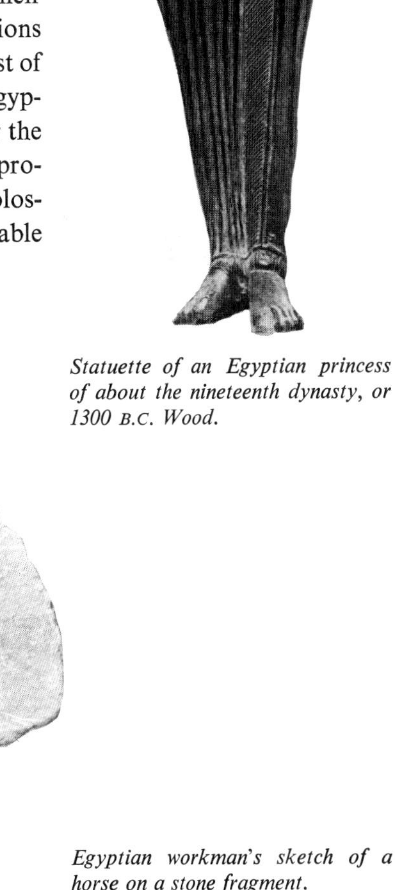

Statuette of an Egyptian princess of about the nineteenth dynasty, or 1300 B.C. Wood.

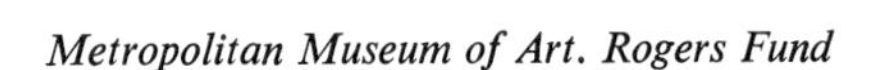

Egyptian workman's sketch of a horse on a stone fragment.

Metropolitan Museum of Art. Rogers Fund

Gudea, lugal *or ruler of the city-state of Lagash stands in respectful praise of Ningursu, his city's god. Gudea was also Ningursu's* ensi *or chief priest, unlike the rulers of Egypt who were gods in their own right. Mesopotamia, also unlike Egypt, was a cluster of independent city-states often at war with one another. This statue, of hard close-grained diorite, has been broken at the middle and has lost its inlaid eyes. It still conveys Gudea's devotion to his god.*

Civilization Develops in Mesopotamia

The Fertile Crescent, the name commonly given to the land which curves in a 1200 mile arch over the northern end of the Arabian Desert, seems to have been the first place on earth where man discovered how to live by plant- and animal-farming alone. The starting point for the discovery seems to have been somewhere near the apex of the arch. Here men first developed one of the world's great food complexes: soft-kerneled wheat (called bread wheat), barley, dates, grapes, together with domesticated animals—cattle, goats, pigs, and wool-bearing sheep with spiral horns.

No one yet knows exactly how long ago this complex was developed. We do not know at what time, or how, tribal organization based on loyalty to family ties disappeared, to be replaced by organization based on loyalty to place and to a god symbolizing a place-rooted community. What we do know is that such a change must have taken place in prehistoric times, and that in the place of tribes there emerged the *city-state. A city-state can be described as a wide extent of farmland, administered from a fortified central community, whose citizens were active not only in farming but also in trade.*

Near the western end of the Fertile Crescent are the remains of Jericho, the oldest known town in the world. Its age is perhaps 10,000 years. It covered an area of about eight acres, was fortified with a wall and a watch tower, and was occupied by different peoples at different times. When Joshua commanded his host to blow their trumpets, "and the wall came tumbling down," Jericho was already ancient and had fallen before invaders time and again.

Skull from Jericho, to which features have been added in plaster. About 6000 B.C.

Courtesy Professor Kathleen Kenyon

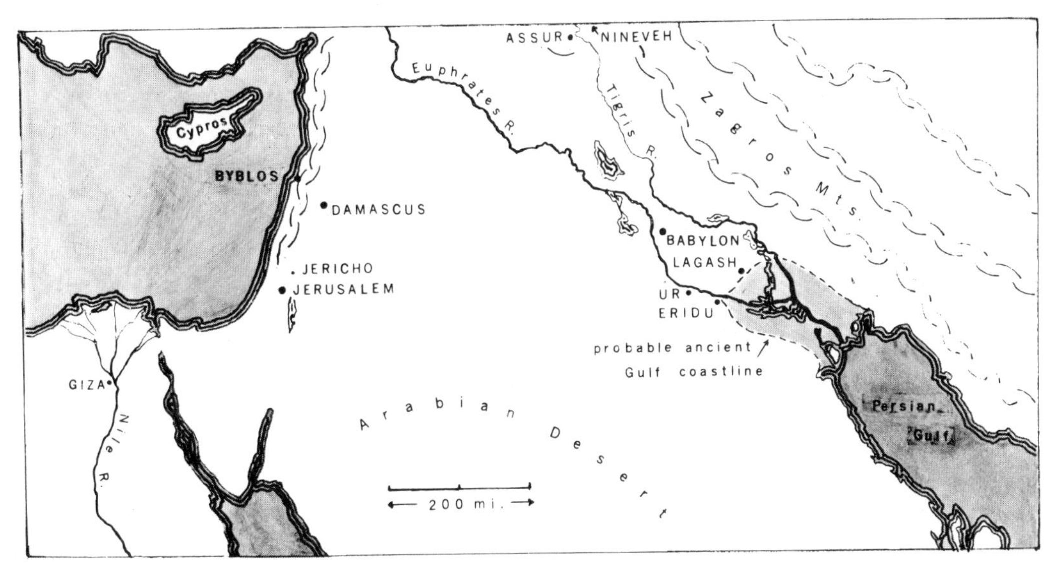

Ancient Mesopotamia. Sumeria, the center in which an agrarian civilization in this area began, lies between the lower Euphrates and Tigris Rivers, below the point at which they run closest.

Under the soil of the Fertile Crescent untold other cities wait to be found and excavated. Each city, as it is uncovered, will tell us more about this part of the world where civilization seems first to have appeared.[11] The part of which we now know most, and which produced a way of life which seems to have affected all the rest, is Mesopotamia, at the Crescent's eastern end. Let us now take a swift look at it.

The Land

Like the Nile valley, the valley of the Euphrates and Tigris Rivers, called Mesopotamia, is suited to farming and raising animals because of soil-bearing river water descending from mountains into a plain. On that plain men learned, as in Egypt, the art of irrigation, the source of life for their crops. These were the likenesses between the two regions. Let us now consider the differences.

The two rivers run faster than the Nile, especially the Tigris, whose ancient name was *Idiglat*, or arrow. Masses of silt are therefore steadily carried all the way to the river's mouth in the Persian Gulf. The rivers, which now have but one mouth, once had two, and the ancient city of Eridu, formerly a seaport, is now 150 miles inland, a deserted mound. At the opposite end of the valley, near the Zagros Mountains, the impetuous Tigris sometimes carries down tons of gravel, clogging its channel and producing unpredictable floods.

While rain in Egypt is a rare and minor occurrence, in Mesopotamia the skies can open in an occasional cloudburst. The desert shielded Egypt from its ancient invaders for hundreds of miles on both sides. But Mesopotamia is an exposed land. Mountain tribes could pounce on it from the north. From the south other tribes could come raiding in from the desertlike pasture lands of upper Arabia.

Except for soil, river water, and, in some places, tar pits, Mesopotamia is poor in raw materials. Stone and metals are scarce or nonexistent. Everything has to be a farm product, made from the soil itself, or imported. Trade with the outside world, therefore, became vital to Mesopotamia. *Uruttu*, the ancient word for copper, was at one time the name of the Euphrates River, the route down which traders brought the metal needed for weapons and tools from distant mines in another land.

From C. L. Woolley, Ur Excavations *V, 1939*

Reconstruction of the ziggurat *or artificial mountain which was once the center of the Mesopotamian city of Ur. It is crowned by a temple to the goddess Nanna. About 2250* B.C.

The Mesopotamians as Builders

Given these conditions, the civilization which evolved in Mesopotamia was consistent and logical. The usual building material was sun-dried mud brick for walls, floors, and platforms. Tree trunks, probably palm, were laid on these and covered with mud for roofs. For permanence the brick walls were sometimes cemented with tar or sheathed with fire bricks or tiles. But these were costly devices, reserved for holy places.

In a fitfully rainy climate such buildings could be treacherous. Houses would collapse, be leveled off, more bricks brought in, and a new home put up, on a slightly higher level. Thus gradually rose the *tell* or platform on which many of Mesopotamia's older cities rested, and still rest (Damascus, for example). Digging a trench through such a mound is like cutting an archeological cake. The layers tell the story of passing centuries, each with its own style of living.

The temple, where the god-ruler of each city dwelt, was worthy of special treatment. At intervals, when a temple was deemed old, it was filled solid with mud brick, even to its courtyard walls. On this high platform a new temple, following the plan of the original temple, would be erected. As this process was repeated, the temple rose ever higher and higher upon a great brick hill or *ziggurat*, the lofty center of each Mesopotamian city. The ziggurat itself, as it rose into prominence, was often given a carefully planned design of its own, with outsloping walls and ascending flights of steps.

Clustered around the base of each ziggurat was a maze of storehouses, offices, record files, schoolrooms, courtyards, and the living quarters of priests. And around these ran a high wall, defining a city within a city.

Each temple crowning a ziggurat, where the god lived, was brilliantly decorated with the best materials the citizens could afford. Cones of fired clay, the flat outer ends painted red, white, and black, were sometimes driven into the walls in patterns. Or sometimes the mud walls were merely painted white and other strong colors.

Mesopotamian Religion and Its Contributions

Just as the sheltered Nile valley, with its regular, gently flooding river and clear, rainless skies, produced a religion whose spirit was *maat*, or order and peace, so the Mesopotamian valley, constantly periled by flood, cloudburst, and ruthless invader, developed religious beliefs in which conflict, fear of the unknown, and materialism were prominent.

Compared to the Egyptians, the Mesopotamians were vague about the fate of a man after death. What concerned them was the present. The god of each city presided over a temple to which people went to ensure *success*, whether in business, farming, love, or war. The high priest of each god controlled the city's irrigation system, the ordering of work crews in the fields, the gathering of taxes, the issuing of food, tools, and other supplies to the citizens, and the marshaling of manpower in time of war. What is fascinating here is that we see the *city* appearing for the first time in history. We see it to have been a center of security so strong and evoking such a loyalty as to possess for its citizens a personality of its own, made visible in the image of the city's god. The Mesopotamian's intense loyalty to his city is proved by his almost inexhaustible will to rebuild after the most hideous experiences of defeat, looting, and massacre by the armies of jealous neighboring cities or foreign invaders. We shall see the city-state appearing again repeatedly, later in history.

Statuettes of worshippers, reassuring a god of their constant devotion; found in the ruins of a temple at what is today Tel Asmar, Iraq. Mesopotamian religion does not seem to have been concerned with man's soul or conscience. One obtained what one wanted from the gods by praise, money, or magic.

Oriental Institute, University of Chicago

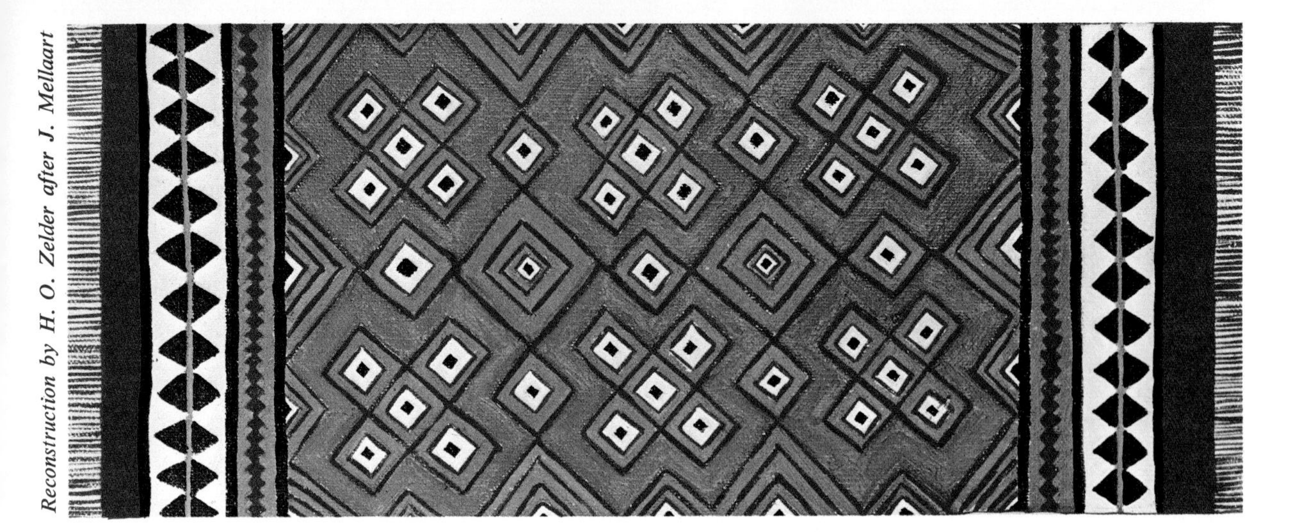
Reconstruction by H. O. Zelder after J. Mellaart

The world's oldest wool pile carpet yet to be discovered, as restored from fragments found in the tomb of an unknown ruler, western Turkey, about 2500 B.C.

Mesopotamian Weaving

The Mesopotamians made the most of their every resource. One of these was the wool from their flocks of sheep. They spun this into thread, dyed it with vegetable dyes, and started a tradition of weaving for which the Near East, thousands of years later, is still famous. For they wove not only cloth for their garments, but carpets to cover their mud-brick floors; and the Oriental carpet is to this day one of the world's most beautiful art forms.

Along with the specialized profession of carpet weaver went another, that of carpet merchant, the man of enterprise who bought the carpets and transported them far from their place of manufacture in the hope of trading them at a profit for copper, sky-blue turquoise, deep-blue lapis lazuli, and other precious materials which Mesopotamia lacked.

Mesopotamian Economics: The Merchant as Full-Time Specialist

The Mesopotamian city-temple was responsible for the community's farming success and therefore for its food supply. The elaborate irrigation system required someone in authority to run it. This is probably why agriculture seems to have been so rigidly controlled by the authority of the city's high priest.

Oriental Institute, University of Chicago

Women from the Near East in their richly patterned garments, as seen through Egyptian eyes. Wall painting from a tomb of the twelfth dynasty, recording a visit by foreigners to Egypt.

Lowie Museum of Anthropology, University of California, Berkeley. Photo John Bridgman

The necessary tools of Mesopotamian business life. 1. Clay tablets covered with cuneiform *(wedge-shaped) writing. Important documents were often enclosed in clay envelopes bearing written descriptions of their contents. Documents of permanent value were made rock hard by firing. 2. Cylindrical seals of carved stone, and (below left) their imprint when rolled on soft clay. Every man carried his own seal, and its imprint was his personal signature.*

But there was another aspect of city life, that of trade. That full-time specialist, the *merchant*, was needed to bring into the city many necessities and luxuries from the outside world. Here again the temple played a vital role. But this time less in a spirit of control and more in one of opportunity.

The temple, as the center of the city's treasure, was the place to which a merchant would go to finance an enterprise in trade (such as, perhaps, the purchase of a load of dates, hides, or wool, and of a donkey on which to transport it). Therefore, temples became banks. Some of the world's most fundamental economic practices were originated here, such as (a) the creation of a *hard currency* in the form of small weights of gold or silver, each bearing the stamp of the temple issuing it. They were still thought of as weights rather than coins, and were probably weighed and reweighed at each transaction. But their circulation lifted trade above the cumbersome barter level and made possible sale and purchase through a medium of exchange which a man could easily carry. The gold *shekel*, worth about $10, and the silver shekel, worth about 75c, were standardized late in Mesopotamian history over large areas, as the names *Babylonian shekel*, *Syrian shekel*, *Phoenician shekel*, etc., indicate. (b) the creation of a *note currency*, in the form of clay tablets stamped with a temple seal, and stating that the temple would redeem the tablet for so much gold or silver. (c) the *loan* of currency for a specific time at a specific rate of interest, secured by collateral,[12] the whole arrangement recorded in writing.

Mesopotamian Mathematics

Such operations as these required the continual use of arithmetic and accounting. This perhaps explains the much greater advance in this science made by the Mesopotamians over the Egyptians. The remains of temple schoolrooms have been found, complete with practice tablets. From these we gather that they developed a number scale based not on 10 but on 60, from which we seem to inherit the 60 minute hour, the 60 second minute, and the 360° circle. They also had discovered elementary algebra. The Egyptians, however, were apparently far superior in geometry, as their methods of design show.

Mesopotamian Astronomy

In a land where life was subject to unforeseen violence in so many forms, there was an intense desire, it seems, to find security by controlling the future and foretelling events. In an effort to *control* future events, magic was extensively practiced. To *foretell* events the Mesopotamian priests attempted to find a connection between the motions of the sun, moon, planets, and stars and the events of men's daily life; they practised astrology, the ancient forerunner of the science of astronomy. The practice led to the first, and, to this day, longest unbroken series of scientific observations known to the world. For 360 years the astronomers of the city of Babylon, who were priests of Marduk, the city's god, kept detailed records of the observed motions of the heavenly bodies. (All observations were made with the naked eye. The telescope was still 2000 years in the future.) From this veritable "great pyramid" of scientific achievement, brilliant priest-astronomers such as Nabu-rimmanu and Kidinnu drew conclusions which laid the foundations for later discoveries by Greek astronomers.

To Mesopotamia also we owe the origin of that time-division which rules our lives, the week. The astronomer-priests divided the lunar month, or span of time from one new moon to the next, into fourths, each seven days long, and named these days respectively in honor of the seven major heavenly bodies then known (Sun, Moon, Jupiter, Venus, Mercury, Mars, Saturn).

Mesopotamian Law

Of all the kings who sought to bind the Fertile Crescent under one rule, only some were even temporarily successful. One of the greatest of these was Hammurabi, whose long reign of forty-three years stretched from 1948 to 1905 B.C. One of his many duties as king was to make decisions on a host of problems brought to him by his subjects from all over the land. Of these decisions records were kept on clay in the king's archive. Toward the end of his reign he ordered his scribes to make a study of this collection of decisions and from it to prepare a series of laws which might have general application throughout his kingdom. Thus came into being what was perhaps the world's first *legal code*. When completed it was carved in hard stone and set up in various parts of the land, so that everywhere men might see the laws by which they were governed. This was a great step forward in justice.

British Museum

The forces of King Assur-bani-pal storming the city of Charnamu. A stone slab from the Assyrian king's palace ruins at Nineveh. About 600 B.C.

Assyria, Mesopotamia's Curse

As Mesopotamian culture spread outward from its starting point at the lower end of the Euphrates valley, it took on new forms, determined by local neighborhoods. When it spread northwest into the foothills of the Zagros Mountains (see page 117) rather late in Mesopotamian history, the results were startling. We might perhaps say that the Mesoptamian ideal of success in material enterprise was there carried to an insane extreme. For the upland peoples centering about the provincial city of Assur, who were chiefly peasants and traders, produced a series of kings who remade them into a war machine such as the world had never before seen.

For three centuries, between about 900 and 600 B.C., the Assyrians entered upon a series of campaigns of conquest which carried everything before them from one end of the Fertile Crescent to the other. They even took on Egypt, defeating its hitherto unconquerable army deep within its own territory. To this success there were several keys. (1) Never before had an army been so thoroughly armed, defensively and offensively, with metal. *Iron* had at last been mined in large quantity in the mountains north of Assyria. Iron is much more easily worked than copper or bronze, and the fitting out of whole armies with it therefore became practical. (2) Never before had an army been so thoroughly specialized to meet the different problems of warfare. The Assyrian kings created heavy and light infantry, efficiently armed cavalry, heavy and light archers, and engineers, who invented siege machinery such as the battering ram and the siege tower. (3) Never before had the conquered been treated with such savagery. Right hands were hacked off. Defeated rulers were impaled on stakes outside their burning cities. Most effective of all, whole populations were moved from one end of the Assyrian empire to another, far from their native lands, so that their will to rebel might be broken.

With the wealth of plunder from these campaigns, Assyrian kings made gigantic display. Each of the later ones felt himself called upon to found an entire royal city, complete with walls, palace, ziggurat, and dwellings for citizens.

The outcome of this burst of murderous energy was that Assyria had no friends, at home or abroad. She finally went down before invading Medes and Chaldeans, from the great world north of the Fertile Crescent, with no ally to stand at her side. When Nineveh, the last royal Assyrian city to be built, fell in 610 B.C., the destruction of city and people was so complete that two centuries later the very name of Assyria, where Nineveh's ruins still stood, had been forgotten.

What remains today of Assyrian art is chiefly royal art, whose original purpose was the glorification of a ruler and the satisfaction of his royal will. The ruins of the great Assyrian palaces, while largely built of perishable mud-brick, contained also enduring stone reliefs which lined the walls of each palace's focal point, the throne room. For Assyria, being a mountain country, had access to stone as no city in lowland Mesopotamia itself ever did.

These reliefs display whatever would most contribute to kingly self esteem: the king's favorable relationship with his gods, his triumphs in hunting and war, scenes of the king sitting at ease with his queen, while the severed head of an enemy ruler comfortingly hangs from a tree bough before him, and so on. As one looks at the longs rows of slabs, now preserved in the British Museum, or at their photographs, one must try to imagine their appearance when the dull stone was alive with color, as once it certainly must have been.

But even without color, one is aware that just as the wall paintings and reliefs of Egypt have a style of their own, so do these works from Assyria. Each in its own way has a certain uniformity. Yet these uniformities, one Egyptian, the other Assyrian, are distinct. Each is the mirror of a culture whose traditions were stronger than the individual artist-craftsmen who lived and worked within them. After looking at as many examples of the two art traditions as you can find, try to determine for yourself wherein the differences between the two styles lie.

Assur-bani-pal hunting lions from his chariot. The wheel was a Mesopotamian invention. Horses were introduced there from the north about 1700 B.C., and did not reach Egypt until sometime later. Wherever it was introduced, the horse revolutionized human transport and methods of warfare.

British Museum

Near Asiatic Museum, Berlin

The great Ishtar Gateway of Babylon, as excavations have revealed it. The gateway was built of fired brick in the sixth century B.C. Two technical advances are of importance here. First is the semicircular arch, a structural device already old in Mesopotamia, but unused elsewhere, apparently, until Roman times (see Chapter 5). Second is the large-scale use of glaze *as a way to color fired clay.*

Babylon, Mesopotamia's Glory

As the centuries rolled by, Babylon gradually emerged as the greatest city in the Mesopotamian plain. The rulers of this city succeeded in creating a great canal linking the two rivers. From this canal, water poured into a complex network of smaller canals, steadily nourishing mile upon mile of land.

Wealth from farming and from commerce made Babylon a fabulous city whose name captured the imagination of the ancient world, so that Mesopotamia and *Babylonia* came to mean the same thing. It was also the center and rallying point for everything Mesopotamians cherished in political power, religion, science, and art. Who held Babylon therefore held the whole land. Repeatedly besieged and sacked by conquerors, it was just as repeatedly rebuilt in ever grander style. Its last and most spectacular revival was under the reign of Nebuchadnezzar in about 600 B.C. This was the king whose engineers constructed one of the wonders of antiquity, the "hanging gardens of Babylon," a marvel now lost to us. In this its final form of glory the city existed until about 300 B.C., when it gradually declined in importance and was at length abandoned. Neglected for 2000 years, archeologists explored its site between 1899 and 1917 and reconstructed the chief of its great gateways for display in the Near Asiatic Museum in Berlin.

The Literature of the Fertile Crescent

The clay tablets so far found in Mesopotamian ruins contain some genuine literature, not just the records of business deals. Much of it consists of myth; some of it is history. But whatever its kind it is far outshone by the literature originating in one ancient city outside Mesopotamia in the western arm of the Fertile Crescent, Jerusalem. The rich collection of prose and poetry, matter-of-fact history, magnificent allegory, and spiritual teaching which was produced in that city has come to be part of our own heritage. This literature, produced over centuries of time by this people whose God was not made with hands, and whose center was a city, we erroneously think of as a single book, the Old Testament.

The Bible can be read for its spiritual content. It can also be read as the record of an age, written down by people who were there, who saw Egypt as she was, Babylon as she was, and Assyria as she was. As such it illuminates history. As a single example, read the Book of Nahum to see how the people of the entire Fertile Crescent apparently reacted to news of Assyria's fall.

The Old Testament is perhaps easiest to read in *The Modern Reader's Bible* (MacMillan, 1926). This preserves the beauty of the King James translation, but frees it from the artificial construction of numbered verses.

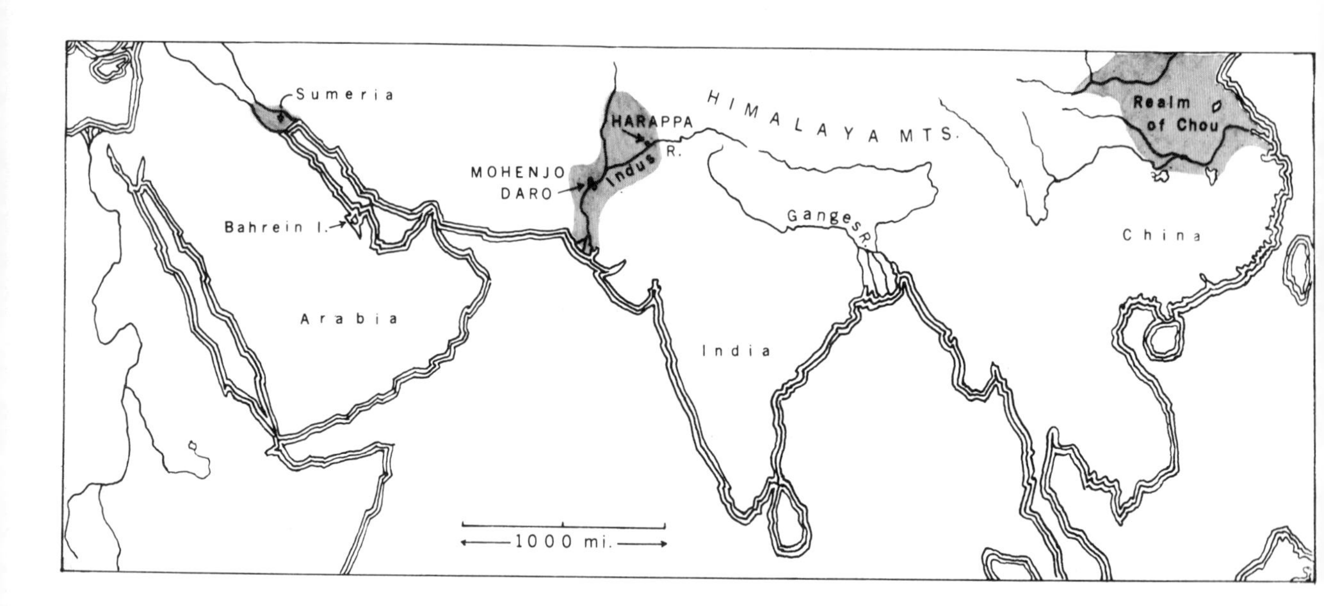

Ancient India and the sea route connecting it with Mesopotamia. The men of 4000 years ago must have been able to make the long sea voyage from the mouth of the Indus River to those of the Euphrates and Tigris, using the island of Bahrein as a stopping place, or perhaps a meeting point for merchants coming from opposite directions. What the main bulk of goods traded both ways was is today a mystery.

Agrarian Civilization Develops in India

Far to the east of Mesopotamia, 1300 miles by ship down the Persian Gulf and beyond, lies the vast subcontinent of India, a triangular tongue of land jutting south into the Indian Ocean. East and west of this triangle two of the world's mightiest rivers, the Ganges and the Indus, carry the melted snows of the Himalayas to the sea. The western river, the Indus, flows through a far more fertile land than Mesopotamia. Here some years ago archeologists uncovered the remains of a civilization based, like the Mesopotamian, on river irrigation. The men of this long-dead world seem to have raised wheat and

Department of Archaeology, Government of India

Statue of a man of importance, perhaps a ruler, found at Mohenjo-Daro. The eyes originally contained fillings like those made in Mesopotamia. But the expression is totally different, withdrawn and thoughtful rather than wide-eyed and staring.

barley, field peas, melons, and dates. They kept dogs, cats, and chickens and used buffaloes as draft animals. They were the world's first known users of cotton for cloth, knew how to work copper and make the alloy bronze, and formed their pottery on a wheel.

The remains of two great cities 400 miles apart, near the present villages of Mohenjo-Daro and Harappa (see page 126), show that these people could build with brick as the Sumerians could, but they were not of the same culture. They had created their own system of writing. Their streets were more skillfully drained than those of eighteenth century Europe! Their sculpture, as nearly as we can judge from scattered remains, had a distinct, thoughtful quality of its own.

In spite of these differences, there seems to be evidence that this civilization owed its basic ideas of farming and engineering to Mesopotamia. Apparently, it came into existence quickly about 2500 B.C., without the long period of trial-and-error discovery which produced Sumeria. It is as if certain basic ideas about crop farming by irrigation, animal husbandry and dairying, building construction, and perhaps political organization had been learned somewhere else and applied anew, with changes suited to a different setting. One of these changes was the greater use of fire-baked rather than sun-dried brick. The land, richer than Mesopotamia, supported more trees, so that there was more wood to burn in brick kilns. And the fierce floods of the Indus demanded a permanent building material which water could not dissolve.

This culture lasted about 1000 years. Then, sometime between 1600 and 1500 B.C., invaders who seem to have come through the mountains northwest of the Indus fell upon the peaceful valley and destroyed its two cities. Even their sites were gradually forgotten. When agrarian civilization bloomed in India, it was to center elsewhere.

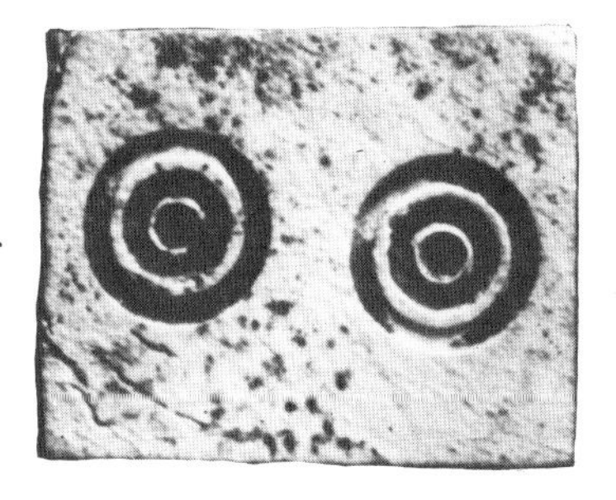

Two carved seals found in the ruins of Mohenjo-Daro, India's oldest known city. Age about 4000 years, writing still undeciphered. Such seals have been found also on the island of Bahrein and in the ruins of Mesopotamian cities, perhaps lost by visiting merchants or acquired through trade. See map opposite.

Department of Archaeology, Government of India

Avery Brundage Collection, San Francisco. Photo John Bridgman

Bronze ting, *or ceremonial vessel for food, cast in northern China, probably before 900* B.C., *during the period known as Western Chou.*

Agrarian Civilization Emerges in China

While the Indus civilization was living out its history, another culture was taking form over 2000 miles further east, in northern China. No one so far knows exactly when Chinese civilization came into being. Archeologists have been at work on the problem for barely 40 years. But it seems likely that in China the cultures passed through the same order as on other parts of the Earth. Hunting or paleolithic societies may have developed first, their people living in little hordes, sparsely scattered through China's primeval jungles and forests. In a few favorable places, especially along river banks in the heart of northern China, some of these hunters were able to take a forward step and form hunting-farming or neolithic societies, organized, it can be surmised, in clans and tribes. These tribes, with their larger populations, next probably began to push the simpler hunting societies back into more remote areas.

Then, in one region where a combination of rich soil and rivers made farming unusually easy and productive, men built a food complex which could completely support the population, freed themselves from the need to hunt, and thus took the first step toward an agrarian civilization. According to Chinese tradition, a single warlike ruler named Shang built a kingdom, perhaps by uniting many tribes, sometime near 1500 B.C. His people learned to focus their loyalty on him and his successors, and on the land where they dwelt, rather than on the blood ties of clan and tribe. Step by step they developed crafts to a high level. Trade increased, especially along the rivers. A system of writing was invented. The agrarian civilization's population began to expand. Men ambitious to farm cleared the forests from ever broader stretches of land and pushed neighboring neolithic tribes back into the wilderness, just as these had once pushed back the still more primitive paleolithic hordes.

The Shang dynasty, again according to Chinese legend, stayed in power for about 500 years. A warrior from Western China, reputedly a barbarian with the name of Chou, dethroned the last member of the Shang line in 1027 B.C. This is regarded as the first authentic date in Chinese history.

It is a remarkable fact that basic characteristics of the Shang kingdom have remained true of Chinese culture as a whole ever since. Nowhere else in the world today does any people exist with such an immensely long record of consistent civilization. Other cultures, though very old, have undergone violent changes because of foreign invaders. The Chinese have absorbed their occasional invaders and continued to maintain their own way of life. Today, when civilization on the Chinese mainland is at last undergoing a violent remaking along the lines of a Western ideology, it is the Chinese who are doing it to themselves and in their own way, with certain age-old features of Chinese political management and belief still in practice.

Why have the Chinese been so stable? Probably because of their location, protected from the rest of the world by the Himalayas on the west, jungles on the south, and the vast Pacific on the east. They have been open to invasion only from the north, where China merges into the plains of Siberia. It is from there that invaders have usually tried to enter, sometimes successfully.

At the same time, China's size is so vast that the constant interchange among millions of people, communicating easily along her great rivers, stimulated the formation of a rich, many-sided culture. But even this was not enough to prevent a stagnation from descending over China for centuries, something like that in Egypt, a stagnation to be shattered only when western powers with new inventions of weaponry and transportation crossed the Pacific, while others spanned Siberia with a railway, and jolted the ancient empire out of her sleep. (See Chapters 9 and 10.)

But let us go back to the China of the Shang rulers 3500 years ago and look more closely into how the civilization started. It grew up at the junction of the Wei and Hwang-ho Rivers. (See page 253.) Thousands of years previously, wind sweeping down from Siberia had deposited topsoil in dust form over this and other parts of northern China. By the time China's remote history began, this dust had been transformed by rains and the passage of time into a solid layer 300 feet deep, a nearly bottomless source of nourishment for growing plants. What the Nile still does for Egypt every year, the wind did for northern China in ages past.[13]

Here the men of the Shang kingdom raised barley and another grain, *millet*. They herded sheep and camels, and later horses, using their meat, milk, wool, hair, and hides for food, shelter, and clothing. The camels and horses also served them for transport. They were familiar with the spoked wheel, and used the two-wheeled chariot in warfare. They knew how to smelt copper, tin and lead, silver, and gold. They could make and cast bronze. They created pottery vessels on a fast-spinning wheel. Already the technical excellence and the imaginative strength of their creations in these materials possessed a distinction which has been typically Chinese ever since.

Bronze vessel for wine, in the shape of a rhinoceros. Chinese, late Shang period, 1200 to 1000 B.C.

Both objects on this page from the Avery Brundage Collection, San Francisco. Photo William Abbenseth

Bronze chia, *or ceremonial vessel for wine, late Shang period, height about 30 in.*

Seated figure, probably of a ruler. Mexican, possibly second century A.D.*, about 30 in. high, of dark grey unglazed earthenware.*

John Ahlsberg Collection, Berkeley. Photo John Bridgman

The Americas: Aztecs, Mayas, Incas

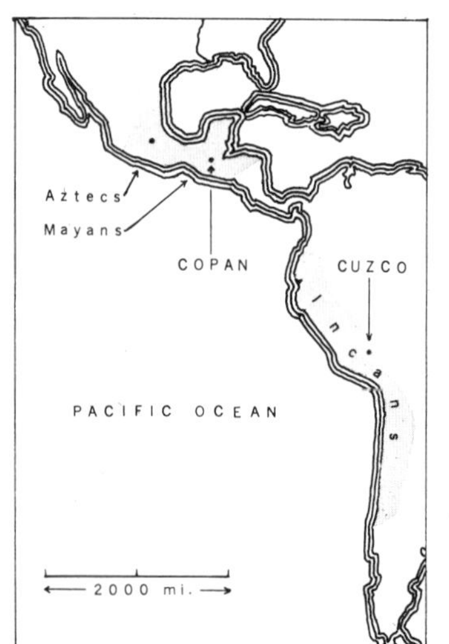

Ten thousand years or more ago, at just about the time that man was learning the art of farming in the Fertile Crescent, it is believed that other men were entering the North American continent, perhaps by way of the neck of land which once probably connected Siberia with Alaska. For the next several thousand years man's energies in the Americas went into travel, and the gradual exploration of the land's resources for food and shelter. This was a necessary prelude to cultural progress. Civilization, therefore, developed late in the new world. Early in the sixteenth century A.D., when Spanish explorers forced their way into Mexico and Peru, they found peoples who were developing ways of life suggestive of First Dynasty Egypt (3200 B.C.), or early Mesopotamia, when the men of the Nile and Euphrates, civilized in other ways, were still practising human sacrifice.

What strides these civilizations would have gone on to make we will never know. They were utterly destroyed by their Spanish conquerors. But from what they left behind we can trace many characteristics which we have already discovered in the two early civilizations described in this chapter. These can be summarized as follows:

Characteristics of Agrarian Civilizations

1. The development of a satifactory food complex produced by plant- and animal-farming alone;
2. The dominance of one people over its neighbors by conquest, and the enrichment of the conqueror from the payment of tribute taxes;
3. The appearance of rulers who were regarded as divine, either because they were themselves called gods (as in Egypt) or the high priests of gods (as in Mesopotamia);
4. The worship of gods who represented a local region rather than a tribe; the erection of enormous monuments in their honor; the appearance of a priesthood dedicated to their worship, whose members were in turn responsible for advances in writing, numbering, astronomy, and an accurate calendar;
5. The appearance of full-time craftsmen and resulting technical advances, especially in metal working, stone working, weaving, ceramics, gem cutting, and materials for record keeping;
6. An increase in trade and commerce, though still on the barter level;
7. The emergence of what we would call art, even if the inhabitants did not recognize it as such, chiefly in the service of religion, funeral practices, and the adornment of the nobility;
8. The establishment of a fairly permanent society, uniting peoples over a large area, administered by an organized central government, and maintained by complex cooperation among persons of a wide range of special skills.

Collection of Philip E. Siff, Santa Barbara. Photo R[illegible]dulpho Petschek

Ceramic figure of a ball player, ancient Mexico. The game was a grim religious ceremony, the losers being slain in honor of a god. Height about 18 in.

Painting by Carlos Vierra. Photo courtesy of Museum of Man, San Diego

Ruins of a great complex of Mayan temples at Copan, Honduras. Dates carved on the stone buildings indicate that they were erected between 600 and 800 A.D. The site covers twelve acres. Besides temples and altars, it includes a ceremonial ball park. Such a complex of stone structures strongly suggests that the Mayans had created their own form of geometry, and used it in planning and proportioning their sacred buildings.

John Ahlsberg Collection, Berkeley. Photo John Bridgman

Ancient Mexican jar of highly polished earthenware. Width about 15 in.

NOTES

1 This is true to the Second Cataract of the Nile, above Abu Simbel. To the First Cataract, near Aswan, the length is about 550 miles. To Khartoum, where the White and Blue Niles become one, the distance is 1200 miles.

2 An old Egyptian name for their own land was *Kemet*, or black.

3 Today an Egyptian *feddan* produces 5 ardebs of wheat. Translated into our units of measure, one acre produces 27½ bushels. (Source: H. Kees, *Ancient Egypt, A Cultural Topography*, University of Chicago Press, 1961.)

4 We consider that *history* began when men started to make and preserve explicit records of events. *Prehistory*, on the other hand, has to be reconstructed entirely from the things which men carelessly or accidentally left behind.

5 *Soul* is an untrustworthy word to use here, though no other does as well. Different peoples have vastly different ideas of the spiritual part of man, though all recognize it. For example, some primitive tribes have arrived at a far more complex, carefully analyzed idea of the "soul" than have more supposedly civilized peoples.

6 The royal court also maintained a school for scribes and an army academy.

7 Several such plans still exist. One is shown in Plate X of the Encyclopedia Britannica's article on *Architecture*.

8 They may have worked on a surface of leveled wet sand, and used a cord, held taut between two slender pegs and snapped against the sand, to produce a straight line. The same cord, pegged down at one end only, could also be used to describe a circle or arc. Large geometrical experiments could thus be worked out and the results reproduced later, on a smaller scale, on papyrus.

9 There is also just one right triangle whose sides are in *arithmetic* progression. This is the 3:4:5 right triangle. This also was known to the Egyptians, who used it as a means to determine the angles of buildings and plots of ground.

10 Selections from a wide assortment of Egyptian writing can be found in *Never to Die, The Egyptians in Their Own Words*, selected and arranged by Josephine Mayer and Tom Prideaux (Viking Press, New York, 1938).

11 Some of these sites, such as Jerusalem and Damascus, cannot be studied because they are still thriving, fully occupied cities.

12 *Collateral* is some of the borrower's property, which the lender may seize if the debt is not repaid. The lender is thus made *secure* in getting back his loan.

13 This thick soil deposit is called *loess*. It seems once to have covered the Gobi Desert.

BOOKS ON EGYPTIAN CIVILIZATION AND ARTS

HISTORICAL AND GENERAL

The Cultures of Prehistoric Egypt (2 volumes), E. J. Baumgartel (Oxford, 1960).

Archaic Egypt, W. Emery (paperback, Pelican Book No. A462).

The Egyptians, C. Aldred (paperback, Praeger, New York, 1961).

Land of the Pharaohs, L. Cottrell (World Publishing Co., New York, 1962).

The Culture of Ancient Egypt, J. A. Wilson (paperback P11, Phoenix Book, University of Chicago Press, 9th printing, 1963).

The Scepter of Egypt, W. C. Hayes (Harper, New York, 1953—59). Volume I: Beginnings to 1675 B.C. Volume II: 1675—1080 B.C. Egyptian history and culture as illustrated by the Egyptian collection of the Metropolitan Museum of Art, New York City.

The Home Life of the Ancient Egyptians. A Picture Book, N. E. Scott. Metropolitan Museum of Art, New York City.

The National Geographic Magazine, October 1941. Two articles, richly illustrated in color, on Egyptian everyday life, history, and achievements.

The Story of Man, by the editors of *Life*, pp. 66—137.

The Nile, photographs by E. Elisophon, text by L. van der Post (Viking Press, New York, 1963).

Lost Land Emerging, W. B. Emery (Scribners, New York, 1967). Archeology of Ancient Nubia, now submerged beneath waters of the second Egyptian dam.

The White Nile, A. Moorehead (Harper & Row, New York, 1962; Dell Paperback 9516).

The Blue Nile, A. Moorehead (Harper & Row, New York, 1964; Dell Paperback 0636).

EGYPTIAN TECHNIQUES, ARTS, AND LITERATURE

Ancient Egyptian Materials and Industries, A. Lucas and A. R. Harris (Edward Arnold, Ltd., London, 4th ed., 1962).

Ancient Glass, R. H. Brill (Scientific American, November 1963). Shows how to make Egyptian faience.

The Art and Architecture of Ancient Egypt, W. S. Smith (paperback, Pelican History of Art, Baltimore, 1958).

Egypt: Architecture, Sculpture, Painting in Three Thousand Years, K. Lang and M. Hirmer (Phaidon Press, London, 1962). A large, richly illustrated book.

Tutankhamen, C. Desroches-Noblecourt (New York Graphic Society, 1963).

Egyptian Architecture as Cultural Expression, E. B. Smith (Appleton-Century, New York, 1938).

The Pyramids of Egypt, I. E. S. Edwards (paperback, Pelican Book No. A168). See especially Chapter Seven, "Construction and Purpose," for a discussion of surveying, engineering, and transport problems.

Living Architecture: Egyptian, J. L. de Cenival (Grosset and Dunlap, New York, 1964).

The Ancient Egyptians, A Sourcebook of Their Writings, edited by A. Erman (Harper paperback TB1233P, 1923—1966).

The Egyptian Book of the Dead (the papyrus of Ani), E. W. Budge (Dover, New York, reprint of 1895 edition).

Egyptian Ornament, M. Vilimkova (Allan Wingate, London, 1963).

Egyptian Art, W. Forman and B. Forman (Peter Nevill, London, 1962).

Egyptian Art, I. Woldering (Crown, New York, Art of the World Series).

Egyptian Wall Paintings from Tombs and Temples (paperback MQ 457 Mentor-Unesco, New York, 1962).
The Literature of the Ancient Egyptians, A. Erman (London, 1927).

RELIGION

The Priests of Ancient Egypt, Serge Sauneron (paperback, Evergreen Profile Book 12, Grove Press, New York, 1960).
Ancient Egyptian Religion, H. Frankfort (paperback, Harper, New York, 1948).
Egyptian Mythology (Tudor, New York, 1965), finely illustrated.

FILM

Ancient Egypt, sound, color, 10 minutes, Corona Film, 1952.

BOOKS ON MESOPOTAMIA AND NEIGHBORING CULTURES

The Story of Civilization, W. and A. Durant (Simon and Schuster, New York), *Vol. I: Our Oriented Heritage, being a history of civilization in Egypt and the Near East to the death of Alexander, and in India, China and Japan from the beginning to our own day; with an introduction on the nature and foundations of civilization.*
Four Thousand Years Ago, G. Bibby (Knopf, New York, 1961). History in Egypt, Europe, and Mesopotamia viewed as an interrelated whole and as seen through the eyes of people who lived between 2000 and 1000 B.C. A remarkable book, not to be missed.
Land of the Two Rivers, L. Cottrell (World Publishing Co., Cleveland and New York, 1962).
The Birth of Civilization in the Near East, H. Frankfort (paperback, Doubleday Anchor Book No. A 89).
National Geographic Magazine, January 1951, pp. 41—105. 35 color illustrations.
Mesopotamia and the Middle East, L. Woolley (Art of the World Series). A book on art.
The Walls of Jericho, M. Wheeler (paperback, Arrow books G 32).
The Archeology of Palestine, W. F. Albright (paperback, Pelican A 199).
5000 Years of the Art of Mesopotamia, E. Strommінger, Hirmer photos (Abrams, New York).
The Art of the Middle East, L. Woolley (Crown, Art of the World Series, 1961).
The Art and Architecture of the Ancient Orient, H. Frankfort (Penguin, 1955). Sumeria to fifth century Persia.
The Sumerians, Their History, Culture, and Character, S. N. Kramer (University of Chicago Press, Man and His Culture Series).
Babylon, A. Champdor (Elek Books, London, 1958).
Assyrian Palace Reliefs, R. D. Barnett (Batchworth Press, Ltd., London, about 1960). Includes photographs of bronze doors from an Assyrian temple.
The Ancient Near East, An Anthology in Text and Pictures, J. B. Pritchard (Princeton paperback).
The World History of the Jewish People, Vol. I, At the Dawn of Civilization, 19 volumes to follow, ed. by B. Natanyahn (Rutgers Press, New Jersey, 1965).

FILM

Ancient Mesopotamia, color, sound, 10 minutes (Coronet, 1953).

BOOKS ON EARLY INDIA AND CHINA

Acres and People, the Eternal Problem of China and India, E. V. Wilcox (Orange Judd Pub. Co., New York, 1947).
The Dawn of Civilization (McGraw-Hill, 1961), Chapters VIII and IX.
Prehistoric India to 1000 B.C., S. Piggott (Pelican A205).
The Religion of India, M. Weber (MacMillan paperback 93453, 1958).
Hinduism, R. C. Zachner (Oxford paperback GB173, 1962—1966).
A Short History of Ancient India, W. H. Moreland and A. C. Chatterjee (Longmans Green, New York, 4th ed., 1957).
A History of China, W. Eberhard (University of California Press, 1960).
The Chinese, Their History and Culture, V. S. Latourette (MacMillan, New York, 12th printing, 1961).
Science and Civilization in China, Vol. I, introduction, J. Needham (Cambridge Press, 1954).
The Art of India, H. Goetz (Crown Art of the World Series, 1959).
The Art of China, W. Speiser (Crown Art of the World Series, 1960).
The Art of India Through the Ages, S. Karnvisch (Phaidon, 1955).
The Art and Architecture of China, L. Sickman and A. Soper (Pelican History of Art, 2nd ed., 1960).
China's Geographic Foundations, A Survey of the Land and Its Peoples, G. B. Cressey (McGraw-Hill, New York, 1934).
The Culture and Art of India, R. MuKerjee (Praeger, New York, 1959).
The Arts and Crafts of India and Ceylon, A. K. Coomaraswamy (Noonday Press, New York, 1964).
Gandharan Art in Pakistan, I. Lyons (Phaidon, 1957).
The Ajanta Caves: Early Buddhist Paintings from India, B. Rowland (Mentor UNESCO paperback).
Myths and Symbols in Indian Art and Civilization, H. Zimmer (Harper Torchbook 2005, 1962—1965).

BOOKS ON NATIVE AMERICAN CIVILIZATIONS

The Ancient Past of Mexico, A. M. Reed (Crown Publishers, New York, 1966).
The Aztecs of Mexico, C. G. Vaillant (Pelican paperback No. A200, 1951), describes also the civilizations that preceded them.
The Chinampas of Mexico, M. D. Coe (Scientific American, July 1964), describes the agricultural origins of Mexican civilization.
The Daily Life of the Aztecs on the Eve of the Spanish Conquest, J. Soustelle (Weidenfield & Nicolson, London, 1961).
The True Story of the Conquest of Mexico, Bernal Diaz de Castillo (paperback, Dolphin Book C25, Doubleday, New York, 1956).
Broken Spears: The Aztec Account of the Conquest of Mexico, M. Leon-Porfilla (paperback BP230-Bea).
Pre-Columbian Architecture, D. Robertson (Braziller, New York, 1962).
An Album of Maya Architecture, T. Proskouriakoff (University of Oklahoma Press, 1963).
Living Architecture: Mayan, H. Stierlin (Grosset and Dunlap, New York, 1964).
The Conquest of Mexico, W. H. Prescott (Bantam RM 104).
The Art of Ancient Mexico, 109 photographs by I. Groth Kimball, text by R. Feuchtwanger (Thames & Hudson, London and New York, 1954). Beautiful book; 109 illustrations.
The Art of Ancient Mexico, P. Westheim (Anchor paperback); 100 illustrations.

The Art of the Ancient Maya, A. Kidder (Crowell, New York, 1959).
Guatemala Art Crafts, P. de Lemos (Pauls Press, Worcester, Massachusetts, 1950).
The Art of Ancient America, H. D. Disselhoff and S. Linne (Art of the World Series, Crown, New York, 1960).
Indian Art in Middle America, F. J. Dockstader (New York Graphic Society, 1964).
Early Metallurgy in the New World, D. T. Easby Jr. (Scientific American, vol. 214, No. 4, April 1966).
The Sun Kingdom of the Aztecs, and Maya, Land of the Turkey and the Deer, V. von Hagen (World Pub. Co., Cleveland and New York).
Ancient American Painting (paperback, Crown, New York); all illustrations in color.
Peru, G. H. S. Bushnell (Praeger paperback, 1963).
The Conquest of Peru, W. H. Prescott (Dolphin C166).
Ancient Arts of the Andes, W. C. Bennett (Museum of Modern Art, 1954); 208 illustrations.
Gold and Gods of Peru, H. Bauman (Pantheon, 1963).
On the Royal Highways of the Incas, H. Ubbelohde-Doering (Praeger, 1966—1967).
Textiles of Ancient Peru and Their Techniques, R. d'Harcourt (University of Washington Press, Seattle, 1962).
Peruvian Textiles (Museum of Modern Art, New York).

Pair of dancing figures from Vera Cruz, ancient Mexico, hollow polished earthenware, height about 22 in.

Collection of Dr. Harold Stratton, Fresno, California. Photo Rudulpho Petschek

Bronze life-size statue of a young charioteer, found among the ruins of the holy city of Delphi. The statue seems to have stood in a bronze chariot, drawn by four bronze horses, their bridles held by grooms. The group probably depicted the tense moment just before the start of a race. Fragments of the other figures have been found, and so has the stone base. It bears an inscription stating that the group was dedicated to Apollo by Polyzales of Syracuse, Sicily. The holy women who dwelt in Apollo's temple at Delphi were often asked to prophesy the future. Perhaps Polyzales was told by them that he would win the chariot race in the Greek Olympic games held every four years in honor of Zeus, king of the gods. When the prophecy came true, Polyzales may have expressed his thanks by donating the group statue. Experts on Greek style date the figure at about 470 B.C. *The sculptor is unknown.*

Photo Alison Frantz, Athens

4 THE MEDITERRANEAN CITY-STATES

Phoenicia, Crete, Hellas, North India. In the Mediterranean City-States Men's Mastery of Sea Trade Frees Some from the Burden of Food Production. In the Ganges Valley a World Religion Is Born.

Preview

The Fertile Crescent lies between two seas, the Mediterranean and the Persian Gulf. Men from her cities, not content to be landlocked, ventured out in ships, both east and west. Eastward they seem to have sailed as far as western India, trading with people of the Indus River valley. There they met a great river civilization of farms and brick-built cities, resembling their own. The island of Bahrein seems to have been a way station for ships moving between the two peoples.

Westward the men of Mesopotamia probably first sailed the short trip to Cypros for copper, and then perhaps to farther islands. But here there was no complex civilization already established, only primitive people ready to learn new ways. In time these people discovered and mastered the skills and the political and economic devices on which the older civilizations were founded. Going on from there they then created a civilization of their own.

But whereas the older cultures were largely hemmed in by deserts and mountains, and irrigated their crops with water from rivers, the new ones opened almost entirely outward, from coasts and islands, upon the sea. And for the irrigation of their crops they relied on rain, in the moist climate which that sea produced. These people sailed forth, in ships of their own, ever farther and farther westward, connecting different regions each rich in its own special resources but perhaps poor in others, so that all were ready to trade. Some places of rich soil produced grain in excess. Others with poor soil had metals, ceramics, woven goods, or salt fish to offer in exchange. Thus, there slowly came into being an active commerce, so active that some cities learned to depend on trade at least as much as on producing their own food. The *mercantile state* came into being and with it a new freedom for citizens, who found themselves controlling the wealth and power which formerly only kings had known.

Photo Universal Color Slide Company

The Aegean Sea, from the shore of Rhodes, one of its host of islands. Gone are the stately Greek temples which once crowned the headlands, and so are the forests which once made such islands an earthly paradise. But white-walled villages still nestle close to the harbors, as they have for thousands of years.

This sequence of events, and the human achievements which directed them, are in some ways unique in history. Still more remarkable were their results. For through them man's life, especially his creative life, found a new direction. What it was is the subject of this chapter.

The Sea

The Nile flows north into the Mediterranean Sea, "the sea in the middle of the land," as its name signifies. For that is what it is, one of the most landlocked seas in the world. On the map it looks small, like a lake. But it is enormous, almost as long as the United States is broad. From Gibraltar in the west to the coast of Syria in the east, the Mediterranean stretches 2400 miles. The United States at the 40th parallel (which runs from northern California through Washington, D.C.) is hardly 300 miles wider.

It is a beautiful sea. Its clear, clean water, breaking in snow-white foam on beaches and rocks, turns to a turquoise blue close to shore, and within one hundred feet changes again, this time to an intense deep ultramarine, almost as if it had been dyed. Out of this rich colored sea rise the dramatically steep shores of peninsulas, islands, and islets. Their jagged cliffs and promontories are enough to waken the imagination of myth makers. For much of the year the sunshine is warm and mellow and the winds gentle, until, from seemingly nowhere, a storm will swoop down with gales and lightning, bringing havoc to small shipping. And then the rocks, which are so picturesque above water, can be treacherous beneath it. In the Mediterranean it is easy to believe in Zeus, the capricious sky god, who in a second can fly into a rage and hurl a thunderbolt, or in Poseidon, god of the sea, with his deadly, stabbing trident.

Nevertheless, the eastern end of the Mediterranean is a wonderful sea in which to learn the arts of shipbuilding and navigation. Sheltering harbors, necessary as starting points, are common, and in ancient times these were surrounded by trees good for shipbuilding. Out to sea, islands and the headlands of distant shores beckon the adventurous to come and explore them. If you look at the map, you will see that as one moves westward in the Mediterranean, conditions change. Islands become fewer, stretches of sea become greater, indented coastlines, good for sheltering small ships, become scarcer. So, although the eastern end of the sea was an excellent school for sailors, the western stretches were certainly their testing ground. Before men became masters of the whole sea, centuries had to pass.

The creation of the Mediterranean civilization was gradual and complex. In its simplest terms it can be reduced to three phases. In each of these a different people made discoveries and created innovations without which the next phase would have been impossible.

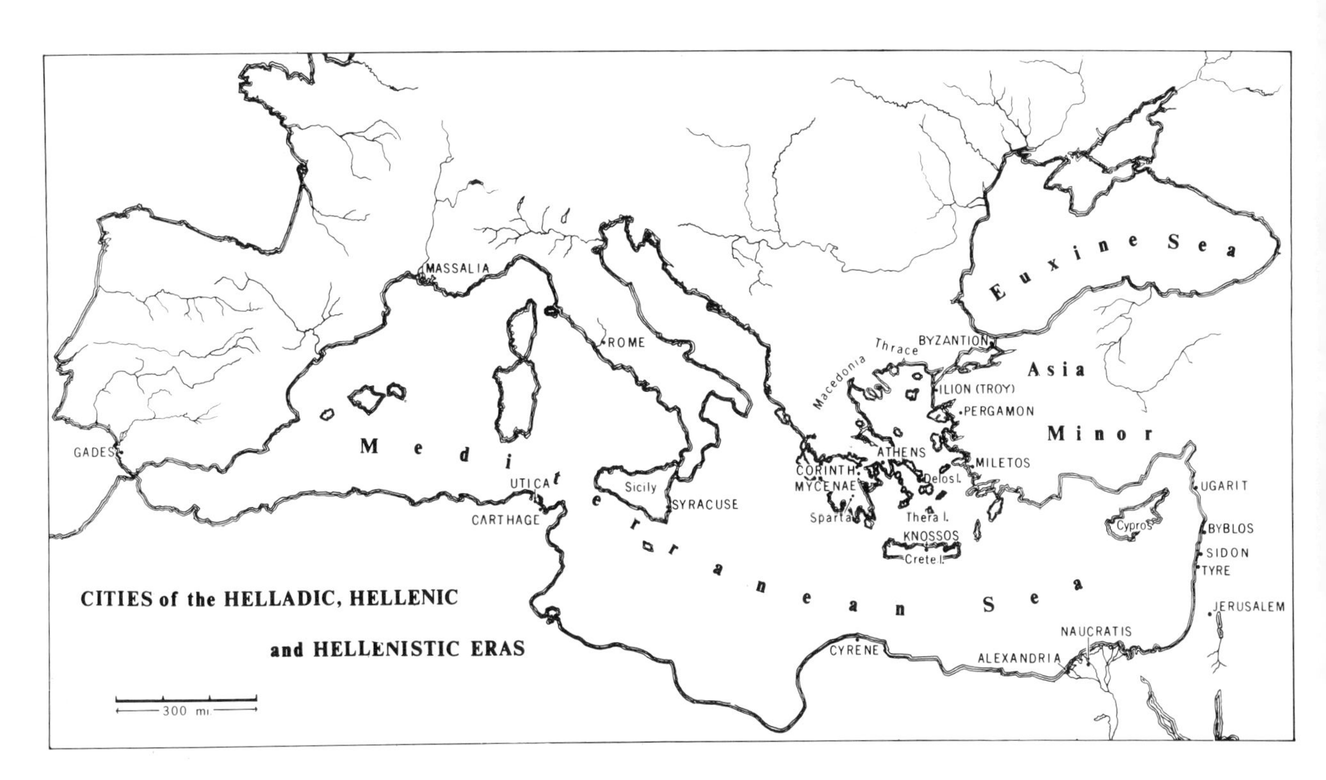

CITIES of the HELLADIC, HELLENIC and HELLENISTIC ERAS

Photo Superintendent of Antiquities, Florence

A Phoenician silver bowl, made for export. Designs are of mixed origin, outer ring Assyrian, inner ring and center Egyptian. Silver, raw material of the bowl, was imported, perhaps from Egypt, Greece, or even Spain. The bowl was found in northern Italy, in the tomb of an Etruscan prince who died in the seventh century B.C.

Civilizers of the Eastern Mediterranean

The Phoenician Cities

The eastern coast of the Mediterranean, called the Levant, runs north and south for over 300 miles. It is a narrow strip of land, hardly ten miles wide, crowded into the sea by a mountain range rising just behind it. This range rises to 8000 feet at the northern end near Asia Minor, but sinks to low desert hills at the southern end near Sinai. In the northern part, from prehistoric times, a few Fertile Crescent communities nestled between the sea and mountains, making their living as best they could from their fields, the mountains, and the sea.

The earliest mention we have of these places is from Egypt. In the reign of King Sneferu about 2700 B.C., it was recorded that forty ships brought cedar from Byblos for the king. Great cedar rafters, each one an entire tree trunk, can still be seen in Sneferu's pyramid tomb. The ships that brought them were probably built in Egypt. But by 2700 B.C. Byblos was already a city.

From at least this time on, contact between Egypt and the Levant was continual. At one time the kings of Egypt's eighteenth dynasty moved their armies northward and possessed the entire area, coastal cities and all. The tomb decorations of Egyptian kings of this period show men in Levantine dress humbly bearing tribute, chiefly vessels of gold, to the royal court. But the cities of the Levant were in spirit Fertile Crescent cities, not Egyptian.

Each was independent of the other. Each had its own city god and its ruler who was the god's servant. Each also had a sharp eye for trade. Travel routes through the mountains behind them kept these cities in touch with Mesopotamia. For the next two and a half thousand years, first one, then another of these cities rose to power: first Byblos, then Ugarit, then Sidon, and finally Tyre.

From their involvement with two civilizations, the Levantine cities —Phoenicians as the Greeks later called them—reaped their advantage. They possessed at least three resources which the rest of the world desired: cedar wood from the mountains, crimson-purple dye obtained from a sea snail called the *murex*, and fish which they knew how to dry and salt. Phoenician merchants carried these and other products abroad, southward by ship to Egypt, eastward by caravan through the mountains to Mesopotamia, and westward, again by ship, to trading places in the eastern Mediterranean. They brought back a wide range of materials: copper from Cypros, grain, ivory, ebony, and gold from Egypt, to mention a few. The grain helped support the home population. As for the other materials, Phoenician craftsmen, using techniques learned from Egypt and designs copied from Egypt and Mesopotamia, worked them into weapons, vessels, jewelry, boxes, and toilet articles. These products the merchants then exported to every point where they could find a market for articles of luxury, in daring ventures by sea and land which, when successful, must have brought immense profits.

The demands of sea trade drove them to improve their ship construction and their methods of navigation. Long voyages required sailing at night. They learned how to hold their ships on course by observing the North Star, or Phoenician Star, as the ancients called it.

Extensive business required written records. The Phoenicians rejected the cuneiform script of Mesopotamia written on clay. Instead they chose the Egyptian script written on papyrus. They stripped it of about 600 needless symbols, kept the signs for consonants, simplified all the forms, and produced the world's first phonetic alphabet. It remained for the Greeks, later on, to add vowels and thus to bring this series of remarkable inventions to completion. Our own alphabet is a distant but direct descendant of theirs.

Examples of ten ancient letters from three neighboring civilizations: 1) Egyptian formal letters (called hieroglyphics*) used in inscriptions carved in stone or precious materials. 2) The letters as made over by Egyptian scribes into swift handwriting (called* hieratic *writing). 3) Phoenician letters, based on hieratic writing, and written right to left. 4) Greek letters, based on Phoenician, and written left to right.*

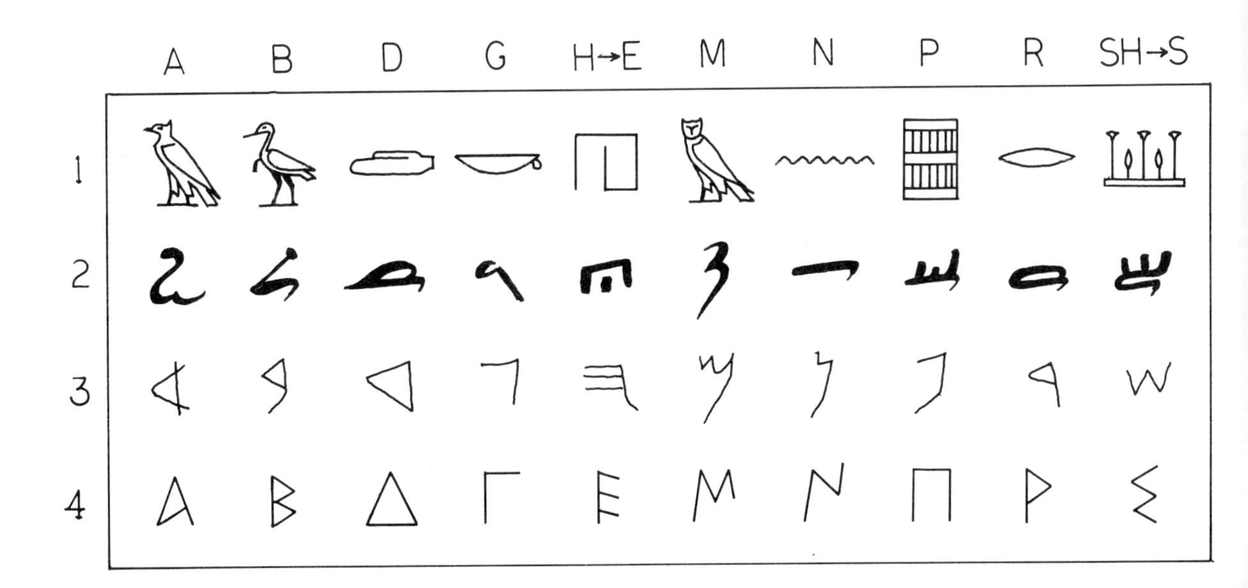

A flight of stairs within the great palace at Knossos, as revealed by excavation and reconstruction. The peculiar columns with bulging black capitals and red shafts tapering downward are found nowhere else in the world. On the wall, top left, is a restored fresco showing a Cretan shield, covered with dappled oxhide and shaped like a figure eight.

Hirmer photoarchive Munich

THE HELLADIC, HELLENIC, AND HELLENISTIC WORLDS

The Minoan-Mycenaean Culture

The next signs we can find of the western spread of civilization are on the island of Crete. This long, rocky island acts like a southern wall hemming in the Aegean Sea. Crete seems first to have been discovered by hunting-farming people who probably came from Asia Minor, perhaps 6000 years ago. For centuries they apparently lived by themselves in a cluster of tribal societies spread over the island, trading only with nearby islands for materials such as obsidian.

Eastern Crete, closest to the Levant, awoke first. Contact with Levantine cities, and then with Egypt, seems to have been made by 2200 B.C. or before. Food plants—wheat, barley, olive trees, grape vines—were somehow imported. Then the series of events occurred which we have already witnessed elsewhere: chiefs with talents in politics and war probably conquered neighboring tribes. Crete appears to have become a number of kingdoms. Among these, one kingdom became supreme, bringing the others under its will. We have as evidence for this the ruins of palaces, at least four, at widely spaced intervals on the island. Of these, one, by far the greatest, is at Knossos near the center of the island's north side.

Sixty years of patient excavation at Knossos, largely by the English archeologist Sir Arthur Evans, have revealed the oldest known city of Europe, with a probable population of over 80,000. It was a city confident of its power, for it had no walls. It consisted of three concentric areas: the outer one, where about 70,000 craftsmen, sailors, and other ordinary citizens lived; an inner, select area, where dwelt perhaps 12,000 persons of wealth; and at the heart of it all the luxurious palace, a maze of offices, workshops, and storerooms, plus a throne room and private living quarters of royal style, all centering on a great open courtyard.

At times the palace had a stormy career. At least twice it had suffered destruction, the first time perhaps by earthquake, the second time apparently by looting and then burning. After the first disaster, in about 1700 B.C. it was rebuilt. After the second, three centuries later, it was deserted and lay thus for over 3000 years.

We can surmise the greatness of ancient Crete from the wreckage of this marvelous palace, whose walls were once alive with painted pictures. Fragments of these, pieced together, show us tall, slim-waisted men carrying great drinking horns, and large-eyed women, glamorously dressed, dancing or watching acrobats do back-flips over the horns of charging bulls. Two differences separate these wall paintings from those of Egypt. They are for the enjoyment of the living, not the dead, and they seem to have been created with a free, spontaneous hand, unbound by any methodical geometric design-plan.

Then there is the astonishing Cretan pottery, skillfully turned to great thinness on a fast-spinning wheel and decorated with vivid designs in colored slip, beautifully suited to the pottery form. Much of this ware was clearly made for export, for it has been found in many places, some as remote as Spain at the opposite end of the Mediterranean.

Two examples of Cretan pottery. Left, 1600 B.C. or later; above, 1500 B.C. or later.

Candia Museum, Crete

Hirmer photoarchive Munich

The citadel of Mycenae as it looks today.

MYCENAEAN CULTURE, OFFSHOOT FROM THE MINOAN. The best proof of the power of Cretan culture, called Minoan (after Minos, its greatest king), is that it was copied by foreigners. Two hundred miles away, on the Greek peninsula, the ruins of towns have been found which look much like Knossos and which seem to have been lived in at about the same time. Mycenae, Argos, Tiryns, Pylos, Thebes, to mention five out of about twenty so far discovered, are all within easy sailing distance northward from Crete. But others have been found as far west as Sicily and as far east as Syria (and distant traces of what appears to have been Cretan culture have turned up even in England). At many of these places are the ruins of palaces, surrounded by traces of towns. The palaces have a different plan from that at Knossos. They are simpler, and each centers around a great hall, rather than an open courtyard, though the courtyard is still present. And the massive stone walls which still surround them show that the men of those times were worried about self-defence. For since they were on the Greek mainland, they were not protected on all sides by sea.

Of these cities the richest and most powerful was Mycenae. Its palace and walled citadel stood on a knob of rock overlooking mile upon mile of fertile lowland, the Argive plain. On the slopes just below the walls crowded the buildings of a good size town. Behind rose a mountain range, whose copper mines must have been one source of Mycenae's wealth. Outward from the city, down into the plain, and backward into the mountains, carefully built roads radiated, their beds made level or gently sloping with roughly squared stones, so that chariots and wagons could travel them safely.

A study of Mycenae's ruins reveals that a wealthy, powerful people once lived there. They had a taste for Minoan art and Minoan ideas, but their attempts to copy them were crude. Mycenaean pottery is far inferior to

Minoan. The style of Mycenaean goldwork, found in the royal tombs, is primitive by comparison. Fragments of wall and floor paintings, found in the palace ruins, suggest that painters may have been brought from Crete to decorate the palace. But in one area the men of Mycenae seem to have been masters for their time.

This was as stone masons. The men of Mycenae must have learned from Crete how to quarry and shape stone by sawing, probably with great copper or bronze saws used with an abrasive. Such saws have been found in the Minoan ruins of Crete. Saw-cut blocks have been found at Mycenae. The best samples of Mycenaean stonework still to be seen are the great tombs laid out on a plan (called the *tholos* plan) learned from Crete. In the side of a hill a horizontal stone-walled tunnel leads inward to a beehive-shaped chamber, also stone-walled, where once lay the body of some illustrious personage, surrounded by his wealth.

These structures must have been built by engineers who knew the construction problems of *corbeling*, as the mode of constructing the circular chamber is called. Their decorations, judging from fragments, harmonize much detail to give richness without confusion.

The Minoan-Mycenaean culture, while it dominated the Aegean world, constituted what we today call the *Helladic Age.*

The Invaders from the North of 1150 B.C.

When the great palace at Knossos was destroyed in 1400 B.C., never to be rebuilt, the island seems to have sunk back into a land of farmers and pirates. But the cities of the Greek mainland, whose people had learned civilization from the Minoans, went on leading a prosperous life. Some believe it was they who turned against the old mother city, robbed her of her rich trade, and, by invading her from the sea, finally gave her the death blow.

A more likely explanation is that a major eruption of the volcano of Santorin, on the Greek island of Thera, in about 1400 B.C., destroyed the cities of Crete. This catastrophe, it is now believed, marked the end of Cretan ascendancy, and its gradual replacement by that of Mycenae and other fortified cities on the Greek mainland.

But the prosperity of these other cities did not last long. The stones of the palace-centered towns of ancient Greece are blackened with fire. In the middle of the twelfth century B.C., a conquering foe must have swept over them. After that there was a cultural blackout. Judging from wretchedly scarce remains, life under the new conquerors must have been hard, rough, and without refinements. Greece took four centuries to recover. Not until the eighth century B.C. do we see the return of a life that might be called civilized.

Who were these invaders? The Greeks believed, and archeologists agree, that they came from the north, and that they were a primitive people grouped in tribes. They seem to have moved down the Greek peninsula in a slowly rising tide, rather than a rush. And they could not have come from far away, for, strangely enough, they spoke dialects (called Dorian and Aeolian) of the very Greek language which was already being spoken in the Mycenaean towns. Their mastery of the land must have been far from complete, for the native Greek dialect (Ionian) continued to be spoken in some areas long after the invasion was history. There is a tradition that some Ionian speaking people fled this invasion and settled on the coast of Asia Minor and on islands in the Aegean Sea. Thus began such great cities as Miletos and Ephesus.

Another strange fact about this invasion was that it was only part of a greater upheaval of peoples, which disrupted life all over the eastern Mediterranean between 1200 and 1100 B.C. In the eighth year of the reign of King Rameses III, shortly after 1200 B.C., Egypt repulsed with difficulty a wave of invaders who attecked the Delta by land and sea. Coming from no one knows where, another strange people, the Phillistines, seized the Levant's southern half, giving it the name of Palestine which it still bears. A little later, northern barbarians overran an entire empire, that of the Hittites, in the northern Levant and Asia Minor.

After this upheaval came a period of settlement and adjustment. In Greece (Hellas, as its people called it) the period between perhaps 1150 and 750 B.C. was one in which tribes of roving, illiterate people from the north, speaking Dorian Greek, settled among the ruins of a culture which they had largely destroyed, and slowly learned its ways. But through this dark period there was miraculously preserved a record of the glory that had gone before. It was preserved in the form of poetry.

Sometime before the Dorians had appeared, the kings of Mycenaean Hellas had mobilized their ships and armed men and sailed for Asia Minor on an invasion enterprise of their own, there to besiege Ilion (or Troy), a walled settlement close to the Hellespont. According to legend, the siege lasted ten years. Of the kings who shared in it few returned to be happily reunited with their wives and resume their reigns. Greek tradition of later centuries fixed the time of this war at two generations (or about 60 years) before the great invasion of Dorian speaking tribes. This would place it sometime near 1200 B.C.

The great Mycenaean expedition, its success, and the tragic fate of its leaders, was one among several heroic tales and mythical accounts of the actions of the gods which fired the imagination of Greek speaking people everywhere. They wanted to hear such stories again and again. In the long dark evenings, kings and men of wealth must have sat in their great dining halls listening to minstrels sing the tales in poetry, accompanied by the sweet, stirring clang of the lyre. Decade after decade new poets kept creating new versions of them, or revising the old. The Dorian invaders, when they came, found themselves pleased by the same songs, which had been passed on from one generation of poet entertainers to another by memory, in an age when the Mycenaean art of writing had been lost.

Homer

Sometime after 800 B.C., Homer, a man of higher poetic genius than all the others, learned the great poetic stories from other minstrels and retold them in his own way. Thus perhaps (for we can only surmise) came into being the *Iliad*, or the tale of the capture of Troy, and the *Odyssey*, the story of one Mycenaean king's return homeward. Homer's followers, recognizing the greatness of his works, may then have put them into writing, an art the eighth century Greeks were adopting from the Phoenicians.

Courtesy Department of Classics, University of Cincinnati. Restoration by Piet de Jong

A minstrel plays upon the lyre, and his song flies out from him like a bird. The favorite evening entertainment of the great lords of Mycenaean Greece was to listen to the folk singers of their time. This restored fresco from a palace at Pylos, burned about 1150 B.C. shows such a singer. Homer, born nearly four centuries later, describes a minstrel as follows:

> *A servant presently led in the famous bard Demodocus, whom the muse had dearly loved, but to whom she had given both good and evil, for though she had endowed him with a divine gift of song, she had robbed him of his eyesight. The servant set a seat for him among the guests, leaning up against a bearing-post. He hung the lyre for him over his head, and showed him where he was to feel for it with his hands. He also set a fair table with a basket of victuals by his side, and a cup of wine . . . The company then laid their hands upon the good things that were before them, but as soon as they had had enough to eat and drink, the muse inspired Demodocus to sing the feats of heroes.*

Odyssey, Book VIII. Butler translation.

The *Iliad* and *Odyssey* are many-sided creations, and as such they can be enjoyed from more than one angle. Above all, perhaps, they are studies of human beings in action. Achilles, hero of the *Iliad*, deepens and broadens as a person through bitter experience, as his life moves on to its violent, untimely close. Odysseus meets endless trials with tireless courage and ingenuity, and at last comes home to rewin his bride. Characters stand out vividly, and both the Greek and Trojan side in the great struggle of the Iliad are told with an astonishing combination of sympathy and detached even-handedness. These great stories, and the ringing language in which they are told, moving with a rhythm like galloping horses, seem possessed with a timeless power. This is their marvelous side, or one of them.

Another is the complexity of their structure. The incidents actually occurring in both the Iliad and the Odyssey cover a short span of time, only about six weeks each. But through the ingenious use of flashbacks, introduced by men recounting past experiences, and through glimpses of the future issuing as prophesies from seers, each epic conveys the sweep of events over a decade.

Viewed from another angle, the *Iliad* and *Odyssey* are like historical movies, whose appeal to the audience is more important than their historical accuracy. No poet of those days even knew what historical accuracy was. Each reverently kept many lines of the poems as he learned them and, as he saw fit, added others suited to his own time. When Homer in his turn inherited this poetic patchwork, he seems to have made the characters behave as his own experience told him they would act in his own day and age, instead of four centuries earlier. That is, he described the behavior of the Dorian invaders, not the Mycenaeans who had fought the Trojan War. At the same time he kept many words and lines from the earlier versions when their quality suited him.

Since writing was still a rarity and was to remain so for generations, Homer's followers appear to have learned his great serial songs by heart and by ear, and to have continued the old tradition of altering them at will. Soon there were various versions of his epics. Not until the sixth century B.C., at Athens, was there a serious attempt to establish, from men who claimed to be Homer's descendants, what the great man's original words had been.

Eighth Century Hellas as Homer Saw It

Homer's Hellas[1] is a land where the clan, or enlarged family, and after that the tribe are still the strongest ties binding men into groups. The Dorian speaking invaders, that is, are still primitive, even though their chiefs like to call themselves "kings." These chiefs and their kinsmen are fine heroic types, generous when it suits them, but with the ideals of highwaymen. Crime exists only if committed against a member of one's own clan. Everyone else, except a few persons made sacred by the gods, is fair game. Odysseus himself "excelled all men in thievery and perjury." Homer states that the god Hermes bestowed these blessings upon him!

But these robber types and their followers have learned how to live the good life of the people they conquered. The have learned to raise and tend grain, orchards, and animals. They have learned to ride and drive horses, build houses and palaces, use towns as centers of government and trade, build and sail ships, work metals for use and ornament, weave cloth, and make wheel-thrown pottery. If they do not do all these things themselves, they dominate people who do them for them. For these Greeks have found that during pirate raids they can seize men and women, boys and girls, bring them home, and put them to work or sell them as slaves. Food is now so easily obtained as to make the terrible practice of slavery seem profitable. Slavery becomes a Greek institution, and remains so for centuries.

Traders come and go with their goods, but two great conveniences of the merchant, money and writing, are not known. One has not yet arrived; the other has been lost in one form, or is just being learned from Phoenicia in another. The conquerors view the traders with contempt. When Odysseus is shipwrecked among the Phaeacians, and is treated with hushed respect until he tells everyone he is not a god in disguise, one of his hosts, during an athletic contest, taunts him as follows: "I suppose you are one of those grasping traders that go about in ships as captains and merchants, and who think of nothing but their outward freights and homeward cargoes. There does not seem to be much of the athlete about you."[2] (This so infuriates Odysseus that he outthrows everyone with the discus.) It is perhaps the Greek superstition of regarding guests and visiting strangers as sacred that makes trade in the eighth century B.C. possible at all.

The religion of the time is strongly colored with magic. A man wins the favor of a god or goddess by performing the correct sacrifice at the proper time (a form of bribery), and can then rely on the god's help in carrying out a pirate raid on some sleeping town, producing rich plunder and the slaughter or enslavement of its citizens.

The gods themselves are supermen and superwomen (often claimed as ancestors by living chiefs and heroes). Their conduct is much like that of the chiefs, for they are persons of touchy dignity and personal beauty, who expect humility and gifts from underlings, that is, mankind. They excel humans in perception (for they can see everything that happens), in travel (they can move wherever they wish on land, sea, or air), in ability to assume any form they choose, and in power over men, whom they can make or break at will. Besides the great gods—Zeus, Hera, Ares, Aphrodite, Athena, Hermes—there are a host of lesser ones. Every gushing spring has its own gentle goddess or *nymph*, every forest its *dryads*, and the sea is alive with *nereids*. Of all these, men must ever be conscious, building little altars to them on which to pour out sacrifices of oil and wine, before they water their flocks, fell trees, or fish.[3]

Such was the world that Homer's ringing poetry made spring to life for his listeners. From that time on, its effect on the Greeks was profound. As he pictured them, so the Greeks saw themselves. As he pictured their gods, so the Greeks believed those gods to be. The Greeks revered Homer not merely as the greatest of poets but as a teacher of men. Centuries had to pass before the primitive conduct of men and gods as pictured by Homer was criticized by the philosopher Socrates. Even at that late date, near 400 B.C., so great was the public respect for Homer that Socrates' wise criticism contributed to costing him his life.

Homer, in short, effectively influenced the life-style of the marvelous culture which was to follow him, and which we today call the *Hellenic Age*.

A wine jar from Athens of the eighth century B.C. On it is scratched the earliest known piece of writing in the Greek alphabet. The sentence, a line of verse, reads, "He whose performance is best among all the dancers shall have me." At the time Athens was still an unimportant place, but its potters had developed their own distinctive style.

National Museum, Athens

Lowie Museum of Anthropology, University of California, Berkeley

A plate from Corinth of the sixth century B.C. At the time Corinth was a leading center for the making and exporting of pottery ware. In the next century Athens successfully competed with her for this leadership.

The Artist Wins Recognition and Respect

The Greek reverent attitude toward Homer as a revealer of the nature of man, the world, and the gods, couched in the organized form of stirring poetry, marks a great step forward in the history of art. For the first time, as nearly as we can tell, we find the people of a culture recognizing the role of the artist as a revealer of men to themselves. For it was not just as a skillful minstrel that the Greeks respected Homer. He was to them vastly more; he was an inspired innovator. As is often an artist's fate, recognition came long after his death.

As the history of Hellas continued to unfold, other men were revered for the same reason. The mighty poets of tragic drama and comedy, who could move an audience to weeping or roaring laughter as human sorrow or absurdity were revealed upon the stage, the great sculptors and painters who brought into being ever more marvelous images of gods, heroes, and perfect-bodied athletes, the architects of exquisitely proportioned buildings, all these too won public acclaim and gratitude.

As we shall see, the Greeks found a conservative way, rooted in ancient belief, for interpreting and explaining the bold creations of their artists. Such men, the Greeks surmised, did not originate their ideas. Rather it was the gods who chose to speak through them, guiding their tongues or their hands, using them as instruments for revealing eternal truths to mankind.

The Greeks of the Seventh Century: The Colony Founders

So, looking at eighth century Hellas through Homer's eyes, we see a young, still primitive people discovering and mastering forms of civilized living which had taken many centuries to create. What were the results?

First, a better food supply and better living conditions made the population mushroom. In the eighth and seventh centuries, more and more Greek children kept surviving to maturity. But the lands where the Greeks lived were restricted. The many-fingered Greek peninsula is rocky and mountainous. Except for a few wide plains, its farmland occurs in patches. The land became glutted with people, many without land. What was to be done?

The Greek answer to the challenge was adventurous. Released by their mastery of shipbuilding and navigation, people set sail from the crowded towns looking for new shores. Wherever they saw a good combination of harbor and fertile land which they could take from the native dwellers by diplomacy or force, there they settled. They planted grain, grapevines, and olive trees, built homes, erected temples to their gods, and started new towns.

They brought to life the shores of Thrace. Southern Italy became so fringed with Greek seaport colonies that it was called Great Greece (*Magna Graecia* in later Latin). The side of Sicily nearest to the Greek peninsula came alive with Greek colonies. The Egyptian kings allowed a Greek city, Naucratis ("Ruler of Ships"), to be set up on one arm of the Nile delta, and trade was resumed after a break of four centuries. Another Greek town, Cyrene, was started on the coast of Libya. Over 2000 long sea miles away a Greek colony called Massalia (modern Marseille) was started at the mouth of the Rhone. At the Sea's opposite end, the Black Sea (or Euxine as the Greeks called it) was successfully entered. Soon it was ringed with Greek settlements. The people there found they could grow grain and catch fish in surprising surpluses. Miletos alone, on the coast of Asia Minor, planted ninety such colonies!

The Greeks began to find themselves running into competition. Tyre, the great Phoenician city of the Levant, was also sending out ship-borne colony founders. Since they were more experienced sailors, the Phoenicians sailed greater distances, even out of the Mediterranean. They explored the coast of Africa and sailed up the headlands of Europe as far as Britain, where they traded for tin, the bronzemaker's necessity. In Spain they founded the first civilized town facing the Atlantic, Gades (modern Cadiz). They seized Gibraltar, and rammed any non-Phoenician ship caught venturing past that rock. Facing the Mediterranean, they made friends with the men of the Spanish town of Tartessos, which was rich in silver. On the north coast of Africa they founded a farming and trading colony, Utica, which, in its turn, founded another one nearby, Carthage. The latter town, surrounded by rich coastal lands over which its people quickly spread their farms, proved to be a fountain of humanity, much like the Greek Miletos. Soon she in her turn was sending out colonies to dominate the islands of Corsica, Sardinia, the Balearic Isles, Malta, and the western half of Sicily.

Thus, in a century, the Mediterranean shores were seized by complexly civilized peoples. Inland, the natives were stirred from their more primitive patterns of living by contact, through trade and fighting, with the more civilized newcomers. Only in northern Italy, a people of unknown origins, the Etruscans, were strong enough to keep control of their own coasts. They took from the Phoenicians, and especially the Greeks, what ideas and luxuries they wished, but proudly continued to hold their few seaports and to maintain their own way of living.

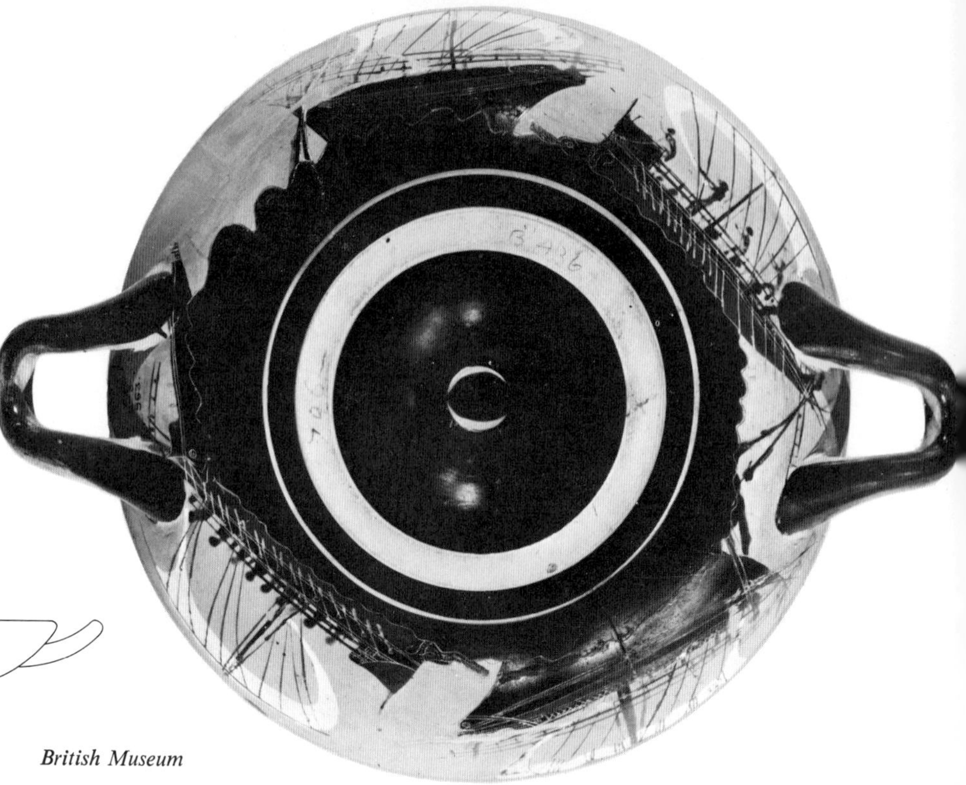

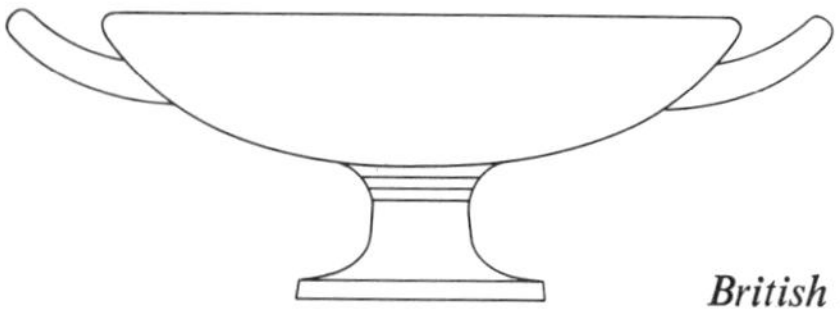

British Museum

A two-handled wine cup (viewed from beneath) made at Athens, about 550 B.C. On it are painted two broad-hulled merchant vessels for carrying cargoes, and two swift war vessels (biremes) to protect them at sea. Cups like this, and other pottery, were shipped overseas by the Athenians in exchange for grain which their own poor soil produced meagerly. The line drawing shows the cup in profile.

How the New Network of Colonies Changed Greek Life

To this world of new seaports the Greeks responded swiftly. The mixing of people through travel had made the old tribes and clans outmoded. Place of residence, rather than ties of blood relationship, became the basis on which men felt loyalty to a community. And foreign shores became less attractive as places to raid for plunder. They were now the homes of kinsmen, who needed all kinds of useful equipment, such as clothing, pottery, tools, and weapons from the home towns, and in exchange could offer grain and raw materials. The Greeks discovered that trade was more profitable than piracy. Though they never quite lost Homer's haughty attitude toward commerce, they were quick to seize upon it as a means to gain. In the home towns of Greece, workshops and households were busy producing goods to ship abroad. In return, new supplies of food came in from the colonies to feed the home populations. Towns grew into cities. In response to these new demands, the Greeks began to improve their techniques as weavers and potters. They became the world's masters at working bronze and the new metal, iron. To expedite trade they adopted a second convenience from the Phoenicians: money. And to protect their trading vessels they adopted the Phoenician style of war vessel, propelled by rowers and armed with a bronze ram.

Soon the Greeks were reaching out to new places to trade, even beyond their own colonies. As the wealth of their cities everywhere increased through trade and the new device, money, so did the demand for articles of luxury, from Phoenicia and farther east. Richly embroidered fabrics, perfumes, rare wines, and carved ivory were eagerly sought. The ingenious Greeks were also trying their hands at making some of these themselves, first copying Asiatic designs, then creating their own.

In spite of all this activity by sea, with ships coming and going between dozens of ports, sailing was still cautious. Open stretches of sea, which look inviting on a map, were shunned because they took vessels too far from ports, leaving sailors nowhere to flee from storms. Other areas were avoided because of tricky winds and hidden rocks. One such area was around the jagged southern end of the Greek peninsula. Shipowners preferred to have their vessels hauled on wheels across the narrow neck of land connecting the peninsula's northern and southern halves! Therefore a city located at this point was bound to benefit from the funneling of an enormous amount of east-west sea trade, as well as from land trade from north and south.

Such a city was Corinth. She was the first Greek city to become a great commercial power. She had not one but three harbors, one on the Corinthian Gulf and two on the Saronic Gulf. The control of the ship-hauling business alone might have made her rich. But her market place was a natural meeting point for the exchange of wares and raw materials from Asia Minor, the Greek islands, Italy, Sicily, and the Greek mainland. Furthermore, she was her own center of production. Corinthian cups, bowls, bottles, jars, and tiles were turned out by her potters and exported far and wide. She was famed for her metal products; her bronzeworkers gave Greek armor its definitive style. Her shipbuilders invented the bireme and trireme, war vessels with double and triple driving power. Syracuse, the mightiest city on the island of Sicily, was her colony. The wealth and luxury of Corinth became Greek bywords.

But Corinth had a rival. The island-city of Aegina controlled the entry of ships to her harbors from the east. Aegina was a commercial city in her own right, reputed to be the first Greek city to coin money. To the Corinthians she was a thorn in the side.

The Greek cities were independent of each other, and quick to enter into rivalry and war. True, they were forever forming alliances, swearing on the altars of the gods that the bond should last "until iron floats." But seldom could the oaths stick, and never was the union complete. Competition was in their blood: the lands were everywhere too constricted, the sources of wealth too meager and hard to win, and men's energy of body and mind too keen to make peaceful coexistence possible. Here lay the seeds of Greek ruin.

Part of the old ship-hauling road across the Isthmus of Corinth, with the ruts worn by heavy-laden wheels still showing in its stone pavement.

Courtesy Firos Verdelis, Athens

A Greek City-State in the Seventh and Sixth Centuries

Let us look at these cities (or rather city-states, for each controlled some land). All had a basis of wealth resting first of all on farming and farm products: grain, flax, wool, hides, cheese, wine, and olive oil. Farming land was the most respected form of wealth, because it was not only the most necessary to life, but the oldest. Each Greek city was surrounded by farm lands (much of it worked by slaves) which had been owned by the same families, sometimes, for generations. The heads of these families were persons of power, who freely gave of their wealth to the building of the city's walls, market places, and temples. Such men were recognized as *citizens*, with the right to guide city government and policy. Inland cities, far from access to the sea, were wholly controlled by their land-owning, farming citizens.

After these in importance came the manufacturers. They ran modest workshops, usually manned by about a dozen slaves. Here pottery, leather goods such as sandals and harness, rope or sailcloth, furniture, tools and weapons, or articles of recreation such as flutes and lyres were made. (Weaving in linen and wool was the work of the women in each household, who often produced a surplus for sale over and above family needs.)

And then, if the city was a seaport, there were the merchants, whose ships brought in cargoes from far away places, and took others outward, always in the hope of making a profit through the exchange.

Last of all there was a rising class of bankers, who dealt in nothing but money. These made possible the work of the merchant, by financing his ventures at a high rate of interest, or *usury*, as it was called.

If men of these last three groups had fathers who were citizens, they too were citizens. If not, they were "foreigners," or, to use the Greek term, *metics*. These were admitted to the city under the ancient Greek tradition of the guest being sacred. They might rent real estate, but not buy it. They did not share in the government, and neither did women, nor, of course, the army of slaves, who carried on much of the hard labor inside the city and out on the farms.

City-Gods of Hellas, and Their Temples

In some respects the city states of Hellas were like the much older ones, far to the east in the Fertile Crescent, in that each city was personified to its citizens by a god or goddess, the city's soul and symbol as it were, whose temple was the city's greatest pride, and on whose guidance and protection the citizens relied. And this deity was served by a group of priests, whose business it was to offer regular sacrifices, to interpret the deity's will, and to administer temple affairs. The priests of Hellas did not control irrigation, banking and education as did those of Mesopotamia. But they were responsible for storing in a temple treasury the annual tribute which citizens respectfully paid to their deity, as if to a ruler.

In primitive times the god or goddess was believed to inhabit some object found in nature, perhaps a tree trunk or a stone (today known as a *cult object*, or object of worship). Then, as the Greeks became more sophisticated and began to conceive of their gods as having distinct personalities, images were required which would make this personality seem real to worshipers. Such images would either replace, or stand in front of, the primitive cult object which was the god's original home (a practice like the older Egyptian one described page 97). The image in turn required a shelter. The Greeks gradually developed the simple shelter into a temple, its roof supported by great tree-trunk columns, its gable ends gaudy with terra cotta images of savage creatures acting as temple guardians. Then, as Greek tastes reached still higher levels, wood and terra cotta were replaced first by limestone and finally by marble, carved and polished with great refinement. At the same time the image of the deity within was given greater and greater majesty and serene dignity, as the Greeks became increasingly interested in these qualities as ideals of conduct.

The fact that the city-gods and goddesses of Hellas were all worshiped by Greeks everywhere helped somewhat to unite the Greeks as a people. Certain cities were particularly respected by all Greeks as the favorite home of a particular god. Of these the greatest were Olympia in the south, as the home of Zeus, and Delphi in the north, as the home of Apollo. It was at Olympia that the great Olympic games were held every four years in honor of the king of the gods. And it was at Delphi that, as the Greeks believed, Apollo revealed the secrets of the future by speaking through the mouth of his high priestess in reply to questions asked by mortal men.

Greek Temples: Votive Offerings

The temples of Hellas were storage houses of wealth, partly because the cities paid the gods yearly tribute, partly because single citizens, with their strongly personal attitude toward the gods, were continually presenting them with gifts. These, sometimes, were in thanks to a god for answering a prayer, sometimes in the hope of getting a prayer answered. The gifts took many forms. The wealthy sometimes gave gold or silver, to be stored in the temple treasury. Often instead they gave works of art dramatically symbolic of the reason for the gift. The bronze charioteer given to Apollo in thanks for victory at the Olympic games is an example. The poor gave what they could. A sailor who had escaped drowning would give the clothes he was wearing when rescued. A man who had regained use of a paralyzed leg would give a small wood model of it. These modest *votive offerings*, as they were called, were often hung up in the temple, row on row. In contrast the magnificent works of art, chiefly sculpture in metal or stone, stood, some within the temple, some on its porch or steps, some in the sacred walled precinct surrounding it. In time the more famous or popular temples became thronged about with such gifts, each temple a veritable museum. See the illustration, page 168.

Gorgon, from a temple of the goddess Artemis, on the island of Corfu, early sixth century B.C. With her terrible gaze which supposedly could turn men to stone, she was placed on the temple's west front in the pediment *or triangle under the gable roof to ward off evil. Compare with the pediment sculptures shown on page 171 to see what strides in taste the Greeks were to make in the next 150 years.*

Greek Temples: Statues of Athletes and Maidens

Of this wealth of sculptural art only rare specimens remain today, preserved by accident. And among these there appear again and again statues of youths and girls in their late teens, standing proudly erect. Why such statues were placed in temple precincts we are not sure (not all are found near temples; some have been found in cemeteries as grave markers). But they tell us much about the Greek ideals of young manhood and womanhood. The girls are discreetly clad in long embroidered robes; they stand with arms bent at the elbows, as if respectfully serving someone. But the youths are completely naked. With arms at their sides they stride forward, splendidly confident of their physical development. They are obviously athletes.

The statues of the youths far outnumber those of the girls. The earliest are rather rigid, the details of muscle, facial features and hair all reduced to conventional patterns, suggestive of what we have already observed in tribal art (see page 69). Later ones show a progressively deeper comprehension of the human body and its mechanics, its modeling and its freedom of pose. When we compare such figures with the rigidly inhibited temple figures of Mesopotamia, or the splendid but relatively unarticulated statues of Egypt, we find ourselves asking Why? What impelled the Greeks to be the first to carry the study of the human body close to its limits of naturalism? No one can finally answer such a question. But it must have had a strong connection with the Greek awareness that as human beings they were free, free from the rigid constrictions of the older cultures which narrowly bound a man's conduct and thought from birth to death. This Greek freedom was only relative, for the Greeks too had their deeply ingrained customs, to be violated at great peril. And freedom, it seems, was fully experienced only by members of a fortunate leisure class who could perfect their bodies through gymnastics, and their minds through uninhibited inquiry. The results of their gymnastics is revealed to us in the athlete statues. The results of their use of intellect is revealed in a host of ways. One is the lucid comprehension of human structure which those athlete statues reveal. Another is the great variety of inventive political solutions which the Greeks attempted in managing their city-states.

Metropolitan Museum of Art, Fletcher Fund.

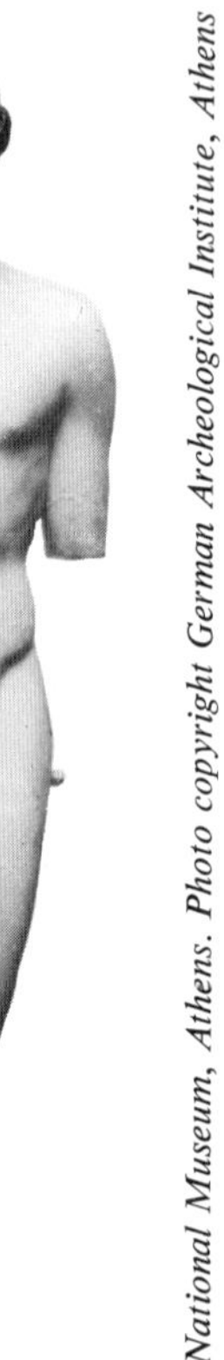

National Museum, Athens. Photo copyright German Archeological Institute, Athens

Greek City-States as Political Experiments

The citizens of each city-state managed civic affairs in their own way; their governments were real experiments in politics. The most conservative were the land-locked ones, where the citizens were all or chiefly land owners. And the most conservative of all, deep in the heart of the Peloponnesus, was Sparta, protected by Ares, god of war. She even clung to the rule of kings (two at a time, in fact, descended from the twin sons of Hercules!). But she behaved less like a kingdom than a conquering tribe. Her citizens specialized in nothing but war; their battle tactics of frontal attack were considered unbeatable. Thus about 7000 men kept their neighbors in terror, and ensured a steady flow of tribute sufficient to meet all the wants of the Spartan state. Tense vigilance was the Spartans' way of life. They refused to surround their city with a wall, lest they be tempted to relax in security behind it. The medium of currency was declared to be iron, so that its massive weight would discourage a love of trade. Once a year, as a matter of form, they declared war on all their trembling neighbors. Thus Sparta remained, as hard as rock, and as rigid—a reminder, or caricature of a reminder, to the rest of Hellas, of a fortunately outlived past.

Opposite page, top: life-size statue of a Greek youth, marble, 600 B.C. or before. Bottom: another statue of marble, 34 in. high, carved about 125 years later.

At the opposite extreme, and barely sixty miles away, was wealthy, relaxed Corinth, protected by Aphrodite, goddess of love, governed by a clique of merchant princes, and facing the sea on two fronts, ever in the forefront of adventurous trade and inventive change. Or nearly in the forefront. For she was soon to be out-maneuvered and outshone.

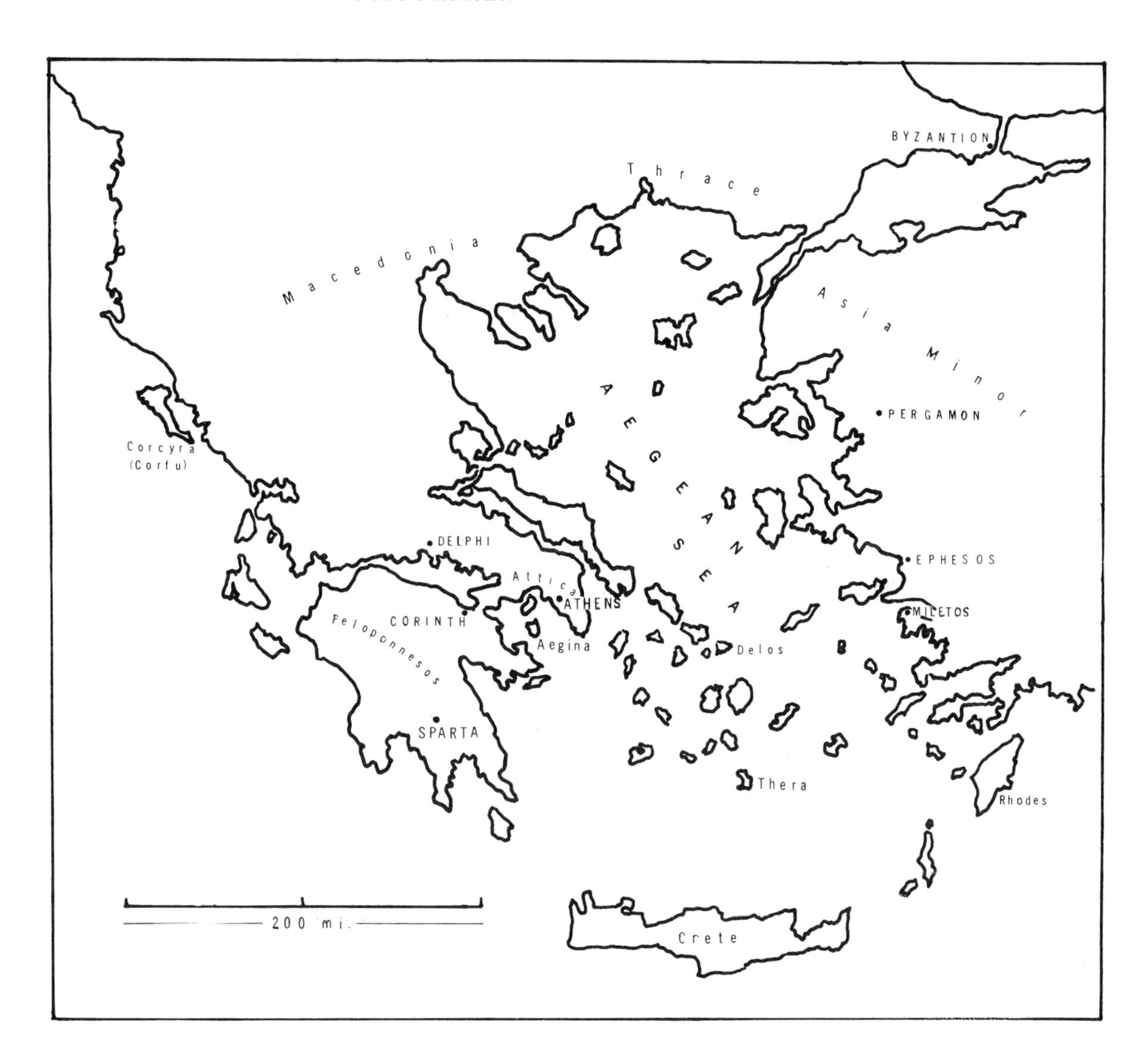

Fifth-Century Athens Makes Herself Powerful

Jutting out eastward from Corinth and Aegina lies the lean, barren peninsula of Attica. Its area of 1000 square miles is about that of Rhode Island. The great philosopher Plato, writing 2300 years ago, describes his native land:

National Museum, Athens. Photo Alison Frantz

Athena, guardian goddess of Athens, revered as governing prudent wisdom in warfare, and therefore usually shown wearing a helmet. She is here shown reading a city law or edict engraved on the stone before her. The Athenians kept all public documents displayed in this manner so that citizens might readily consult them. This is a votive relief, fifth century B.C.*, found on the Acropolis.*

> "Attica may accurately be described as a mere relic of the original country . . . All the rich, soft soil has been moulted away, leaving a country of skin and bones.. . . There are mountains in Attica which can now keep nothing but bees, but which were clothed, not so very long ago, with fine trees producing timber . . . The annual supply of rainfall was not lost, as it is at present, through being allowed to flow over the denuded surface into the sea, but was received by the country, in all its abundance, into her bosom . . . and so was able to discharge the drainage of the heights into the hollows in the form of springs and rivers . . . The shrines that survive to the present day on the sites of extinct water supplies are evidence of the correctness of my hypothesis."[4]

In other words, Attica in ancient times had already been ruined by erosion, caused by unwise lumbering. She was a poor land. But besides her poverty she had pride. There was a tradition, borne out by modern archeology, that she had successfully resisted the Dorian invasion of 1150 B.C. Her single important city, Athens, was built around a formidable citadel, or *acropolis*, like a towering ship of rock. The people of those parts still spoke Ionian Greek, going back to pre-Dorian times.

How did this wretched land become the mightiest of its time? How did it manage to give a new direction to civilization, which we feel even today? These victories were won by feats of human intelligence, which turned misfortunes into advantages and obstacles into springboards to success.

The remarkable city claimed a fitting deity for its protector, Athena, goddess of wisdom in war and peace, and of skill in arts and crafts, There was a legend that Athena competed for possession of Athens with Poseidon, god of the sea. Poseidon smote the great rock of the Acropolis with his trident and opened a salt-water spring. Athena planted an olive tree on its summit. Zeus and the other gods awarded the city to Athena, and the name of the city, whose Greek form is *Athenae* (meaning Belonging-to-Athena) was the result. This charming myth seems to symbolize the fact that Athens had to resort first to her land resources before she could become a sea power. Be that as it may, the city's acropolis had from ancient times been crowned with a temple to Athena, repeatedly rebuilt on an ever grander scale.

Shortly after 600 B.C. the men of Attica began planting grove on grove of olive trees. These thrive on poor soil and scant water, but produce a valuable crop. Digging into the subsoil, potters located new deposits of clay, from which they turned out storage jars for the export of olive oil. For olive oil was everywhere in demand in the ancient world for three reasons: it was the butter of the period; it was burned in lamps; and it was used as a cleansing rubdown after labor, athletics and fighting. Soon olive oil was being exported at a profit to ever more distant markets.

A special quality of Athenian genius now appeared. The potters were not content to turn out jars for utility only. They began to create cups, bowls, dishes, jugs, and jars of such quality and style as to compete with the Corinthians. Athenian ware began to push that of Corinth off the foreign market. *Ceramics* (from the Greek word *keramos*, potters' clay) became a major Athenian industry.

This ceramic ware was remarkable in two ways: first, for its elegant shape; second for the manner in which its rich ornamentation fits that shape. Using chiefly three contrasting colors—terra-cotta red, black, and white—they brought to life the swelling shoulders of jars and the floors of dishes with scenes from the *Iliad*, the *Odyssey*, and the Greek myths. Strangely enough, most of these potters were not native Athenians, but metics. The names they proudly signed to their wares were those of foreigners. And when they naïvely labeled the pictures of gods and heroes, the spelling was often inaccurate, suggesting an alien pronounciation. So "Athenian genius" did not depend on one's being a native. It can only be explained by the atmosphere in which men in Athens could work. What was this atmosphere?

Athenian Political Life

Over the century from about 560 to 460 B.C., the government of Athens was one of ever increasing *democracy*, or rule by all the mature male citizens. Step by step a succession of remarkable statesmen, beginning with Solon, succeeded in reshaping that government. It had once been solely in the hands of wealthy, aristocratic heads of families. Between these and the unrepresented poor there had been a bitter division. Gradually the poorer citizens were given more and more chance to be heard in government, first by being permitted to vote, then actually to hold office. By degrees, the concept of democracy was pushed to its logical extreme. The Athenians began to fill many public offices not by voting, but by lot!

Above: Athenian amphora *(storage jar), early sixth century B.C. The black formal figures against a red clay background create a strong design harmonizing with the shape of the jar. Museum of Fine Arts, Boston. Below: Athenian* hydria *(water jar) of about 120 years later. Red figures are now silhouetted against black, drawing is natural, and a new, freer relationship between figures and shape of jar has been found.*

Metropolitan Museum of Art

Here the Greek thinking was different from ours. Since all their civic duties were regarded as a kind of worship, preceded by appropriate sacrifices and prayers, their approach to the use of lots was a religious one. They believed that the gods, who are above the laws of chance, could thus be free to decide into whose hands the various city offices should fall. Ten thousand judges, for example, were thus selected every year. From these, courts of 501 each (to avoid split decisions) were selected, again by lot, to hear cases and to vote for plaintiff or defendant as they felt the hearings indicated. No one, the Athenians believed, could afford to bribe 251 judges.

Thus, large numbers of citizens were constantly being drawn into civic affairs. To make sure that no one begged off because he had to earn a living, the city itself paid citizens a good wage for every working day they missed: first one *obol* a day, then two, then, as prices soared, three; that is, first about three, then seven, and finally ten cents.

Even so only a fraction of the total Athenian population, perhaps 15%, was politically active. For besides women, minors and metics, there were also tens of thousands of slaves who of course could not participate.

About once a month, all citizens were expected to gather in one spot (in the shadow of the hill called Pnyx) to hear, and debate on, problems of local government and foreign policy. After sacrifices and a prayer to the gods for wisdom, the debates began, presided over by the *archon*, or mayor. Decisions were reached by the voice vote of the multitude. The laws which were thus enacted, and the treaties with other cities thus agreed to, were engraved on slabs of stone, where all might see them.

Lowie Museum of Anthropology, University of California, Berkeley

Athenian silver coin worth four drachmas or about 80¢. This would have been two days' salary for men like Ictinos and Pheidias, who directed the construction of the Parthenon and created its sculpture. The coin bears on one side the profile of Athena. On the other is an owl, sacred to Athena, and a sprig of olive. In ancient times the coins were called "Athenian owls."

While metics might not participate in such civic duties, they were made welcome to Athens if they had something of value to contribute to city life. Men throughout Attica began to breathe the fresh air of freedom as nowhere else, even in other Greek towns. Other states watched the experiment with enthusiasm, cynicism, or concern. Corinth was enraged with jealousy. Sparta was shocked.

How the Athenians Financed Their City Government

Such a city government required funds. Although wealthy citizens were proud to build temples, fortifications, market places, gymnasia, and parks for their beloved city of their own free will, compulsory taxes were not tolerated. The Athenians developed a harbor, Peiraeos, about three miles from the city, facing the Saronic Gulf. There they collected a two percent duty on all imports and exports. When good fortune came their way, and veins of silver were discovered under Attic soil, Athens began to mint her own coins: *drachmas*, worth six obols, and *tetradrachmas*, worth four drachmas. Allowing for the crude methods of metal refining then known, these coins were of remarkably consistent purity and weight. While other cities were shortsightedly using underweighted coins and cheap alloys as a means to cheat foreign merchants, Athens, bent on attracting business, stuck to a policy of honesty in all financial dealings. Officials policed all market places, both in the harbor and in the city, enforcing accuracy of weights and measures and requiring certain standards of quality in the goods sold. To protect the harbor and their own merchantmen on the seas, the Athenians built a navy, first of fifty-oared vessels, then of triremes, with lumber imported from Thrace. They were rewarded for their enterprise and integrity by the growing popularity of their harbor and city as meeting points for traders from other regions. Customs duties filled the city treasury, and Athenians began to enjoy prosperity.

The Panathenaea

While they were building their economic strength and their sea power, the Athenians were just as ambitious to develop other sides of their lives. They were concerned that their sons should grow up to be well-developed and well-balanced men. Education was focused on two widely contrasting fields: gymnastics and music. Gymnastics, taught in the public gymnasia donated by wealthy citizens, included wrestling, bare-knuckle boxing, dancing as performed for the great religious festivals, and finally the ancestors of our modern track and field events. Music, taught privately by masters to small groups, included the learning of many poetic forms then used, singing, and the playing of lyre and flute. It included, also, reading, writing, numbering, and history, for to the Greeks the word *music* meant any form of intellectual or artistic pursuit which they believed men had learned from the god Apollo and his goddess-handmaidens, the *Muses*.[5]

So Athenians tended to reach manhood with strong athletic and literary tastes. The city provided opportunities to keep these interests alive. To honor the city's protecting goddess, Athena, contests were held each year. The

Greeks loved competition, and always arranged it on a religious pretext. The fields of competition were athletic events, poetic composition, and the reciting of Homer's poetry. Every four years the *Panathenaea*, as the annual competition was called, became a tremendous festival, lasting for days. Months before, heralds went out to other city-states inviting them to send competitors, and at the appointed time these came flocking in. The girls of Athens, as their share in the praise of Athena, had helped during the past four years to embroider a great *peplos*, or mantle, for the goddess.

At one point in the Panathenaea a procession of young men on horseback, older men with olive branches, and girls bearing baskets of offerings, wound its way through the city. In the midst of the procession a line of maidens, walking in single file, bore on their heads a long slender chest containing the new peplos for Athena.[6] To the sound of chanting and instruments, this parade, the cream of Athenian youth and citizenry, finally mounted the zig zag road up the west face of the grim Acropolis, passed through its great gateway known as the Propylaea, and entered the sacred precinct at the top of the rock. There, on open-air altars, priests let the rich aroma of roasting oxen and burning incense float upward to please the goddess. The new peplos was borne into the temple and suspended before Athena's statue, replacing the fabric that had hung there for the previous four years. Later, when all had descended once more to the city, a relay race run with torches served as a nighttime close to the festival. The following day the guests from other cities departed, some doubtless bearing away jars of olive oil, which were the prizes for the various events.

Athenian lekithos *(oil flask), decorated with olive leaves and Athena's sacred bird, an owl. Fifth century* B.C.

Collection of Miss A. Jenzer, Winterthur, Switzerland

The Athenians' Use of Drama

One other extraordinary side of Athenian life should be mentioned. This was the annual performance of drama. Here again we find an ancient form of recreation which looks like our own, but which differed in aim. To the Athenians, drama was a way of honoring Dionysos, youngest of the gods, protector of fertility and legendary revealer to mankind of the art of wine making. In his honor four different festivals were celebrated each year. Of these, two had become especially important or popular. One was a time of ribald jollity and dancing, probably with a generous touch of orgy, celebrating the new wine vintage. The other, more serious, celebrated Dionysos' symbolic death (each winter) and rebirth (each spring). Before an assembly of the people a chorus of men and boys, costumed as goat-like satyrs and dancing in a circle around an altar, chanted a series of songs telling the god's life story.

We surmise that these, or something like them, were the simple beginnings from which the Greeks, and especially the Athenians of the sixth and fifth centuries B.C., developed the complex dramatic forms known as comedy and tragedy. Both remained in a sense religious ceremonies whose purpose was to sensitize the audience, whether through violent laughter or tears, to the cleansing voice of conscience. To this end not one but several arts were combined, synthesized to create one dynamically moving experience. First there was the *drama itself*, either hilariously funny, or moving with relentless steps toward heroic doom. The thread of their action was carried by only a few actors who in the earliest dramas appeared singly, in later ones two or three at a time. Next there were the *choruses* for men and boys (traditionally fifty), their words set to specially composed music accompanied by clanging lyres and shrill pipes, woven through the drama to accentuate it in various ways. Their rhythmic motions as they sang were governed by a *choreography* carefully planned to heighten the mood of the play. Supporting these co-ordinated actions and sounds were the developing arts of *stagecraft and costuming*, designed to make the spectacle of the drama carry to an audience whose outer fringes might be over two hundred feet away. Such distances required heroically simple gestures, strikingly vivid costumes and intensely individualized masks to distinguish one actor from another. Last of all there was the *architectural setting*, the open-air theatre, a great semi-circle of stone seats rising tier on tier and focusing not on a stage but on an altar sacred to Dionysos and on the level space around it (the *orchestra*) where the chorus might perform in his honor. The stage where the actors appeared in ones, twos or threes, stood behind the orchestra.

Thus did Athenian creative genius convert primitive ritual into glorious annual festivals, each several days long, at which composers of comedy and tragedy competed on separate occasions for a prize, a simple wreath of myrtle or bay leaves. Scripts were submitted to city officials well in advance, and those judged worthy of participation were produced either at public expense or with funds from private donors. Everyone connected with each production was held in high public honor, especially the dramatists and their most important interpreters, the actors. From such annual experiences the audience was expected to depart with emotions wrung clean of hard heartedness and greed, ready to fulfill another year of civic responsibility.

As the sixth century passed into the fifth, such were the Athenians; inventive, liberal with each other and with strangers, pious toward the gods, and alert to maintain civic health by keeping a balance between business, athletics and art.

The theatre of Dionysos at Athens, as it looks today from the Acropolis. The altar to the god was at the center of the diamond-shaped pavement, and was originally surrounded by a circle, the present shape being the result of Roman alterations. The theatre could seat perhaps 17,000 people.

Photo Alison Frantz, Athens

Photo Oriental Institute, Chicago

Darius, king of the Persians, surrounded by courtiers and guards, and with incense burning before him, gives audience to a foreign ambassador. The scene is from the wall of the treasury in the royal palace, erected in the sixth century B.C. at Persepolis, in present-day Iran.

The Fateful Fifth Century

The Persian Threat and Its Outcome

While the Greeks of the sixth century had been busy developing the power, wealth, and cultural life of their city-states, gigantic forces had been stirring eastward of their little world. Cyrus the Persian, one of the world's geniuses at politics and war, was carving for himself the greatest empire mankind had yet known. To this his son and grandson made additions until the extreme east-west extent of the great land mass was 4000 miles. Eastward, the Persians pushed their borders into India, past the Indus River. Westward, they swallowed up the entire Fertile Crescent. Babylon was theirs, and Tyre. They laid hands on the ancient land of Egypt and made it a province. They moved on to seize Libya in north Africa and the Greek colony-city of Cyrene.

The Greeks began to smart under Persian blows when Cyrene fell. They began to bleed when Lydia, the kingdom of Asia Minor just inland from the Greek cities there, was conquered by Cyrus. For Cyrus then demanded submission from the eastern Greeks themselves. When Miletos refused, Athens, loyal to a fellow city whose citizens spoke Ionian Greek, sent twenty ships to aid her. The Persians took Miletos with much destruction and slaughter. Thereafter, they could not forget that a little city across the Aegean had aided Miletos. In three compaigns (492, 490, and 480 B.C.) they attempted a conquest of revenge.

The three Persian thrusts at Hellas are a study in trial-and-error experiment, using military power on a scale hitherto unknown. The first attempt to move an invading army from Asia Minor across the Hellespont into Thrace and then southward was a disaster. In the second attempt the Persians paid more attention to quality of troops and speed, though perhaps not enough. Using Phoenician ships, they transported a force under their generals Datis and Artaphernes directly across the Aegean toward the coast of Attica. On the way they paused at the island of Delos, sacred to all the Greeks as the birthplace of their beloved god Apollo, and in an effort to win him over to the Persian side, burned eight tons of frankincense on his altars.

Continuing their voyage, and guided by an aged Athenian who bore his native city a bitter grudge, they landed on the shore of Attica at a plain called Marathon, about twenty miles from Athens. Ten thousand Greeks, generaled by the Athenian Miltiades, were awaiting them. The hail of arrows which the Persians expected to break the Greek charge was ineffective. Bronze armour, overlapping shields, and coordinated action won the day. Sixty-four hundred Persians fell, compared to only one hundred ninety-two Greeks whose funeral mound, twenty-five feet high, still marks the field of victory. Apollo apparently had been unimpressed by all the incense. The Persians re-embarked and retreated to Asia Minor.

They bided their time for ten years. When the Persian generals again went into action in 480, it was to launch an operation whose coordination seems incredible for those days of slow travel and hazardous communication. Ambassadors must have worked on it endlessly, not to mention officers of supply. The strategy was to employ a pincer movement. From the west, Carthage, aided by Persian gold, launched an attack from her colony cities in Sicily, aimed at pushing the Sicilian Greeks into the sea. From the east, 700 Phoenician ships—war vessels and transports—swept up into the Aegean, and supported a troop movement, better planned than the first one, moving in from Asia Minor to Thrace and then southward. This Persian horde moved like a tide, burning Greek cities which did not surrender.

The Persians, also moving in directly at Athens from the sea for an expected kill, landed on Attica, only to find it deserted. For the people had taken refuge on the island of Salamis, ringed with Greek triremes. From there the horrified refugees could see Athens, miles away, going up in smoke. It now remained for the Phoenician fleet to crush the Greeks. The following morning, Xerxes, the Persian King, who was directing affairs in person, had a throne set up on a high point of shore to watch the expected victory. But the Greek fleet, chiefly Athenian, had lured the Persians into narrow waters where great numbers of ships were useless. The ship-shattering victory by the Greeks that day was complete.

At the same time the mountains came, in a sense, to the Greeks' aid. In the narrow, strategic pass of Thermopylae, north of the Gulf of Corinth, three hundred Spartans heroically blocked the huge Persian army's advance for a day. But that day was the crucial one. Persia's fleet was now broken and fleeing, and to advance without sea support was unwise. Though another year of hard fighting was required to drive the Persians out of northern Hellas and Thrace, Hellas was saved. Meanwhile, Gelon, lord of Syracuse, was administering a stunning defeat to the Carthaginian army which was striking from western Sicily. Large numbers of the defeated Carthaginian troops were taken prisoner and spent the rest of their lives as slaves tilling Syracusan farms.

The people of Attica presently returned to their fields and to their beloved city. Their houses were blackened walls, their temples ruined and defaced. The Athenians were for the moment destitute, but they were free, and they were victors.

Athens Becomes a Leader, Then a Dictator

The Athenians did not require much time to revive their city, their farming, and their trade. They now had a new reputation. While it was Spartan courage that had stopped the Persian host on land, it was Athenian courage and tactical skill that had defeated them at sea. Thus spurred by success, Athens went on to greater things which Sparta, always fearing a revolt at home, dared not undertake. Athens took the lead in forming an alliance of Greek cities on the Aegean islands, with the aim of driving Persian and Phoenician ships once and for all out of the Aegean Sea. This alliance of about one hundred forty cities was the first of its kind on such a scale. Its administrative center and treasury were on the island of Delos, under Apollo's protection, and so it was called the Delian League. The other cities contributed ships, crews, and money. Athens supplied her share of these and more. One of her admirals, Cimon, led the Delian fleet to victory after victory. Soon not only the sea but the shores of Asia Minor were free from Persians (and from pirates as well). Athens' glory shone ever brighter.

The other cities of the League began to relax their interest. More and more wanted to pay money only, and let others build ships and go to sea. But who were those "others"? Athens, of course. Her harbors were busy building new vessels for the Delian fleet. Her poorer citizens were busy manning the rowing benches, two hundred men to every trireme. In from the Delian treasury came money to pay the ship builders and the wages of the rowers. Athens had a new source of wealth.

A change began to come over Athens. The poorer people, with their newly found income, began to express their wishes more and more forcibly in the Assembly. They were hungry for power and wanted to see Athens supreme. They lacked the restraint of the aristocratic Athenians, whose experience told them to keep the power among the cities balanced.

At length the "popular" part of the Athenian citizenry had its way and elected an archon to its taste. This man, Pericles, an aristocrat but athirst for glory, promptly launched Athens on an aggressive course. In his hands the fleet became a weapon against other Greeks. Cities which let their dues go unpaid, or which wanted to get out of the Delian League, found the Delian fleet, now largely manned by Athenians, riding in their harbors, ready to discipline them. The cities woke up to find themselves no longer members of a league but subjects in an empire. Athens under Pericles' guidance now began to wield her power for her own ends.

Going further, the Athenians dared to use the Delian treasury in ways for which it was never intended. They drew upon it to finance the rebuilding of the temples on the acropolis, and even to defray the expenses of the annual dramas honoring Dionysos. Their argument seems to have been that their city had been destroyed in defence of all the other Greek cities, and that therefore all Hellas owed them something in return. Citizens of integrity protested this dishonest reasoning and this betrayal of trust. They went unheard. In fifteen miraculous years, between 447 and 432, Athena's temple, the Parthenon, was rebuilt. It was the city's crowning glory, and for 900 years remained so. Today its ruin is still a marvel. The fact remains that it was built with funds contributed by other cities, in good faith, for other purposes, namely, the upkeep of the Delian League fleet. The enormous cost of about 30,000,000 drachmae, or $6,000,000, was more than any one city could have managed at the time.

Pericles, archon *(mayor) of Athens for thirty years, the man most responsible for the city-state's policy at the peak of its power. A man acutely aware of his public image, he was said to require that he be shown wearing a helmet to conceal his unusually high forehead.*

British Museum

The acropolis of Athens as it may have looked in the fifth century B.C. The zig-zag road mounting to it, lined with votive statues donated to Athena, leads up to the great bronze-gated entrance called the Propylaea. Above and beyond rises the colossal bronze statue of the goddess presented to the city by the admiral Cimon. In the left distance is the Erechtheion, where once stood the palace of the ancient kings of Athens. To the right is the Parthenon, the supreme architectural creation of the Greek world.

Reconstruction by Marcel Lambert, 1877

The Creation of the Parthenon

The Parthenon was the work of two Athenian architects, Ictinos and Callicrates, Ictinos being the more important of the two. He later wrote a book about the building, unfortunately long since lost. Nearly everything we know about it therefore comes from study of the ruins, and from a few descriptions by ancient writers. We know that, when the architects started planning, there was standing on the Acropolis an already partly completed temple, the most magnificent up to that time, which the Persians had damaged. Ictinos and Callicrates naturally decided to use for the new temple the stone already collected for the old one. This was glistening white marble from newly discovered quarries about four miles from Athens. To haul it had been a costly task, especially the great drums for the columns, six feet across, and the huge marble beams to rest on them, fourteen feet long.

THE PARTHENON'S DESIGN: 1. SIMPLE PROPORTION. In planning the new temple, the architects also decided to alter and refine the old temple's measurements. In this respect they achieved one of the world's masterpieces. For the Parthenon is by no means the largest Greek temple ever built, but among all the buildings of the world it is outstanding for the harmony of its proportions. Men have responded emotionally to this quality in the building ever since it was completed. But it was not until the nineteenth century that archeologists made precise measurements of the ruins to find out just what its proportions are. By far the most thorough study was made by an Englishman, F. C. Penrose, in 1844. His findings were then interpreted by another Englishman, W. W. Lloyd, who recognized that the parts of the Parthenon are united by certain simple ratios, the most frequent one being 9 to 4. Here are some examples:

Ratio of length of temple platform (228.14 ft.) to its width (101.34 ft.), 9 to 4.

Ratio of center-to-center distance between two columns (14.09 ft.) to the thickness of one column (6.25 ft.), 9 to 4.

Ratio of center-to-center distance to height of one column without its capital (31.4 ft.), 4 to 9.

Other ratios also exist. The width of the platform is to the temple's total height (65.18 ft.) as 7 is to 12. The total height is to the platform length as 9 is to 14. Lloyd noticed that these ratios were usually united by one peculiarity—their difference is nearly always 5.

From their study of other Greek temples, Penrose and Lloyd realized that this proportioning was by no means original with Ictinos and Callicrates. They seem, rather, to have applied the principles more consistently than had any previous architects.

THE PARTHENON'S DESIGN: 2. SUBTLE REFINEMENTS. While measuring the Parthenon, Penrose became aware that, contrary to its appearance, few of its lines are straight, but curved, and few of them exactly erect, but sloping. At first this suggested inaccurate building, until he discovered that these slight deviations are consistent, and that they have logical explanations.[7] The name given to such refinements of architectural form is *entasis*.

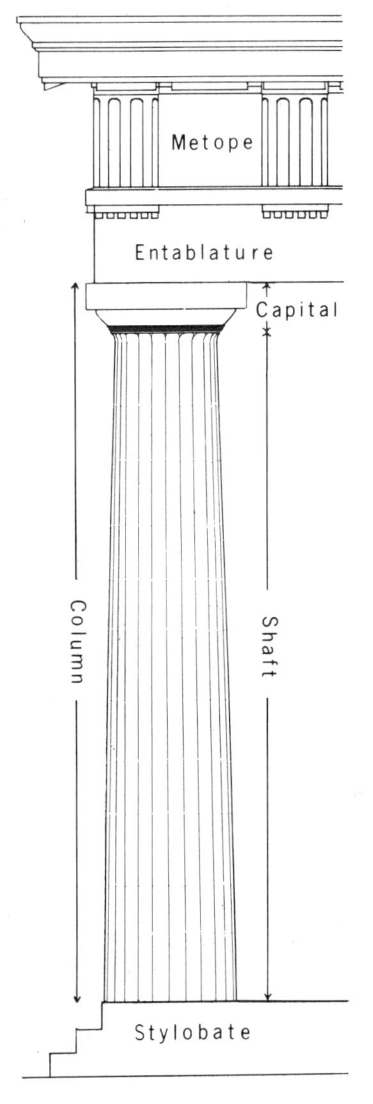

Of the three styles or orders *of architecture which Hellenic architects developed, the earliest and most severely elegant was known as Doric. The order was gradually perfected in the course of a century of temple building, and its supreme example is the Parthenon, completed in the mid-fifth century* B.C. *Important elements of the order and their names are shown above.*

Opposite page, top: The Parthenon today, viewed from the east, its marble, once white, browned with age. For 900 years it was a temple to Athena. Then it became a Byzantine Christian church, and next a Turkish mosque. In 1687, while serving as a powder magazine during a siege of Athens, an explosion partially wrecked it. In 1801 Lord Elgin removed the sculptures from the triangular pediment above the pillars and transported them to England, where they still are, in the British Museum. Middle: The east front of the Parthenon as it may have looked originally, its white marble enriched in places with color (for an example see page 181), and great gilded bronze shields hanging above its columns. The group sculpture in the pediment shows the birth of Athena, springing to life full grown and armed from the brain of her father, Zeus. Bottom: The interior of the Parthenon somewhat as it may have looked 2400 years ago. Pheidias' great statue of Athena, thirty-nine feet tall, was completely sheathed in ivory and gold and decked with jewels. The base was of tinted marble. Contrary to this picture, there was probably no opening in the roof. The dim interior probably added to the majesty of the statue.

Reconstructions by Loviot, 1881

a) The platform (or *stylobate*) on which the temple's columns stand bulges upward toward its center. Across its front the platform rises less than 3 inches in a hundred feet. Along its sides the rise is only about half as great. More remarkable still, as Penrose discovered, these curves are not simply circular, but parabolic, increasing toward the center. Their subtle presence counteracts the optical illusion of sagging which a perfectly straight horizontal line creates.

b) The columns (their surfaces enriched with 20 vertical grooves or *flutes*) not only taper upward; they do so in a scarcely visible consistent curve (1 inch for every 552 inches of length); and again this curve is not a simple segment of a circle, but this time a flat hyperbola. The columns also lean inward, 1 inch to every 148 inches of height. Together these curves and slants heighten the viewer's impression of the temple's monumental strength.

Most of the columns are seen against the solid stone background of the temple. But this is not true of the corner columns, which appear silhouetted against the sky. This creates two optical illusions: the bright background makes each corner column appear exceptionally slender; it also gives the impression that it is detached from the others. Ictinos and Callicrates surmounted this double illusion in two ways. They made the corner columns one-fortieth thicker than the others, and they moved them inward, reducing the center-to-center distance from about 14 feet to about 12.

c) Of the 3 rather shallow steps surrounding the Parthenon platform on all four sides, the top one is $\frac{1}{14}$ higher than the other two. Lloyd noticed that this gives a valuable impression of lift to the whole building.

d) One of the remarkable but unobtrusive aspects of the temple is its mouldings, around doors, roof eaves and column capitals. Mouldings have one purpose—to vary the surface of a building with bands of light and shadow. The clear dry air of Hellas makes the distinction between light and shade extremely clear, and the Parthenon's mouldings exploit this quality to the full. They bulge and recede in highly refined curves, controlling the gradations from sunlit to shaded surface with great nicety.

Again, Ictinos and Callicrates did not invent these refinements. Generations of Greek temple builders had already discovered the need for them and had tested them, some in one temple, some in another. But never before, it seems, had so many been used in one building. Their precision required a rare quality of taste. The resulting exactitude of stone cutting added enormously to the building cost. The final result was an arrogant challenge to the other city-states of Hellas to approach it in perfection, if they could, and if they dared to try.

THE PARTHENON'S DESIGN: 3. MAGICAL AND RELIGIOUS ASPECTS. The simple, consistent proportions of the Parthenon, and subtle curves and slants of its surfaces, were all intended to delight and inspire the human beings who beheld it (and who still do). But the temple had also a superhuman aspect; it was the home of a mighty goddess, whom the people of Athens had worshiped from ancient times. Age-old traditions, some Greek, some perhaps borrowed from older civilizations, seem to be hidden in the temple's layout and design.

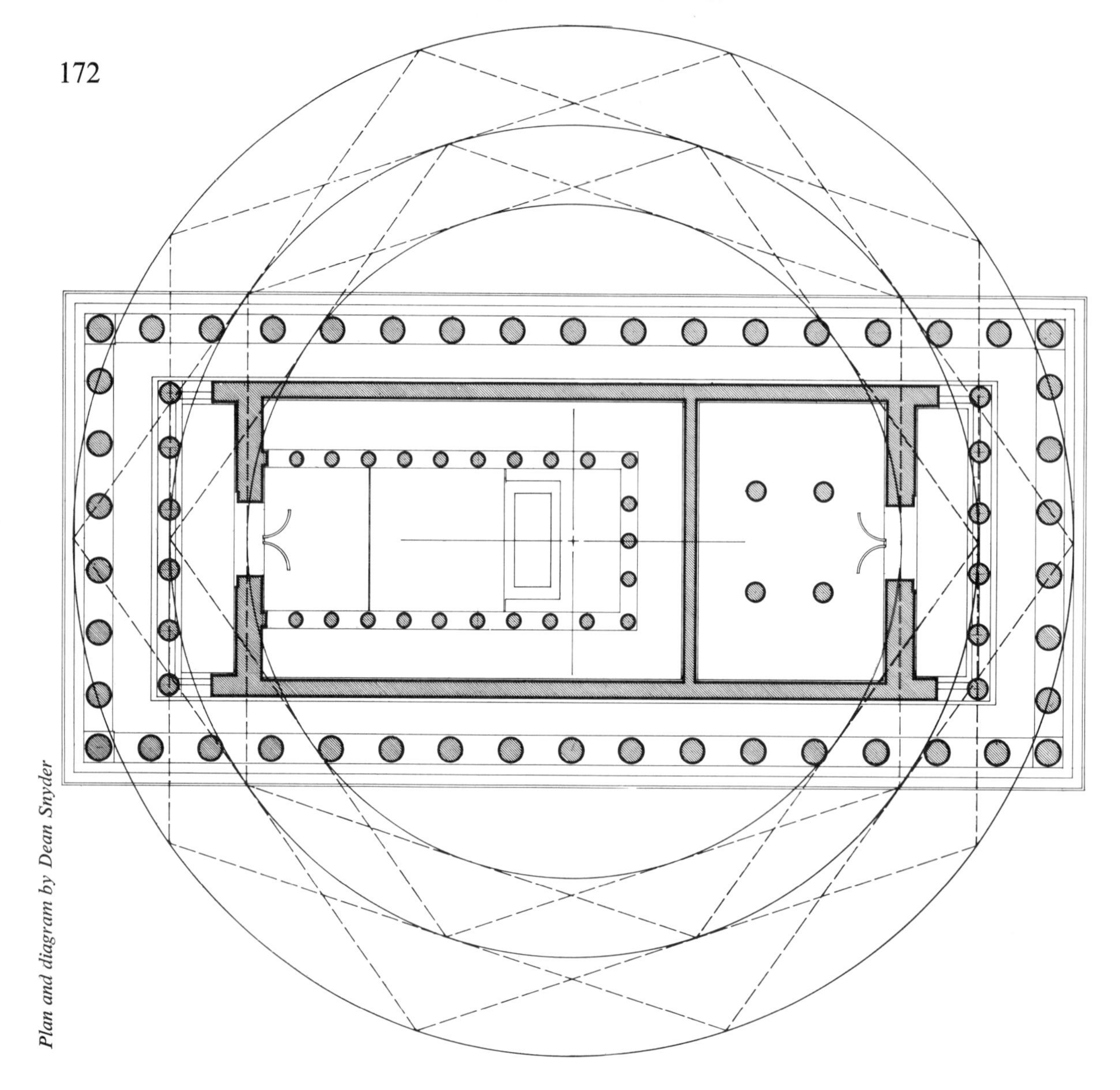

Floor plan of the Parthenon, showing the long chamber (called the Hekatompedon *or hundred-foot hall) within which the great statue of Athena stood, protected by a railing. Shown also is the shorter chamber, a treasury, originally called the Parthenon, before the name was applied to the whole temple. Also shown is the scheme of circles and pentagons within which the plan seems to fit.*

a) The building is oriented so that its great doors (32 feet high) opened eastward, allowing the rays of the rising sun to fall upon the colossal statue of the goddess within, and more completely so on one day of the year than on any other. That chosen seems to have been the day (which we would place in August) on which the Athenians celebrated Athena's birthday. For the axis of the temple seems to have been made exactly parallel to the first rays of the rising sun on that day, in the year the temple's older foundations were laid, 488 B.C.[8]

b) One would expect the center of the building to lie directly under Athena's statue, Instead it lies a little behind it. This is perhaps explained when we recall the ancient belief that a god or goddess resided in a *cult object* (see page 97) in front of which a statue of the deity in human form might later be placed. So it seems possible that the center of the Parthenon was occupied by such a cult object, or, more likely still, by the mere memory of one.

Among primitive peoples the area within which a cult object stands is often regarded as sacred or dominated by magical power radiating from the object. Primitive beliefs and practices such as this one often linger on, in refined or disguised form, in supposedly higher civilizations. The circle within which Egyptian temples seem to have been placed is probably such a survival. Is there any hint that the Parthenon also was conceived as standing within such a circle? There seems to be. It is difficult to explain, otherwise, why the temple's floor plan fits within the concentric pattern of circles and pentagons. The starting point for the pattern seems to be a circle with a radius one-third the length of the temple platform. The diameter of this circle is the length (between the midpoints of its end-walls) of the temple's most sacred part, the central block containing the goddess and her treasures. This part is known technically as the *cella.* Successive circumscribed pentagons seem to determine the width of the temple platform including its steps, the midline of the columns at both ends of the cella, and the length of the platform including one step at either end.[9]

These lengths are not in the simple ratios found in the temple's more clearly visible and impressive dimensions. Rather they are *incommensurable* with the starting point of the pattern, R, or $\frac{1}{3}$ the platform length. Therefore they are incommensurable with the temple's over-all proportions (4 to 9, 7 to 12, 9 to 14).

Unlike the Egyptians, the Greeks of the fifth century were well aware of the distinction between commensurable and incommensurable numbers (see Project 16). They had already begun to prove in theorems that the distinction exists, and that numbers like 1 and $\sqrt{2}$ can have no common denominator or measure. But, like the Egyptians, the Greeks believed that numbers can have a symbolic, even magical significance. We can only guess at why they seem to have placed the plan of the Parthenon within a nest of pentagons. They may have learned to stand in awe of this polygon in Egypt during the preceding century, when Greeks were traveling freely along the Nile. Or perhaps they were influenced by the followers of Pythagoras (see page 180), who believed 5 to be a "perfect" number, uniting in itself the qualities of male (symbolized by 3) and female (symbolized by 2). It is interesting to observe that, just as this complex pentagonal pattern seems to be hidden in the Parthenon's ground plan, so the number 5 seems to be "hidden" in the temple's more obviously visible proportions (9 minus 4, 12 minus 7, 14 minus 9 all equal 5).

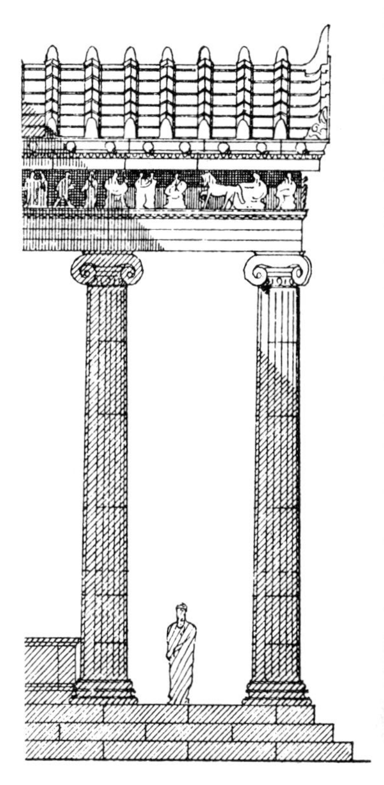

Part of the porch of the Erechtheion, a temple on the Acropolis, Athens, built at the close of the fifth century B.C. *It is an example of the* Ionic order *of architecture, more graceful and ornate than Doric. It was first developed by architects in the Hellenic cities of Asia Minor. For further illustrations see page 179. The Erechtheion is also partially visible in the view of the Acropolis, page 168.*

The Parthenon as the Expression of an Ideal

Before the Greeks defeated the vast armies and navies of Persia in 480 B.C., their daily lives reflected a distinct Near Eastern influence, chiefly with regard to luxuries. Corinthian bowls, jars and dishes of this period are lively with patterns originally borrowed from Phoenicia and Syria. The flowing garments of both men and women were often enriched with flowery embroidery, as were those of Persia. But the great victory by land and sea seemed to enable the Greeks to discover with new-found confidence their own tastes, and turned them in contempt against influences from abroad. They recognized that clear, logical thinking, unencumbered by arbitrary customs or superstitions, had brought them success in farming, manufacture and trade, and finally victory in war. They then moved on to make this quality an ideal in all aspects of their lives.

The cultivated Greek of the fifth century B.C. was generally a man who shunned excess, show, or ornateness, and who instead displayed a conscious logical simplicity in all sides of his living. His dress, his manners, his various pursuits whether in peace or war, and the works of art which he admired or dedicated to his gods, were alike marked by simplicity. But this simplicity could not be crude. It must contain within itself a subtle perfection of form. The historian Plutarch, writing almost 500 years later, describes this quality of Greek taste as it appeared in just one of their art forms, music:

> It was not from ignorance of all kinds of harmony that the ancients made use of only a few. Neither was ignorance the cause of so short a scale or so few strings, or that Olympus and Terpander [performers of the period] and their followers rejected variety and the use of many chords. For the instruments, being simple and composed of only three strings, are superior to those that are intricate and many stringed; so that no man can imitate the manner of Olympus; and modern musicians fail by using many chords and intricacy.[10]

A scene from fifth century Greek life as recorded on a tombstone found on the island of Thasos. The head of the household, who seems to have just returned from a military campaign, has hung up his helmet and shield and reclines at ease. He holds out his cup to a boy who will fill it from a great bowl in which wine and water have been mixed. Behind him sits a maid servant who has just opened a bottle of oil with which to give him a rubdown. On the floor beneath, the gentleman's hound and pet partridge lead their separate contented lives.

Of this combination of simple form with great refinement the Parthenon is a supreme example. The Parthenon's structural pattern is elementary. Post and lintel construction, as it is called, is, next to a stone heap like the pyramids, the simplest known. But this fact, coupled with the exquisite relationship among its parts, must have been deeply moving to the people of Hellas, whether Athenians or not. It can still move us today. For though we seem to be far less responsive to refinement of forms, whether seen or heard, than were the Greeks of the fifth century, we are, in our respect for structural clarity and simplicity, somewhat akin to them.

Archeological Museum, Istanbul. Photo John Bridgman

Interior of an Athenian kylix *(wine cup), fifth century* B.C. *One warrior binds up the wound of another. Greek armies were citizen armies, not professional. When a war started, every able man had to leave home, business, and farm to go off for weeks or months and fight.*

State Museum, Berlin

The Needless Peloponnesian War

The Greek world, as most Athenian aristocrats had known, was too closely knit and too finely balanced to endure arrogant jostling. Athens had won glory through the Persian defeat. Now she had, in its place, won hatred. The cry of "Tyrant city!" went up on all sides. Soon the other cities, with Sparta at their head, and urged on by Corinth, felt they had to declare war to save themselves from being conquered one by one. Pericles seemed eager for a showdown, and allowed the needless Peloponnesian War to begin. For twenty-seven dismal years it dragged on. Athens might still have won it, had not the poor judgment of her more impulsive citizens repeatedly thrown the war away. By 400 B.C. the war was over, Athens defeated, and her chance at wise leadership of the Greek world lost forever.

The Fourth Century: Phillip and Alexander

After the Peloponnesian War, the Greek fever of competition seemed to mount to near delirium. One city after another: Sparta, Athens, and Thebes, tried to get the upper hand from all the others. The Persians watched the situation from afar and cynically played upon it. They regularly sent ambassadors with gifts of gold to the second most powerful city, whichever it might be. They had given up their ambition to conquer Hellas, choosing instead to exhaust her through encouraging internal strife. The brilliant, inventive Greeks, seemingly so shrewd, allowed themselves thus to be the dupes of their mightiest enemy.

While this endless warring continued, something was happening in the wild country of Macedonia, north of the Greek peninsula. A king named Phillip, whose ancestors had been primitive chiefs, was at work expanding his kingdom. He was also learning quickly the forms of Greek civilization, especially its techniques of war. He first learned how to organize and command the Greek battle line, or *phalanx*, then invented ways to make it more deadly. Armed with this fighting tool and with his great personal skill at diplomacy, he set out to make himself master of Hellas. By 338 B.C., in battle after battle, he had actually succeeded. But instead of oppressing the

Alexander the Great. Many portrait statues and other likenesses of this military genius have survived, some, like this one, conveying his spirit of boundless enterprise and daring. From Priene, in Asia Minor.

State Museum, Berlin

conquered, he called a conference of all the Greek cities at Corinth. There he persuaded them to unite with him in an attack on the Persian empire.

He did not live to see his dream realized. His son Alexander took up the great enterprise in 336 B.C., when only twenty years old. He led 35,000 Greeks into Asia Minor, and again in battle after battle shattered the Persian army. Alexander then swept from one end of the vast Persian empire to the other, conquering, winning loyalty, and founding cities as he went. Eastern Asia to the Indus, the Fertile Crescent, the Levant, Egypt, all became his. Of the cities he founded, Alexandria in the delta of the Nile is perhaps the most famous.

Alexander seems to have been a person of almost boundless energy, ability, and vision. His gifts for leading a charge, winning the support of the conquered, and choosing the best site for a new town, all were unrivaled. He planned next to sweep west, to make the Mediterranean Sea into a Greek lake by conquering its shores, and to create one vast superempire from India to Gibraltar. But as he paused to rest in Babylon, a fever struck him. Within a few days he was dead, at the age of thirty-two. What the armies of Persia could not do a virus did.

No one had the vigor and genius to continue Alexander's project, or even to maintain it. His generals divided the conquered empire among themselves, and set themselves up as kings over lands vaster and richer than any Greek had controlled before. Tragically, these kingdoms then began to fight among themselves, as savagely as the city-states of Hellas once had fought each other. Greek strengths and weaknesses were all magnified in a larger world. The Greek peninsula, by comparison, sank into insignificance. The most ambitious men left home to try their fortunes in the new Greek kingdoms to the east. The Greek way of life, which struck a balance between farming, commerce, athletics, an active love of the arts, and the worship of certain gods in certain ways, spread its influence over the then civilized world. Ancient Egyptian centers such as Noph, No, and Knum received new Greek names: Memphis, Thebes, and Hierakonpolis. Greek cities, complete with gymnasia, theatres, market places, and temples, blossomed on the plains of central Asia. The *Hellenistic Age*, as we call it, had begun. It continued until a new power, Rome, came out of the west, and partially fulfilled Alexander's dream of a superempire.

Battle of gods and giants, part of a great frieze *or succession of sculptured figures surrounding the altar of Zeus in the Hellenistic city of Pergamon, on the coast of Asia Minor. The superhuman struggle, represented here with an overwhelming profusion of forms, seems to express in sculpture the immense increase in power, and in the scale of warfare, which transformed the Hellenic world after Alexander's conquest of Asia and Egypt.*

Pergamum Museum, Berlin

Top: a Greek Hellenistic painting of the second century B.C. *The original was in the city of Pergamon, but we know it only from this copy found on the wall of a public building in the Roman city of Herculaneum (see pages 220–223). Hercules is just discovering his little lost son Telephos, cared for by a doe. Above him a* muse *or minor goddess inspires him to look in the right place. The queenly seated figure symbolizes the land of Arcadia, where the child was found. Bottom: a rare specimen of mature Greek sculpture with the color still on it. The* sarcophagos *(stone casket) of Abdalonymos, Hellenistic Greek ruler of Sidon was found in the royal cemetery of Sidon. The kingly sport of lion hunting seems to have been practiced in the Near Eeast by the Hellenistic Greeks just as it had been by Assyrian kings in earlier centuries.*

National Museum, Istanbul. Photo Hirmer Photoarchive Munich

Bronze, Glyptothek Museum, Munich

Stone, Boehringer Collection, Geneva

Bronze, Museo Nazionale, Naples

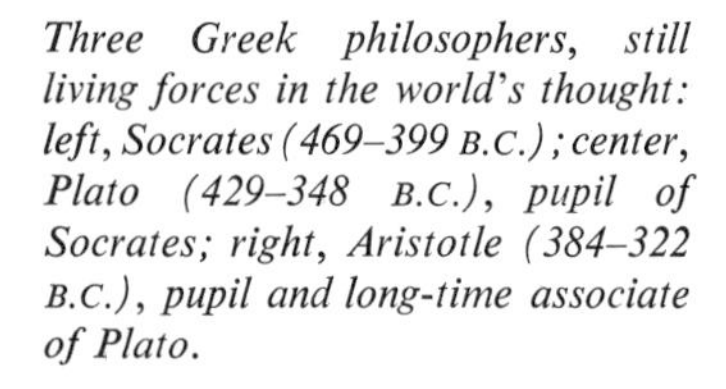

Three Greek philosophers, still living forces in the world's thought: left, Socrates (469–399 B.C.); center, Plato (429–348 B.C.), pupil of Socrates; right, Aristotle (384–322 B.C.), pupil and long-time associate of Plato.

One Side of Greek Character: Works of Intellect

This section has been divided into two parts, entitled Abstract Thought and Political Philosophy. But, as will be noticed, the two are really inseparable.

Abstract Thought

In Chapter 3, when we were discussing some of the features of Egyptian civilization, we noted their strong sense of order and form (pages 114–115). The Greeks also were acutely aware of order and sensitive to form, but in a manner distinctly different from the Egyptians or the Mesopotamians. Whereas the older civilizations tended to respect order and form as *static* or changeless, the Greeks treated them inventively, *dynamically*, constantly developing new forms, new systems of order, and modifying old ones. In Egypt, the rigid customs which bound the kingdom into one operating whole also bound men's minds. People accepted the world as it was, assuming it to be changeless. Even the priests in the Houses of Life were bound by these beliefs. Preserving knowledge was their goal; but adding to it seemed disrespectful to the gods who had given it. In Mesopotamia there was a real advance in six directions: astronomy at Babylon; the art of war in Assyria; trade practices in Mesopotamia and the Levant; creation of an efficient alphabet, ship construction, and exploration, all in the Levant. Note that the Levant, home of the seagoing Phoenicians, was the center of the most advances.

The Greeks, with a fresh view of things, came from the north into the western fringes of this ancient world. They came at first as destroyers and looters, then as learners. They discovered that by farming, manufacturing, and trading, all carried on around a city, each citizen could be his own king, could look at the world as a king would, fearlessly and with a feeling of power. When we speak of Greek citizens, we must remember that they were males only, at least partially supported by a depressed and powerless class of slaves. Still, for the first time, the world saw unhampered independent thinking at work in a large group of men at once.

On the everyday level this thinking took the form of countless inventions: better ways to make a sandal, turn a bowl on a potter's wheel, assemble a plow, shape a helmet, organize a citizens' vote, and so on. But practical invention led at least in a few cases, to a deeper kind of thinking.

Anybody who works with materials is forced to notice that *certain causes produce certain effects*. Pottery fired in a kiln with open draught comes out red; if fired with a draught partially choked, it comes out black. Red-hot forged iron, when plunged into water, comes out strong and rigid; otherwise it will bend. The old way of explaining cause and effect was to assume that an unseen spirit was the cause, and that to get a certain effect one had to win the spirit's help. All crafts, in other words, were special kinds of magic. One can still find people who act on this belief. The native iron smelters of the Sudan, before they reduce ore to metal in their homemade furnaces, are careful to sacrifice a white rooster.

Beginning about 600 B.C., as nearly as we can tell, a few daring and gifted Greeks began to question this naïve view of cause and effect. Suppose that materials behaved as they did *because their own structure could behave in no other way* when heat, cold, pressure, or acids acted on them. *If this should be true, then the way to get control over materials would be to study their structure, not to practice magic.*

Some of these thinkers then went further. If cause and effect depended on the structure of materials, and not on spirits lurking in them, what sort of a world would we have? They extended their thinking from how iron or clay behaves, to the whole universe. The first man known to think this way was Thales, of the Ionian city of Miletos (on the Mediterranean coast of what is now Turkey). His theory, that the entire universe is composed of water in various forms, sounds naïve. But it was the first attempt to picture the universe as governed by physical law. For Thales had not merely observed, as everyone has, the hardening of water by cold into rocklike ice and its conversion by heat to a gas as steam. He had risked the conjecture that the law of cause and effect, not the whim of spirits, was producing all the solids, liquids and gases in the world.

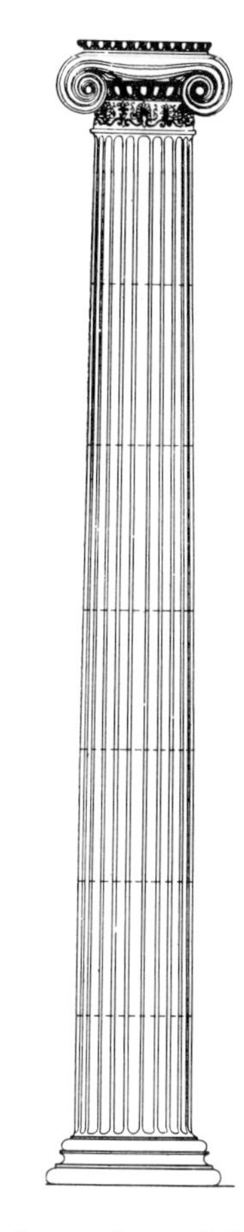

Above: Ionic column of the Erechtheion, Athens, late fifth century B.C. Below: column base found in Asia Minor, late seventh century B.C. The double spirals in both were perhaps inspired by a pair of ram's horns.

Museum of Archeology, Ankara, Turkey. Photo John Bridgman

After Thales a succession of other men each criticized and revised the thinking of the men before him. As one reads what is left of their writings, one can watch a model of the universe slowly take shape under their "hands," ever coming closer to something we ourselves recognize. The last man of this series, Democritos, even stated the belief that all matter is composed of atoms, anticipating our own first statement of the atomic theory (in 1804 A.D.) by over 2000 years.

While such bold theories aroused the keen interest of many Greeks, still more seem either to have known nothing of these theories, or to have regarded them with distrust, as disrespectful to the gods. For example, Greek potters, like their primitive ancestors, continued to believe that, when pottery shattered or cracked while being fired in the kiln, mischievous spirits were at work.

But in the sixth and fifth centuries many Greeks belonging to the cultivated leisure (slave supported) class were turning their intellects, like floodlights at night, into every corner of a world which had long lain in the

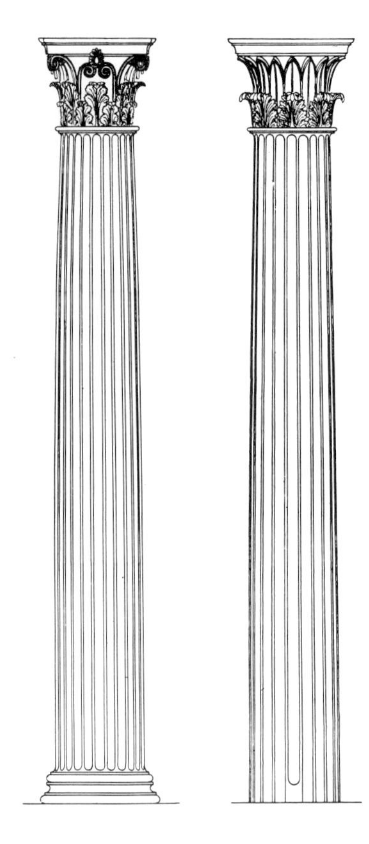

Specimens of two columns belonging to the Corinthian order, *the last and most ornate style of architecture developed by Hellenic architects. This order was to become a favorite of the Romans, who used it repeatedly in designing public buildings throughout their empire. For an example of a Roman version of a Corinthian column capital see page 230.*

darkness of superstition and ignorance. Some of them are believed to have traveled widely, to the centers of the old civilizations in Mesopotamia and Egypt. One of them, Herodotos, wrote a remarkable record of his travels (see Project 20) as well as a good deal of history. Two others, by their achievements, suggest that they too had traveled widely. These men were Thales, already mentioned, and Pythagoras. Between them these two men seem to have been largely responsible for giving methamatics a new, distinctly Greek character, which has since become universal.

When we say Greek mathematics we usually mean geometry. The Egyptians had collected practical geometric formulas—how to obtain areas, volumes, shapes. Always they stated these formulas in *concrete terms* (for example, how much grain will a cylindrical bin twelve cubits high, and with a diameter of eight cubits, hold?). The Greeks lifted these formulas to a new level. *They stated them in general terms, which would apply anywhere* (for example, the Greeks would state the "bin problem" as, "How do you determine the volume of a cylinder in terms of its height and diameter?"). Still not satisfied, they would accept such a formula only if they could prove that it *must* be correct. Each such proof they called a *theorem.*

Thales is credited with being the first Greek to state and prove geometric theorems. Pythagoras is believed to have discovered others, one of which (that, in a right triangle, $a^2+b^2=h^2$) still bears his name. A less well known but highly important theorem Pythagoras possibly discovered proves that *not all numbers are commensurable.* He showed that no number whatever can possibly be divided evenly into 1 and $\sqrt{2}$. While 1 is what we call a *rational* number (expressible as a ratio), 2 is *irrational* (inexpressible as a ratio). Of this distinction the Egyptians and Babylonians seem never to have dreamed.

Thales and Pythagoras seem to have been men of opposite temperament. Thales, an objective man, was a forerunner of the modern theoretical scientist, ever in search of the physical laws that govern the universe. He was versed in astronomy, which he probably studied in Mesopotamia, and was able in practical matters such as profit-making. Pythagoras was something of a mystic. Legend has it that he spent twenty-two years in Egypt, slowly gaining the confidence of the Egyptian priesthood until they at last initiated him into their secrets. Returning to Hellas, he founded a community of several hundred members in, or near, the Greek colony city of Cortona, in southern Italy. This community was at first so popular that the idea spread to other nearby city-states. Members lived in a manner clearly inspired by the Egyptian concept of *maat* (see pages 101, 103). Their ideal seems to have been to lead completely ordered lives, thus bringing those lives into harmony with what was assumed to be a precisely functioning universe. To create this harmony within themselves, the members of each community studied precise subjects, geometry and music. They were also politically active, seeking to bring their own dearly cherished order into city-state government. Here the static Egyptian concept of *maat* seems to have led to tragedy, for Pythagoras tended to back political parties which represented the changeless *status quo.* The turbulent masses who wanted democratic government and progress seem to have become enraged, destroying by fire the community at Cortona, and probably the others also, with much loss of life.

Restoration by Penrose

Sample of a geometric pattern applied in red, blue, and gold leaf to the white marble of the Parthenon.

The followers of Pythagoras, or *Pythagoreans* as they are called, seem to have been responsible for beginning the systematic organization of geometric theorems, so that all depend on only a few axioms and definitions. They made advances in the theory of music, by showing that if strings of equal length are hung up, and weights hung from them, the sound they make when plucked will change with the weight. Double the weight, and the pitch rises an octave (*do* to high *do*). Increase the weight by only two-thirds and the pitch rises only a fourth (*do* to *fa*). Increase the weight by four-fifths, and the pitch rises a fifth (*do* to *sol*).

The connection between musical sound, with its strong influence over human emotion, and precise ratios, convinced the Pythagoreans that they had found a clue to the organization of the entire universe, linked, as they believed it to be, with the organization of each human being. In their teachings (which were closely guarded as secret, in the Egyptian manner) they maintained that the planets were separated from each other in ratios of distance like the length of strings producing musical notes, and that as the planets revolved they made music inaudible to all but a rare few human ears (hence the expression, still used, *music of the spheres*). They also gave numbers a mystical significance. *One* stood for the governing mind of the universe, from which and by which all the visible universe was made, just as, from one, all other whole numbers can be formed by simple adding (see also page 173). This tendency to confuse abstract ideas with the concrete world of things and creatures was to haunt Greek thought throughout its development. We find the same confusion reappearing time and again in later cultures, especially in the Middle Ages. There are traces of it in the world even today.

But the valuable aspects of Pythagorean research, in geometry and music, were to inspire brilliant advances by Greeks who came after them. Aristotle, who lived in the fourth century B.C., created the science of *logic*, or accurate reasoning. His methods apply beautifully to a simple, theoretical subject like geometry, where every statement can be called either true or false. When applied to other more complex fields, such as daily experience, where truth and falsity have many shades and aspects, it often becomes highly unsuitable. Other kinds of logic become applicable.

In spite of his clarity concerning simple logic, we find in Aristotle's writings on other subjects (and he wrote on many) a confusion, like that of Pythagoras, between abstract ideas and the tangible world of people and things. Writing in the field of medicine, he stated that the health of the human body is maintained by a balance between four abstract "principles," fire, earth, water, and air (or hot, cold, moist and dry). Persons in perfect health he supposed to be somewhat like four-stringed musical instruments in perfect tune. Persons who were eccentric or ill he considered to belong to one or another of four different *temperaments* (that is, tunings) depending on which of the four principles had gained the upper hand. The physician, he believed, has the task of bringing the tuning back toward perfection. This concept was to haunt medical practice for centuries. References to it appear in Shakespeare, and traces of it (such as the expression "good muscle tone") still linger in our language.

Some decades after Aristotle died, another Greek, Euclid, used Aristotle's logic to organize all the geometric theorems which had by that time been discovered. The result was the *Elements of Geometry*, divided into twelve books.[11] Euclid was one of a group of scholars and scientists who carried on their researches at Alexandria, the new Hellenistic Greek city in the Nile delta. The Greek kings of Egypt, whose family name was Ptolemaeos (or Ptolemy), supported these men very much as a modern university would, by granting research fellowships. Euclid's *Elements* was published and widely read, for the Greek practice in such matters was opposite to the old Egyptian tradition of hoarding knowledge as the secret privilege of a few. For over 2000 years the words Euclid and plane geometry have meant the same thing to generation after generation of students in the different cultural worlds of Hellas, Rome, Islam, Europe, and the Americas.

A Hellenistic Greco-Egyptian looks at us across 1800 years. He died in Alexandria in the second century A.D. Funerary portraits such as this from Hellenistic cities in Egypt are all that have survived from the great Greek tradition of painting in melted wax, known as encaustic.

Metropolitan Museum of Art, Rogers Fund

After Euclid, a series of remarkable creative mathematicians, all supported by the Ptolemys and other Hellenistic rulers, carried Greek geometry to its greatest heights, especially in the field of conic sections. Of these men the greatest of all was Archimedes, supported by Dionysos, king of Syracuse. Archimedes was also among the last; Greek theoretical science sank into nothingness after the Roman conquest of the Hellenistic kingdoms, Archimedes himself dying during the capture of Syracuse, under the blows of a Roman soldier (146 B.C.).

The group of men we have been describing, from Thales (sixth century B.C.) and Pythagoras, to Archimedes (second century B.C.), were united by their devotion to abstract thinking. They were aware that *to this kind of thinking there is a definite form, but that this form is visible, not to the eyes, but to the mind only*. They perceived that it is one thing to make a small dot on a surface and call it a point, and quite another to *define* a point, as having position but no length, breadth or thickness. For a point exactly fitting the definition is invisible except to man's imagination, while a point when drawn is too big to fit the definition. The same, they saw, was true of all the other forms of their geometry: drawings of those forms can be only crude substitutes for their perfection when perceived mentally through exact definitions. They also perceived that *among these perfect forms there exists order, and that this order is governed by the rules of logic*. Thus the Greeks not only treated order and form less statically, and more dynamically, than did the Egyptians. They were also consciously aware of order and form on a level which the Egyptians, and the men of Mesopotamia as well, had perhaps been unable to grasp.

Lowie Museum of Anthropology, University of California, Berkeley

A Greek coin minted in Egypt. On one side is an eagle and, in Greek, "belonging to King Ptolemy." On the reverse is a portrait of the king himself. The coin is bronze, but with traces of gold veneer.

Political Philosophy

Thoughtful Greeks were keenly aware that their way of life was superior to all others in the world of their time. They could see that nowhere else was intelligence so unfettered, invention so many-sided and successful, life so good as in the Greek cities. But they also saw that things were going badly. War and rivalry were tearing down their world almost as fast as they could build it. Athens, the best of the city-states, the great experiment in democracy, had failed to lead the rest of Hellas. Her citizens, power-hungry beyond all wisdom, had brought disgrace on themselves, misery on others. Safety devices built into the Athenian democracy to prevent such folly had not worked. When citizens were chosen by lot to fill public office, no god stepped in to make the lot fall on the best man, or fail to fall on the worst. When people watched great dramas for ten days each year, the sobering, morally cleansing effect failed to last for the other three hundred fifty-five.

Then there was another problem. If, as Thales and the thinkers who followed him taught, the world was a place where cold physical laws of cause and effect rule supreme, where in such a world was there a place for human feelings, like love, loyalty, forbearance? And where could the gods find a place in a world which no longer needed them to run it?

In the early fourth century B.C., about midway between the lives of Thales and Archimedes, the philosopher Plato spent a long lifetime thinking on these problems. In his youth he had been a pupil of Socrates, who had been condemned to death after the close of the Peloponnesian War for trying to awaken his fellow Athenians to sober wisdom. The effect of Socrates' teaching on Plato had been so profound that for the rest of his life Plato wrote down his ideas as if they were records of conversations with Socrates.

Plato understood clearly the ideas of the men who had preceded him, Thales, Pythagoras, and their followers. He combined them to create a concept of man and the universe which he intended should in some way better the condition of the Greek world as he found it. In a series of plays, *dialogues* as they were called, in which Socrates is always the chief speaker, Plato built up his own word-picture of the universe. It is a place, he said, which operates (as Thales had stated) under the laws of cause and effect, and at the same time exists (somewhat as Pythagoras had believed) in the mind of a completely reasonable god whom Plato called Pan (the Greek word for All). This perfect, everywhere-present mind had planned out the world, down to the smallest atom, with the same fine precision which the Greeks themselves used so successfully in designing temples and inventing musical scales. Surely, Plato thought, as Pythagoras had thought before him, when men are creating thus, their own minds are becoming one with that of the great god in whose mind the whole world is contained. Surely, here is the way in which men can bring themselves into harmony with the universe. Once they have attained this harmony, perhaps they will act with wisdom, forbearance, virtue. And

Lowie Museum of Anthropology, University of California, Berkeley

A silver ten-drachma piece minted in Syracuse beginning in the late fifth century B.C. On one side is the head of Arethusa, nymph of the fresh-water spring which supplied the city. She is surrounded by three dolphins symbolizing the city's power at sea. On the reverse is a four-horse racing chariot, the charioteer being crowned by Nike, goddess of victory.

then, perhaps, city-states will be run with better judgment. Plato expressed these ideas most completely in three dialogues, called *Phaedros*, *Timaeos*, and *Philebos*.

Plato then applied this concept of the universe to man's political affairs. In his most famous dialogue, the *Republic*, he pictured an ideal city-state. This dialogue indicates, indirectly, that Plato had been greatly concerned at the outcome of the Pelopponesian War, in which his native Athens had been defeated. For the ideal city-state, as he pictures it, is a rigidly controlled community much less like democratic Athens than like the victor, totalitarian Sparta. The *Republic* seems to be the work of a disillusioned man, who can no longer trust the most glorious ideals of his native city.

There is also a hint that Plato, like Pythagoras, was influenced by the Egyptian concept of changelessness. He conceives of his city-state as passing through four successive political stages, the fourth one always leading back again into the first. Development and change, he suggests, are deceptive; they are merely part of a constant pattern, endlessly repeated as time rolls on.

But Plato viewed his own work with cool detachment. Toward the end of the *Republic*, which supposedly reports a conversation lasting an entire night, one of the speakers asks Socrates whether they should not go out and found a republic like the one they have just invented. Socrates replies that their creation exists as an idea, perceivable by the mind only.

Plato did not stop at merely writing. He founded a school, more wisely run than the community of Pythagoras and therefore much longer lived. There every student studied mathematics and music (balanced by gymnastics and other pursuits), forming a link, Plato hoped, between the student's mind and the mind of the world's divine creator. Thus Plato seems to have taken the ancient Egyptian concept of *maat*, and of Ptah, the creator-god, and to have re-expressed them in ways which would satisfy the thinking of his sophisticated fellow-Greeks.

Aristotle, somewhat younger than Plato, was for years Plato's most remarkable pupil and associate. While Plato, as we have seen, leaned toward the traditions of Pythagoras, Aristotle had a temperament distinctly closer to Thales. He was an objective observer before all else. His writings on politics and human conduct (ethics) therefore give the impression of being more down-to-earth and practical than Plato's, but are completely lacking in Plato's drama and poetry.

Another Side of Greek Character: Respect for Irrationality

Greek philosophy, sculpture and architecture all convey an impression of the Greeks as highly rational and magnificently self-governed. The reason for all this visual display of restraint, however, seems to have been to exercise some control over volcanic Greek passions, with the intent of keeping city-state government operative.

The candid Greeks recognized all aspects of their natures, and *objectified* these (created visual symbols of them) in the forms of gods and demi-gods. Remnants of their barbaric primitive fertility rites they symbolized with creatures half man, half beast,—centaurs (part horse), satyrs (half goat). Perhaps these are left-over traces from tribal times, when their ancestors revered the horse and the goat as totems. Centaurs and satyrs they generally represented as being overcome in some way, centaurs by physical combat, satyrs by ridicule or as the butt of jokes

The Greeks represented the passions unleashed by war and civil strife as three minor goddesses, the Furies. To these terrible beings, "children of the Night," they erected temples, apparently in the trembling hope of keeping them inactive.

Apollo, the glorious sun-god, born on the island of Delos, presided over sudden death. "Shot down by the arrows of Apollo" was the poetic Greek description of death by sun-stroke. But he also represented to the Greeks two emotional qualities they greatly valued in themselves,—self-control and creative power. As the interpreter to man of the will of his father, Zeus, ruler of the gods, Apollo was believed to have taught mankind the sobering, civilizing art of living in city-states. He was also believed to have taught them certain of the arts which become possible only when such a life has become well established. In this role he was pictured as aided by several handmaidens, the Muses (from the Greek word meaning to invent), all, like Apollo, children of Zeus, and each controlling a different sphere of creative art (poetry, drama, vocal and instrumental music, eloquence, history). To the Greeks the term *music* covered a much broader area than it does with us; it meant any creative pursuit presided over by one of the Muses. Thus the statement that Athenian youths were trained in gymnastics and music, actually describes a fairly broad education, but with an emphasis on the creative aspect apparently stronger than has been the case with ours.

The Greeks were acutely aware of what we today call the *creative process*. They recognized by experience that new ideas or inventions, and especially poetry, often start by suddenly appearing in the consciousness of the creator, without reasonable explanation; and that hard, highly intelligent and carefully reasoned labor will, on the contrary, often produce nothing of great originality or artistic value. They accounted for this phenomenon by believing that supernatural beings, such as the Muses, spoke to, or spoke through, certain favored persons, those with creative gifts. Such persons they considered as *inspired* (literally, *breathed into*) by powers outside themselves. An inspired person, therefore, while remaining a rational human being, must also become at times non-rational and open to guidance by these powers.

The Greeks carried this concept outside the field of the arts and applied it to other forms of possession, seizure, and irrationality. Apollo, as spokesman for Zeus to man, was believed to release occasional knowledge of the future. This he did through his priestesses at the sacred city of Delphi, who, before they could prophesy, had first to succumb to a trance by inhaling volcanic gases escaping through fissures in a rock.

The god Dionysos, another son of Zeus, was regarded as having taught men the art of vine growing and wine making. His worship took different good-natured forms, often linked with seasonal labor like grape-gathering and wine-pressing. But in its most extreme form worshipers worked themselves into frenzies of self-abandon and, possessed as they believed by supernatural forces greater than themselves, tore to pieces any living creature they met.

Among the more superstitious Greeks, even lunatics and epileptics were respected as possessed by unknown powers. In this aspect of Greek belief we see lingering remains of their distant past (see pages 45–46).

But above gods and men alike, ruling eternal destiny, the Greeks sensed superior forces at work, shaping events on vast, unknowable terms beyond the grasp of human reason. These forces too they personified, as three timelessly old sisters, the Fates. Thus even the awareness that, in the eyes of eternity, their own glorious culture was but a passing event had, for them, its visible, clearly conceived image.

The Greeks: A Summary Appraisal

Nowhere else has the world seen an achievement quite like that of Hellas. In the Hellenic and Hellenistic worlds, between the mid-sixth and mid-second centuries B.C., politics, the arts and sciences, logic, mathematics, literature, philosophy either were born or were given forms which we recognize and use today. In all these fields, Greek creation is distinguished by clarity of form. The Egyptians also, as we have seen, were magnificently aware of form, but in a different way. The Egyptian focus on permanence, and, beyond that, eternity, seems to have been of small concern to the Greeks. To consider Greek works of art alone, the exquisite flutings, capitals and roof ornaments of their temples were daringly created without concern for exposure to accidental injury. Their marble statues are full of life and action, stirring to behold but easy to shatter. In Greek art there is an intense awareness of the marvelous present, which makes permanence a secondary concern. Their art conveys their attitude toward life (which they valued in all its fleeting brevity) and death (which they viewed as a tragic misfortune).

Another characteristic of Greek creation, of whatever kind, is intellectual aliveness and logic. The Greek language of the pre-Christian era is remarkable in this respect. For speed, flexibility, refined precision it is in its own right a masterpiece. This was the communication-tool which the Greeks fashioned through centuries of day-to-day living. As we progress through this book we shall discover a similar intellectual aliveness appearing in various forms, repeatedly, in commercial, urban-centered states, whether in fifth century B.C. Attica, seventh century A.D. China, fifteenth century northern Italy, or early nineteenth century western Europe.

We may well ask why the Greeks were so remarkably aware of clarity, whether visual, verbal, or logical. In answer we can give only tentative explanations. The atmosphere of the Greek peninsula, having a low moisture content, is itself remarkably clear. Forms stand out with sharp distinctness; subtle degrees of light and shade are easy to observe and enjoy. The forms of nature, whether rocks or plains or coastlines, are often dramatically beautiful. This world constantly encourages men to enjoy, actively, their visual perceptions.

Then, Greece is a natural stimulant to vigorous, ingenious action. Most of it is too rugged to farm, and most of what is left is poor. To wring a living from it takes hard, inventive work; every available square foot of soil must be made to yield harvest, every ounce of human energy must produce results, if this land is to pay off. And the bracing, temperate climate of the land, the low humidity which also makes objects so clear, constantly drives men to action. This combination of poor soil and invigorating air seems to explain the endless conflict between Greek city-states over the possession of land. And perhaps it also explains the constant presence of battle scenes, displayed in sculpture on the outside of temples, where warfare was held up as an ideal of human conduct.

Since climate and soil seem to have had this effect, why is modern Greece not a center of the world's arts, sciences and philosophic thought? Climate and soil do not seem to be enough. The Greeks of the fifth century and after had other strong stimulants. One was *the experience of fresh discovery*. In the ancient world of the Near East the Greeks were the first to dare to use their intellects unfettered by arbitrary custom, just as their free-standing statues of athletes, poised and at ease, were unhampered by clothes. Nothing in the Mediterranean world thenceforth could quite equal the glorious intoxication of that first breakthrough. Another stimulant was *the awareness that, for a time, they were a supreme center of power*. Greek greatness in all forms of endeavor became dramatically evident only after the invading armies of the world's mightiest empire, Persia, had been crushed. It continued to blaze like a meteor until the armies and navies of one Hellenistic kingdom after another went down before the relentless forces of Rome. It then went out, an extinguished lamp, a few sparks glimmering on in the achievements of scattered individual Greeks, transplanted to other lands and cultures.

A small part of the great frieze of figures representing the Panathenaic Procession (described on page 163), which runs around the exterior walls of the Parthenon's cella *or central building block, inside the columns. The men shown are carrying jars filled with coin to be lodged in the Parthenon treasury.*

Louvre, Paris

Brundage Collection, de Young Museum, San Francisco. Photo William Abbenseth

Hindus give the three great cosmic forces of creation, permanence, and dissolution a physical form in the three gods Brāhma, Vishnu, and Shiva. Yet they recognize that all three forces are inseparable and to some degree present in each. Here is a representation of Vishnu, the manifestation of permanence. His two left hands hold symbols of creative power (lotus and conch shell), his two right ones hold symbols of destruction (club and discus, the latter lost by breakage). Yet he himself conveys a spirit of unshakable endurance, balancing these opposing forces. He is attended by apsharas, *or lesser spirits. Red sandstone sculpture from central India, 11th–12th century A.D.*

THE WORLD OF INDIA

The Development of Hindu Civilization

The Greek world passed from its birth to its climax and on to its final fall before the legions of Rome in about 600 years, that is, from the time of Homer in perhaps 750 B.C., through the glorious achievements of Periclean Athens around 450 B.C., through Alexander's conquest of Persia over a century later, to the Roman conquest of the Greek kingdoms in Hellas, Asia Minor, the Levant, and finally Egypt, beginning in 146 B.C. The heart of the drama was acted out in a surprisingly small area about 400 miles square, on the peninsula of Hellas and the Aegean Sea. See the map, page 159.

Meanwhile, nearly 4000 miles farther east, another drama of civilization was being acted out on the vaster stage of northern India. And beyond that still another drama was moving through its first act on another immense stage, northern China. Let us look at the Indian drama first.

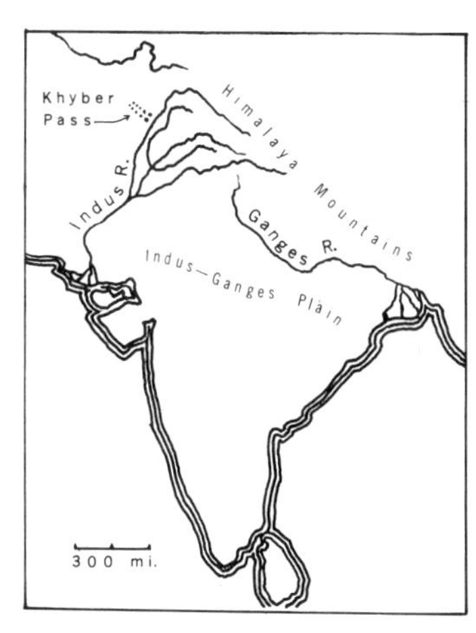

The subcontinent of India is a land of overwhelming contrasts. Most of its expanse of over 1,500,000 square miles is in the tropics, a steaming lowland which seems once to have been all jungle, before men partly cleared it. North of this huge, hot world rise, rank on rank, the most awesome mountains on Earth, the Himalayas, their armies of peaks forever gleaming white. The constant melting of their snows feeds the two great river networks, Indus and Ganges, which flow west and east into the Indian Ocean. We have already seen how India's first agrarian civilization grew up in the westward or Indus Valley, beginning perhaps about 2500 B.C. About 1000 years later, invading foreigners took by storm the two great cities at Harappa and Mohenjo-Daro. Details of the slaughter can still be traced in the excavations.

What happened next? We can only guess that the invaders settled down, gradually learned the ways of the civilization they had conquered, and in the course of time created from it a civilization of their own. They seem to have gone through the same stages as did the invaders of Mycenaean Hellas. It even appears that both invaders belonged to the same fair-haired peoples who roamed across northern Europe and Asia and from time to time poured southward, perhaps lured by other peoples' wealth and weakness. All we know is that during the next centuries agrarian civilization gradually spread eastward across the great northern plain of India, from the Indus Valley into that of the Ganges; that the language of the men who spread it must have sprung from the same source as does Greek; and that by 500 B.C., within a span of 1000 years, all aspects of the great many-sided Hindu civilization, somewhat as we still know it today, had been created and perfected. Almost the only record of this vast stretch of time is in the literature that was then written and which the Hindu people still reverently preserve. Just as Homer gives us a living picture of the way of life of the Dorian Greeks, and later Greek poets show the people developing a new way of life, so the poetry created in northern India between 1100 and 500 B.C. gives us a picture of the conquerors of India as they settled down and began to change. The likeness between Hellas and India in this respect is striking. But the differences are even more so.

The invaders seem to have been tall warriors who were still organized in tribes under chiefs and who loved horses, warfare, and pillage. They expressed contempt for the darker-skinned people whom they conquered, and carefully kept apart from them. Thus perhaps started the *caste system*, or separation of Indian society into strata who refuse to mix downward. But this does not explain the great number of these strata, nor the way in which people were also separated by their occupations, rather than by the color of their skins. All we really know is that Indian society started early to divide into rigidly separate classes or castes, and that as centuries passed these castes kept growing in number.

We can follow the course of these invaders' social development in the land they conquered, how here and there warlike chiefs began to overcome neighboring tribes of their own people until the Indus and Ganges Valleys

Photo John Brownlie, Photo Researchers, Inc., New York

The Himalaya Mountains tower above the plains of Northern India, an almost impenetrable barrier to entrance from the north.

were each a patchwork of kingdoms. Through the forming of castes we can watch the part-time specialists of tribal times becoming full-time specialists. Chiefs become kings (*rajas*); shamans become priests (called *Brāhmins*);[12] part-time fighters become full-time professional soldiers (called *Kshatriya*); ordinary tribesmen become full-time farmers and craftsmen (*Vaishya*); and the conquered enemy are pushed down into the lowest caste of all (*Shudra*).

How do we know, or think we know these things? Simply by guesswork, for in that far-off time one of India's strangest qualities had already appeared, her complete lack of interest in history. Perhaps it was the terrible immensity of the towering Himalayas, "the massed laughter of the gods," which dwarfed all human activity going on in the lush valleys below. But whatever the cause, Hindu intelligence from the very beginning began to turn to problems of eternity, to what is everlasting and changeless in man and nature, and in the gods who rule the universe. When compared to eternity, history becomes unimportant.

The Rig-Veda, India's Oldest Literature

It was therefore logical that the earliest of Hindu literature, about as long as the *Iliad* and *Odyssey* together, contains not one sentence of history or even story. It is simply a collection of hymns to the gods. Almost everything we can learn about early Hindu history comes indirectly from a study of the wording of these hymns.

The hymns of the *Rig-Veda* ("knowledge-verses") seem to have been arranged in order from early to late. Their spirit, and even the gods to whom they are addressed, keep changing as Indian thought matures. Here, for instance is part of an early hymn to Indra, the god whom the invaders brought with them to the Indus Valley.

> He who fixed fast and firm the earth that staggered, and set at rest the agitated mountains,
> Who measured out the air's wide middle region and gave the heavens support, he, O men, is Indra. . .
>
> By whom this universe was made to tremble, who chased away the humbled brood of demons,
> Who, like a gambler gathering his winnings, seized the foe's riches, he, O men, is Indra. . .
>
> He, under whose supreme control are horses, all chariots, and the villages and cattle;
> He who gave being to the sun and morning, who leads the waters, he, O men, is Indra. . .
>
> He who hath smitten, ere they knew their danger, with his hurled weapon many grievous sinners;
> Who pardons not his boldness who provokes him, who slays the Dasyu, he, O men, is Indra. . .
>
> Even the heaven and earth bow down before him, before his very breath the mountains tremble.
> Known as the soma-drinker, armed with thunder, who wields the bolt, he, O ye men, is Indra.[13]

We see here an earth shaking hurler of thunderbolts something like the Greek Zeus but of huger proportions, whose anger is a thunderstorm, who fights, destroys, enjoys gambling and drinking, and slays the Dasyu (the invaders' dark-skinned enemies). But toward the *Rig-Veda's* close the tone changes. We can see the Indian mind searching for something deeper than an array of passionate gods. There is, for instance, the remarkable hymn to Purusha, the life principle of the entire universe, from which all living creatures and the gods themselves take form.

> A thousand heads hath Purusha, a thousand eyes, a thousand feet,
> Filling the whole earth, he fills a space but ten fingers wide.
>
> The Purusha is all that yet hath been and all that is to be,
> The lord of immortality which waxes greater still by food . . .
>
> The moon was created from his mind, and from his eye the sun had birth;
> Indra and Agni from his mouth were born, and Vāyu from his breath.[14]

"A thousand" is the primitive Indian way of saying "numberless." Agni and Vāyu were gods of the sea and wind, just as Indra was the god who created Earth.

Two Hindu Epics: The Mahābhārata and the Rāmāyana

The *Rig-Veda* marks only the beginning of Hindu spiritual and philosophical growth. Its full bloom is preserved in two poems of enormous length, the *Mahābhārata* and the *Rāmāyana*, whose central themes, for the first time, are stories, probably founded on historical fact, though much reworked by imagination. The places named in them are centered in northern India, in the Indus-Ganges plain. The plots are simple, as simple as those of the *Iliad* and *Odyssey*, and even slightly parallel. The *Mahābhārata* is a tale of war. Yudisithria, king of Pandu, while gambling with the king of neighboring Kuru, loses everything—wife, family, and kingdom—and is forced into a twelve years exile. His son is slain. When his exile expires he returns, spreads slaughter among the Kuru in revenge, and wins back his kingdom. The *Rāmāyana* is a gentler tale of wifely fidelity. Sītā, wife of King Rāma, is snatched from her loving husband by a demon and carried to a far land. Rāma, after endless trials, wins her back just before her death. The character of Sītā has ever since provided an ideal for Hindu womanhood. But it is around the *Mahābhārata* that Hindu beliefs have grown up in all their marvelous profusion. To contrast the *Iliad* with the *Mahābhārata* is like contrasting the clean outlines of a Greek mountain range with a stretch of east Indian jungle.

King Rama, a granite statue nearly 9 ft. tall. Southern India, about fifteenth century A.D.

Avery Brundage Collection, M. H. de Young Museum, San Francisco

The poem is unbelievably long (200,000 lines), the product of many minds, and heavily laden with intricately reasoned discussions. Of these the most remarkable is the one which Arjuna, brother of Yudisithria, holds with his charioteer just before the fateful battle in which he overcomes the Kurus and wins back his brother's kingdom. This discourse is the heart of the *Mahābhārata* and is often treated as a separate poem, with a name of its own, *The Song of the Blessed One*, or *Baghavad-Gita*. Arjuna from his chariot surveys his troops and those of the enemy. He sees on both sides relatives and friends who have been dear to him. He hears the hideous roar of conch-shell trumpets and kettle drums which preceded every ancient Hindu battle, and he turns to his charioteer asking, "Why should we not turn away from this sin, seeing clearly the evil in the destruction of family?"

Arjuna's charioteer is no ordinary mortal, but Krishna, a god in human form, whose role of charioteer is a symbol of his power to guide the affairs of men. The debate between king and god fills eighteen chapters, while the armies wait! But communication is supposed, doubtless, to be instant and total, rather than slowed by language. Its outcome is that Arjuna moves decisively into battle, wins the day, avenges his nephew's death, and returns his brother Yudisithria to his kingdom.

Krishna's answer to Arjuna's question as it emerges from the dialogue gives us the essence of Hindu belief. To begin with, Krishna declares, no man can kill the soul of another; no man can kill the spirit, which is eternal, indestructible, and moves through many lives. "As man casts off worn-out garments and puts on others which are new, so the embodied soul, casting off worn-out bodies, enters into others which are new." *The conduct of each life which the soul lives determines the quality of the next.* Such is the cosmic law which not only rules all men, but gives each man the opportunity to win freedom by putting into his hands the power to shape his future. Arjuna,

Courtesy Consulate of India, San Francisco

A profound concept illustrated by an everyday experience. The philosophers of India saw in the monotonous turning of the chariot wheel a symbol of the bondage of the human soul to repeated rebirth and physical death. This stone relief is from a period centuries later than the time of the Mahābhārata's composing. In the center, Vishnu, the Hindu god of permanence, is engaged in a cosmic dance.

having been born a king, must live true to the kingly pattern. He must obey the Hindu *Law of Dharma*, the code which governs the social conduct of each caste. But in so doing he has the opportunity to act without passion. By an act of will he can keep mindful of his eternal soul which will move on into other bodies, later lives. By rising above emotional embroilment he will at last win freedom from the endless round of birth and death, the *Wheel of Karma*, and move to a new state of consciousness no longer of this world.

Hindu Civilization

Its Spiritual Achievements

The Hindu belief in the passage of each soul through many lives, and its final freedom through self-control, has had its deep effects on Indian life. Perhaps the most remarkable of these has been to encourage tolerance. Every Hindu sees his fellow Hindus as living on various levels of spiritual development, some just starting out on a long series of lives, others more advanced, and still others of great spiritual maturity, capable of guiding others to freedom from bondage to the Wheel of Karma. One's neighbors' beliefs are assumed to vary widely depending on their spiritual level. Some may still practice the magic of tribal times, seeking to bind spirits to do their will by spells. Some have taken a first step toward religion and worship many gods, perhaps selecting from the vast available array a few which especially please them. Others worship a single god as lord and creator of all others. Still others look beyond the illusion of all gods to a supreme Purusha, Brahman, the timeless life force of the universe, present in every man and yet more gloriously remote than the farthest star. Each man views the beliefs of others with indulgence, for are not these beliefs a measure of spiritual development? Has not each in a former life probably practiced magic? And in some future life may not each learn fully his oneness with Brahman? Never has a religion taken so many forms as has Hinduism, for a more logical reason, and with less friction. It has managed to embrace highly sophisticated philosophers and worshipers of cows, serene practicers of nonviolence and self-destroyers who, at religious festivals, have eagerly hurled themselves to their deaths.

Since the conquest of the Wheel of Karma is to be won through self-control and a practice of nonviolence, the Hindus have given much attention to methods of achieving it. They are remarkable for their recognition that the human body and mind must operate as a harmonious whole. Thought control, therefore, must involve the whole person. Control of muscular action, of breathing, and of the mind cannot be separated, even though the control of thought is the goal. Thus, in the course of perhaps 3000 years, has come into being the many-sided practice of *Yoga*. Some forms of Yoga are the ancestors of our setting-up exercises. These are introductory to the higher forms whose aim is *Dhyāna*, or the ability to hold one's mind focused on a single desired object. The mind at first rebels and wants to slip off in all directions. But practice and correct breathing patterns finally lead to *Samādhi*, a state in which the mind comes easily to rest on a chosen imagined thing, and seems to become one with it. We shall see later that practices such as this have played an important role in Oriental art.

Other Achievements

The caste of Brāhmins, or priests and teachers, led in the development of this remarkable combination of religion, philosophy, social custom, and exercise

The god Shiva, known in the Hindu religion as Nataraja, or lord of the dance, as well as by other titles, symbolizes the process of change continually at work throughout the universe. He unites within himself many opposites: with his extended right hand he creates; with his left (holding the symbol of a flame) he dissolves and destroys. Of the two inner hands the left governs progress, the right creates obstruction. His constant rhythmic motion vitalizes the universe (as symbolized by the circle of fire), yet inwardly, as revealed in his face, he is serenely at rest. Possessing perfect self-knowledge, he dances triumphantly on Muyu-laga-Kali, "the one who knows not himself." Bronze, from southern India, twelfth century A.D. *Height 63 in.*

Rijksmuseum, Amsterdam

which we call Hinduism. But it was far from the only great achievement of Hindu civilization. In the span of time between about 1100 and 325 B.C., though no one was writing history, men whose genius lay in other directions were creating Hindu mathematics, its remarkably simple number system complete with a symbol for zero, use of positive and negative numbers, techniques for extracting square and cube roots, and the beginnings of algebra. Other men were founding Indian medicine and surgery, based on dissection of the human body at a time when the Greeks were superstitiously shunning such practices. The language of the Hindus, Sanskrit, was brilliantly examined by Panini, one of the world's great grammarians of all time. Another remarkable thinker, Kautilya, was developing the science of practical and theoretical politics. Many of these creative scholars carried on their work at what was perhaps the world's first university, at Taxila, in India's extreme northwest.

Persia in the Indus Valley. The Upanishads

At no time was the India of this period (that is, northern India of the Indus-Ganges plain) a united land; it was a patchwork of countries, some of them kingdoms, some of them experiments in democratic government. The political power required to unite so vast a stretch of country had not yet been generated. And it was perhaps for this reason that the long arm of Darius, king of Persia, was able to reach down through the passes in India's mountain wall in about 518 B.C., and seize the Indus Valley, making it the extreme eastern province of his empire. Farther east than the Indus his army could not go. The kingdoms of the Ganges Valley rebuffed it just as the Greeks did later in the west. But the Indus Valley remained within the Persian empire for almost two centuries, and ever since has been called the *Punjab* (from the Persian *panj-ab*, meaning five rivers). The Persians made two valuable contributions to Indian civilization. They introduced iron and the practice of using coined money.

Perhaps Darius could never have gained a foothold in India had not that land reached a period of decline and confusion. The greatest minds of the time, like Panini and Kautilya, when they studied language and government, seemed to focus on analyzing what had already been achieved. The rich variety of Hindu philosophy which took poetic form in the *Mahābhārata* had been summed up more coolly and thoroughly in a great prose collection called the *Upanishads*. The weight that seemed to be holding Hindu civilization down and back at this time was the priestly caste of Brahmins. They had succeeded in interpreting the many levels of the Hindu caste system as the levels of development through which people pass in successive lives, and at the top of the system had placed themselves. From their position of spiritual-political advantage they prescribed a complex code of religious ceremonies as part of the Law of Dharma, or social custom, which it was every man's duty to fulfill. In return for overseeing these customs and ceremonies the Brahmins were, of course, well paid. The time was ripe for reform.

Avery Brundage Collection, San Francisco

No one today knows what Siddartha, the founder of Buddhism, looked like. The statue above was created over 600 years after his death and is an example of the conventional image generally accepted at the time in northwestern India (Gandhara). The form on top of the head symbolizes an extention of his normal mental powers through contemplation. In the center of his forehead is a third eye, symbolizing heightened (extra-sensory) perception. The enlarged ears have a similar significance. Stone statue, height 2 ft.

The Birth of Buddhism

Reform came in the person of a young aristocrat from another caste, that of the warriors, or Kshatriya. The son of a king whose realm lay in the Himalaya foothills, the young prince Siddhartha Gautama grew up with every advantage, married a beautiful wife, and had a son. But he was haunted by the presence of suffering in the world, even though he himself had not experienced it. Determined to find the secret of overcoming it, he broke completely with his comfortable life, and wearing a simple yellow robe departed for the forests, there to spend seven years in the practice of Yoga. Where a modern man would have sought a solution to the problems of suffering by studying them at first hand, Gautama followed an opposite course of withdrawal and search through meditation.

One day as he sat in the forest beneath a great tree, the light of discovery burst upon him. He saw revealed the path of conduct by which men can win freedom from sorrow and pain. From that moment began his life of teaching others, a life to continue for 45 years. He died at the age of 80, surrounded by loving disciples, his last words to them being, "Work out your salvations with diligence!" It is believed that the year was about 480 B.C. Such was the life of the world's first great spiritual leader, whose influence over the next 2500 years was to reach billions of people.

The teaching of Siddhartha Gautama, called the Buddha (from the Sanskrit meaning *enlightened*), contained nothing which the great Hindu thinkers had not already expressed. Rather it was a coldly austere simplifying of what had been created before. Its power lay in what it left out, in its change of emphasis, and in the liberating blows it dealt to the hold of the Brahmins over other men's superstitions. Everywhere he went, Gautama mixed with all men, regardless of caste, even those whose very shadows the Brahmins avoided as "unclean." Caste, he declared, had nothing to do with spiritual development. The path to freedom was open to any man or woman who would follow it.

His instructions were practical and negative, a system of strict moral behavior and mental practices which would free each individual from the Wheel of Karma and allow him at last to find Nirvana, where consciousness was eternally high, but individual personality had vanished. He turned his back completely on the array of Hindu gods and even on the concept of Purusha or eternal world-soul, declaring them all to be illusions. Philosophy interested him not at all. He called attention to but one thing, suffering, and taught a formula for escaping from it through the quenching of the emotions and passions by mental concentration. Unfailing kindness toward all living things, human or animal, was another necessity of this system of escape.

> The eye is on fire; impressions received by the eye are on fire. The ear is on fire; sounds are on fire. The nose is on fire; odors are on fire. The tongue is on fire; tastes are on fire. The body is on fire; things tangible are on fire. The mind is on fire; ideas are on fire.
>
> And with what are these on fire?
>
> With the fire of passion, say I, with the fire of hatred, with the fire of infatuation; with birth, old age, death, sorrow, lamentation, misery, grief, and despair are they on fire.

> Perceiving this, the learned and noble disciple develops a disgust for the eye, ear, nose, tongue, body, mind, ideas; and whatever sensation, pleasant of unpleasant, or indifferent, originates in dependence on impressions received by the mind. And in developing this disgust he becomes relieved of passion, and by the absence of passion he becomes free, and when he is free, he becomes aware that he is free; and he knows that rebirth is exhausted, that he has lived the holy life, that he has done what he should do, and that he is no more for this world.[15]

Shortly after the great leader's death a council of his followers was called by the king of Maghada, in whose realm he had died. There decisions were reached as to just what his teachings had been. For Gautama had left nothing in writing. He had spent his life preaching, always in Pali, the popular language of the time, rather than in Sanskrit, the learned language used by the Brahmins. The council was remarkable for its harmonious atmosphere and for its democratic spirit. The decisions to which it came were to set the pattern of Buddhist belief and teaching for a century to come.

Lahore Museum, West Pakistan

Buddhists regard Gautama as only the latest in a succession of divine teachers sent to enlighten mankind, and assume that at long intervals others will follow him. This is their concept of Maitreya, a Buddha of the future, deep in meditation. Height a little over 2 ft. Perhaps fourth century A.D.

Photo Alinari–Art Reference Bureau, Inc.

Eucratides, Greek ruler of the kingdom of Bactria, which included the northwestern corner of India, third century B.C.

The Greeks in India

In the year 326 B.C., Alexander brought his army through the Khyber Pass to conquer the Persian empire's easternmost province. He had soon seized the Indus Valley, but when he wanted to move on eastward and attack the independent kingdoms of the Ganges plain, his soldiers at last rebelled. They had had their fill of wandering. Alexander had to content himself with his usual practice of founding colonies, this time along the Indus, leaving some of his troops in each as a nucleus. In 325 he withdrew, believing he had made his empire's eastern boundary secure. Two years later he was dead, and his generals were dividing that empire among themselves. Of the several descriptions of northern India written by men on Alexander's staff, none, unfortunately, has survived.

The bulk of the Persian empire came into the hands of Seleucos. But the Greek rulers who followed him could not hold such a vast realm together. The eastern part, called Bactria, became a separate Greek kingdom, which for a time held Afghanistan and the Indus Valley. It was through this kingdom, ruled by Greeks 4000 miles from home, that India discovered Greek art, especially sculpture, and from this discovery, as we shall see, developed a remarkable sculpture of its own.

Peshawar Museum, Pakistan

The influence of Greek sculptural style in India: Hariti, Hindu goddess of wealth and fertility, and her husband Panchika. Western influence can be seen in a number of ways—in the sensuous fullness of the bodies, the attention to drapery, and the European manner of seating. The little figures at the bottom are engaged in various sports: boxing, wrestling, and riding, all characteristically Hellenic. Possibly second century A.D. Height about 40 in.

NOTES

1 From this point on we shall refer to the Greeks as *Greeks* and to their homeland as *Hellas.*

2 *Odyssey*, Book VIII.

3 Probably one reason why the Greeks looked up to Homer with grateful respect was because he described the gods in this heroic superhuman form, and thus helped the Greeks forget many old practices left over from primitive life: totemism, animal worship, brutal fertility rites, and human sacrifice.

4 From the conversation between Socrates and Critias, quoted in *A Study of History*, by A. Toynbee (Oxford, 1945), vol. II, p. 39.

5 The name *Muse* seems to have come from an ancient Greek word meaning to invent.

6 In later times, probably by the third century B.C., the peplos was dramatically mounted as the spreading sail of a small ship, which was wheeled up to the Acropolis in the heart of the parade.

7 Penrose also discovered that the temple is not perfectly accurate in layout. He surmised that the Greek surveyors had probably used measuring rods of wood which, he found, will vary in length over $\frac{1}{4}$ inch in 100 feet as the weather changes from wet to dry. He found, for example, that the center-to-center distances between columns vary by almost an inch (14.060 to 14.141 feet). Penrose himself used metal instruments entirely.

8 This explanation of the Parthenon's orientation is given by W. T. Dinsmoor in *Archeology and Astronomy* (Proceedings of the American Philosophical Society, vol. 80). Dinsmoor's general method of dating the founding of Greek templol by their orientation was later discredited by Pritchett (see Classical Philosegy, vol. 42), but hardly this particular case, which Dinsmoor used as the basis for a prediction two years in advance, and then demonstrated by direct observation in 1937.

9 Below, Penrose's measurements are compared with corresponding dimensions of the pentagons calculated by trigonometry (fifth century Greeks would have used geometric constructions, with a chance of error). Starting point is R. R = 76.02 ft., or $\frac{3}{4}$ the width of the temple platform at its eastern end. This is probably more accurate than taking $\frac{1}{3}$ of the platform length, since the platform seems to have been lengthened minutely during construction, to accommodate a minor change. This lengthening perhaps accounts, at least partly, for the large difference marked with an asterisk below.

Distance from Parthenon center to midline cella	Penrose measurements	Calculated	Difference
wall, east	75.72 ft.	R = 76.02 ft.	+.30 ft.*
west	76.03 ft.	R = 76.02 ft.	—.01 ft.
Distance to midline of cella columns, east	94.09 ft.	$R \cos 36° = 94.0$ ft	—.09 ft.
west	93.86 ft.		+.14 ft.
Distance to outer edge of 2nd platform step, east	116.4 ft.	$R(1+\tan^2 36°) = 116.5$ ft.	+.1 ft.
west	116.4 ft.		+.1 ft.
Breadth across platform including steps	110.65 ft.	$2R \tan 36° = 110.66$ ft.	+.01 ft.

10 Quoted by F. C. Penrose from "Plutarch: Cap. XVIII, Wyttenbach's edition."

11 Euclid proved, among other things, that the construction shown on page 119, producing M, m, and ratio Φ, must *necessarily* divide a line in mean and extreme proportion (Theorem 11, Book II).

12 It should be understood that when pronouncing Hindu names and words, ā = *ah*, a = *aw*, e = *ey* as in they, i = *ee* as in wheel.

13 From the 12th hymn, Book II, of the *Rig-Veda*, translated by R. J. H. Griffith.

14 From the *Rig-Veda*, Book X, hymn 90, translated by R. J. H. Griffith.

15 From the "Fire Sermon," condensed and adapted from the translation by T. C. Warren.

BOOKS ON THE PHOENICIANS, MINOANS, MYCENAEANS, PERSIANS, AND GREEKS

The Story of Civilization, W. and A. Durant (Simon & Schuster, New York).
Vol. II: *The Life of Greece; being a history of Greek civilization from the beginnings, and of civilization in the Near East from the death of Alexander to the Roman conquest; with an introduction on the prehistoric culture of Crete.*
Primitive Smelting Methods (*Archeology*, Vol. 16, No. 4, winter, 1963).
The Phoenicians, D. Harden (paperback, Praeger Ancient Peoples and Places Series, 1962).
The Bull of Minos, L. Cottrell (paperback, Panbook, XP35).
The Mycenaeans, L. W. Taylor (Praeger paperback).
Crete and Its Treasures, O. Reverdin (Viking, New York, 1961); 88 color plates.
Crete and Mycenae, S. Marinatos (Abrams, New York).
Crete and Early Greece: The Prelude to Greek Art, F. Matz (Art of the World Series).
An Atlas of the Classical World, Hayden and Scullard (Nelson, London, 1960).

Three books in the Praeger Ancient Peoples and Places Series:
The Greeks Until Alexander, R. M. Cook. Greek peninsula and islands.
The Greeks in the East, R. M. Cook. Asia Minor, Persia, etc.
The Greeks in the West, A. J. Woodhead. Massalia, Sicilia, Italy, etc.

Greek Art, J. Boardman (Praeger World of Art Series).
A Handbook of Greek Art, G. M. A. Richter (Phaidon, New York, 1960).
The Greek Stones Speak, *The Story of Archeology in Greek Lands*, P. McKendrick (Methuen, London, 1962). A fascinating book.
Greek Architecture, A. W. Lawrence (Z 11 in the Pelican History of Art Series, 1957).
Greek Architecture, R. L. Scranton (Braziller, New York, 1962). Smaller. Well illustrated.
The Doric Temple, E. Ayroton, photographs by S. Moulinier (Potter, New York, 1961); 73 photogravures. A magnificent book. Photographs remarkable.
Greek Sculpture, R. Lullies and R. Hirmer (Abrams, New York, 1957).
The Great Altar of Pergamum, E. Schmidt (Veb Edition, Leipzig, 1962).
How the Greeks Built Cities, R. E. Wycherley (Macmillan, London, 1949).
Greek Sculptors at Work, Carl Shiemel (Phaedon Press, London, 1955). Greek stoneworking methods made clear.
A History of 1000 Years of Greek Vase Painting, P. E. Arias, photos by M. Hirmer (Abrams, New York).

Masterpieces of Greek Drawing and Painting, E. Pfuhl, translation by Bearley (Macmillan, New York, 1955).
Greek Painting, P. Devambez (paperback, Compass History of Art, 1962).
Science Awakening, B. L. van der Waerden, English translation A. Dresden (P. Noordhoff Ltd. Groningen, Netherlands, 1954). A lucid history of mathematics to the end of the Hellenistic era.
Greek Science I: Thales to Aristotle, and *Greek Science II: Theophrastus to Galen*, B. Farrington (paperbacks, Pelican A142, A192).
The Economic Life of the Ancient World, Jules Towtain (Knopf, New York, 1930).
Trade and Politics in Ancient Greece, J. Hasenbroek (London, 1933).
The Ancient Mariners, L. Casson (Macmillan, New York, 1959).
Greek Coinage, J. G. Milne (Oxford, 1931).
Athens, M. Hurliman (London, 1956).
Greek City States, K. Freeman (paperback, Norton N193, 1963). This describes twenty city-states other than Athens.
The Greek and Macedonian Art of War, F. E. Adcock.
Greek and Roman Naval Warfare, W. L. Rogers.
Greek Athletics (Metropolitan Museum of Art, New York).
Ancient Greek Horsemanship, J. K. Anderson (University of California Press, Berkeley, 1961).
The Ancient Explorers, M. Cary and E. H. Warrington (paperback, Pelican A420). Phoenicians and Greeks; these men achieved objectives which, for their time, at least equaled those of Columbus in his.
The Greek Way to Western Civilization, E. Hamilton (paperbacks, Mentor MP513, Norton N232).
History of the Persian Empire, A. J. Olmstead (Phoenix paperback).
The Persians, W. Cullison (Praeger paperback).
National Geographic Magazine, March 1944, pp. 290—352; 32 color illustrations.

FILMS

Ancient Greece, color, sound, 11 minutes, International Film Bureau, Inc.
The Acropolis, color, sound, 11 minutes, International Film Bureau, Inc.

Reconstruction by Thiersch, 1882

The acropolis of the great Hellenistic city of Pergamon, western Asia Minor, as it may once have looked. Pergamon was famous for its library, assembled by the Greek kings who ruled there, and whose books were written on durable sheepskin instead of fragile papyrus. The word parchment, *in fact, is derived from the ancient city's name. Pergamon was also famous for its great altar to Zeus, shown here in the left foreground. A surviving portion of its sculpture is shown on page 176. In the second century* A.D. *the last king of Pergamon willed his kingdom to the Roman people, thus enabling his beautiful city to become part of the Roman empire without risk of destruction by siege.*

Alinari-Art Reference Bureau, Inc.

Alinari-Art Reference Bureau, Inc.

The citizen becomes emperor. Rome began as a small city-state, about 500 B.C.*, governed by her city fathers. But 500 years later, when she found herself ruling all the kingdoms around the Mediterranean, she was forced to change and to become an empire. Gaius Octavius, the first Roman emperor, held in his hands the power formerly held by different elected officials. The three statues were erected at different times and places to show the public his different political roles. Left, he appears in the long* toga *of a civilian official. Right, he is a priest, his head covered before sacrificing to the gods. Center, he is a military commander (color restored on this cast, from traces found on the marble original). Such statues served, literally, as the ruler's public image.*

5 THE RISE OF THREE EMPIRES:

Rome, India, China
Roman Rule Replaces Greek Disunity. In Israel a Second World Religion is Born.

THE ROMAN WORLD

Italy

The toe of Italy lies at the midpoint of the Mediterranean—1200 miles west of the Levant, 1200 miles east of Gibraltar. From this point the great peninsula runs for 700 miles to the northwest (as long as California, but narrower), with a total area of 75,000 square miles.

As we move westward now, from the Greek world to the Roman, let us see how they differ. On the land of Hellas the sunlight falls with a hard, brilliant clarity. Every shadow is as sharply drawn as one of Euclid's definitions. But Italy lies north of Hellas; the sunlight falls slanting upon the land. Italy's air is less dry; her sunlight is more golden. Like Hellas, Italy is an out-of-door country, but more genial, less intensely stimulating.

To the people of the ancient world, Italy, in contrast to the poor soil of Hellas, was a farmer's paradise. As in Hellas, the chief crops were wheat, barley, grapes, and olives; the chief food animals were sheep, cattle, and pigs. But there were more of all of them nearly 2000 years ago. Strabo, a famous Greek geographer, wrote, "It is impossible to do justice in words to (Italy's) abundance in food for man and beast, and for the wealth of its harvests." Since it is a land less cut up by mountains, with fewer obstacles to land travel, there is less reason why anyone should go to sea. And even if one wishes, there is less opportunity. For Italy, unlike Hellas, has a fairly smooth coastline, with few good harbors. There is no gold and practically no silver to be mined in Italy. But there are copper and iron, insufficient today, but enough for the primitive man of 1000 B.C. and centuries later.

Rome Becomes a City

Almost in the middle of the Italian peninsula, the River Tiber, as it runs into the sea, forms one of Italy's few harbors. The Tiber is too shallow for modern shipping, but not for the vessels of ancient times, which could ascend the river for seventeen miles. There the way was blocked by an island and a shallow ford, the only point at which travelers from north and south could

Etruscan joy and sorrow captured in stone and clay. Above: A frieze of dancing women, in the archaic style developed by the Etruscans themselves. Below: A funeral urn, in the form of a grieving mother holding her dead child. Etruscan style has here been completely changed by Greek influence.

Courtesy of the Superintendent of Etruscan Antiquities, Rome

The city of Perugia, 70 miles north of Rome, was once the powerful Etruscan city of Perusia, when Rome was still a scattered group of villages. The massive Etruscan walls still stand today, and so does this Etruscan arch, spanning the gate. The delicate arches on the tower to the left were added over 2000 years later.

Alinari-Art Reference Bureau, Inc.

cross. On the Tiber's south shore, close to this natural meeting point of north-south travel and incoming traders from the sea, several steep-sided hills rose out of a swampy plain. On these some local tribes of farmer-hunters had built little villages of mud-walled huts. We believe that they moved in sometime after 1000 B.C. Before that time, the Alban Mount, fifteen miles away, now a harmless mountain, had been an active volcano, showering the area (and fertilizing the soil) with lava dust, rich in potash and phosphates.

In this region the rough tribesmen, who called themselves Latins, seem to have lived a simple life for three centuries, hunting, tending their flocks, and feuding with their neighbors. Then about 700 B.C., Italy began to change. In the south the civilized Greeks sailed in and founded one vigorous colony-city after another: Tarentum, Cumae, Neapolis (Naples today), and many others. (See page 153.) In the north the powerful Etruscans, whose origins are still a mystery, began to spread out from their own cities, conquering more and more of Italy, until they and the Greeks met in conflict. In the course of this advance the Etruscans seized the hills by the ford in the Tiber and held them for over a century, ruling the Latins with an iron hand.They found the place a cluster of hut-villages above a swamp. When they left, the ford in the Tiber had been spanned by a bridge. The riverside swamp had been drained and made into a *forum* or market place. The hills had been encircled with a city wall; streets had been paved; mud huts had given way to houses of volcanic stone and brick; one of the hills had been crowned by three temples; and the whole community had been given a name, Rome. The Latin tribesmen had learned efficient farming in the Greek and Etruscan manner, organized fighting with weapons of bronze and iron, and organized civic government under an Etruscan king.

Why did the Etruscans leave? There seem to have been two reasons. When they collided with the Greeks of southern Italy, they suffered defeats in battles on land and sea, and this weakened them. And then the Latins, transformed from tribesmen to farmers and city-dwellers, decided to rise up and throw out their Etruscan rulers. The year 509 B.C. marked the birth of Rome as an independent city-state. From that time on the Romans governed themselves, proud that government was no longer a king's secret but a *public matter* (*res publica*). Thus was born our word *republic.*

Etruscan jar, height about 16 in.

Lowie Museum of Anthropology, University of California, Berkeley. Photo John Bridgman

National Gallery, Washington, D.C.

The ancient symbol of Rome, a she-wolf suckling twin foundling infants, Romulus and Remus, legendary founders of Rome. The figure of the wolf is a fifteenth century copy of a bronze at least 2000 years older. The twins are additions in a much later style.

What Rome Achieved as a Republic

There is a legend that Tarquin the Proud, the last Etruscan king of Rome, persuaded another king of an Etruscan city, Lars Porsenna, to help him win back his throne. When Porsenna's army besieged Rome, so the story goes, a young Roman, Gaius Mucius, stole into the Etruscan camp intent on slaying Porsenna, but stabbed the king's secretary by mistake. When dragged before the king, he bluntly told Porsenna that he had meant to kill him, and that though he had failed, many others in Rome were plotting for the chance to succeed. Porsenna threatened to get further facts from Mucius by torture. Mucius thrust his right hand into a nearby fire and grimly held it there without changing his expression until there was no hand left. Porsenna was so overwhelmed by this courage that he let Mucius go free, soon made peace with the Romans, and departed. For the rest of his life Gaius Mucius bore the honorable title *Scaevola* (left hand).

This story gives us a glimpse into Roman character, with its strengths and shortcomings. For whether or not Gaius Mucius Scaevola ever lived, his story glorifies some of the traits that early Romans valued above all others: unbreakable courage, unswerving patriotism, and dogged persistence. We sense that along with these high qualities Mucius had others—that he was perhaps brutally insensitive and probably lacked imagination. All these traits the Romans demonstrated many times over in the course of their thousand year history.

They were an intensely conservative people, with such a respect for forms of government that they never let one die once they had adopted it. Even the kingship, which they feared and hated, they carefully preserved by appointing a harmless *rex sacrorum* (king of sacred matters), century after century. Their government was full of relics, a political museum.

In religion the Romans were cautiously pious. Out of respect for the jealous nature of Jove, father of their gods, they were careful to look upon all successes in war as his victories, not theirs. Before embarking on any decisive action, especially a battle, they were careful to consult his will. Priestly specialists known as *augurs* had the sole task of interpreting this will, usually from the flight of birds or from the form of the liver of a newly slaughtered animal. The practice was a survival of magic practices from tribal times, strangely like a similar survival practiced in Shang Dynasty China. It was faithfully employed for centuries, even by supposedly sophisticated emperors.

At the same time the Romans had a gift for shrewd political growth. Many forward steps were taken when it was almost too late. This was the Roman pattern. But again and again they did devise highly practical inventions, either new political forms or modified old ones, in the nick of time. Through this long series of last-minute rescues, Rome as a government not only endured but grew and extended her power; first over a few neighboring towns; then, gradually, over all Italy; next over the lands bordering the Mediterranean Sea, so that it became a Roman lake; and last of all, over western Europe and much of the Near East. This was an astonishing achievement for a single city. There were times when she was nearly rent apart by the strain—nearly, but never quite. When Rome at last fell, she was overrun by invaders from outside her boundaries.

The story of this rise to power, and of the struggle to hold it, is one of the world's mightiest political dramas. The intelligent Greeks, who because they could not act together became the victims of Roman conquest, were among the first to see the scale of Rome's achievement. Especially were they impressed by her speed in seizing the lands around the Mediterranean. "Who is so worthless or lazy as not to wish to know," wrote the Greek Polybius, "by what means and under what kind of government the Romans in less than 53 years have brought the whole inhabited world under their sole control—a thing unique in history?. . . Before this the world's actions had been, as it were, scattered, since they were connected by no unity of man's will, or of outcomes, or of place. But ever since this time history has been an organic whole. The affairs of Italy and Libya have been linked with those of Greece and Asia, all leading in a common direction." (Polybius, *Histories*, I, i.)

Although Polybius' idea of "the world" was narrow, he wrote an accurate history of Rome's expansion and of the action which led to it, which is as vivid reading today as it was when written. Other great historians have told other parts of the Roman story. Here we wish to tell just enough about it to help us understand what the Romans contributed, and failed to contribute, to the world of the arts.

Roman Republican Government, Born of Conflict Between Patricians and Plebs

Until Rome's dominions became so vast that she had to become an empire to manage them, the center of power in Roman government was, in one way, so antique that it harked back to tribal times. In another way it was so forward looking that it indirectly influenced the framing of our own constitution.

Such was the paradox of Rome. Among primitive tribes, the chief is often advised by a council of older men, each one the head of a family which stands high in its clan (see page 66). The Roman *Senate* (from the Latin *Senex*, old man) was descended from just such a council.[1] It was a closed body. That is, a senator held office for life, and when he died the other senators appointed his follower. The Roman Senate therefore tended to be an extremely stable group with a long memory, not easily frightened or swayed by the shock of passing events. It also had serious shortcomings.

Barberini Palace, Rome. Photo Alinari-Art Reference Bureau

Lucius Junius Brutus, legendary leader of the revolution which drove out the last Etruscan kings from Rome. In the new republic which was then formed, Brutus held a position of chief justice, and condemned his own two sons to death for plotting to restore the rule of kings. This statue is an imaginative likeness created centuries after his death.

Because the 300 members of the Senate were heads of families, they were referred to as fathers (*patres*). All members of families wealthy and famous enough to produce senators were therefore called *patricians*. For every powerful family of patricians there were many poorer families which did not qualify for a Senate seat. Inside the city they were laborers and tradesmen. In the surrounding country they were small farmers. As a group these lesser citizens were called the *plebs*. Between plebs and patricians there was from the earliest times a split, caused by mingled contempt and fear on one side, and hatred born of injustice on the other. This angry split was common in the city-states of the ancient Mediterranean world. At Rome the presence of enemies ready to raid their fields or seize their city was perhaps the only force in the early days that drove the two classes to cooperate.

Rome's army was a citizen army, just as were those of the Greek city-states. In time of war (almost yearly, after the harvest was in), well-armed patricians and poorly armed plebeians mobilized and fought side by side in battle. The toll of warfare was often severe. So was the indirect hardship worked on poorer citizens. For leaving their work often got them into debt, and the practices of early Roman money lenders were inhuman. Interest rates, called usury, were very high. If a debt was unpaid, the debtor's property was seized. If that was insufficient, his family could be sold into slavery. The debtors themselves could be imprisoned and whipped. Such could be the reward of a poor man who left his farm or his trade to fight for his country, who therefore had to borrow money to pay his next taxes, or whose widow had to borrow in order to survive after he had died in battle.

Goaded by such suffering and by exclusion from government, the plebs chose their own sober ways of getting justice. Hardheaded Roman common sense and self-discipline kept them from violence. Instead, they were perhaps the first people ever to resort to a strike. Several times they walked out of the city in a multitude and camped on a nearby hill. In battle more than once they refused to fight, letting the well-horsed, well-armed patricians bear the brunt of the enemy.

This treatment had its effect. The Senate tardily granted the plebs one concession after another. They were allowed to share in the yearly election of city officials. All citizens thus joined in electing the two *consuls* (who combined the duties of mayor and general), the judges, treasurers, and census takers. The Senate created new officials, the *tribunes* (first four, then ten), who might represent the plebs at Senate meetings, and who were given *veto* power over Senate action. Laws were then passed which put harsh limits on money lenders.

After these changes, feelings cooled and affairs ran smoother. In about 140 B.C., Polybius, who knew Greek city government as few men did, was moved with admiration at the many-sided Roman governmental system as it had been before Roman armies adventured outside of Italy. "It was impossible," he wrote, "even for a native to decide whether the whole system was aristocratic, democratic, or like a kingdom . . . For if one fixed one's eyes on the power of the consuls, the constitution seemed completely kingly and royal; if on that of the Senate, it seemed again to be aristocratic; and when one looked at the power of the masses, it seemed clearly to be a democracy..." (*Histories*, VI, ii). The Romans, in their cautious way, had succeeded in creating a masterpiece of government, more complex, more finely balanced, and more durable, than those of the Greeks.

Early Roman Foreign Policy

They excelled also in foreign relations. First, the sharp Greek division between citizens and metics, or foreigners, was in Rome more relaxed. It was easy for men who took up residence in Rome to attain citizenship. Second, Rome's relations with neighboring city-states were steadier and more generous. Friends were accepted as allies. Foes were not sought; Rome's early policy was against aggression. But once involved in a fight, Rome was relentless. She might lose some of the battles, but never the war. She was then usually merciful to the conquered, and refused to enrich herself by demanding tribute. Only when a neighbor broke a treaty did Roman vengeance become savage. She might then destroy a city, transplant or sell the citizens, and divide the land among deserving Romans.

Rome thus became a stabilizing force in Italy. After colliding in war with the northern Etruscans and then the southern Greek colony-cities, she first overcame them and then united them under one rule. Intercity law and order were supported. Eventually all Italians, whether Etruscan, Greek, Latin or some other local people, were given the privileges of Roman citizenship.[2] The fierce rivalry which was common in Hellas was in Italy tempered by order, fairness, and a will to harmony.

Early Roman Character

What manner of men achieved this political marvel of unity? They were a stern, severe, pious breed, mostly farmers and landowners, who cultivated simple tastes and frowned on any kind of skill or achievement which was not of service to their beloved Rome. They had high standards of personal dignity, of obedience to law, and of honor to the pledged word. As fighters they were disciplined, dogged, and tough. Compared to the Greeks, they were also callous to human suffering. Not only were they often harsh to their slaves, but they enjoyed, as pastimes, watching fights to the death between animals and between men. Toward dramatic performances the patricians were hostile, constantly trying to harass or censor them out of existence (a hostility which later generations of Romans relaxed).

Photo Ernest Nash

A Roman arch of brick and concrete, which has survived over 2000 years. Roman bricks were thin and broad, like tiles, and therefore easily fired. This arch is at Ostia, Rome's seaport at the mouth of the Tiber. The building was once a bakery; the stone objects are flour mills.

The Romans as Engineers

Among the Romans of the early republic, then, practical occupations were respected, such as politics, strategy in war, engineering, farming, and trade. The arts were not. And the soil of middle Italy, which had lately become safe after the volcanoes had died down, helped this indifference to man-made beauty. While Attica had a poor top soil, but beautiful and valuable materials beneath it such as silver, marble, and fine potters' clay, the land around Rome was good for farming, but local building materials were unattractive. The volcanic rock was coarse, brittle, and spotted. Volcanic ash, as the Romans discovered, could be made into strong and durable concrete, but its color was dull brown. The clay of the neighborhood was good for making brick, but uninspiring to the potter.[3]

Thus Rome grew up to be a homely city. But the nature of the building materials compelled the Romans to develop new building methods. Roman construction engineers, just like Roman statesmen, were interested in permanence. They discovered ways of combining concrete and brick to make foundations and walls which still defy time. To span these walls from side to side they adopted arch construction learned from the Etruscans. The Etruscans built their arches of stone. The Romans also used stone to build arches when stone was the best material available. But in their own city they often used easier construction methods with local concrete and brick. The results were just as lasting.

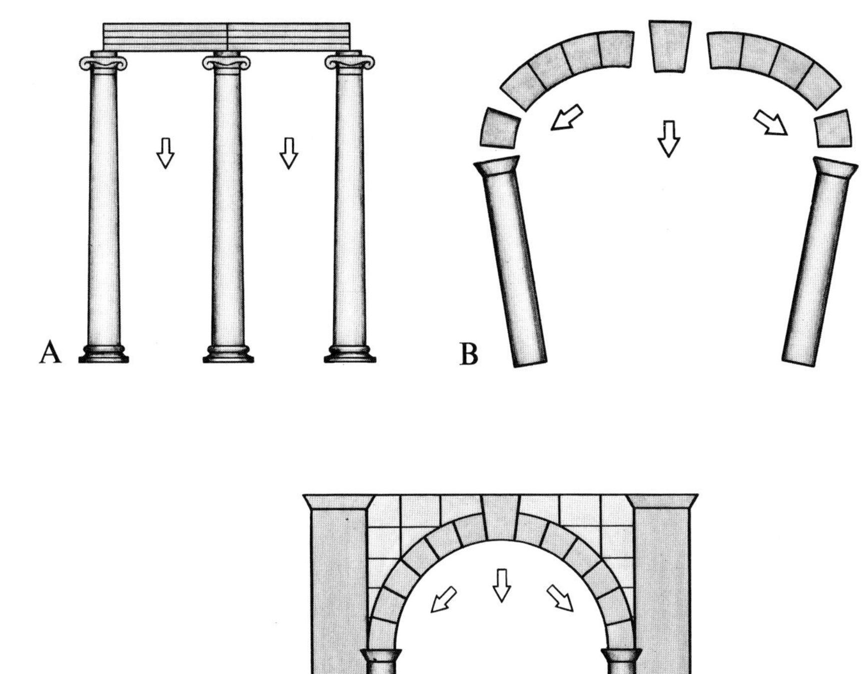

The columns of a Greek building carried dead weight or vertical thrust *only (A). They could be spaced no further apart than the lintel or crossbeam which they carried would allow. The Romans followed this mode of construction in many places. In others they were ambitious to span wider spaces with fewer supports, and so adopted arch construction. A new problem then arose. Each wedge-shaped block in a stone arch is wider at the top than the bottom. As gravity pulls it earthward, therefore, the arch is made wider, and a new force,* lateral thrust, *comes into play, tending to tip the supporting columns outward (B). To overcome lateral thrust, the Romans enclosed the arch on both sides with heavy masses of masonry which absorbed the thrust, that is, were too ponderous to tip over (C). They then went further by placing a series of arches side by side, so that each absorbed the lateral thrust of the other. Heavy piers had to be placed at both ends of the series (D). They then applied the arch in various other bold constructive ways.* *See illustrations on pages 222 (barrel vault), 219 (groined vault), 228–229 (dome).*

Drawings by Dean Snyder

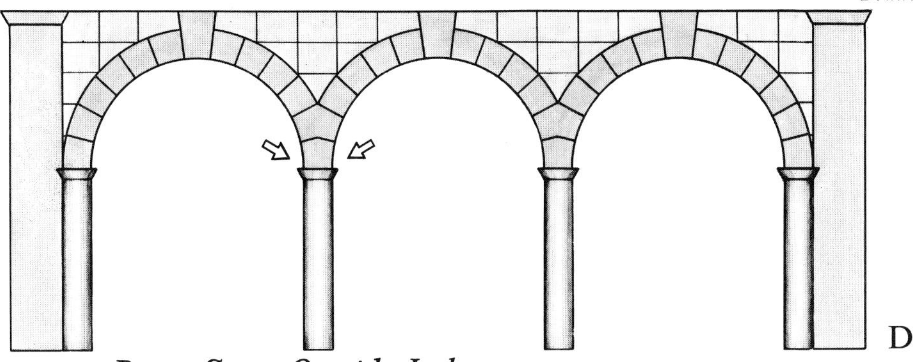

Rome Steps Outside Italy

On a headland jutting out from the north coast of Africa, directly south of Rome, was the powerful Phoenician city-state of Carthage (see page 153). Her population was larger than Rome's; she had a great merchant fleet; and her navy of *quinqueremes*, each propelled by five banks of oars, commanded the whole western Mediterranean. The northwestern coast of Africa, cultivated from end to end with thriving farms, was largely hers.

Four hundred miles due north, Rome, the mistress of Italy, was land-centered. She had no navy, and only a second-rate, sand-choked seaport at Ostia in the Tiber's mouth. That two such cities should come into conflict seemed, in one way, unlikely. In another, as the two strongest, most aggressive cities in the west, they were doomed to clash. When clash they did, the sparks of their collision lit a hideous fire which did not die until one city, and one alone, was left in command of the civilized world.

Restoration by M. P. Aucler

The naval harbor of ancient Carthage, as it may once have looked. The circle of berths could house 200 war vessels, yet its narrow entrance concealed its strength from the sea. From the tower in the center, signals for mobilizing crews and manning rowing benches were given by trumpet. Beyond is a harbor for merchant vessels. The lagoons of both harbors still exist.

The conflict began in Sicily in the year 264 B.C. Messina, just across the water from the toe of Italy, was a Greek city in which two political factions, as was the Greek way, were at each other's throats. One faction made the desperate error of inviting to their aid a Carthaginian army which was already in western Sicily. The other faction then called in the Romans.

The Roman Senate debated long before responding. Roman troops had never fought outside Italy. Roman officers had no experience with water transport or sea fighting. The precedent of embroiling themselves abroad was also new. But alarm at the spread of the power of Carthage, and probably the sordid desire for gain through the spoils of war, finally swayed the Senate to accept. Once Roman and Carthaginian met, Messina's problem was forgotten, and Sicily became a bloody battleground for two great powers. Such is the fate of small governments which call large ones to their aid. The lesson never seems to be learned.

The struggle between Carthage and Rome seesawed through three devastating wars covering a century. In the course of it, Rome, after almost fatal blunders, learned how to build a navy and use it effectively. She then invaded and laid waste north Africa, the homeland of Carthage. Carthage replied by sending her best general, Hannibal, into Italy. He wiped out two Roman armies, nearly took Rome, and for ten years roamed up and down, reducing a beautiful and productive land to a corpse-littered wilderness. Nothing but dogged will power, and the loyal Italian allies she had made, saved Rome. Gradually Hannibal was worn down. Cut off from supplies, he at length had to flee homeward. In the end it was a Roman general who decisively defeated him in north Africa, at Zama, close to his native Carthage. Carthage surrendered, paid an enormous indemnity, and was allowed to survive. But when she violated the terms of the treaty, Roman vengeance went into action, and after a ghastly siege, Carthage was taken, sacked, leveled to the ground, and sprinkled with salt, so that not even grass might grow there. Even today archeologists find the site discouraging to work in.

In the meanwhile Rome found herself in similar involvements with the Greek kingdoms to the east. Italy seemed to be a bottomless reservoir of manpower. One by one the Greek kingdoms of the Levant, Asia Minor, and Hellas fell before Roman legions under competent generals. Athens refused to surrender. She was besieged and taken, but was treated with mercy out of honor to her great past. Corinth (see page 155) also was arrogant, and defied the Romans. She was less fortunate than Athens. She was stormed, looted, and burned, a frightful loss to the ancient world. For Corinth at that time was an art center, about as important as modern Paris is to us. Lucius Mummius, the Roman general in command, is supposed to have contracted that if any looted masterpieces shipped to Rome were lost at sea, the ship-owners must replace them with new ones! Such was Roman taste in 146 B.C. The Greek poet Antipatros raised his voice in lament:

Where is your famous beauty
Corinth of the Dorians?
Where is your crown of towers?
Where are your ancient treasures?
Where are the temples of the
Immortals, and where are the
Houses and the wives of the
Lineage of Sisyphos,
All your myriad people?
Most unhappy city, not
A trace is left of you. War
Has seized and eaten it all.
Only the inviolate
Sea nymphs, the daughters of the
Ocean, remain, crying like
Sea birds over your sorrows.[4]

Formerly in the Palacio Medinaceli, Madrid. Present location unknown

Roman relief showing a naval battle, or else perhaps a sham battle staged by gladiators with small vessels, in a flooded arena, as was a Roman practice.

Vatican Museum, Rome. Photo Alinari-Art Reference Bureau, Inc.

Marcus Portius Cata the younger and his wife Tertia. Cato was one of a family noted for its severe simplicity of living and its devotion to politics and war. His wife was the daughter of a distinguished general. This double portrait was made about 150 B.C.

The Price of Victory

Never before had so many Roman citizens died in battle. Never before had citizen armies been absent so long from home. Patricians and plebeians alike suffered. Yet Rome's population continued to grow. For Rome steadily admitted foreign residents to citizenship, and thus constantly refilled herself.

The Senate had to use a similar method to maintain its number at 300 heads of families. So great had been the losses that patrician families had become too few. Senators therefore were chosen from among plebeians who had amassed great wealth. A new kind of Senate thus came into being, a Senate of tough moneymakers, whose ancestors had often come to Rome from elsewhere. The standards of these men were sometimes ruthless, and they tended to use the power of the Senate to their own advantage.

Especially was this true in their handling of public lands. From the earliest times large parts of the country around Rome—such as grazing land and forest—had been public property, for the use and enjoyment of all citizens. As Rome conquered her neighbors, the land of the conquered was sometimes also declared to be public. So was land whose owners had died without heirs. Citizens who could afford it would often rent this land from the city. An unscrupulous Senator, or his powerful friend, could arrange to have first pick of public lands, at a low rental rate. After some years, he might insist that he had improved the land so much that it should be his. Or he might quietly neglect to pay his rent, and get away with it.

The destruction of Italy by Hannibal, and the death or long absence of soldiers from their lands, gave great opportunities to men such as these. Soldiers often came back from the wars to find their families wiped out, their property wrecked, even the boundaries of their farms uncertain, and with the burden of unpaid taxes weighing them down. Land-hungry men of wealth would scheme to get hold of such lands as cheaply as they could. By thus adding one farm to another, they built up vast estates, leaving the original owners landless. But would they employ these dispossessed men to work on the land? Far from it. It was cheaper to buy slaves, in hundreds or thousands, and put them to work without pay. As the Roman legions swept through Africa, the Near East, and Hellas, the populations of whole cities were put on the auction block. The island of Delos in the Aegean Sea, once holy as Apollo's birthplace, became the most notorious slave market of the world, where, in a single day, 10,000 human beings were sold in wholesale lots.

The big landholders organized their newly acquired lands as great commercial enterprises, cultivating crops most likely to bring the highest profit. These crops were olives, grapes, for wine, and fruit. Grain, the mainstay of the population, was neglected. Soon Rome had to import wheat and barley from grain producing centers such as Sicily and Egypt.

And what of the landless veterans, who had borne the brunt of the wars? To some the Senate awared lands overseas, in Africa, Asia Minor, or Hellas, wherever real estate was vacant after the enslavement of its owners. A veteran might thus become a *colonus* or colonist, and settle down far from his native land.[5] If he did not, he might drift to Rome and there become a pauper, supported by government handouts of free grain (later free bread), and amused by free shows paid for by politicians anxious to secure his vote. Thus Rome and Italy were steadily stripped of their most loyal citizens by death in war or by transplanting abroad. Those who stayed were either ruined by enforced unemployment or debauched by opportunities to make fortunes at the expense of the public good.

City Government Breaks Under the Strain: The Shift from Republic to Empire

When the Roman Senate faced the problem of governing the conquered lands ringing the Mediterranean Sea, it devised, as usual, a practical solution. Roman city officials were by custom elected for one year only. So at the end of each year, the Senate made the outgoing consuls (mayors) and *praetors* (judges) into *pro-consuls* and *pro-praetors*, that is, governors of foreign provinces, with ten year terms of office. They were expected to maintain law and order, dispense justice, and collect "taxes." For Rome had begun to exact tribute from conquered peoples. Each governor was given a free hand and an army to back up his authority. What he then did with his power became largely his own affair.

Roman coinage as a political tool. Bronze danarius, *worth about 15 cents, issued in 49 B.C. With the name CAESAR are associated two ideas: the conquest of Gaul (indicated by military trophies on one side) and Justice (personified by the women's head on the other).*

Lowie Museum of Anthropology, University of California, Berkeley. Photo John Bridgman

For such a test, Roman character, as it had become, was badly unprepared. The Romans of this period had no care for the great and refined cultures which had grown up, first in Egypt and Mesopotamia, then in the Levant and Hellas. Their schooling had closed their eyes to it. They viewed the conquered peoples merely with contempt, and therefore as a source of loot. Taxes were overcollected, the governors pocketing the excess. Bribes of various kinds were accepted. The almost boundless wealth of art—paintings, furniture, vases, and sculpture in marble and bronze—which had slowly gathered in and around the temples and public buildings in Hellas and the Near East began to be stripped away as governors shipped specimens off to Rome, either for their own estates of to be sold at a profit.

A racket with a distinct pattern took shape. Election to high office at Rome had become a matter of winning the votes of the degraded Roman populace. Candidates for office won popular favor by putting on immense public displays, which often included combats of the most brutal kind between men and wild beasts. The cost was colossal. Many a politician thus went deeply into debt to win office, became consul for a year, and then later paid off his debts by plundering a province, of which he had become governor. Rome was politically and morally sick. Misgoverned provinces revolted in agony, only to be savagely punished and their people sold into slavery by thousands.

The wrenching strain on Rome's city government began to show. Governors with armies at their command, and the wealth of a province to draw upon, could become more powerful than the Senate itself. They could influence Senators from afar, through friends and with money, and could thus control Senate decisions. When two governors struggled for Senate control, civil war could result. For years such a tug of war went on between two governors, Marius and Sulla.[6] First one, then the other, would march on Rome with an army, compel the terrified Senate to make him consul, and then decree the murder of all his enemy's friends. More than once Rome's streets ran with blood. Rome was crying for a stronger government. No one yet had the gifts to create it.

At this point a member of one of the few patrician families left, Julius Caesar, went through the usual steps to power. After serving as consul he shrewdly chose to govern a frontier province in southern France, just beyond the Alps. It was not a rich province; instead it offered other opportunities. In ten years he did what the Senate generally disapproved. Aggressively, without real excuse except conquest, he pushed his province's boundaries north until he had conquered all of what is now France. He then turned around and marched his now unbeatably tough army homeward across the Alps. When ordered by the Senate to resign his command, he refused; instead he marched south to Rome. Troops sent out to check him were useless. He entered the city, seized the government, and proceeded to reform it. The frightened Senate did as he ordered. Out in the provinces, governors everywhere rose in revolt against him. In a series of lightning campaigns Caesar conquered them all and returned to Rome in triumph. The year was 46 B.C.

Among the few surviving patrician families the ancient fear of kings sprang to life. Junius Brutus, whose distant ancestors had thrown out the Etruscans, and who now confused the distant past with the burning present, led a conspiracy of Senators, who murdered Caesar in the only unguarded place available, on the Senate floor itself. They paid the penalty for their blindness. The need for strong central government was so obvious that it had won powerful supporters, at whose head was a young man, only twenty years old, Julius Caesar's great-nephew, Octavius. Helped by his temporary ally Marcus Antonius, he defeated the conspiring Senators in battle after battle, assumed his uncle's one-man rule, and proclaimed himself Rome's first emperor. From that time on governors of provinces were accountable directly to him for their actions. The Senate became merely an honorary body. For the Roman world, in the year 31 B.C., a new era began.

Bronze danarius issued after Caesar's assassination. With the name BRUTUS it associates two ideas: on one side the image of Brutus himself as consul walking to the Senate surrounded by lictors; on the other, Liberty.

Lowie Museum of Anthropology, University of California, Berkeley. Photo John Bridgman

Rome Becomes a Hellenistic City

This era which Octavius launched lasted for over 400 years. Of these the first 200 were among the most peaceful and prosperous the world has ever known. Governors of provinces became responsible public servants. The Western civilized world, centering at that time on the Mediterranean, was united. From Spain to the Levant, trade and travel went on freely in all directions. Perhaps most surprising of all, the Romans, having conquered the Greeks on the field of battle, became conquered by them in the field of culture and the arts. Octavius himself led the way. As a boy he had spent a year in Greece. Perhaps that accounts for his excellent taste. After placing the power of the Roman government firmly in his own hands, he began to encourage all the arts. And the arts as they then existed were Greek, especially Hellenistic Greek.

First, Octavius began to make Rome into a beautiful city.[7] The wealth pouring into Rome from all the provinces as taxes gave her greater resources than any yet known.[8] It was said of Octavius that when he became emperor he found a city of brick and that when he died 45 years later he left one of marble. More accurately, he left it covered with a marble veneer. The practical Romans continued to use their own unattractive but sturdy building materials for foundations, walls, and arched ceilings. But they began to import marble of many beautiful colors from Africa, Syria, and Hellas. Slaves were put to work to saw this into thin sheets, with which the brick and concrete walls of public buildings, the emperor's palace, and the town houses of the wealthy were sheathed. Brick and concrete floors were concealed beneath precise patterns of marble tiling, or beneath vivid pictures in marble *mosaic*. Only the marble columns were solid. So great became the demand for marble from abroad that one whole quarter of the port of Ostia was devoted to docks and warehouses for receiving, storing, and shaping it. When needed, the stone was carried up the Tiber in barges to special docks and warehouses at Rome. From there it was hauled and installed by slave labor.

But not even a Roman emperor could afford to sheath an entire palace in marble. Even the imperial palace was partly walled with smooth white plaster, which artists were employed to decorate with rich colors and refreshing designs. This practice was also followed by ordinary citizens who could not afford marble at all. Plaster walls, decorated in the Hellenistic Greek style, by Greek slaves working for Roman decorating firms, became common.

Museo delle Terme, Rome. Fototeca Unione

Marble panel from a great altar, known as the Altar of Peace, erected in the Roman Forum in honor of Octavius. In the top panel Italy is shown as a woman, surrounded by symbols of plenty.

For Rome was in many ways taking on the aspect of a Hellenistic supercity. Greek architects are known to have designed some her buildings. But Roman architects seem to have been men of taste and ability, first mastering the Doric, Ionic and Corinthian orders, then combining these with arched construction to create a distinctly Roman development of Hellenistic building style. The proportions and sculptural detail of Roman temples were Greek-inspired. Within them the Roman gods were represented by Greek statues, sometimes imported from Hellas, sometimes created at Rome by skillful (if sometimes uninspired) Greek sculptor-slaves.

From Architecture of Ancient Rome, *Anderson & Spiers (Batsford, London)*

Groined vaulting, produced by making barrel vaults intersect at right angles. A reconstruction of the great hall of the Baths of Caracalla, Rome, erected shortly after 200 A.D.

The very people who enjoyed all these beautiful buildings were often descendants of foreign families which had become Roman citizens. Of these foreigners some had at one time been slaves, many of them Greeks, who had luckily won or bought their freedom from kindly masters. It was in some-ways hard to say what was still Roman about Rome. The emperors themselves often had foreign backgrounds. The greatest emperor of all, Marcus Aurelius, had a great-grandfather who came to Rome as a poor man, from far away Gaul, and who then built up a fortune making bricks.

An artist dreams of Pompeii as it once was. The Italian painter Fanfani, who lived about a century ago, shows himself leaning against a broken pillar in the Pompeian forum, while his imagination reconstructs the buildings and fills the place with people of 1800 years earlier.

Two Buried Cities Brought Back to the Light

In the year 79 A.D., 65 years after the death of Octavius, a strange calamity befell two neighboring cities on the coast of southern Italy, a few miles from Naples. One was Herculaneum, a resort full of villas belonging to wealthy Italians. The other was Pompeii, a more ordinary town, with a forum or market place, temples, public baths, a theatre, a city wall, docks, and a fishing industry. One August afternoon, Vesuvius, an old volcano which everyone believed extinct, awoke to life and began to shower the two towns with ashes and mud.

There was just time for most of the citizens to escape with their lives and little else. Almost everything they owned was left behind. Before the eruption was over, Herculaneum, which was nearer to Vesuvius, had been buried to an average depth of 90 feet, Pompeii to about 12.

The two town sites lay abandoned, untouched, and at last forgotten for almost 1700 years. In the eighteenth century first Herculaneum and then Pompeii were discovered by sheer accident. The excavation which was begun over 200 years ago is still in progress. What the digging has revealed is a complete, intimate picture of Italian life as it was being lived when Hellenistic-Roman civilization was close to its height. What kind of houses people lived in, what they ate and drank, what they wore, what furniture they used, how they amused or defended themselves, did business, shared in politics—all is there to see or to reconstruct. The picture that emerges from these two rediscovered towns is that living, even in this provincial spot, had reached a level which in some ways is hard to equal even today. In some ways only, for the easy, refined life was made possible by the presence of thousands of slaves on whom the dangerous, exhausting, and dirty labor rested.

Above and right: Two examples of the wealth of wall paintings with which the Pompeians enriched the walls of their rooms. Above is an imaginary landscape. In the other a lady practices the cithara, *Roman ancestor of the guitar, while her little daughter, or perhaps a slave girl, watches. Below: Mosaic copy of a celebrated Hellenistic painting by the Greek artist Dioscorides, depicting a group of street entertainers, all masked (except for the small boy).*

Universal Color Slide Co.

Above: The enclosed garden or peristyle *of a Roman house, Pompeii. Roman houses were somewhat like Roman constitutional government. While adjusting to the present, they never forgot the past. The peristyle was, for the Romans, a Greek innovation, which they attached to their more conservatively designed homes. Below: Pompeian dining room, with barrel vaulted ceiling.*

Right: This bronze bust of a Pompeian banker was found in his house. An inscription states that it was given to him by a grateful former slave. Below: Silver wine goblet found in a Pompeian mansion.

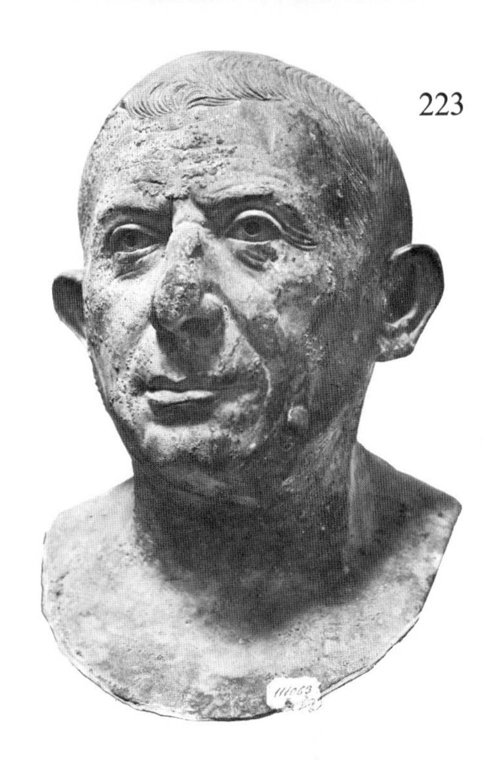

Gladiator's bronze parade helmet, discovered in Pompeii's amphitheatre. The sculptured scenes on it depict the sack of Troy.

Few living creatures seem to have been trapped in Pompeii. This struggling hound did not make it. He was buried in volcanic ash and mud, enabling excavators to make this cast.

All Photos Alinari-Art Reference Bureau, Inc.

Right: Plan of the Forum of Trajan, Rome, as reconstructed by the Italian archeologist Canina, 1838. The main entrance was through the great triumphal arch at the top of the plan. The temple shown at the plan's bottom was erected after Trajan's death, in his honor, by the Emperor Hadrian. Below: Canina's reconstructions of the front elevation of the Basilica Ulpia, the main entrance to the Forum, and the section down its long axis.

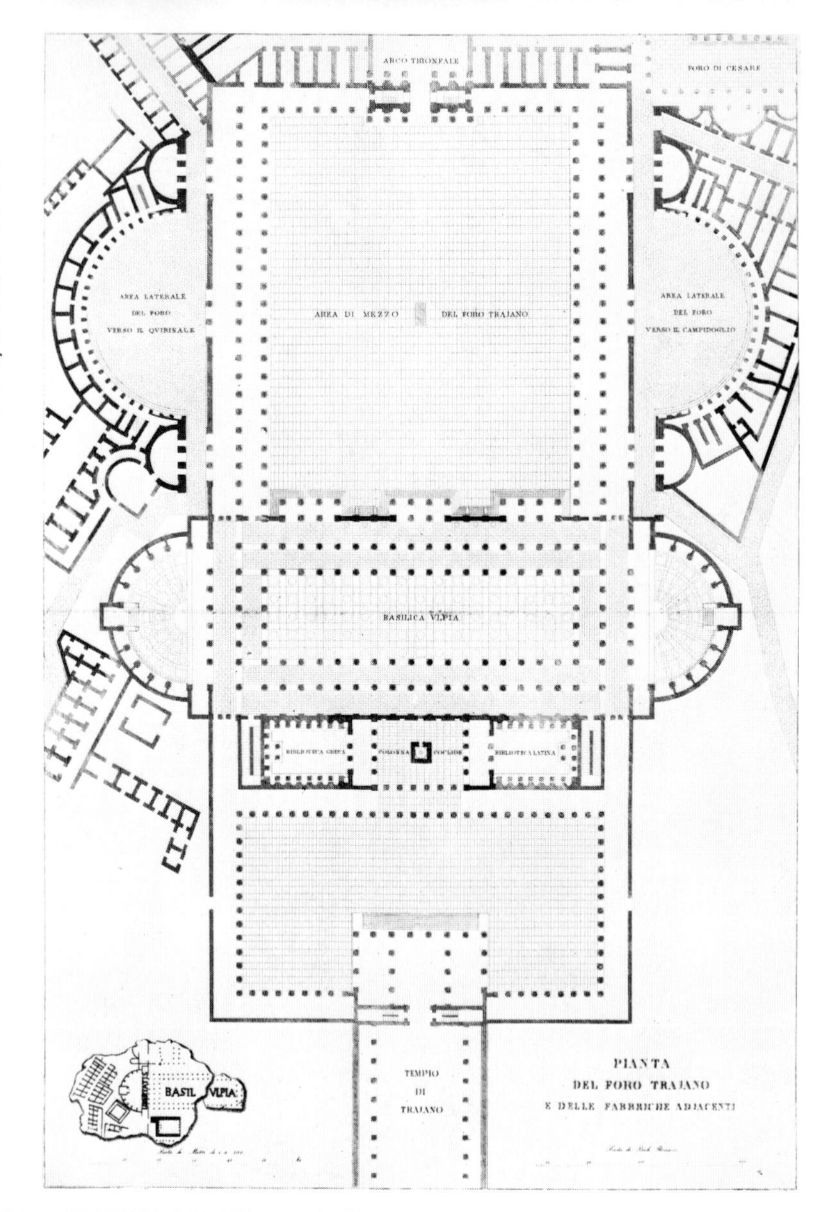

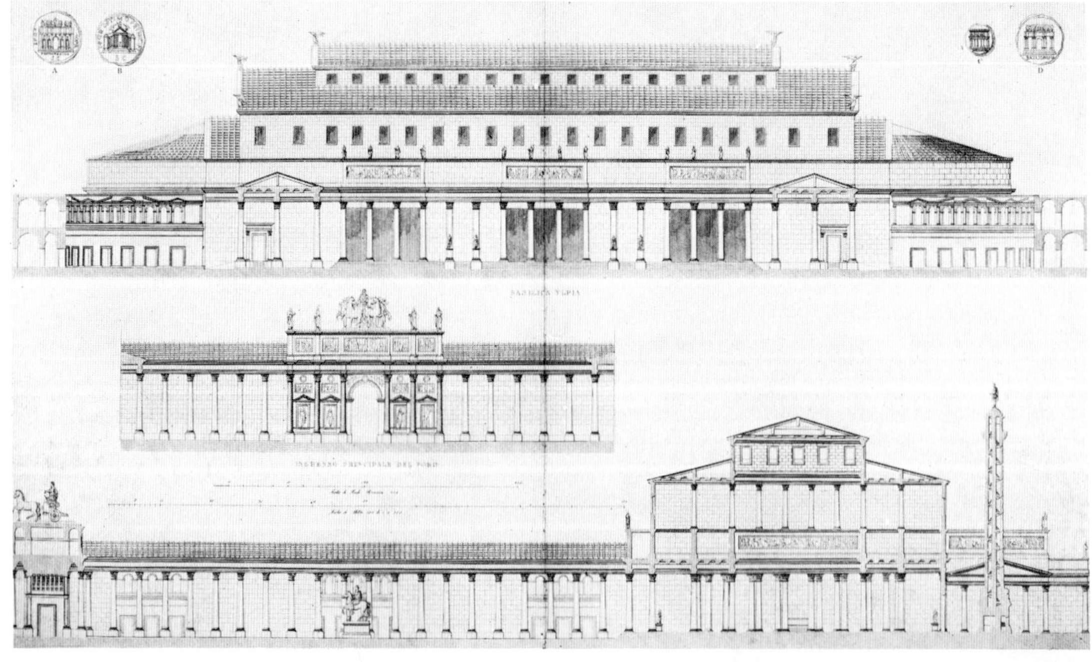

Archeological Museum, Ankara. Photo John Bridgman

Above: Bronze bust of the Emperor Trajan. Below: Trajan's Column, seen through the ruined columns of the Basilica Ulpia.

The Emperor Trajan, Glorifier of Rome

As emperor after emperor followed Octavius to power, many, like Octavius himself, were hard working public officials. Of the others, some were weaklings. Some were sensual monsters. A few were victims of jealousy and suspicion, capable of murdering their own sons. At least one was a dangerous lunatic. At least one other, Marcus Aurelius, came close to being a philosopher-saint. But almost all had some hand in shaping the appearance of Rome.

They were inspired to do this by the sight of the marvelous Hellenistic cities whose Greek rulers had made them glorious: Alexandria with her great library and her lighthouse nearly as tall as the Washington Monument; Syracuse with her palaces; Ephesus with her temple of Diana, a forest of decorated columns; Antioch with her roofs of gilded bronze; Pergamon with her gigantic altar to Zeus; and Athens, the queen of them all for austere beauty, crowned by the Parthenon, the most perfect structure of the ancient world.

After Octavius, the emperors who perhaps did most to make Rome beautiful were Trajan and his successor, Hadrian. During the 40 years that these two men governed the Roman world, from 97 A.D. to 136, some of Rome's most remarkable buildings were erected.

It was sometimes the custom of emperors to encourage business life in Rome by building an open forum or market place for shopping and trading. A suitable place in the city would be chosen, the real estate would be bought, buildings would be demolished, and a well-planned arrangement of open space surrounded by shops and shaded walks would then be built.

Close to a forum, as part of its plan, stood a building for law offices, financial transactions, and the trying of cases before judges. These one or two storey buildings came to have a special design, suited to Roman needs, and were called *basilicas*. They were oblong, with plenty of floor space, the roof usually being supported by rows of columns. At one end, or both, was a semicircular alcove, or *apse* as it was later called, in which judges could hold court hearings.

Trajan brought to Rome a distinguished Greek architect, Apollodorus of Damascus, and entrusted to him the designing of the greatest forum Rome was ever to see. Apollodorus probably knew the planning methods which Greek architects had used for the Greek kings of Asia, who would sometimes order similar large civic projects. He was also familiar with the geometry of Euclid. On Trajan's instructions, he developed an elegant bilaterally symmerical plan combining all the elements which the emperor wished brought together in one place. These were: (1) an open forum, ringed with shops and markets for all kinds of goods, and shaded at the sides with columned walkways; (2) a great basilica with much office space and two law courts; (3) two libraries to house state documents, one for those in Latin, the other for those in Greek; (4) a vivid record of the emperor's successful wars in eastern Europe.

Note the ground plan of the Forum of Trajan as Apollodorus planned it and a view of what is left of the forum today. It lies between two of Rome's hills, and the two semicircular rows of shops on either side of the open forum

Fototeca Unione, Rome

Alinari-Art Reference Bureau, Inc.

Close-up of the lower portion of Trajan's Column. The complete spiral frieze, over 600 ft long, tells the story of two campaigns conducted by Trajan north of the Danube. Here the river god symbolizing the Danube watches in wonder as Roman troops cross his river on a military bridge.

rose six stories high against the hills, which had been hollowed out to receive them. As one entered the Forum through a great archway, one saw directly before him on a pedestal in the Forum's center a gilded bronze statue of Trajan on horseback. As the visitor moved forward past this statue, either across the sunny open space or in the shade of one of the columned walks along either side, he next came to the great Basilica Ulpia[9], with its outside columns of golden yellow marble. Entering its great hall, he found rows of red and grey columns capped with white. Crossing the basilica's marble floor and going out the opposite doorway, he came face to face with the record of Trajan as a general. This is the only part of the Forum, and one of the few monuments of Rome, which remains intact, even though the pure white of its stone and the color and gilding on its figures have long since been dulled to tired grey. It is a hollow column of Cararra marble about 130 feet high crowned by a statue, originally of Trajan, but now of St. Peter. Within the column a spiral stone stair winds upward to the top. On the column's outside surface a continuous sculptured picture-record of Trajan's battles beyond the Danube mounts the column in 23 turns. Today only the lower part of the column can be viewed easily. In Trajan's day people could mount to the roof of either the Latin or the Greek library, both two storeys high, which stood one on each side of the column.

Such was the center which Trajan created for the Roman people, and to his own glory. He also caused a great public bath to be built, thus adding one more to the hundreds already operating in Rome. For Romans of all social levels had developed an intense love of bathing. For them, bathing had become a form of recreation, a luxurious process in which contrasts between hot, cold, and tepid water were enjoyed at length, followed by a rubdown with perfumed olive oil, and a careful skin scraping, all by slaves, in an age before the invention of soap.

Still another of Trajan's gifts to Rome was the redesigning of the port of Ostia. The clogging of the harbor and its openness to storms had always been problems. Trajan's engineers, probably led by Apollodorus, solved these problems for a long time to come. A new basin was dug, just inland from the coast, and a new channel cut, connecting it with the Tiber. Today such a project would be a major one, even with power shovels, bulldozers, and diesel trucks. In Trajan's day it was achieved entirely by men with spades, and by other men with baskets on their backs, all moving under the slave driver's cold eye. The form of the harbor was a perfect hexagon, surrounded by rows of columns and made beautiful with statues. Beyond the columns were storehouses and well-planned streets, a triumph of classic architecture and geometry.

British Museum

Marble bust of the Emperor Hadrian.

Hadrian Continues Trajan's Work

On Trajan's death, Hadrian, his cousin, succeeded him, and took up the great work of glorifying first Trajan's memory, then Rome, and last but not least himself. Since the new emperor could not endure Apollodorus' candid mode of speech, the great architect fell from favor, was banished, and later killed.

Hadrian first put the crowning touch on Trajan's Forum. Beyond the libraries and the great column, he caused a temple to be built to Trajan's memory. The worship of emperors as gods was beginning to find acceptance at Rome, following a practice developed in Egypt 3300 years before. In keeping with the Roman style, the new temple of Trajan stood at the top of a great flight of steps. The column shafts supporting the roof of the temple porch were of grey granite, sixty feet tall, each column shaft a single stone! The Greeks had never done such things. As temple builders their aim seems to have been to inspire awe, rather than to overwhelm the spectator with a sense of imperial power.

The supreme building achievement of Hadrian's reign was the completion of the only large Roman structure tough enough to have survived in a roofed condition to the present day. This is the Pantheon, a glorious replacement of earlier structures bearing the same name. At one time, a century earlier, it is believed to have been an oblong temple by the emperor Agrippa. Its wooden roof had burned more than once. Hadrian commanded that it be rebuilt as a circular temple honoring Jupiter, Mars, Venus, and other divine personages. Out of respect for Agrippa's memory, the beautiful façade of his temple was preserved. The new architect, a Roman known as Valerius of Ostia, performed a miraculous feat of unifying the square portico and the cylindrical mass behind it in a single harmonious scheme, as recently deduced by George Lesser. In ancient times the portico and dome alone seem to have been visible from outside, the bulk of the cylinder having been concealed by magnificent structures on either side. These have long since disappeared. The

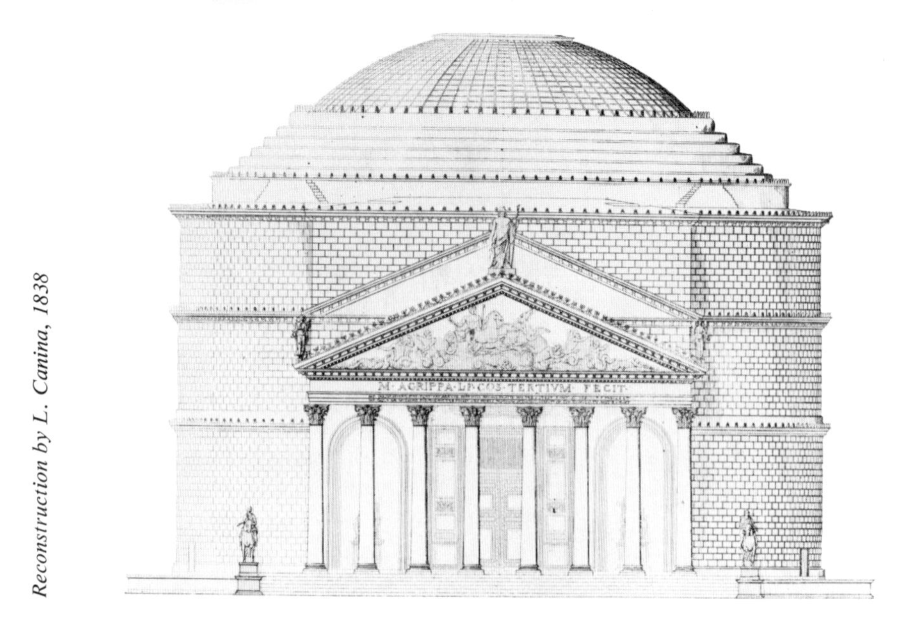

Reconstruction by L. Canina, 1838

The Pantheon as it may have looked in the time of the Emperor Trajan. The original bronze doors are still in place today.

great columns, each a single granite shaft capped by a white marble capital, are now discolored; and the broad sweep of seven steps which once led up to them has been buried by a raised street level.

The bronze reliefs which once filled the great triangle above the columns were stripped away as early as the seventh century. For over the years the great building has been repeatedly plundered.

It is only when one steps inside, past great doors which have never been replaced since Hadrian's day, that the Pantheon's greatest glory makes itself felt. 142 feet across, and 142 feet from the floor to the highest point of the dome, its beautiful proportions have moved architects with wonder for 1800 years. Michelangelo, the genius of the Renaissance, who planned St. Peter's much as it is today, declared it "angelic, not merely human."

Structurally the Pantheon is a Roman arch rotated to form a hollow hemisphere or dome. This rests on a hollow drum with walls over twenty feet thick where not hollowed out in niches, as a precaution against outward thrust, a problem attending all arch construction. It was built in the usual Roman manner of concrete and bricks, brick arches being set into the walls at intervals with the intention of relieving and distributing the dead weight of walls and dome. For 1700 years it was a challenge to architects. Not until about 100 years ago did anyone successfully create a dome with a wider span.

Concrete and brick were originally completely concealed by costly sheathing. White marble stucco covered the outside walls, bronze tiles like fish scales, gleaming with gold leaf, clothed the dome. Within, richly colored marble and reddish-violet porphyry covered the walls, and sculptured sheet silver filled the *coffers* or rectangular recesses of the domed ceiling. In alcoves and niches around the cylindrical wall stood statues of the gods, beautifully lighted from above by a circular opening, twenty-nine feet across, open to the sky, in the great dome's apex.

The temple once contained still another marvel. The roof of its great portico was once supported by girders of bronze, the first example of metal used *structurally* on a large scale, of which we have knowledge. For the fate of these bronze girders see Chapter 9.

Section by von Godetz, 1795

Hadrian's final act as creator of large architectural projects was to order for himself and his successors a splendid tomb, to be the marvel of all mankind. On a square platform almost 250 feet wide there rose a marble-sheathed cylinder capped by a conical roof—an artificial mountain planted over with a forest of pine trees, and crowned by a colossal pine cone of gilded bronze.[10]

Above: Cross section of the Pantheon. Three diagrams below: The geometric scheme which apparently determined the planning of the Pantheon. The size and placement of every major part of the building is accounted for, even the diameter of the circular opening in the dome.

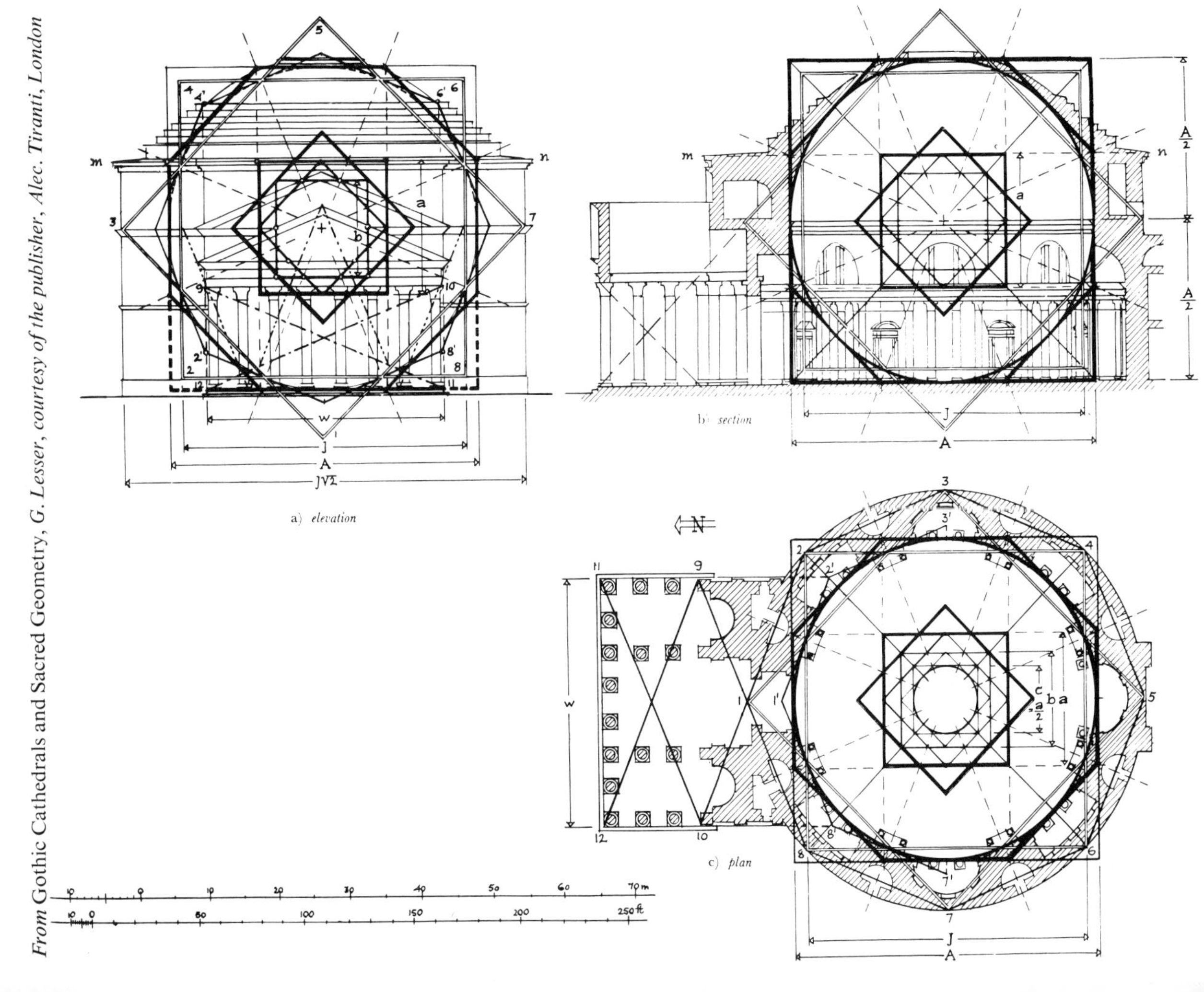

From Gothic Cathedrals and Sacred Geometry, *G. Lesser, courtesy of the publisher, Alec. Tiranti, London*

Above: Corinthian capital, a favorite Roman architectural detail, borrowed from the Greeks. Below left: Triumphal Arch of the Emperor Septimius Severus, Rome. In Roman times it was crowned with bronze statues, and its marble reliefs were probably alive with color. Below right: Analysis of its design, showing a reliance on mean and extreme proportion.

Analysis by E. Moessel, 1938. Courtesy Deutsche Verlag-Anstalt, Stuttgart

The tomb stood across the Tiber from Rome; a specially constructed bridge, its parapets enriched with statues, led to it. The bridge is still there. The cylinder, stripped of its marble and its conical forest-roof, and with gun emplacements added, is now the grim Castel Sant Angelo, the one-time fortress of the popes.

Vitruvius, Teacher of Europe's Architects

Besides Greeks like Apollodorus of Damascus, there were other architects, like Valerius of Ostia, who were Roman or Italian. The only book on architecture which has survived from the ancient world to the present was written by a Roman, Marcus Vitruvius. Vitruvius had been a military engineer in the army of Octavius. Later he became inspector of the public buildings of the city of Rome, and found time to write a work on architecture and related subjects, even town planning, in ten volumes. To a Roman a "volume" was usually a papyrus scroll 50 or 60 feet long when unrolled. The whole of Vitruvius' work, in English translation, fills one paperback book.

Vitruvius reduced to orderly, simple form a good part of the knowledge of building construction then known. He presented the three great systems of building design developed by the Greeks; stern, simple Doric; graceful, elegant Ionic; and richly ornate Corinthian. To these systems he added another which Roman architects had devised: Tuscan, simpler than Doric.[11] Together these styles were called the *orders* of architecture. They set the standard of human taste and practice in building for a long time to come. Architects of the sixteenth to nineteenth centuries leaned heavily on a knowledge of Vitruvius, or rather on the knowledge which he had brought into one book from many other sources. In every modern city of the world[12] buildings can be found which show signs of one or more of Vitruvius' four orders, either used directly or adapted. Only within the past few decades have

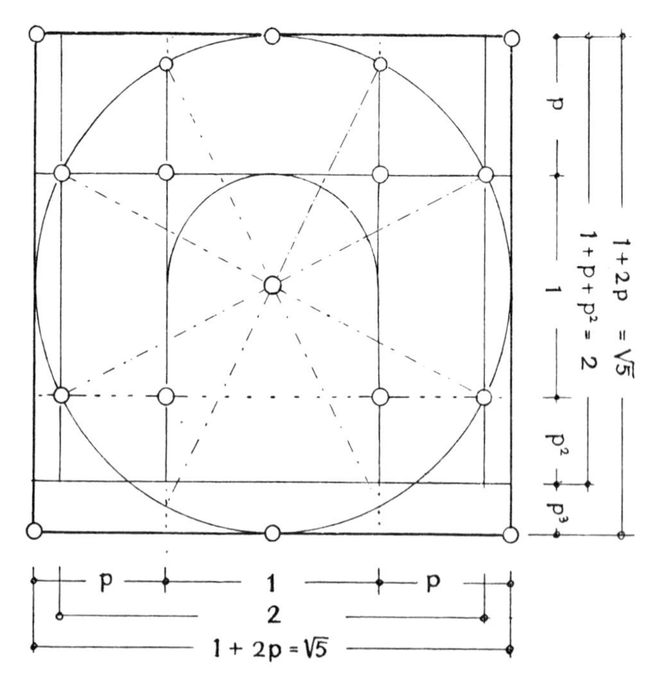

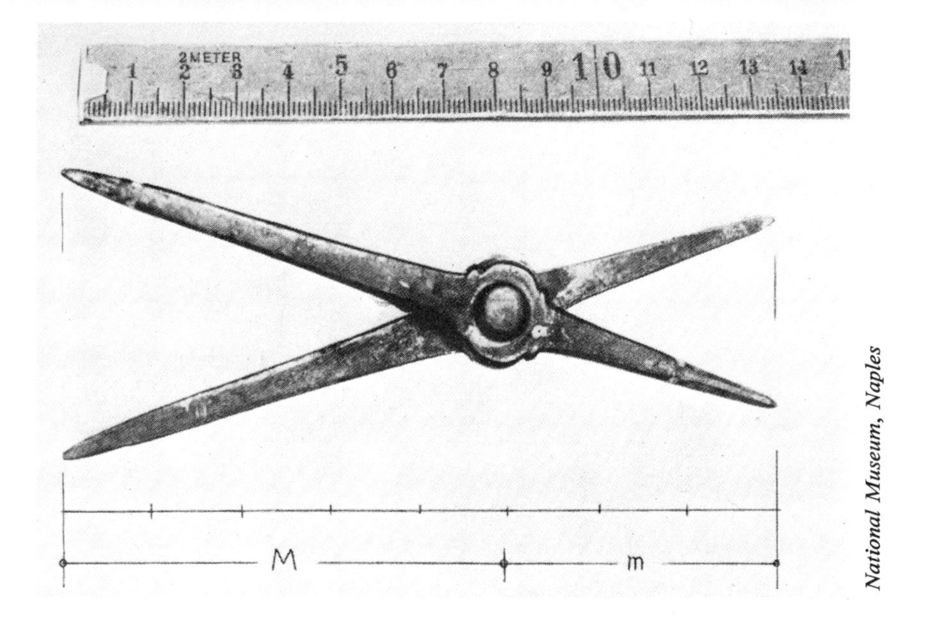

National Museum, Naples

Bronze dividers, belonging to an unknown Greek or Italian architect, found in Pompeii. The smaller dividers always open to Φ times the openings of the larger.

architects freed themselves from these ancient styles and developed new ones suited to the building materials, methods, living habits, and world outlook of a new age.

One or two of Vitruvius' ideas can interest us even today. For example here is what he had to say about proportion in building design.

> The design of an edifice consists in obtaining symmetry, the principles of which the architect should diligently study. They are due to proportion, called by the Greeks *analogia*. Proportion is the fitness of measure between the members and the whole work with reference to one part used as a standard, and it is thus that symmetry is obtained. Without symmetry and proportion there can be no proper design, as in the well-drawn human form, where the ratio between the members is exact. (Book III, Chapter I.)
>
> There is nothing to which the architect should devote more care than to the exact proportions of the building with reference to a certain part taken as a standard. After symmetry has been calculated and expressed in figures, the next consideration is the nature of the site with reference to use or beauty, adding or subtracting, but without apparent change, leaving nothing in appearance to be desired. (Book VI, Chapter II.)

What Vitruvius is saying here is that all parts of a building should be thoughtfully interrelated by being made multiples of a *module*. He then states that after the building has been designed, the architect should adjust its measurements slightly, to harmonize it with its future surroundings Notice that Vitruvius thought of a building as a self-sufficient unit conceived within the architect's mind and *then* fitted somehow into its surroundings. Today there are thoughtful architects to be found who work the other way round, starting with the site and devising a building to harmonize with it.

Vitruvius included much more information in his book, as you will find in reading it. In Appendix B you will find his brief statements on human proportion, followed by Leonardo's interpretation and illustration of it.

Reconstruction by A. de Giovanni

A view across imperial Rome, as reconstructed in a model. In the foreground is the Circus Maximus, for chariot races, with its two-level royal box, and with a total seating capacity of perhaps 250,000. Beyond rises the vast complex of the imperial palace, covering the Palatine Hill, Zigzagging toward it from the upper right is the aqueduct which brought fresh water to the palace from miles outside the city. At the top left is the Flavian Amphitheatre, or Coliseum, for gladiatorial combats, with a seating capacity of 87,000.

Roman Life in the Empire

Where and how did the people in Rome live? The emperors dwelt in their palaces, high on the Palatine Hill, the spot from which Rome had started. Persons of rank and wealth lived in lesser "palaces" or town houses. But the great mass of the people lived in apartments and tenements, usually one family to a floor. No building code regulated their construction. They were often six or seven storeys high, without plumbing of any kind, or fire escapes, and were often subject to collapse. Emperor Trajan limited their height by law to 70 feet on the side facing the street! The "street" might be a mere alley between buildings, only ten feet wide. When operating at its best, the Roman city government supplied much that the tenement builders did not. Fresh water flowed in by aqueduct to Rome's countless pools and fountains. At these, housewives could fill their bronze pails and pottery jars, and then go trudging up flight after flight of stairs to their apartments; it was accepted as part of life. Comfort stations, connected with efficient sewers, were everywhere maintained. The public baths assured everyone with a small coin in his pocket a chance to bathe in luxury. To preserve order and add to the public safety, police and fire stations were located throughout the city. But at night Rome must have been hard to police, for there seems to have been no public lighting of streets. And if a fire broke out in an apartment, ther was little hope for the people on the floors above.

The wealthy in their private houses were more fortunate. They could arrange with the city officials for a special line of lead pipe to bring them water straight from one of the aqueducts. When the city became hot or unwholesome they could leave for a country villa, often any one of several, each in a different part of Italy. They had their large staffs of slaves, a different slave for every household chore, from social secretary to pot scrubber.

In our own age of machine production, it is hard to realize how completely hand crafting was present in every square foot of the city. Not only was each bit of ornament on each building hand chiseled and drilled, but every brick in every public building bore a stamp naming the owner of the brickyard, often the slave who managed it, and the date of manufacture (that is, the names of the public officials for the year). Lead water pipe was never mass produced. It was custom built for each job, and bore stamps naming the plumber who installed it and the family for whom it was laid. Skilled labor was cheap. And nobody invented labor-saving machinery when a good slave could be bought and put to work. Slavery discouraged invention.

Roman writing during the empire. Part of four lines from the Aeneid, *an epic poem commissioned by Octavius Augustus, hoping thereby to compete for eternal fame with Homer. This fragment is from an ancient costly edition written on* vellum *or calf skin.*

There was no effective way to spread news, at least by our standards. As in many parts of the world today, it went largely by word of mouth. But books were easy to buy. The Roman method of publishing was to gather hundreds of skilled slaves in one great hall and to dictate the book, sentence by sentence. The slaves sat writing endlessly on papyrus imported from Egypt. The written pages were then glued in a series to form a scroll.

Entertainment, when it came, was lavish. One could sit in a theater and watch a Greek or Roman play, go to the Circus Maximus and bet on the races, or enter the huge amphitheater and watch men and animals slaughter each other. The barbaric atmosphere of these spectacles was heightened by the weird sounds of musical instruments created to penetrate the vast space of the arena: the hoarse blast of bronze trumpets; the clang of lyres "as large as chariots;" and the bubbling hoot of the newly invented *organum*, a pipe organ whose airflow was maintained by water pressure.[13]

And then there were parades. When a Roman general returned from a successful campaign, a *triumph* was held, a procession of the homecoming troops and of the spoils of war, including long lines of captives in their native garb. The climax of the triumph was the general himself, standing erect in a great chariot, a golden wreath held above his head. But at his side stood an attendant whose duty it was to keep whispering, "Remember, you are only a mortal." And the triumph was always declared to honor, not the general, but Jupiter, father of the gods, who had achieved the victory by using the Romans as his instrument.

Shrines and temples of the gods were everywhere, and invited practices still close to tribal magic (attempts to bind the gods through bribery). If a man wanted success in business, he would sacrifice a rooster at a nearby temple of Mercury. If a girl wanted success in love, she would seek out a temple of Venus and offer up a pair of doves. Other gods and goddesses had their own areas of influence and their own requirements for sacrifice. People who believed in the gods lived in superstitious fear of their anger, and in the hope of successfully winning their favor with gifts. The number who no longer believed steadily increased. And everyone, believer or not, looked on death with dread. What would it bring? A shadowy, pleasureless life in Hades? No one felt sure. Men of power and talent attempted to achieve immortality by deeds which they hoped men would remember for all time. Such achievements were beyond the grasp of the powerless masses. Whither could they turn for comfort and reassurance?

Head of a despairing old woman, a fragment of Hellenistic sculpture.

Vollmer Collection, New York

The Empire is Peacefully Attacked from Within

Museo delle Terme, Rome. Photo Alinari-Art Reference Bureau, Inc.

Jesus as the Roman Christians thought of him in the fourth century A.D. He is shown here as a beardless youth, in Graeco-Roman clothes, and in the act of teaching or persuading in a traditionally Roman pose.

The vast Roman empire was a world of many peoples and many contrasting religions. In the forests of western Germany, savage tribes of warriors were still practicing human sacrifice. In Egypt, prayers to the animal- and bird-headed gods still were offered, day after day, year after year, as they had been since time began. In Hellas, and in the provinces once ruled by Greek kings, the images of Zeus, Athena, Apollo, and the other gods still stood in their temples, feared by the common people but viewed with amusement by educated Greeks who had left the old religion and found their comfort in philosophy, such as that created by Plato, Aristotle, and their followers. In the provinces of Asia the Persians worshipped Mithra, god of light. Among all these religious practices and philosophies the Roman people could choose almost at will. The government was lenient, so long as citizens gave an oath of allegiance to the emperor. Only two religions offered a threat to Rome, and these stood to each other in the relation of father to son.

In the heart of the Levant, inland from the Phoenician seaports, stood the mighty city of Jerusalem, one of the most strongly fortified centers of the ancient world, crowned at its highest point by its temple gleaming with marble and gold. This city was the capital of the kingdom of Israel. Here, in the great temple, the Jews worshiped Jehovah,[14] a God who despised sacrifices and magic.

> I will take no bullock out of thy house, nor the goats out of thy folds. For every beast of the forest is mine, and the cattle upon a thousand hills. If I were hungry, I would not tell thee: for the world is mine, and the fullness thereof.

Thus, in one of the great Jewish hymns, or *psalms*, was Jehovah envisioned as speaking to his people. And thus, in the following psalm, did the people reply.

> Behold, Thou desirest truth in the inward parts: and in the hidden part Thou shalt make me to know wisdom . . .
> For Thou desirest not sacrifice; else would I give it: Thou delightest not in burnt offering.
> The sacrifices of God are a broken spirit: a broken and a contrite heart, O God, Thou wilt not despise.[15]

And how was "truth in the inward parts" to be achieved? By obedience to the Holy Law which Jehovah Himself had given through Moses to His people. Of this law, the Ten Commandments were the core:

> Accept no god but Jehovah.
> Make no image of any god.
> Use not Jehovah's name with disrespect.
> Devote each seventh day to worship.
> Honor your parents.
> Murder not; commit no adultery; steal not.
> Testify falsely against no one.
> Covet no other man's possessions.

The second of these Commandments was to have a fateful, far-reaching effect on the art of not merely one, but three, of the world's greatest religions.

To the Ten Commandments many other practices had been added, such as those set down in the Old Testament's Book of Leviticus; the life of a devout Jew was not easy. His was the purest religion of the ancient world, just as it is among the purest today, but it was exclusive, a religion chiefly for one people only, though they did accept foreigners (*gentiles*) as converts to Judaism. The Jewish religion was in one way still a tribal religion, and the conservative Jews, civilized city-dwellers though they were, still held to an ancient tribal organization. They divided themselves intwo twelve clans, each named after a different grandson of Abraham, whom they regarded as their common ancestor.

When the Romans conquered the Levant, the kingdom of Israel fell under their control, and a Roman governor and garrison were stationed at Jerusalem. There they encountered a people who claimed as their ruler the unseen God, under whom was a senate (or *Sanhedrin*, as it was called). The Roman governors did not intend to interfere with religion. Their concern was to collect taxes and to maintain what the Romans considered to be law and order. They insisted only on deciding certain cases at law, such as those involving life and death. To the proud Jews this was not only humiliating, it was an act of impiety against Jehovah whose earthly representatives, the Sanhedrin, had had full charge of such cases. They looked for their God to send them a new leader, a Messiah, who would deliver them from this foul oppression.

Passage from the Pentateuch, *or first five chapters of the Old Testament (*Exodus, *chap. XX, verses 1–5). An example of Hebrew manuscript, date uncertain, ninth century or earlier.*

British Museum

But when a man arose among them who spoke with a Messiah's authority, they refused to believe him. He was no Jewish aristocrat, capable of leading an armed revolt to break the power of the Romans, as the Jewish hero Judas Maccabeus had once broken the power of the Hellenistic Greeks. Instead he was a young man from one of the poorest parts of Judaea, who went about quietly but fearlessly preaching a life of peace, love for one's enemies, and adaptation to force:

> Blessed are the peacemakers: for they shall be called the children of God.
>
> Ye have heard that it hath been said, Thou shalt love thy neighbor, and hate thine enemy.
>
> But I say unto you, Love your enemies, bless them that curse you, do good to them which despitefully use you, and persecute you . . .

Thus did Jesus speak to a people in the grip of Rome, a conqueror mightier than any the world had yet seen. For the times, his was the highest kind of political realism. But Jewish pride, with its long record of stubborn resistance to every gentile foe, would not accept it. Jesus cried:

> O Jerusalem, Jerusalem, Thou that killest the prophets, and stonest them that are sent unto thee, how often would I have gathered thy children together, as a hen gathereth her chickens under her wings, and ye would not!
>
> Behold, your house is left unto you desolate . . . Verily I say unto you, There shall not be left here one stone upon another, that shall not be thrown down.[16]

A generation later this prophecy was ruthlessly fulfilled by a Roman army under the Emperor Titus, who stormed and sacked Jerusalem, demolished the temple, and temporarily ended persistent Jewish revolt by scattering the people to the four corners of the earth.

But Jesus did far more than preach kindly nonresistance. He dared to declare that he spoke for Jehovah, whom he taught his followers to address as Father in a new and loving manner. He spoke not to Jews only but to all men. He declared that any man on earth could attain everlasting life in another world, provided he lived in a certain manner in this one. This manner of life was in one way less demanding than that required of the Jews. It was less burdened with endless minor rules of conduct. In another way it was vastly harder; it required obedience to Moses' Commandments, plus a constant will to love all other men, regardless of their rank or nation. Jesus' teaching was not inconsistent with the faith of his fathers. He was a Jewish reformer who attacked the rigid formalism, materialism, and self-satisfaction which were afflicting certain ruling classes of Jews (Pharisees and others) in his day. They repaid him with hatred, partly on this account, partly, perhaps, because they misjudged him as a revolutionary, who might disturb the temporary arrangements which some powerful Jews may have reached with their Roman conquerors.

Said the Pharisees to the Jews, "He hath a devil and is mad; why hear ye him?" And when they saw his gentle power growing, they contrived his execution like a criminal or runaway slave, by crucifixion. So ended a life whose period of teaching seems to have lasted perhaps three years. The power that might have enlivened an older faith was cast out to become the creator of a new one.

But never has so astonishing an effect been created in so short a time. The new religion grew slowly at first, then with the mounting power of a flood. Word spread that here was a new purpose for living, a new hope for life after death. Jesus was hailed as the Messiah, the *Christ*,[17] for whom the Jews had been looking but who had come for all men. It was reported that three days after his crucifixion he had risen from the dead. As time passed, Converts by the thousands appeared on all levels of society, first in Israel, and then in Asia Minor, Greece, Egypt and Rome itself. Christians everywhere were recognizable by their cheerful gentleness, honesty, and obedience to law. In only one respect were they a problem. They would not swear loyalty to the Roman emperors, whose worship as gods had by that time begun. And this made a terrible difference.

How the Romans responded to this quiet resistance depended on the will of particular emperors and governors of provinces. Some treated the Christians with urbane tolerance, shrewdly recognizing their superior qualities as citizens. But for nearly three centuries the common practice, especially at Rome, was to punish Christians as if for treason, by the more cruel forms of death. The religion was repeatedly outlawed. In response the Christians went literally underground. In order to worship in freedom, and to give their fellow Christians decent burial, they tunneled for miles beneath the city. The *catacombs* still bear witness today to the endless energy and the vast numbers of Roman Christians in those early years of oppression.

On the whole, the Roman government's approach to Christianity was typical of its approach to new problems throughout its history: arrogant resistance to change until it was almost, but not quite, too late. When penetration of every level of society by the new religion had become so universal that even an emperor's own mother was a Christian, the emperor Constantine at last took the step of declaring Christianity legal, and then made it the official state religion of the Roman empire. Thus, in the year 323 A.D., nearly three centuries after Christianity's gentle but fearless founder had died a criminal's death for preaching that a pure and loving heart is the key to eternal life, his successors suddenly found themselves raised to a position of high prestige by the greatest political and military power in the West.

The Roman empire at its greatest extent, 117 A.D. Under Roman domination, Latin versions of place names replaced Greek (e.g., Byzantion became Byzantium, Miletos became Miletus), and in western languages have remained so ever since.

The Empire is Forcefully Attacked from Without

If we look at a map of the Roman Empire at the time of Hadrian, about 125 A.D., we see an area stretching from Britain east to the Persian Gulf, and from the mouth of the Rhine south to the Sahara Desert. Throughout this vast region were many flourishing cities, each one a lesser Rome, each with its own forum, basilicas, temples, theaters, amphitheater, and baths, all built with a skillful blend of Roman arched construction and Greek columnar design. Each city had its own city government and bustled with its own social and business life. Connecting these cities was an efficiently maintained network of stone-paved roads, all eventually leading, directly or indirectly, to the center of power in Rome. Ringing the frontiers of the great empire, armies were stationed, totalling nearly a quarter of a million men, armies which had long since ceased to be civilian-manned, and had become professional, finely organized and equipped, and well paid and housed. And wherever invaders were especially dangerous, as in northern Britain and in Germany, ramparts and forts had been built along the borders, as if the empire were a huge supercity.

Museo delle Terme, Rome. Photo Alinari-Art Reference Bureau, Inc.

A battle between Romans and barbarians, as shown in a Roman relief, second century A.D.

For to maintain the Roman empire required constant resistance to pressure from outside. Picts, Scots, Franks, Germans, Dacians, Galatians, Parthians, Persians, Arabians, Ethiopians, Numidians: these were the names of the empire's near neighbors, completely encircling her land borders; and every one of them was hostile. To hold back such a tide required constant vigilance, a strong army, and an unfailingly effective central government. Unfortunately, the imperial government of Rome contained more than one fatal flaw.

Perhaps the most serious of these was the lack of any reliable way to determine the succession of emperors. The two founders of the empire, Julius Caesar and Octavius, had come to power through force of arms in civil wars. The Roman Senate was then compelled to act as a rubber stamp and approve the victor. This had set an ugly precedent. Later emperors had avoided bloodshed by choosing successors, whom they sometimes actually placed in power before their own deaths. But when no such provision was made, the title of emperor was his who had the largest army.

An invitation to trouble occurred in about 190 A.D., when the emperor Commodus, a particularly loathsome ruler, was murdered in his palace. Three different generals out on the empire's frontiers then claimed the title of emperor. When the resulting civil war was over, one of them, Septimius Severus, emerged on top. But barbarian Parthians had siezed the opportunity to invade the empire; statesmen of ability who had sided with the wrong general had been murdered; and towns which had also made the wrong choice had been sacked and ruined. The same tragic struggle for power that had ended the republic appeared all over again, but on a larger scale. Severus, after securing the power in his hands, turned upon the invading Parthians and routed them. Rome could still indulge in bloody power struggles within and repel invaders from without.

But not forever. Once started, the evil practice of seizing the title of emperor by aid of the army continued in headlong succession. Emperor after emperor rode to power on an army's shoulders, at the expense of the empire's lifeblood and the weakening of its human walls of defense. Something had to give, and when it did the hostile outsiders came roaring in at not one but many breaches. Cities, farms, and estates which had known peace for generations were burned, looted, and strewn with corpses. Rome, which had stood proudly for centuries without a wall, was hastily ringed with fortifications, expecting a barbarian siege. The empire seemed doomed. But once again, Roman generals and their legions rose to the crisis and drove the invaders back.

In 285 there came to power a soldier-emperor strong enough to hold back all invaders, and politically shrewd enough to reorganize the empire from top to bottom. This man was Diocletian. He found the empire half ruined and bitterly impoverished by civil wars, invasions, and looting. Coin had become so scarc that taxes were often collected in grain and other materials, as if the land were Egypt. Still worse, great stretches of land had been made temporarily sterile by shortsighted overfarming.

Diocletian's solution was typical of what he was, a lifelong soldier. First, he made the frontiers secure by nearly doubling the size of the army. Turning his attention within the borders, he then everywhere reorganized the chain of command. He streamlined Rome's custom ridden, inefficient provincial administration into a pair of completely separate pyramids, one military and the other civil. At the apex of the military pyramid and responsible to the emperor was a *magister militum* (master of troops), beneath whom were a number of *duces*, each responsible for defense of a section of the empire. Under each *dux* in turn were several *comites*, each responsible for a still smaller area, and so on down.

At the apex of the civil pyramid was a group of *praetorian prefects*, each responsible to the emperor for some aspect of civil government. Beneath these were twelve *vicars*, each in charge of what was called a *diocese*. These in turn were divided into provinces, over 100 in all, each ruled by its governor. And every province was divided into thousands of smaller districts, each rigidly responsible for producing its quota of taxes. No one was spared, not even the previously privileged citizens of Rome. To operate, the new system required a larger bureaucracy than the empire had ever seen, but it had to be created when finances were at their lowest ebb.

The emperor himself was of course the real center of power, who could make, break, or revise bureaucratic pyramids at will. Diocletian shrewdly aimed at strengthening this power by adopting methods which Persian and Babylonian rulers had already found successful in ruling empires. He appeared seldom in public, surrounding himself with aloofness and mystery. When he did appear, it was as a superior being, richly robed, gloriously crowned, and seated on a lofty throne, a true god-emperor. That such an appeal to superstition would succeed suggests how greatly the population of the empire had changed from the days of the republic and early empire.

The Emperor Diocletian, as shown on a bronze denarius minted during his reign. He chose to appear holding an olive branch (for peace) and a scroll (for law).

Lowie Museum of Anthropology, University of California, Berkeley. Photo John Bridgman

Near Eastern peoples and barbarians had become more important than Italians and Greeks.

To make sure that the new governmental machine worked, Diocletian converted the empire into a vast military camp, in which everyone was under orders. No soldier might leave the army; no farmer might leave his land; no townsman might leave his profession or trade. Every son must follow his father's occupation. In towns and cities, civic duties became cumpulsory. The price of literally everything, down to a dozen eggs and a pound of cheese, was fixed by imperial decree. The penalty for violating any of these regulations was conveniently uniform: death. Diocletian's idea of enabling the dying empire to fight for what was left of its life was to freeze it, like a block of ice.

Diocletian assumed that the new structure would operate only if it had divine approval. He suspected that the gods had for some time been angered by the toleration of strange religions. First he conducted one more ruthless suppression of the Christians. Then he ordered everyone in the empire to sacrifice to the ancient gods. It was a little like universal compulsory inoculation.

Last of all, Diocletian, always the soldier, gave himself an avenue of retreat. On the coast of Dalmatia, where he was born, he commanded the erection of a palace fortified with walls and towers to withstand a long siege, and so big that today its ruins enclose the entire modern town of Spolato (Yugoslavia). There he retired, in 305, leaving the empire to a successor, and peacefully lived out the last nine years of his life, raising vegetables (as he wrote to a friend) with his own hands.

Some of Diocletian's "reforms" were ineffective. His attempts to stabilize the position of the emperor, and to ensure orderly succession, were short-lived. His financial policies did not work; even the threat of death could not fix prices or make farmers produce taxes from worn-out land. And the Christian religion was too vital, too comforting to the desperately unhappy masses, to be killed by a law. But his changes in organization had a lasting effect on the history of Europe. In the military "*pyramid*" lay the beginnings of the medieval feudal system, the Roman *duces* and *comites* eventually becoming *dukes* and *counts*. And from the civil "pyramid" later developed the structure of the medieval Catholic Church.

Fragment of a colossal statue of the Emperor Constantine, which must have been at least 40 ft high, erected in Rome during his reign. Few works of art could better convey the dismal condition of the late Roman empire than this vulgarly huge statue with its mediocre workmanship and its vacant, lifeless stare.

Alinari-Art Reference Bureau, Inc.

Constantine

In spite of all Diocletian could do to prevent it, civil war sprang up after he abdicated. Not until 319 did a new man, Constantine, after overcoming five other men on various battlefields, get a firm hold on the empire. Once he had attained this hold, he achieved three things that shaped Europe's future.

As we have already seen, he raised Christianity to the dignity of a state religion. And thereupon he discovered a new tangle of problems. He found the leaders of the Christian religion debating intensely among themselves as to the exact relation of Jesus the Christ to God the Father. To settle such debates, Constantine called a great conference of these leaders, at Nicea, where the differences were temporarily settled, thanks in part to the emperor's awe-inspiring presence.

Next, Constantine solved one of the empire's most serious problems, that of getting plenty of metal coin back into circulation. Barbarian looters had carried off a great deal. Shipwrecks had lost some. Great sums had been shipped to India and China in exchange for luxuries. Much had been protected from looting by hiding and hoarding. Constantine's remedy was to seize what hoarded gold was available and not privately owned. These hoards lay in the sacred temple treasuries and sheated many images of the pagan gods, who were now no longer the official gods of the empire. The store of precious metal thus confiscated was melted down and issued as a new coin, the gold *solidus*, worth about $5.50 today. This did not restore fertility to worn-out soil. But the money shortage was eased, and the solidus remained the standard coin for centuries.

Last, to honor the new religion and to give the empire a new administrative center, Constantine founded a second capital (a New Rome, as it was sometimes called) named Constantinople (from the Greek, meaning Constantine's city). He ordered it built at the mouth of the Black Sea, on the site of the ancient Greek colony-city of Byzantium. Here Constantine erected a palace, administrative offices, and a number of splendid places for the worship of God in a Christian manner. He enriched the city by collecting in it some of the most glorious works of art from other parts of the empire. He even commanded the great statue of Athena by Pheidias to be removed from the Parthenon and set up in one of Constantinople's forums.

A gold Solidus, struck about 150 years after Constantine's death. On one side the emperor Valentinian is shown. On the other the city of Constantinople sits on a lion-headed throne, her right foot resting on a ship's prow.

Collection of Mr. Ed Gans, Berkeley

The End of the Story

After Constantine, the struggle to hold the empire together became steadily more and more desperate. At length, in 370, two brothers, Valentinian and Valens, agreed to divide the empire between them, one taking Rome as the capital of what he called the Empire of the West, and the other ruling the Empire of the East from Constantinople. The official language of the former was Latin, and of the latter, Greek.

The Empire of the West, under constant pressure from barbarians moving westward across the Rhine, steadily declined in strength. Barbarian tribes were actually allowed to settle within its borders, and their fierce chieftains were allowed to call themselves kings. Within these borders the Roman sense of government and style of life became more and more diluted, finally to sink out of sight in 476, when Rome was taken by barbarians and sacked, and the last pathetic weakling of a Western emperor abdicated.

But the Empire of the East moved in an opposite course. Its strength for a time increased. Constantinople was to remain a world center of government, culture, and religion for another 1000 years. Its history, therefore, is part of a new age.

One final act, however, belongs in the era we are leaving. In 530, Justinian, Emperor of the East, commanded the most seasoned legal experts in Constantinople to make a study of the mass of court decisions and legal opinions which had been collected during Rome's previous 1000 years of history. He desired them to reduce this legal mass to a simplified, briefer statement which would convey the substance and spirit of Roman law. A committee of 17 men under the leadership of the great jurist Tribonian set to work and in three years produced a legal masterpiece, a summary or *digest* of Roman law to which judges, lawyers, and lawmakers could refer. The Digest of Justinian, as it was called, was the last flower on the tree of Roman creative power, a dower which had spent itself on government and lawmaking. The Digest was the summary of an era, and in a way its epitaph. And it had a profound influence on the future of Europe, whose laws to this day acknowledge a Roman origin.

The Romans: A Summary Appraisal

The outstanding successes for which the Greeks are remembered were all won at the cost of different kinds of human exploitation. The Athenian democracy, built with imaginative thought and effort, required citizens free to exert such effort. This freedom existed in part because the citizens owned slaves, who could be relied upon to run farms and trades in the masters' absence. The crowning symbol of all Hellenic culture, the Parthenon, could be erected in all its exquisite perfection only because Athens seized the treasury of a league of over a hundred cities, appropriating it to her own use. Another, totally different, Greek state to win lasting fame, Sparta, achieved her military supremacy through her cruel domination of neighboring city-states, who were compelled to feed and clothe their Spartan lords, thus freeing them for statesmanship and battle practice. Finally, the Hellenistic kingdoms founded by Greeks in Asia were based on heavy taxation of conquered peoples, the proceeds going into wars of aggression, spectacular public buildings, and the personal extravagances of rulers.

Personified image of one of the Roman provinces, under the empire.

Alinari-Art Reference Bureau, Inc.

The Romans carried these forms of exploitation to a greater extreme on a vaster scale. Through the wholesale enslavement of some conquered cities' populations and the taxation and ravaging of others, they concentrated at Rome enough wealth and manpower to feed and bathe a large city population, launch colossal building programs, defray the monstrous extravagances of emperors, and finance insanely bloody power struggles between would-be heads of state. This endless milking of many provinces to enrich one city and its power elite gradually produced a living desert, in places, of human beings starved by overtaxation, and land starved by overproduction. The physical state of the empire in its final centuries was mirrored by its cultural state. Except for a few immense structures, such as baths and basilicas erected at an emperor's command, creation in art, literature, music, science, higher mathematics, and all those activities that spring from an inspired mind and spirit was nonexistent. It was one of the most dismally sterile periods in history.

But this is only one aspect of the Roman story. Roman history can be looked on as a long series of creative experiments in government, applied to political groups of different sizes: first a single town, then all Italy, and finally the entire Mediterranean basin plus western Europe and the Near East. The experiments were perhaps most successful at their earliest, when applied to the smallest political group of all, Rome itself. The larger the area over which Rome exerted her governing will, the more she allowed herself to resort to warfare, resulting in the death and demoralization of the very citizens for whose well-being the state was supposed to exist. Other areas of Roman creation were in a sense the handmaidens and supporters of her political interest. These supporting activities were military organization, structural engineering, architecture, city planning, and oratory.

The Roman legion and its modes of warfare, both of movement and position, were logical developments from Greek discoveries in these fields, and were supremely effective (when properly generaled) until new developments made them in their turn obsolete. When horse breeders succeeded in developing horses big enough and strong enough to carry a heavily armed man, and cavalry experts had developed the effective management of such heavy troops, the infantry legion could no longer withstand a cavalry charge. From then on the roles were reversed. Infantry was to remain of secondary importance until a new deadliness of firepower, in the fifteenth century, enabled it once more to come into its own.

Roman structural engineering relied chiefly on a bold, practical use of arch construction. The arch was known to Mesopotamians, Egyptians, Greeks, and Etruscans. But the Roman use of it, not only as an arch but in barrel vaulting, groined vaulting, and domes, was unprecedented for scale and wide application. Through the use of arch construction, Romans were able to span great areas of 100 feet and more, to build bridges, aqueducts, palaces, baths, and temples such as the world had not seen. In all such work they had to rely on trial and error alone, and on the customs thus slowly and painfully developed. No scientific methods for the testing of structures and materials were known, nor would they be until the time of Galileo and later . . . When it came to erecting such structures with elegance of proportion and refined taste, Roman architects seem sometimes to have proved themselves the rivals of the Greeks. Perhaps many were actually of Greek ancestry. But architects of the Roman empire had heavier tasks to face than had those of the Greek city-states, and greater resources of wealth and slave-power with which to work. In North Africa, Gaul and Germany whole cities had to be laid out-each complete with forums, temples, theaters, baths, basilicas and gymnasi, ums, plus the pattern of surrounding streets. At Rome itself the great public structures were often oppressive in their size, thanks to the ambitions and wealth of the emperors. The arrangement of groups of buildings was often bilaterally symmetrical, a ponderously impressive symbol of Roman imperial power. In contrast Greek arrangement had often been refreshingly asymmetrical.

Photo German Archeological Institute, Rome

A Roman aqueduct leading to the city of Segovia, Spain, still intact after 1800 years.

Roman oratory, still one more Roman child of a Greek father, was indispensible to Roman political life.

Romans and later Hellenistic Greeks seem to have been alike in their apathy toward mechanical invention. The cause seems to have been a disdain for manual labor, that is, slave labor. The practice of slavery thus laid its dead hand on human inventiveness, as well, of course, as on human sympathy. This hand was not to be lifted until a new age brought some small advances in mutual human respect, or until the population had shrunk to such a degree that labor-saving devices such as water-driven mills became desirable.

Archeological Survey of India, Government of India

Buddhist stupa, *or shrine, at Sanchi, central India, believed erected during the reign of Asoka, third century* B.C. *Pilgrims visiting the sacred spot entered one gate and made a slow counter clockwise circuit.*

THE GREAT HINDU EMPIRES

While Rome was growing from a tiny republican city-state to become the master of Italy, and on to a Mediterranean empire, India's own first great empire was rising, spreading downward over nearly the whole subcontinent, then disintegrating, to be followed by others, no two with the same boundaries. Between 322 B.C. and 647 A.D., three such empires thus emerged, each the work of a single conqueror, each ably continued by one or more successors, and each at last falling apart. All three empires started in the north. Here the rulers would make their realm secure before facing the task of fighting southward through rough mountainous country into middle India, called the Deccan, lying between the Narbada and Kistna Rivers. The southern tip of India, where the peoples who spoke Tamil lived in the mountains, was the hardest of all to conquer. In these exploits large armies seem to have been involved—foot soldiers in ten thousands, cavalry in thousands, and war elephants in hundreds.

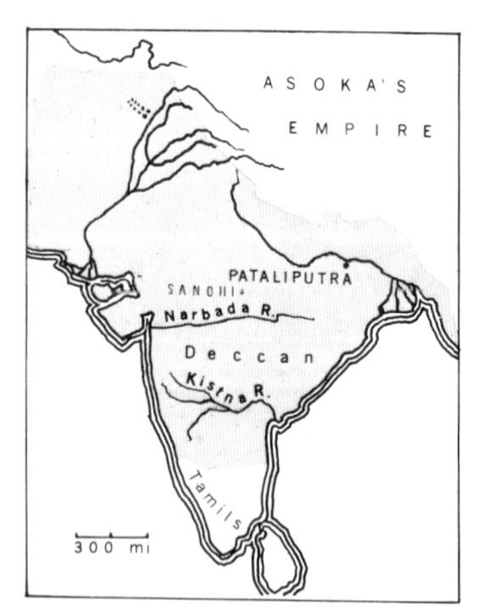

Asoka's Empire, Third Century B.C.

The first of these empires, founded in 322 B.C. and successively enlarged by three men, father, son, and grandson, endured for over a century. Its capital was Pataliputra, the modern Patna, overlooking the Ganges. As an empire it was remarkable for two reasons: it was the largest of all the early Hindu empires; and one of its emperors, or *Maharajas*, was perhaps the most enlightened ruler the world has ever seen.

Asoka came to power in about 273 B.C. He inherited from his father the whole of northern India and part of modern Afghanistan. Starting out as a conqueror, he added land southward by force of arms until all but the land of the Tamils was his. The war was a bloody one. The effect on Asoka was profound. Already a devout Hindu, he became converted to Buddhism and for the rest of his forty year reign resolved to govern according to the Law of Dharma, or rule of earthly conduct, as laid down by the Buddha.

Following a Persian custom (which they, in turn, had learned from the great Mesopotamian kings), he caused his laws to be carved in stone in many places throughout his vast empire, where some still exist to this day. They are remarkable because they are more than laws. Some are earnest instructions in personal conduct; some are records of what Asoka did. They were intended, apparently, as an example to his subjects:

> Everywhere has His Sacred and Gracious Majesty the King made two kinds of curative arrangements, to wit, curative arrangements for men and curative arrangements for beasts. Medicinal herbs also, medicinal for man and . . . beast, wherever they are lacking, have been imported and planted; roots also and fruits, wherever they are lacking, everywhere have been imported and planted. On the roads both wells have been dug and trees planted for the enjoyment of man and beast.[18]

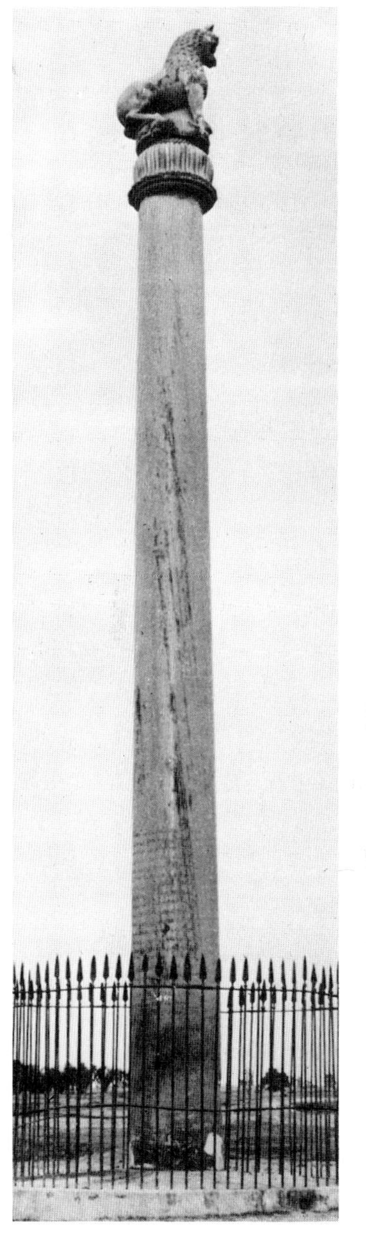

Archeological Survey of India, Government of India

An edict column of Asoka still standing after 1700 years.

Thus did Asoka uphold the Buddhist rule of unfailing kindness to all living things, whether human or animal. In Europe and the United States the humane treatment of animals was ignored until the late nineteenth century.

To make his policies consistent, Asoka abandoned the royal sport of hunting, discouraged all primitive forms of animal sacrifice, and enforced the kind treatment even of criminals. But perhaps his most remarkable reforms were in international relations. He gave up completely the usual aggressiveness of Hindu rajas (and kings all over the world) toward their neighbors. In his first edict he expressed the wish "that the unsubdued borderlands should not fear me, that they should trust me and should receive from me happiness, not sorrow."

Although completely tolerant of all men's beliefs, Asoka believed in the positive spreading of the Buddha's teachings. He called a second council of Buddhist monks at his capital city of Pataliputra to clarify once more the substance of those teachings, for the Buddha had died well over two centuries earlier. Then he encouraged the sending of missionaries not only throughout India but into foreign lands, even the Levant, Egypt, and Hellas. We have no record of how these missionaries fared in the west. But they seem to have had great success in southern India, Ceylon, and Burma. In a later age when the Brahmans attacked Buddhism in order to regain their prestige, and effectively caused its death in India, these outlying countries preserved it in its original form, as they do to this day.

Archeological Survey of India

Cave-temple interior at Karli, near Bombay, hewn from solid rock. Early Buddhists never represented the Buddha by an image. His role was simply that of an enlightened teacher. The placing of a stupa within a temple, as here, was the first step toward worship of the Buddha as a divine being. This temple was completed 80 B.C., *midway between the reigns of Asoka and Kanishka.*

ART IN ASOKA'S REIGN

Asoka gave a strong impulse to Indian art. In order to provide a physical object which would somehow symbolize the Buddha's teachings, he encouraged the building of *stupas.* A stupa is a shrine, a large mound, sometimes containing a relic of the Buddha, perhaps a lock of hair or a bone. Its shape is intended to resemble a bubble, as a reminder that all things in this world are short-lived. It is crowned with an umbrella, a symbol of royalty in hot countries, as a further reminder that the Law of Dharma, as the Buddha defined it, rules supreme in human life. Stupas were not intended as objects of worship, but as reminders to mankind of the necessity of following Buddhist practices to attain spiritual freedom. In the course of time, however, superstition began to have its way. People began to look on the Buddha as a divine being, and on his relics as having miraculous power.

In later invasions, especially by the Muslims, much Indian art of this period was destroyed. Nearly all that remains are some of Asoka's edicts beautifully carved on columns of hard stone, some stupas with their stone gateways, and some astonishing cave-temples carved into solid rock.

PESHAWAR
Khyber Pass
KANISHKA'S EMPIRE
MATHURA
300 mi

Kanishka's Empire, Second Century A.D.

The next great Indian empire to arise was in the northwest, with its capital at Peshawar, on one of the branches of the Indus River. It took form under invaders, a primitive tribal people known as the Kushanas, who came down through the Khyber Pass from the north in the first century A.D. and swept over the Greek kingdom of Bactria which at this time covered the Indus plain. This was one more of those waves of roving peoples from northern Asia which at intervals burst in upon the eastern and western civilizations. In the course of time Kushana chiefs became kings, and the son of one of these, Kanishka, is believed to have carved out a large empire in northwest India and the Deccan beginning in about 120 A.D.

Gai Collection, Peshawar

The Buddha image evolves into that of a divine being. Left: A statue of the second century A.D., from Ghandara, northwest India, shows strong Hellenistic and Roman influence. The pose suggests a Roman orator; the robe is draped like a toga; the hair is worn in something like a late Roman style, as shown in the small picture below (but the halo is of Persian origin). Right: A fourth century statue from Mathura, 500 miles east of Ghandara, shows how Indians have transformed the image. The gaze has become completely remote and inward. Folds of the robe have become an abstract design in dynamic rhythm. Body proportions have been slightly changed to fit an ideal rather than human standard (described on page 249).

Archeological Survey of India, Government of India

THE RISE OF MAHAYANA BUDDHISM

The facts of Kanishka's rule and personal life are vague. It seems that he too was converted to Buddhism and did much to encourage its spread, even issuing gold coins bearing the Buddha's likeness. But by this time Buddhism had undergone a gradual change to suit people's craving for a religion. The Buddha had been converted into a divine savior of mankind, who, it was claimed, had willingly given up *Nirvana*, or an existence completely outside the Wheel of Karma, in order once more to enter a human body and show mankind the path to freedom. It was also believed that by his act of winning freedom for himself he had made that path easier for others to travel—a comforting thought to those who found his instructions hard to obey.

Roman relief, empire period.

From this belief other comfortable ones easily followed. Since the Buddha was a divine being who had responded to human need once, he must surely be ready to do so again. Temples containing his image were erected to him. Here he was worshiped somewhat like a Hindu god; gifts and incense were offered to him in the hope that worship could thus interest him in granting favors. Of the many forms of Buddhism which now began to blossom, all had the central characteristic of looking on the Buddha as divine. Thus came into being what is called *Mahayana* (literally "great vehicle") *Buddhism.* It was a far cry from the simple, austere form of personal self-discipline which Gautama had left behind him, and which came to be called *Hinayana* ("lesser vehicle") *Buddhism.* When his teachings spread eastward through China and on to Japan, they were to do so altered into the Mahayana form.

Since the empire of Kanishka contained the former Greek kingdom of Bactria, many Greeks still lived there, and their influence seems to have been strong. It was made stronger by overland connections, by long caravan routes across Persia to the Levant, and by sea routes which merchants had discovered across the Indian Ocean. For centuries traders had made the long, cautious voyage along that ocean's coast, always in sight of land, carrying silk, pearls, and pepper to the ports of south Arabia. The Arabs would buy these luxuries for gold, then carry them up the Red Sea for resale to the lords of the Greek and Roman world. But daring Greek navigators discovered that they could sail down the Red Sea, bypass the Arabian ports, and at the right time of year sail directly across the Indian Ocean before a prevailing wind, returning later when the wind reversed. Thus grew up a luxury trade between the two empires, Roman and Indian, of Indian silk and pearls in exchange for Roman gold. Greek artisans must also have made the journey, by sea or land. So we must conclude from the scattered remains of buildings, sculpture, bronzework, and even jewelry from the place and time of Kanishka's empire. Everywhere they show a style sometimes Hellenistic, sometimes Roman. The first statues of the Buddha created within this empire, during the second century, are draped in a garment like a Roman toga.

This Greco-Roman sacred sculpture had its strong effect on Indian artists. Rather than tamely copying it, they seem to have recognized in it the presence of a culture alien to their own, and they did not rest until they had subdued it and made it over to express their own feeling.

The Empire of the Guptas, Fourth to Seventh Centuries A.D.

India's third great empire seems to have risen out of the confusion following the Kushana empire's collapse. Beginning in 320 A.D. a succession of strong maharajas, each with a name ending in -gupta (meaning *protected*), forged a strong empire out of the Indus-Ganges valley and then conquered the Deccan, returning the land to its ancient traditions before the time of the foreign invasions. The capital was once more Pataliputra on the Ganges.

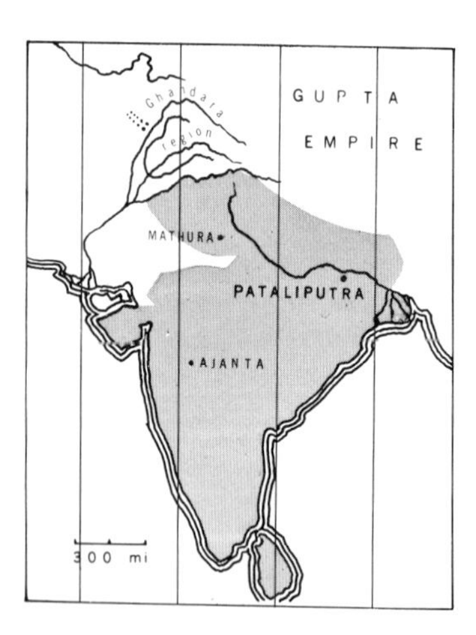

This empire was a final flowering of Hindu civilization, a period of great elegance and refinement, in spirit something like that of aristocratic Europe in the eighteenth century, even though of a remotely different civilization. In this age lived Kalidasa, India's most renowned poet and one of the world's great dramatists. The painting of the period is preserved on the walls of rock-hewn temples at Ajanta in central India, its sculpture in fragments from many places.

It was a time in which all past influences, whether foreign or local, became fused and remade into a single thoroughly Hindu civilization. Of the host of Hindu gods, three had become favorites: Brahma, god of creation; Vishnu, god of preservation; and Siva, god of destruction. And of these Vishnu and

Siva had become the most popular of all, some people preferring one, some the other. The Buddha, now converted into a god, was worshiped on an equal footing, and, like Vishnu and Siva, had his own temples. Indian artists had welded the Greek, Roman, and Persian influences into an art-form of their own, true to a strictly Indian spirit.

Late in the fifth century A.D. this great empire suffered from yet one more invasion through the mountain passes of the northwest, seemingly from the very same Huns, northern barbarian horsemen who were at the same time overrunning the Western Roman Empire, 4000 miles further west. In India the Huns seem to have gained a foothold for only about 70 years before they were defeated. But the power of the great Gupta dynasty had by that time become a thing of the past, and for the next centuries was succeeded by lesser dynasties, ruling lesser realms.

ART IN THE GUPTA EMPIRE AND AFTER. Whereas the Greeks considered the world's supreme example of beauty to be the human body, the Hindu artist regarded man simply as one of the many marvelous forms of nature: human, animal, and plant. And whereas the Greek artist, when he created an ideal form to represent a god, brought together the best he could find from many human beings, the Hindu went further and *sought to represent a god by assembling in one work of art beautiful form drawn from many places in nature.*

Thus in creating a statue or painting of the Buddha a tradition grew up which governed the shaping of various parts of his body. His hips were to suggest the slim loins of a lion and his shoulders the broad forehead of an elephant. His head must be broadened, approaching a sphere, but with the smoothness of an egg. His lips were to suggest the fullness of the ripe mango, his eyelids lotus-petals, and his brow the curve of Siva's bow. The proportions of the body were determined by exact rules of measurement, probably learned from the Greeks but altered and interpreted to fit mystical meanings.

Out of this collection of natural forms and arithmetical measurements, a formula was developed which was to influence images of the Buddha down to the present day. The poses in which he was displayed were few, either standing, or seated with the legs locked as if practicing Yoga. The hands sometimes suggest preaching, sometimes blessing, sometimes meditation. The eyes indicate intense inward-turned concentration, the means by which the Buddha had overcome the world of pain by escaping from it into Nirvana.

Each Hindu god was conceived in a different way, each a composite of many aspects of nature, and it was the artist's task to assemble these in a single image. But a mere patchwork was not enough. *The artist was expected to penetrate past the forms to the spirit of the god of which they were merely a suggestion, to become one with that spirit, and to create only on the basis of that experience.* Through the practice of Dhyana, a form of Yoga described on page 194, he was expected to focus on the nature of a particular god until he had attained a state of *samadhi,* and to use this experience of being mentally one with the god himself as a starting point for creating his image. It is perhaps this practice which gives remarkable power to the best Hindu and Buddhist religious art.

Opposite page, top: Reconstruction of a small Hindu temple, built in about the ninth century A.D. in western India (province of Gujarat). It has a mountainous form over the sacred chamber, has an ample porch in front, and stands on a high platform with complex molding. Originally it was richly encrusted with jewels. Rulers and people alike contributed to its building, and the construction was carried out by craftsmen's guilds under the direction of master masons.

At the same time, in the Hindu treatises on art which are preserved we find repeatedly the requirement that the artist be familiar with the principles of the dance. In India dancing was much more than a recreation. It was believed (and still is) to represent the rhythmic motion which maintains the harmony of the universe. Dance thus became a form of worship. Every important Hindu temple had not only its staff of Brahmin priests but a corps of dancers and an orchestra. And it was assumed that unless an artist had made the harmonious grace of the dance physically a part of himself he would be unable to import harmony to his creations.

HINDU TEMPLE ARCHITECTURE. The men who designed Hindu temples during the Gupta empire and for the following centuries are believed to have gained certain basic concepts from Hellenistic and Roman architects who came to India by way of the Greek kingdom of Bactria. In both West and East, builders chose the site and orientation of each temple according to rules governed by religion and magic. And in East and West alike they used geometry as a sacred device, mirroring the thinking of the gods themselves, in shaping the dwelling places of the gods on earth. For the Hindus, like the Greeks and Romans, looked on a temple as such a dwelling, rather than as a place for people to worship in. Each was a holy chamber (called *cella* in the West, *garbha griha* in India), before which was a porch, and the whole was raised on a platform mounted by steps. This basic form seems to have been Greek-inspired.

So much for the likenesses. The vast differences reveal how completely the same basic plans can be transformed by different cultures in pursuit of differing ideals. A typical Greek temple housed the god-protector of a city-state whose people looked on the logical clarity of the temple structure as just one aspect of the same clarity which ordered their own city government, its laws, and its relations with other city-states. It was set in a usually rather austere landscape, in which the greatest height (some 8000 feet) is Mount Olympus.

The Hindu temple, by contrast, seeks to interpret and bring order into a world of bewildering variety, vast distances, and incredibly towering heights. Each is an image of the universe as seen through spiritual eyes, represented as a mountain rising in ordered and complex stages to a peak which at one and the same time presses *against* heaven and is a door through which the human spirit may be released *into* it. Originally they seem to have been snowy white like the Himalaya peaks which inspired them, though today only the stone color remains. Without and within, the temples rise in a multitude of layers or strata suggesting the multitude of Indian social castes, and the layers swarm with dynamic figures, monsters and beasts on the lower levels, human beings higher up, and the gods (sometimes many gods, sometimes many aspects of the same god) higher still, the great mountainous form of the temple dominating all.

Opposite page, bottom: Hindu temples at Pattadkal, India. The large one, left background, is dedicated to the god Siva. The smaller one, right foreground, is for Nandi, the sacred bull who carries him on his travels (that is, symbolizes his power to travel throughout the universe).

The complex geometric principles governing the construction of these temples was refined over the course of centuries. But whereas in the West Vitruvius alone preserved an imperfect record of Greek and Roman principles, in India several manuals for temple construction, known as *shastras*, have been carefully preserved right down to the present day.

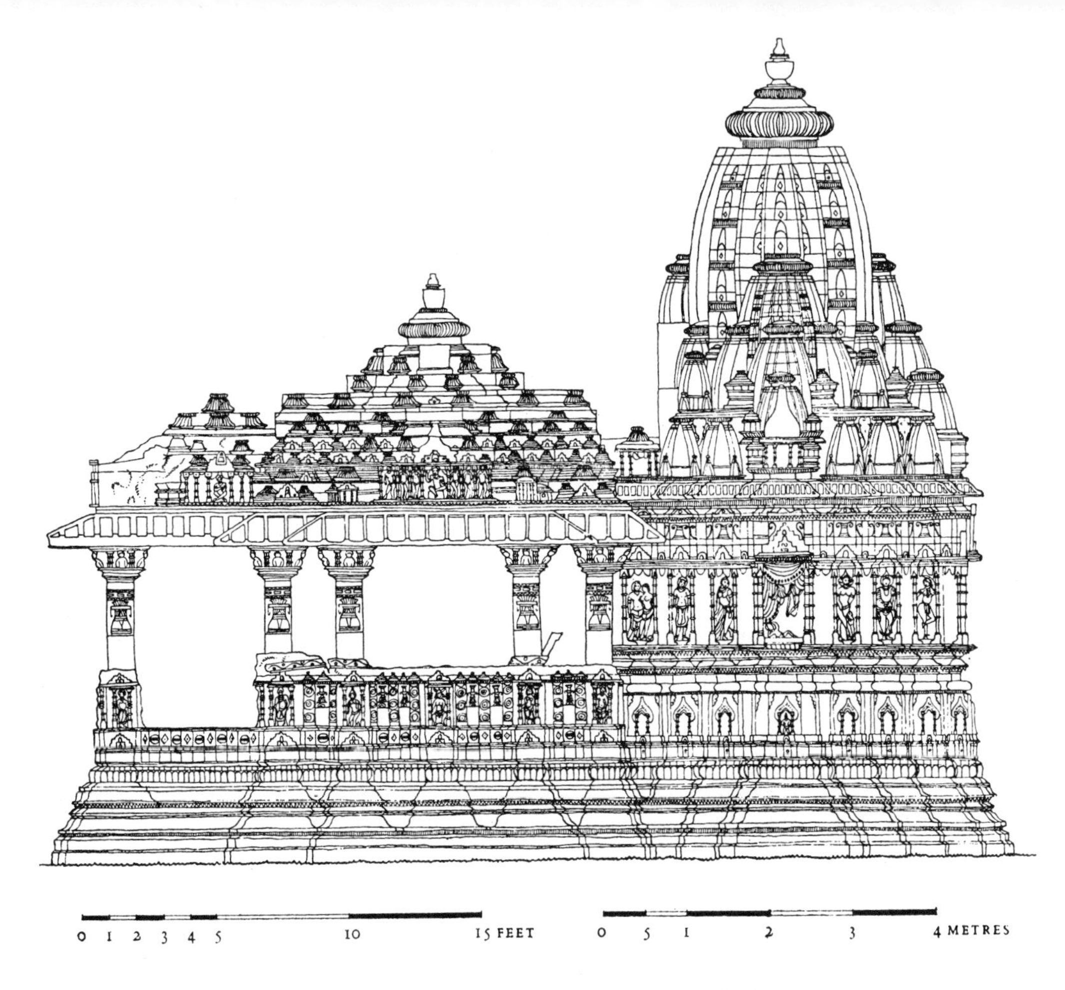

Archeological Survey of India, Government of India

The Great Wall of China, a marvel of human labor and engineering, which was once effective in stopping nomad invasions from the north. Its remains can still be followed along 1500 miles of China's northern borders.

THE FOUNDING OF THE CHINESE EMPIRE

The land mass of China dwarfs that of India. Its total extent is 4,000,000 square miles. From the great curve of its Pacific shore line the country mounts slowly westward through broad coastal lowlands upward in great steps, higher and higher into mountains ever more rugged until these become part of the Himalayas and the plateau of Tibet, the highest land in the world. Northward from China lies desert and the endless grassland of what is today Siberia.

Most of this vast country lies farther north than India and is therefore cooler. But, like India, China's river valleys have been the centers of her civilization; the northernmost, the Hwang-Ho, was its starting point and its dynamic center. China's other great river, the Yangtze, sometimes called the Long River, divides the land into halves, each with its own character. North

Avery Brundage Collection, San Francisco. Photo John Bridgman

This austerely elegant ceremonial disc of jade, a symbol of the perfection of Heaven, was carved during one of China's most terrible periods of civic upheaval, known as the Warring States.

China is the land of crops such as millet, barley, and wheat. South China is a semitropical land of rice, a crop with a heavy yield of grain, but laborious to raise. Its seedlings must be transplanted, and since it was originally a marsh grass, it must spend its growth period with roots under water. South China is also the home of tea, which the northern Chinese learned to enjoy only after centuries.

We have already seen in Chapter 3 how, in about 1500 B.C., men of a family called Shang founded a small kingdom in northern China near the meeting of two rivers, the Wei and the Hwang-Ho, and that this kingdom lasted for about 500 years. Let us now see how, from these small beginnings, one of the world's most remarkable civilizations took permanent form.

Like many another society when it masters the raising of food, or farming, the people of the Shang kingdom seem to have undergone a population explosion. They began to push outward north, west, and south, converting forest and wasteland into farms. This was a pioneering time, a time of battle against untamed nature and against primitive tribes fighting to save their hunting grounds from invasion by farmers. It bred ever growing multitudes of people toughened by work and fighting, who, as they spread outward over more and more of northeastern China, began to lose touch with each other and with the center of government, An-Yang, the royal city of the Shangs. At the same time the Shang kings seem to have been undergoing a change which was to repeat itself time and again in Chinese history. Court life was converting them from strong rulers to soft lovers of luxury, who still retained a

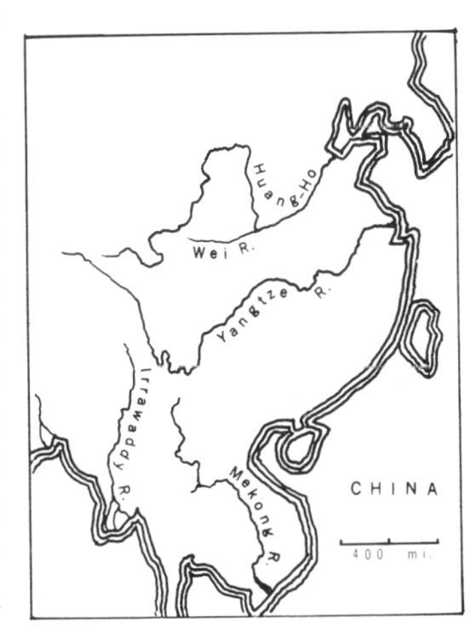

Opposite page, top: The Tae-kei, *traditional Chinese symbol of the Tao, containing Yang and Yin, opposites yet eternally independent. The dot in each symbolizes that each springs from the other. Center: The Pa-kua, eight symbols for the interaction between male and female elements in the universe, represented by an unbroken bar and a broken one. They stand for eight aspects of nature, eight points of the compass, and have philosophical meanings as well. We see here the Chinese love of many interpretations clustered in a single symbol. Bottom: Tae-kei and Pa-kua combined in a symmetrical symbol of the universe, the forces at work in it, and its main directions.*

trait of many Chinese rulers, enormous cruelty. While the outer parts of the expanding kingdom grew in rugged strength, its heart and nerve center was turning soft and treacherous. It is not surprising that the outlying areas became semi-independent under leaders of their own, and that one of these finally turned on the last Shang ruler, forced his suicide, and founded a new dynasty, that of Chou (pronounced Jo), which ruled a much expanded kingdom. The date is believed to have been 1027 B.C. See the map, page 126.

The period of nearly 800 years that followed has been recorded in detail, like the rest of Chinese history down to the present. As historians the Chinese have from early times been the complete opposite of the Hindus. The Chinese concern with eternity has been minor, but their interest in the events of this world has been permanently strong, and as historians Chinese scholars have been superb. Even the human soul, they have commonly believed, lives on after death only so long as a man's descendants on earth remember him as an ancestor and nourish his memory with respect.

The Realm of Chou, A Chinese Feudal Kingdom

The tangled 800 year period from 1027 to 246 B.C., that started with an era of elegance and chivalry and ended with wars of unbelievable brutality, is perhaps best regarded as China's school of self-organization. From the first the Chinese had shown remarkable gifts in technical discovery, art, and the life of the detached intellect. But their society was still close to the primitive state of tribal times, in which loyalty to clan, leadership by chiefs, and reliance on magic practiced by shamans was the way of life. How would such a remarkable people, spreading outward over ever vaster areas, transform such simple customs to meet new complex demands? How could they build an empire on the social foundations of a tribe? These were the problems which required eight centuries of invention, experiment, meditation by thinkers, and bloodshed by rulers to solve.

The founder of the Chou dynasty followed the logical course of dividing his new kingdom among the men who had been loyal to him in the fighting which overthrew the Shangs. He made them, in other words, into landowning nobles. Thus he established in his far-spreading kingdom nearly 1800 strong points of local government, On the land there were already peasants, descendants of the men who had first cleared the land. These became the vassals, almost the personal property, of the new noblemen. Thus came into being a *feudal society*,[19] in which a toiling lower stratum of peasant farmers supported and were in turn protected by a higher, smaller stratum of lords who in turn were bound in loyalty to obey the *Wang* or king and to supply him with tribute in time of peace and troops in war.

The person of the Wang had an awesome, sacred quality. He had the power and duty to perform every year certain ceremonies which would ensure, supposedly, the success of the crops and therefore the life of the kingdom. Every spring equinox, at his capital city, wearing the yellow robes of the Son of Heaven, as he was called, he opened the farming season with the solemn sacrifice of a red bull. Every fall equinox he celebrated its end with the sacrifice of another bull, this time black. Besides being a ruler he was a priest, or rather a supermagician whose spell-like rituals of sacrifice could bind the forces of weather and luck to man's will.

Yang, Yin, and Tao

The rhythmic division of the year in halves was one of many things into which the thoughtful Chinese read a pattern of opposites, dramatically contrasting, yet dependent on each other. One half, the vigorous farming season managed by men, was active and dominant. The other half of the year, in which the women's work of weaving took first place, seemed by comparison gentler and more passive. From such simple experiences as these the earliest Chinese thinkers developed *the dual principles of Yang and Yin*, which they imagined they could see at work in every occurrence, great or small, in the entire universe: day-night, warm-cold, wet-dry, sun-moon, man-woman, and so on. But above the vigorous, active principle of Yang and the gentle passive one of Yin they respected a still greater one, *the principle of their unity in eternal interaction*, called *Tao*.

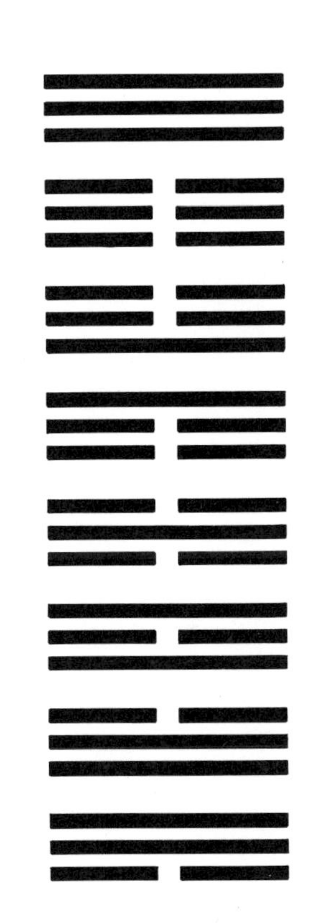

The magical ceremonies which the king practiced to ensure good crops were only one part of the formulas or *rites* which all Chinese were constantly practicing in order to win success or maintain harmony in their personal lives. Many of these rites were modes of behavior toward each other. The elaborate systems of courtesy and etiquette which the Chinese developed thus seem to have had an origin in superstition. To learn these systems was not merely a social grace; it was a magical necessity.

So elaborate were these codes surrounding the Wang that he required specialists (*scholars*) to advise him on proper conduct in a host of situations. Since some of these situations were bound to be new, the scholars came in time to act as counselors. They even relieved the king of administrative tasks. Thus seems to have grown up one of China's most remarkable institutions, a body of civil servants or *mandarins* who had successfully passed examinations in China's traditional literature, and whom the ruler employed to fill administrative posts. For good or ill the practice (revised, as we shall see, by Confucius) was to continue until 1912 A.D.

Technical Advances

The recording of literature required writing. The astonishing system of written Chinese has an unbroken history of over 3000 years. The Chinese writing tool is a pointed brush dipped in ink, which when it touches paper or silk can leave anything from a line as fine as a hair to a massive ribbon, depending on the writer's control and desire. Chinese writing has, visually, a wealth of variety and expressiveness unknown in the West.

Every Chinese word in represented by a complete symbol, or group of two or three symbols, each packed into a square. Of these symbol-squares, or *characters*, there are 40,000, of which a cultivated Chinese scholar was expected to know at least 10,000. The elegant beauty of each character, some simple, some complex, is such that merely to look at a page of them is a delight. Of this the Chinese have always been aware. One of their most respected arts is that of the *calligrapher*, who has studied the great styles of writing created in the past, has developed his own, and has left examples of his writing as masterpieces to be enjoyed by future generations. A Chinese landscape painting will often contain a poem, so placed as to balance the forms of the painting and to be enjoyed with it as a total work of art.

Drawings by Dean Snyder

The emperor Nan Sung Li-tsung, who ruled China for 40 years, 1224 to 1264, is believed to have composed this couplet of 10 characters, 5 to each line, and to have set it down in his own strong handwriting on this oval of silk. The gourd-shaped stamp, left, indicates imperial ownership. Other stamps are those of later owners. Translated word for word (right column first, top to bottom) the characters mean:

Autumn deep, clear reach bottom.
Rain pass, blue connect sky.

Mr. Charles E. Hamilton, who gave this information, also gives this free translation:

Deep in the autumn the water is clear to its depths.
Rain has passed, and the blue of the water joins that of the sky.

The emperor may have composed the poem to honor a landscape painted by one of his courtiers.

Calligraphy from the collection of John Crawford, New York

The Chinese language has a strong individuality; verbs have no tenses. As one reads the characters (from the top down or from right to left) one's mind receives a row of concrete meaning-images (no abstractions) which one must then connect and interpret. Chinese genius has created from such an unpromising device a language which can convey precise, subtle meaning, dramatic action, and profound thought.

While the Chinese were developing their written language, a number of other crafts, distinctively Chinese, were being perfected. Women had discovered methods of *spinning and weaving silk*. Men had discovered the process of lacquering. They had found that the sap of a local tree, a kind of sumac, could produce a waterproof, acidproof, heatproof surface capable of taking a high, lustrous polish. An object of wood or even paper, when properly coated with lacquer, thus could become an almost timelessly durable thing of beauty. The oldest lacquered wood cups and boxes that have so far been found have survived burial in damp soil for 2500 years. Still another craft which was to become typically Chinese was the carving of fine-grained, semiprecious stone—marble, crystal, and especially jade.

Grove surrounding the ancient tomb of Confucius. Two stone sages stand watch. Shantung Province, China.

Form the earliest times the Chinese looked on jade with reverence. Its beautiful color ranging from white through lettuce green to golden brown, its hardness combined with its fine texture suitable for carving, and the ringing musical sound which can be struck from thin slabs of it, all were marvels which moved them to call it the Stone of Heaven. The most sacred objects used in magical ceremonies were carved from it. And when the Chinese developed their five-tone musical scale, they played it on pieces of free-hanging jade, whose pitch never changed. Such were the beginnings from which the Chinese went on to create one prodigy after another over the ensuing centuries.

Confucius

Although the first rulers of the Chou dynasty were strong, the luxuries of court life slowly softened them into ineffectuality. The feudal lords, uncontrolled in the great sprawling land, began to turn on each other, the stronger forcing the weaker to submit to their rule. China became a cluster of small semikingdoms, whose number kept dwindling as the greater gobbled the lesser. Their rulers recognized the Wang for his ceremonial duties and little more.

For the superstitious concern for the magical value of correct practices was as strongly alive as ever. The new rulers of the many small kingdoms had to maintain their own practices of ancestor worship and etiquette. They needed the services of specialist scholars to counsel them on such matters. Experts in traditional customs were therefore in demand. So, also, were the teachers of such experts. It was from among this group of experts, and teachers of experts, that China's first and most influential men of thought arose.

Kungfu-tzeh,[20] whose westernized name is Confucius, lived between 550 and 480 B.C., a period surprisingly parallel to that of Gautama Buddha, 2000 miles away in India. His background was a proud one, for he belonged to the family of the Shangs. Brought up in the manner of a young nobleman, well trained in archery and in music (which he loved all his life), he married at 19, separated himself from family life at 23, and began to devote himself to scholarship, the study of China's literature, and the mastery of China's intricate codes of ceremonies.

He examined the written record of China's partially legendary history and prepared his own edition of it. He stressed the virtuous acts of past rulers, changing the record at times to create finer examples of kingly conduct than history could show. For in an age before rules for accurate scholarship had been invented, his intent was to hold up to men an inspiring ideal of conduct. From the great mass of over 3000 poems preserved from China's past, he selected about 300 which he believed had moral value and might, for example, soften the hearts of rulers toward the sorrows of their people. When it came to the complex codes of ceremonies and rites, he breathed life into them by stating that they were more than magical formulas, that they were the means for maintaining right relations between human beings, between the members of families, between the heads of families and the ruler, and between the ruler and Heaven. He laid endless stress on manners, courtesy, and self-control as devices for maintaining a frictionless society.

Confucius was deeply disturbed at the dog-eat-dog behavior of the men of his age. He was looking for a device for controlling such behavior, and he believed he had found it in the respect with which the Chinese held the written record of their past. But in his own age few of the many rulers trusted him; they had no interest in having their consciences awakened. At the age of 70, Confucius is reported to have said, "No intelligent ruler rises to take me as his master, and my time has come to die," and he wept.

But the younger generation found in him a mighty source of inspiration. They flocked to him to study. It was not as an expert, but as a teacher of experts, that Confucius triumphed. After his death his editions of the Chinese classics—history, poetry, and ceremonies—came into tremendous demand. They became the basis for the education of all scholars, and in the course of time for all civil servants. His insistence on formal family relations, on the supreme power of the head of the family, and on the secondary place of women, had the effect of freezing Chinese society in archaic patterns. His belief that his own class, the aristocrats, had privileges which the

The lid of a round lacquered box, from China of the late Chou dynasty. The brilliantly complex pattern of phoenixes, vigorous yet refined, indicates the high level of culture which the Chinese had already attained 2500 years ago.

common people did not, helped to make that society one of double standards. His grand examples of serene, peace-loving rulers drawn from the mythical past had a beneficial influence on some future emperors, though far from all.

Lao-tzeh

The opposite extreme to Confucius among Chinese men of thought was Lao Yang, called Lao-tzeh. Born about 20 years earlier, around 570 B.C., he too seems to have been a scholar. But instead of being rejected by the rulers of his day, Lao-tzeh rejected *them*. Sometime in his middle years, after long service as adviser in various kingdoms, he rose up in disgust, mounted his chariot drawn by black oxen, and drove off westward, toward China's still untamed wilderness. At the border the commander of a guardhouse respectfully asked him for a summary of his wisdom. Lao Yang paused long enough to set it down in 5000 words, then climbed into his chariot and went his way out of sight, never to be heard of again. The *Book of Tao* which he left with the officer has ever since been one of the guiding lights of Chinese thought.

Such is the legend. But just as the records about Confucius are clear and apparently accurate, so those clinging about the memory of Lao-tzeh are as indefinite as clouds. Students of literature have suggested that he may have been several men, writing years apart. All we can say is that the *Book of Tao* represents a single point of view, even if difficult to capture in words, which opposes Confucius' endless concern with public and personal relations.

Lao Yang's concern was with the inner man, not the outer; with the secret of finding deep in one's self the Tao, the unity which comes from the interacting of seemingly conflicting forces. Live thus, he said, and your outer relations will take care of themselves. The secret of successful living is to find harmony with the world of nature, rather than remake it to your will. Keep inwardly relaxed; refuse to be hungry for power.

> He who is on tiptoe does not stand;
> He who hurries does not walk;
> He who reveals himself is not luminous;
> He who justifies himself is not far-famed;
> He who boasts of himself is not given credit;
> He who prides himself is not chief among men.
> These in the eyes of Tao
> Are called the "dregs and tumors of Virtue,"
> Which are things of disgust.
> Therefore the man of Tao spurns them.
>
> Rather than jingle like the jade,
> Rumble like the rocks.
>
> Nothing is weaker than water,
> But nothing is stronger in conquering the hard . . .
> That weak overcomes strong
> And gentle overcomes rigid
> Everyone knows;
> No one can practice.

Lao-tzeh then applied this principle to the government of a kingdom.

> He who by Tao purposes to help a ruler of men
> Will oppose all conquest by force of arms.
> For such things are wont to rebound.
> Where armies are, thorns and brambles grow.
> The raising of a great host
> Is followed by a year of dearth.
>
> Therefore a good general effects his purpose and stops.
> He dares not rely upon the strength of arms;
> Effects his purpose and does not glory in it;
> Effects his purpose and does not boast of it;
> Effects his purpose as a regrettable necessity;
> Effects his purpose but does not love violence.
> Things age after reaching their prime . . .
> And he who is against the Tao perishes young.[21]

In the following centuries more than one emperor was to be driven to fury by scholarly mandarins quoting to him lines such as these.

Shih-Hwang-ti, China's First Emperor

For all their influence on later ages, Confucius and Lao-tzeh had scant effect on their own times. China was undergoing one of her darkest periods. The kingdoms kept devouring each other until they numbered only five (with the ringing names of Ch'in, Ch'u, Chao, Han, and Wei). Locked in

Avery Brundage Collection, San Francisco. Photo John Bridgman

Chinese warrior-ruler, of the kind who helped forge a new empire out of China's warring kingdoms and clans. This ceramic figure, 30 in. high, was made in the turbulent time between the Han and T'ang dynasties (200 to 600 A.D.).

a deadly struggle for survival, each victor seemed to feel secure only if he exterminated his defeated enemy. After each military success, heads rolled by the ten thousand. Chivalry was forgotten. To add to the country's woes, Huns from the northland, making the most of the confusion, came raiding southward and devastated great stretches of the northernmost kingdoms.

At last but two kingdoms remained, Ch'in and Chao. In the year 246 B.C. there came to the throne of Ch'in a boy of 13 who was destined to become China's first emperor. In 234 B.C., when he was 25, the last army of Chao was destroyed and he received from his generals a gift of 100,000 severed heads. This gift seemed fitting for a ruler described by an eyewitness as "a man with a prominent nose, large eyes, the chest of a bird of prey, the voice of a jackal, and the heart of a tiger or wolf."[22] Utterly ruthless, he

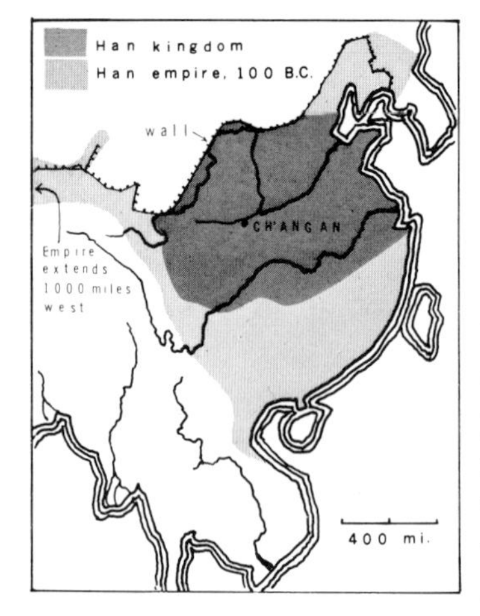

nevertheless knew how to govern. Before his death in 210 B.C., at the age of 49, he had given China a sense of unity which it was never again to lose. He bore the name and title of Ch'in Shih-Hwang-ti (literally First Emperor of Ch'in).

He pushed his armies south as far as Canton, opening up southern China and planting pioneering colonies who began the task of clearing its limitless forests for farming, a process which was to go on for centuries. He ordered laws, the calendar, weights, and measures to be standardized. He made the language uniform by enforcing everywhere the use of the same written characters. If any region insisted on its local ways, he transplanted the population wholesale. Exasperated by the conservative moralizing of Confucian mandarins and by their loyalty to the old feudal system, he marched them off to the north where, with thousands of other conscripted workers, they were worked to death or exhaustion erecting the Great Wall, 1500 miles of fortification intended to block forever the entry of northern nomads. He ordered all copies of Confucius' carefully edited works seized and burned. Henceforth, China was to be ruled by the emperor's will and the laws he chose to enact.

With the exception of his destruction of the writings of Confucius, Shih-Hwang-ti's reforms became permanent. After his death, when a new dynasty, that of Han, arose, one of its emperors more than made up for the burning. In the year 195 B.C. he ordered the remaining copies of Confucius' works brought out of hiding and restored to their position of authority. With solemn ceremonies he offered sacrifices to the memory of the great man, thus lifting him to the level of a god. With this act Confucianism became a state religion.

Two Great Dynasties, Han and T'ang

Based on a new security born of unity, the achievements of the Han dynasty were so glorious that for 1800 years, long after it had vanished, the Chinese proudly referred to themselves as "sons of Han." The emperors' armies marched westward, north of Tibet, all the way to the borders of the old Persian empire, thus opening the Silk Road, a caravan route connecting with the Near East and what was soon to become the Roman empire. After improving their native breed of horses and mastering the art of archery from horseback, the Chinese felt prepared to counterattack the ever threatening Huns, invaded their homeland, and smote them hip and thigh. At home peace reigned; the government was fair and efficient. The practice of educating future mandarins in the classics had been restored and was producing a remarkable body of civil servants, men of practical affairs who had been trained in the high standards of literary and musical taste which Confucius himself had possessed. Painting, once the profession of simple craftsmen, became an accomplishment expected of gentlemen.

Such a state could not last in China, where court life, with all its exquisite delights, eventually undermined the character of the imperial families. As the hold of the Han emperors weakened, venomous court intrigues sprouted, the administration of the land was neglected, the policing of the borders relaxed, and once more in poured invading nomads (this time a new people, ancestors of the Turks). Such was the Chinese pattern.

Ceramic sculpture representing a Chinese farmhouse of 2000 years ago. Han dynasty.

Avery Brundage Collection, San Francisco. Photo William Abbenseth

Avery Brundage Collection, San Francisco. Photo William Abbenseth

Dragon incised and painted on a long tile, white touched with red on a dark grey background. Han dynasty, 37 in. long.

The confusion that followed resembled the fate of the later Roman empire when generals fought for the right to the emperor's title. A whole series of short-lived dynasties came and went. Civil war raged until a victorious general gave himself the title of emperor T'ai-Tsung, founder of a new and long-lived dynasty, that of T'ang. The dynasties of Han (206 B.C.–221 A.D.) and T'ang (618–906 A.D.) were to be China's greatest.

NOTES

1 The Romans never entirely forgot that their families had once been grouped in clans. Every Roman of distinction had a middle name, supposedly his prehistoric clan name!

2 This was another case of Roman brinkmanship. General citizenship was granted only after much of Italy rose in revolt, with a loss of 300,000 lives.

3 The only attractive building stone found near Rome was a cream colored limestone, called *Travertine*, quarried at Tibur, five miles up the Tiber. This became popular after the Romans developed taste in building. Abandoned quarries at Tibur show that over 5,000,000 cubic feet were removed in Roman times.

4 From *Poems from the Greek Anthology*, translated by Kenneth Rexroth (Ann Arbor paperback, 1962), by permission of the translator.

5 These colonists later proved to be one of Rome's greatest strengths, even though far from home. In strategic places throughout the conquered lands they established towns and farming communities which were loyal to the mother city, and helped "Romanize" the surrounding aliens.

6 Sulla was a patrician; Marius was one of the plebs. The age-old split between classes had broken open again.

[7] For another side of Octavius' work in the advance of Roman culture, see Project 26.

[8] Immense wealth became centered in Rome, both in the public treasury and as private fortunes. In 20 B.C. Crassus, a real estate dealer specializing in Roman apartment buildings, had a fortune equal to $7,000,000. This was larger than the treasury of the entire Delian League, 400 years before, to which many Greek cities had contributed.

[9] Ulpia was derived from Trajan's family name.

[10] By some miracle this huge bronze object has been preserved. Today it stands in the Vatican gardens.

[11] Later Roman architects invented a fifth order: Composite, more fussily ornate than Corinthian.

[12] Except the most completely modern of all, such as Brazilia.

[13] Its construction is described by Vitruvius, Book X, Chapter 8, *On Architecture.*

[14] Some scholars now agree that the correct form of this Hebrew name may be Yahveh.

[15] Psalms 50:9, 12 and 51:6, 16, 17, King James version of the Bible.

[16] Matthew 5:9, 43, 44; 23:37, 38; 24:2, King James version of the Bible.

[17] *Christ*, or Christos, is a Greek word which can be translated as *Messiah* (Hebrew for *anointed*), and signifies one sent from God to rule the Earth.

[18] *The Edicts of Asoka*, V. A. Smith, ed. (Essex House, London, 1909), pp. 7, 8.

[19] Or a revision of an older one.

[20] The ending -tzeh, or -tzu, is a title of respect.

[21] Adapted from *The Book of Tao*, sections XXIV, XXXIX, LXXVIII, and XXX, as translated by Lin Yutang in *The Wisdom of China and India*, edited by him (Random House, New York, 1942).

[22] Quoted in *The Rise and Splendor of the Chinese Empire*, R. Grousset (University of California Press, 1962), p. 42.

BOOKS ON THE ETRUSCANS AND ROMANS

The Story of Civilization, W. and A. Durant (Simon and Schuster, New York). Vol. III: *Caesar and Christ; a history of Roman civilization and of Christianity from the beginnings to A.D. 325.*

The Etruscans, D. Bloch (Praeger paperback).

The Etruscans, Their Art and Civilization, E. H. Richardson (University of Chicago, Man and his Cultures Series).

Art of the Etruscans, M. Pallottino (Vanguard, New York, 1955).

Etruria and Early Rome, G. A. Marselli (Crown, Art of the World Series).

The Origins of Rome, D. Bloch (Praeger paperback).

The Civilization of Rome, D. R. Dudley (Mentor, MD308). A concise history.

The Birth of Western Civilization: Greece and Rome (McGraw-Hill, 1964). Beautiful and expensive.

Roman Architecture, F. E. Brown (Braziller, New York, 1961).

Roman Art and Architecture, M. Wheeler (Praeger World of Art Series, 1964).

Roman and Etruscan Painting, A. Stenico (Compass Books, CA).

Roman Painting, A. Maiuri (Skira Great Centuries of Painting Series).

Roman Art, G. M. Hanfmann (NY Graphic Society, Greenwich, Connecticut).

The Art of Rome and Her Empire, H. Kahler (Crown, Art of the World Series, 1963).

The Roman Cookery Book, for Use in Study and Kitchen, translated by B. Flower and E. Rosenbaum (Harrap, London, 1958).
Roman History from Coins, M. Grant (Cambridge, 1958).
The Roman Letter: A Study of Notable Graven and Written Forms from 20 Centuries, J. Hayes (Donnelly & Sons, Chicago, 1951–52); 54 pages, illustrated.
Roman Lettering: A Book of Alphabets and Inscriptions (Her Majesty's Stationery Office, London, 1958).
Roman Life, M. Johnson (Scott-Foresman, Chicago, 1957).
The Roman Legions, H. M. D. Parker (Barnes and Noble, New York, 1958).
The Roman Soldier: Some Illustrations Representative of Roman Military Life, A. Forestier (London, 1928).
The Roman Triumph, P. S. R. Payne (Abelard-Schuman, New York and London, 1962–63).
The Roman Mind at Work, P. McKendrick (Van Nostrand paperback No. 35). Particularly valuable for its collection of passages from Roman writers.
National Geographic Magazine, "Ancient Rome Brought to Life," November 1946, pp. 567–633, 32 color illustrations.
Pompeii and Herculaneum: The Glory and The Grief, M. Brion (Crown, New York; Elek Books, London, 1960).
The Art of Roman Gaul, M. Probé, photos J. Roukien (University of Toronto Press, 1961).
Art in Roman Britain, J. M. C. Toynbee (Phaidon, 1962); 260 illustrations.
Roman Art in Africa, M. Vilimkova (Paul Hamlyn, London, 1963).
Empire, R. Koebaer (Grosset & Dunlap, UL179).
Mithras, the Secret God, M. J. Vermasseren (Barnes & Noble).

FILM

Buried Cities (*Pompeii and Herculaneum*), color, sound, 14 minutes, International Film Bureau, Inc.

BOOKS ON INDIA

The Sources of Indian Tradition, ed. W. T. deBary (Columbia University Press, New York, 1958); 2 Vols., paperback.
A History of India, Volumes I and II, P. Spear (Penguin A770, 1965).
India, a Short Cultural History, H. G. Raulinson (Praeger paperback, 1937–1967).
Indian Mythology, Veronica Ions (Paul Hamlyn, London, 1967).
Indian Thought and Its Development, A. Schweitzer (Beacon Press paperback BP37, 1937–1967).
The Art of India, H. Goetz (Crown, New York, 1964).
The Art and Architecture of India, B. Rowland (Penguin Books, Inc., Baltimore, 1956).
The Hindu Temple, S. Kramrisch (University of Calcutta, 1946); 2 Vols.
The Dance in India, E. Bharnani (D. B. Taraporevala Son & Co., 210 Naoroji Road, Bombay 1, India).
The Dance in India, F. Bowers (AMS Press, Inc., New York).
The Upanishads, a One-Volume Abridgment, S. Nikhilananda (Harper Torchbook 114).
The Quest for Sita: Central Section of the Rāmāyana, retold by M. Collins (Capricorn 254).
The Bhagavad-Gītā, F. Edgerton (Harper Torchbook 115).
Teachings of the Compassionate Buddha, ed. E. A. Burtt (Mentor 884).
Mahayana Buddhism, A Short Outline, B. L. Suzuki (Collier paperback AS551, 1959–1963).

Colossal bronze statue of Heraclius, Emperor of the East from 610 to 641 A.D. This stern-faced ruler spent most of his reign driving back the enemies of the eastern Roman empire, chiefly the Persians. Shortly before his death, when he was worn out with the cares of governing, he learned that the Arabs, inspired by their great religious leader, Mohammed, were overrunning Egypt, the Levant and Mesopotamia, undoing years of war and diplomacy. Only the head, body and arms of this statue are original. The hands and legs are clumsy fifteenth-century restorations of lost parts. It stands in the Italian town of Barletta, on the Adriatic coast.

Alinari-Art Reference Bureau, Inc.

6 *THE WORLDS OF BYZANTIUM, ISLAM, AND CHARLEMAGNE*

In Arabia a Third World Religion Is Born.
Indian Civilization Spreads North and East

THE BYZANTINE WORLD

Constantinople

The Mediterranean Sea receives water from only four important rivers: the African Nile, the Spanish Ebro, the French Rhone, and the Italian Po. The sea loses water by evaporation from its vast surfaces faster than these rivers can feed it. Water to make up the difference flows in from the Atlantic past Gibralter, and from the Black Sea through the Dardanelles. The incurrents thus created have always made the Mediterranean difficult for small vessels to sail out of, and thus have helped to keep it a closed sea.

The incurrent to the Mediterranean from the Black Sea is especially strong—five to six miles per hour. But Minoans, Greeks, and finally Romans learned that there were rewards to be won from bucking this current. For ships which entered the Black Sea could then go on across it, enter the mouths of the Danube, Don, or Dneiper Rivers, and then sail up these great waterways, deep into the continents of Europe and Asia, trading as they went.

The narrow channel to the Black Sea is about 160 miles long. Leaving the Mediterranean, ships first enter the Dardanelles, which widens after 40 miles into a lake (the *Sea of Marmora*). About 15 miles from the Black Sea itself the channel narrows again to form the *Bosporus.* Overlooking this channel, on a point of land above a harbor known as the Golden Horn, stands the city of Constantinople, for 2000 years a center of population and power.

In ancient times, when this great city had another name, Byzantium, the Greek historian Polybius wrote:

> The site of Byzantium is, as regards the sea, more favorable to security and prosperity than that of any other city in the world known to us . . . It completely dominates the mouth of the Black Sea so that no one can sail in or out without the consent of the Byzantines. Thus they have complete control over the supply of all products furnished by the Black Sea which people require in their daily life . . . The fullest supplies and best qualities of cattle and slaves reach us from the countries surrounding the Black Sea . . . with plenty of honey, wax, and preserved fish, while of the excess produce of our countries they take olive oil and every

Courtesy Turkish Information Office, New York

The modern city of Istanbul, Turkey, in ancient times called Constantinople, capital of the eastern Roman empire. Here Europe and Asia nearly meet, separated only by a narrow stretch of water, the Bosporus.

> kind of wine . . . The Byzantines themselves are the people who derive most profit from the position of their town, since they can readily export all their excess produce and import whatever they need on favorable terms and without risk of hardship . . .[1]

Polybius then described how the zigzag currents flowing from the Black Sea through the Bosporus carry ships easily into Byzantium's natural harbor, the Golden Horn. Strabo, another Greek writer, told how these same currents carry great shoals of fish close to the harbor, where they are easily caught.[2] To crown all this the country spreading out inland from the Byzantine promontory is ideal in soil and climate for farming.

This was the place which Constantine, the first Christian emperor of Rome, wisely chose as a new and second capital for the Roman empire in 323 A.D. Soon the old city took on a different name, Constantinople. Constantine lived for 14 more years to see his city crowned with churches, great public buildings, and typically Roman places of amusement. The soundness of his choice was proved after his death. The life of the empire became centered there. Rome's importance gradually declined; but for nearly 1000 years Constantinople was the western world's leader of civilization.

Gold nomisma *or* bezant, *standard coin of the Byzantine empire for centuries. For significance of the images on its two sides see opposite page.*

Leu & Co. Bank, Zurich. Courtesy Mr. Ed Gans, Berkeley

Byzantine Civilization

The Time Span

The way of life which took form about Constantinople as a center was in many ways a continuing development of Roman civilization. But it had a distinct character of its own, now known as *Byzantine*. We think of Byzantine civilization as having been born in the fourth century A.D., and as having finally died in 1453, when Constantinople was captured by the Ottoman Turks, who hold it to this day. Within that span of over 1000 years there was a shorter 700 year period during which Byzantine power was greatest. This was from the 40 year reign of the emperor Justinian in the sixth century until the sack of Constantinople by the Normans in 1204. Throughout its history the official language was Greek. Literary men and court officials took pride in keeping it "pure" Greek of a kind once spoken and written at Athens.

The Emperors and Religion

The rulers of the Eastern Roman empire, or Byzantine empire as we shall henceforth call it, were emperors with absolute power. Each surrounded himself with ministers. Of these some managed a beaurocratic system like that of Diocletian (see page 239). Others had charge of foreign relations, and conducted the complex diplomacy needed to control the outside forces pressing on the empire from all sides. Others were treasurers, and still others were generals. But supreme over them all was the will of the emperor, who ruled with godlike pomp, in the manner first adopted by Diocletian. The long life of the Byzantine empire, century after century, as it met new dangers and flexibly adjusted to new times, seems to have depended at least in part on this administrative structure, frought though it frequently was with complex, savagely intense court intrigue.

For some comments on the music of this general period see Appendix A, pages 600–601.

From the old Roman Empire the Byzantine emperors inherited certain traditions; they were responsible for upholding the law. Beginning with Constantine they were also part of a new tradition. Each regarded himself as Christ's delegate on earth, maintaining the empire as an earthly version of the Kingdom of Heaven, and therefore responsible for upholding religious law and teachings. Thus the gold coins minted at Constantinople bore on one side, century after century, an image of Christ the Universal Ruler (or *Pancrator*), and on the other a corresponding image of the current emperor.

Greek writing from the fourth or fifth century A.D. (Old Testament, Book of Esther, chap. xx, verses 4–8). The ancient manuscript was preserved in a remote Greek monastery at the foot of Mt. Sinai. This style of writing was the basis on which the modern Russian alphabet was later developed.

National Library, Leipzig

The empire needed strong rulers. Not only was it under repeated attack from without. Tensions and frictions continually threatened it from within, and one of the most abrasive of these centered around the Christian faith. The universal love and compassion which Jesus had preached and lived were disfigured almost beyond recognition by converted Romans eager for a religion which could make armies victorious, by converted Pharisees to whom their religion had always been an exclusive privilege, and by converted Greeks whose most intense interest was precise definition supported by the rigid either-or logic of Aristotle. What emerged instead was a state religion which mirrored governmental policy, viewing all people outside it as subject to aggressive conversion by missionaries, just as the empire's enemies must be subdued by the sword. Within the religion itself battles raged between theologians over the reduction to correct human language of superhuman mysteries such as the nature of God, of Christ, and of their exact relationship. To settle such bitter disputes the emperors called one counsel of Church fathers after another. Woe to those whose beliefs and definitions were rejected. They were declared guilty of heresy and their followers persecuted in thousands, even to death, in what amounted more than once to civil war.

In the year 787 a counsel at length arrived at definitions for correct Christian belief which were judged perfect. The Christian accepted them all and was safe within the spiritual fortress of the faith, or he disagreed with any of them and was an outcast heretic. The character of Christianity thus became established in a pattern which was to endure for centuries. Positively its earnest concern was to spread correct doctrine; negatively to stamp out what was judged incorrect.

The arts of this period can best be understood as extensions of the policies of Emperor and Religion. Of the pomp which surrounded the emperors, enhancing the impression of their worldly power, only traces remain. Of the arts supporting the Christian faith, creating an atmosphere of spiritual power, and everywhere advancing its teachings through vivid pictures or other means, much is left. It is to religious art, therefore, that we shall turn our attention.

Interior of the church of San Clemente, Rome. Its appearance has changed little since the fourth century A.D. The sanctuary lies behind the further of the two low marble walls. The altar stands under the stone canopy supported by four columns. Behind it, in the curving apse, can be seen the bishop's throne.

The New Church Architecture

WHAT EARLY CHRISTIAN WORSHIP WAS LIKE, AND WHY IT REQUIRED NEW BUILDINGS. The typical pagan temple, which was the home of a god and whose doors were opened at certain times so that the god might look out and see the sacrifices performed in the open air before his house, was totally unsuited to the new religion. Worship no longer centered on burnt sacrifices in the open air, but on the condition of the worshiper's soul, attained through worship of an invisible God, inside a building which shielded worshipers from distraction.

While Jesus was alive, his words, as people heard them and as his followers later wrote them from memory, were simple, direct, informal, and charged with spiritual insight and love for mankind. And after his death, all those who believed his teachings gathered in little groups to worship one God in a simple, direct, and informal way, addressing God in prayer as a father, confessing their sins, partaking together of a sacred meal of bread and wine, singing psalms, and listening to discussions (sermons) on the meaning of Jesus' teaching. Such services were led by a selected member of each group, a man who had been *ordained*, or blessed, by one of Jesus' closest followers and was therefore entitled to serve as a priest of the new religion. Since the first Christians were all Jews, these early gatherings followed a Jewish pattern of worship. The melodies to which they sang hymns were sacred Jewish melodies. The Jewish practice of keeping Saturdays holy was changed to keeping Sundays, the day of the week on which Christ had risen from death, as a holy day. As the new religion spread among Greeks and Romans, they too followed these customs. A new rhythm entered the lives of former pagans, who had never thought of the passing days as being grouped into weeks.

As time went on the simple gatherings for worship became formalized into set practices, through much repetition in many places. And when Christianity became the Roman state religion, these formal practices became elaborate. The sacred meal of bread and wine became a ceremony conducted before a congregation of worshipers by a priest whose every act and spoken word were eventually to become fixed by custom.

The religion also acquired an organization. The churches of the empire, each under the direction of their priests, were grouped into *diocese*, each governed by a higher church dignitary, a *bishop*. Each bishop's center of administration within his diocese was always a central city or town, and here was his own church, in which stood his throne or *cathedra*. The bishop's church thus came to be called a *cathedral church*, or simply a cathedral.

Another important Christian ceremony was that of the initiation of new members into the faith. This was a sacred bathing of the body, a symbol of the washing away of sin from the soul (the rite of baptism). Among early Christians every baptism was particularly dramatic, since it marked the conversion of adult unbelievers and their families to a new way of life. A special building, known as a *baptistry*, centering around an indoor pool of water, was therefore needed for this single purpose.

BASILICA AND BAPTISTRY. To meet these new religious needs, Roman architects of the fourth century, working in different parts of the empire, made changes in already known types of public buildings. For the celebration of the Mass they adapted the basilica. The great columned hall was suited to the gathering of a large congregation. In the curved alcove, or *apse*, at one end, the high seat, where once a judge had sat as he heard cases at law, was preserved as a throne, a cathedra, on which sat the bishop when he visited the church. Before his cathedra stood a permanent stone table, or *altar*, at which the holy bread and wine were prepared. At some distance in front of the altar a barrier or railing was placed to keep the space needed for the holy ceremony free from intrusion. This space before the altar was called the *sanctuary*, and was the most sacred part of the church.

Entrance doors to the basilica were placed at the far end of the building, opposite the altar, and this end thus became the building's front. Before it, in the earliest churches, was an outdoor courtyard having at its center a fountain or pool.

As new kinds of building rose, new styles of architecture were createa for them. This column capital from a Byzantine building is an example. *See also pages 281, 284.*

Archeological Museum, Istanbul

Sectional view of an early Roman baptistry, with place for baptisms at its center.

Near the church stood the *baptistry*, for the admission of new members. Here the Roman architects adapted a different kind of structure, a round building housing a pool and covered with a dome, of a kind which Romans had commonly used for baths and summer houses. The Pantheon had been a huge enlargement of this kind of building.

THEIR DECORATION. The earliest Christians, who were first mostly Jews, knew by heart the commandment of Moses that they should neither make nor worship any statue or image of God. But as Greeks and Romans also became converted, they had no prejudices against images. Also, how were these crowds of new Christians to be taught all there was to learn about the new religion? And once they had been taught, how was all they had learned to be kept fresh in their hearts and minds? There was a great deal to learn. There was the full story of Jesus' life, as his followers had come to accept it: his birth, his growth to manhood, the miracles he was believed to have performed, his heroic death, and his glorious resurrection. And there were the names and likenesses of the martyred saints. There was only one way to make all this come alive, especially to all people whether or not they could read, and that was through pictures. Roman architects and artists of the fourth century found a way to make these pictures vivid, permanent, and beautiful. They created them, not with mere paint, but with *mosaic*, that is, colored stone, and even with gleaming gilded glass, high on basilica walls and baptistry domes, where all might look up and see them; and thus a former Roman method of decorating floors and the bottoms of pools horizontally became lifted vertically to a new and finer purpose. The rest of the interior was also made beautiful. Below the mosaics, the church walls were sheathed in colored marble slabs. Marble columns, often the same ones which had stood in temples to Roman gods, supported the roofs and upper walls. Marble inlaid patterns covered the floors.

But there were ideas in the new religion which were hard to put into visible form, and very early we find symbols being created to stand for such ideas. The most important of these symbols was the cross. Originally a device used by the Romans to inflict a slow, cruel death, it came to stand not merely for Jesus' death, but for his triumph over that death. In a somewhat similar way, the simple symbol of a wheel means for the Buddhist a triumph over the suffering of repeated rebirth into this world.

The Influence of the East

If we look at the remains of Christian art in its first centuries, before and shortly after it became a state religion, we see that the forms which appear, for example, in the carved reliefs that have survived, are a natural outgrowth of the Roman art forms of the period. In the illustration below the three youthful, beardless images of Jesus wear a toga, and in the upper two panels his pose is determined by a tradition developed for statues of Roman senators, orators, attorneys and philosophers, the pose of the wise persuader. This may also be seen in the illustration, page 234. Moreover, the highly articulated human forms, their draperies, the animals and trees, all sensuously pleasing and rich in the interplay of light and shade, are a part of a still older tradition established by Greek sculptors, Hellenistic and Hellenic. The ornate architectural decoration of columns and friezes belong to the late Roman Empire.

When we look at the Byzantine shrine carved perhaps 600 years after the sarcophagus, we see a new outlook revealed. Figures are more vertical, more uniformly front-facing, less flexibly articulated. The space in which they

Marble sarcophagus of an early Roman Christian, Junius Bassus, who died about 360 A.D. The scenes from left to right are: 1) above, Abraham prepares to sacrifice Isaac; below, Job endures his sufferings; 2) above, Peter is led to martyrdom; below, Adam and Eve have eaten of the forbidden fruit; 3) above, Jesus sits enthroned between Peter and Paul; below, Jesus enters Jerusalem; 4,5) above, Jesus stands before Pilate; below, Daniel endures the lions' den, and Paul is led to martyrdom. 8 ft × 3 ft 10 in.

Vatican Grotto, Rome. Photo Hirmer Verlag Munich

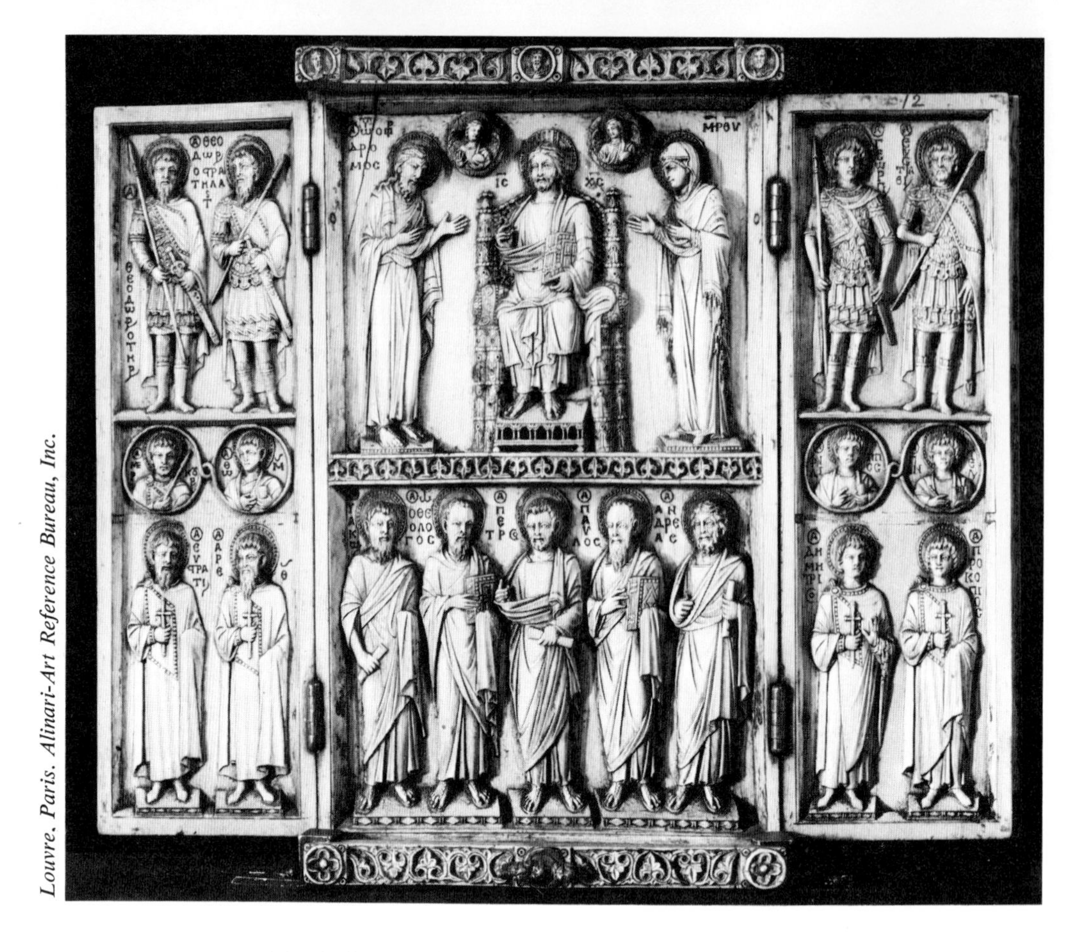

Louvre. Paris. Alinari-Art Reference Bureau, Inc.

Byzantine portable shrine of carved ivory, showing Christ as Pancrator or ruler of the world, flanked by John the Apostle and Mary, and surrounded by saints. Tenth century A.D., 9½ × 11 in.

stand is shallower, the modeling flatter, less sensuously pleasing. Every one is fully clothed from head to foot, and we sense that, beneath the robes and armor, bodies are more shaped by spiritual pursuits than physical ones. Holy persons now have halos and every one is labeled. Above all, Jesus is no longer a persuader but a ruler, a bearded man seated on a throne fit for an emperor, one hand raised in a restrained gesture of blessing, the other holding the New Testament as a source of authority.

To understand these changes we must realize that the Byzantine Empire was heavily influenced by its eastern regions, especially Syria—which at that time included Palestine—and Asia Minor. Syria especially commanded respect, for it contained the most holy cities of the Christian world, Jerusalem and Bethlehem. Long before Hellenic sculpture was even thought of, the people of this region had been part of a vastly older civilization with its roots in Mesopotamia. To these people the human figure was always robed, its poses were stiff and vertical, and male authority was identified with a beard. It was in the Fertile Crescent of Syria and Mesopotamia that the now universally accepted image of Jesus as a tall bearded man in flowing robes was born. It was there also that other conventions of Christian art originated, such as those in the illustration opposite. For centuries they were to be repeated with endless variations, their flattened, rigid style gradually dominating the sensuously pleasing style originated by the Greeks. The reason for the domination would appear to be the intent behind it. This intent was the presentation through visual images of severe inflexibly authoritative spiritual doctrine.

Out of the Byzantine Empire's eastern regions came also another tradition, a strong respect for rich, ornate materials. This was to give a distinct character to Byzantine arts of all kinds, from personal apparel to the interiors of palaces and churches. The sober white toga of the Roman senator was replaced by gorgeously dyed robes, often of silk, intricate in pattern and broadly bordered with embroidery. Precious stones, heavily mounted in gold, appeared in new color combinations, and in new places, such as on crowns, on the stems of goblets, and even on the covers of that new invention, the book, which was beginning to replace the less convenient scroll. The ancient Egyptian art of *enameling*, or filling compartments on a metal surface with opaque colored glass by a process of melting, took on new life in Byzantine workshops. Creamy-hued ivory, imported at great cost from Africa, replaced plainer materials for carving. The dim interiors of Byzantine churches and palaces glinted with soft-hued polished marble and gold mosaics.

Page from the New Testament, written and illustrated in northern Mesopotamia in 586 A.D. We see here early examples of forms which have since become common everywhere. Among others are: a bearded Christ enclosed in an oval (known as a mandorla*), and winged angels with halos. The figure of Mary (dressed in purple), her arms outspread in praise, was to be repeated in Byzantine churches for centuries.*

Laurentian Library, Florence. Photo Hirmer Verlag Munich

Photo Giraudon, Paris

Silk woven at Constantinople about 975 A.D.; eagles and rosettes of gold thread on a blue background, with details in black. This magnificently designed textile was executed on a grand scale; each eagle is nearly 20 in. high. Some facts about silk: a single thread of silk has 2/3 the tensile strength of an equally slender iron wire. But it is lighter, has greater elasticity, and much less heat conductivity. Silk therefore makes a tough, elastic, light cloth which insulates the wearer against temperature change. It absorbs moisture better than any other natural fabric. It is therefore easier to dye, and display color brilliantly. One ounce of eggs laid by the silk moth will produce about 30,000 "silkworms" or caterpillars. As these grow to maturity, they will devour a ton of mulberry leaves. From their cocoons about 12 lb of silk can be unwound, from which can be woven about 50 square yards of cloth.

Photo Hirmer Verlag Munich

A glowing example of Byzantine goldsmithing, jewelry and enamel work, made about 960 A.D. *at the command of an emperor. The door of a* reliquary *or sacred treasure box for containing the bones or other remains of saints.*

Courtesy Turkish Information Service, New York

The Church of Hagia Sophia, or Holy Wisdom, as it looks today, 1400 years after it was built. The four slender minarets are Turkish additions, erected when the church was converted to a mosque about 500 years ago.

Justinian

After Constantine, the next great Byzantine emperor was Justinian, whose long reign lasted nearly 40 years, from 527 to 565.

> Justinian was easy of access, patient of hearing, courteous and affable in discourse, and perfect master of his temper. In the conspiracies against his authority and person, he often showed both justice and clemency. He excelled in the private virtues of chastity and temperance; his meals were short and frugal; on solemn fast he contented himself with water and vegetables, and he frequently passed two days and as many nights without tasting food. He allowed himself little time for sleep, and was always up before the morning light. His restless application to business and to study, as well as the extent of his learning, have been attested even by his enemies. He was, or professed to be, a poet and philosopher, a lawyer and theologian, a musician and architect; but the brightest ornament of his reign is the compilation of Roman law, which has immortalized his name . . .[4]

JUSTINIAN AS CONQUEROR. Justinian set about winning back the empire of the west from the barbarian hordes that had overrun it. His remarkable general, Belisarius, subdued the Vandals in north Africa, and the Goths in Spain and part of Italy. The city of Rome, sacked and already partially in ruins, was brought back for a time into the empire. Western Europe (Gaul, Britain, Germany) could not be recovered. See the map, page 285.

Justinian also carried on the struggle which every Byzantine emperor had to face: keeping the Persians at bay in Asia Minor and the Levant, and holding back the barbarians endlessly pressing down around the Black Sea from the north. The cost of such wars was great, both in wealth and in human suffering. A historian of the time has left this black picture of Photius, one of Justinian's officials:

> In all the provinces of the East . . . he seized on every man . . . if he found that he had bread for a single day, and such persons he

> plundered, he imprisoned, hung them up and tortured them . . . . For always he took his cut, and said, "Give many pounds [of gold]; the Emperor needs money for his wars."[5]

JUSTINIAN ADVANCES THE EMPIRE'S PROSPERITY. But Justinian, in spite of the brutal methods of his tax collectors, wished to restore and increase prosperity. By winning back Africa, Italy, and Spain from the Vandals, Goths, and other northern barbarians he was restoring these lands to the rule of Roman law. He was reopening the Mediterranean Sea to the peaceful coming and going of merchant ships. Only when law and peace prevail does business permanently thrive.

He took steps to encourage new industries. Of these the most remarkable was the starting of silk manufacture in the west. For centuries silk had been imported from the Far East by ship and caravan at great cost and risk. Justinian managed to have cocoons of the oriental silk moth smuggled out of China. At the same time groves of mulberry trees, on whose leaves the caterpillars of the silkworm live, were started in Greece and the Levant; silk caterpillars multiplied on their leaves, and soon a thriving new industry of silk thread manufacture was launched. The thread was then shipped to Constantinople where skilled weavers converted it into fabrics of rich color, design, and texture to be sold at a high profit to persons of wealth and power all over the western world.

Justinian also knew how to economize. He stopped the old Roman practice of free public games and free public bread, which Constantine had brought to Constantinople from Rome. When this produced riots, he suppressed them ruthlessly and established permanent police forces in the empire's chief cities, such as Constantinople, Alexandria, and Antioch. He put thousands of men to work by spending government funds on an astonishing amount of building: fortifications for cities, palaces for himself, and churches everywhere. After 1400 years a few of these churches miraculously still stand intact. Some are in the Italian city of Ravenna, once an important Byzantine city. The greatest of them all and one of the world's architectural marvels, is in Justinian's capital city of Constantinople.

By Justinian's time the basilican type of church had been in use for over 200 years. But their timber roofs were subject to fire. The solution was to build a church all of stone or all of brick, whose wide ceiling would be spanned by a dome. Besides being fireproof, a domed church had another, even greater advantage. When one entered it, one's gaze and one's thoughts soared upward as if toward heaven. This was the experience of everyone who entered the great Pantheon at Rome, or even a smaller domed church such as a baptistry. When one entered a basilica, on the other hand, one's gaze and one's thoughts moved not upward, but forward like an arrow to the apse at the far end, and to the altar within the apse.

Justinian must have been ambitious to build a church which would last forever, and whose dome would out-soar that of the Pantheon. He summoned two renowned Greek architects, Anthemius of Tralles and his assistant, Isodorus of Miletus, and set them to work designing the greatest church the world had ever seen. By the year 532 their plans were complete. Five years later the church itself was finished.

Ivory portrait panel from sixth century Constantinople; the Byzantine empress Ariadne, carrying a scepter *or wand of authority, and an* orb *or sphere symbolizing the Christian world over which she ruled. The heavy jewelry and rich embroidery which she wears, and the costly ivory in which her likeness is carved, are all characteristic of Byzantine taste.*

Bargello, Florence. Photo Hirmer Verlag Munich

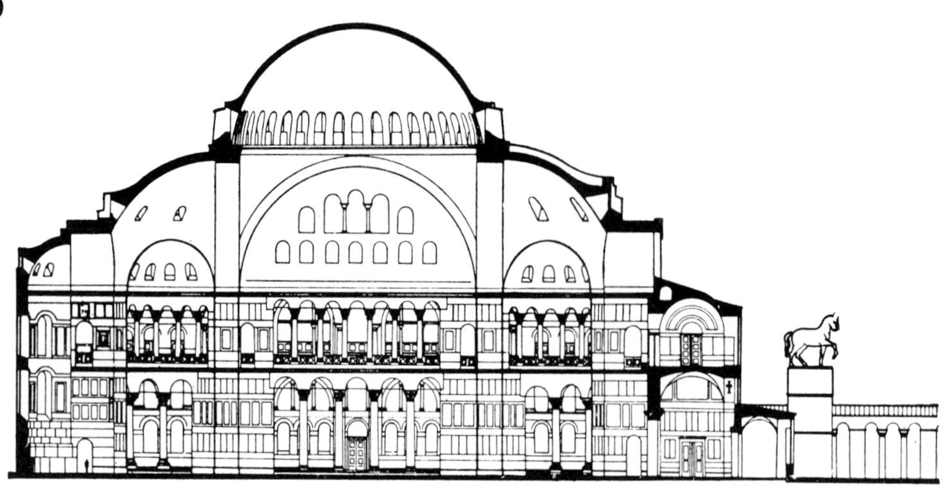

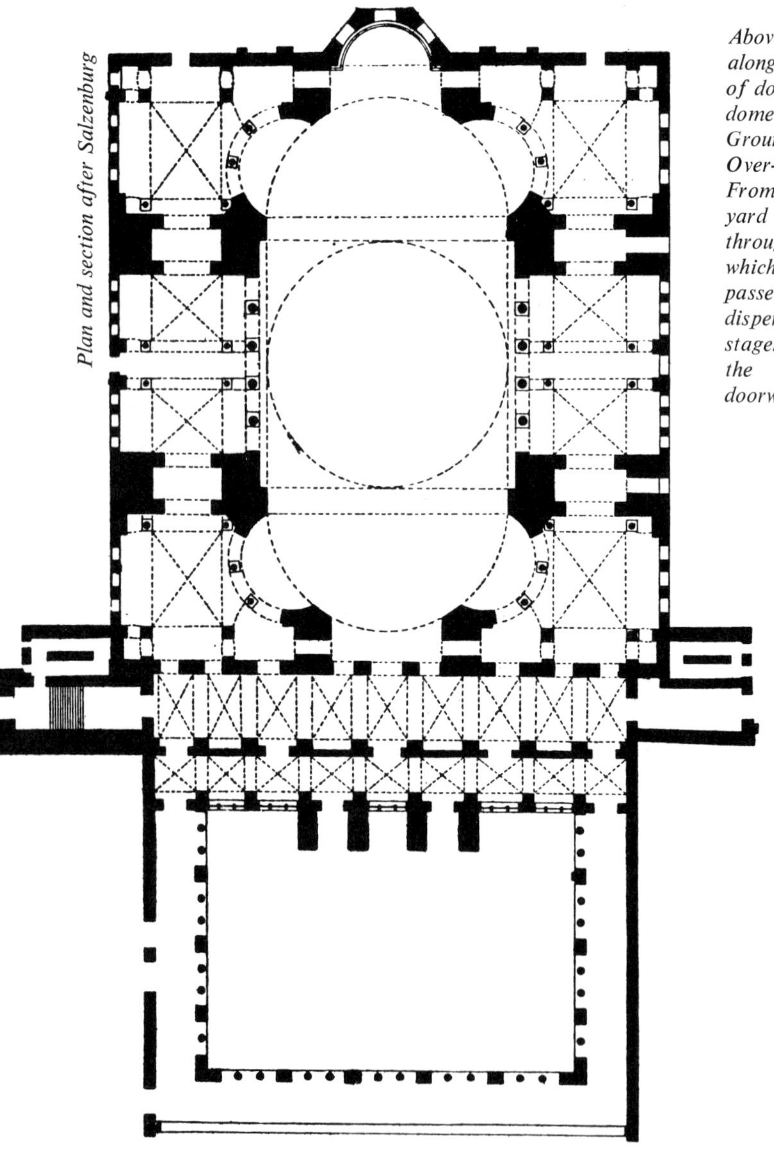

Plan and section after Salzenburg

Above: section of Hagia Sophia along east-west axis. Height to apex of dome about 190 ft. Diameter of dome slightly over 100 ft. Left: Ground plan of Hagia Sophia. Over-all dimensions, 500 × 350 ft. From the fountain-centered courtyard people entered the church through three great bronze doors, which are still in use. They then passed through two vestibules which dispersed the entering crowd by stages, so that worshippers entered the church itself through nine doorways.

Courtesy Turkish Information Service, New York

Interior of Hagia Sophia, looking southeast. In each pendentive, *below the dome, can be seen the mosaic image of an archangel, fitting the description in the book of Isaiah: "Each one had six wings: with twain he covered his face, and with twain he covered his feet, and with twain he did fly." The great circles containing Arabic passages from the Koran are recent additions.*

Hagia Sophia Through Sixth Century Eyes

We are fortunate to have a vivid description of the great Church of Holy Wisdom (*Hagia Sophia*, as it is called in Greek), from an eyewitness who knew it when it had just been completed, Procopius of Caesarea, a Greek historian:

> . . . it exults in an indescribable beauty . . . and it abounds exceedingly in sunlight and in the reflection of the sun's rays from the marble. Indeed one might say that its interior is not illuminated from without by the sun, but that the radiance comes into being within it. . . . The upper part of this structure . . . rises . . . marvelous in grace, but by reason of the seeming insecurity of its composition is altogether terrifying. For it seems somehow to float in the air on no firm basis, but to be poised aloft to the peril of those inside it. Yet actually it is braced with exceptional firmness and security . . . But even so . . . observers are still unable to understand the skillful craftsmanship, but they always depart from there overwhelmed by the bewildering sight.
>
> The whole ceiling is overlaid with pure gold, . . . yet the light reflected from the stone prevails, shining out in rivalry with the gold . . . Who could recount the beauty of the columns and stones with which the church is adorned? One might imagine that he had come upon a meadow with its flowers in full bloom. For he would surely marvel at the purple of some, the green tint of others, and at those on which the crimson glows and those from which the white flashes . . . And whenever anyone enters this church to pray . . . his mind is lifted up toward God and exalted, feeling that he cannot be far away . . .
>
> Furthermore, concerning the treasures of this church—the vessels of gold and silver and the works in precious stones, which the Emperor Justinian has dedicated here . . . I shall allow my readers to form a judgment by a single example. That part of the shrine which is especially sacred, where only priests may enter, which they call the Inner Sanctuary, is adorned with 40,000 pounds' weight of silver.[6]

During Procopius' lifetime, when the Patriarch of Constantinople, standing before the high altar, surrounded by clouds of incense, celebrated divine services for a huge congregation which stood on the marble floor in this great building, the lofty space must have resounded with singing. How it sounded we can only guess from fragments of Byzantine music that have survived.

Hagia Sophia as a Structure

Hagia Sophia is the supreme example of man's daring use of the round arch. In it this form of construction in stone and brick is pushed as far as it can go. Its architects put to use all that the Romans had discovered about arched and domed construction since the Pantheon was built, 400 years before. In those years important steps had been taken. (1) Instead of raising a dome on a solid cylinder of masonry, architects had learned to raise it on a ring of arches, thus reducing the dead supporting mass. (2) They had learned to reduce the outward thrust of an arch or dome gradually, through supporting

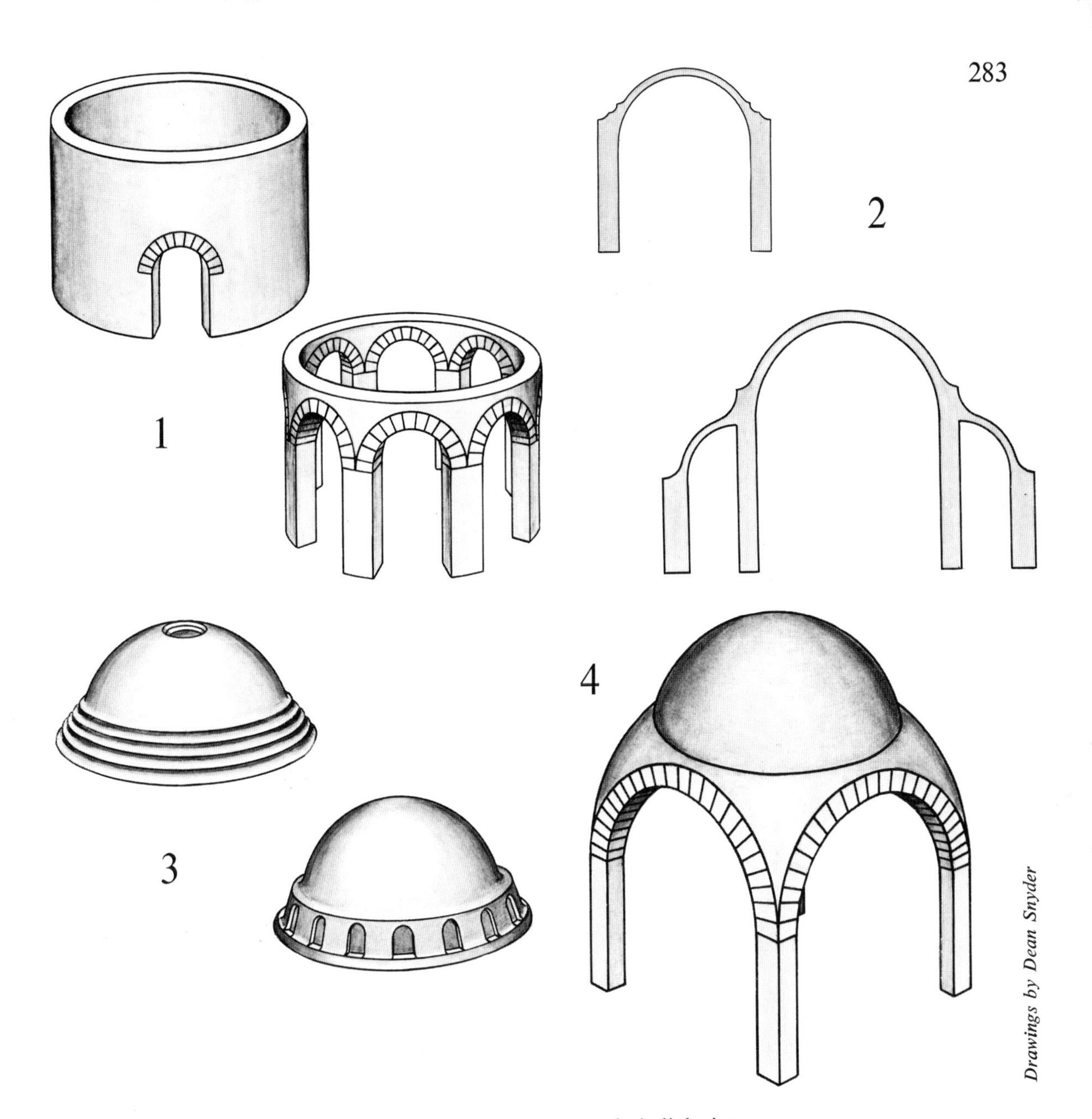

half arches or half domes. (3) They had learned how to admit light into a dome without having to leave its apex open. Their alternative was to place a ring of small windows around the dome's base. (4) By inventing a structural form called a *pendentive*, they discovered how to place a round dome on a square building.

These four constructional devices were put to use in the building of Hagia Sophia. The great central dome rests on four huge arches. Two of these arches, those on the left and right, are supported by walls (pierced though they are by many windows and columns). But the other two arches stand completely open, in order to give a long view through the church to the altar.

The tremendous outward thrust of these arches is met by counterthrusts from lower arches bracing them from each side. In later times, architects doubted the strength of these supporting arches to withstand earthquakes, and buttressed them with great additional blocks of masonry.[7]

Justinian, a Final Comment

The Emperor Justinian died in 565, in his 84th year, after a long, effective, many-sided life which is still the subject of controvery. In one respect it bears a mark of tragedy, in that the emperor officially supported religious persecu-

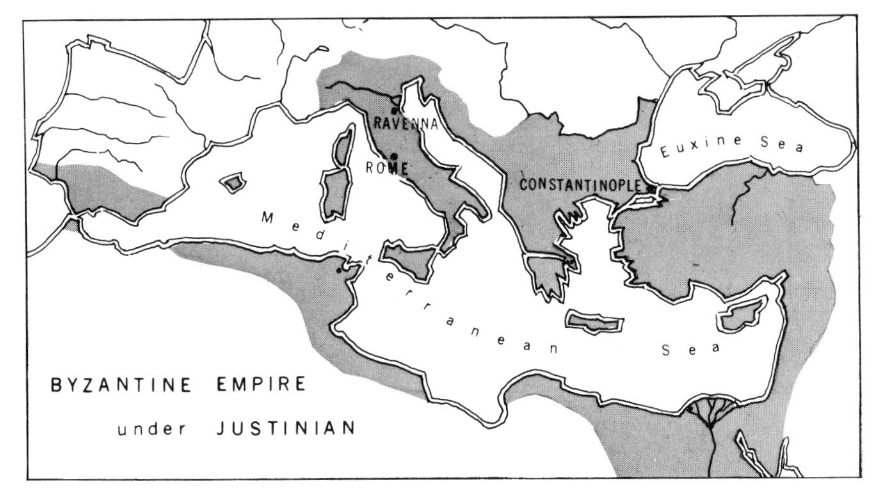

Oposite page: interior of the church of San Vitale, Ravenna, northern Italy, built by Justinian. In the lower extreme right can be seen the mosaic, shown below, of Justinian himself surrounded by high officials of the empire. The strong individuality of the seven most important faces suggests that they are portraits from life.

tion of his Jewish subjects. The Jewish religion, from which Jesus never separated himself, teaches that the human soul is pure. Those who came after Jesus, beginning with Paul the martyr, held the view that the soul can be made pure only through the grace of God, and that this grace may be won only by those who hold certain beliefs, among others that Jesus was divine, not merely human. The Jews regarded him as a teacher only, and for this difference they were made to suffer not only then but repeatedly since.

In other respects Justinian's reign was the high point of early Byzantine civilization, whose strength was soon to be challenged, for shortly after Justinian's death there loomed up from the south an ominous threat to the Byzantine way of life.

Universal Color Slide Co.

A member of the bodyguard of the Sultan of Azzan, extreme southern Arabia, photographed about 35 years ago. His manner of living and costume had hardly changed in 2000 years. His dagger sheath is enriched with silver and carnelians.

Photo Freya Stark, before 1938

Bedouin encampment in the Arabian Desert, preparing to move at sunrise.

Photo Carl Raswan, before 1935

THE BIRTH OF THE MOHAMMEDAN FAITH

Arabia

The great peninsula of Arabia, barren desert though it largely is, has supported millions of people since history began. Water holes are far apart. Grass, wherever it can grow, is tough and resistant to drought. In most of this wilderness man could never survive if it were not for that strange, arrogant beast, the camel, which can withstand broiling midday sun and midnight frost, drink water no human can stand, feed on thorn-bushes, and travel for days living off the fat stored in its hump. Arabian life depends largely on the camel, whose meat and milk give food and drink, and whose hide and wool give leather and cloth. This life depends also on the date palm, for dates are the bread of Arabia.

In a few green spots, around large oases and along the southern coast, Arabians can lead settled lives as farmers among their date palm gardens, and can even build towns and cities. But over the rest of the land Bedouin herdsmen move restlessly from one poor pasture to another, living off their droves of camels, sheep, and goats. There is always too little to go around. A man's chance to survive depends on his ability to seize and hold pasture land for himself, even for a few days. Fighting, therefore, has always been part of the Arab way of life.

The Arabian peninsula, showing its two distinctly different regions: Arabia Deserta, *largely barren, and* Arabia Felix, *its more fertile southern rim.*

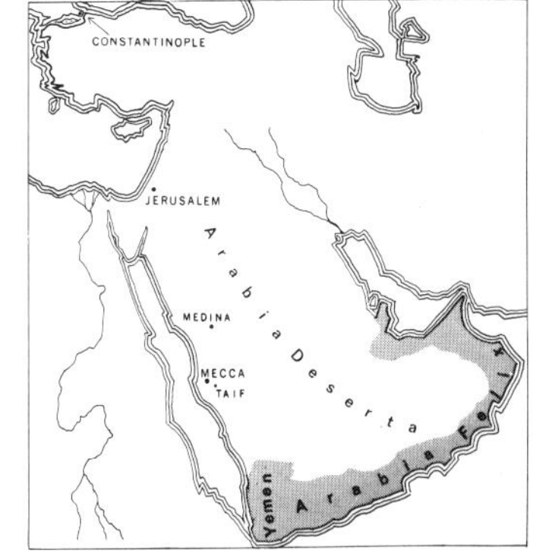

Long ago the shrewd Arabs discovered how to make a profit from their wandering life. They found that goods bought (or plundered) from one town on the desert edge could often be sold at a profit somewhere else. Gradually they developed trade routes crisscrossing the great deserts between cities and towns. Along these paths plodded *caravans,* long lines of laden camels protected by armed guards mounted on racing camels and fiery horses. Arabian towns, finding their wealth increased by the trade, built inns to house visiting caravans. These *caravanseries* enclosed great courtyards where dozens of camels could be laden, unladen, housed, and fed. Around the courtyard were sleeping rooms for merchants and camel drivers, and warehouses for their goods. The whole structure was surrounded with a high wall against marauders.

A fortress of the Sultans of Azzan, southern Arabia. The architecture is believed to have been inspired by that of ancient Mesopotamia, and to have changed little if at all in thousands of years. The materials are wood and unbaked mud brick, decorated with whitewash.

Photo Freya Stark, before 1938

All this trade was not limited to Arabia alone. For Arabia's desert plants produced aromatic gums of marvelous fragrance, valued in other lands where they were known as *frankincense* and *myrrh*. While most of Arabia remained permanently poor, its southern edge grew wealthy on the export of such luxuries, westward to the kings and temples of Egypt and later Hellas and Rome, and eastward to the princes of India. This bleak, proud land, ruled by the sharp sword and the shrewd bargain, has always repelled invaders. Augustus Caesar in 25 and 23 B.C. sent two Roman armies to conquer it, lost the armies and their general, and never tried again.

Arabian Social Structure

While Egyptians, Mesopotamians, Greeks, Jews, and Romans were moving up from life dominated by clan and tribe into one of more complex civilization, the Arabs in their isolated pocket of land remained rigidly attached to a tribal way of life. Each band of Bedouin herdsmen was bound together by blood ties of kinship and ruled over by a patriarch, or *sheik*. These clans in turn were grouped in tribes. Each tribe controlled an area of the country, jealously guarding it from invasion by other tribes. Where tribal land contained a town, the tribe, or part of it at least, would become stationary, devoting itself to farming and trade rather than herding.

Along the southern coast, where a better water supply encouraged farming, a more advanced form of society was possible. A few tribal chieftains succeeded in conquering surrounding tribes and thus became kings, or *sultans*, ruling sizeable kingdoms. Of these, Yemen, Oman, and Muscat are modern examples. Although the fierce tribal structure of society never disappeared even in these kingdoms, it was along the southern coast that Arabian art and Arabic writing first took form.

The Birth of Islam

Halfway down the western side of Arabia, less than fifty miles inland from the Red Sea, is a shallow, barren valley. At its bottom is a well, called Zem-Zem, whose mineral-laden, terrible tasting water was in ancient times valued by the Arabs as medicine. It may have been the well that attracted permanent residents to this place. Or it may have been a black meteorite, a "stone that came down from Heaven," which the ancient Arabs worshiped as a goddess, and which made the spot a religious center. Again it may have been because the place is a halfway point for caravans moving between the kingdom of Yemen in the south and the lands of Palestine and Syria in the north. Perhaps for all these reasons a city has existed there since before men can remember. It has survived because Taif, a farming town some miles away across the desert, has enough water to raise and export dates and other food crops for the neighboring city. This city, Mecca, lies in the land of the tribe called Quraysh (pronounced koo-rEYEsh). Here, about the year 569 A.D., shortly after the Byzantine emperor Justinian's death, a child was born who was to remold the Arab world and change the course of history.

Except that he was born of the tribe Quraysh and the clan Banu Hashim (ha-SHEEM), little is known of the early life of Mohammed. Delightful legends are numerous. But it does seem clear that he grew up knowing both the settled and the roving side of Arab life, and that he was experienced with trade and caravan travel. He must have had the chance to meet Jews, many of whom had fled from the Roman empire into Arabia. He must also have met early Christians, who visited Arabia as traders or missionaries. Thus, probably, he learned that, outside Arabia, people lived united by a belief in one God, while his own people fought each other endlessly and worshiped desert rocks.

Not until he was forty years old did Mohammed first emerge as a spiritual leader of men. He had for some time found himself eager to withdraw for a month each year from Mecca's busy life, to be alone with his own thoughts in the wilderness. Here, one day, Mohammed had the decisive experience of his life. In his own words, there appeared to him "one terrible in power . . . gifted with wisdom. With even balance stood he in the highest part of the sky. Then came he nearer and approached—and he revealed to his servant (Mohammed) what he revealed."[8] From that time on until he died 23 years later, Mohammed was seized with many fits of inspiration. It is reported that when the revelations came to the Prophet "they pressed hard upon him and his countenance darkened," and that "he groaned like a camel's colt." The results of these experiences Mohammed put into words. They became the Koran, the holy book of a new religion, Islam (is-LAHM).

The Teaching of the Prophet Mohammed

Perhaps the most burning message of the Koran is that a Day of Judgment is coming when the souls of all men shall be sternly judged by an all-powerful God, Allah, the one and only.

> In the name of the merciful and compassionate God . . . verily the torment from thy Lord will come to pass;—there is none to avert it! The day when the heavens shall reel and the mountains shall move,—woe upon that day to those who call [the prophets of God] liars! . . . On the day when they shall be thrust away into the fire of Hell,—this is the fire which ye used to call a lie! Is it magic, this? or can ye not experience it?—broil ye in it, and be patient or not patient, it is the same to you; ye are but rewarded for that which ye did do!
>
> Verily, the pious [shall be] in gardens and pleasure, enjoying what their God has given them; for their God will save them from the torment of Hell. "Eat and drink with good digestion, for that which ye have done!" Reclining on couches in rows; and we will wed them to large-eyed maids.[9]

In vivid word-pictures like these the Koran again and again presents Judgment Day as a terrible coming reality, rewarding good and evil as they deserve. Mohammed believed that through him was revealed the path of conduct which men must follow to be saved on that day. For he was convinced that the angel Gabriel was dictating to him, sentence by sentence, from a heavenly book, of which the Koran was therefore a copy. He also believed that once the book was dictated, no more would ever be revealed. He was, he believed, God's last prophet on earth. Prophets and religious leaders, such as Moses and Jesus, had come before him, but none, he believed, would come after.

True to his visions, Mohammed taught that in order to be saved a man must declare openly his belief in Allah, must pray five times a day touching his forehead to the ground, fast once a year, and give one-fortieth of his wealth to widows and orphans. He must treat all fellow believers as brothers and must settle disputes before a judge rather than by fighting. But unbelievers deserved to be conquered by force. War against them, in order to spread belief in Allah, was a holy undertaking. This stern religion with its simple, clear-cut code of conduct, had a center, Mecca, made holy by the angel Gabriel's visits. Mohammed instructed all believers to face Mecca when they prayed, and to journey to the city at least once during their lifetimes. But no image of Allah, the almighty, invisible and unknowable, must ever be made.

Islam Spreads Halfway Around the World

After years of hardship for Mohammed, Islam suddenly caught the Arab imagination. Before he died at Medina, 200 miles north of Mecca, Mohammed was to see all Arabia converted. The effect was astonishing. All the intense energy which Arabs had poured into fighting each other was suddenly united and turned outward upon surrounding lands of unbelievers. In a wave Arabian armies swept across Egypt and north Africa and up into Spain, tearing away from the Byzantine empire the lands which Justinian's generals had lately won back. Moving eastward, other Arabian armies overran Syria, conquered the great Persian empire, and swept on straight across to northern India. Never had a religion traveled so fast so far.[10]

One reason for this rapid spread was that Islam offered a refreshing contrast to the Byzantine empire of the seventh century. Byzantine taxes had become crushingly heavy, especially on the poor (see page 278). Byzantine church leaders, completely losing sight of Jesus' great command that all men should love each other, constantly argued over the precise meaning of his words and the correct definition of his nature. The Holy Church was divided into factions by these frivolous matters, each faction calling the others *heretics,* that is, holders of false beliefs, who therefore deserved eternal punishment. Behaving thus to each other, they were still more savage toward the Jews, whose long and senseless persecution by Christians was a persistent disgrace to the Byzantine empire.

By contrast, the conquering *Muslims,* or followers of Mohammed, were not only united in belief but were at first tolerant to Jews and Christians alike, provided they submitted to Muslim government and paid heavier taxes. Here, as in all other matters, they were guided by the recorded words of Mohammed. The numbers of Arabians in the vast new empire must have been everywhere fairly small. They seem to have conquered not only by warfare but by winning respect. In some places whole cities and stretches of country went over to them without loss of a life.

Islamic Civilization

Government and the Attitude Toward the Conquered

It is astonishing that men fresh from a primitive desert life of feuding and camel herding could manage to govern many widely different peoples, each with their own civilized customs. But they did it with surprising success. What had happened was that Mohammed had given the Muslims not only a religion but a governmental system as well. The two could not be separated. Islam is a total way of life in which religion, politics, and one's personal behavior are one. It is the most political of the world's great religions. The ruler of the Muslim empire was the *Caliph* (ka-LEEF), a successor to Mohammed and therefore the chief religious authority of the land. The various governors of provinces under him were also political and religious authorities in one. Taxation, as Mohammed had already created it, was a form of religious contribution. Taxpayers became spiritually interested in paying it, tax collectors in collecting it fairly. For, watching both, was Allah, who missed nothing and would forget nothing before Judgment Day.[11]

The first wave of conquering Muslims who swept eastward and westward from Arabia were inclined to be narrowly fanatical when they met the literature and science of other peoples. The conqueror of Egypt calmly ordered the burning of the great library at Alexandria, declaring with simple logic that those books that disagreed with the Koran were untrue, and those that agreed were unnecessary. But later this attitude was completely changed, in keeping with a saying of Mohammed's, "Wisdom is a stray camel; lay hold of it where you find it." The Arabian approach to foreign literature was selective. They loved their own marvelous poetry too well to find that of other peoples interesting. But works on philosophy, science, and mathematics

Opposite page: ceramic tile arabesque *from the Muslim palace of Al-Hambra, Granada, Spain, late fourteenth century. Since the religion of Islam forbids the use of any image of a living creature, Muslim genius has been focused on the creation of abstract pattern. The rediscovery of Euclid's geometry by Muslim mathematicians in the tenth century gave an added stimulus to this art form.*

Above and left: ceramic bowl from Kushan, Muslim Persia, thirteenth century. Diameter 9 in.

Avery Brundage Collection, San Francisco. Photos John Bridgman

Right: ceramic bowl from Nishapur, Muslim Persia, tenth century. Diameter 13 in.

Photo Wim Swaan

were sought out everywhere and eagerly translated into Arabic. Thus Muslim scholars not only discovered Euclid's geometry, but they discovered also that 4000 miles away in India men of equal brilliance had been at work creating a different kind of mathematics known as algebra, and a number system more efficient than any known to the Greeks. To this day algebra is commonly regarded as Arabian in origin. We also speak of "Arabic numerals." Both were actually Hindu creations introduced by Arabian Muslims to the western world.

The Mosque and Its Purpose

It was not long before artists and artisans in the new Muslim empire began to create beautiful things in keeping with the spirit which everywhere gave that empire its character. And since religion was its inspiration, architects were soon at work designing religious centers for worship. Thus came into being the *mosque*, a building unique in the world.

If a typical mosque suggests any building it is a caravanserie (see page 287), with its open courtyard surrounded by shaded rooms and protected by a wall. It is not a temple, not a church. No priest conducts services there. It is first of all a house of prayer, as its name suggests. For the word mosque comes from the Arabian *masjid*, meaning to adore. It is also a men's building, women being expected to pray at home. Daily, from a tower, or *minaret*, of the mosque comes a ringing, singsong summons to give praise to Allah, and for a few minutes life in the surrounding town comes to a halt as men everywhere unroll their prayer rugs, kneel facing Mecca, and recite a verse from the Koran. Every mosque is so aligned that all believers can tell where Mecca lies, for one faces Mecca as one enters its gateway. Continuing inward across its open court, one can wash one's hands at a pool or fountain before

Interior of the mosque of Al-Azhar, Cairo, Egypt, completed 972 A.D. (Muslim date 361 H.). The mihrab can be seen at the far right. The columns, as their different thicknesses and capitals show, have been taken from various older Roman and Byzantine buildings. The original stucco patterns still remain on the walls; quotations from the Koran can be seen as borders over the arches.

By permission of Professor K. A. C. Cresswell and the Clarendon Press

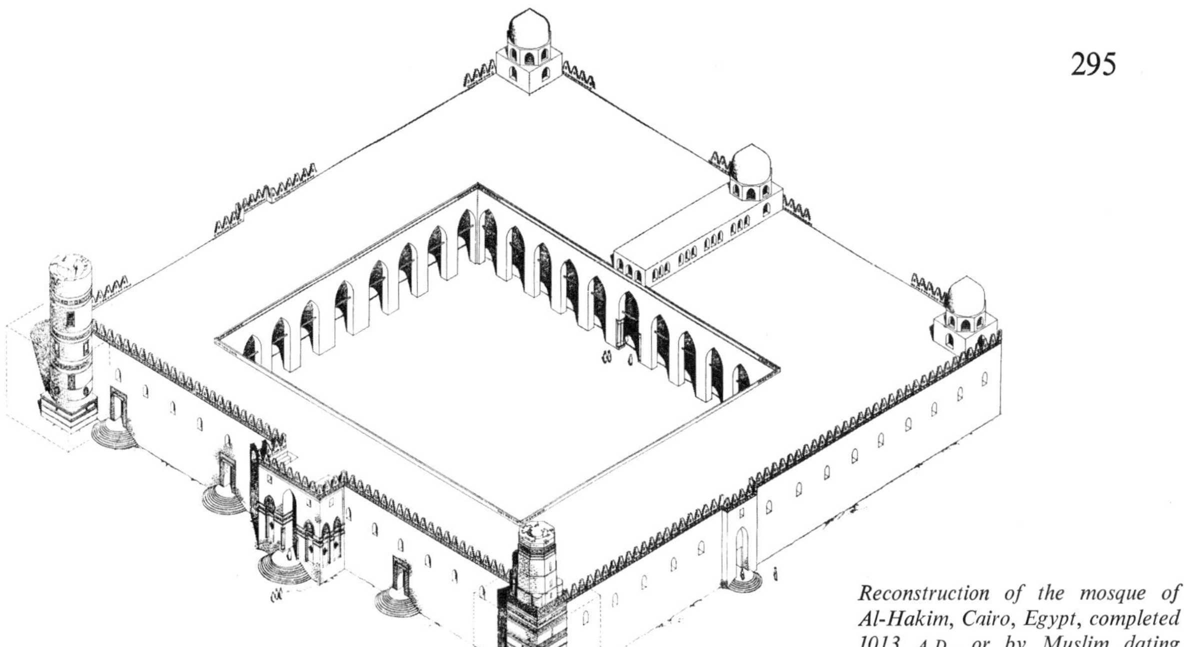

Reconstruction of the mosque of Al-Hakim, Cairo, Egypt, completed 1013 A.D., or by Muslim dating 404 H., that is, 404 years after the Hegira. Hegira, *the Arabic word for flight, refers to a famous journey made by Mohammed from Mecca to Medina, an act which launched Islam as a religion. The drawing is by Dr. Farid Shafei, professor of Muslim Architecture, Cairo University, and is used with his permission.*

touching the holy Koran, if one intends to read from it. Continuing on into the cool of the prayer house beyond, one finds no altar, no image of any kind, merely an empty niche in the far wall, the *mihrab* (me-RAHB), pointing the way to Meca. The space just in front of the mihrab is often crowned with a dome. On Friday, the Muslim holy day, men gather here to pray together and to hear readings from the Koran and perhaps a sermon by the local *imam* (ee-MAHM), a fellow citizen who has this duty.

The mosque has another function. It is a school. Boys gather in the courtyard daily for instruction in reading, writing, logic, grammar, the Koran, and related subjects. In ancient times this education broadened the mind. But as knowledge and ideas advanced, the old unchanging pattern of schooling began to have the opposite effect. In progressive Muslim countries state schools are replacing those in the mosques, but such schools still exist.

Muslim architects, borrowing from the Romans and Byzantines, made no *structural* advances in the use of the round arch and dome, for there were no more to be made. But they explored ways of using them to create new *effects*. They experimented with interlacing arches and with arches of daring new contours, of which one was the pointed arch, later adopted in Medieval Europe.

Muslim artisans at first found inspiration in the world of plant life for the decoration of mosque walls. Then, when the geometry of Euclid became known to them, they began to invent intricate geometric patterns in Allah's honor. But one of the greatest sources of decorative inspiration was the text of the Koran itself. The rhythmic Arabic writing was skillfully redesigned into friezes and borders so that everywhere men might read Allah's word, even if forbidden to look upon his image. Special loving attention was lavished on the mihrab, the niche facing Mecca, and on the mosque wall surrounding it.

Dome interior, in the Great Mosque, Cordova (Spain), built 961–5 A.D. The building is now a Christian cathedral.

صدق الله العظيم الحي القيوم الحي
لا إله إلا هو وبلغت الرسل ونحن
على ما قال ربنا ومولانا من الشاهدين
وصلى الله على سيدنا نبيه محمد
وعترته الطاهرين وسلم عليهم
أجمعين ولا قوة إلا بالله رب العالمين

كتب هذا الجامع علي بن هلال بمدينة السلام
سنة إحدى وتسعين وثلثمائة حامدا الله
تعالى على نعمه ومصليا على نبيه محمد وآله

Last page of a copy of the Koran, written on Chinese paper, in the handwriting of Ali ibn Hilal, perhaps the Muslim world's greatest calligrapher. According to one Muslim critic, the letters are accurately arranged so that they look "as if they smiled at each other and showed front teeth." Ali also enriched each page with delicate floral designs and gold borders. He completed the manuscript at Baghdad in the year 391 H. (1000 A.D.).

Library of Sir Chester Beatty

Calligraphy, Woodcarving, Metalwork, and Weaving

The art of *calligraphy*, or beautiful writing, was lavished on copies of the Koran itself. Parchment, or treated sheepskin, a writing surface first developed at Pergamum in Asia Minor, was adopted by the Muslims. On it the Koran's pages were copied in faultless script, often made beautiful with abstract or flowered designs in color and gold. Later, when the Muslims learned the art of making paper from Chinese they met in Central Asia, they adopted paper as a writing surface, thus introducing it to the western world.

No Muslim home was complete without its heavily screened balconies, where the women of the household might look out without the risk of being defiled by being seen. The creation of these screens inspired the ingenuity of Muslim woodcarvers. In another department of life, the constant need for armor and weapons inspired metalworkers to advance the craft of steel-working and to create swords and daggers of great strength and keenness, often with a text from the Koran delicately engraved and inlaid along the blade. Damascus became the western world's steelworking center. In the Near East, especially Persia, carpet weavers produced richly colored, intricately patterned floor coverings, one of the Near East's great arts since the most ancient times.

Islam Reaches Its Limits in the West: Iconoclasm

The tide of Muslim conquest ran east and west. But when it started to flow north it was blocked. When a Muslim army and fleet made a supreme effort by land and sea to storm Constantinople in 717, Byzantine troops under Emperor Leo III gave them a crushing defeat. Sixteen years later, far in the west, when a Muslim army moved north from Spain over the Pyrenees into southern France, a northern army under Germanic barbarians led by Charles Martel ("the Hammer") defeated them at Poitiers. The Muslim caliphs and generals then gave up trying to move in either of these regions. Instead they developed their land possessions in Spain, north Africa, the Levant, and the great plains of Iran. The capital of the Muslim world was moved from Medina in Arabia, first to Damascus in the Levant, and then, as the great stretches of Iran and beyond were conquered, to Baghdad, 500 miles farther east. Other great cities, such as Cordova and Sevilla in Spain, Tangier, Marrakech, and Tunis in north Africa, and Cairo in Egypt, took form as centers of Muslim government, learning, and the arts. It is probable that during this time Muslim civilization was the most refined and broadminded in the world, certainly in the west.[12]

The terrible collision of empires, involving both sides in costly victories and crushing defeats, seems to have shocked Byzantine and Arab alike, stirring both to a strange kind of reform. Searching (independently, of course) for some spiritual cause fo the reverses each had suffered, rulers in both empires fixed on one commandment of their respective religions. This commandment was derived from a basic one of Judaism, the parent religion of both Christianity and Islam: "Thou shalt take unto thyself no graven image; . . . thou shalt not bow thyself down to them nor serve them."

Shortly after the year 720 the Muslim Calif Yazid began a purge of all sacred statues and pictures containing a human likeness. These were chiefly in the Christian churches which had come under Arab control. But the Arabs themselves had at first been somewhat lax in enforcing Islam's restriction against images. From this time on it was strictly observed and is to this day.

In the year 730 the Christian Emperor Leo III commanded that henceforth throughout the Byzantine Empire images should be excluded from churches. His reasoning, and that of the church fathers advising him, seems to have been that in some places sacred statues and paintings had actually been worshiped or had been believed to possess miraculous powers, thus bringing down the wrath of Heaven upon the Empire. For over a century the policies of various emperors wavered on the subject. By the year 843 the ban on images of saints and angels in churches was permanently lifted, but not before the *iconoclasts*, or enemies of images, had destroyed or defaced sculptures, paintings, and mosaics in churches everywhere, replacing them with abstract forms such as simple crosses. The rare examples of representational church art surviving this period were preserved by accident in remote corners of the empire, or because they were temporarily hidden under whitewash.

While events such as these were transpiring in the Eastern Mediterranean, other changes were under way, in Italy and western Europe.

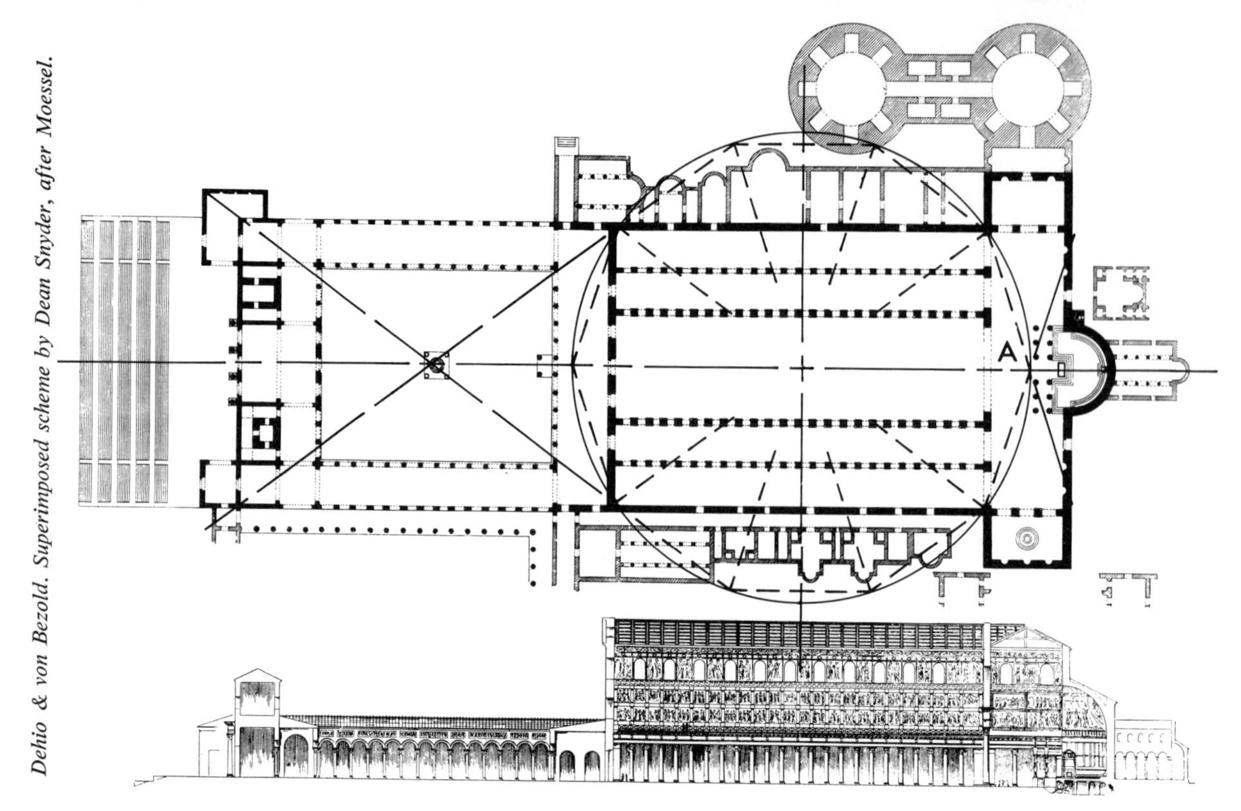

Dehio & von Bezold. Superimposed scheme by Dean Snyder, after Moessel.

Plan and section of old St. Peter's basilica, Rome. This building, erected by the emperor Constantine in 324 A.D., was placed over what had been one side of the Circus Maximus (see page 232). The two circular buildings shown in grey marked the spots at which Saints Peter and Paul were believed to have been martyred in the Circus, during a public entertainment in the year 64 A.D. It is believed that St. Peter was later buried beneath the intersection marked A on the basilica plan. In the sixteenth century, after standing for 1200 years, the building was demolished to make way for the present St. Peter's. The proportions of the plan seem to have been determined by a regular decagon, as shown.

THE REBIRTH OF THE WESTERN EMPIRE

Rome Becomes a Center of Religion

Rome, whence men once went forth to build empires, was no longer a city of any political power. She was too hard to reach from Constantinople, whose ships, instead of going halfway around Italy, could easily sail up the Adriatic Sea to the port of Ravenna. After 500 A.D. Ravenna therefore became the center of Byzantine government in Italy, while Rome sank back to being a small town, its vast complex of palaces and public buildings disused and plundered. Still the memory of her past was never lost. Even in those days of difficult travel, men from distant lands seem to have journeyed there to view the crumbling temples and meditate on the city's former greatness, much as serious minded tourists do today.

But in one way Rome had never lost a certain power, far from political, which she had gained late in life. She had become a major administrative center of the Christian religion. There was a tradition that, at the command of the emperor Nero, in about 64 A.D., two great Christian saints, Peter and Paul, had died the death of martyrs there. Throughout the early days of persecution, when to be a Christian required almost superhuman courage, the spiritual prestige of Rome steadily grew. She remained a center of religious authority even after her fall from political power.

By the sixth century the affairs of the Christian religion had come to be administered from five centers: Rome, Constantinople, Jerusalem, Antioch, and Alexandria. In each of these cities dwelt a prince of the clergy, a *Patriarch* (Greek for father-in-chief), often called by the endearing term of *Papa*. Under the authority of each Patriarch were *archbishops* or *metropolitans*, and under each of these were bishops, each governing a diocese.

In the seventh century, three of these great centers, Jerusalem, Antioch, and Alexandria, fell before Muslim armies, reducing the administrative cities to two. Each of these had won its own kind of reverence from Christians. The Patriarch of Constantinople, in his powerful position close to the emperor, had immense authority. His counterpart at Rome, whom Italians to this day call "il Papa," had a different kind of prestige; he was a successor to Peter, the apostle and martyr. Jesus was believed to have said to Peter on one occasion, "On you I will build my Church." The problem as to which of the spiritual rulers, Pope or Patriarch, had the higher authority was never settled. Eventually, in the eleventh century, the two separated, one to become the leader of the Greek Orthodox Church in the East, the other to govern the Roman Catholic Church in the West. The heavy duties resting on each holy man kept both fully occupied, each in a different way. The Patriarch of Constantinople was surrounded by old, civilized countries, heavily populated and full of cities. The Pope at Rome was close to western Europe, which had once been a civilized part of the empire, but which was now overrun by barbarian tribes from northern Eurasia.

CUMAUTEMINMUN.
DUSSPSEXIERIT
ABHOMINE
AMBULATPERLOCAARIDA
QUAERENSREQUIEMET
NONINUENIT
TUNCDICIT
REUERTARINDOMUM
MEAM
UNDEEXIUI
ETUENIENSINUENITEA
UACANTEM
SCOPISMUNDATAMET
ORNATAM
TUNCUADITETADSUMIT
SEPTEMALIOSSPS
SECUMNEQUIORESE
ETINTRANTESHABITANIBI
ETFIUNTNOUISSIMA
HOMINISILLIUS

Latin as written in the sixth century A.D. (New Testament, St. Matthew, chap. xii, verses 43–45). This kind of lettering influenced the formation of alphabets in western Europe, just as Greek writing influenced those in the east (see page 269).

British Museum

The Taming of the Barbarians

Out among these pagan invaders moved fearless Christian missionaries from Italy, dedicated to making converts even at the risk of becoming martyrs. Some did their work in Gaul; others went farther afield. One of them, Patrick, who lived in the fifth century, journeyed as far as Ireland. The Christian religion, thus planted in that far-off island, had an amazing cultural effect. It nourished the growth of a magnificent Irish civilization, with an art and literature of its own, from which missionaries and men of learning traveled outward in their turn, spreading the Gospel as far as western Germany.

Thus the rough invaders of what are now France and western Germany became enthusiastic Christians. At the same time they were learning to respect Roman civilization, for they had settled in a land where the memory of the Roman empire and its language, laws, and customs was strong, where the remains of Roman cities still stood, and where merchants from the Eastern Roman empire still came sailing up the Rhone to sell luxurious articles from the Byzantine world. The barbarians became ambitious to live as the Romans had. Their first attempts at this were crude, but they improved with time. In matters of religion they respected Rome, where the Pope dwelt. They also respected the power of far-off Constantinople, the capital of the Eastern empire.

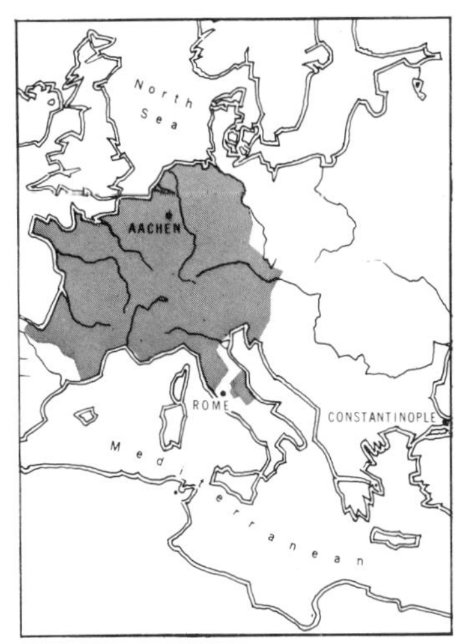

Charlemagne's empire. The zig-zag region cutting across its southern extremity was ruled by the Popes and was known as the Papal States.

The Emperor of the West Reappears

The most powerful Christianized people in western Europe were the Franks (ancestors of today's French people), who had united so many neighboring tribes under them that the Frankish chiefs deserved to be called kings. It was a Frankish general, Charles Martel, who had defeated the Muslims in 733 and had gradually driven them back to Spain (see page 297). About 50 years later another Charles became king of the Franks. But this Charles excelled

The glory of a Frankish craftsmanship under the reign of Charlemagne. The cover of a book on church law, gold set with pearls and precious stones, made at Reims, in what is today Northern France, in the mid-ninth century. In the center Christ sits in majesty. On either side sit the four Evangelists, Matthew, Mark, Luke and John. Above and below are four scenes from the life of Christ. This rich display of gold and jewels was inspired by the example of Byzantium.

Staatsbibliothek, Munich. Photo Hirmer Verlag Munich

Emperor Charlemagne, a bronze statuette, possibly from life. The horse is a more modern substitute for a lost original.

Louvre, Paris

Charles Martel, his own grandfather. He was one of those many-sided geniuses in government, an ideal for future rulers, who fully deserved his name of Charles the Great (in Latin *Carolus Magnus*, or *Charlemagne*). A living word-picture of Charles (in middle age) has come down to us, written by Einhard, the king's personal secretary:

> Charles was large and robust, of commanding stature and excellent proportions, for it appears that he measured in height seven times the length of his own foot. The top of his head was round, his eyes large and animated, his nose somewhat long. He had a fine head of gray hair, and his face was bright and pleasant, so that, whether standing or sitting, he showed great presence and dignity . . . He wore a blue cloak, and was always girt with his sword, the hilt and belt being of gold and silver . . .[13]

He was an expert rider and swimmer, temperate in his habits, could speak and understand Latin and Greek, was deeply interested in learning, and surrounded himself with scholars, the best of whom came from Ireland. But he never could find time to learn to write.

This was the man who spent his long reign uniting Europe as it had not been united since Roman times. Years of fighting and diplomacy crowned Charles' labors with success. He organized the government of the land into counties and appointed to each a count, who was responsible to Charles himself for public safety and justice within the county. He declared slavery unlawful in Europe, thus putting his kingdom morally ahead of the Byzantine and Muslim empires. He supported religion and the authority of the Pope. Everywhere in the land churches were built, and to each was given a piece of farmland, so that the priests and deacons who ministered to the neighboring people could be supported by the produce from it. He encouraged the founding of schools and the spread of knowledge. The orderliness and security of his kingdom encouraged trade. The coins which circulated everywhere were the gold solidus and the silver denarius as established nearly 500 years before by the emperor Constantine.

British Museum

Celtic design, pre-Christian era. Bronze object, purpose unknown, from Ireland. Diameter about 1 ft, cast about the second century A.D.

In the year 800 Charles journeyed south through a pass in the Alps to Italy. He went first to Ravenna to solve problems of government, and then to Rome to pay a respectful visit to the Pope. When he arrived, Pope Leo, surrounded by his retinue of bishops and priests, stood on the steps of his great cathedral church of Saint Peter to receive the Frankish king. Charles dismounted from his horse, and followed by his counselors and lords-in-waiting, greeted the Pope as his spiritual father. Leo in his turn greeted Charles as his spiritual son. The distinguished gathering then moved into the basilica church to hear the celebration of the Mass. Some days later, on Christmas Day, as Charles again knelt in prayer before the altar during the Christmas service, Leo placed upon his head a crown which was supposed once to have belonged to Emperor Constantine, and proclaimed Charles emperor. Once again, after over three centuries, there were two Roman emperors, an eastern and a western one.

For the last 14 years of his life, Charles rose nobly to the challenge of his new title (though he was believed to be displeased at receiving it at the Pope's hands, rather than claiming it for himself). He tried to unite the two empires by peaceful means, but without success. Their borders no longer even touched, but were separated by a great stretch of barbarian kingdoms in eastern Europe. Their closest link was by sea, along the Adriatic, from Ravenna to Constantinople. Both empires, east and west, taken together, were also smaller and weaker than the Roman empire at its height. Spain, north Africa, Egypt, and the Levant had all been seized by the Muslims. Britain had been abandoned to self-government. The complex network of trade which had flowed through the great empire like blood through a circulatory system, giving it life, had been partially destroyed. No man could restore in a few years what many men had put together in the course of centuries.

After Charles died and his body was laid to rest in the church he had built at his favorite town of Aachen, not even his grandsons could preserve the great kingdom he had won and held together by sheer genius. They were lesser men, divided by jealousy. And new hordes of invaders were soon to bring on Europe another time of sorrows.

Celtic design, Christian era. Page from an Irish manuscript copy of the New Testament. This marvel of ingenuity is the work of an unknown Irish monk in the seventh century. Three Greek letters, XPI, the beginning of Christ *in Greek, fill the page.*

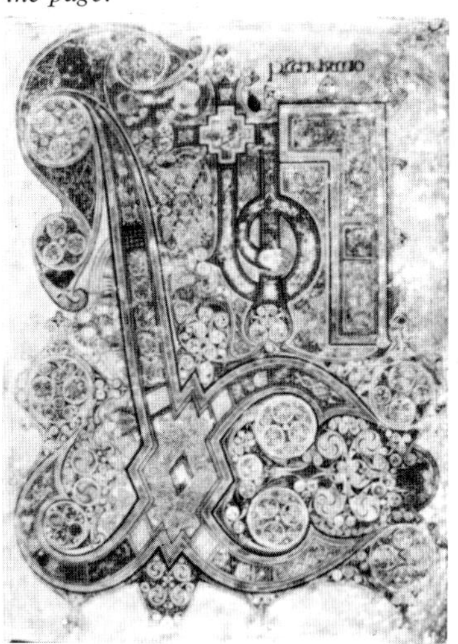

Trinity College Library, Dublin

Djakarta Museum, Republic of Indonesia. Photo Jean O'Meara, Paris

Head of a devata, *or divine being, found in an abandoned Buddhist temple in the Javanese jungle. About ninth century A.D.*

THE SPREAD OF INDIAN CIVILIZATION

The Spread Southeastward

By 650 A.D. Arabian armies inspired by Mohammed had swept across Persia and had spilled down the Khyber Pass into the Indus Valley. Like other invaders before them they made the land west of the river theirs. This land became the extreme easternmost province of the new Muslim empire whose capital was Damascus, and the Mohammedan faith thus gained its first foothold on Indian soil. But 500 years were to pass before that foothold was enlarged.

Meanwhile, the rest of India went its way. Kingdoms and empires came and went, separating and merging, their boundaries and dates made uncertain by the Indian indifference to keeping historical record. As centuries passed the center of empire in northern India shifted eastward, into the region of Bengal, where the Ganges and Brahmaputra rivers nearly meet. Here Hindu civilization had been free from repeated invasions, and here was centered the last of India's native empires, the Pala empire.

Long after Buddhism had died out in the rest of India, it continued to thrive in Bengal, in strangely altered forms, laden with symbolism and even magical practices which would have revolted its great founder. Nevertheless it was in this form that Buddhism was soon to spread, as one part of Hindu civilization, northward into Tibet and southeastward into the Malay Peninsula and Indonesia.

The men who carried the civilization seem to have had various motives. Some were Indian soldiers of fortune who carved out kingdoms for themselves in such places as Cambodia, Sumatra, and Java. A few others were perhaps missionaries. Many must have been merchants, for it seems likely that by this time India had become a center for the weaving and export of cotton cloth to markets throughout Southeast Asia. Many a merchant colony must have dotted the coasts of the Indonesian islands.

View up one of the great stairways leading to the summit of Barabudur.

Photo Jean O'Meara, Paris

Of all these various people it was probably the conquerors who did most to spread the Hindu practices, and the belief in Hindu gods, which still persist in parts of Southeast Asia today, for instance on the Island of Bali. In the past century explorers making their way through the jungles of Cambodia and Java have come repeatedly on the ruins of Hindu temples. At least two of these have proved to be astonishing human achievements, unequaled in their way. These are the temples of Barabudur in Java and Angkor Wat in Cambodia. Both were erected at a king's command.

Both structures are more monuments than temples, gigantic masses of masonry, intricately planned, gorgeously enriched with sculpture, of great external expanse, but with only limited interior space. Each has its own distinctive style of design and ornament, but the basic plan of both has a common origin, the simple stupa, with its central mound and its surrounding wall pierced by four gates, facing north, south, east, and west. (See page 246.) Extensive study has revealed that these two immense temples were designed as interpretations of the universe, each in its own way. Such was a stupa's function also.

Photo Jean O'Meara, Paris

Barabudur, Java. Temple to the Buddha and memorial to a Hindu king. The huge structure is here reconstructed in small model form.

The vast temple-city of Angkor Wat, Cambodia, as it appears today, cleared of jungle.

Cambodian troops and their allies from Thailand on parade. One part of a great wall relief which runs along one of the corridors of Angkor Wat. Ninth century A.D.

The temple, or rather the religious city, of Angkor Wat, whose outer circuit exceeds $2\frac{1}{2}$ miles, was built to the glory of Vishnu, god of preservation, whose statue was placed within the central tower. Directly beneath it is a well 120 feet deep, believed to symbolize the world's center.

Barabudur in Java, on the other hand, was built to honor the Buddha and Mahayana Buddhist teaching. The building's foundations, richly carved with plant and animal forms, were intentionally buried, apparently as a symbol of the Buddhist triumph over the world of the senses. From this the levels of the great monument mount up and up, adorned with ever simpler and more severe sculptures conveying the life of the Buddha and his teachings. At last one comes out on the top level. Here 72 images of the Buddha in meditation are sheltered each by its own encasement of stone. In the center is a great spire containing still another statue of the meditating Buddha.

The king who commanded the building of Barabudur is believed to have belonged to a dynasty of Hindu rulers founded by a certain Saitendra,

"King of the Mountain and Lord of the Isles," who created an empire in Java, Sumatra, and the Malay Peninsula in the eighth century A.D. The builder of Angkor Wat was Suryavarman II, who lived in the first half of the twelfth century and ruled the kingdom of the Khmers, a people whose way of life had been influenced by earlier Hindu conquerors.

At Angkor Wat the central image of Vishnu is believed also to be a portrait of the king as an earthly incarnation of the god. The sculpture on the walls of the long halls surrounding it depict Hindu myths which symbolize events of the king's own life, in a counterclockwise series. In the same way, it has been conjectured that the central image at Barabudur represents a king as incarnation of the Buddha, and the story-sculpture in its galleries are also arranged in counterclockwise order. Thus visitors to both temples seem to have been expected to make counterclockwise tours, just as pilgrims to the stupas in India do to this day. No one today knows why these immense masterpieces, once the centers of crowding civilizations, were abandoned to the jungle.

A chakra *or symbol of the Wheel of Karma, in the Tibetan holy city of Lhasa. In the background is the Potala, palace of the Dalai Lama, the spiritual ruler of Tibet prior to his flight to India in 1959, to avoid capture by forces of the Communist Chinese government. The chakra is flanked by two deer (one visible in the picture) as a reminder that the Buddha's first sermon, in which he discussed the Wheel of Karma, was delivered in a deer preserve or park.*

Buddhism in Tibet

When Buddhism was carried north to Tibet from India in the seventh century A.D., through the high passes of the Himalaya Mountains, it went in what was then its latest form (described pages 247–248), enriched with myth and magic absorbed from the traditions of the Hindu religion. From this wealth of teachings the Tibetans, under the guidance of their own Buddhist saint Padma-Sambhava (eighth century), developed a third variety of Buddhism, known as *Vajrayana*. The Tibetans soon became ardent followers of this form. For centuries perhaps a third of the male population of Tibet have been Buddhist monks. Tibetan art has been chiefly religious art, created in her great monasteries, in accordance with ancient rules and conventions.

In 1959 this seemingly changeless land was occupied by Communist Chinese troops. Ever since, the government of mainland China seems to have been intent on shattering Tibet's centuries-old cultural patterns. Some of her people have succeeded in escaping to India and other countries.

For further illustrations see page 309.

NOTES

[1] Polybius, *Histories*, Book IV, 38.

[2] Strabo, *Geography*, Book VII, Chap. 6, Sec. 2.

[3] At a later date it was usually placed to the right of the altar.

[4] Anthon's *Classical Dictionary* (Harper, New York, 1849), p. 707. The description is derived from the writings of men who lived during Justinian's reign. It is difficult to tell how much of it is truth and how much flattery.

[5] John of Ephesus, *Ecclesiastical History*.

[6] Procopius, *Concerning the Buildings of the Lord Justinian*, I, i (28–48, 53–64).

[7] Earthquakes have caused partial collapse of the dome three times: in the sixth, tenth, and fourteenth centuries.

[8] *Koran*, Chapter 53, adapted from E. H. Palmer's translation (Oxford, 1928–54).

[9] *Koran*, Chapter 52.

[10] The religion later spread on into Mongolia, parts of China, and southward into Indonesia and the Philippines. Today there are over 300,000,000 Muslims, or followers of Islam.

[11] Today the great divisions in Islam are not over questions of religious belief, as in Christianity. Instead they are political, the point of difference being how the leader of the religion is to be selected. The Shia, Sunni, and Khawarij sects each have their own views on this.

[12] It was not until after the Crusades (described pages 317–8) that the Muslim attitude of fierce intolerance toward Christians and Jews appeared. It has remained ever since.

[13] As quoted in Robinson, *Readings in European History*, Vol. I.

BOOKS ABOUT THE JEWISH, BYZANTINE, MUSLIM, AND FAR EASTERN WORLDS

The Story of Civilization, W. and A. Durant (Simon & Schuster, New York).
Vol. IV: *The Age of Faith; a history of medieval civilization (Christian, Islamic, Judaic), from Constantine to Dante (325 to 1300 A.D.).*

JEWISH CIVILIZATION

The Book of Jewish Knowledge, an Encyclopedia of Judaism and the Jewish People, Covering All Elements of Jewish Life from Biblical Times to the Present, N. Ausubel (Crown, New York, 1964). One Vol.
My People, the Story of the Jews, A. Eban (Random House, New York, 1968).
A History of the Jews, C. Roth (Schoeken Books, New York, 1954–61).
Masada, Y. Yadin (Random House, New York, 1966).
Jewish Art, an Illustrated History, ed. C. Roth (McGraw-Hill, New York, 1961).
Jewish Art from the Bible to Chagall, L. Gutfeld (Th. Yosaloff, New York, 1963–68).

BYZANTINE CIVILIZATION AND ITS OFFSHOOTS

A History of the Byzantine Empire (324 to 1453), A. A. Vasiliev (2 paperback volumes, University of Wisconsin).
Fourteen Byzantine Rulers, M. Psellus (Penguin paperback).
The Art of the Byzantine Era, D. T. Rice (Praeger paperback, 1963).

Early Christian Painting (Compact Books).
Early Christian to Medieval Painting (Golden Series, Art of the Western World).
The Age of Charlemagne, D. Bullough (Putnam, New York, 1966).
A Concise History of Russian Art, J. Talbot-Rice (Praeger paperback).

ISLAMIC CIVILIZATION

A History of the Islamic Peoples, C. Brockelman (Capricorn Books 204, New York, 1962).
The Social Structure of Islam, R. Levy (Cambridge paperback, 1965).
Mohammed, the Man and His Faith, T. Andrae (Harper Torchbook 62, 1960).
The Meaning of the Glorious Koran, An Explanatory Translation, M. M. Pickthall (Mentor paperback).
The Story of Moslem Art, C. Price (Dutton, New York, 1964).
Islamic Art, D. T. Rice (Praeger paperback, 1963).
Islamic Art, W. Pinder (Crown, Art of the World Series).
Seen in the Hadramaut, F. Stark (Dutton, New York, 1939). Almost entirely photos.
Mecca the Blessed, Madinah the Radiant, E. Esin, photos by H. Doganbey (Crown, New York, 1963). Beautiful illustrations, fascinating text.
Western Islamic Architecture, J. D. Hoag (Braziller, New York, 1963).
Moorish Spain, E. Sordo (Crown).

FILMS

The World of Mosaic, sound, color, 28 minutes (University of California).
The Mohammedan World, Beginnings and Growth, sound, black and white, 11 minutes (Coronet).

FAR EASTERN ART

The Temples of Angkor, D. Griswold (Tudor Press).
The Art of Indonesia, F. A. Wagner (Crown, Art of the World Series).
The Art of Indochina, B. P. Groslier (Crown, New York).
The Art of Burma, Korea, Tibet, D. Griswold (Crown).
Buddhist Art, D. Seckel (Crown).
Secret Tibet, F. Maraini (Evergreen, E-211).
Tibetan Religious Art, A. K. Gordon (Paregon, New York, 1952).
Tibet's Terrifying Deities, F. Sierksma (Tuttle, Rutland, Vermont, 1966).
The Tantric Mysticism of Tibet, a Practical Guide, J. Blofeld (Dutton D 270, New York, 1970).

Photos Donald Ferris

Tibetan thonka, *or sacred painting, symbolizing Samsara, the circular world into which souls are repeatedly reborn. That this world is a delusion is shown by the forbidding monster who supports it. At the circle's center are the three forces which draw souls into it: ignorance (pig), craving (cock), and passion (serpent). Just outside is a ring of souls, half serenely rising as they overcome themselves, half descending as they become their own victims. Outside that are shown the six kinds of inhabitants of this world of delusion (dwellers in hell, ghosts, animals, humans, dwellers in heaven, gods). The outermost ring shows twelve kinds of human experience which keep souls attracted to this world. Outside and above, two images of the Buddha imply that his teachings enable souls to escape from this endless round. Right: Rahula, a guardian of the Buddha's doctrine. His ten faces symbolize his alert awareness in all directions at once.*

Courtesy of the Nyingmapa Meditation Center, Berkeley, California

The grim uncertainty of life in Dark Age Europe, caught between onslaughts of Viking and Muslim marauders, is eloquently conveyed by this grave relief of a French count, Girard de Vaudemont, and his wife, Heduerg von Dagsburg.

Chapelle des Cordeliers, Nancy. Marburg Fotoarchiv

7 THE MIDDLE AGES, WEST AND EAST

Medieval Europe

Europe's Dark Age

For nearly 200 years, from the early ninth century to the end of the tenth, western Europe was caught in the jaws of a gigantic vise, slowly, ruthlessly crushing her, snapping her lines of connection with the outside world, and shattering all but her toughest links with the past.

The southern jaw of the vise was the Muslim empire in the Levant, Africa, and Spain. The great caliphs of this empire, having made their hold firm on all the land around the southern half of the Mediterranean, turned their ambitions toward making that sea a Muslim lake. From naval bases on the African coast their fleets of war galleys ventured forth to seize one Mediterranean island after another, each one larger than the last, first the Balearic Isles, then Corsica, Sardinia, and finally even Sicily. From the same African ports, as from so many hornets' nests, came swift pirate vessels, singly and in groups. Greek and Byzantine merchant vessels were no longer safe. Neither were the coasts of Italy and southern France. Wherever they found a coastal town outside their own empire, the pirates would strike. They would appear out of nowhere, slay, plunder, burn, and seize prisoners for future sale as slaves, and be off to sea before the local count, miles away, could raise his county army and come to the rescue. They dared to ascend the Tiber and attack Rome. The seaport of Marseille at the mouth of the Rhone lost its trade with the east and shriveled to unimportance, unable even to prevent Muslim pirates from sailing up the Rhone and plundering inland France. Other pirates sailed out through Gibraltar, circled Spain, and struck at the French coast from the Atlantic.

The northern jaw of the vise was a barbarian people who up to this time seem to have been fairly quiet and unawakened, the Vikings of Scandinavia. These people had developed a rude culture of their own, even a form of writing, but it was a culture far different from anything known in Frankish Europe.

Oseberg Museum, Norway

A Viking ship, excavated from a Viking chieftain's burial mound, and now preserved in the Oseberg Museum, Norway. This vessel, a beautiful example of axe-hewn planking, shows the elegant lines and shallow draft characteristic of Viking ships. It was equipped with oars, and a mast which could be quickly stepped or unstepped.

A Description of the Baltic World

The peninsula of Denmark thrusts north from the European continent somewhat as the Greek peninsula, over 1000 miles away, thrusts south. Both are heavily indented with deep harbors, and off shore are many islands, inviting men to sail out and explore them. And just as the inland Mediterranean Sea encouraged Greek sailors to make ever bolder voyages farther from home, so the Baltic, another inland sea, offered a like opportunity to Danish sailors, once they had mastered the art of sailing from island to island. And once they had mastered sailing on the Baltic, there was a larger, more difficult sea lying to the west, the North Sea, with the green shores of Britain over the horizon to lure adventurers.

North from Denmark, across 60 miles of water, is the great Swedish-Norwegian peninsula, its shores pierced by still other natural harbors (fjords) and heavily forested with tall, straight cone-bearing trees, ideal for ship building. But many of these harbors face outward on the Atlantic with its rough weather and enormous tides, a savage challenge to sailors rather than an invitation, just as the Atlantic beyond Gibraltar was once a forbidding challenge to men of the Mediterranean. The great difference between these two land-sea worlds, the Mediterranean and the Baltic, is, of course, the weather; that of the first is mild and open all year round; the other is partly frozen over and buried in snow for several months in every twelve.

For centuries the men of Scandinavia had no ancient civilization to learn from as had the primitive Greeks of 1000 B.C., who "grew up" next door to the Minoans, Phoenicians, and Egyptians. Perhaps this explains why the Greeks were stirred to become aggressive shipbuilders and navigators 1700 years before the Danes. It was not until the Danes in their turn had found themselves the neighbors of advanced civilizations, first the Roman and then the Frankish, that they too began to stir. And their stirrings in turn awakened the men of more northern Scandinavia.

The Viking Tide Rises

In the year 800, Einhard, Charlemagne's secretary and historian, recorded that "When spring came again, about the middle of March, King Charles left Aachen and journeyed toward the coast of Gaul. Off this coast, which was being devastated by the piratical Northmen, he built and manned a fleet." This invasion by sea was the beginning trickle of a future flood. After Charlemagne's death, the Vikings, or Northmen as the Franks called them, came in ever greater hordes. They had developed a beautifully seaworthy type of vessel, with a draft of only about three feet, in which they could mount even small rivers for miles inland. Penetrating the land ever more and more deeply, they started the most savage kind of looting over the extreme northwest of Europe and gradually worked south, like an epidemic.

But northwestern Europe was only one part of the land that suffered. The Northmen also struck westward across the North Sea. Britain was overrun. The marvelous civilization which Patrick had inspired in Ireland was destroyed, never to reappear in the same form. Eastward the Northmen sailed along the Baltic and up every river they could find, into what are today Germany, Poland, and Russia. Everywhere kings, counts, and other local strong men raised armies and fought them, sometimes with temporary success. But the Northmen never gave up. With endless bravado they kept coming back in wave after wave, always thirsty for the joy of battle, slaughter, burning, and plunder. A high spirit of adventure must also have stirred them. For at the same time they were venturing out onto the Atlantic in their "long ships"—hardly more than rowboats—discovering Iceland, then Greenland, and finally the New England coast!

In western Europe the climax of this invasion came in 885, when the Northmen even tried to capture Paris, at that time an island city protected on both sides by the River Seine. In Russia, at the same time, Northmen were setting up permanent armed camps ever deeper in the land, first at Novgorod, then at Smolensk, and finally at Kiev, in Russia's very heart.

British Museum

Temporal and spiritual rulers in an age of fear. Three chessmen of walrus ivory, two kings and a bishop. Tenth century, possibly English.

A New Civilization is Born

By 900 A.D. the condition of western Europe, caught between Muslim and Viking plunderers, was utterly deplorable. Slaughter and famine had shrunk the population. Travel was almost nonexistent. Everyone lived inside a walled community, or *borg*, maintained by a count or a bishop, or near one to which he could flee when he heard the cry, "The Northmen!" or, "The Moors!" Coin vanished from circulation; some was looted, the rest hoarded. The condition of trade sank not merely as low as in ancient Egypt, but lower. For in Egypt, even though no one had used money, there had been trading by barter along the whole Nile Valley. Here, in some places, there was not even barter. Few dared to risk carrying goods to a point of trade. Centralized government completely broke down. True, from Charlemagne's time onward there was a so-called emperor who had been officially crowned by the Pope. But he moved his seat of government to a safe place deep within Christianized Germany, or rather what is today Germany. The counts in western Europe were ungoverned, and one after another they coolly seized as their own the counties they had been trusted to govern. It was not long before counts were at each other's throats over county boundaries, and a new sorrow tore Europe: civil wars everywhere.

Out of such wretched chaos it would seem impossible that order, health, and prosperity could ever again arise. But mankind is an endlessly enterprising breed. And as Aristotle had remarked over 1000 years earlier, he is a political animal, who sooner or later creates system out of anarchy. The society that the men of the tenth century began to create, and those of the eleventh and twelfth carried forward, was like none the world had yet seen. In some ways it was, in comparison to the best periods of Greek and Roman civilization, naïve and ignorant. But in others it towered gloriously above them. And within it lay the seeds from which modern Europe and modern America have sprung.[1]

The New Medieval Society

Its Feudal Structure

For some comments on the music of this general period see Appendix A, pages 602–3.

Just as had happened in China under the Chou dynasty (see page 254), so in this time of European confusion there developed a feudal society. The conditions were somewhat the same. A strong ruler (in this case Charlemagne) had distributed the responsibility for local government among many counts. These men later took advantage of weak central government and the general state of lawlessness to seize their counties as their own and even to make war on neighboring counts. On the land were farm workers, or *serfs*, who had been born there and might not leave it, riveted to it much as in the time of Diocletian. The counts provided for the armed horsemen or *knights* who comprised their private armies, by granting to each a piece of county farmland, each knight becoming lord of the serfs on his land in return for a promise to serve the count in war. The whole social structure was bound together by oaths of loyalty, oaths made holy by the one power everyone feared most, that of God to give or take away everlasting life. Serfs swore loyalty to their overlord, whether knight or count; knights swore loyalty to counts, counts to kings, and kings, in theory at least, to the Holy Roman Emperor.

Each oath had a material basis. In this age of confusion each neighborhood had to be self-sufficient, relying on little from outside. Men were compelled to cooperate, whether in combatting enemies or in producing food, clothing, and shelter. Thus serfs pledged a fraction of their crops to the knights and counts in exchange for their armed protection. The knights pledged loyalty to the counts in exchange for their land. The counts supposedly had a similar relation with the king, and the king with the emperor. But a strong and arrogant count, especially if he lived far from the seat of government, might ignore the king, just as a self-willed king might ignore the emperor. Thus later on, in the twelfth century, a strong king, Philip Augustus, was to begin the creation of a unified kingdom of France by compelling the counts, one by one, to obey him, at the same time defying the emperor.

A similar structure of men and oaths of allegiance grew up around the bishop of each diocese. Over the years pious kings and counts, sometimes as an act of penance for past crimes, or in thanks for some victory, had bestowed on every diocese large pieces of land, each with its serfs. The serfs swore allegiance to the bishop in return for his protection. The bishop distributed some parts of his land to support churches and priests. Other parts he granted to knights. For even a bishop needed a private army in those grim times. Priests and knights then swore loyalty to the bishop. But each bishop had been placed on his cathedral throne by an archbishop or cardinal, and therefore swore loyalty to him. Archbishops and cardinals in their turn swore loyalty to the Pope himself, from whose hands they had received their power.

Such, in brief, was *feudalism*, a form of society permitting a high degree of organization with a minimum of money, trade, or travel. It consisted of two great social pyramids, one devoted to government, the other to religion, the lands held by each interlocking with the other in an intricate pattern.

West front of Wells Cathedral, Somersetshire, England

A king as envisioned by a thirteenth century sculptor. Compare the self-assured majesty of this ruler with his anxiety-ridden counterparts from two or three centuries earlier, pages 310 and 314.

The feudal system can be described as a large number of laboring human beings who fed, clothed, and housed several levels of human beings privileged with leisure, in return for their pledge to protect, govern, and minister to the laborers. It has been estimated that ninety percent of the population at this time were serfs.

The basis of both pyramids and of everybody's survival was the land. There grew the grain which made man's bread; there grazed the sheep and cattle which supplied man's meat and the wool and leather for his garments; there grew the trees from which he shaped his tools, furniture, and dwellings; and thence came the stone and metal for his protective fortifications and weapons. The *psychological* basis of the system was first the need to cooperate for survival, and next *the belief that human beings were not equal but were "born" to belong to just one level of society and no other.* Such a society, though undemocratic, marked a certain social advance: it contained no slaves.

Originally developed in France, feudalism gradually spread eastward through Germany, middle Europe, and beyond. By the time it was beginning to disappear in the west it was taking hold in eastern Europe, where it clung stubbornly for centuries as the accepted way of life. Its lingering effects have affected even our own times. One of the causes of the Russian Revolution of 1917 was the inability of the Russian empire to free itself by peaceful means from the remains of a feudal form of society.

Some Invaders Are Tamed, Others Are Counterattacked

But perhaps these feudal pyramids could never have arisen unless the fury of the plundering invaders had begun to cool a little. The Northmen got what they wanted: new, larger, better lands to live in, with conquered peoples to work for them and pay them tribute. In France, for example, a weak willed descendant of Charlemagne known as Charles the Simple presented them with a region which ever since has been called Normandy and its inhabitants Normans. The former wild men settled, and in about a century gave the outward appearance of complete conversion to Frankish ways. They quickly learned to speak tenth century French, adopt French manners, customs, and clothes, master Roman law, use the Roman arch in buildings, and fight on horseback. They became ardent Christians; some even became monks, priests, and bishops, who learned to speak, read, and write Latin, the scholars' language of the period. But all this was chiefly on the surface. Rather than calming down, the Normans were inclined to use their new culture as a tool for gaining what they wanted. Whether they used weapons or legal argument, it was aggressively, to expand their power. William of Normandy, for example, invaded and conquered England under a ridiculous legal pretext (a more socially acceptable course than the outright seizure practiced by his ancestors). The Normans were trouble makers in a troubled land, where fighting disrupted everybody's daily life.

In this crisis, when emperors seemed helpless, the popes rose to creative action. They forbade battles on all but three days in the week! Violators were threatened with *excommunication*, an especially powerful weapon in that age of ardent worship and belief. For no priest might grant absolution or celebrate the Mass for an excommunicated man, who therefore believed himself doomed to a future life in Hell.

The popes then guided the restless energies of the fighting men of the north in a drive against the Muslim threat in the south. In this drive the Italien city of Pisa, facing the Mediterranean, had already proudly led the way. In 1015, with a fleet of only 60 galleys, she seized the islands of Corsica and Sardinia back from Muslim control, and then began to free the Mediterranean from Muslim pirates. Soon merchant vessels from Pisa were sailing safely to the Levant for rich cargoes, and the wealth and power of Pisa began to mount.

But Muslim rulers still held Sicily and Spain, perilously close to Europe. And presently a new war threat arose in the east. The Turks, an Eastern people, who had lately been converted to Islam, were moving westward from inner Asia, conquering even the Arabian Muslims in the Levant, and invading the Byzantine empire in Asia Minor. The Byzantine Emperor Alexius desperately appealed to the Pope, Urban II, for aid. The pope responded by declaring that any man who would go to fight the Turks and free the holy city of Jerusalem from Muslim rule would receive absolution for all his past sins, no matter how black.

The response was tremendous. Beginning in 1096, and over the next 200 years, eight waves or *Crusades* of European fighting men poured eastward to fight in "holy" wars. In a way these were an answer in the eleventh and twelfth centuries to the "holy" wars the Muslims had waged in the seventh, eighth, and ninth. Everywhere in these campaigns the ambitious, undisciplined Normans were in the forefront of the action. Some of the campaigns

West front of Wells Cathedral, Somersetshire, England

A thirteenth century bishop, spiritual counterpart of the ruler on the opposite page.

Photo Dr. Harald Busch

In a time when strife and housebreaking were uncontrolled, no man of substance was secure unless he owned a castle. In harsh contrast to the churches of the period with their geometrically controlled proportions, castles were planned with one aim in view, to make them impregnable. This is the Castle of Eltz, on the lower Moselle River, western Germany.

Photo Istvan Racz (Courtesy Thames and Hudson, Ltd., London)

Shoulders such as these bore the weight of the feudal system. Man in the garb of a serf. Finnish, fifteenth century.

attained their goal. The sacred city of Jerusalem was freed for a time from Turkish and Muslim rule. Sicily was freed, and a Norman king sat on its throne. But in other ways the results were disastrous. The Normans, with no superior force that could control them, took whatever they could seize. One carved himself a kingdom from southern Italy. Another assumed the title of King of Jerusalem. Others tore land from the weakened Byzantine empire and gave themselves fantastic titles, such as Duke of Athens. The government they had gone forth to help became their victim.

This anarchy reached its height (or depths) in the year 1204, when an army of Crusaders, acting as the ignorant tools of the wily city fathers of Venice, actually seized Constantinople and pillaged it. The loot in precious objects was carried back to every part of Europe, where it is still preserved in countless churches and museums. Constantinople never fully recovered. Venice attained the commercial supremacy over Constantinople she had desired. In the rioting at Constantinople that followed the looting, the great statue of Athena by Pheidias, which Emperor Constantine had removed from Athens and set up in Constantinople's chief forum, was shattered, even its fragments lost forever. Men had gazed upon her grandeur for over 1600 years. But she was not to be spared for our time.

New Breakthroughs in Food Production

What was eastern loss was western gain. With her most ungovernable fighters drained off, Europe had a chance to catch up with herself. But the key to the immense burst of energy and the surge of new population that now began to bloom in Europe seems to have been the invention of new, cheaper, and better sources of food. One of the first to recognize these new inventions had been the emperor Charlemagne.

The Greek and Roman grain farmers had plowed, sown, and reaped only half of their fields each year. Half was always *lying fallow* (plowed but not sown), recovering its fertility from the decay of weeds turned under by the plow and from the dung dropped by grazing animals. When farmers departed from this routine and overplanted, they wore out the soil, as occurred, for instance, before Diocletian's reign.

But the men of medieval Europe put to work a new farming principle, that of renourishing the soil through extra crops and extra plowing. One year they would plant wheat, barley, and oats, which impoverished the soil. The next year they would plant beans, peas, or lentils, which partially enriched the soil. In the third year they would plow the same land twice but plant nothing, allowing rotting plant growth and dung to ready it for a new sowing and reaping of grain. The men of the time did not know why this system worked; soil chemistry was unknown. But experience had shown that it did.

By dividing the land on a farm into three parts, and planting one to grain, another to beans or peas, and leaving the third fallow, one farm could not only raise a third more food each year than before, but there were even greater advantages. For beans and peas contain more and different proteins than grain, and together with grain therefore make a more energizing diet for man. And oats feed horses, a faster animal with longer endurance than the plodding, grass-eating ox.

So the supply of better food gave men more energy, and as horses replaced oxen to pull plows, the year's plowing was done faster. Also, farmers mounted on horses could now "commute" farther to their fields each day, and could therefore live in larger, centralized villages instead of being scattered all over the countryside in small hamlets. In Chapter 2 we saw how human living advanced when primitive men were able to gather in larger living groups. For the same reason Europe's serfs now led better lives. Under stimuli such as these, western Europe's population began to grow. A new, better fed, more energetic kind of man began to press outward against the untilled parts of the land. Forests were felled, swamps drained, and abandoned fields replanted.

Photo Istvan Racz (Courtesy Thames and Hudson, Ltd., London)

Woman in the dress of a housewife (although few could read). Finnish, fifteenth century.

Travel and Trade Revive

With more settled times, travelers ventured out on the roads again. Pilgrims came and went, bent on visiting the holy shrines and relics of the saints. A new invention, the horse-drawn heavy-load wagon with pivoted front axle reduced the cost of transporting goods by land. Merchants had learned how to travel in well-armed bands, thus protecting their merchandise. They took bold business risks by carrying what was plentiful in one place to another where it was scarce, buying cheap here and selling dear there. Counts and bishops had discovered that by protecting roads and waterways for travel they could collect a toll from the travelers. They were finding, also, that excess grain, wool, and hides produced by their serfs had a use beyond feeding and clothing the men who produced them. They were finding that merchants would buy these materials, paying them in coin.

For not only had barter revived, but so had the demand for metal coins to speed up exchange. Prospectors found and mined new veins of gold and silver to meet the new demand. Many counts and bishops began to mint their own local coinage. A money confusion reigned. The professional money changer appeared, the specialist who knew his way around among the 1000 or more different coins in circulation.

As the men who controlled the land began to build up a treasure in coin from the sale of excess farm products created by the labor of their serfs, they began to demand luxuries: spices for their food, fine steel weapons, silk as clothing for themselves and their families, or as gifts to churches for the vestments of bishops and priests. But in the tenth century, the source of such luxuries was far away in Constantinople and the Levant.

In the tenth century, before the Turks had arisen, before the Crusades, and before the fleets of Pisa had cleared the western Mediterranean of pirates, Constantinople was still queen of the East. In this period the safest route for merchants from Europe lay through passes in the Alps to the head of the Adriatic Sea, and thence to Constantinople by ship.

The old Byzantine seaport of Ravenna, from which the emperors of the East had ruled Italy, had been made useless by natural forces. Her harbor had become hopelessly silted up (today the city is miles inland). A new city, Venice, on a cluster of offshore islands further north, had replaced her.

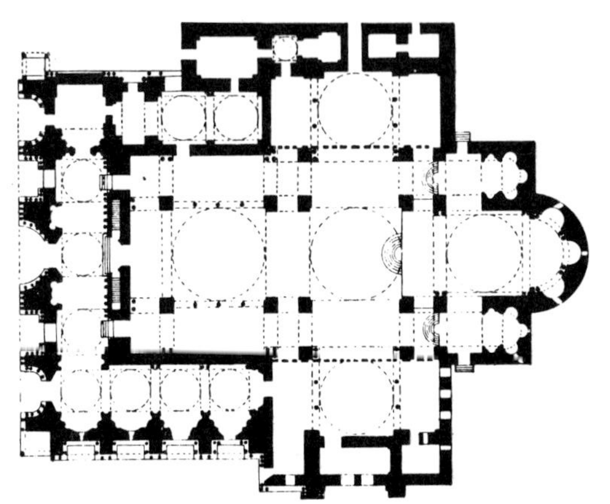

St. Mark's Venice, view of the west front, section, and floor plan.

VENICE, GREATEST BYZANTINE CITY IN THE WEST

At the extreme western tip of the Byzantine empire, Venice started out as a dependent of Constantinople. She was one of the many cities in the great sea trade network which the emperors of Constantinople, in the eighth, ninth, and tenth centuries, controlled for Byzantine profit and protected with the Byzantine navy. This region included the Adriatic Sea and part of its shores, the Greek peninsula, the Greek islands including Crete and Cyprus, Asia Minor, and the southern shores of the Black Sea. This region Muslim galleys and pirates had learned to avoid, lest they be destroyed by Byzantine naval vessels hurling Greek fire, a secret chemical weapon so jealously guarded at Constantinople that today its formula is unknown. The wealth of the Byzantine sea empire was fabulous. In the tenth century, taxes and import duties collected within it are believed to have poured $500,000,000 a year into Constantinople's imperial treasury. Everywhere the standard of exchange was the gold *bezant*, minted at Constantinople. While the Eastern empire was in this stable, prosperous state, western Europe was struggling back from primitive anarchy.

While other cities in the Byzantine empire were producing goods of different kinds, Venice was also producing merchants, shipbuilders, and sailors. From the first she was a *commercial* city. Companies of Venetians would pool their capital and send a ship, or a small fleet, eastward to pick up cargoes of luxury goods. When these came safely home to port, the Venetians would sell their cargoes at a huge profit to bands of merchants from western Europe. These would load their pack mules for the long, hazardous journey up through the Alps and then down again into France or southern Germany. There they would sell at a still greater profit to feudal lords whose wealth came from their farmlands.

Venice was the first Europen city in the tenth century to become a center of wealth. She was therefore the first able to build a great church (between 975 and 1050), partly from religious devotion, partly from sheer civic pride. At the time, Venice was part of the Byzantine empire. So the Cathedral of St. Mark is also Byzantine, the largest, richest, best preserved of its kind in western Europe. In all ages the Venetians have enjoyed enriching their city's crowning jewel. The four bronze and gilded horses above its main entrances are believed once to have drawn the bronze chariot in which stood a statue of the Roman Emperor Titus, on top of his triumphal arch. The great false domes, the mosaics above the doors, and their ornamental gilded frames are later additions.

Courtesy Italian Consulate, San Francisco

Merchants Create Their Own Towns

These merchants required a home base, a permanent dwelling for their families, for the storing of goods and wealth, and for the outfitting of new ventures. They chose, of course, the places of greatest security, the walled refuges, or *borgs*, built by bishops and counts,[2] and of these chose the borgs most conveniently close to the roads they had to travel. The merchants, once they had settled around these strong points, attracted other men with different skills whose services they needed: blacksmiths, carpenters, weavers, tailors, shoemakers, and so on. Soon what had once been a fortress became the center of a teeming community, which required a new defense wall of its own, and new, sensible laws to protect the rights of its merchants. Thus sprang up along the merchants' routes leading into Europe a whole series of prosperous towns, like stars in a dark sky. And of these the brightest was Venice, at the eastern end of the galaxy.

NORTHWESTERN EUROPE AWAKENS. At the same time other stars were appearing in Europe's northwest corner. The country at the mouths of the rivers Rhine and Scheldt, even in the Roman period, had been the center of a great woolen and weaving industry. With more settled times this trade revived. The demand from other parts of Europe for wool cloth became so great that the Flemish weavers even bought raw wool from merchants bringing it across the North Sea from Britain. Later Flemish fishermen caught and salted fish. To a land of devout religion, fish was a near necessity every Friday. By river boat, wagon, and pack mule, merchant companies carried the products of Flanders deep into Europe. By ship they carried them out onto the North Sea and the Baltic. One by one, prosperous towns developed in the north; and as the merchants, both north and south, grew in wealth, their little protective bands grew into larger, permanent organizations: brotherhoods, guilds, and leagues.

Medieval western Europe and some of its important cities:

1. Pisa	*11. Nurenburg*
2. Genoa	*12. Mainz*
3. Florence	*13. Trier*
4. Milan	*14. Ghent*
5. Trent	*15. Bruges*
6. Geneva	*16. Antwerp*
7. Bern	*17. Cologne*
8. Zurich	*18. Bremen*
9. Augsburg	*19. Lubeck*
10. Strassburg	*20. Barcelona*

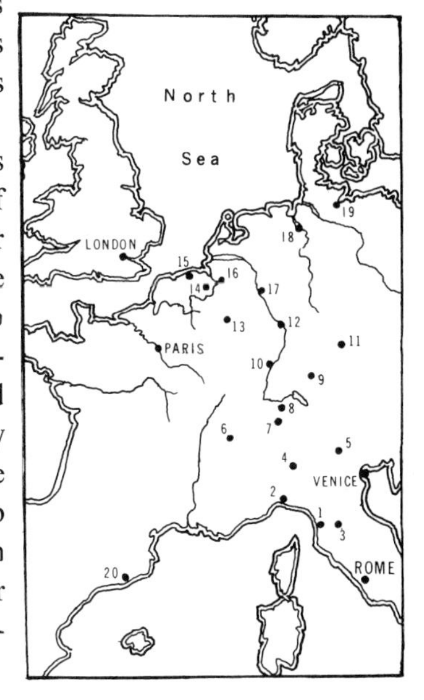

Courtesy Consulate of France, New York City

Gate of the French town of Carcassonne, whose medieval defense walls still stand, with nineteenth century restorations.

WHAT A MEDIEVAL TOWN WAS LIKE. By the year 1100 there was a whole galaxy of free towns spread across Europe from the North Sea coast south all the way into the Alps, each with its own government and its own personality. These towns sprang up on the property of counts and bishops, but their whole character soon became anything but feudal. The merchants who built them were boldly independent, had traveled, and held fluid wealth, that is, money. They had small sympathy for men whose lives were spent in one spot, whose wealth was in land, and who tried to keep society frozen with a system of arrogant feudal oaths of loyalty. Their towns were a haven for serfs, who, once they had escaped to "breathe the free air of the town," were their own masters, provided they could make a living. Small wonder, therefore, that the citizens of the towns found ways to shake off ownership by feudal lords, sometimes peacefully, sometimes by open revolt. They were a distinct new class, or rather a return to importance of one already existing from Roman times. They were called, from the old French word for borg-dwellers, the *bourgeoisie*.

These free towns were in some ways (and without knowing it) surprisingly like the city-states of ancient Hellas. Each was a highly organized unit, a political work of art created by its own citizens, who had banded together to provide themselves with a city government, fair courts of justice, and the maintenance of town walls for defense. To all these problems they brought creative good sense. But between old Hellas and the new Europe there were vast differences.

MERCHANT GUILDS AND CRAFT GUILDS. Nowhere in a medieval town could one find a slave. No man was ashamed to labor with his hands. And the working citizens grouped themselves into brotherhoods, or *guilds*, each piously organized unter the protection of some saint, but each with intensely practical aims. There was at least one local guild of merchants whose presence had created the town, and who had shaped the local government and laws to fit their interests. Following their example, other professions and crafts in the town had organized their own guilds. For security in those troubled times the members of these craft guilds often grouped themselves compactly in one quarter or along one street, weavers in one place, fishmongers in another, goldsmiths in another, and so on. Since patent laws did not exist, each craft guild wanted to protect its own trade secrets; and since almost nobody in town could read or write, unless he were a priest or monk, the guilds wanted to find ways to pass on these trade secrets to each new generation of craftsmen. The way they chose was the apprenticeship system, already in existence since the Roman period.

Medieval mason's mark and the grid on which it was constructed. Hundreds of such marks have been found carved on stones in European cathedrals and churches. But they fit into only a few grids. It is believed that the grid identified the guild in which the mason served his apprenticeship, whereas the mark was distinctive of the mason, who was awarded it when he had earned the rank of journeyman.

THE CRAFT GUILDS AND THEIR APPRENTICES. The word for craft knowledge at this time was, literally, *mystery*. When a boy was about 14, his father, having considered his talents and ambition, would seek to place him as an *apprentice*, or student of the mystery of a particular craft, such as tailoring, carpentry, blacksmithing, goldsmithing, painting, or the like, under a recognized master. The boy would move into the master's household, usually with a few other apprentices, and would live there for several years, serving the master's family in return for his craft training (home and workshop were always under one roof). Anything he produced, or helped produce, was the master's property. Training in a craft was thus an intimate, personal affair which the apprentice received as part of a family. The master craftsman became, in a way, his second father. In the course of time, if the boy satisfied his master, he was freed from his apprenticeship and became an independent craftsman, admitted to the guild and entitled to be paid by the day: a journeyman (from the old French word *journée*, meaning daily). Later, with luck and hard work, he might marry and set up his own household as a master craftsman.

Each craft represented a highly regulated industry. The guild members allowed no one man to monopolize it. Raw materials were fairly distributed; prices were fixed; the number of apprentices to each master was limited. Intense competition might exist between different towns, but within one town the craftsmen themselves would not permit it.

Men Harness Natural Energy with Machines

When Charlemagne abolished slavery in his empire, he helped to set a new value on human labor. In medieval Europe, for the first time in the world, we find men seriously directing their ingenuity to labor-saving devices. No longer could heavy tasks be passed off on some slave. Consequently the heavy monotonous tasks, such as grinding grain, sawing planks for lumber, even the wielding of heavy hammers in smithing, over which slaves had worn themselves out for centuries, were at last handled in many places by water power.

A page of machine drawings from the notebook of a French thirteenth century architect, Villard d'Honnecourt. Some of the machines are misunderstood; others are believed to have magical power; all are naively simple. They are important because of the real interest which they show in such devices. The interest had to come first. Real understanding and achievement followed later.

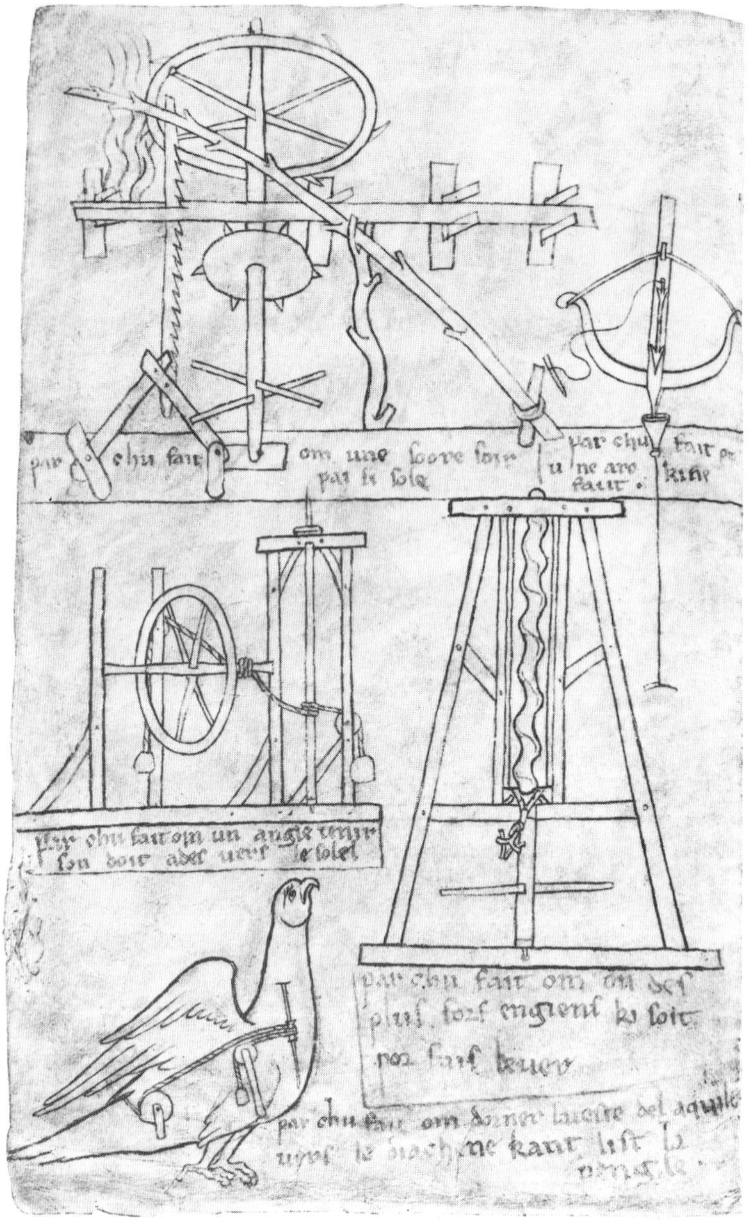

Courtesy Anton Schroll, Vienna

In the eighth or ninth century, a simple invention, the stirrup, *added to the deadliness of fighting on horseback. The horseman firmly seated in a high saddle and braced with stirrups could now charge with a lance gripped under one arm, converting himself and his galloping horse into a heavy projectile. The effective use of the lance, singly or in well-drilled group attacks, required constant training from boyhood. The* tilting yard *became a necessary area in or near every castle. The* knights *or* chevaliers *of Europe became a special class with their own standards of fighting and lovemaking, both romantic. The word* chivalry *had its birth at this time (from the word* cheval, *a horse!).* Jousting *was a sport developed by the knights of Europe to keep themselves in fighting trim, but with amorous overtones. Ladies were present, to inspire their lovers, to rejoice when triumphed or to grieve when they were unhorsed. Thirteenth century manuscript.*

Heidelberg University Library

The idea of a water mill was not new. Vitruvius, writing in the time of Emperor Augustus, described such a mill, even including the gears needed.[3] But now, nearly 1000 years later, men were at last applying it everywhere. At the same time they advanced the ideas of Vitruvius and invented the windmill,[4] for use where water currents were too slow to turn a mill wheel.

In northwestern Europe, in response to the mounting demands for woolen cloth, mechanical devices were created to speed the spinning of thread and the weaving of thread into cloth. Thus in the twelfth century came into being a simple form of spinning wheel, and the foot-treadled loom.

Several simple inventions made possible a more effective use of horses. The rigid horse collar increased four-fold the power horses could exert to pull plows and wagons. Introduction of a pivoted front axle made horse-drawn wagons easier to steer. Stirrups put riders in more secure control of their mounts.

Pinacoteca Sabauda, Turin, Italy

Mary, mother of Jesus, as medieval men envisioned her, surrounded by adoring angels. This painting, by the Italian artist Duccio di Buoninsegna (about 1260–1318), is obedient to Byzantine tradition in its flatness, its gold background, the rigid pose of Mary, and the throne on which she sits. But the infant Jesus and surrounding angels have a lifelike quality which belongs to a new age.

Intellectual Creation

But no one can experience a magnificent building just by looking at its foundations. And merely to picture these achievements of medieval men—the breakthroughs in food production, the rebirth of trade and town living, the emergence of the bourgeoisie as a social class, and the new control of horse power, water power, wind power, and foot power—fails to give a full picture of what was happening in that great age. A new civilization, a new way of life, was coming into being. Every man had a part in it, great or small, and every man must have felt the thrill of it in the air. There is no other way to explain the superhuman achievements of that age.

Christ judging the world on the Day of Resurrection. Sculpture above the center door of the Cathedral of Notre Dame, Paris. Christ, flanked by Mary, John, and two angels, sits with the world of mankind beneath his feet. Below him souls are being weighed by the recording angel. In the bottom panel, all men, whether king, queen, pope, bishop, knight, or common man, awake and rise from their tombs on Judgment Day.

The center of this developing world was the city of Paris. Here, between 1180 and 1223, dwelt the strong king, Philip Augustus, as he tamed the arrogant counts and forged from a disunited land the beginnings of the French nation as we know it today. Here, in the person of the king, was the pinnacle of that French creation, the feudal system. Here dwelt another feudal prince, the Bishop of Paris, with authority over many priests. Here also was a natural meeting place between merchants from the south with their luxuries and those from the north with their plain staple goods. And here, besides all these, beginning in 1000, was one of the great new expressions of the age, a university.

In the Europe of this age education was conducted by the only really educated men, the clergy. Thus it happened that in each of Europe's great cathedral towns was a school under the special protection of a bishop. The university of Paris began as the school protected by the Bishop of Paris, and its director was the administrative officer, or *chancellor*, of his Cathedral of Notre Dame. But various pious noblemen from time to time had added other schools to it, financing the buildings and donating farmlands complete with serfs to provide for their upkeep. At length the chancellor organized these schools into four divisions, or *colleges* (theology, law, medicine, liberal arts), and thus the university was born. Its reputation soon spread throughout Europe. There students from far and wide might attend lectures by the greatest thinkers and men of learning of the day. All lectures were given in Latin, the only common language everyone could understand. What those lectures were about gives us a glimpse of the absorbing interests, the intellectual brilliance, and the amazingly limited knowledge of that day.

A young man (occasionally even a mere woman) would spend years earnestly studying Latin grammar and rhetoric, logic, arithmetic, the elements of geometry, rudimentary astronomy, and the simplest kind of musical theory. He was then a person of superior education, and declared to be a bachelor of arts. Nowhere was there a study of the forces of nature, of science as we understand it.

Clearly, medieval men had a keen interest in controlling the power of nature, but not one of them would have dreamed of studying the subject in a university. One learned such things as a common apprentice. To the thoughtful medieval man, the greatest power in the world was spiritual, not physical, and its origin was not in this world, but in God. Since God's power had created the world, the way to understand the world must be to understand God. The power of God to grant to each man an eternal life of happiness after death was known as God's grace, or Divine grace. When one compared one's eternal life after death with one's short life on earth, what could be more necessary than to understand and win God's grace?

The most important lectures at the University of Paris, therefore, were devoted not to a knowledge of matter and this world, but to an attempt at a knowledge of God, that is, *theology*. The problem was, how was one to study God? To the medieval man the answer was simple: God, being all-powerful, had chosen to reveal himself to mankind at certain times, through certain men. The *revelations* of God's nature made by these men were the whole source of man's knowledge of God. And who were these men? The most important were enshrined in the Bible. Jesus himself was looked on as the perfect revelation. On a lower level were such sources as the two great Greek philosophers, first Plato and later Aristotle. In the twelfth century, Plato was known through a part of just one of his dialogues, the *Timaeus*.

In this dialogue Plato describes God as a mathematician, supremely logical, who had created every part of the universe on geometrical principles, so that all its parts were united in perfect harmony, just as are the individual notes in a piece of symphonic music. Plato maintained that a man who studied geometry and musical theory would thus come to understand something of God's mind, and would begin also to understand how the universe had been put together. (See pages 183–184.)

This one dialogue of Plato's had a profound effect on the thinking men of the twelfth century. It was in part for this reason that they gave logic, geometry, and music so high a place in university education. And the great theologians of the day, using logic as an intellectual tool, attempted to construct on a narrow foundation of knowledge and ideas (Holy Scripture, Plato's single dialogue, and a few other sources) a noble picture of the entire universe, created by God, in which all created things were contained.

The men engaged in this mighty, even if impossible, attempt were in their own way completely in harmony with the rest of medieval society. For the great desire of most men of this time seems to have been to bring their world back from confusion and anarchy to a state of unity in law, order, and government. In their way the theologians were fighting to create this unity *intellectually*, just as valiantly as King Philip Augustus was *politically*, when he compelled rebellious noblemen to swear loyalty to him as a king blessed by the pope and therefore by God.

This great effort toward unity, in which so many men were caught up in so many different ways, seemed to require something dramatic in which all men could share, thus finding among themselves the unity they craved. Perhaps only in this way can we explain the glorious churches which were to spring up in the cathedral towns of France, and later the rest of Europe,

Thirteenth century handwriting. From the notebook of Villard d'Honnecourt (see also pages 324, 331).

Courtesy Anton Schroll, Vienna

Photo Jose Echaque

Above: Gothic building at its simple beginning. The Cistercian monastery of Santa Maria de la Huerta, northern Spain, built 1142. The pointed arch seems first to have been developed by Muslim architects. Europeans probably derived the form from this source. Opposite page: Gothic building at its most daring height. The interior of Beauvais Cathedral, built 1272.

in the two centuries between 1150 and 1350. For grandeur of scale, ingenuity of construction, costliness in relation to limited resources, and above all sheer beauty, the world has rarely if ever seen such an achievement, before or since.

The cathedrals of France were a project in which all men shared in one way or another. Not only did everyone, whether bishop, nobleman, merchant, craftsman, or simple pilgrim, give what he could to finance them, but men of high rank, even princes, occasionally took token part in hauling stones to the building site. The great driving force unifying these men was a desire to express adoration to God, to that aspect of God called Christ, and to Mary, whose purity had made possible the birth into this world of Christ in the human form of Jesus. Such was the medieval center of absorption. Men were especially fascinated by Mary, the unifying channel, as it were, between God in Heaven and man on Earth. One after another, cathedrals rose dedicated to Mary, *Notre Dame*, Our Lady.

Though wealth and labor came from all the people, the actual planning of the cathedrals was strictly in the hands of the clergy, and, of course, their highest thinking, and the total sum of their knowledge, went into this planning. It is only through an attempted understanding of the thinking of the medieval theologians that we can understand a medieval cathedral as a work of construction, as design, as art, and as an expression of medieval man's idea of the universe.

Photo Th. Seeger

Church Architecture

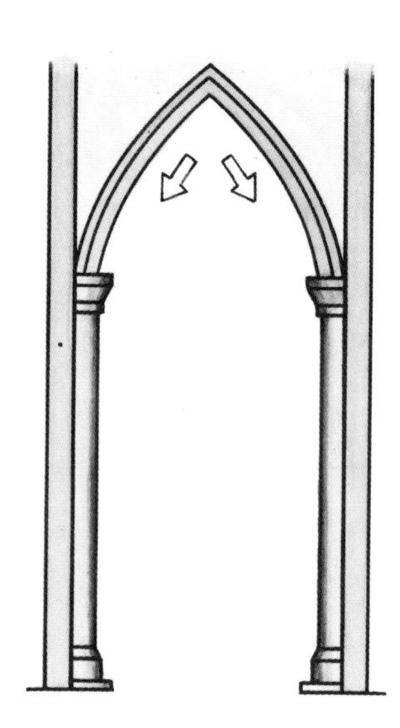

ADVANCES IN ENGINEERING. In the eleventh and twelfth centuries the monks of the Cistercian and Benedictine Orders (see page 333) were active in many ways, including the building of new monasteries and churches in a style using round arches.[5] Out of all of this action came three advances in building construction, the first to be made in 500 years:

1. *The lateral thrust of an arch can be reduced by pointing it,* and therefore less masonry will be needed to keep it from pushing the walls outward. Perhaps even more vital to the devout men of that time was the way in which such an arch pointed upward, heavenward.

2. *What remains of this outward thrust can be effectively counterbalanced by a flying buttress,* a column of masonry standing free from a building, but connected with it by a half-arch at the point requiring the counter thrust.

3. More daring construction can be achieved through using the *groined arch.* This was a new way of looking at an old Roman constructional device, the *groined vault.* The Roman groined vault was an intersection of two tunnels, or barrel vaults. (See the picture of the Baths of Caracalla, page 219). But architects using the *groined arch* fixed their attention on the lines of intersection rather than the tunnels. Instead of two tunnels, they saw two intersecting arches, the space between them being filled with masonry; they made the ribs of those arches stronger. It was a matter of emphasis. But the new emphasis led to new inventions: a more complex intersecting of vaults and a practice of making several arches spring in different directions from a single column. It sometimes pays to look at a familiar object or idea in a new light.

These three advances, the pointed arch, flying buttress, and groined arch, can be seen only in their modest, cautious beginnings in monastery churches. It was not until they were picked up and applied to the proud construction of city churches and cathedrals that they came into their own. The new style of construction had a practical advantage. It reduced the mass of stone required for a building by as much as one-half, a great saving in an age when every block was hewn by hand and drawn by horse or ox.

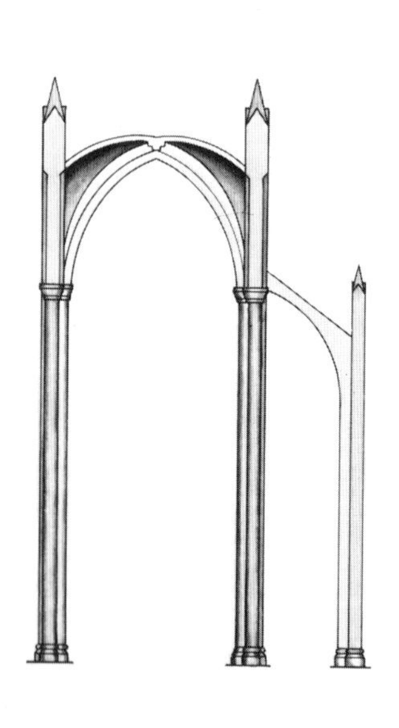

RADIAL SYMMETRY AS A DESIGN FORM. It would be untrue to say that medieval architects invented the design scheme known as *radial symmetry.* That honor probably belongs to the inventor of the spoked wheel, or, long before him, to nature, where one can find an endless variety of radially symmetrical structures and patterns. It would be more correct to say that men of the Middle Ages used this design form as a basis for creating a new kind of marvel, the great rose windows usually placed at the west end of their churches. To the medieval mind everything in a church must be a symbol of something divine. The rose windows were a symbol of Mary, mother of Jesus, of whom it was said, "I am the rose of Sharon."[6] To us the familiar type of rose is the "double" rose with its thickly crowded petals. But medieval men seem to have known the "single" rose, whose structure of five or ten petals radiating from a center was simple and clear. The rose window was only one of various radially symmetrical structures which architects of the period created.

A radially symmetrical structure created by a medieval architect. The central column of the chapter house, Salisbury Cathedral, England, thirteenth century.

Marburg Fotoarchiv

A favorite subject for radially symmetrical composition on a flat surface in the Middle Ages was the Wheel of Fortune. In those troubled times the spectacle of a man rising from being a nobody to become a person of fame and power, only to fall and to sink back out of sight into unimportance, disgrace, or death, was a common one. The whole tragic sequence was conveyed by picturing man as caught up and then cast down by a wheel ruled by Fate, Chance, or Fortune. A plan for such a composition was created by Villard d'Honnecourt, the thirteenth century architect whose machine drawings are shown on page 324. In the center is the image of Fortune, the changeless ruler of human affairs. Around the outside are six images of a king, blessed and then cursed by Fortune's whim.

A radially symmetrical design can be divided into identical mirror-image parts by any of several (two or more) axes, which intersect at just one point, the design's center. The geometrical pattern on which the seven figures are placed, has three such axes shown in the drawing, and three others not shown.

A thirteenth century scheme for a "Wheel of Fortune," described on this page. A thousand years or more earlier, Buddhist missionaries are believed to have carried the message of their faith as far as the eastern Mediterranean. One of the indirect results may be this symbol, which is perhaps a greatly altered version of the Wheel of Karma (pages 193, 306). From the notebook of Villard d'Honnecourt.

Courtesy Anton Schroll, Vienna

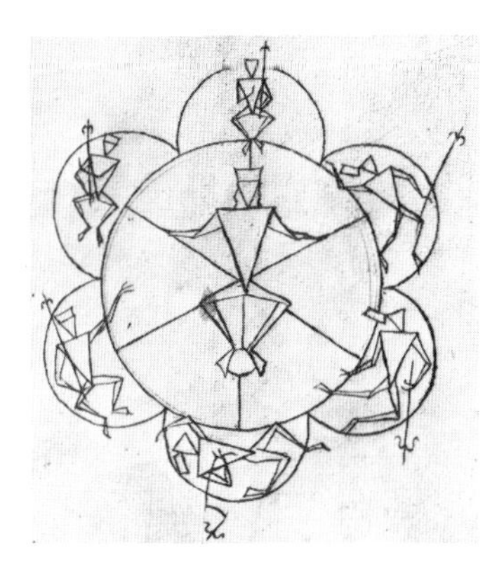

Courtesy J. K. St. Joseph, Selwyn College, Cambridge, England

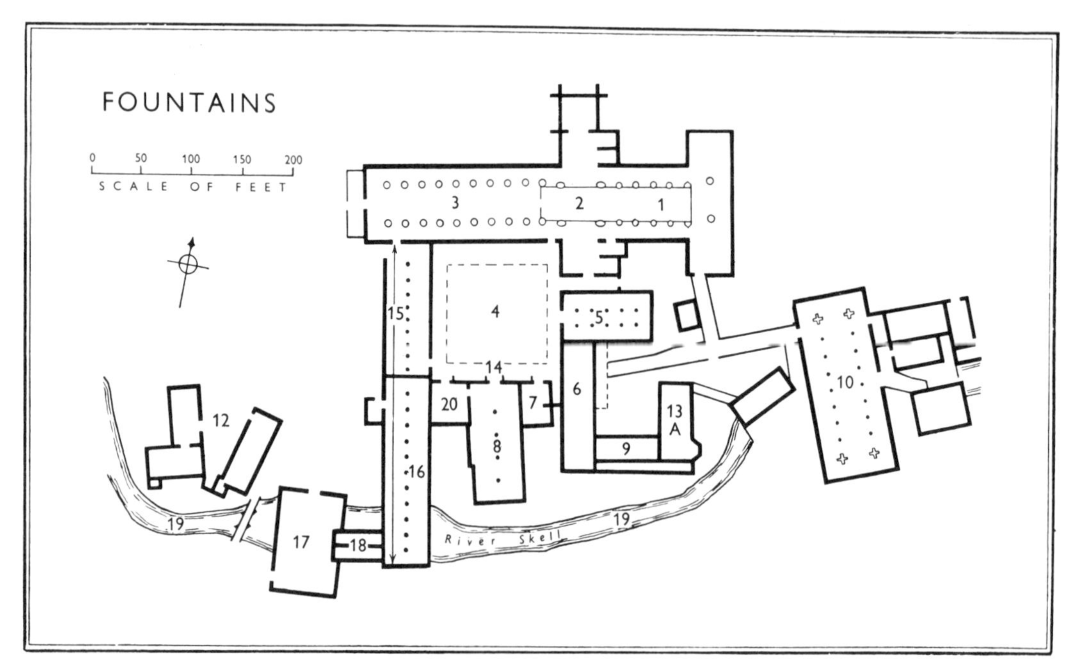

1. Presbytery
2. Quire
3. Lay brothers' quire
4. Cloister garth
5. Chapter-house
6. Dorter (on first floor)
7. Warming-house
8. Frater (on subvault)
9. Rere-dorter
10. Infirmary
11. *Cellars*
12. Guest-house

13A. Abbot's Lodging

13B. *Prior's Lodging*

14. Washing-place
15. Lay-brothers' Dorter
16. Lay-brothers' Frater
17. Lay-brothers' Infirmary
18. Lay-brothers' Rere-dorter
19. Stream or Drain
20. Kitchen

MONASTICISM. In the sixth century a mighty spiritual leader, Benedict of Monte Cassino, an Italian, had developed rules of living for men and women who wished to devote the rest of their short lives on earth to prepare for eternal life in the hereafter. This had satisfied a great popular hunger of the time. Everywhere men took vows to become monks, and women to become nuns. They devoted themselves to lives of prayer, work, and charity in monasteries and convents as members of the *Benedictine Order*. For support they relied at first on the work of their own hands, and later on gifts from kings, noblemen, bishops, and pilgrims.

In the tenth century another remarkable man, Bernard of Clairvaux, a Frenchman, established another order of monks and nuns known as the *Cistercian Order*. It proved to be an improvement on the Benedictine system; Bernard created monasteries which were self-supporting, relying on efficient farming and stock raising. The Cistercian pattern of living was outstanding for its simplicity. All ornament was forbidden in its churches, whose beauty relied entirely on their fine proportions, an intellectual beauty which Bernard believed was akin to that of Heaven.

The monks and nuns of the tenth, eleventh, and twelfth centuries made an immense contribution to the recovery of Europe and the formation of its new civilization. They formed havens of peaceful industry when the land was in turmoil. They helped reclaim land and spread new farming methods. They provided homes for orphans, hospital care for the sick, and charity for the poor. They conducted schools, and in their *scriptoria*, or writing rooms, monks patiently copied what few books were available.

THE NEW SPIRIT. Discoveries in structural engineering fail to explain the astonishing use which church architects soon made of them. A totally new spirit was abroad. Church walls were no longer hidden behind mosaics or plaster. Now the aim was to show the clean structure of the building—the work done by every pointed arch, even by every carefully placed stone. If a column supported several arches, its surface was carved to resemble a *cluster* of columns, each supporting its own arch, its purpose made crystal clear.

At the same time the lines of the structure were aimed at carrying the eye upward. Columns were made longer, more slender, with smaller capitals. The pointed arches springing from them were made ever taller. To display this structure, great windows, made glowing with rich color, were opened in the walls. A use of glass on a scale no one before had dreamed of was created to flood church interiors with soft light.

Nor was this enough. The vast interior must not be silent. A marvelous new space-filling way of making thunderous music was created. The *pipe organ*, that device used by the Romans to add a thrill to scenes of horror in their amphitheaters, was given a new and holy use, and a more complex form than the Romans had ever attempted. For at least 1000 years, from the tenth century to the present day, the organ has been the musical instrument most closely linked to worshop, and over that long span of time it has undergone continual change and development, each age making of it what it desired. In the church towers were hung devices to make the *outside* air resound, great bells, single or in groups *(carillons)*.

Opposite page, above: Aerial view of Fountains Abbey, an English monastery, now in ruins, but whose plan is still clear. In the great monastery church, services were conducted nine times daily, starting at 2 A.M. On the material side, English monasteries like this did much to build up England's wool trade by raising wool-bearing sheep. Opposite, below: Plan of Fountains Abbey and a list of its structures and their purposes.

A spiritual leader of the Middle Ages, Francis of Assisi. In the thirteenth century he founded the Franciscan Order *of monks, "the little brothers of the poor," whose purpose, among others, was to help the poor in cities. As the centuries passed, new religious orders were continually being founded in Europe, each intended to fit a particular need of the times. This intensely expressive piece of wood sculpture is an imaginary likeness, made over 100 years after Francis' death.*

Finnish National Museum, Helsinki. Photo Istvan Racz (Coutesy Thames and Hudson, Ltd., London)

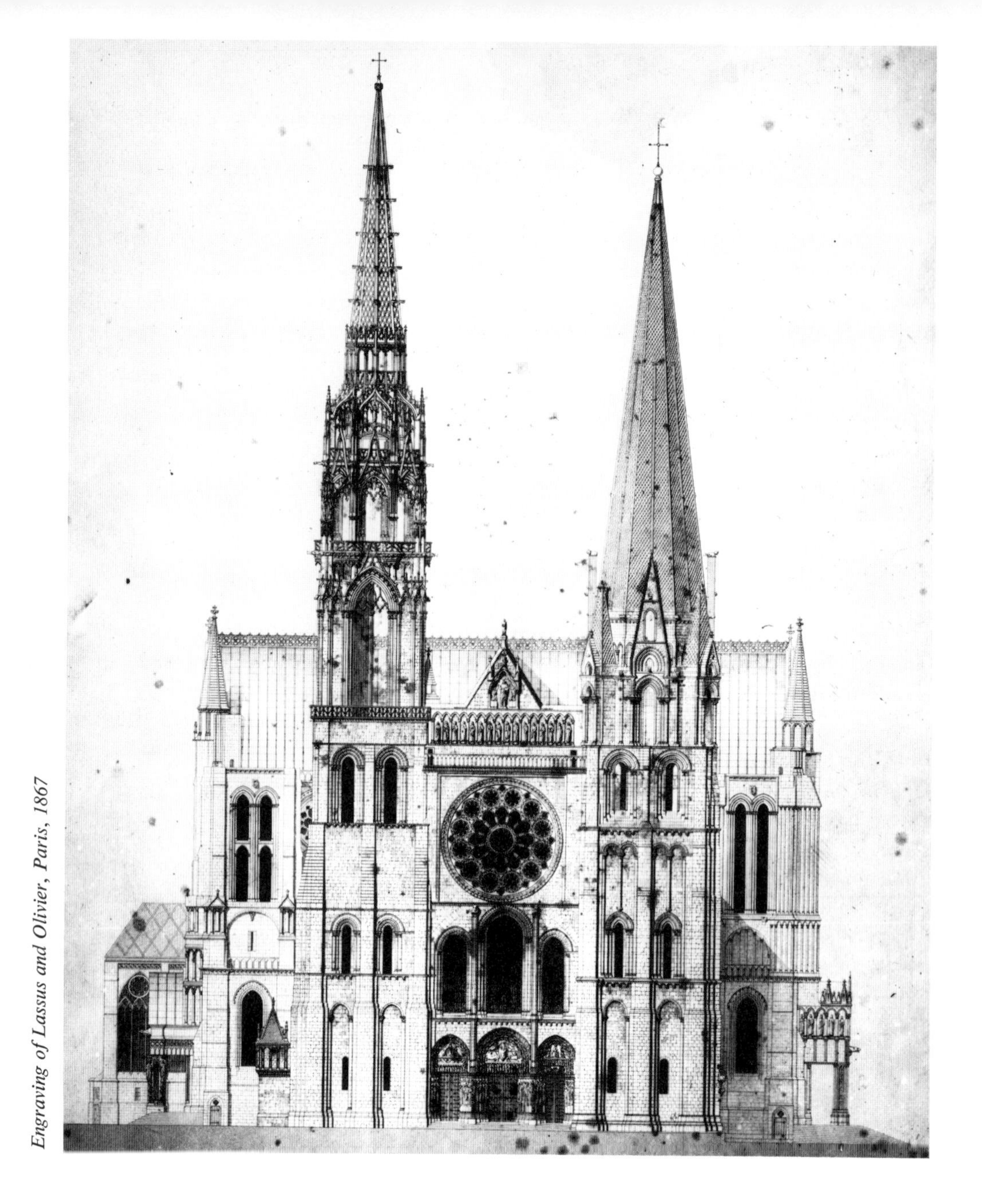

Engraving of Lassus and Olivier, Paris, 1867

West front of Chartres Cathedral.

THE CATHEDRAL OF OUR LADY OF CHARTRES. The total effect of moving through a great medieval church whose glass is still intact and in place defies description. One of the few which has been thus fortunate is the Cathedral of Our Lady of Chartres[7] about 45 miles southwest of Paris. As one approaches this great building with its two spires, one can sense in a glance the whole history of medieval architecture. For the right-hand (or south) spire was completed in the later twelfth century, just as the new style was taking form. The left-hand (north) spire was finished almost 350 years later, when the style had been pushed to its limit.

Between the great towers are three tall doors, each set in an arched frame enriched with complex, many-figured carving. Above these are three arched windows, taller than the doors. And above these rises a great *wheel window*, or *rose window*, larger still.

If we enter by the center door, under the serene image of Christ, surrounded by the four Evangelists, blessing the world, we find ourselves in the vestibule between the towers. This is the oldest part of the church, the only part not ruined by an accidental fire which destroyed the rest of the building in 1194.

Moving on into the church, we enter the immense, softly lighted world created by some medieval architect whose name is forever lost, but who seems to have lived to see his dream of form and color made real in stone and glass, for the cathedral had been rebuilt according to his designs by about 1220. The distance from the entrance to the east end is about 432 feet, and from the floor to the apex of the arched ceiling 108 feet. But it is not size alone which gives the visitor such an experience of quiet excitement, nor is it just the soft colored light from the windows. There is something else: the remarkable way in which the walls and the space within them have been proportioned.

THE DESIGNING OF CHARTRES. The unknown architect of Chartres Cathedral, just like Ictinos who had planned the Parthenon over 1500 years before, faced a number of problems, but his were far more difficult. Not only is Chartres almost twice as long as the Parthenon, and (without even considering its spires) three times as high. It is a far more complexly articulated building. He had to deal with forces which never plagued Ictinos at all. For the Parthenon stands by reason of dead weights, or vertical pressures only. Chartres is full of lateral thrusts which can knock over walls unless counter-thrusts are brought into play, or buttresses placed to absorb them.

He was working in an age still without scientifically precise engineering knowledge. Its substitutes were a mixture of what we may call "building sense" acquired through experience, heavily mixed with tradition, superstition and symbolism. It is easy for us to laugh at this mixture, for we live in an age whose technical knowledge enables us to calculate the stresses within and upon a building before it ever leaves the draughting table. But have we created, can we create, a magical architectural presence for our time as miraculous as Chartres was for *its* time? The answer is no, at least not yet.

It can, therefore, be absorbing to try to conjecture the thinking of this unknown master builder who conceived Chartres and steered it to completion.

That he had building sense in a high degree is obvious. The building stands beautifully firm after 750 years.

As to tradition, we can only assume that he had attained the rank of master in the stone masons' guild whose center was probably Paris. Thus he was well schooled in the quarrying, hauling, hewing, hoisting and mortaring of stone. He probably had learned, besides, the closely guarded secrets of his guild, namely a number of geometrical plans on which to base the design of sacred buildings. This was an age in which such plans were everywhere relied upon in the creation of religious works of art, whether great or small. In the past seventy-five years art historians have made some progress in the rediscovery of these secret plans. Two examples of their rediscoveries are shown. One is the floor plan of a German cathedral, the other the design scheme of a little ivory shrine less than four inches high. Both rely on a

From Medieval Cathedrals and Sacred Geometry, G. Lesser (Courtesy Alec Tiranti, Ltd., London)

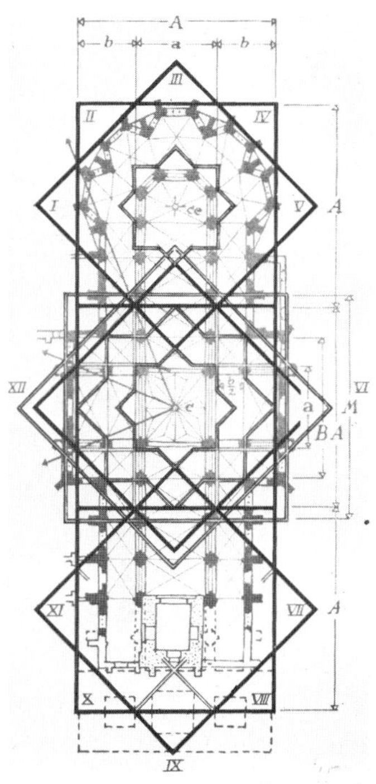

Two examples, one on a large scale, the other minutely small, of the medieval craftsman-designer's use of geometric patterns to guide his plans. Above, apparent design scheme of Schwerin Cathedral, nearly 300 ft. long. Below, design scheme of an ivory portable shrine, about 3 in. high.

De Young Memorial Museum, San Francisco, California

Courtesy Msg. Roger Michon, Bishop of Chartres

Tree of Jesse window, Chartres Cathedral, a triumph of bilaterally symmetrical design.

favorite medieval basis for such designs, the star octagram. For other examples of medieval geometric planning see Project 40. Projects 37 and 38 give you opportunities to test your own detective skill in this direction.

The tradition of which this kind of planning is a part seems to be of enormous age, extending backward in time in a more or less unbroken line, through the designers of imperial Rome to those of the Greek world, and beyond these, perhaps, to the priest-designers of Egypt. It is possible that this tradition included the custom of laying out a sacred building within a circle. The original church of St. Peter in Rome, erected in the fourth century A.D., seems to have been conceived within such a circle, as was the Parthenon. And Chartres itself seems to lie within such a circle.

Besides being a master mason, the architect of Chartres must have been under the direction of learned clergy who had studied geometry, logic, music and theology at the University of Paris, or at the similar school at Chartres. These men, almost certainly, had read the fragment of Plato's *Timaeus* mentioned on pages 184 and 327. To the skill and traditional training of the master builder these men must have brought a theoretical, philosophical approach. They would perhaps have conceived of the building as an attempt to realize in stone an idea existing in the mind of God himself, God the divine geometer and musician who has created the universe, so they believed, on principles of geometry and musical harmony, principles invisible except to the eyes of human reason, just as God himself is invisible except to the eyes of human faith.

It is perhaps a combination of thoughts such as these, stemming partly from masons' traditions, partly from the thinking of theologians, that accounts for the complex geometric scheme which seems to underly the proportions of Chartres Cathedral. The plan of the building, whose internal length is 400 medieval French feet (just under 13 modern inches) lies within a great circle of slightly greater diameter. If a decagon is inscribed in this circle, and another circle is inscribed within the decagon, diagonals thus created seem to define important proportions and divisions of the plan. This seems to be apparent in spite of irregularities in the building's layout, due perhaps to the shortcomings of medieval surveying.

If a square is also inscribed within the circle, as shown, certain diagonals formed by both square and decagon seem to determine still other important boundaries of the building.

If we look next at the section of the cathedral through its transepts, we find its proportions determined by a similar pair of circles, circumscribing and inscribing a decagon, and by the diagonals within them. The internal height from floor to apex of vault is 100 medieval feet (108 modern) or one-fourth the building's length. In both cases the agreement of geometric pattern with the actual building seems to be so consistent that it is hard to consider it accidental.

We may well ask the question, why were these particular patterns chosen as invisible determiners of the stone structure? We can only surmise. The tradition of placing a sacred building within a decagon is as ancient as Egypt itself. But to a medieval theologian such a plan would have particular significance. To medieval men a favorite symbol of Mary, mother of Jesus,

Courtesy Msg. Roger Michon, Bishop of Chartres

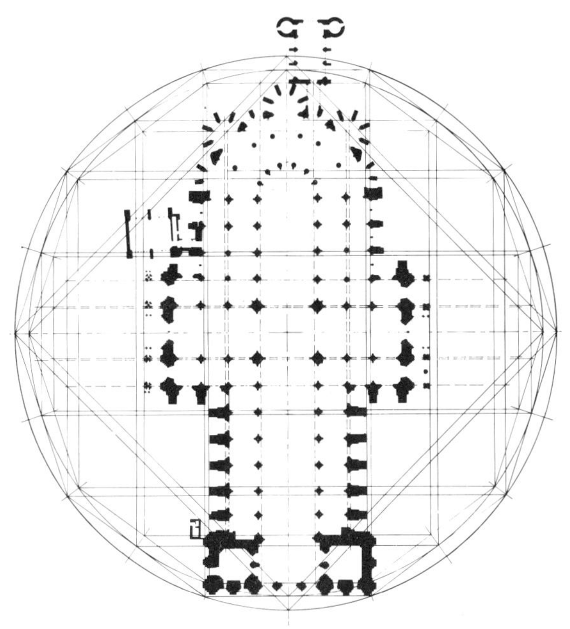

Above, left: rose window in Chartres Cathedral's north transept, a glorious example of radially symmetrical design. Above, right: ground plan of Chartres Cathedral. Superimposed is a modern conjecture as to the medieval geometric scheme which may have determined the plan, discussed opposite page. Lower right: section through the transepts of Chartres Cathedral (engraving by Guillamot, 1867, after drawing by Adam). Superimposed is a conjectural geometric scheme which apparently accounts for the proportions.

was the five- or ten-petaled rose. It would therefore be logical to plan a church sacred to her so that it harmonized with the pattern of her flower.

To medieval men a square was often the symbol of God the father and his unity with Christ. To place a square within the great circle of the church plan, and to allow some of the plan's proportions to be determined by interaction between God's square and Mary's decagon seems not unfitting to the thought of the period.

M. H. de Young Memorial Museum, San Francisco, California

Reliquary, which at one time held the relic of a saint, perhaps a bone from his forearm. Such relics were sometimes believed to work miracles of healing, and persons who sought their aid often went on pilgrimages to visit them. Copper coated with gold, Italian, fourteenth or fifteenth century.

Artist and Craftsman in Medieval Society

If we ask, what was the life of an artist like in the Middle Ages? the answer is simple: artists as we understand the word did not exist. The concept of an artist as someone who is a revealer (see page 152) would have struck a medieval man as dangerous. Matters of revelation were under the firm control of the Church. In order to create anything, a man must not only have mastered the use of some material, whether wood, metal, cloth, leather, glass or stone. He must also have mastered the one style which everyone in his world accepted. Inventiveness within that style was limited; society was stronger than its members, and individual men needed the assurance of that strength as symbolized by that common style.

The men that we would call artists were therefore submerged beneath the surface of medieval society as craftsmen, and were thought of as such. All started as apprentices, passed upward into the rank of journeyman, and perhaps at last succeeded in becoming full masters of their craft. Of these a rare few had the talent, or the luck, to plan a cathedral such as Chartres, or develop the scheme of its great windows, or devise and complete the cross and candlesticks of its high altar, or the sacred jewelry worn by its bishop. But if such opportunities to be an artist-craftsman on a grand scale were scarce, the chances of being a craftsman at all were many. This was an age when machine production and mass production were unknown. Everything that was made at all came from human hands. And unlike the factory employees in our own age of parts assembly, every man saw his product through from start to finish. Each product, whether a scythe or a pair of shoes, a bench or a water jar, a trimming knife or a sword, was an individually created object, in certain ways unlike any other. So not only did craftsmen have to be present in every community; they also had the chance to make their own thought and feeling show in their work, so long as they stayed within the narrow limits of popular taste. The scattered few objects that have somehow survived the past six or seven hundred years, the pieces of furniture, the bowls, jugs and goblets, the tools and weapons, show a vigor of form which seems to say, "A human being created me!"

To the hand-craft way of life there were drawbacks. Labor-saving devices as we know them hardly existed. Working hours were long; men aged fast; death often came early. But a vastly larger proportion of working men and women were masters of their product, of the place where they worked (their homes), and their tools, than today. And then life was simpler. Possessions, because they took such labor to make were fewer, and no one had learned to expect more. Even to a great lord's banquet every guest brought his own knife and spoon. And even at a lord's table no one expected the dishes to match; nobody had yet become obsessed with uniformity. If life in a great castle could be so modest, imagine what it must have been in a peasant's hut.

Medieval Society: Climax and Decline

The great cathedrals of medieval Europe, of which Chartres is but one, are somewhat like glorious flowers—flowers bursting forth from the vigorous

National Library, Vienna

Above: *God as geometer and architect, designing the universe with a compass. Medieval men accepted this idea of God from Plato and from a verse in the Old Testament: "Thou hast ordered all things in measure and number and weight." (Wisdom of Solomon, Chapter 11, Verse 20; to be found in the Apocrypha).* Right: *The medieval architect as he saw himself, humbly following God's example by using compass and set square. A hardwood carving from a church or cathedral choir stool.*

National Museum, Munich

tree of medieval civilization. But that culture, born of such stress and struggle, did not remain at its climax long. Its turning point was in sight even as Chartres was being completed. Of the many causes for that change and eventual decline we can guess at a few.

Mary grieving at her son's death. Wood carving, early fourteenth century.

Turku City Historical Museum, Finland. Photo Istvan Racz (Courtesy Thames and Hudson, Ltd., London)

The intense desire for unity, which was one of the great drives behind medieval culture, had a negative side, namely a fear and hatred of deviation. Christianity was a splendid facade freshly plastered on a recently pagan society—pagan Frankish, pagan Italian—some of whose customs were still rooted in a pagan past. A core of fanatical high clergy stirred the people to fear what lay behind that facade.[8] For them the greatest crime was not murder or treason but incorrect belief. Any challenge to priestly authority, any appeal to the inner light of conscience as opposed to the official teachings of the Church, was therefore rewarded with death by burning. The idea, it seems, was to purge society completely, with fire, of its "unclean" members. Original thinking in the field of philosophy and religion was thus extremely dangerous. But this was an age of vigorous minds, well schooled in logic, and it was also an age of high courage. Great movements of independent religious belief therefore appeared. Of these, the Albigensians in the south of France were the strongest in the twelfth and early thirteenth centuries. The pope, finding these men and women unmoved by his warnings that they avow their error, preached a crusade against them. The movement was crushed by force, and the Albigensians were literally exterminated in hideous fashion, screaming among smoke and flames. Thus France lost a precious possession: many vigorous, independent minds; timid conformity was encouraged.

The two great feudal pyramids, one crowned by the emperor, the other by the pope, were supposedly cooperative, one ruling the political world, the other the spiritual. Actually both held great political power and were therefore doomed to clash. Each drew to itself a political faction, and for a time part of Europe was divided between Guelphs (for the pope) and Ghibellines (for the emperor), as the parties were called. This power struggle had its destructive effect. Men began to regard the office of pope with cynicism. And the behavior of many medieval priests and monks added to this cynicism.

King Philip Augustus, the strong willed king of France, was determined to rule his own land without interference from either emperor or pope. In this respect he was looking forward beyond his own times to the Europe of the future. When Otto IV, the ruling emperor, united with Philip's rebellious lords to subdue him, he met their united forces and at the battle of Bouvines in 1214 gave them such a beating that no one dared challenge him again. The battle of Bouvines was a turning point in French history. As late as 1956, it was honored with a great "action painting" by the French painter Mathieu.

Philip was just as firm with the free merchant towns, though in a different way. He wisely respected them, granted them much freedom in running themselves, and even preferred to select sober minded bourgeoise merchants as his counselors, rather than power hungry feudal lords. But in return he demanded, and won, the towns' allegiance. Neither would Philip stand interference from the pope. By sheer force of will he demanded, and won,

Schnütgen Museum, Cologne. Photo Dr. Harald Busch

Head of Jesus. Wood carving, about twelfth century.

the right to share in selecting bishops to rule each diocese of France. This was a blow to papal authority, one of a series that were to follow over the next 300 years.

But the greatest blow of all was a calamity which befell Europe in the early fourteenth century. The continent was beginning to crowd with population, especially the towns, which ignored the sanitary measures once practiced by the Romans. The people were thus easily exposed to epidemics. In the year 1348, and on at least eight successive occasions, the bubonic plague, brought, it is believed, from the Near East on ships docking at Marseille, swept across Europe. In one year alone between one-fourth and one-half of the population died. Nothing was ever the same again. When Europe emerged from this horror with a restored population, it was in some ways another Europe, with the beginnings of new aims and outlooks.

National Palace Museum, Taiwan

A Eulogy on Pied Wagtails, *copied in the handwriting of an emperor, T'ang Hsuang-Tsung. He was the subject of Tu-Fu's poem on the opposite page, and was later to lose his throne. The stamp marks are the seals of owners through whose hands the page has passed in the course of twelve centuries.*

MEDIEVAL CHINA

The T'ang Dynasty

The rulers of the T'ang dynasty went through the usual Chinese cycle, or rather the cycle common to great dynasties everywhere. The first T'ang emperors tended to be strong, clear-eyed, and aggressive. Then, as later princes were brought up in luxury, surrounded by courtiers who hopelessly spoiled them by fawning, the dynasty lost its vitality. In an emperor, vitality was a necessity. To dominate a country larger than the United States in a time of poor communication, to control ambitious governors of distant provinces, to deal with famines caused by floods and droughts, to keep northern nomads at a distance by force or diplomacy, to maintain an effective army without making generals all-powerful, to maintain a smoothly running civil service without letting the mandarins get out of hand, and at the same time to guard against *coups* by one's own relatives: such was the business of a Chinese emperor. It was no job for a weakling. When a weakling or a man of poor judgment sat on the throne of the Son of Heaven, the vast, complex political machine began to tear itself to pieces, with hideous results.

The T'ang dynasty's founder (T'ang T'ai Tsung) became emperor in 621, and established the empire's capital at Ch'ang-an. For the next 130 years China's history was one of expansion. Emperors or their generals hurled back the Turkish nomads and made them Chinese vassals. North of Tibet they reopened the Silk Road all the way to Persia. When Persia fell to the Muslim Arabs, the Arabs found their advance east of Bactria blocked by Turkish nomads fighting under the emperor's orders.

The T'ang period was brilliant in other ways as well. Toward its beginning lived a remarkable many-sided scholar named Hsuan Tsang (602—664). The teachings of Buddhism had reached China some centuries before, and had inspired him to learn about them at first hand. Against the wishes of the emperor he set out for India in 629, alone and without a passport. Fifteen years later, in 644, he was back in China with a knowledge of Sanskrit in his mind, and, in his hands, copies of India's leading treatises on philosophy.

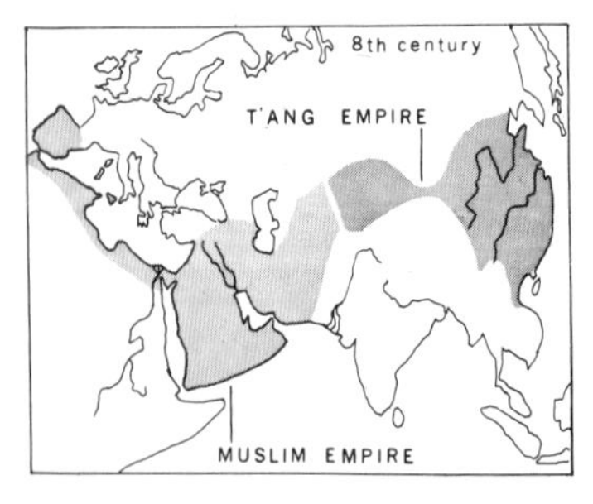

This time the emperor welcomed him with respect and urged him to write an account of his travels. Hsuang Tsang prepared a remarkable, comprehensive report, in its way equal to his other work of translating philosophy. To the latter he devoted the rest of his life; in so doing he gave the Chinese language and thought a new dimension. He enriched it by adding to it the greatest products of the Hindu mind.[9]

At the same time missionaries from the west had introduced an early form of Christianity (Nestorian Christianity) to China. Toward both religions the Chinese emperors were tolerant. But the mandarins with their strong Confucian training and tough practicality disapproved of them, especially Buddhism. Wrote one of them: "The doctrine of the Buddha is full of absurdity and extravagance . . . This sect numbers more than 100,000 monks and the same number of nuns, all vowed to celibacy. They would form 100,000 families and provide soldiers for the future."[10]

Two T'ang Poets

Toward the close of this 130 year period lived two of China's greatest and best loved poets, both supported by the emperor at his court. Li-Po was a lyrical dreamer, a loving observer of nature. To his friend Tan Ch'iu he wrote:

> My friend is lodging high in the Eastern Range,
> Dearly loving the beauty of valleys and hills.
> At green Spring he lies in the empty woods,
> And is still asleep when the sun shines on high.
>
> A pine-tree wind dusts his sleeves and coat;
> A pebbly stream cleans his heart and ears.
> I envy you, who far from strife and talk
> Are high-propped on a pillow of blue cloud![11]

By contrast, Tu-Fu was a thoughtful observer of human affairs. He watched the growing laxness of the emperor Hsuan-tsung:

> On a throne of new gold the Son of the Sky
> sits among his Mandarins. He shines
> with jewels, a sun among stars.
>
> The Mandarins speak gravely of grave things;
> but the Emperor's thought has flown out
> by the open window.
>
> In her pavilion of porcelain the Empress
> sits among her women, a bright flower
> among leaves.
>
> She dreams that her beloved stays too long
> at council. Wearily she moves her fan.
>
> A breathing of perfumed air kisses the Emperor's face.
> "My beloved moves her fan, and sends me
> A perfume from her lips."
>
> Towards the pavilion of porcelain walks the Emperor,
> shining with jewels, and leaves his grave Mandarins
> to look at each other
> in silence.[12]

Long necked jar with dragon handles. Chinese, T'ang dynasty.

Avery Brundage Collection, San Francisco. Photo William Abbonseth

A Chinese image of Gautama the Buddha. It is of gilded bronze, the earliest such Chinese image known which bears a date, the equivalent of 338 A.D. At that time, although the great Indian seer had been dead for 800 years, Buddhism and its ideas were only recent arrivals in China. Height nearly 16 inches.

Every Brundage Collection, San Francisco, Mike Roberts Color Reproductions, Berkeley.

He watched the injustice which supported this luxury:

At court they are distributing rolls of silk
Which the women of the poor have woven.
To extort it from them and offer it to the emperor
their husbands have been beaten with rods.
Moreover I have heard it said that all the gold plates
in the imperial palace
Have passed, one by one, into the hands of the family
of the favorite.
In the palace there is such abundance that meat is
allowed to go bad and wine to turn sour,
While in the streets people die from poverty and cold.[13]

And the effects of the endless wars roused Li-Po:

The Great Wall, which separates China from the desert,
Winds on into infinity.
Above the whole frontier
No towns now stand.
Here and there scattered human bones
Cry their everlasting hatred.

Three hundred and sixty thousand men, dragged
  from their homes,
Weep as they bid their families farewell.
Since it is the order of the prince, they must obey,
But who will cultivate the fields?[14]

Li-Po died just before revolution swept the land, but Tu-Fu lived to witness it. It started with a palace coup. One of the emperor's trusted generals, a soldier of fortune from the nomad north, decided to seize the royal power. The emperor fled; the beautiful empress, who had seduced him from his duties and had given palace treasures to her own family, was strangled. To restore the emperor's son to the throne, loyal Chinese generals stooped to calling on the nomad Turks for help.

The eight year civil war which followed had an apalling effect on China. Destruction by fighting, famine, and disease, the interruption of farming and trade, and an inhuman tax burden to meet the costs of war brought such misery that the population shrank by at least half—26,000,000 or more people seem to have met unnatural deaths. The T'ang dynasty never succeeded in restoring prosperity to China. After another wretched century and a second revolution (this time a popular uprising of landless, starving peasants and ruined businessmen) drove the family from power in 874. Again Chinese generals called in the Turks, granting them, as a reward for their aid, large pieces of northern China (on which they settled and became completely Chinese in culture). But this did not prevent the murder of the royal family in 904, the collapse of central government, and the dismemberment of China into nine pieces, eight under different warlords, the ninth a pitifully shrunken empire with a capital at Kaifeng. There, ruler followed ruler. One general, in order to make himself emperor, called in a new wave of barbarians, the Tartar Khitai, to help him, and as a reward gave them China's northeast corner. Here was the town of Peking, at that time a minor place, later to become the empire's capital. Thus did the Tartars gain a first foothold on China's soil, an event fateful in history.

Two court ladies of the T'ang period practising the art of falconry. The hawks once mounted on their wrists have been lost. These ceramic figures, whose overall length is about a foot, were recovered from a T'ang dynasty tomb. The carved wood supports are modern.

University of California Museum of Anthropology, Berkeley. Photo John Bridgman

National Palace Museum, Taiwan

Eight Chinese characters executed by Emperor Sung Hui-Tsung himself, in a style of calligraphy (called slender gold *script) which he himself created.*

The Sung Dynasty

Permanent peace returned when a general arose who was strong enough to reconquer the land, humane enough to regain the people's confidence, and sufficiently practical to start healing the sick economy. This man was Sung T'ai-tsung, founder of the great Sung dynasty, perhaps the most famous in China's history. Its reign was to last for three centuries, from 960 to 1279, of which, as usual, the early period was successful, the latter part increasingly disastrous.

The Sung rulers were not to be famous as conquerors. The Khitai held northeastern China around Peking as an independent kingdom. An aggressive Tibetan king had seized for himself a piece of China's northwest. The rest of the empire, still an enormous area, was governed by the Sung emperors from their capital, Kaifeng. Wisely they appointed ministers whose chief concern was economic reform. Among these mandarins there was intense controversy over policy, much as we find among economists today. Experiments were tried, guided by the remarkable Chinese historical sense. Some remind us of the Roman Emperor Diocletian, especially an attempt to fix the price of everything. Others were remarkably modern. Public granaries were set up, of two kinds. One supplied the needy, a sort of unemployment insurance. The other was a device for regulating prices and keeping prosperity at a level; when there was a bumper crop and grain prices tended to drop, the government bought grain at a fair price. When grain was scarce, the government kept prices from soaring by selling, again at a fair price. A system of farm loans was set up by which farmers could borrow from the government in the spring and pay back after the harvest, thus rescuing them from loan sharks who had been charging one hundred percent interest. The government regarded twenty percent interest as fair, an error in judgment which led to this policy's failure. But in economic thinking the Chinese of this period were far ahead of medieval Europe.

In the field of commerce the Chinese were just as forward looking. Merchants and craftsmen had long ago organized themselves into guilds. The art of banking (whose rise in Europe we shall watch in the next chapter)

was developed to a high degree. The imperial government, 700 years ahead of Europe, had even taken the daring step of issuing paper banknotes. Business was intensely active and prosperous. The great southern ports of Canton and Hankow were centers of international trade, where coastal and river junks swarmed. There Muslim and Persian merchants, whose ships transported goods both ways through the Malay Straits and across the Indian Ocean, maintained colonies and warehouses. South China, after centuries of labor clearing forests, was beginning to find many people living on its land. The population of the empire mushroomed to over 90 million.

The Chinese of the Sung dynasty, like those of preceding ages, seem to have been highly inventive. To meet the new opportunities of ocean commerce, they developed the mariner's compass and constructed a type of ocean-going junk equipped with a stern-post rudder, remarkable for its stability and ease of handling. A host of other inventions from this and previous times were to reach Europe by various channels and to stimulate technical growth in the West. Paper had already been transmitted by the Arabs. Among other inventions which followed were the canal-lock gate, deep well drilling, efficient harness for draught horses, the crossbow, gunpowder, the wheelbarrow, printing by movable type, the kite, cast iron, and finally (late in the eighteenth century) the iron chain suspension bridge.

But it was in the field of art and philosophy that the Sung dynasty won special distinction. The emperors were men of great refinement, deeply interested in cultural matters. Their taste set the pattern for the rest of the land.

Shrike, *painted about 1110 by the Sung dynasty artist Li An-Chung. Li was a member of the Emperor Hui-Tsung's Academy of Painting. Former owners have stamped it with their seals. Size 10 inches square.*

National Palace Museum, Taiwan

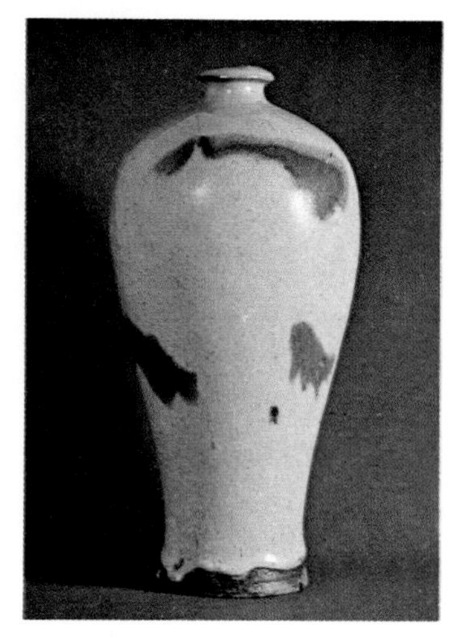

Sung Dynasty Ceramics

Chinese potters had discovered a kind of hard white clay, known everywhere today as *kaolin*, from the location of the Chinese clay pits at Kaoling. This, when fired at a great heat, produced the beautiful ceramic ware *porcelain*. The Chinese had already discovered the technique of *glazing*, or coating pottery with powdered glass, which melted in the kiln and when it cooled sealed the pores of the clay vessel. They had also learned to use glazing as a coloring device and a means of giving texture. The Sung emperors supported pottery centers and cherished their finest products. The vases, bowls, and dishes of this period, made to please an emperor or persons of rank and wealth who copied the emperor's taste, have never been equaled anywhere for beauty of shape, delicacy of coloring, or purity of texture. Chinese ideals in this field were high. For example, they specified that one kind of porcelain (Ch'ai ware) should be "thin as paper, ringing as jade, and blue as the sky seen between clouds after rain."

Sung Dynasty Painting

Ceramic ware from the age of Sung. Above: "Mei P'ing" vase, pale blue, touched with dark rose. Height about 14 inches. Below: bottle vase from the late Sung or early Yuan dynasty, with a floral design.

Both Avery Brundage Collection, San Francisco. Photos John Bridgman

The emperors encouraged the arts of painting, calligraphy, and poetry by bestowing titles of distinction on outstanding artists and men of letters, by conducting contests and sponsoring exhibitions, and by practicing these arts themselves. Chinese painting reached perhaps its greatest height in this age, setting standards for later times and for its development in Japan.

Every artist started his career with a long apprenticeship during which he mastered many different brush strokes, each with its own name and its particular effect. Next he was trained in copying from memory the works of various masters. After examining a painting at length he would go home and try to reproduce it. Then, just as in the West every artist concentrates on drawing the human figure, so in China the focus was on plant forms, chiefly the bamboo, in all its moods, seasons, and stages of growth.

At last the artist was considered ready to compose. His subject (unless it was a portrait, or on a religious theme) was almost certainly some aspect of nature, ranging from a study of a single flowering branch to the sweep of a massive mountain range. The scene was never painted on the spot. Creation took place at home, after the artist had spent long periods of meditative study of the scene, in a Chinese version of the Indian practice of Dhyana, in which spiritual unity was reached between artist and nature. Without such an experience the work would be mechanical and contrived. But without the previous training the work would be weak, without style, faulty in composition, and lacking in richness of detail and contrast. The Chinese connoisseur who enjoyed the finished painting would respond emotionally to its total impact. He would then take additional pleasure in studying the use of the different brush strokes, which he knew by heart. Thus, by a rather distant parallel, an experienced modern listener at a symphony concert enjoys the sweep of the music as conceived by the composer, while he critically appreciates the relationship maintained between instruments, the handling of phrasing, and even individual performances within the total *ensemble*. And

just as in an orchestral performance no player can go back to erase a false note, so the Chinese artist could never remove or paint over an error. His piece of silk, spread out on the floor before him, instantly absorbed every touch of ink and made every stroke permanent.

Human beings, when present in Chinese landscapes, are insignificant in scale, but in a relationship of enjoyment, conscious or unconscious, with their surroundings. Whether one sees a sage contemplating a view, an emperor on a journey, a fisherman asleep in his boat, or a plowboy riding his waterbuffalo, one senses that the Tao of harmonious interaction between man and nature is complete. Nature majestically dominates man; and man, recognizing that fact, is at peace. But man, in the person of the artist, quietly dominates nature. He interprets it in a work of art. He selects from nature only what he needs, then combines what he selects into a serene picture-world which is new. Thus he interprets nature with his own personal vision, and his own unique control of the complex technique learned from his masters.

Classical Chinese painting took three customary dimensions. There was the vertical oblong, intended for display on walls, but rolled up when not in use. Then there was the album page, suitable for placement in a book, where it could be enjoyed as part of a collection. The form of these is often a compromise between square and circular, as if intended for mounting on a Chinese fan. Last of all there was the scroll painting, sometimes 50 feet long, which was to be enjoyed by slowly unrolling, as if one were on a journey through ever changing scenery. The sense of the viewer being in motion is also created in the largest of the vertical wall paintings. As one's eyes mount the landscape the angle from which it is represented tends to be constantly level, as if the viewer were physically climbing, looking and enjoying while he climbs.

An Emperor-Artist

Of all the Sung emperors the most famous is perhaps Sung Hui-Tsung (1082—1136). Not only did he form a royal academy of painters, entitled to wear robes of purple silk and to bear insignia of jade and gold; he also attempted to find a philosophical link between the three great Chinese religions of the period, Confucianism, Taoism, and Buddhism. But when he entered the field of power politics he brought ruin on his empire and tragedy on himself. He dreamed of ousting the Khitai from China's northeastern corner, never stopping to think, apparently, that these former Tartars had completely absorbed Chinese culture and had become loyal allies. He made the fatal error of enticing another Tartar people who were still savage nomads into attacking the Khitai from the north. The operation was successful; the Khatai were overrun. But the nomad Tartars presently turned on the Chinese (stirred by a second diplomatic error of the Emperor's). They rolled back the Chinese armies, entered and looted the capital of Kaifeng, and took the Emperor himself captive. The great Sung Hui-Tsung died nine years later, still a military prisoner. His successor moved the capital south, across the Yangtze to Hangchow.

National Palace Museum, Taiwan

Snowy Peaks at Dusk, *by an unknown artist of the early Sung period. About 40 × 22 in. High above a river a temple nestles among mountains.*

China's astonishing vertical mountains, which inspired the great landscape painters of the Sung and other dynasties.

The Coming of the Mongol Horde

This was but a prelude of sorrows to come. The Tartar tribes of Siberia had up to this time only just begun to awaken from their endlessly routine life as herdsmen in the northern wilderness. Now a new wave, the *Golden Horde*, who called themselves Mongols, under a great leader, Genghis Khan, were to erupt in the greatest nomad flood of all time, spilling across the civilized world wherever the land was open to cavalry, in a surge which did not subside westward until it had washed across Russia and into Hungary as far as the Danube. The mountains blocked their way into India. The Great

Wall saved the Chinese empire for two years. Then, in 1211, the Mongols were through it, and nothing could stop them until they had reached the banks of the Yangtze.

The invaders understood only one use for land: as pasture for herds of horses and camels. Cities and carefully tilled fields, one surrounded by walls and the other by fences and irrigation ditches, were alike merely a nuisance, impeding the grazing of livestock. The Mongols wiped them out and leveled them, often massacring the inhabitants. The first inroads of the Mongols were therefore everywhere utterly destructive of advanced civilization. The great cities of Persia and the Arab empire were left desolate. The canal system of Mesopotamia, which had functioned for 4000 years, was wrecked, never to be restored. In the Far East the same fate befell parts of northern China. Peking was reduced to a wilderness of covered mounds.

At the same time Genghis Khan knew how to appreciate a valiant enemy. He spared the lives of a few and in time even listened to them. Such men provided an opening wedge of understanding through which some awareness of the material advantages of Chinese civilization gradually entered his mind. In his son this understanding had widened. His grandson, Kublai Khan, was, as we shall see, an enlightened ruler.

Fate of the Sung Dynasty

Prior to 1233, the Mongols conquered northern China only. The Sung emperors, in their new capital of Hangchow, south of the Yangtze, had once more set up a court in which they resumed a refined mode of living. The beauty of the country surrounding Hangchow, the dramatic mountains, cultivated plains, and exquisite flowers (azaleas, roses) which they found there proved a fresh inspiration to court artists and poets. South China, with its endless stretches of rice paddies and its prospering multitudes of merchants, was a splendid source of imperial revenue.

But the Sung pattern was to repeat itself. Once again the emperor needlessly aroused the invaders' anger, just as Hui-Tsung had. Beginning in 1233 the Mongols launched an invasion which was to continue for over 40 years. In the course of it they adapted themselves to new ways of fighting in situations where cavalry had proved useless: rice paddy fighting, mountain fighting, and even fighting at sea. In 1276 the last Chinese center of resistence fell and the great empire was a Mongol possession. The Mongols had learned much besides improved methods of fighting. They had learned to respect farmland and cities. Kublai Khan, who was to govern this empire until 1290, was a wise ruler who set about healing the wounds of war. These were grievous; again the population had shrunk by nearly half, as shown by the Chinese' own census reports of the period.

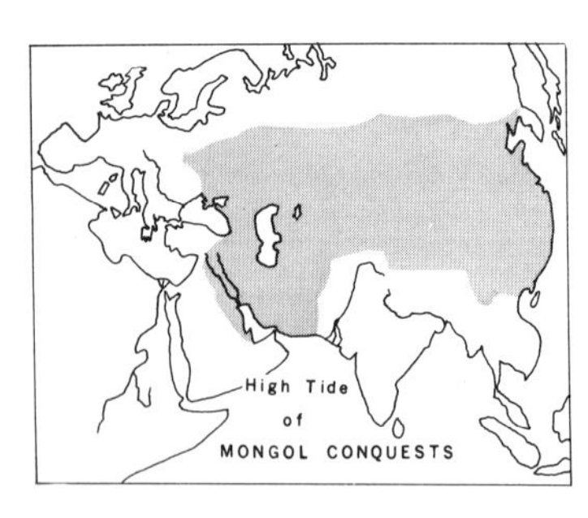
High Tide of MONGOL CONQUESTS

Into this world of conquest, in the year 1273, came a traveler from the West, Marco Polo the Venetian, then still in his late teens, and in the company of his father and uncle, merchant-explorers who bore a letter from the pope, 6000 miles away. All three men were to stay 18 years, starting homeward in 1291, the year after Kublai Khan's death. Years later, while he was a prisoner of war in Genoa, Marco Polo collaborated with a fellow prisoner in preparing an account of those fabulous years, describing China as the empire then was, and the routes to and from it which in themselves took years to travel. Perhaps the most striking quality of this sober, reasonably accurate work is the amazement with which a Venetian, from the wealthiest medieval city of Europe, beheld the greater wealth, larger populations, and more advanced modes of living which were characteristic of the Chinese, even in that period of confusion and warfare.

NOTES

1 This civilization is usually called *Medieval*, or the *Middle Ages*, as it was assumed to fill a sort of gap between the fall of the Roman empire and the Italian Renaissance (see next chapter). The name does this remarkable culture an injustice.

2 The names of some modern European cities still indicate that they grew up around borgs: Nurnberg, Augsburg, Salzburg, Strassburg, Bourges, and Edinburgh are examples.

3 Vitruvius, *The Ten Books on Architecture*, Book X, Chapter V.

4 Or brought the idea home from the Crusades. Windmills were already in use among the Persians.

5 This style is today commonly called either *Romanesque* (in continental Europe) or *Norman* (in England). Toward the end of the twelfth century it was replaced by a new, more daringly ingenious style which is generally called *Gothic*. (Actually the Goths had nothing to do with developing it.) The Gothic style is described on the following pages.

6 Song of Solomon, II, 1.

7 Of the wealth of stone sculpture on the cathedral's exterior, two examples are shown in Illustration IX. They and the two royal heads from Ife, west Africa, shown in Illustration X, were created at about the same time, i.e., in the thirteenth century.

8 The persecution of witches (the "descendants" of tribal shamans), which was to go on for centuries, was one example of this fear.

9 The travels of this great scholar appealed to Chinese imagination. They became the subject of folktales, in which Hsuan Tsang was transformed into a mythical character called Tripitaka (actually the Sanskrit name for the chief writings on Buddhism). Tripitaka, riding his magic white horse, had many adventures in his search for the jewel of wisdom. The tales were collected in a Chinese classic, recently translated into English under titles such as *Monkey* and *The Monkey King*. (See the reading list at the end of the chapter.) The legends are still popular favorites, especially for children, acted out by puppets in the street theatres of Taiwan, and presumably also in mainland China.

10 Quoted in *The Rise and Splendor of the Chinese Empire*, by R. Grousset (University of California Press, 1962), p. 139.

11 Translation by Arthur Waley.

12 Translation adapted from E. Powys Mathers.

13 Translation by Rene Grousset.

14 Translation adapted from Rene Grousset.

BOOKS ON MEDIEVAL WESTERN EUROPE

Medieval Europe, A Short History, C. W. Hollister (Wiley paperback, New York).

PRECURSORS

Ireland, Harbinger of the Middle Ages, L. Beeler (Oxford). Beautifully illustrated.
Irish Art (to 800 A.D.): Irish Art (A.D. 800—1020), F. Henry (Cornell University Press, 1967).
The Anglo Saxons, D. M. Wilson (Praeger, Ancient Peoples and Places Series).
Art of the Anglo Saxon Age, E. Jackson (R. R. Smith, Peterborough, New Hampshire).
The Vikings, H. Arbman (Praeger, Ancient Peoples and Places Series, New York).
Viking Art, D. M. Wilson and O. Klindt-Jensen (Cornell University Press, 1967).
Westviking: The Ancient Norse in Greenland and North America, F. Mowatt (Atlantic-Little Brown, 1965).

ROMANESQUE PERIOD

William the Conqueror, O. C. Douglas (University of California Press).
The Bayeux Tapestry, F. Stanton and others (Phaidon, 1947); 100 illustrations.
Count Bohemond, A. Duggan (Pantheon, 1965).
Romanesque Painting, J. Ainaud (Compass Books, CA5, 1963).
Early Medieval Art, J. Beckwith (Praeger, New York).
Carolingian and Romanesque Architecture, K. J. Conant (Pelican History of Art, 1959).
Romanesque Europe, H. Domke (Batsford, London). One of series. All photos of buildings.
Medieval Architecture, H. Saalman (Braziller, 1962).

GOTHIC PERIOD

The Medieval World, 1150—1350, F. Heer (Mentor paperback MQ524).
The Medieval Scene, An Informal Introduction to the Middle Ages, G. C. Colton (Cambridge paperback, 1960).
Medieval Technology and Social Change, L. White, Jr. (Oxford, 1962).
The Renaissance of the 12th Century, C. H. Haskins (World paperback M44, New York).
Medieval Village, Manor and Monastery (Harper TB1022, 1925—1965).
Medieval People, The Story of Six Ordinary Lives, E. Power (Doubleday Anchor A32).
Six Medieval Men and Women, H. S. Bennett (NY Atheneum paperback 3).
Arts of the Middle Ages, D. Robb (Doubleday Arts of Man Series).
Mt. St. Michel & Chartres, H. Adams (Anchor paperback A66).
Gothic Architecture, R. Brannan (Braziller, 1961).
Gothic Europe, H. Domke (Batsford, London). All photos of buildings.
Gothic Architecture, P. Frank (Pelican History of Art, 1962).
Gothic Sculpture, M. H. von Freeden (NY Graphic Society, Greenwich, Connecticut, 1962).
Gothic Painting (Compass Books).
Knights of the Crusades, J. Williams (American Heritage Publishing Co., 1962).
Gothic and Roman Manuscripts (Compass Books).
Art of the High Gothic Era (Crown, Art of the World Series, New York).
The Rise of the Universities, C. H. Haskins (Cornell University paperback, Ithaca, New York).

The Growth of English Representational Government, G. L. Haskins (Barnes, New York, 1948).
The Crusades, 3 Vols., S. Runciman (Cambridge University Press, 1951–54).
The Crusades, N. Pernoud (Capricorn Books 109, 1960–65).

FILMS

The Medieval World, sound, color, 10 minutes (Coronet, 1950).
The Meaning of Feudalism, sound, color, 10 minutes (Coronet).
The Medieval Crusader, sound, black and white, 27 minutes (Enc. Brit.).
The Medieval Guilds, sound, black and white, 21 minutes (Enc. Brit.).
The Medieval Knights, sound, black and white, 22 minutes (Enc. Brit.).
The Medieval Manor, sound, black and white, 21 minutes (Enc. Brit.).
Images Medievales, sound, color, 18 minutes (Film Images, Inc.). Remarkably beautiful film, entirely pictures from late medieval manuscripts.

BOOKS ON CHINA AND CHINESE ART

The Sources of Chinese Tradition, ed. W. T. de Bary (Columbia University Press, New York, 1964), 2 Vols., paperback.
The Tiger of Ch'in, L. Cottrell (Holt, Reinhart & Winston, 1963). Biography of China's first great unifier.
The Rise and Splendor of the Chinese Empire, R. Grousset (University of California Press, 1962).
Chinese Art and Culture, R. Grousset (Grove Press paperback, 1951–1961).
Chinese Art, L. Hajek, photos by W. Forman (Spring Books, London).
Chinese Painting, J. Cahill (Skira, 1960).
Painting in the Chinese Manner, Chang Shu-chi (Viking, New York, 1960).
Principles of Chinese Painting, rev. ed., G. Rowley (Princeton University Press, 1959).
The Chinese on the Art of Painting, translated by O. Siren (paperback, Schocken Books, New York).
The Evolution of the Buddha Image, B. Rowland, Jr. (Abrams, New York, 1963).
The Art of the Chinese Sculptor, H. Munsterberg (Tuttle, Rutland, Vermont and Tokyo, 1960).
Early Chinese Pottery and Porcelain, B. Gray (Faber and Faber, London, 1953).
The Silk Road, L. Boulnois (Dutton, New York, 1966).
Jade, Stone of Heaven, R. Gump (Doubleday, Garden City, New York, 1962).
The Travels of Marco Polo, new translation by R. E. Latham (Penguin paperback L57).
Marco Polo's Adventures in China, M. A. Rugoff (Horizon Books, 1964).
Marco Polo, Venetian Adventurer, H. H. Hart (University of Oklahoma Press, Tulsa, 1967).
Genghis Khan, The Emperor of All Men, H. Lamb (Garden City Pub. Co., 1927).
Science and Civilization in China, J. Needham (Cambridge University Press), 4 Vols.
Heavenly Clockwork: The Great Astronomical Clocks of Medieval China, J. Needham (Cambridge University Press).
The Monkey King, a New Translation of the Chinese Legend (Paul Hamlyn, London, 1961–64).
Folk Tales of China, W. Eberhard, ed. (University of Chicago Press, 1965).
The Art of Chinese Poetry, James J. V. Lin (University of Chicago Press, 1962).

Palermo Museum

Eleanora of Aragon, by Francesco de Laurana, about 1460. Although this portrait is that of a Spanish queen by a sculptor from Dalmatia, it seems nevertheless to capture perfectly the spirit of the Italian Renaissance. We see here reverence for a human being as living in this world rather than the next, coupled with a superb sense of form.

8 RENAISSANCE EUROPE MING DYNASTY CHINA EARLY JAPAN

Fifteenth Century Italy

Italy, Source of the Renaissance

The medieval way of life, based on the feudal system and the rigid teachings of the Catholic Church, and expressing its soul in gothic architecture, was a creation which came to birth in twelfth and thirteenth century France. From there the culture spread in all directions, but with varying success. Flanders, Germany, and Austria embraced it and made it theirs for centuries. So did England and Spain. Italy, at the opposite extreme, gave it only passing recognition. The causes for this appear to have been two. First, the Italians were in experience richer than the Franks and Normans, whose ancestors had been rough tough tribesmen when Rome was a mature empire. The Italians had been part of that empire, many of them with ancestors who had helped rule it.

The Italians, also, had not been forced back on themselves, cut off from the rest of the world, as the Franks had been in the ninth and tenth centuries, when they were caught between the jaws of Muslim and Viking invaders and pirates. Traffic between Italy and the Byzantine empire by way of the Adriatic never ceased; money and goods flowed. Therefore, Italy depended less on the rigid forms of feudal government created to operate with scant money, travel, and trade.

In the twelfth century, when medieval civilization was taking shape in northern France, the two great centers of power in Italy were Rome and Venice. The power of Rome was religious; the power of Venice was its wealth. We have already seen how these two centers, each in its own way, influenced all western Europe. Let us now look at their influence in Italy.

The Pope as a Power in Italy

The pope, though a spiritual ruler, was also a powerful earthly ruler. All the land in central Italy, right across the boot, was his. From it the pope drew wealth in taxes. To protect it he maintained his own army. At Rome his palace, known as the Vatican, whose protecting fortress was the Castel Sant Angelo, was a center of still greater wealth drawn as tribute money

Alinari-Art Reference Bureau

Above: Procession of Venetian citizens in the Piazza San Marco, as seen by the artist Gentile Bellini in 1496. Below: Venetian gold zecchino. Each bore on one side an image of Christ blessing the world, and on the other that of St. Mark, the city's protecting saint, giving a wand of office to the city's elected ruler, or doge. *Because each coin bore the word DUX (the Latin version of* doge*), the coins were commonly called ducats.*

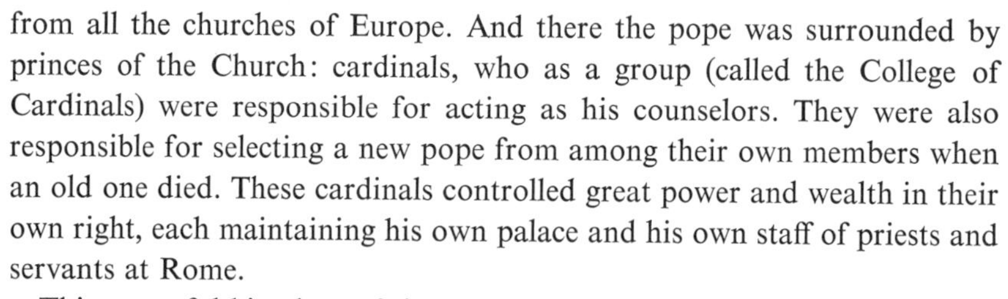

from all the churches of Europe. And there the pope was surrounded by princes of the Church: cardinals, who as a group (called the College of Cardinals) were responsible for acting as his counselors. They were also responsible for selecting a new pope from among their own members when an old one died. These cardinals controlled great power and wealth in their own right, each maintaining his own palace and his own staff of priests and servants at Rome.

This powerful kingdom of the popes, known as the Papal States, divided the rest of Italy into a northern and a southern part, each with a character of its own. The part lying south of the Papal States belonged entirely to the Kingdom of "the Two Sicilies" (Sicily and southern Italy), whose center of government was Naples. North of the Papal States lay a whole constellation of independent city-states, of which the brightest was Venice.

Collection Mr. Ed Gans, Berkeley

Venice as an Influence in Italy

The citizens of Venice, in their island city two miles off the north Italian shore of the Adriatic, became in the tenth century the richest men in Italy, and the most worldly wise. They knew the civilized ways of their mother city, Constantinople. Partly from her, partly from their own experience, they learned to respect the power of money. While the great feudal lords of France and Germany in their gloomy castles were looking with contempt on anyone who bought or sold for a living, every Venetian was proud to be a merchant. While the popes were preaching that any man who collected interest on the loan of money (usury) was a sinner, the Venetians were making and accepting loans at interest (ingeniously concealed in various ways) as the only way to finance merchant ventures on the sea. And while the lords of northern Europe were forever setting out on Crusades against the Muslims as agents of the Devil, the Venetians were learning to trade with Muslim merchants in the Levant, and to respect them as men of learning, culture, and honor.

Anyone who visited Venice in the Middle Ages found a city humming with activity, her head bowed to no outside ruler, and her harbors full of ships. Men of all classes were well employed and well clothed; their beautiful wives and daughters were adorned with jewels; their houses were finely built and furnished; great public buildings were going up; and money was changing hands everywhere. The marvelous results of the Venetian freedom from snobbery, from strict obedience to the pope, and from fear of the (Muslim) Devil himself were there for all to see.

For some comments on the music of this general period see Appendix A, pages 603–4.

The Venetians, therefore, set a pattern of conduct for other independent cities in that part of Italy which lay north of the Papal States. North Italian noblemen, instead of staying on their country estates, used the profits from farming those estates to set themselves up as merchants in the nearest city. According to the humble standards of those times, these cities began to grow rich. Their citizens, having found wealth from living boldly as merchant adventurers, much as the Venetians did, developed a self-reliance and a freedom of thinking which was far superior to that in any other part of Europe.

The first north Italian cities to follow the example of Venice, and to move aggressively into the life of sea traders, were situated on the sea just as she was, but in places where they were safe (at first) from her ruthless competition. These cities were first Pisa and then Genoa. Both cities had fine harbors which faced the Mediterranean, not the Adriatic. But before the Pisans and Genoese could prosper as merchants, their first task was to clear the neighboring seas of Muslim pirates. This they did in the eleventh century, as we have already seen (page 317). Soon both cities had established their own connections with the Levant, Egypt, and Byzantium, and were importing luxuries to Italy in their own ships. The resulting prosperity of these cities can be measured by the beautiful public buildings which their citizens proudly and thankfully erected in the twelfth and thirteenth centuries.

But these coastal cities were merely members of a whole network of towns spread across northern Italy, each with its own skillful and aggressive merchants and craftsmen. Of these, names such as Milan, Padua, Ferrara, Lucca, Florence, and Siena stand out, but they are hardly one-tenth of the total number. These cities were in turn part of the great chain of merchant

The cathedral at Pisa, with its round baptistry and leaning bell tower, begun in the twelfth century and completed in the thirteenth and later. The cathedral was, for its time, a bold experiment in combining Eastern and Western church architecture. It is a basilica of the Western type, but at its center, where nave and transepts meet, an Eastern type of dome has been erected. The walls of the dome have been made steep to avoid lateral thrust.

Photo Enit, Rome

Photo Enit, Rome

The Cathedral, Florence, crowned by its great dome. Before it, right, stands its octagonal baptistry. The bell tower, as at Pisa, is a separate structure.

cities which, as we have already seen, stretched all the way across medieval Europe (see page 321). We have already remarked that medieval cities resembled the Greek city-states of the sixth century B.C. and later. In Italy the resemblance was even closer. Led by the example of Venice, the Italian cities were far in advance of the cities beyond the Alps, financially and intellectually. Even the climate, similar to that of Greece, favored the same kind of outdoor living and working. And the actual connection with the ancient world was more direct; everywhere one could find beautiful ruins which had been erected, once upon a time, by Romans who had in turn been inspired by Greeks.

Of these Italian cities certain ones were more favorably placed than others, and so rose to greater prosperity and power. But there seems to be no satisfactory way to explain why the citizens of just one of these cities became the intellectual leaders of the rest of Italy.

Florence, Where It Lies and How It Grew

Florence, an inland city 45 miles from the Mediterranean Sea, is an inviting place. She lies in the broad, shallow valley of the winding River Arno, with beautifully dramatic hills rising on all sides. She is a very old city, at the heart of that part of northern Italy called Tuscany, home of the ancient Etruscans, and her oldest church stands on the foundations of a Roman temple to Mars. The climate is so kind to flowering plants that the city's very name comes from the Italian word *fiore*, or flower; for centuries the civic symbol has been a single iris bloom. From a more sternly practical standpoint, Florence is well placed for trade. Three important passes through the hills make her a natural center of roads leading to other cities. The Arno gives her access to the Mediterranean, although in the Middle Ages Pisa controlled the river mouth, and therefore had the upper hand. Thus forced back upon their land resources, the restless, energetic Florentines resorted to ingenuity to better their condition.

The history of medieval Florence is a violent one. There were wars without and wars within. Without, Florence was often fighting other cities, either to enlarge her lands whence came the grain and meat which fed her citizens, or for less practical reasons. Within, Florence was constantly experimenting with her form of government, as different social classes or different powerful families struggled to gain control of the city. Families that lost were usually sent into exile.[1] The process of casting out groups of citizens because they had disturbed the civic peace seemed to be endless. Dante, one of the world's great poets, who belonged to one of these exiled families, bitterly compared his native city to a sick woman who lies constantly shifting her position to ease her pain.

It is hard to imagine such an uneasy place as a center of industry, trade, and banking, all of which need peaceful times to thrive. But that is just what Florence managed to make of herself. She was first of all a medieval merchant city, ruled by guilds of merchants and craftsmen who would take no meddling from noblemen unless they became guild members. The jewel-like beauty of her churches and palaces, rich with sculpure, painting, and metalwork, the long list of geniuses who created great art, great literature, and great scientific discoveries in or near that city, all were financed or supported by wealth contributed by guilds or by rich citizens. That wealth had first to be built up by human labor and brains. The marvel of Florence is two-fold: first, that so many men of great talent in the arts, sciences, politics, and finance developed there, and second, that the men gifted in finance were so ready to support the men gifted in other fields.

Seldom, if ever, has a city been so conscious of itself during its short period of greatness, for surely no city has had so many historians. The first of these, Giovanni Villani, began to write in 1300 and continued until the plague epidemic of 1348, the Black Death, carried him off. His son then continued the story. After him, Leonardo Bruni wrote history of a different kind, comparing Florence to the great city-states of ancient Hellas and to the early Roman republic. But the greatest of all was Niccolo Machiavelli, famous all over the world today as the first known Western writer on power politics. He brought the city's history down to the year 1492.

The city of Florence began to mint gold florins *in 1252. Each bore on one side an iris, and on the other the image of St. John, the city's protecting saint. Florins were soon respected everywhere for their purity and uniform weight. Even today four nations mint a coin called* florin.

Collection Mr. Ed Gans, Berkeley, California

Sources of Florentine Wealth

Wool and Silk Weaving

From early times Florence seems to have been a center of wool processing, weaving, and dyeing. The river supplied the abundant water needed for washing the wool before weaving, and for fulling and dyeing afterwards. The wool came, at first, from sheep pastured on the neighboring hills. But as time went on, and the demand for Florentine goods increased, Florence began to import raw wool by ship from far-off places, chiefly England and Flanders. Pisa's hold on the Arno River mouth became intolerable, and in 1406 the Florentines broke this bottleneck to their trade by defeating the Pisans in battle.

Alinari

Lion supporting the civic shield of the city of Florence, with its single iris flower. Sandstone statue by the Florentine sculptor Donatello, about 1404. For other examples of Donatello's sculpture *see page 367.*

The production of wool cloth is more involved than one might suspect. From the sheep's back to the finished cloth, about twenty different steps are involved, each requiring a separate skill. In Florence in this period, each step was usually handled by a different craftsman working in a different place, often in his own home. To coordinate all these steps, to steer the wool through many different hands, was a skillful business in itself. Any man so involved was the nearest approach, to be found in those times, to the modern manufacturer; and for want of a better word we shall so call him.

Not content with turning out wool cloth, the enterprising Florentines began to buy raw silk from neighboring towns whose people had invested in silkworms and mulberry groves. From this they began to manufacture luxurious silk brocades and velvets. Silk processing and weaving require fewer steps than does wool—for one thing, the silk is already spun by the silkworm. But these steps are more difficult. Much more complicated looms and much higher weaving skill were needed to produce the intricate patterns of silk brocade. The profit from such materials was therefore higher.

Banking

A Florentine manufacturer of silk or woolen cloth required capital—money to invest in raw wool or silk, and in the labor of many craftsmen. He got his money back when he sold the finished cloth, usually to a merchant adventurer of the type we have already seen operating between the towns of northwestern Europe. The Italian merchant adventurers bought cloth in order to carry it by mule, wagon, or ship to other markets, perhaps to a nearby town, perhaps to a French city across the Alps, or perhaps to a port over the sea, such as the Christian city of Barcelona in Spain or the Muslim city of Tunis in North Africa. The merchant adventurer, in his turn, needed capital to invest in the cloth. This he could win back only after his hazardous trip to a foreign market, where he sold, hopefully, at a good profit.

The merchant adventurer had other problems besides transport. Wherever he traveled he was likely to find a different kind of coin in circulation. If he bought goods in Florence he paid out *florins* issued by that city. If he sold in Venice, for example, he received Venetian *ducats*. If he carried his hard-won ducats back to Florence, risking highway robbery on the way, he needed the help of a money changer to exchange his ducats back to florins.

The banks of medieval Italy, and especially Florence, came into being to meet all these problems: *to supply manufacturers and merchants with capital, to exchange different coins for them, and to help them avoid the risk of carrying money over thief-infested roads.*

BANKING INVENTIONS: PARTNERSHIP, TIME DEPOSIT, BILL OF EXCHANGE. The bankers of the period usually started out as money changers. This explains why a bank was called a *tavolo*, or table. For the money changer sat at a table, usually in an open doorway, with his simple equipment of a pouch of assorted coins, a pair of scales, and a ledger in which to keep records of exchanges. As the green cloth which covered his table indicated, he was a respected member of the money changers' guild, whose officers policed his practices, lest he bring discredit to the profession. Each exchange of coin was a service for which he charged a fee. Since a family could live well and keep a servant on only 100 florins a year (about $250), a skillful and reliable money changer could, in the course of time, build up a supply of excess capital. It was natural, therefore, that manufacturers and merchant adventurers should approach him for loans. The money changer at this point became a banker.

Since there was no profit in making a loan unless the borrower paid interest, and since the Church declared usury to be sinful, bankers resorted to various ways of avoiding sin. One was to form a partnership. The banker put up the money, the manufacturer or merchant did the work, and both parties agreed by signed contract to share the profits. The banker was usually a *sleeping partner*, liable only to the extent of his investment; his active partner could not get him into debt. Bankers also avoided usury by arranging with borrowers that a gift would be forthcoming when a loan was repaid. Such arrangements were often hard to defend in a court of law. Still, properly managed banking became a highly profitable business. In skilled hands, money begat more money.

Presently other men who had somehow gathered excess capital would ask the banker to use his skill in putting their money to work for them. They would *deposit* it with him, usually for an agreed number of years. (Today we call this a *time deposit*, as distinct from the *demand deposit*, withdrawable at will, which most of us use.) The banker would make a profit from investing these deposits, but pay only part of the profit to the depositors, keeping the rest for himself.

Medieval bankers also worked out devices for converting metal money to *credit*, expressed only on paper. A merchant in Florence (let us call him Angelo) would pay his banker, say, 100 florins (plus a commission), stating that he wished to spend that money in Venice. The Florentine banker would write to a trusted banker friend in Venice instructing him to pay Angelo 90 Venetian ducats (90 ducats = 100 florins). Angelo would journey to Venice, present his letter to the banker there, draw his money, and invest it in merchandise as he thought wise. Such a letter was called a *bill of exchange*, or *letter of credit*.[2]

A bill of exchange written at the Medici branch bank in Venice, July 20, 1463. A merchant, Girard Chanixani, paid the bank 500 Venetian ducats, and in return received these written instructions to the Medici branch bank in London to pay him 2,350 English sterling (or pence), supposedly equal to 500 ducats. The money was to be paid October 20. The London bank refused to pay, stating that 500 ducats were worth only 2,200 sterling. The bill of exchange itself, in informal handwriting, occupies merely the lower right-hand edge. All the rest is the refusal to pay, prepared in elegant handwriting for the London bank by an English notary, William Slade.

State Archive, Florence. Courtesy Harvard University Press

All photos Alinari Art Reference Bureau, Inc.

Five generations of the Medici family, master bankers of fifteenth century Florence and of western Europe. I. Giovanni (1360–1429), founder of the bank. He shrewdly avoided the errors (too many branches, lending to kings) which had ruined the Peruzzi bank. Relief by A. Bronzino (Palazzo Medici Riccardi, Florence). II. Cosimo (1389–1464), who made the bank internationally great, but still avoided the Peruzzi mistakes. He was a leader in Florentine government, supporter of artists, sculptors, architects, and men of letters. His iron grip on the bank's affairs began to slip in his last years. Marble relief by Verrochio (formerly in Kaiser Friedrich Museum, Berlin).

A device like this would also work between much more distant cities, such as Florence and far-off London. But it could work anywhere only if merchants in both cities trusted each other and could recognize each other's handwriting (samples were kept for this purpose). Also, *it could work only if credit was moving both ways in about equal amounts.* If it was all moving one way, credit could be restored only if one merchant risked shipping real coin the other way to restore the balance. Such adjustments were known to occur.

To make their connections with other cities more reliable, Florentine bankers began to establish branch banks in the important trading centers of Italy, France, Spain, Flanders, and England. The greatest bank of all, owned by the Peruzzi family, had sixteen such branches and was the financial counselor of kings and cardinals.[3] Florence had become the financial powerhouse of western Europe. About the year 1420, 2,000,000 florins changed

III. Piero (1416–1465) of little influence, due to illness. Bust by M. de Fiesole (Museo Nazionale, Florence).

IV. Lorenzo (1449–1492) called "The Magnificent," was a brilliant statesman and patron of the arts, but was educated as a gentleman and did not concentrate on banking. He once said, "I have three sons; one is foolish, one is clever, and one is kind." The clever one, Giovanni, was made a cardinal (at 13!) and later became Pope Leo X. The foolish one, Piero, inherited the family bank. Terra cotta bust by Verrochio (Kress Collection National Gallery of Art, Washington, D.C.).

V. Piero (1472–1503) completely wrecked his family's reputation in Florence in just two years. The bank failed, never to reopen. Bust (Bargello, Florence).

hands daily in her banks and money changing offices. She was also still a textile center; 120 wool manufacturers were producing 20,000 pieces of finished cloth a year.

AN INVENTION IN CIVIC FINANCE: THE MUNICIPAL BOND. When the city of Florence went to war with a neighbor, she had to spend more in a year than she could collect in taxes. The problem was how to raise the money to pay this public debt (which the Italians picturesquely called *monte*, or mountain). The city fathers' solution was to sell citizens a piece of parchment for, say, 100 florins, in which the city promised to pay the buyer five percent interest until the 100 florins were repaid. The city could then repay gradually during years of peace, when income from taxes was greater than the cost of government. Thus was invented the municipal bond, or city bond, a device much used today to pay for schools and other civic improvements.

Two panels from a choir balcony, Florence cathedral, showing boys singing in concert. The balcony, created by the Florentine sculptor Luca della Robbis in nine years (1431–1440) contains ten such panels, as well as much rich decoration. The Renaissance appreciation of living human beings, expressed through forms inspired by Roman sculpture, here achieves one of its highest expressions. Renaissance artists were keen observers of children, as shown here, and on the opposite page, in the cherubs by Donatello (Cavalcanti Chapel, Florence, about 1440).

Florence, Center of Fifteenth Century Italian Art

If you travel inland from the Mediterranean coast today, up the Arno Valley, you first leave behind the city of Pisa with its beautiful cream colored cathedral and baptistry and follow the winding course of the river for about an hour, a distance which once took travelers two days. Soon you can see spread out far ahead the city of Florence, dominated by the vast dome of its own cathedral, which seems to say, "I am greater than anything Pisa can build!"

Like Chartres, in northern France, the Cathedral in Florence was built to honor Mary, "Saint Mary of the Flower" (Santa Maria del Fiore). The two great churches were started only a century apart (Chartres in 1194, Florence in 1294). But what different human passions created them! Chartres was first of all a work of piety to replace an accidental loss by fire. It was financed by pilgrims from all over Europe, but its design was directed by a small group of holy men *for* the people of the time. Florence's Cathedral was a civic enterprise, financed and built *by* the people of a single city as an expression, not only of their piety, but of their power and their pride.

Unlike Chartres, built in about 25 years under the eye of a single unknown architect, work on the Cathedral at Florence was directed at different times over a span of 140 years by nine different architects, every one of whom is known. (One of these, the great painter Giotto, designed the richly inlaid bell tower.) Some idea of the impetuous planning methods of those times, and the spirit of intense competition which must have hovered over the whole construction process, can be glimpsed from the situation that developed in 1420. By this time the church was nearly finished except for the great dome. No one seemed to have thought how it was to be constructed! To make matters worse, every distinguished architect in town was watching every other like a hawk, ready to pounce on any hint of a good method so that he could make it his own.

Filippo Brunelleschi, Architect of the Dome

The man who had both the genius to plan the construction and the shrewdness to outsmart his competitors was a plain looking little man, Filippo Brunelleschi (BrooneLESki). "Many whom Nature creates small and insignificant in appearance have their souls filled with such greatness and their hearts with such boundless courage that even if they undertake things of almost impossible difficulty they bring them to completion to the wonder of all beholders." With these words Giorgio Vasari began his biography of Brunelleschi about 75 years after the great architect died.

Brunelleschi's father wanted to make him a public notary, but in despair finally apprenticed him to a goldsmith. The boy rapidly mastered this complex craft, moved on to the ingenious construction of clocks, then to sculpture, and finally to architecture. He collected enough money to go to Rome,

> where at the sight of the grandeur of the buildings and the perfection of the churches, he was lost in wonder, so that he looked like one demented . . . He attentively observed all the difficulties of the vaulting of the Pantheon . . . He drew every sort of building, round and square and octagonal, churches, basilicas, baths, arches . . . Two great ideals possessed him—the one to bring to light good architecture, of which he should be the creator and discoverer,. . . the other was to find a method, if possible, of vaulting the dome of Santa Maria del Fiore.[4]

When at last his time came, and the woolen manufacturers' guild wanted to finance the dome's construction, Brunelleschi was ready with plans and a scale model, but, knowing his competitors, he kept these out of sight. When he appeared at public hearings of the cathedral board of governors, he resorted to gamesmanship.

> They wanted Filippo to declare his plan . . . but he refused, and proposed to the masters assembled that whoever should make an egg stand upright on a flat marble surface should make the dome, as this would be a test of their ability. He produced an egg and all the masters tried to make it stand but no one succeeded. Then they passed it to Filippo, who lightly took it, broke the end with a blow on the marble and made it stand. All the artists exclaimed that they could have done as much themselves, but Filippo answered, laughing, that they would also know how to vault the dome after they had seen his model.[5]

By such devices he won private hearings before the cathedral board, convinced them, and won the contract to construct the dome. For the next sixteen years he supervised every step of its building. To everyone's amazement it slowly rose without scaffolding to support its incurving walls—only scaffolding for the workmen. The great vault was finally closed in 1436. The crown, or *cupola*, was completed after Brunelleschi's death, by other men, following his plans. The whole cathedral ever since has been lovingly nicknamed *il Duomo*, the Dome.

Brunelleschi's dome is an engineering marvel. Its internal diameter is 138 feet, not much less than the ancient Pantheon which he had studied so

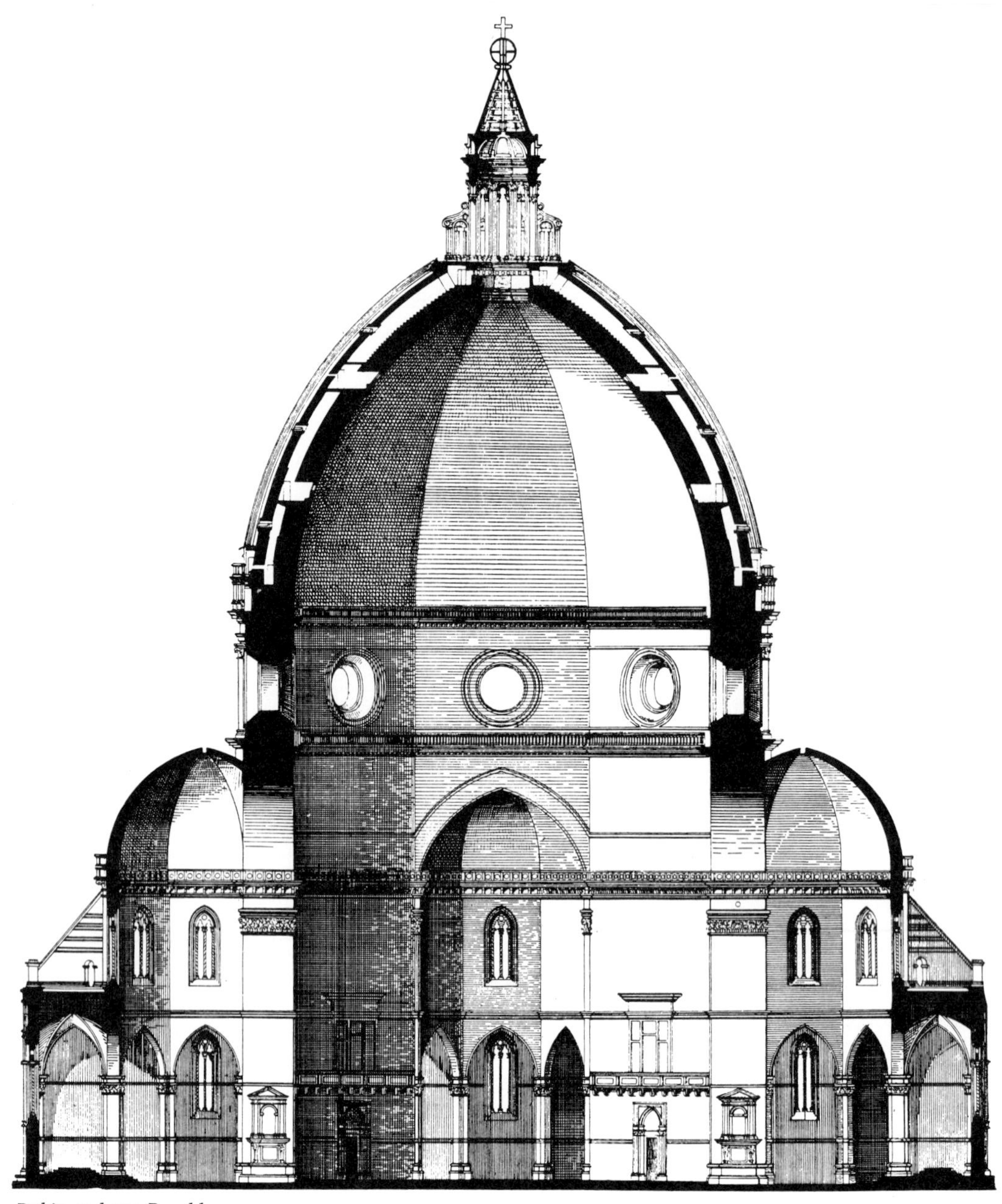

Dehio and von Bezold

Section of Florence Cathedral dome. Brunelleschi designed the dome and supporting drum with circular windows. The remainder was already built. Height from floor to apex dome (interior), 287 feet. Height from street to top of cross, 387 feet. Diameter of dome (interior) 138 feet.

thoroughly in Rome (but note that his dome is octagonal, not circular). Its inside height is much greater: 287 feet, outsoaring even Hagia Sophia. Its construction has the following features.

1. It is a double dome, one inside the other, the two being bonded together at regular intervals.

2. The inner dome is partly constructed of pumice, a very light and porous rock, to reduce weight.

3. At each of its eight angles it is strengthened with a rib, as in Gothic vaulting.

4. To reduce the outward thrust which might tip over its supporting walls, the dome's height is increased in a Gothic or pointed arch.

5. To counteract the outward thrust within the dome itself an iron chain, imbedded in the masonry, encircles the dome about $\frac{1}{8}$ of the distance down from its top.

6. The stone cupola crowning the dome acts as a counter weight without which Brunelleschi predicted that the pointed dome would eventually collapse.

7. The thinking involved was remarkably comprehensive. Brunelleschi "put in the least dangerous places the channels for carrying off the water, showing where they should be covered, and where uncovered, arranging spaces and apertures to break the force of the winds, and to provide that tempests and earthquakes should not injure it . . ."[6]

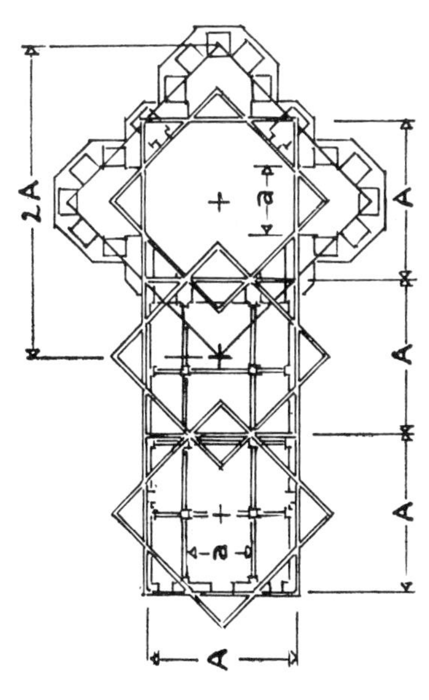

Ground plan of Florence Cathedral.

From Gothic Cathedrals and Sacred Geometry, G. Lesser (Courtesy of Alec Tiranti, Ltd., London)

So much for the engineering aspect of this structure. Men of the time were even more deeply impressed by another side of his creation: *it marked a return by the Italians to their ancient Roman heritage of architectural design*, free from the northern influence of Gothic, which they had never really enjoyed or mastered. Before Brunelleschi the architects at work on the Cathedral had created a fascinating but jarring mixture. *Inside*, the structure is simple, watered-down Gothic, all *pointed* arches and vaulting. *Outside*, its flat, almost windowless walls are brought to life by patterns of white and colored marble dominated by rectangles and *round* arches. On this exterior, exquisite but out-of-place little Gothic window frames appear at intervals, looking as if glued on. (Note that Italy's brilliant sunshine makes large windows unsuited to the dim interior of churches.)

Brunelleschi cut through this charming hodgepodge. He used two Gothic building principles in designing the dome: he made it somewhat pointed, and he strengthened it with eight ribs. He did these things because the construction of such a dome on existing foundations required them. But he never forgot that a dome is a Roman form, not a Gothic one. He made Gothic behave, as it were. Wherever possible the dome is built according to classic Roman principles of design and decoration, which Brunelleschi's tireless labor had rediscovered at Rome. When planning decorations, he dispensed with flat surfaces of inlaid marble except as these were needed to make his dome harmonize with what was already built. Instead he introduced beautiful sculptured festoons of fruit, and Roman half-columns, whose light and shadow have a quality of their own, richer and more subtle than bald light and dark stone patterns.

All this was intensely exciting to the men of Brunelleschi's time. "Filippo..." said Vasari, "was given by Heaven to invest architecture with new forms, after it had wandered astray for many centuries . . . He abandoned himself to his studies . . . studying the good orders and not the barbarous Gothic then in use."

When Brunelleschi thus turned his back on medieval building styles and instead drew his inspiration from Roman ruins, he was only one part of a great burst of enthusiasm for the Roman and Greek past which was sweeping Italy at that time. Scholars were rediscovering pagan Latin literature, learning to read Greek, opening themselves to a refined but earthy outlook on life which the early Christians had dreaded as sinful. They began to criticize the medieval disrespect for any kind of knowledge except that of Holy Scripture and the Church Fathers. For it was an alert knowledge of the world, not of scripture, which had brought the northern Italians commercial power and wealth.

Filippo Brunelleschi, Experimental Painter

Brunelleschi was in the forefront of this desire to advance knowledge. He did it in his own individual way, and in harmony with one of his own deep interests, the impact of buildings on the human eye. Choosing as a subject the oldest building in Florence, *he painted an exact study of its appearance from a fixed point of view.* Strangely enough, such a precise study of how the world looks was unheard of in his time. The building he chose was the beautiful eight-sided baptistry of Florence Cathedral. Selecting a spot about six feet inside the cathedral doorway, with the baptistry straight ahead, he painted his minutely exact picture on a polished silver mirror about a foot square, leaving the sky unpainted. In the frame of the finished picture he bored a small hole which widened, funnelwise, from front to back. Anyone who wished could sit in the doorway with the picture in one hand and a hand mirror in the other. By holding up the painting, facing away from him, he could look through the hole with one eye and see the real baptistry. With the other eye he could look at the reflection of the picture as shown to him by the mirror held in his other hand. The polished silver sky in the picture would reflect the actual sky and clouds! Thus anyone who wished could critically compare his own view of the baptistry with Brunelleschi's.

This little picture, known to us today only from fifteenth century descriptions,[7] was one of the milestones in man's cultural history. In its way, one can compare it to the Wright brothers' first flying machine, which could fly scarcely 100 feet, or to Lawrence's first atom smasher, which could be picked up with one hand. It was great, that is, not for what it was in itself, but for the direction it pointed out to others. It was especially great because it foretold not just one course of human development, but three.

1. As a careful study of the way the human eye takes in the outside world, it was the forerunner of technical advances: *perspective drawing*, developed in Brunelleschi's own time, and eventually *the invention of the camera* (an adapted model of the human eye) 400 years later.

2. One of the basic principles of the scientific method, on whose discoveries our present civilization partially rests, is that *any scientist reporting a new discovery must give others the opportunity to repeat the experiments on which the discovery rests.* The advance must be impersonal, open to anyone's testing and criticism. Brunelleschi's little picture was just such an experiment in vision, especially designed to be tested by anyone. As such it was probably the first (certainly among the first) of its kind.

3. Prior to this time, medieval Christian men had not thought of themselves as the center of anything. God was the center; eternal life in God's kingdom of Heaven was the permanent goal toward which all men desired to move. The Earth, and man's life on it, was simply a short testing place, whence some souls were graduated upward, others demoted downward. Medieval art, therefore, had its center in the images of God, the saints, and the Devil. *These were fixed, changeless beings to be viewed by spectators who were moving about.* But for Brunelleschi's painting *the human spectator was the motionless center, and so was the spot on the earth's surface where he sat.* If that painting was seen from too far or too close, the perspective lines

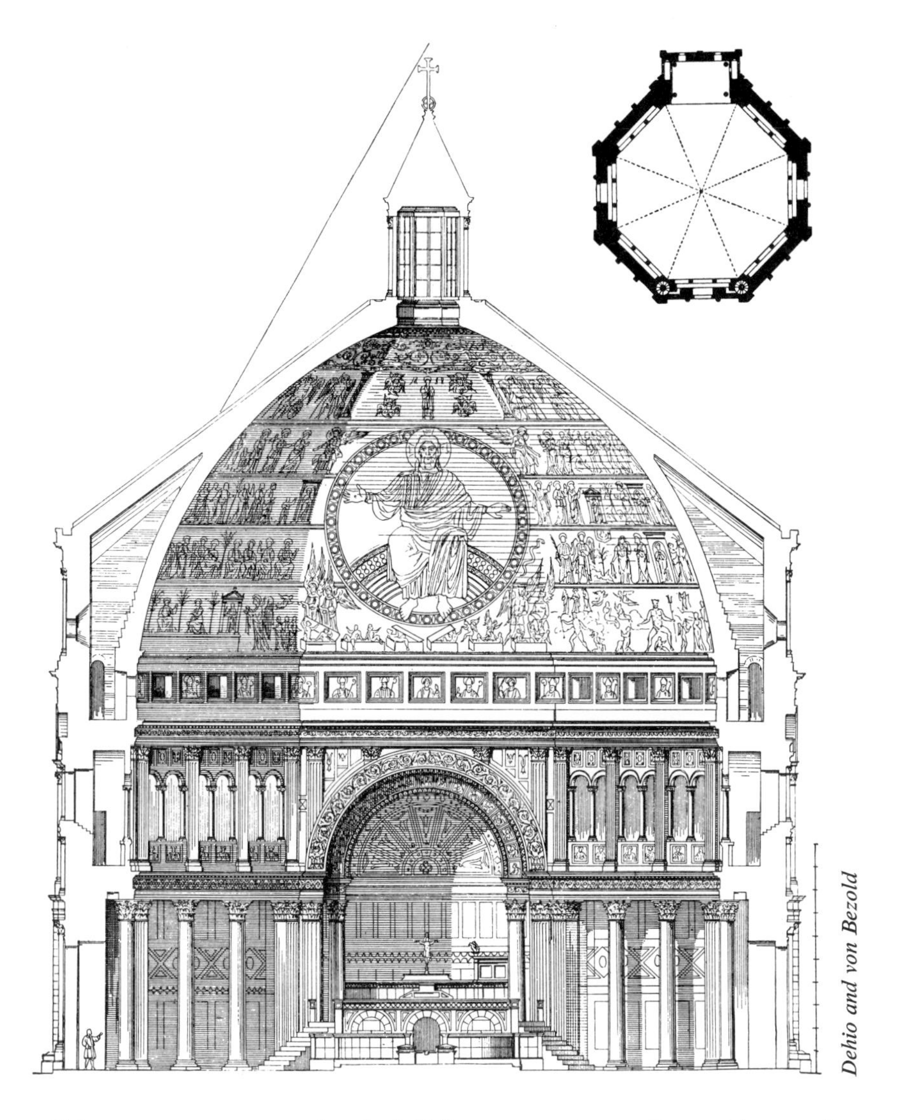

Section through the Baptistry of Florence cathedral. This octagonal building is believed to be the oldest still standing in Florence (eleventh century). Its exterior is dramatically patterned in white and dark green marble. The interior of its dome gleams with gold mosaic. It can be seen in the aerial view, page 360.

did not converge properly. And if it was seen in another setting, such as indoors, the silver mirror sky gave back the wrong reflection. The picture, in its quiet way, declared that *man can be an important center in his own right*, and that *the Earth which surrounds him is, in its own right, worthy of loving study*. This is the attitude known as *Humanism*. It had its origin among the Greeks, and after them the Romans. Its rediscovery and further development by the north Italians of the fourteenth, fifteenth, and sixteenth centuries therefore made that period one of rebirth, or (in French) *Renaissance*. And that is why the name for this period, the *Italian Renaissance*, given to it over a century ago, still sticks.

Leon Battista Alberti

Brunelleschi's experiment in making pictures was a modest one, seen by only a few friends. One of these was Leon Battista Alberti, a member of a once powerful Florentine banking family. A political feud, so common in Florence, had forced his father to flee to Genoa, where the family maintained a branch bank. So it was in Genoa that Leon Battista Alberti was born, in 1404.

Advances made during one century in the mastery of representing depth. Opposite page, above: St. John Raising Drusiana, *by Giotto, about 1325. Giotto's painting (fresco) was commissioned by the Peruzzi family of bankers for their private chapel. Opposite page, below:* St. Peter Preaching, *by Masaccio, about 1425. This too was commissioned for a private chapel (by the Brancacci family, for the Church of the Carmine, Florence).*

Alinari-Art Reference Bureau, Inc.

Alberti's father gave him a superb education for that time. The boy read the great pagan authors of prose and poetry which scholars were eagerly rediscovering. He kept a balance between study and physical exercise, which medieval educators had thought unimportant. Later he studied law at the northern Italian university of Bologna, read the speeches of the great Roman lawyer Cicero, and mastered his methods of persuasion. But Alberti was a many-sided genius, a painter, a sculptor, and above all an architect. Young though he was, he was brought to the attention of the pope, who invited him to Rome to survey the city and recommend its replanning. City planning had become nearly a lost art.

In 1434, when Alberti was just 30, he accompanied the pope on a visit to Florence. His father had left the city as a fugitive; the son entered it in triumph. What he found was a new world of artistic creation. Rome was the center of power, of great churches, and of mighty Roman ruins. But Florence was the center of *avant garde* art[8] where new things, using the broken remains of Roman art as an inspiration, were being created such as had never before been seen, by men like Donatello, Ghiberti, and above all Brunelleschi.

Fired with wonder and delight at what he saw, Alberti gained permission from the pope to remain in Florence for a time. Combining his powers as a persuader and an artist, he then wrote a little book called *On Painting*, in which he stated with clarity and force the new aims for art which he saw emerging all around him. He wrote the book in two versions. One was in Latin, full of learned references to great Roman authors, such as Pliny the elder. This was aimed at scholars and educated men of wealth; it lifted painting above the level of a mere craft and made it a subject for cultivated discussion; it also encouraged rich men to support artists as persons worthy of high respect. The other version was in Italian, a more straightforward statement intended to interest practicing artists, and affectionately addressed to Brunelleschi.

> I say the function of the painter is this: to describe with lines and to tint with color on whatever panel or wall is given him . . . surfaces of any body so that at a certain distance and in a certain position from the centre they appear in relief and seem to have mass. Know that a painted thing can never appear truthful where there is not a definite distance for seeing it.[9]

Thus wrote Alberti, firmly turning his back on all the flat looking paintings of the Middle Ages. He went on to say, ". . . first of all, about where I draw, I inscribe a rectangle . . . as large as I wish, which is considered an open window through which I see what I want to paint."

Alberti then described what he called a "veil," a semitransparent cloth of fine weave, divided into squares by thicker threads. When he hung this up before a landscape or a motionless human group, he could locate accurately the outlines of everything before him, and could draw these outlines on a sheet of paper, also squared off.

But what of the painter who wanted to *invent* a scene? How could he be certain that objects in it appeared as they would if real? To meet this need, and to go beyond Brunelleschi, whose little painting merely copied what was already there, Alberti stated the first known rules for perspective drawing.

Looking on the scene which the artist was creating as contained in a box with its front wall removed, he described how to draw on a flat surface desired persons or objects to accurate scale, larger or smaller, depending on whether near or far.

"No matter how well small bodies are painted in the picture," wrote Alberti, "they will appear small or large by comparison with whatever man is painted there." He therefore used man as his unit of measurement, by dividing the floor of the box into squares, each with a side (for convenience) one-third of an average man's height, that is, about 2 feet.[10]

On a drawing surface he then made a picture of this box, showing its squared floor accurately foreshortened. If he then wished to show a man standing, say, 4 feet within the picture, he would count 2 foreshortened squares inward and draw him with his feet on the inner boundary of that square. He would know how *tall* to draw him by measuring the *horizontal width of 3 squares* at that point.

The problem was, how to make the foreshortened drawing of the box with the squared floor? Alberti's method for doing this, as improved upon by his illustrious friend Piero della Francesca, will be found in Appendix I of the Projects Manual.

Alberti and Piero were not the only men of their time who were mastering the technique of perspective. Among the others was the remarkable Paolo Uccello, who devoted himself chiefly to complex perspective problems. One of his drawings, now in the Uffizi Gallery, Florence, is reproduced on the cover of this book.

Alberti also discussed other important matters: the need to study human proportion and anatomy, the need to understand how light falls on bodies, and the value of beautiful color combinations. All these had their effect on later painters. But his deepest interest lay beyond these technical problems.

A room 8 feet wide, deep, and high, as seen at a distance of 8 feet from its front edge, and 4 feet above floor level. One man stands 2 feet inside the room, the other 4 feet. Construction lines leading to the left are to place the horizontal lines bounding the foreshortened squares. The diagonal line AB can also be used to determine these horizontal lines.

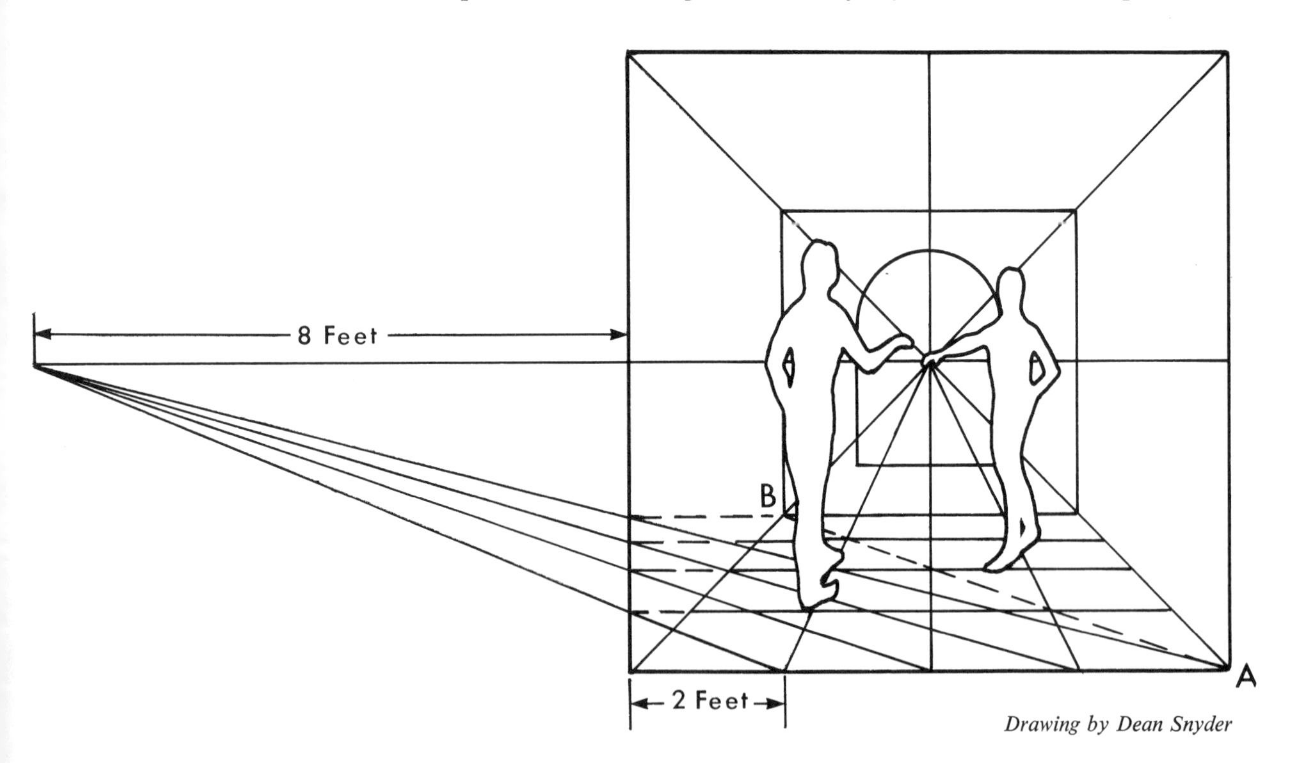

Drawing by Dean Snyder

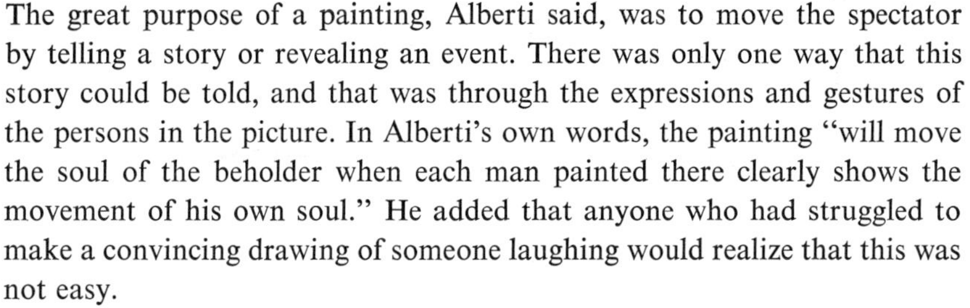

The great purpose of a painting, Alberti said, was to move the spectator by telling a story or revealing an event. There was only one way that this story could be told, and that was through the expressions and gestures of the persons in the picture. In Alberti's own words, the painting "will move the soul of the beholder when each man painted there clearly shows the movement of his own soul." He added that anyone who had struggled to make a convincing drawing of someone laughing would realize that this was not easy.

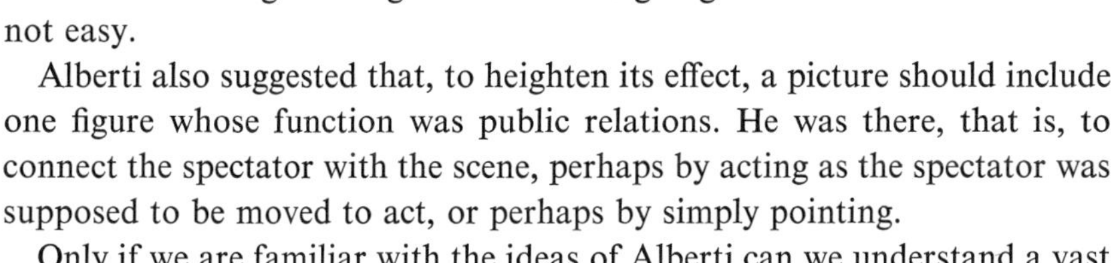

Alberti also suggested that, to heighten its effect, a picture should include one figure whose function was public relations. He was there, that is, to connect the spectator with the scene, perhaps by acting as the spectator was supposed to be moved to act, or perhaps by simply pointing.

Only if we are familiar with the ideas of Alberti can we understand a vast number of paintings, chiefly religious, produced during the ensuing two centuries. He seems to have written a sort of prophetic summary of Renaissance and later painting.

Photo Enit, San Francisco

The facade of the church of Santa Maria Novella, Florence, designed by Alberti. The superimposed diagram shows how this facade fits into a square (allowing for some photographic distortion), and how its parts may be interpreted as halves and fourths of this square.

Alberti's Influence on Architecture

When he left Florence and returned to Rome, Alberti wrote several other books, each with its own far-reaching effect. One of these was on architecture. He carefully modeled it on the work written by Vitruvius nearly 1500 years before, even dividing it into ten books. In it he pays careful attention to classic Roman building styles. Gothic is ignored, in keeping with the Italian taste of the period. He gives a clear statement of the time-tested theory that *the most vital problem in designing a beautiful building is to work out its proportions, which should be related like the notes in a musical harmony.*

Using Plato as an authority, Alberti then goes on to discuss the square and the circle, and their solid forms the cube and sphere, as the most perfect of bodies, and therefore most suited to represent the perfection of God. He praises the dome, or hollow hemisphere, as finely suited to crown a church, since it leads the thoughts of the worshipers to soar upward with wonder, as if toward the sky, and hence toward Heaven. Here again Alberti had an enormous influence, by intensifying, through clearly worded statements, a trend toward which other men were feeling their way. For the next 150 years the ground plan of new churches was often to be *radially* symmetrical rather than *bilaterally* symmetrical.

Alberti stated another principle of architectural design. He scarcely mentioned the ancient tradition, stretching back into the dim magic-ridden past, which seems sometimes to have based the proportions of sacred buildings on the pentagon, decagon, and mean and extreme proportions. Instead he followed his master Vitruvius, who never made any reference to the proportion Φ, but related the parts of his buildings in simple ratios, such as 1 to 2, 2 to 3, etc. Note the illustration which shows the facade of the Church of Santa Maria Novella in Florence, which Alberti himself designed (the rest of the church is much older). It also shows his apparent design scheme based on squares within squares. Alberti's purpose seems to have been two-fold. He perhaps wished to make the proportions of the building instantly clear to the beholder, instead of subtle and concealed. He also certainly wished to give buildings proportions which agreed with the ratios of simple musical harmonies ("innate with harmony itself," to use his own words): 1 to 2, 2 to 3, 3 to 4, and so on. In this attempt to find a link between architecture and music, Alberti was completely unlike his hard headed master Vitruvius. But, unknowingly, he was in one way like the men who had planned Chartres, over two centuries before. Like them, he was being influenced by Plato. For the Italians of Alberti's time were discovering Plato's dialogues for themselves, much more fully than the men of Chartres had been able to, and were reading him with intense interest—more interest, perhaps, than understanding.[11]

Alberti launched a tradition which another architect, Andrea Palladio, living in the next century (1508–1580), was to continue. Palladio, famed for his design of north Italian country houses, attempted to reduce to simple ratios the proportions of every part, within and without, using a single unit of measure, or *module*, for each building. He in turn wrote his own book on architecture,[12] in which he publicized his ideas with great clarity, giving many examples of his own designs. He was to have a strong, if rigid, influence on architects until well into the eighteenth century.[13] (See pages 406–407.)

A Painting by Piero della Francesca

Alberti's influence on the artists of his age can be surmised from a study of the picture opposite. We see there a painting by Alberti's close friend and student, Piero della Francesca. Like many another great work of Renaissance art, this painting, Piero's last, is complex, much more complex than meets the eye.

To begin with, what *does* meet the eye? A group of hushed, motionless persons, some seemingly unaware of the presence of others, stand in a beautifully designed Renaissance chapel, bathed in warm light coming from the left. The sleeping infant Jesus, whose existence is the cause of the whole painting, lies in the lap of his young mother, who sits erect, deeply absorbed in prayer. She and the four angels behind her are all on a higher floor level, thus separating the picture's heavenly beings from the earthly ones. Above and behind Mary a single white egg hangs from the tip of a great scallop shell.

History

Behind the painting there is a story. Federigo, Count of Urbino, who kneels in armor at the right, had a beautiful brilliant wife, the Countess Battista, much younger than he, who by 1470 had born him eight children. Unfortunately they were all daughters. The Count needed a son to carry on the family name. The Countess, greatly concerned, at last made a pilgrimage to a nearby shrine and there offered to sacrifice her own life if only she could bear a son worthy of her husband. Shortly afterwards she became pregnant, and in January 1472 gave birth to a beautiful boy. Every one in the Count's domain was overjoyed. All went well until the end of June, when the Countess contracted a fever and died within a few days, at the age of 27.

Photo SCALA

The grief-stricken Count did not marry again, but for the rest of his life took great pride in his only son. As a solemn record of what he believed was his wife's sacrifice of her life to give him a male heir, the Count requested Piero della Francesca, his friend for many years, to paint this picture for the Church of San Bernardino, in Urbino, where the Countess was buried.

Piero at the time was nearing sixty. He had spent many years as an artist, but his interest in mathematics, which had always been strong, was steadily increasing. At the time, 1472, he was at work on a book on perspective in which he was treating the subject more thoroughly than Alberti ever had. He seems to have torn himself away from his studies to paint this, his last picture. When he had finished it he retired to devote the rest of his life to mathematics, finally dying in 1492 when nearly eighty.

Mary and the infant Jesus, surrounded by holy men and angels, by Piero della Francesca, artist, mathematician, and close friend of Leon Battista Alberti. Originally it hung over the altar in the Church of San Bernardino at Urbino. Brera Gallery, Milan. (The painting is here shown framed. On pages 379 and 381 it is shown with the frame removed.)

Piero placed three saints on each side of Mary. On her left stand St. Francis of Assisi, St. Peter the Martyr (identified by the wound on his head), and a saint who is perhaps St. Andrew. On her right stand St. John the Baptist, St. Bernardine (in Italian, San Bernardino), and St. Jerome. Two of these indicate the dramatic center of the painting, as Alberti recommended, by eloquently pointing to the sleeping infant. St. Andrew, who was patron or protecting saint of the Count, looks benignly down upon him. St. John the Baptist was patron saint of the Countess. His face looks grim with grief, and his pointing finger can also be interpreted as indicating the empty space where the Countess would have knelt if she were alive.

The Count, who was a distinguished professional soldier, kneels with his marshal's staff, gauntlets, and helmet neatly laid out before him. Years before he had been blinded in the right eye while jousting, and all portraits of him show his left or undisfigured side. The great dent above the left eye slit of his helmet hints that in some battle or other he had nearly lost his left eye as well.

What is the meaning of the white suspended egg? It seems to be a thank offering, hung up after prayers for success in childbirth had been answered. Such seems to have been the Italian custom, perhaps inherited from pre-Christian times. And why does it hang from a great scallop shell? Probably because such a shell was a symbol of pilgrimage, and on the Countess' pilgrimage to the shrine, it was believed, hung her success in bearing a son.

Human Proportion

St. John the Baptist, the standing figure with the least foreshortening of any in the painting, has a head which is one-eighth of his height. His pointing hand is one-tenth of his height. So is his face from chin to hair line. This and other measurements on the standing foreground figures indicate that Piero was probably following Vitruvius' rules of human proportion. See Appendix B. But the Count kneeling in the foreground departs from Vitruvius' ideal proportions. Piero painted him as he was, a small man with a large head.

Perspective

The illustration opposite shows how the lines of the architectural setting converge to a focal point slightly to right of the painting's center line. From them, and from the spacing of the architecture, it is possible to reconstruct the scene from the side and from above, as shown in the diagrams opposite. One diagram shows an imaginary spectator, his eyes slightly below the eye level of the standing saints in the painting. Alberti's squared-off floor has been indicated, each square representing a *braccio*, or one-third of a man's height.

If Piero, like Alberti, thought of his painting as an open window through which an actual scene could be viewed, where, between viewer and actual scene, would that window (or painting) be? If close to the viewer, its scale would be small; if close to the scene, large. The figures in the painting are three-fourths life size. The window, therefore, would be three-fourths of the distance from viewer to scene.

Photo SCALA, with perspective lines superimposed by Dean Snyder

Left: Perspective scheme of Piero della Francesca's Urbino Madonna. The painting was removed from its frame for photographing. Below: Side elevation and plan of the architectural setting of the Urbino Madonna. The diagrams assume that the lines MN, M'N', and M''N'' in the illustration above are spaced at equal distances. They also assume that the arch supports which appear just within the edges of the painting originally extended downward to its bottom edge.

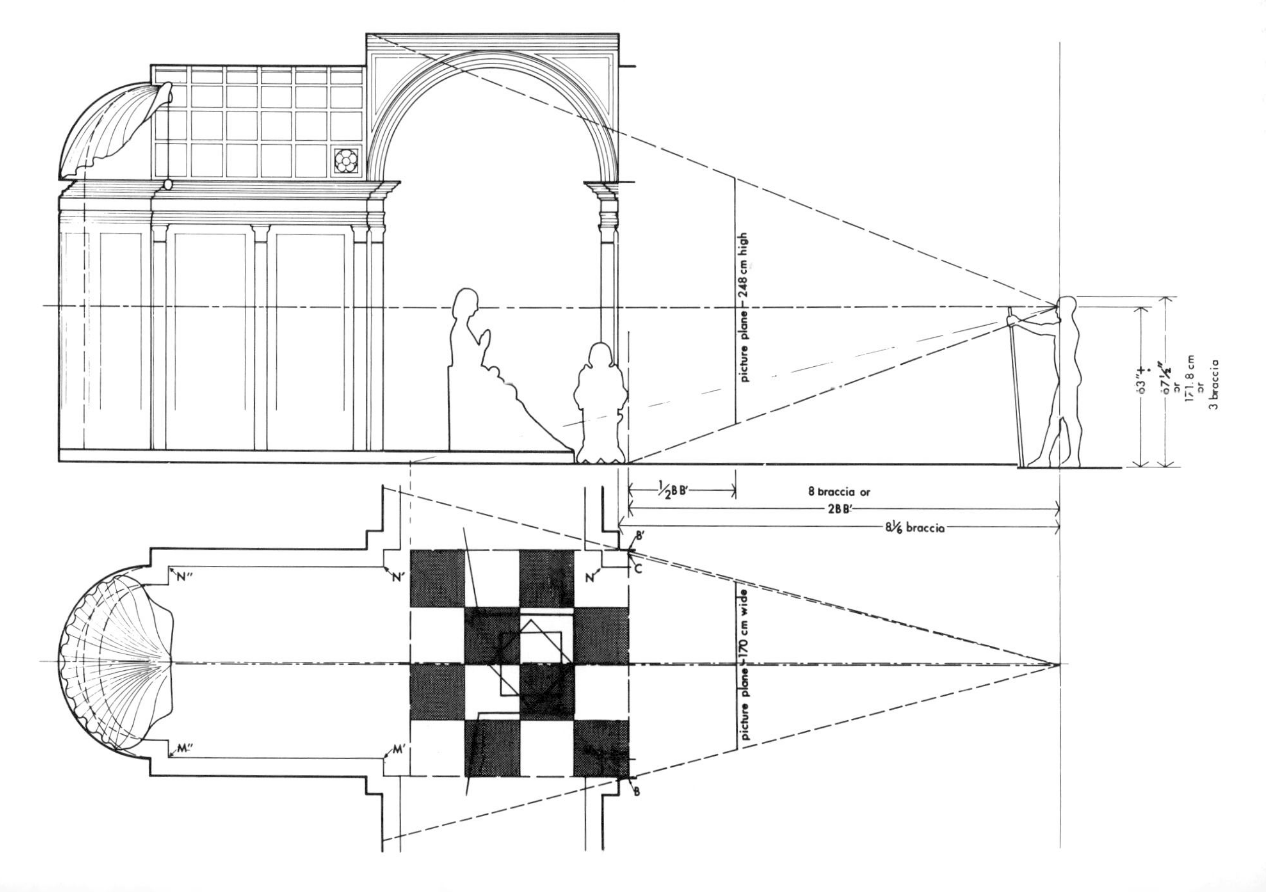

Let us next look at the marvelous chapel which Piero has created to enclose the group surrounding the infant. Not only is it made of precious marble exquisitely wrought and fitted. Its proportions are simple and symmetrical, as would have pleased Alberti. We would therefore expect the pilasters supporting the arches to be as far apart as they are tall, enclosing an invisible square. For such was Alberti's ideal, as he not only wrote in his book on architecture, but practiced when he designed churches. If the two nearest pilasters were extended downward to the bottom of the picture they would be as tall as far apart, plus the thickness of the step beneath Mary. But these pilasters have been shortened, which in effect pushes them back behind the group. Why? No one, perhaps, will ever know. Piero may have decided that they interfered with the people. In the illustration, page 379, the building appears as if the pilasters had not been shortened, possibly as Piero first intended them to be.

The depth of the chapel behind Mary turns out to be surprisingly great, and the suspended egg turns out to be a huge ostrich egg, seen at a distance. It is also surprising to discover that Mary herself, if she stood up, would be much taller than the other figures. In his earlier paintings Piero more than once painted Mary larger than life, surrounded by smaller figures. But this time he has skillfully concealed her height, and the size of the ostrich egg, by placing them at some distance within the painting. Their size makes us believe they are near the front of the picture, when they are not. The French have a term, *trompe l'oeil* ("fool the eye") for such innocent trickery. This is perhaps the first known example of *trompe l'oeil* using perspective.

Design on the Picture Plane

We have been thinking of the picture as a copy of a "real" scene (though in smaller scale). But as a work of art it is also a creation free from such narrow interpretations and existing in harmony with its own flat surface. This flat surface is called by artists the *picture plane*. When one studies and enjoys the picture plane of a painting, one forgets about depth, even about the picture's meaning, and thinks of it as a complex of forms and colors. Today we often turn a painting upside down or on its side, in an attempt to see past its content to its design or *composition*. Was Piero also concerned about the placement of forms and colors on the picture plane? Obviously yes, even though his approach must have been far different from that of an artist living today.

The illustration opposite shows that Piero, when it came to composition, perhaps inherited certain design traditions from an earlier century. He appears to have determined the dimensions of his painting and the placement of its forms on principles like those used in designing the ivory carving shown in the illustration on page 335. Here again we see what appear to be octagrams and Φ divisions combined. The beautiful egg seems to be just as long as the bands forming the great octagrams are wide. The small diagram (right) shows how this width seems to have been determined. If we look at this diagram in another way, as one of the small octagrams in the carpet border, it shows how the egg just fits into one of them. The suspended egg itself, as if swinging, does not lie on the painting's center line. Its own line,

Photo SCALA, with design pattern superimposed by Dean Snyder

Left: Conjectural design plan of the Urbino Madonna. Clues to the scheme are the small octagrams in the carpet border, the proportions of the egg, and the line, extended, of St. John the Baptist's staff. The Virgin's left foot is just above one of the border octagrams, while her right touches the midline of the large octagram beneath her. Below: Relationship between the egg and the octagram in the carpet. AB is the base of a $1:1:\sqrt{2}$ *triangle. AC is the base of a* $1:2:\sqrt{5}$ *triangle. The point G divides AC in mean-and-extreme proportion, or* Φ.

Diagram by Dean Snyder

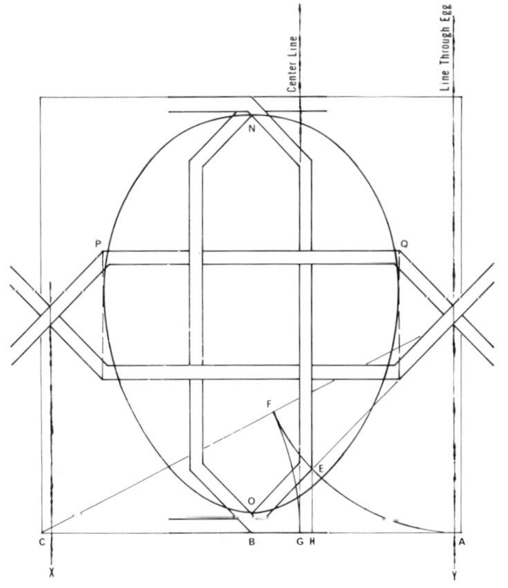

extended downward, cuts the bottom of the painting just one-half egg width away from the center line.

Color

The soft cool greys and grey-blues in the painting, as shown in the illustration, make the warm reds stand out with extra strength. Between these moderate extremes of color the shades of brown ranging from brownish grey to soft orange serve as connecting links.

Some Possible Hidden Connections

The infant Jesus, sleeping in the Virgin's lap, is a distinct individual. He seems to be at least a year old, and is golden haired, just as the Countess was. This, perhaps, is a portrait of the very child the Countess offered her life to bear. If so, it fits into a pattern: every other portrait of the Count painted after this child was born includes the child also.

Let us next look at the two pairs of saints standing on either side of Mary. On her right (the viewer's left) St. Bernardine looks like St. Jerome, but older. On her left (the viewer's right) St. Peter looks like St. Francis, but older. We seem to have here a pair of disguised double portraits. Oddly enough, the face of St. Peter has for some time been recognized to be that of a person who actually lived. This person was a Franciscan monk named Luca Paccioli, who as a young man studied mathematics under Piero and later wrote a book on arithmetic dedicated to him. The likeness was discovered by comparing the face of St. Peter with the known portrait of Paccioli. But there is something strange about this. The known portrait was painted in 1495, when Paccioli was about fifty. Piero painted his Urbino Madonna over twenty years earlier, when Paccioli was still under thirty. How could Piero have known how Paccioli would look over twenty years later? To this mystery the logical solution seems to be that St. Francis is a portrait of Paccioli as he looked in about 1473, while St. Peter is Piero's shrewd guess at how Paccioli would look after he had aged by two decades, a shrewd guess indeed. It is likely that Paccioli played an active role in assisting Piero work out the complex measurements of the painting's design. Perhaps that is why, as St. Francis, he holds the elegantly precise little cross. He was later to make an entire career of the mathematics Piero taught him. The known portrait of Pacciolo is shown on page 390.

And whom do we have on Mary's right? Between the gesturing hand of St. Jerome and the praying hands of the Count the Infant lies in a direct line. Is not the grey-haired man Piero's own self-portrait? If so, he has painted himself as a saint who in middle age retired to a life of sacred study, just as Piero was about to retire from painting to a study of mathematics. As Jerome he points to the Infant Jesus. As Piero he gives the Count this portrait of his son. And behind himself has Piero placed, in the person of St. Bernardine, a guess at how he himself would look in two decades? He was actually to die before two decades had quite passed.

So the painting seems full of double meanings. Such was the manner in which many a great artist of the Renaissance developed his works. Beneath the glorious impact which the painting was devised to make on the beholder lay hidden interpretations, based on various fields of knowledge,—a many-faceted creation from the hands of a many-sided man, not just a simple craftsman proud of his single skill.

Leonardo da Vinci

The next man to make great progress in the art of painting, and to write about it, was one of the world's towering geniuses, Leonardo da Vinci. Whereas Alberti wrote to be published, Leonardo wrote for himself, even making his notes illegible to the casual eye by jotting them down backwards

Windsor Castle, Royal Library

Five imaginary men, an ink drawing from one of Leonardo's notebooks, about 1490. The stern-faced man (wearing the wreath) appears over ninety times in Leonardo's notebooks, and has been conjectured to be his father.

with his left hand. What he put down on page after page in the course of perhaps 40 years is still the marvel of the world. Every side of human knowledge and thought came under the searchlight of his mind, and what he had to say was often centuries ahead of his time. On a single page, for instance, one can see a delicate drawing of a violet, to its left a geometrical construction, and below it a device, with sketches and notes, for welding sheet metal. On another, a drawing of a gentle mother and child is close to a plan for shrapnel-firing cannon. Elsewhere are endless drawings of men in action, horses, a whole page of cats, studies of problems in optics, physics, the action of flowing water, the structure of the Alps, an air-conditioning machine, at least three flying machines, and so on. Today hundreds of these priceless pages are treasured by a few of the world's greatest libraries.

Leonardo, the natural son of a Florentine notary, was born in a little village in the mountains behind Florence, and spent his boyhood there. When he was not attending the little local school, he was out in the beautiful Italian countryside, drawing and studying whatever met his marvellously penetrating eyes. When he was 17 his father moved into Florence and apprenticed him to an excellent artist, Verrochio, a man of broad abilities not just in painting but also in sculpture and engineering. Here Leonardo became one of a group of able students, all working in a large, busy workshop where commissions of all sorts were being completed. He soon distinguished himself. He completed in two years the apprenticeship training which usually took six, and was admitted to the painters' guild at 19. Verrochio retained him as a valued assistant for six more years.

Leonardo's First Important Painting

Soon Leonardo attracted the attention of Lorenzo de Medici, "The Magnificent," the most illustrious member of the powerful banking family (see page 365). He invited Leonardo to study his private art collection, a privilege he extended only to the best of Florentine talent. He also began to nudge painting commissions in Leonardo's direction. This is why the monks of a nearby monastery decided to request Leonardo, then 29 years old, to paint for them the *Adoration of the Kings*. The painting was to be paid for in installments, with cheese and wine produced on the monastery's farm.

Two of Leonardo's studies for the Adoration of the Kings. *Right: An early sketch. Below: Perspective study for the painting's top half. Note how the idea of the double stairway with arches keeps developing.*

Photos Alinari.

Louvre, Paris

Uffizi, Florence

Leonardo's Adoration of the Kings *(49.2 inches × 48.6 inches), as it exists today. This stage is known as* underpainting, *in which the artist concentrates on placement, form, light, and shade. Only when these satisfied him, would Leonardo have gone on to add color. Near left: The perspective scheme of* Leonardo's Adoration of the Kings, *and, far left: what seems to have been his plan for the chief divisions of the picture plane.*

The painting was never finished. The following year Leonardo was summoned by a powerful friend of Lorenzo de Medici, the duke of far-away Milan, to enter his employ as artist and engineer. But the incomplete painting of the *Adoration of the Kings* still exists in Florence, with Leonardo's studies and drawings for it. So we can see what is perhaps more absorbing than the finished picture—a glimpse into his mind at work bringing it into being.

Leonardo was at work on this painting in 1481–1482,[14] nearly ten years after Piero della Francesca, many miles away, had worked on his painting in memory of the Duchess of Urbino. What a difference in outlook divides them! Piero's is the work of an old man who looks back to the patient, devoted study of a lifetime. Leonardo's is young; it looks forward, like the words of a prophet, to the course art will take for years to come. His painting is full of restless, tumultuous motion; it takes us out of narrow indoor limits into the great outdoors and leads our eyes, behind the figures, off into a distant landscape of the kind Leonardo grew up with and loved. It is also much better organized and unified as a composition. One could cut Piero's painting across the middle and have two pictures, one of people, the other of architecture. Leonardo interlocks the two.

To make any sense out of all the restless action of men and horses in this painting, one must think back to the brilliant Florence of Leonardo's time and imagine what it was like to see some visiting nobleman come clattering into town surrounded and followed by his showily armed and dressed friends, bodyguard, and servants, all on horses more or less spirited according to the rider's rank. When such a party came to a halt and its chief members dismounted, grooms sprang forward to take nervous horses by the bit, and the whole street was full of noise and surging motion which sometimes started a brawl or two. To any Florentine of the period, three kings converging on one spot would produce such a tumult as a matter of course!

There is something else surging here too, of course, and that is Leonardo's imagination, seething with all the possibilities offered by his first important painting. If we look at the studies he made, those still existing, we see that he was following Alberti's perspective plan, even though the great spread of outdoor space makes this difficult. The illustration shows his perspective scheme (later changed) for the painting's upper half, divided into foreshortened squares, each measuring in width one-third of a man's height. These he had used as a guide to the scale of the buildings, men, and horses spread over the plan. (Notice, however, that whereas the buildings follow perspective laws exactly, the people do not.)

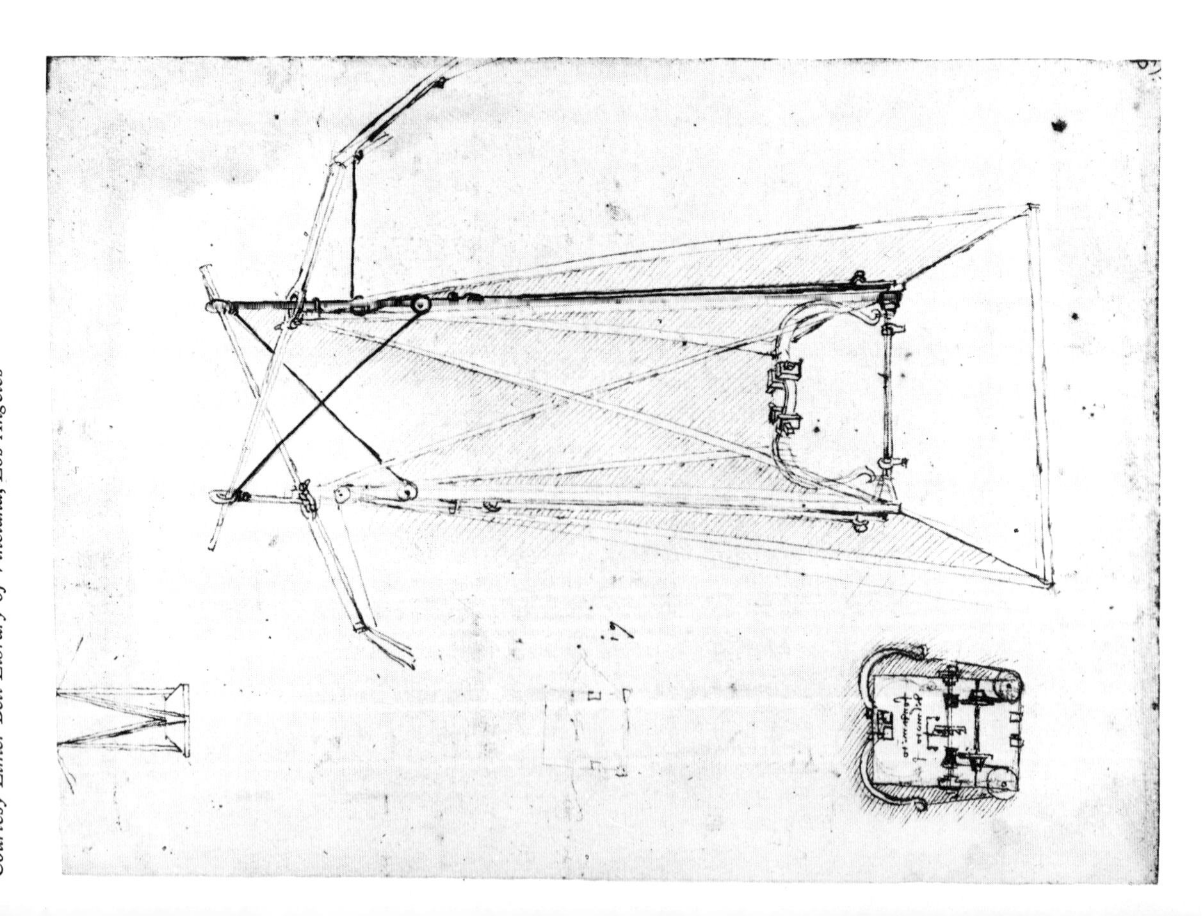

One of Leonardo's plans for a flying machine. Compare this with the drawings by Villard d'Honnecourt, page 324, to see how far machine drawing had advanced since the thirteenth century.

Courtesy Elmer Belt Library of Vinciana, Los Angeles

At the lower right he has followed Alberti's advice and placed a figure who connects the painting with the spectator by pointing. This figure is believed to be a self-portrait of Leonardo as a young man.

If we look next at Leonardo's awareness of the picture plane and its divisions, we find him using the same technique as Piero, but in a more elegantly simple and unified manner. The painting, to begin with, is an almost perfect square (perhaps respecting the square as a symbol of God's perfection).[15] The diagonals of this square intersect behind Mary's head, and help determine the placement and direction of forms leading toward her from all sides. If we then divide the square's sides in mean and extreme proportion, and then divide the shorter leg of these divisions once more, we find that these determine lines which separate the foreground from the background, help place the large tree, and locate the horizon and vanishing point of the perspective scheme.

All his life Leonardo had trouble finishing works of art. So aware was he of the understanding of nature required, and the problems involved, always new for each work, that each one became a starting point for study which often took years. For example, the Duke of Milan wanted to erect a bronze statue of his father on horseback, and engaged Leonardo to do it. Leonardo, before he could even begin, felt impelled to write an entire book (now lost) on the anatomy of horses. He then set to work on model after model. The work was interrupted by war and was never completed. Leonardo's best known work, the *Mona Lisa*, a portrait of a Florentine banker's wife, took four years to complete, during which time the sitter must have aged noticeably.

Leonardo's Contribution to Perspective

When Leonardo turned his attention to a close study of perspective, he went more deeply into the subject than Alberti had. To begin with, he saw a flaw in Alberti's method. Something, he noticed, had been overlooked. What this was he showed in a diagram.

If it is true that a picture is a flat surface (*F—F*) intersecting converging lines to the human eye from a real scene, why would Columns 1 and 3 appear larger on such a plane than Column 2 does? His answer is that the plane surface, to be accurate, should actually be curved (*F′—F′*), and that the best way to meet the problem is to treat a painting as if it were such a curved surface flattened out. The difference is slight, but important. Alberti's method, however, is simple, and near enough to the truth to be usable most of the time.

Leonardo then went on to say that *linear* perspective, which governs the receding *size* of objects, is only part of the science of perspective. As bodies recede, he wrote, they not only grow *smaller*, they change in two other ways: *they become less distinct*, and *they change in color*, *becoming bluer*. If you study the background landscape in the *Mona Lisa* or in some other of Leonardo's paintings, you find the mountains there following this triple rule, just as he stated in his notebooks that they should.

(a) Alberti's method and (b) Leonardo's method of perspective.

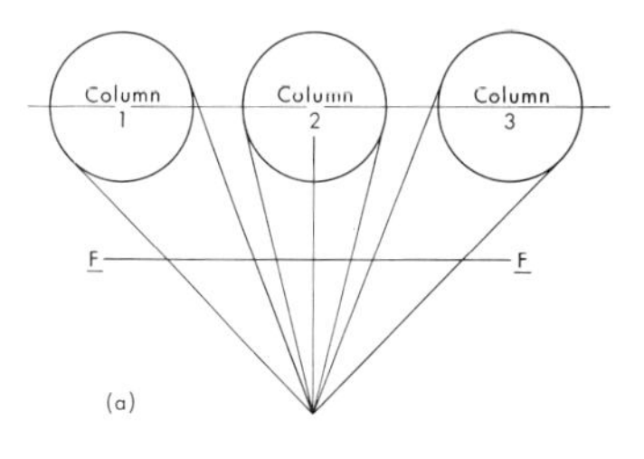

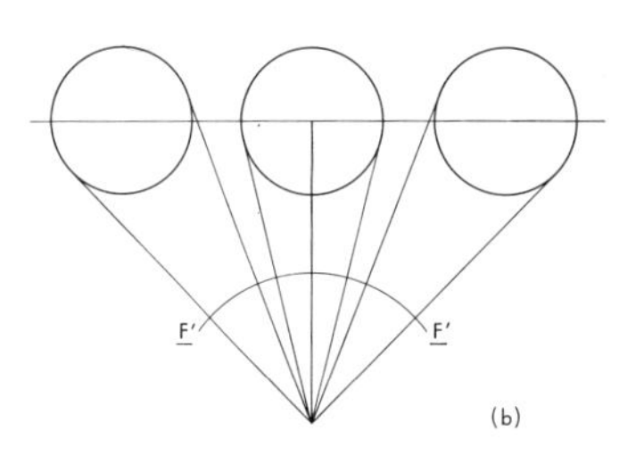

A Painting by Botticelli

The *Adoration of the Kings* by Sandro Botticelli was completed somewhere near 1490. It is believed to have been influenced by Leonardo's painting of the same subject begun, though never finished, nearly ten years earlier. The illustration shows a space division scheme by which Botticelli seems to have organized both the picture plane and the illusion of depth (perspective) in his painting. To begin with, the painting's width is to its height as three is to two. Botticelli apparently divided the width into eighteen equal parts and the height into twelve, for a number of important forms, especially the ruins and the horizon line fall on vertical and horizontal lines determined by these divisions. The divisions also seem to determine the perspective. Botticelli's approach to perspective seems to have been like Leonardo's: while his buildings follow perspective laws exactly, his human figures, while decreasing in scale with distance, do so irregularly. On this formal abstract framework, a scene alive with drama, motion, color, light, and shadow has been created, full of devices for intensifying the viewer's enjoyment and attention. Note, for example, that Mary's face, although one of the smaller ones in the picture, holds the center of attention because it is the lightest face against the relatively darkest background.

Our particular point of interest is the manner in which the painting is, and is not, bilaterally symmetrical, even though the *invisible* plan on which it was devised is definitely so. The visible painting obviously is not. Apart from the distribution of the colors, the great gable is off center. The whole ruin surrounding the Holy Family is not only placed left, but it leans slightly in that direction. A force is thus set up, a force of unbalance, intensified by the leftward lean of Joseph, Mary, the child and all the royal visitors on the right half of the painting. This force Botticelli has carefully balanced by three counterforces: the arched ruin on the left with its counterjutting stone, the massive group of kneeling and standing men on the left who are purposely placed extra far left, and the white horse with red trappings at the far right who in turn is stabilized by the horse confronting him.

The painting therefore is balanced, but in a far more lively way than if it had been exactly symmetrical along its center line, like its design-plan. It is deliberately thrown off symmetry by leftward displacement and tipping. Balance is then restored by other than symmetrical means, that is, by *asymmetrical* means. Now turn the painting upside down and study it. See how basically symmetrical it is, with its broad, weighty base of brilliantly colored figures pointing upward to the airy, central apex of the gable.

Botticelli's painting, then, is still a bilaterally symmetrical Renaissance painting. But at the same time it suggests in two ways a breaking away toward the future. (1) Its design relies on the simple obvious proportions proposed by Alberti, instead of the age-old reliance on more subtle *phi* relationships. (2) It gives a prophetic hint of a change in taste, which will cause painters to give preference to more dynamic forms of composition. In the seventeenth century we shall see artists of the Baroque period creating boldly asymmetrical paintings. In the nineteenth century we shall see Paul Cézanne repeatedly use tipping as a tension-producing device.

Opposite page, above: Adoration of the Kings, *by Sandro Botticelli (1445–1510), painted 1485–90. Below: Perspective of the painting, and grid on which it appears to have been composed.*

National Gallery, Washington

Naples Museum. Photo Alinari-Art Reference Bureau, Inc.

Above: The monk and learned mathematician, Fra Luca Paccioli, pupil of Piero della Francesca. This portrait (probably by Jacopo da Barbari) is dated 1495. When it was painted Paccioli was therefore at least 20 years older than when Piero was completing the Madonna of Urbino (page 377). Paccioli, who lectured on mathematics at the University of Rome, is still famous for two written works. One was the first surviving book to discuss the use of mean and extreme proportion in art. The other was the world's first known description of double entry bookkeeping. The first looked backward to an ancient practice, the other looked forward to the business world of today. Left: Page from Paccioli's manuscript book, Concerning the Divine Proportion. *The polyhedron shown was drawn for Paccioli by Leonardo da Vinci, as were the other illustrations of the manuscript. Paccioli and Leonardo were close friends when both were living in Milan, after Leonardo left Florence. The precious manuscript is still at Milan. It later appeared in printed form, but today even the printed version is hard to find. Reproduced courtesy Sr. G. Mardersteig, Officina Bodoni, Verona.*

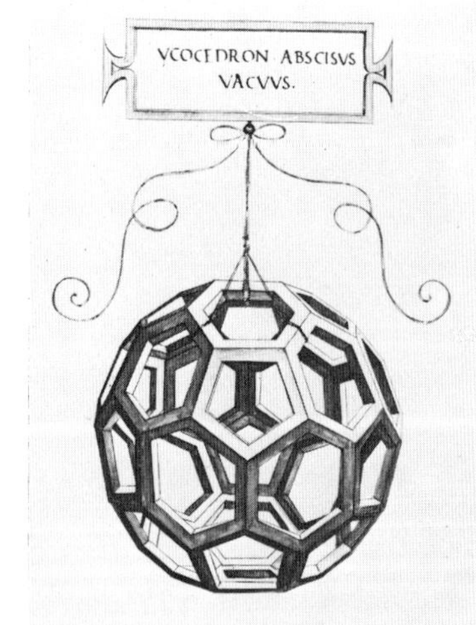

Florence in the Fifteenth Century

Such was Florence in the fourteenth and fifteenth centuries, a center of dazzling achievement in art, literature, politics, and finance. Before we leave her, let us look at the city in terms of its total population. How good was life for everybody in it? Of this we can form a clearer picture than for any other city of its time. The Florentine tax records are still on file, complete with the reports prepared by the head of each family, from which his tax was calculated.

In the year 1457 the city listed about 10,600 families, representing a total population of perhaps 100,000. Of these, the Medici family were over four times richer than any other, paying nearly 600 florins a year in taxes. But only ten other families (0.1% of the population) paid a tax of over 50 florins. Eighteen percent paid a tax of from 1 to 50 florins. Fifty-four percent paid less than 1 florin, and were probably feeling the pinch of poverty. Twenty-eight percent (3,000 families) were judged paupers, too wretched to pay any tax at all. Thousands seem to have been forced to beg. The great guilds of bankers and manufacturers of wool and silk used force and even torture to prevent unskilled laborers (chiefly wool combers) from organizing their own guilds, and thus fighting effectively for decent wages.

Wealth in fifteenth century Florence, in other words, was in the hands of a few men, who had also taken control of the guilds, and of the Palazzo Vecchio or City Hall. The citizens had ceased to serve in the army, but had begun instead to hire mercenary soldiers from distant places for the city's defense. When the city fathers saw fit, they used these troops to quell riots of desperately unhappy and impoverished Florentines. The situation was better than in the slave-supported Greek and Roman civilizations, but not much better.

But forces were at work to rob Florence of some of her power. In the Near East, the Turkish empire was steadily growing, engulfing the once great city of Constantinople, the Levant, and at last even Egypt. To the west, Portugal and then Spain were opening sea trade routes around Africa and across the Atlantic to the New World. The whole balance of Europe's trading power was eventually to shift, leaving the cities of northern Italy in a backwater, brooding over past glory.

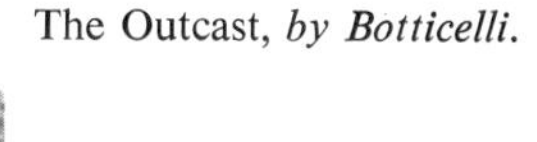

The Outcast, *by Botticelli.*

Pallavicini Collection, Rome

Cathedral of St. Bavon, Ghent

The Ghent altar piece by Hubert and Jan van Eyck, completed 1432. When open it reveals 12 panels. Top center, Christ sits enthroned as ruler of Heaven. On his right sits Mary who bore him, on his left John the Baptist, who foretold his coming. To their right and left angels make heavenly music. On the outside stand Adam and Eve. Below, Christ, symbolized by a lamb, is surrounded by angels and many saints and holy men. Dimensions when doors are open, about 11×14 feet. Christ, Mary and John are nearly life-size.

NORTHERN EUROPE IN THE FIFTEENTH CENTURY

Flanders

While these great advances in art were going forward in Florence, there was another center of European wealth, 700 miles northwest by land travel. The country of Flanders had awakened to become an active trade and manufacturing center in wool and other goods during the Middle Ages (see page 321), and had remained so ever since. The great cities of Bruges and Ghent were rich merchant towns, by the standards of the times, just as Florence and her sister cities were in the south. But the Flemish cities were not so independent. They had lost their freedom to the Dukes of Burgundy, who ruled a large part of what is now Holland and Belgium, as well as part of eastern France.[16] These dukes were practically uncrowned kings in their own territory. The wealth coming to them in taxes and import duties on wool, cloth, fish, wine, and other goods was enormous. With an arrogant disdain for anything like thrift, they often squandered their wealth on their own personal glory and entertainment. Some of this wealth, fortunately, found its way to artists, for the taste of these aristocrats could sometimes be excellent. The same can be said about the taste of the merchants of the richer cities. We find, therefore, that Flanders was an art center in its own right.

The artists of Flanders gave to their work a distinctively quaint character which was in some ways far behind the Italians. These simple men were still a part of Gothic Europe, close to its very heart and place of origin in northern France. They had tasted no daring break with tradition as the

Florentines had, but were still devout, humble members of workmanlike craft guilds. They had never heard of Vitruvius or his classic rules of human proportion, never seen a Roman statue or perhaps even a Roman arch, and knew nothing of the new science of perspective. But they were men of shrewd intelligence and sensitive eye. They were creating works of art for persons whose wealth and power had given them leisure, and whose leisure had given them a new taste for the sensual enjoyment of this world. But while enjoying the here and now, these men of wealth kept a cautious eye on their future lives in Heaven. And they employed the painters to help them get a foothold there, by paying them to paint pictures for churches.

Late medieval (fifteenth century) Flemish paintings, therefore, were a charming mixture, full of religious piety and also full of tempting things belonging to this earth. Stimulated by their patrons' taste, the artists struggled with the problem of making people, objects, buildings, and landscapes look invitingly real. Their paintings began to have depth. The people shown there took their place within a space instead of being applied to a flat surface, and around them appeared animals, birds, plants, buildings, and landscapes. All this was executed with a craftsman's thoroughness. But it was all the result of close observation, not of theoretical planning. In their paintings perspective lines never converge to a vanishing point, nor do human proportions follow any classic rule.

The greatest of the Flemish artists was Jan van Eyck, who lived between about 1380 and 1440. He was not only a master craftsman and draftsman, but he must also have had a gift for reading to their depths the character of his fellow men. Several portraits by him still exist, including one of his own wife. In each one a complete personality comes across to us, as if 500 years ago, and more, were yesterday. It seems to have been this power of his which made van Eyck stand in high favor with the Duke of Burgundy, known as Philip the Good. The duke sent Jan on confidential journeys to the courts of several European kings, once even to Portugal. Why? So that Jan might paint portraits of the kings' eligible daughters. The duke had ambitions to marry a princess, complete with the lands that came with her, and wanted to see whom he might be marrying. Jan, in other words, was valued as a sort of court "photographer." None of his royal portraits has survived. The duke at last succeeded in marrying Isobel of Portugal, and gratefully rewarded Jan with an honorary position and a pension for life.

But Jan van Eyck is chiefly remembered for two things. First, he was a great painter of exquisitely jewel-like pictures for churches. The greatest of these, and the most astonishing Flemish painting of his time, at least that has survived, is an altarpiece which was commissioned by a merchant of Ghent (named Jodocus Vydt) to hang in his private chapel in the Church of St. John.[17] Jan's elder brother, Hubert, was first in charge of the work, but presently died. Jan then completed it; such a painting was a labor of years.

Jan's second claim to fame was as an inventor. He discovered a way to use oil successfully in painting, thus giving paintings a new brilliance and permanence, and paving the way for future technical advances.

St. Barbara, *by Jan van Eyck. This is the underpainting (called imprimatura) for an unfinished picture. The drawing, on a grey tinted panel, appears to be in metal-point, strengthened with ink applied with a fine pointed pen. Some color has been applied to the sky; there, for some reason, the overpainting stopped. Painting in this formal manner, once it has begun, must proceed as preplanned, with few if any alterations of forms.*

National Museum, Antwerp

The German town of Erfurt, with its two Gothic churches and steep roofed houses, looks much as it did, probably, 500 years ago.
Photo Anton Schrall Verlag

Germany

So far we have said little about the great Holy Roman Empire, including Germany, Austria, and other lands, lying east of France and directly north of Italy. This land was under the rule of emperors who looked on themselves as successors to the Romans. Everywhere in the country the society was feudal. Lesser lords swore loyalty to greater ones, the greater ones swore loyalty to the emperor. Parish priests swore loyalty to their bishops, and bishops swore loyalty to the pope. Supporting both pyramids were the toiling serfs, leading their monotonous lives bound to the land on which they were born.

Scattered throughout this feudal pattern was a network of cities and towns, crowned by great cathedrals and churches, and governed by guilds of merchants and craftsmen. These cities, once free, had been subdued and forced to swear allegiance to various great feudal lords and bishops, except in one fiercely independent corner, Switzerland. The tough citizens of Bern, Zurich, Geneva, and Basel, led by patriots like William Tell, had kept their independence, and have to this day.

The manufacturing and trade that were the lifeblood of these cities had several sources. In the south was the luxury trade coming across the Alps from Venice. In the north lay the Baltic Sea (see page 312), a sort of northern Mediterranean for ease in shipping, its waters a source of herring, its shores strewn with amber and (more rarely) emeralds. Overland from the east came Polish furs, valued by the wealthy. By ship from the west came English and Flemish woolen goods. The great Austro-German heartland lying in between was in several places rich in metals: iron, in constant demand for armor, weapons, tools and horseshoes; copper, used everywhere for pots and pans; and precious silver and gold, always in demand for minting coin.

So the northern ports of Hamburg and Lubeck and the more southern inland cities such as Cologne, Frankfurt, Nurnberg, Mainz, Strassburg, and Augsburg had plenty of material for commerce and for what was then called prosperity. They tended to be proudly independent of influence from western Europe; Florentine bankers who tried to start branches in German cities were rebuffed. The Germans gradually developed their own methods for supplying merchants with capital and credit. In the course of time they too developed their own great banking families. The greatest of these were the Fuggers, and in that family the greatest member was Jacob Fugger (1459–1525). In his lifetime he performed some astonishing feats of finance, including the placing and maintaining of a Holy Roman Emperor on his throne.

The Germans of the fifteenth century began to display a quality which has characterized them ever since: a gift for technical inventiveness and excellence. German armor was the best produced in northern Europe (just as that of Milan was the best in the south). So at one time were German clocks. Germany was also in the forefront of the development of firearms: first the *bombard*, or seige gun, throwing a stone cannon ball, which by 1450 had made obsolete the medieval castle with its vertical walls; and then the hand gun, which was soon to render body armor ineffective and shorten the days of chivalry and knighthood.

Jacob Fugger, the greatest financier in sixteenth century Europe, as painted by Albrecht Dürer in 1523. This dynamic face could well belong to a man of our own age.

Bavarian State Museum, Munich

Printing

But the greatest technical advance of all, because of its liberating influence on men's minds, was the perfection of the art of printing by Johann Gutenberg and his associates at Mainz in the mid-fifteenth century. Prior to this time a book, its every word shaped by a quill pen in a human hand, was a rare, costly possession. So was the knowledge which books contained. The printing press soon changed all that.

CHAIN OF NECESSARY STEPS IN THE DEVELOPMENT OF PRINTING

1. Discovery of the element antimony: in the eighth century, by the Muslim alchemist Jabir-ibn-Haiyan.
2. Type metal: a hard alloy of lead, tin, and antimony, with low melting point, undistorted by cooling, and inexpensive.
3. Movable type: first developed in Europe (Holland) in a crude sand-cast form in about 1400, though it was known in China before that date.
4. Type mold: for precision casting, in large quantity. The letter was first carved in steel. This *matrix* was then repeatedly punched into brass, each punched impression becoming a mold, when properly mounted and enclosed. *This was Gutenberg's contribution as an inventor.*
5. Making paper: a method imported from China by the Muslims and spread through Europe from Muslim Spain. By 1320 there were paper mills at Mainz, the city in which Gutenberg worked to perfect the printing technique.
6. Printers' ink: a strongly colored liquid which will quickly dry solid and become permanently part of the paper without smudging, fading, or leaving an oily ring. The ink was boiled linseed oil containing lamp black, and was probably developed in Flanders or Holland at about the same time Jan van Eyck was perfecting a boiled-oil technique in painting (perhaps about 1400).
7. Printing press: probably developed from the bookbinders' press used in assembling hand written books.
8. Public demand: the rise in Germany of a large class of independent minded *bourgeois*, i.e. merchants and craftsmen, taught in local schools to read, and suspicious of a Church controlled from Italy, created a market for books (especially the Bible) which could be produced faster and cheaper than by pen.

Printing, aside from being an enlightening influence, was significant in another way. Industrially speaking, it was a beginning step in *mass production.* And it was not the only example of it. There were at least two others, both closely related to printing as a process. Both were connected, however, not with words, but with art and especially illustration: woodcut and engraving.

A page from Gutenberg's 42 line Bible, first published in 1457 on six hand presses, all in simultaneous operation. Still unsurpassed for excellence of design, workmanship, and materials. This was Gutenberg's great triumph as a craftsman: to manage to make the first also the best.

omne tentoriũ ⁊ cunctam supellectilē.
et homines huiuscemodi contagione
pollutos: atq; hoc modo mundus lu-
strabit immũdũ tercio ⁊ septimo die.
expiatusq; die septimo lauabit et se et
vestimēta sua: ⁊ immundus erit usq;
ad vesperam. Si quis hoc ritu nō fue-
rit expiat⁹. peribit anima illius de me-
dio ecclesie: quia sanctuariũ dñi pollu-
it: ⁊ nō est aqua lustrationis aspersus.
Erit hoc preceptũ legitimũ sempiternũ.
Ipse quoq; qui aspergit aquas. lauabit vestimenta sua. Omnis qui tetigerit aquas expiatōnis: immũdus erit
usq; ad vesperam. Quicquid tetigerit
immundus. immũdum faciet: ⁊ anima que horum quippiam tetigerit. im-
munda erit usq; ad vesperum. XX

Veneruntq; filij israhel et omnis
multitudo in desertum sin mense
primo. ⁊ mansit pp̄ls in cades. Mortu-
aq; ē ibi maria: ⁊ sepulta in eodem lo-
co. Cumq; indigeret aqua popul⁹ con-
venerunt adversum moysen et aarō:
et versi in seditionē dixerūt. Utinam
perissemus inter fratres nostros corā
domino. Cur eduxistis ecclesiā dñi in
solitudinem: ut ⁊ nos ⁊ nr̄a iumenta
moriamur? Quare nos fecistis ascen-
dere de egipto. ⁊ adduxistis ad locum
istũ pessimum qui seri nō potest: q̄ nec
ficũ gignit. nec vineas nec mala gra-
nata: insup ⁊ aquam nō habet ad bi-
bendũ? Ingressusq; moyses ⁊ aaron
dimissa multitudine in tabernaculũ
federis. corruerunt proni in terram: cla-
maveruntq; ad dominũ atq; dixerunt.
Domine deus audi clamorē populi
huius. ⁊ aperi eis thesaurũ tuũ fontē
aque vive: ut satiati cesset murmura-
tio eorũ. Et apparuit gloria dñi super
eos. Locutusq; ē dominus ad moysen
dicens. Tolle virgam et congrega po-
pulum tu ⁊ aarō frater tuus. ⁊ loqui-
mini ad petrā coram eis: ⁊ illa dabit
aquas. Cumq; eduxeris aquā de petra.
bibet omnis multitudo ⁊ iumenta eius.
Tulit igit moyses virgam que erat in
conspectu dñi sicut preceperat ei. cōgre-
gata multitudine ante petram: dixitq;
eis. Audite rebelles ⁊ increduli. Num
de petra hac vobis aquā poterimus
eicere? Cumq; elevasset moyses manũ
percutiens virga bis silicem. egresse sunt
aque largissime: ita ut popul⁹ biberet
et iumēta. Dixitq; domin⁹ ad moysen
et aaron. Quia nō credidistis michi
ut sanctificaretis me coram filijs isrl:
non introducetis hos populos in terram quā dabo eis. Hec ē aqua contra-
dictionis. ubi iurgati sunt filij israhel
contra dñm: ⁊ sanctificat⁹ est ī eis. Mi-
sit interea nūcios moyses de cades ad
regem edom. qui dicerent. Hec mādat
frater tuus israhel. Nosti omnē labo-
rem qui apprehendit nos. quomodo
descenderint patres nr̄i in egiptũ. ⁊ habi-
taverim⁹ ibi multo tempore: afflixerunt-
q; nos egiptij ⁊ patres nostros: ⁊ quomodo clamaverim⁹ ad dñm et exau-
dierit nos. miseritq; angelũ qui edu-
xerit nos de egipto. Ecce in urbe cades
que ē in extremis finibz tuis positi: ob-
secramus ut nobis transire liceat per
terram tuā. Non ibimus p agros nec
per vineas: nō bibemus aquas de pu-
teis tuis: sed gradiemur via publica.
nec ad dexteram nec ad sinistram decli-
nantes: donec transeamus terminos
tuos. Cui rn̄dit edom. Non transi-
bis per me. Alioquin armat⁹ occurrā
tibi. Dixeruntq; filij israhel. Per tritā
gradiemur viā: ⁊ si biberim⁹ aquas
tuas nos et pecora nostra. dabimus

Library, University of California, Berkeley

Technical progress in German woodcut rendering in the course of a century. Right: Sower, by an unknown craftsman, fifteenth century. Far right: trumpeter, by Jost Amman, sixteenth century. Command of sculptural form, foreshortening, depth of landscape, and wealth of detail have been greatly advanced. But the earlier one has its own simple strength.

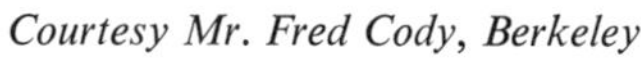

Courtesy Mr. Fred Cody, Berkeley

Woodcut

One of these was wood-block printing. The idea of printing a picture defined by black lines from a carved block had been known for a long time, but it did not come into common use until after 1400. Perhaps this was because it was only then that a usable printing ink was discovered. The first known block prints (or *woodcuts*) are simple and strong, resembling the lead patterns in a stained glass window. Later the technique became more refined. But the strength of the first woodcuts was never surpassed.

The great German painter, draughtsman, and engraver, Albrecht Dürer (1471–1528). This is a self-portrait, executed in 1497, when he was 26 years old. He lived most of his pious, hard-working life in his native city of Nuremberg, where he was a respected member of the painters' guild. For examples of his work see pages 399–400.

Louvre, Paris

Engraving

The other technique was copper-plate engraving. This way of repeating a drawing many times seems to have been worked out by German gold- and silversmiths. By 1400 the art of *chasing* metal, or grooving a fine design in it, had been well advanced. Goblets and other vessels, bearing chased designs or inscriptions, were owned by many noblemen and wealthy merchants. Goldsmiths who wished to keep a record of the designs they had chased would rub some material like printers' ink into the grooves, wipe the rest of the surface clean, and then press a sheet of paper, softened by moistening, against the surface so hard that it would pick up the ink in the grooves. This is just about all there is to making a simple engraving. Soon pictures, not just designs, were being engraved by artists using a *burin*, or chasing instrument, on flat metal plates. Each plate was then inked and wiped. A sheet of moistened paper was laid on the plate, and both were placed in a press under great pressure to obtain an *impression*. If you touch the surface of an engraving, you can feel each line slightly raised by having been forced into the plate's ink-filled grooves.

Metropolitan Museum of Art, New York

Melancholia, *engraved by Dürer toward the end of his life. Dürer achieved for the art of copper-plate engraving very much what Gutenberg achieved for printing. He brought it to a high degree of perfection never since surpassed.*

Besides Dürer's engravings, woodcuts, and paintings, much remains of what he did probably just to please himself (all from the Albertina Archive, Vienna). Right: plant study, watercolor. Bottom right: portrait, charcoal. Below: drapery study, black and white inks on dark gray.

British Museum

Left: Early Italian copper-plate engraving (1497). A copy by one artist of a painting by another (Andrea Montegna). Below: Some of the first Italian printing. A page from the first Italian translation of Euclid's geometry, printed in Venice in 1482. The theorem shown (Book II, Proposition 11) proves the construction for dividing a line in mean and extreme proportion.

THE HIGH RENAISSANCE IN ITALY

Raphael

While northern Europeans were thus awakening, the Italians were carrying forward the advance of their own culture to near perfection. Whenever word of a technical discovery made in Flanders or Germany trickled south over the Alps, the Italians laid hold of it and made it over for their own use. Antonello da Messina, in about 1460, learned the painting secret of van Eyck which employed boiled oil, and experimented with it until he had changed it to his liking. Shortly after that, other Italian artists were experimenting with copper-plate engraving to create compositions in their own style. In 1490 the Aldi family set up in Venice the first publishing company in the world devoted to printing scholarly works, such as Aristotle, Plato, and Dante's *Divine Comedy*. The Aldi are credited with designing the first italic type.

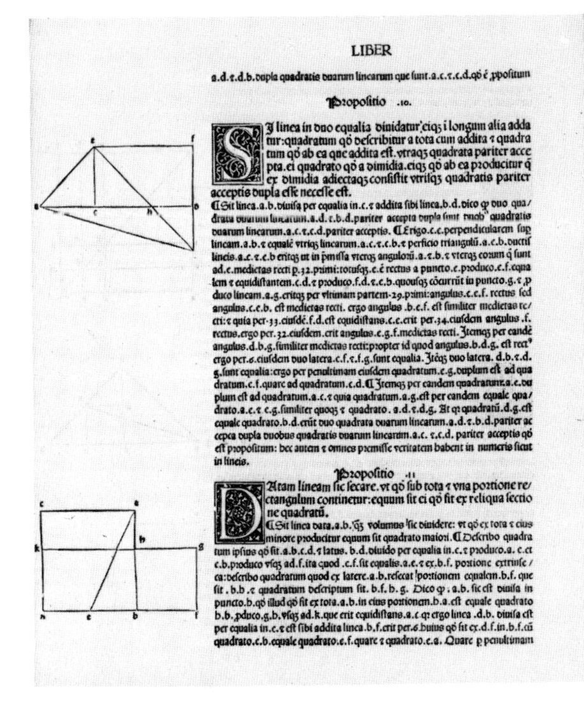

LIBER

Propositio .10.

Propositio .11

II

Propositio .12.

Propositio .13.

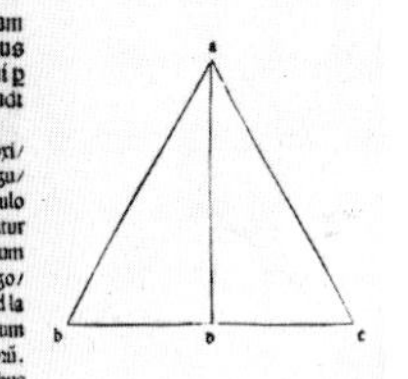

b4

Library, University of California, Berkeley

All these technical advances, oddly enough, were made by Italians outside the city of Florence. The Florentines themselves, it seems, were chiefly absorbed in other directions—finance, high politics, and the creation of ever more magnificent sculpture and painting. For artists, the atmosphere of the city was at this time still intensely inspiring. One of those to respond to it was a young man from the northern Italian town of Urbino, who, in the course of a short life of 37 years, was to express in his painting the supreme ideals toward which not only all Renaissance artists, but the whole culture, seemed to be striving. Rafael Sanzio came to Florence in 1504, when he was 21, and after Leonardo and Michelangelo had already left the city. He came well trained as an artist, but what he saw in Florence showed him that he was still a provincial.[18] Thanks to his great natural talent and intelligence, he taught himself other men's styles so swiftly that word of this young genius soon reached the pope. Rafael, therefore, was summoned to Rome in 1508, and was there engaged to decorate the walls of certain great rooms in the Vatican. He was still at work there when he died of a sudden "fever," perhaps virus pneumonia, before his talent had reached its full flower. The entire city mourned his death, and he was buried in the most glorious spot the Romans could imagine, the Pantheon itself.

Rafael seems to have been a living example of all that the men of this period aspired to be. He was, that is, *a fully developed person*, physically strong, gracious and considerate in his human relations, morally excellent, well read in both sacred and pagan literature, and a master at drawing and painting. To those who knew him he gave a personal impression of quiet, unassuming perfection. At Rome he lived like a prince, surrounded by poets and philosophers. He corresponded with other great men of his time, even with Albrecht Dürer in far-off Germany. In his painting he managed to sum up the ideals, and the learning, of his age.

How Rafael achieved this can best be seen by looking at two great wall paintings which face each other in one of the rooms of the Vatican. Their full meaning emerges only if they are examined together. In one painting all the great thinkers of pre-Christian times, as far as they were then known, are assembled. In the center stand Plato and Aristotle in deep conversation, Plato pointing heavenward, Aristotle, the scientist, pointing toward the world of here and now. In the lower left foreground Pythagoras sits devising geometry's first theorems. In the lower right, Archimedes demonstrates conic sections. Every other figure represents some great pagan thinker. But the identity is double. Some, perhaps all, are also portraits of the great men of Rafael's own time. Plato, for example, is believed to be Leonardo in his later years. A full record of all identities has long since been lost.

Everywhere there is a feeling of intense life, the excitement of intellectual discovery, and the thrill of its transmission from man to man. All this action goes on beneath vast barrel-vaulted ceilings suggestive of Imperial Rome, the architectural ideal of the period.

If we turn around and face the opposite wall, we see a brilliant even though wordless statement of the other half of Renaissance men's ideal. In this painting there is no man-made ceiling, but an open sky. The center of attention has shifted from the pagan past to the Christian Renaissance present, from the lower level of Earth and history to a higher one of Heaven and belief. Here, in visual form, is expressed the concept of the Trinity. God appears in his three forms, distinct, yet somehow one. At the apex of the painting God the Father, creator of the Universe, blesses the world. Below him Christ, or God the Son, who on earth took the form of Jesus, sits between Mary and John the Baptist, holding up his hands pierced by nails to remind all men that through his suffering they have been saved. Below Christ's feet appears, in the form of a flying dove, God the Holy Spirit, or that aspect of God which enters human hearts and speaks as the voice of conscience or divine inspiration. Directly beneath the Trinity, on an altar, stands a *monstrance*, or device for displaying the sacred bread of the Christian Mass to worshipers.

On either side of the Holy Spirit, small angels hold up the four divinely inspired Gospels of the New Tastement. Above them, seated in a great heavenly semicircle, are the fathers of the Church who helped to develop the concept of the Trinity. Below, on Earth, popes, cardinals, bishops, and other worthies stand in quiet, eloquent wonder at the miracle of man's salvation.

When we study the designs of the two paintings we find that Rafael seems to have used older geometrical conventions to reinforce the idea behind them. The shape of the paintings was already fixed by the structure of the building. So he began with what was given him. It seems clear that he then ingeniously used a circle divided into ten parts, by a regular decagram as the basis for his divisions of the picture plane. Note for example, the line AB in the illustrations. As if to show that the content of one painting is pagan and earthly, the other Christian and heavenly, everything important in the first fills the space below, and, in the second, the space above it. Both paintings, in this and other ways, seem to be planned on an age-old pattern for laying out sacred buildings.

Personification of an earthquake, a drawing by Rafael in metalpoint, actual diameter 4½ inches. Rafael grew up in the north Italian town of Urbino, where his father was court painter to Duke Guidobaldo (whose father, Duke Federigo, can be seen kneeling in the Madonna of Urbino, page 377).

Collection Mr. Janos Scholtz, New York

Photo SCALA

Rafael's School of Athens *(Vatican), conjectural divisions of picture plane and perspective.*

Rafael's use of perspective in the two paintings is also worth noticing. In the heavenly painting, the vanishing point and the center of the design-circle are one. In the earthly one the vanishing point has been raised. (How is its position determined?) Rafael's intention here was probably to give

Photo SCALA

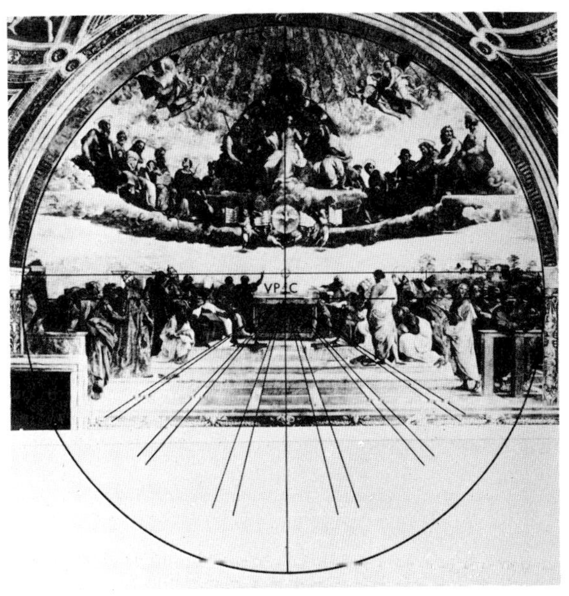

Rafael's Disputa *(Vatican), conjectural divisions of picture plane and perspective.*

the foreground more importance. In both paintings he has used perspective more grandly than any man who preceded him. The possibilities suggested in Leonardo's *Adoration of the Kings* are here carried to fulfillment.[19]

Photo Alinari-Art Reference Bureau, Inc.

Right: One of many churches built in keeping with Alberti's ideas, resorting to cube and sphere as much as construction requirements and the use of building will allow. Santa Maria della Consolazione, Todi, built in 1508. The ground plan is radially symmetrical. Below: Design for a trussed bridge, the oldest surviving plans for this kind of construction. The plans appear in The Four Books of Architecture, *by Andrea Palladio, the sixteenth century's leading publicizer and formalizer of Alberti's concepts. For an example of his architecture see opposite page.*

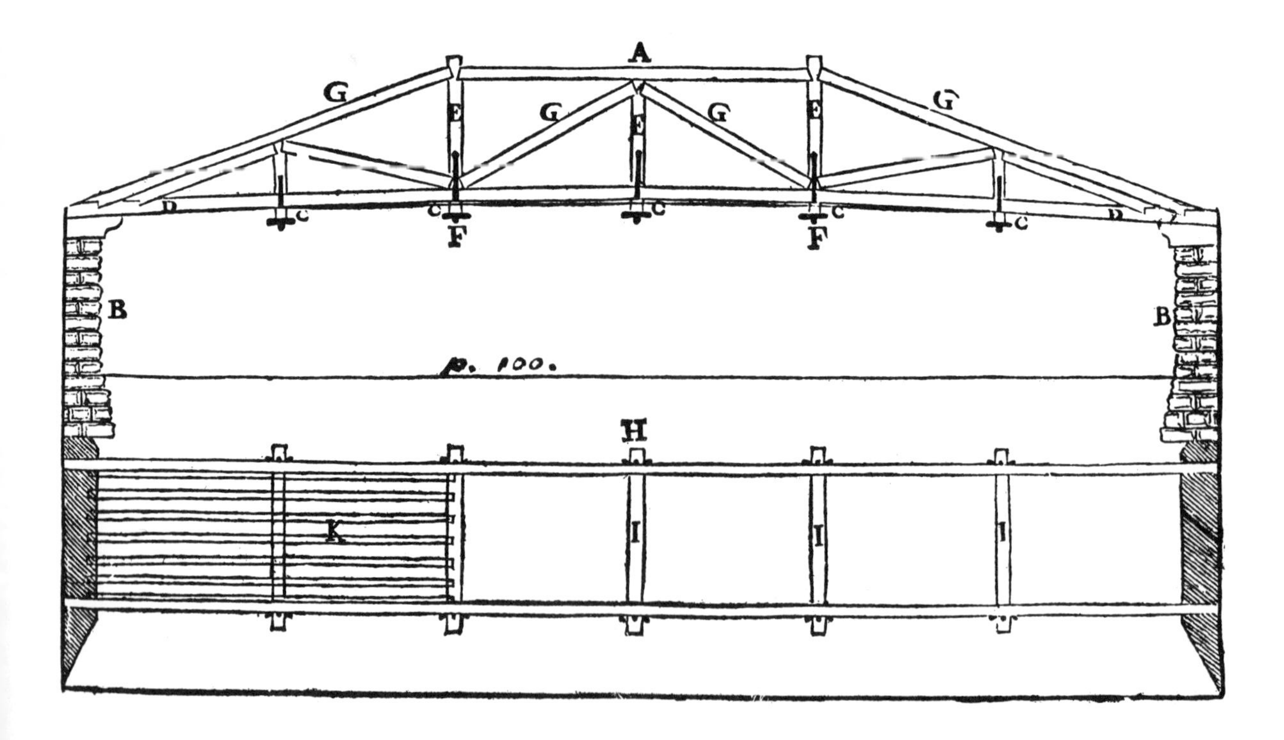

Photo Alinari-Art Reference Bureau, Inc.

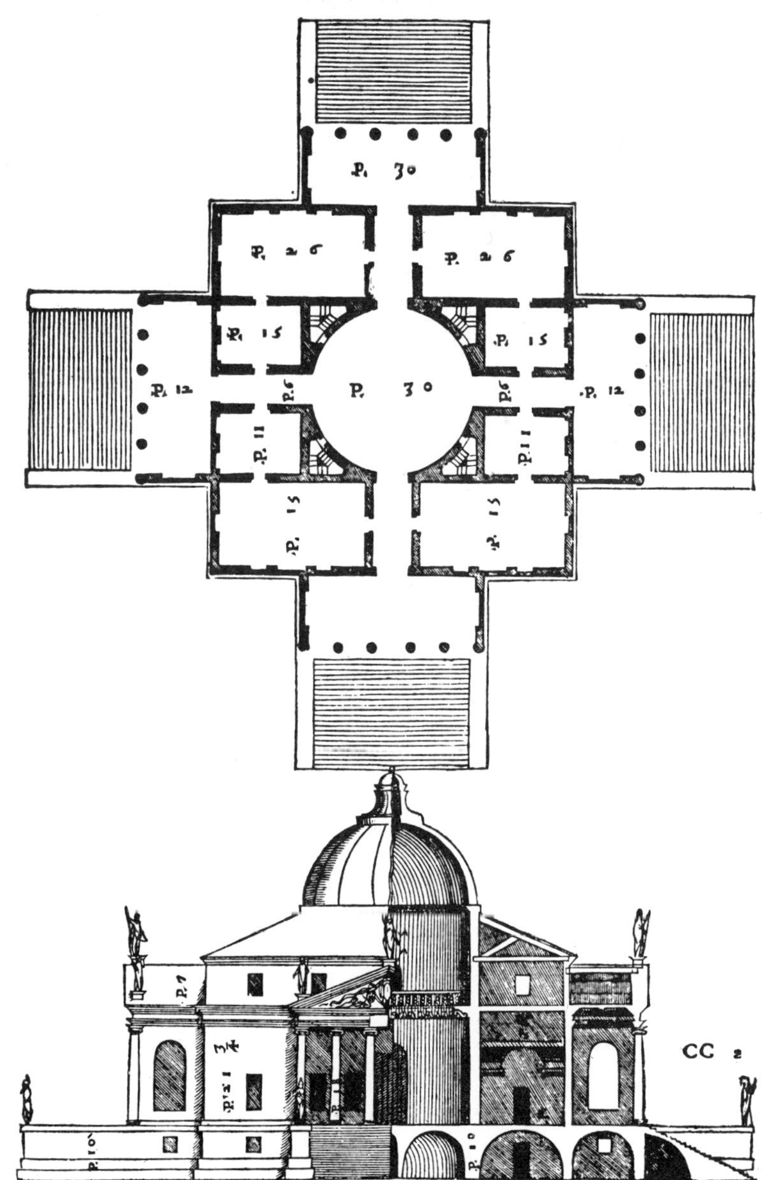

Above: Example of Palladio's achievements as an architect. The facade of the Villa Rotonda, built in 1550, one of his finest country houses. Right: Palladio's own plans for the Villa Rotonda, together with the proportions expressed in simple whole numbers. From Palladio's own work, The Four Books of Architecture *(English translation, eighteenth century).*

Right: Chinese architecture, with its rich colors and formal design, was created to dominate the world about it, a physical symbol of the human will and energy required to bind together a vast and intractable country. This monastery in Chinkiang province, eastern China, is crowned with a pagoda, a Chinese development of the stupa of India. Below: Plan and elevation of a Chinese temple, eighth century A.D. *The construction, designed to enable a wood frame to support a heavy tile roof, continued in practice for over 1000 years. Proportions were aimed at harmonizing the building with the Chinese concept of the universe.*

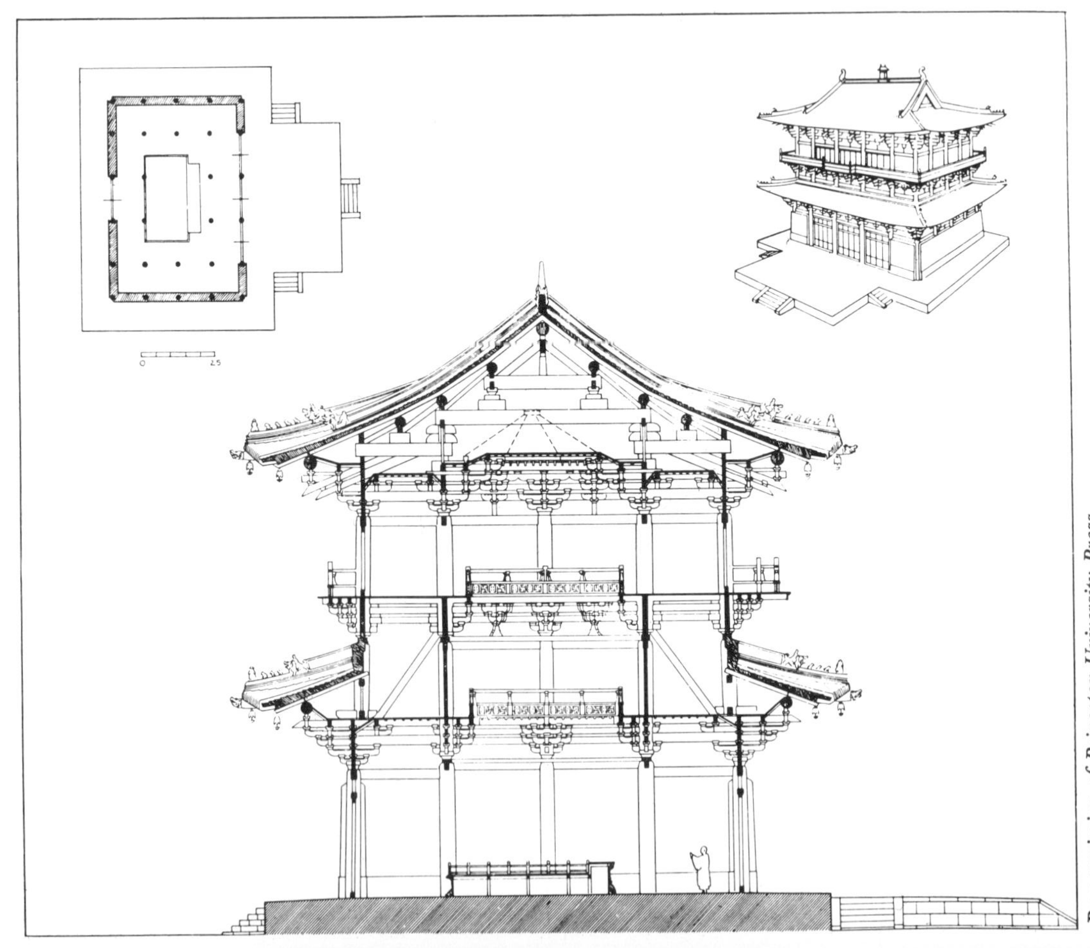

Groom currying his horse, carved jade from the Ming dynasty (fifteenth century). Length 6 inches.

Avery Brundage Collection, San Francisco. Photo John Bridgman

CHINA RESTORED TO HERSELF

From Yuan to Ming

Khublai Khan, one of China's truly great emperors, even though an alien Tartar Mongol, was the founder of a new dynasty, whose Chinese name was Yuan. The Yuan dynasty was to remain in power, in name at least, for about a century (1260–1368). It followed the usual Chinese pattern. The early Yuan emperors, Khublai and his grandson Temur, were conscientious, energetic rulers. Then came a short series of worthless successors, weakened by the luxuries of Chinese court life but still limited by Mongol primitivism. Their crude religious sense attracted them to the magic-ridden, debased forms of Buddhism; the lofty, seasoned schools of thought evolved by great Chinese sages were beyond them.

Politically the later Yuan rulers were blind except to the most childishly glittering aspects of power. Relatives quarreled for the title of emperor while the empire as a well-governed state dissolved. Once more China fell back into chaos, its vast expanse divided among bandit warlords who fought each other and plundered the land and its defenseless people.

Hope for the grievously sick empire lay in the coming of a strong man. Fortunately he appeared, an orphaned farm boy turned Buddhist monk who, at 25, left his monastery near Nanking to head a band of marauders or revolutionaries, it is not clear which. Whatever their origins, under the leadership of Chu Yuan-chang, they developed discipline, humanity, and a sense of mission. Wherever Chu overcame a local warlord he forbade pillaging of the common people. Soon wherever he went he was hailed as a liberator. Eleven years later the whole of south China was in the hands of just two men, Chu and another leader of humble origin whom Chu later overcame and slew. In 1368 Chu turned northward to rid northern China of the Tartar control which had gripped it for centuries. In the same year he entered the Tartar capital of Peking a complete victor. By the time he was 40 the simple farm boy and monk had outperformed all the Sung emperors.

Ceramic ware characteristic of the Ming dynasty. Above: blue and white porcelain bowl, width 9 inches. Below: stoneware jar, height 14 inches.

Avery Brundage Collection, San Francisco. Photos John Bridgman

Chu Yuan-chang, founder of the Ming (literally *brilliant*) dynasty, was to rule for 30 years. Once more China was united under a native Chinese, for the first time a south Chinese, who made Nanking his capital, and whose ambition was to restore Chinese greatness as it had been in the far-off times of T'ang. Chu's strong successor, Yung-le-ti, was to push beyond mere restoration. Keeping Nanking (literally *South Capital*) as a secondary center of government, he moved his court north to Peking (*North Capital*), the first Chinese to rule from a point so far north. From this center, perhaps in a spirit of revenge, he carried on destructive warfare against the now weakened Tartar Mongols. At the opposite extreme of the empire, in the far south, Yung-le-ti seized control of Annam (modern Cambodia, Laos, and Vietnam) and in 1407 organized it into provinces.

Since the days of T'ang, China had developed a new arm, her ocean-going merchant marine. From this Yung-ti-li forged a navy which, for the only time in China's history, performed extraordinary feats. The emperor's intention was to establish naval control over the South China Sea and the Indian Ocean. In his lifetime he achieved half of this. His fleets were supreme as far as Ceylon and the entire Bay of Bengal. As for the western half of the ocean, his war vessels sailed as far as Arabia (on voyages of exploration), going up the Red Sea as far as Jeddah, the port of the holy city of Mecca.

All these expansionist programs were viewed with intense disapproval by China's civil administration, the Confucianist mandarins. Nearly 600 years earlier they had opposed a similar power drive by the T'ang emperors. Probably they were partially right on both occasions. The empire, in spite of its enormous resources in manpower and wealth, was driven to overstrain itself. But this state of overstrain was soon to cease. After the death of Yung-le-ti in 1424, the inevitable pattern of ever weaker emperors once more became clear. The concern of the mandarins shifted from "What to do with the emperor's overambition?" to "What to do about his indolence?" The next emperor abandoned China's policy on the high seas. On land, in the north, Chinese armies and diplomats retreated from involvement in the affairs of Mongolia. In the south the Chinese yielded to persistent guerilla warfare carried on by the native Annamese, and withdrew from Annam, abandoning (in 1428) their administrative center of Hanoi.

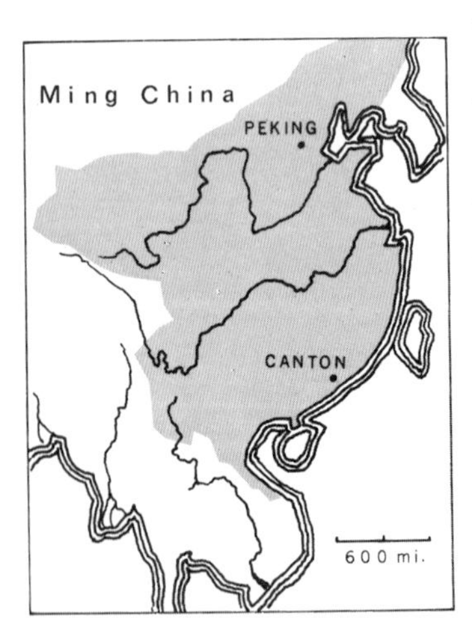

Yung-le-ti and his ministers, although their policies had been opposite, had both probably been equally limited in vision. The emperor seems to have had his eye on glory; he was ambitious to outdo the T'ang emperors. The mandarins were probably thinking in terms of Confucius' teachings and their long standing jealousy of the other half of the administration, the military. But there was one area in which the emperor's policy seems to have been right, even if perhaps for the wrong reason. This was his plan to make China a sea power. About 70 years after his death the Portuguese rounded the Cape of Good Hope, sailed across the Indian Ocean, and entered the China Sea unopposed. As we shall see in the next chapter, they were little better than pirates. If a superior naval force had been on hand to oppose them, it would have been better for Southeast Asia and eventually China. China, rather than Portugal, would have controlled the trade route linking Asia by sea with Europe.

Freer Gallery of Art, Washington, D.C.

The poet Shih-teh laughing at the moon. An ink painting on silk, height 5 ft, by the Ming dynasty artist Chang Lu.

A century later, when the grip of the Ming dynasty had weakened, a new and more serious threat arose from overseas, this time from Japan. The soldier-statesman, Toyotomi Hideyoshi, having learned of the Chinese empire's decay (from the ease with which Japanese pirates were raiding the China coast), was seized with an ambition to conquer it. He gathered a navy and a force of 100,000 men, then crossed to the Korean peninsula, believing this to be an adequate bridgehead from which to advance on Peking. Korean resistance delayed him, the Chinese army was larger than he had expected, and he had to retreat. A second attempt was defeated by the Koreans themselves, who resorted for the first time in history to metal-sheathed war vessels. Even these events failed to awaken the last Ming emperors to the need for sea power. However, it was not invasion from the sea, but revolt from within which, 50 years later, in 1644, was to topple the last of the dynasty from the throne of the Son of Heaven.

Photo Ken Domon, Tokyo

Japanese interpretation of the Buddha. Mid-ninth century, Muroji Shrine, Nara. Wood, height 5½ ft. The pose conventionally conveys the concept of banishing fear.

THE RISE OF JAPAN

The Land

Japan, the island nation which threatened China with invasion in 1582, was, compared to China, a newcomer to advanced civilization. Still, in the sixteenth century, Japan's history was already 1500 years old. Prior to that she had passed quickly through the more primitive cultural stages and had managed to preserve in her religion certain traces of all of them. That religion, Shinto, was a form of ancestor worship, as it is to this day.

The curving chain of the Japanese islands extends 1500 miles north and south opposite northern China and Manchuria. Their total area is 150,000 square miles, about that of California.[20] Of this most is mountainous; only one-fifth of the land can be farmed. But it is astonishingly beautiful, perhaps the most beautiful land in the world. Everywhere forest-covered mountains and hills stand above deeply indented bays and coves. And man, though everywhere intruding his rice paddies and farmhouses, has maintained a respect for the natural beauty around him, cooperating with it rather than dominating it.

Japan's archeology, like China's, has come under study only lately. But it seems clear that from remote times paleolithic hunters roved its woods and mountains. For up to 10,000 years ago Japan was part of the Chinese mainland, and the Japan Sea was merely a lake. Then, as the Ice Age ended, the world's glacial ice cap melted, the seas rose, and Japan became what she is today, a cluster of 3000 islands, of which Honshu is larger than all the others together.

The Ainu, Japan's Aborigines

Sometime later the islands seem to have been invaded from Siberia by neolithic hunter-farmers, who gradually spread southward over the whole island chain. The people, the Ainu, are today a vanishing race, long since driven back into the northernmost islands by the pressure of Japanese civilization. They lived by hunting with bow and arrow, and by an extremely primitive form of millet farming. They had no knowledge of metal, and the women (who tattooed their faces and arms) wove fabric from elm bark thread. The people lived loosely organized in clans and tribes governed by chiefs. They depended on shamans to control the unseen spirits (believed to dwell in trees and rocks) which could give or take away luck and good health. Their belief in the presence of an eternal soul in man and, in fact, in all things, was intense, so much so that they had no fear of death. This belief extended even to their simple, gable roofed, thatched huts, which were given "life" by magic charms when built, and which were often burned after the owner's death, thus releasing the soul of the house to shelter him in another world.

A simple farming people, the Ainu had a religious respect for millet grain. To them the oblong granaries, around which their little thatched hut villages clustered, were holy places. Beside each granary doorway a sheaf of millet, the first to be harvested, was hung each year as an offering to the unseen spirit which had made the fields fertile. These thatched, gabled granaries, unlike the people's houses, were raised well above the ground on posts to protect them from rodents, and could be reached only by a notched log ladder.

The Ainu spoke a language with an Indo-European origin from which, apparently the Hindu, Persian, Greek, Latin, and western European languages also sprang. A number of important place names in modern Japan have an Ainu origin. Of these perhaps the most important is the now quiescent volcano Mt. Fugi, whose name in Ainu means fire.

When the Ainu were first studied as a people about 85 years ago (by a kindly British missionary, John Batchelor), they appeared to have no knowledge of pottery making. This provides one of the puzzles of Japanese archeology. Many examples of strongly modeled pottery, some of them vessels, some figures like the one above, have been found, whose age, by the radiocarbon test, goes back as far as 7500 B.C. Did the people who made them arrive in Japan before the Ainu? If so, pottery making seems never to have been transmitted from one people to the other. Figures like the one below are believed to have had some connection with crop fertility rites. The culture of which they were a part has been called Jomon.

Photo M. Sakamoto, Tokyo

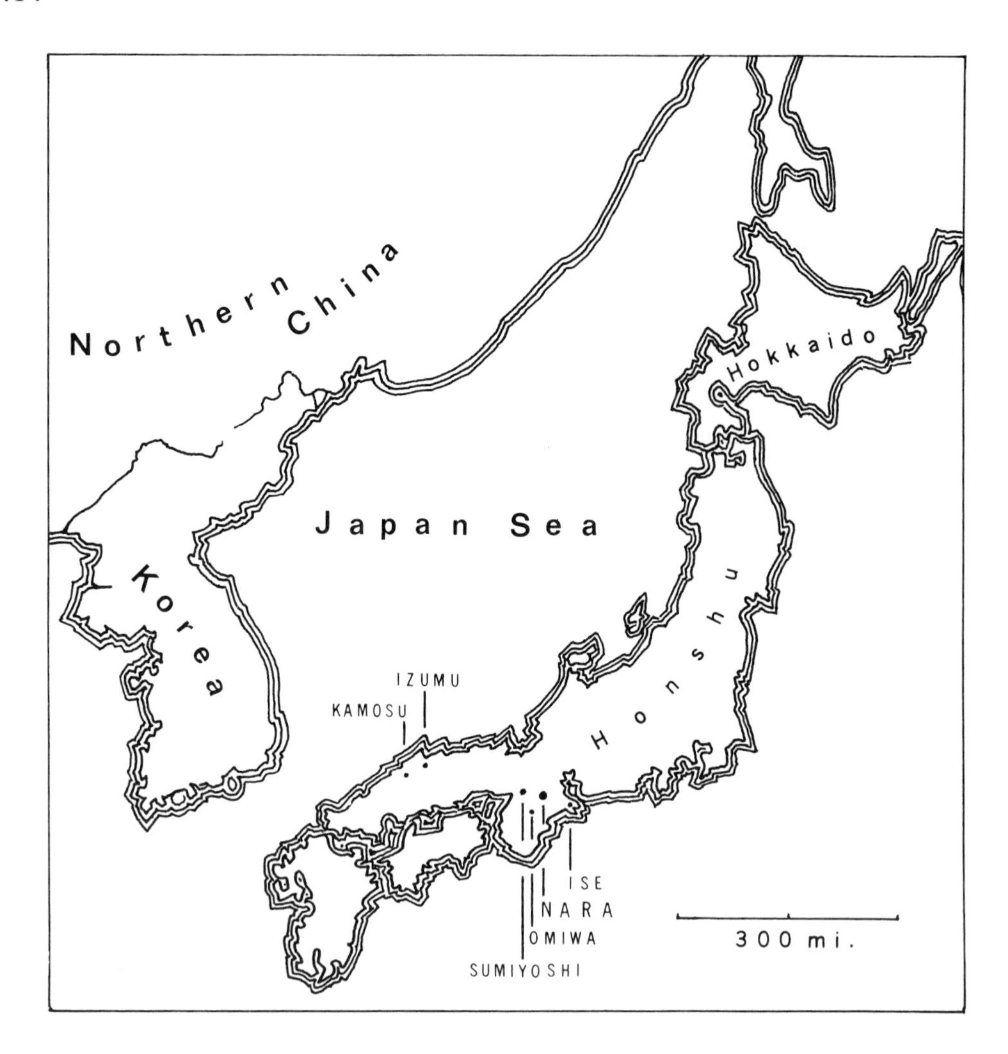

Fifth century Japan. The kingdom and civilization of Yamato had for its center the capital city of Nara.

The Yayoi People

The Ainu were not the only invaders of the island chain. It is believed that in about the fourth century B.C. another human wave (or several) arrived, this time from southeast Asia or from China's southern mainland. Perhaps they were fleeing before the conquering Chinese, who at that time were beginning to colonize southward into the Yangtze Valley. Wherever they came from, the prevailing ocean current seems to have carried the newcomers up the western side of the Japanese islands, enabling them to land along the southern coast of Honshu, on the Pacific Ocean side.

Thus in a limited area on southern Honshu Island was planted the seed of a new era in Japanese civilization. For the new settlers brought with them new complex techniques: rice growing, fishing, metalworking, carpentry, and slabwork pottery. They had solved the food production problem; they could make effective tools and weapons; and they were therefore prepared to make great social advances, of the kind described in Chapter 3. But this was to come slowly. First came a period of survival in a foreign land, where they found themselves strangers among natives. Homes had to be built, land cleared for rice farming, and sources of clay and metal discovered and mined. In the course of three or four centuries the farming newcomers and hunting-farming Ainu seem to have intermingled, in the part of southern Honshu called Yamato, to form a new mixed culture superior to that found anywhere else on the islands. This has been named the *Yayoi culture*. As it gained in strength and produced its own local population explosion, its people must have started pressing outward on the more primitive Ainu who lived on the rest of Honshu. A conflict thus began which was to go on for 1000 years. Japanese civilization was born in conflict.

Conflict was also internal. The process of tribe warring upon tribe went on within the Yayoi culture, the stronger conquering the weaker. We can surmise the process from the relics of the period, the great mound-tombs still to be found dotted all over southern Honshu, erected, presumably, in honor of dead war chiefs. To heap up such mounds must have taken multitudes of toiling humans, perhaps a conquered people working for its conquerors. Within the mounds have been found terra-cotta figures of warriors, maidservants, horses, houses, and boats supposedly to serve the great men in the next world. But these mounds are dwarfed by a few giants, surrounded to this day by double and triple moats, erected for the first rulers who made themselves masters of all other chiefs and united the land of Yamato into a single kingdom. These are Japan's Great Pyramids.

Avery Brundage Collection, San Francisco

Above: Terra-cotta warrior, from a mound-tomb, fifth or sixth century A.D. Height 4 ft. These figures (called haniwa*) are made hollow, the openings of the eyes, and sometimes of the mouth, being cut right through the clay wall. They perhaps replace an earlier practice of sacrificing human lives at the funerals of rulers.*

Left: Mound tomb of the Japanese emperor Nintoku, fifth century A.D.

Courtesy M.I.T. Press, Cambridge, Massachusetts

The Naiku Shrine at Ise, seen from the air, showing its buildings and its four fences with their gates. To the rear is the alternative site, on which the present buildings will be reproduced in 1973. The single small building in the center of the site houses the sacred post, which is never removed.

Courtesy M.I.T. Press, Cambridge, Massachusetts

The sacred gateway, or torii *in the outermost fence surrounding the Geku Shrine, Ise.*

First Contact with China

But now a new outside force was stirring, to give the still primitive land of Yamato a great forward push. This force was applied through the peninsula of Korea, which juts within 160 miles of Japan's southernmost island, Kyushu. The Chinese empire under the guidance of the great Han dynasty (206 B.C.–221 A.D.) had conquered northern Korea and made it a Chinese province. Soon there began an interchange of ambassadors and other travelers between the land of Yamato and the Chinese-Korean administrative center of Lolang. The rulers of Yamato sent abroad eagerly for men of various skills. Silk breeders and weavers, physicians, musicians, and men skilled in writing, numbering, and calendar making were to help create a new, complex, refined culture by leaps and bounds. The men of Yamato absorbed this wealth of techniques and made them over into something entirely their own, an integral part of what was by that time their own long tradition.

Japan's Most Ancient Shrines

We have already seen the great difference between magic and religion: whoever practices magic tries to force or bribe supernatural beings to do his will, but whoever practices religion does the opposite; he tries to conform his own will to that of some supernatural being. The drives in both these directions are present in primitive societies. Primitive men sense that the forces of nature can be controlled, but they have as yet no scientific knowledge or any awareness of it, and resort instead to spells and other magic devices. The opposite or religious drive is also present; men realize that their survival depends on submitting themselves to their tribe or clan, with all its customs and conventions. Any being who stands for the tribe thus easily becomes an object of submission, reverence, or worship. A chief can be a living embodiment of the tribe. So can the ancestors from whom the tribal members learned the skills by which they live and the customs by which they live in harmony. As we have already seen in Chapter 2, ancestor worship and the worship of a tribal ruler are thus often the beginnings of religion.

Japanese calligraphy, twelfth century, on paper already decorated with a faint landscape design. A passage from perhaps the oldest novel in the world, The Tale of Prince Genji, *composed about 1000* A.D.

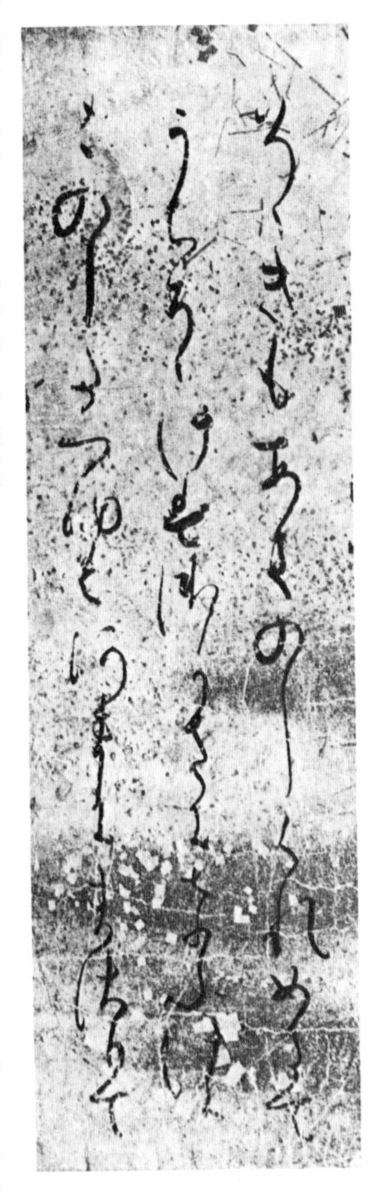

East Asiatic Library, University of California, Berkeley

Shintoism contains both of these forms, ancestor worship and ruler worship, as well as others more remote, reaching back into the realm of magic. The remarkable Japanese people, so swift to seize and adapt ideas from outside their culture, have miraculously kept unbroken a connection with their primeval beginnings, like a completely supple wrestler with a backbone strong as iron. This gift for permanence in change takes dramatic form in Japan's most ancient shrines, still reverently preserved and visited amid their sacred forests. Their very location seems to bear witness to man's beginnings as a forest hunter. The shrines, as clearings in those forests, seem to record the steps by which he rose above hunting to a freer life.

The holy shrines of Japan—Kamozu, Izumo, Sumiyoshi, Omiwa, Ise—are to be found in the Yamato region in southern Honshu, close to the place where Japanese civilization began. Of them all, Ise (EEseh) is the most sacred: the spot to which the Japanese go as pilgrims to revive their union with their most ancient past.

It is really a double shrine: two open spaces (called Naiku and Geku) in the deep forest, four miles apart on opposite banks of a small crystal clear river, not far from where it flows into the sea. Around these two open spaces, standing half hidden among the trees, are rocks whose spirit inhabitants have been revered from prehistoric times. And here are nearly 100 little shrines to minor gods or spirits, reminding us of the Ainu belief that everything in nature has its own soul. These shrines contain no images. Sometimes they house a stone, sometimes nothing visible. But the real centers of the Naiku and Geku, respectively, are two clusters of buildings sacred to two important goddesses. Geku is the shrine of Toyouke, goddess of grain. Naiku is the shrine of Amaterasu, goddess of the sun and legendary grandmother of the first ruler of Yamato. He in turn is believed to be a direct ancestor of the present emperor of Japan.

Each shrine is an oblong gravel space, containing a group of unpainted cypress wood buildings, surrounded by four fences. Beside each space an identical space stands empty. At intervals of 20 years the buildings of each shrine are completely reconstructed on an empty site. The other structures are then reverently dismantled. In the year 1973 this rebuilding process will be repeated for the 60th time. The practice began in the year 773, but the shrines were erected for the first time perhaps centuries before that. The buildings are thus always so new that their precisely shaped cypress beams, rafters, walls, and floors are still fragrant. And they are so old that they reveal to us the origins of Japanese architecture. They have been called the Parthenons of Japan.

Courtesy M.I.T. Press, Cambridge, Massachusetts

Left: building containing the sacred mirror of the Sun goddess Amaterasu, in the Naiku Shrine, Ise, Japan. It is believed to be patterned after a Japanese ruler's palace of the fifth century. The building is of cypress wood, the roof thatched with cypress bark. The great logs on the ridge pole were once intended to hold the roof down in a high wind. Later they became symbols of royalty. In the whole building the only signs of Chinese influence are the metal ornaments. Below: The ancient monastery of Horyujii, Japan's oldest Buddhist shrine, designed on formal Chinese lines, complete with pagoda, and using methods of wood construction developed by the Chinese to support tile roofs, as shown on page 408. Seventh century A.D. (founded 607).

Courtesy Princeton University Press

Courtesy Professor Yeoung Dae Kim

Korean calligraphy by Ann Kyoo Dong (1969). Korea has a completely phonetic alphabet of 24 letters, devised in 1443 at the command of its then ruling king Se-jong (Vi dynasty), by a group of scholars headed by Chong In-ji. Koreans, however, frequently continue to mix Chinese ideograms with their own alphabet, as is the case here.

On each site the most important building is the home of the goddess, built, it is believed, as were the palaces of the rulers of Yamato, 1500 or more years ago. The shrine-palace of Amaterasu contains nothing but an ancient bronze mirror, magic symbol of the goddess' authority, laid within a boat-shaped container. Close by each palace stand two store houses, holding the goddess's personal treasures. At a greater distance is a hall with open sides, in which Shinto priests may perform their daily ceremonies when the weather is bad. Still farther off stands a small building in which food, prepared by special ritual, is offered to the goddesses twice daily. Near it stands another small treasure house. At the north and south gates in the outermost fences are guard houses; for none but a few Shinto priests may enter the sacred area.

Under the floor of each palace-shrine a sacred post has been driven which is never removed even during rebuilding, and which is carefully enclosed in its own small house. One is reminded of an Ainu custom of driving into the ground close to the hearth two sacred posts symbolizing husband and wife. The form of the store houses suggests an origin in Ainu granaries; one even has the portable steps shaped from a single piece of timber. The roofing of the buildings with finely shredded cypress bark, rather than tiles, also suggests an ancient origin.[21]

But it is another aspect of these buildings, the perfection of their proportions, the beautiful spacing between the buildings, the variety in the decorative rhythms of the four fences—their vitality as works of art—that make them objects of wonder. Each building is like a piece of wood sculpture, or, in the elegance of its joinery and finish, like an enormous piece of furniture or cabinet work. And their construction is at the same time highly logical, made to give with the rocking jar of earthquakes in a quake ridden land. "The entire later course of Japanese architecture starts at Ise. The use of natural materials in a natural way, the sensitivity to structural proportions, the feeling for space arrangement, especially the tradition of harmony between architecture and nature, all originate here . . . The later history of Japanese architecture has never been able to advance beyond it. It has remained the prototype of Japanese architecture."[22]

To a westerner the shrines at Ise shed light on the best in Japanese house and garden design. Every Japanese home is in a way a little Ise. In the garden the reverent attention to the placing of rocks, in a setting of trees or plants and, if possible, flowing water, has its origin in something deeper and more religious than just refined taste. The house itself, carefully considered as a harmonious part of the garden, is constructed on simple lines with great respect for the color and texture of undisguised material, especially beautifully fitted and finished wood. *Everywhere space is respected for its own sake, as much as, or more than, the objects which fill space.* Before each New Year the house is renewed by the gluing up of fresh white paper on the *shojis*, or room partitions; fresh mats on the floor fill the house with the fragrance of grass or rice straw. And the center of each home is traditionally a small Shinto shrine, honoring the family's ancestors and the emperor, whose divine ancestor is claimed to be Amaterasu.

From the Japanese architectural magazine, Kenchiku Bunka, June 1964

Entrance of a modern Japanese home (architect, H. Ban). This city residence, with severely constricted lot space, still preserves the tradition of a carefully designed garden, involving plants and rocks. Note the varied uses of stone: as two kinds of paving contrasting in texture, color, and size; as stepping stones into the miniature garden; as ground cover (pebbles replace water where ponds or streams are impractical); and lastly, in the religious tradition, as objects of beauty for contemplation.

NOTES

[1] These "families" were sometimes really clans, involving near and distant relatives, and headed by the oldest able male member of the entire group. In other words, families of this period were still organized in the Roman manner, which in turn had its basis in the structure of primitive tribes.

[2] The refined differences between these two credit forms is explained in *The Rise and Decline of the Medici Bank*, by R. de Roover (Harvard Press, 1963), pp. 135–137.

[3] That is, until its collapse in 1346. The Peruzzi bank made the mistake of lending King Edward III of England over 1,300,000 florins, which, when his war with France went badly, the king declined to repay. Florence suffered a financial crisis, made worse by the Black Death of 1348. The city later recovered, even though the Peruzzi bank did not. The bank of the Medici family, more shrewdly managed, later replaced it.

[4] *Life of Brunelleschi*, Giorgio Vasari.

[5] This charming tale has somehow gotten wrongly attached to Columbus.

[6] This and earlier quotations from Giorgio Vasari's *Life of Brunelleschi.*

[7] See *The Birth and Rebirth of Pictorial Space*, J. White (Faber & Faber, London, 1957), pp. 113–116. Also *Literary Sources of Art History*, E. G. Holt (Princeton, 1947).

[8] *Avant garde* (literally *advance guard*) is applied to any human activity which is brilliantly experimental, and sometimes ahead of popular taste.

[9] All quotations from *On Painting* are according to the translation by J. R. Spencer (London, 1956).

[10] At this time the Florentine unit of measure was the *braccio*, or arm, about 23 of our inches long. An average man was considered to be 3 *braccia* tall.

[11] The Italian scholar Ficino had translated the then known dialogues of Plato by 1482. Alberti's book on architecture was first printed in 1485, after his death. Previous to that it had been much read in manuscript form, and so had Plato's dialogues.

[12] *The Four Books of Architecture*, by A. Palladio, English translation, with Palladio's illustrations (Dover, New York, 1965).

[13] Karl Wittkower, in *Architectural Principles in the Age of Humanism* (Tiranti, London, 1952), discusses the ratios Alberti and Palladio used in their architectural designs, and shows the connection between the ratios they chose and the musical theory of their period.

[14] Another Italian painting, from nearly the same year, is shown in the second illustration in the Prologue: a portrait of the de Sacrati family, by Baldassare Estense of Ferrara

[15] But the only way to comment accurately on the dimensions of either Leonardo's or Piero's painting would be to study the actual places in the churches for which they were planned.

[16] The two regions were unconnected. Feudal lords often ruled scattered lands in this manner. When a nobleman married he would acquire, along with his bride, a large piece of her father's land, perhaps far from his own domain. Marriages were usually contracted with such land gifts in mind.

[17] Now called the Cathedral of St. Bavon, Ghent.

[18] *Provincial* art is that kind produced in a somewhat backward region, where artists are imitating a style created by original, independent-minded artists living in another place.

[19] The vanishing points of the two pictures are respectively about 16 feet and 17½ feet above the floor. Rafael had discarded Alberti's idea that they should be opposite the beholder's eye.

[20] Prior to 1945, when Japan included Formosa and the whole of Sakhalin Island, the extent was over 1000 miles greater and the total area was nearly 174,000 square miles.

[21] Ainu houses had walls also of thatch. One of the ceremonies in the coronation of a Japanese emperor still requires that he eat sacred meals in two temporary thatch walled and roofed structures.

[22] Kenzo Tange, in *Ise, Prototype of Japanese Architecture* (MIT Press, 1965), pp. 16 and 51.

BOOKS ON RENAISSANCE EUROPE

GENERAL

The Story of Civilization, W. and A. Durant (Simon & Schuster, New York); Vol. V: *The Renaissance; a history of civilization in Italy from 1304 to 1576 A.D.*
The Civilization of the Renaissance in Italy, J. C. Burckhardt (Harper Torchbook 40).
A History of the Italian Republics, de Sismondi (Anchor paperback).
Renaissance Europe, H. Busch (Macmillan, New York, 1962).
The Horizon Book of the Renaissance (American Heritage, Doubleday Distributors, New York, 1961).
The Waning of the Middle Ages, a Study of the Forms of Life, Thought, and Art in France & the Netherlands in the Dawn of the Renaissance, J. Huizinga (Doubleday Anchor A92, 1954).

ROME

The Papacy, a Brief History, J. A. Corbett (Van Nostrand paperback, No. 12).
Renaissance Art in Rome, V. Mariani (Universe Books, New York, 1961); 48 illustrations.

VENICE

Venice, N. Hurlimann (Viking, New York, 1963); beautiful illustrations.
Venice Observed, M. McCarthy (Harper paperback).
Venetian Ships & Shipbuilders of the Renaissance, F. Lane (Johns Hopkins).
Venetian Painting, M. Valsecchi (Golden Press).

FLORENCE AND SIENA

History of Florence and the Affairs of Italy, N. Macchiavelli (Harper TB1027).
Florence, N. Hurlimann and H. Acton (Viking, New York, 1960); fine illustrations.
The Stones of Florence, M. McCarthy (Harcourt Brace, New York).
Siena, City of the Virgin, T. Burckhardt (Oxford).
Painting in Florence and Siena after the Black Death, M. Meiss (Princeton, 1951).
Florentine Painting and its Social Background, F. Antal (London, 1948).
Art Treasures of the Medici, text by A. Morassi (NY Graphic Society, Greenwich, Connecticut, 1963). Illustrations of precious objects in gold, silver, crystal, and stone.

ARCHITECTURE

The Architecture of the Italian Renaissance, P. Murray (Batsford, London, 1963).
Renaissance Europe (Batsford, London). All photographs of buildings.
Architectural Principles of the Age of Humanism, R. Wittkower (Tiranti, London, 1962).
Ten Books on Architecture, L. B. Alberti, translated by J. Leoni (Tiranti, London, 1955).
The Four Books of Architecture, A. Palladio (Dover, New York, 1965). Hard cover; fine illustrations.

PAINTING

Renaissance Painting, F. Rusoli (Compass Books 8, 1962).
On Painting, L. B. Alberti, translated by J. R. Spenser (Yale University Press, 1956).
The Art of the Renaissance, P. and L. Murray (Praeger paperback).
Early Italian Painting, 1250–1500, M. Godfrey (paperback, Tiranti, London).
Flemish Painting, J. S. Held (Abrams paperback).
Piero della Francesca's Madonna of Urbino, a Further Examination, E. Davies and D. Snyder (Gazette des Beaux Arts, Paris, April 1970).

INDIVIDUAL ARTISTS

The Lives of the Painters, Sculptors, and Architects, G. Vasari (Dutton, Everyman's Library Nos. 784–87).
Leonardo da Vinci, L. Goldscheider, ed. (Phaidon, 1944); 150 large and 95 small illustrations.
The Inventions of Leonardo da Vinci, M. Cooper (Macmillan, New York, 1965).
The Notebooks of Leonardo da Vinci, E. McCurdy, ed. (Garden City Pub. Co., Garden City, New York, 1941–42).
Treatise on Painting, L. da Vinci, translated by A. P. McMahon (Princeton University Press, 1956).
Raphael (Phaidon, 1941).
Giotto (2 vols.), *Masaccio*, *Uccello*, *Mantegna*, *Piero della Francesca*, *Antonello da Massina*, *Leonardo*, *Raphael's paintings* (2 Vols.), *Raphael's frescoes* (2 Vols.), *Van Eyck* (Hawthorne Books, New York, All the Paintings of . . . Series).
Fra Angelico, *Botticelli*, *Carpaccio*, *Piero della Francesca* (Skira), small volumes.
Botticelli, *Raphael* (Abrams Pocket Library of Great Art).

DRAWING AND GRAPHIC ARTS

Italian Drawings (Sherwood, New York, Drawings of the Masters Series).
The Drawings of Leonardo da Vinci (Harcourt paperback, New York, HB58).
150 Masterpieces of Drawing, selected by A. Toney (Dover, New York, large paperback, T1032); fifteenth to eighteenth centuries; Italy, Netherlands, France; fine selection.
Early Florentine Designers & Engravers, J. G. Phillips (Harvard University Press, 1955).
A History of Engraving & Etching from the 15th Century to the Year 1914, A. M. Hind (paperback, Dover, New York, 1965).
Dürer, His Life and Work, M. Brion (Tudor Publishing Co., New York, 1960).
On the Just Shaping of Letters, A. Dürer, 1525 (Dover paperback).
The Art of Etching, E. S. Lumsden (Dover, T49, 1924).
An Introduction to a History of Woodcut, 2 Vols., A. M. Hind (Dover paperback, 1965).
The Craft of Woodcuts, J. R. Biggs (Sterling, New York, 1963).

MINIATURES

The Belles Heures of Jean, Duke of Berry (Metropolitan Museum of Art, New York).
The Hours of Jeanne d'Evreux (Metropolitan Museum of Art, New York).

MISCELLANEOUS

The Economic Development of Western Civilization, S. B. Clough (McGraw-Hill, New York, 1959).
Banking through the Ages, N. F. Hoggson (Dood Mead, New York, 1926).
The Rise and Decline of the Medici Bank, R. de Roover (Harvard University Press, 1963).
Arms and Armor, S. V. Grancsay (Odyssey Press, New York, 1964). Small, well illustrated.
Renaissance Diplomacy, G. Mattingly (Houghton Mifflin, Boston).

FILM

The Renaissance, sound, black and white, 10 minutes (Coronet, 1950).

BOOKS ABOUT CHINA

Chinese Monumental Architecture, P. Swann (Viking, New York). Only work of its kind.
Imperial Peking: Seven Centuries of China, L. Yutang (Crown, New York, 1961).
Peking, a Tale of Three Cities, N. Cameron and B. Blake (Harper and Row, New York, 1965).
Ming Pottery and Porcelain, S. Jenyns (Faber and Faber, London, 1953).
Art of China, Korea, Japan, P. Swann (Praeger paperback, 1963).

BOOKS ABOUT JAPAN

The Sources of Japanese Tradition, ed., W. T. de Bary (Columbia University Press, New York, 1964), 2 Vols., paperback.
The History of Japan, K. S. Latourette (MacMillan, New York, 1957).
The Pageant of Japanese History, M. M. Ditts (Longmans Green and Co., New York, 1937–1961).
The Tale of Genji, Lady Murasaki (Modern Library Giant). One of the world's classics. On its pages medieval Japanese court life is vividly revived.
The World of the Shining Prince: Court Life in Ancient Japan, I. Morris (Knopf, New York, 1964).
An Introduction to the Arts of Japan, P. C. Swann (Bruno Cassirer, Oxford, 1958).
Japanese Art (Crown, Art of the World Series).
Japanese Architecture, W. Alex (Braziller, New York).
Ise: Prototype of Japanese Architecture, K. Tange and N. Kawazoe (M.I.T. Press, Cambridge, Massachusetts, 1965).
Japanese Homes and Their Surroundings, E. S. Mosse (Dover, T746).
The Tradition of the Japanese Garden (East-West Center Press, Honolulu).

Alte Pinakothek, Munich

Alexander the Great defeating the King of Persia at the Battle of Issus, by the German artist Albrecht Altdorfer, about 1529. The battle scene has nothing to do with the Hellenic world. Instead it shows two sixteenth century armies battling in the Alps.

9 THE REFORMATION, COUNTER-REFORMATION, AND EIGHTEENTH CENTURY

The Oceans Cease to be Barriers and Become Bridges Between Continents

Michelangelo Versus Leonardo

> As Leonardo . . . was passing the Spini bank . . . several notables were there assembled, who were discussing a passage in Dante, and seeing Leonardo, they asked him to come and explain it to them. At the same moment Michelangelo passed, and when one of the crowd called to him also, Leonardo said, "Michelangelo will be able to tell you what it means." To which the latter, thinking this had been said to entrap him, replied, "Nay, explain it yourself, horse modeller that you are—who, unable to cast a statue in bronze, were forced with shame to give up the attempt." So saying, he turned his back upon them and departed.[1]

This incident probably occurred in Florence about 1501, when Leonardo was a middle-aged 49 and Michelangelo was only a youthful 26. It reveals much about the two men: Leonardo's detached interest in truth; Michelangelo's razor-sharp tongue, his tendency to suspicion, and the hard, penetrating realism with which he seized on Leonardo's chief, and perhaps only, weakness, that of overspreading and overreaching himself in the pursuit of perfection. In those days Michelangelo looked on Leonardo as a competitor whom he intended to outstrip. All his life he took on the best man, or the toughest task, that an artist could find, whether painter, sculptor, or architect. Always, even up to his death when nearly 90, he came out the victor.

How did he achieve these miracles? He did so partly through superhuman talent, and partly by intense concentration of his energies in one field, art. He was too absorbed in it even to marry, just as was Leonardo. But, unlike Leonardo, his interest in science never got the upper hand: all his patient studies of anatomy by dissecting human corpses were merely to increase his knowledge as an artist. In fact, it took three men, Michelangelo the artist, Galileo the physical scientist, and Vesalius the world's first great anatomist, to carry forward the kind of productive life Leonardo had lived. Michelangelo never allowed himself to stray from his one intense love, art.

During Michelangelo's long life, from 1475 to 1564, Europe, which had changed so often, changed again, approaching the climax of new power as a continent. For the first time men discovered that the whole planet Earth was no longer a place of mystery, but a sphere bearing on its surface just seven continents and five oceans. Europeans made this discovery and reaped the power which it brought. They became conquerors of the world—its rulers and its plunderers. The titanic political and economic forces they thus released were beyond anything man had yet known. And it is perhaps as a prophet of this age, and of the ages to follow, that Michelangelo's creations can best be understood. Let us look, therefore, at some of the larger historical events and currents that colored his life.

Right: Leonardo da Vinci (1452–1519), chalk drawing, 1498, perhaps by Ambrogio da Predis. Below: Michelangelo Buonarotti (1475–1564), pen drawing, probably by Bugiardini.

Royal Library, Windsor

Louvre, Paris

Topkapi Palace Museum, Constantinople. Photo John Bridgman

Sultan Mehmet II, "the Conqueror," capturer of Constantinople for the Ottoman Empire. Tempera painting on paper, late fifteenth century.

Sixteenth Century Europe

The Menacing Turkish Empire

In several places so far we have seen migrant, warlike peoples come pouring out from that great reservoir of humanity, northeast Asia, to overwhelm civilized empires. These peoples have borne various names, such as Huns, Kushanas, Tartars, and Mongols. Another such people were the Turks. Like their relatives, the Mongols, the men were expert horsemen and deadly archers. Like the Mongols, their first response to civilization was to attempt to destroy it, as a useless device for cluttering good pasture land. And again like the Mongols, this contempt, on closer acquaintance with civilized living, gave way to respect. Between the ninth and the seventeenth centuries the Turks invaded Western Asia, then Africa, and finally Europe in successive waves. Two of these waves preceded the great Mongol invasion of the thirteenth century; the last followed it and filled its place as it receded. The starting point of the waves was the part of central Asia called Turkestan.

The Ottoman empire at the height of its power, in the mid-sixteenth century.

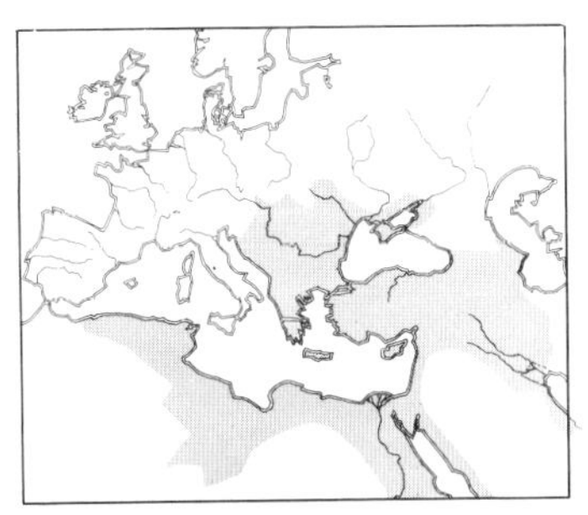

The first of these invasions overran the eastern end of the Arab empire in Persia in the eighth century. Arab armies blocked its progrcss westward. The Turks, settling in what is now Afghanistan, became converted to the Mohammedan religion and Persian culture. From this new starting point they then began to move eastward into India through the Khyber Pass, conquering (as was usual in Indian history) the Indus Valley. In two centuries a succession of strong men with Turkish ancestors then battled their way across all northern India, carving out an empire. The conflict between the two cultures was violent, for they were completely repugnant to each other.

British Museum

Above: Seated Turk, by the Venetian artist Gentile Bellini. Pen drawing, late fifteenth century. Opposite page: Turkish woman, by the same artist.

The Muslim Turks had a puritanical hatred of images and the worship of many gods; the Hindus were horrified at the slaughter of cattle (to them a holy animal) by their beef-loving conquerors. To this day India is grievously split between the two ways of life. The ruined state of India's older temples is chiefly the work of invading Muslim zealots.

In the tenth century a fresh wave of Turks, known as the Seljuks, came pouring out of Asia and again struck the Arab kingdom of Persia. This wave proved irresistible. It swept westward over the Arab capital of Baghdad and on to the Mediterranean.

Europe first became aware of the Turks as a threat in the eleventh century (see page 317) when the Seljuks crushed a Byzantine army in Asia Minor. Europe's response was a series of crusades, which temporarily checked the spread of Turkish power (and helped extinguish that of the Arabs) but did not end it. For a third Turkish wave, that of the Osmanlis (or Ottomans, as the Europeans called them), followed the Seljuks. Little by little, Turkish armies whittled away the once great Byzantine empire until only the city of Constantinople remained in Christian hands. At last, in 1453, Constantinople too fell before a Turkish assault, the last Byzantine emperor, Constantine Palaeologos, dying in the city's defense. The fabulous capital was plundered; most of its precious works of art vanished. If it had not also been plundered by Norman crusaders two and one-half centuries earlier, and the loot spread throughout Europe, we would know far less today about Byzantine art, in its many-sided richness.

British Museum

Year by year after this success the Turkish conquerors kept on spreading, first over the Levant, then into Egypt and north Africa, respecting neither the Christians nor their own fellow Muslims, but intent only on conquest. The Turkish rulers, or *sultans*, next showed a desire to master the Mediterranean Sea. Twice the city of Venice tried to destroy the Turkish fleet, in 1478 and again in 1540. Both times it was the Venetian fleet that suffered. Both times the city made peace and kept on friendly trading relations with the Turks by paying enormous bribes (100,000 ducats the first time, three times as much the second). Even so, Venice managed to prosper. But at last, when the Turks violated the terms of their treaty and brutally murdered the Venetian governor of Cyprus, Venice took to herself two allies whom she ordinarily distrusted, the pope and the king of Spain. Somehow the allies held together long enough to assemble a fleet, the larger part of it Venetian. Off the Greek coastal town of Lepanto, in 1571, they not only gave the Turkish navy its first crushing defeat but broke its power and prestige forever.

But the Turkish tide was also pressing northward and westward by land, engulfing Greece and Bulgaria, and soon pressing on the eastern boundaries of the Holy Roman Empire itself. In 1497 and 1498 they devastated southern Poland. In 1526 they crushed the military power of Hungary. In 1529 then even besieged Vienna, but without success. A century and a half later, in 1683, they were back again before Vienna's walls, and again an Austrian army repelled them. After that the tide turned. But by that time the Turkish threat had been grimly present to Europeans for 600 years.

Fotoarchiv Marburg

Above: The palatial Chateau de Chambord, one of several which belonged to Francis I. This, like the others, was originally a castle, its defenses made obsolete by artillery. Francis spent vast sums converting them into magnificent settings for his public and private life. Below: Francis I in parade armor, on horseback.

The Thirst for Money

As trade flowed ever more freely through Europe, so did money. The kings and great lords quickly recognized money as a source of power and reached out to lay hands on it. They squeezed money from the people by taxes and other means. To create new money they developed gold and silver mines. They even hired alchemists to explore ways of turning baser metals into gold. The alchemists failed, though even their failures laid some of the foundations of modern chemistry.

But though kings and nobles knew how to get money, they were deplorable at managing it. To save and to reinvest were ideas utterly foreign, even contemptible, to most of them. Money was to be spent on one's personal glory, through the ever more costly game of war. Armies were by this time largely hired from certain parts of Europe, especially from Switzerland. Such troops were reliable only when paid. And the cost of arming them, as weapons were improved and firearms developed, went steadily upward.

A ruler's glory and power were also displayed through the palaces and hunting lodges he built, and through the showiness of the court life with which he surrounded himself. To maintain such a court he would spend beyond his income—magnificent in public, behind the scenes bankrupt and worse.

Louvre, Paris

The Renaissance bankers caught in the dangerous game of advancing credit to Europe's kings were often ruined (just as were the Peruzzi of Florence in the fourteenth century) when their royal debtors arrogantly decided not to pay. One of the wisest policies of the wise Medici family was to shun business with nobles and kings. When the manager of the Medici branch bank in Bruges, one Tommaso Portinari, began lending money to the self-willed Charles the Bold of Burgundy (son of Philip the Good), the twilight of the Medici banking chain was at hand. The thirst for money among Europe's aristocrats could be called a measure of their thirst for power, and this seemed bottomless.

Overseas Exploration and Conquest

Forces such as these must have driven Europeans out on the boundless oceans in search of new connections with the fabulous East, that ancient source of luxuries and wealth. They did not go because Europe was overpopulated. The Black Death and later plagues had actually made the population smaller. Rather the causes were partly that the hated Turkish empire had won control of existing trade routes to the Orient, and partly, it seems, because the hunger of Europeans for wealth was growing; money was becoming the key to more and more forms of success, especially success in war.

For some comments on the music of this general period see Appendix A, pages 604–7.

Starting from Europe's outermost bastion, the Spanish peninsula, the explorers followed two directions into the unknown seas, logically the only two. The Portuguese sailed south around Africa, then eastward past Arabia to India, the East Indies, and finally China. Their financial reward was spectacular; the first vessel to return to Portugal with a full cargo from India made a 6000% profit. The Spaniards, led by the Italian navigator Christofer Columbus, sailed westward, aiming at the same lands, but instead discovered the New World. After the explorers came a second wave, among whom were adventurers whose sole motive seems to have been greed.

The Spaniards Cortez and Pizzaro utterly wrecked three young civilizations, the Aztecs and Maya of Mexico and the Incas of Peru (see page 130), in order to plunder them of their gold. In each case the wreckers were at first aided by the natives' naïve belief that they were gods. After that, superior European armor and weapons enabled the invaders to do what they pleased. The greatest exports from the New World to Spain were gold (while it lasted) and then silver. *But of far greater value to man have been two new vegetable foods, Mexican corn and Peruvian potatoes. They have gradually become two of the world's major food crops, equaled in importance only by wheat and rice.*

The Fall of Icarus, *by the Flemish artist, Peter Breughel the elder, painted about 1535. The theme from classical mythology is almost forgotten (Icarus is hard to find). The real subject is the departure of an ocean-going vessel for distant parts, from the mainland of Europe with its highly developed agrarian economy.*

Museum of Fine Arts, Brussels

British Museum

A lidded vessel, probably a Salt cellar, carved from elephant ivory, in the Kingdom of Benin, Equatorial Africa, in the fifteenth century, for export to Portugal. Height about 1 foot.

The Portuguese were as ruthless as the Spaniards, and if they could probably would have plundered the empires with which they traded. But these empires were older, more powerful, and more sophisticated than anything the Spaniards met in the Americas. They had also had a long experience with foreign merchants, chiefly Persians and Arabs. The great Indian Moghul emperors Akbar and Shah Jehan, and the Chinese emperors of the Ming dynasty, took the Portuguese for what they were, pirates. The Duke of Albuquerque, Portugal's viceroy, or royal representative in the Far East, was barely able to make Portuguese dominated cities out of the seaports of Goa and Cochin in India, and Malacca on the Malay Peninsula. The Chinese emperors limited them even more strictly, and with reason. Portuguese misconduct contributed to China's later permanent distrust of the West.

The Effect of More Precious Metal: Prices Rise

The effect upon Europe of the new overseas discoveries was therefore to release upon it a tide of gold and silver treasure beyond what anyone had dreamed. And with this release came a bitter lesson. The more money was in supply, the more the price of everything went up. It was once the common belief that the only thing that made the price of something rise or fall was whether it was hard to get or plentiful. Now the world was to discover what Florentine bankers had known for years. *When money itself is plentiful or scarce, prices also rise and fall accordingly.*

The rise of prices had a cruel effect on Europe's poor. No one seems to have dreamed at that time of adjusting wages to meet the high cost of living. The first effect of the influx of wealth from the New World seems therefore to have been enrichment for a fortunate few and starvation for many.

The Vatican in the Sixteenth Century

Among the fortunate few were the materialistic, cynical popes of the period. As the supply of money mounted, the total paid to the Vatican as tribute from the churches of Europe, especially Portugal and Spain, correspondingly increased. But the popes had devised other ways of increasing even this hoard. We must remember that they were not only religious leaders but rulers of central Italy as well. Being rulers, they were sometimes as eager for glory as any king. Their method of raising funds for their ambitious projects was simply to sell what people of the age wanted.

The popes indulged in *simony;* that is, they sold positions of power within the Church. Two members of the Medici family become popes in close succession. Lorenzo de Medici had procured the rank of cardinal for one of them (his son Giovanni, at age thirteen!), and from cardinal to pope was an easy step. These were only two of endless examples; cardinals, bishops, abbots of monasteries, and ordinary parish priests paid their way to appointments, great and small, and thus gained security and authority for the rest of their lives.

The popes also sold forgiveness of sins, or *indulgences*. It was the theory of the time that Jesus while on earth, and the many saints and martyrs who had followed him, had through their pure lives laid up in Heaven a sort of bank credit of virtue, and that the popes, as heads of the religion, had the authority to pay this out in installments to sinners needing forgiveness.

From the wealth thus gathered at Rome the popes spent splendidly on buildings, sculpture, and paintings. For thus, rather than by war, did the popes usually pursue glory. Their power to command, and to reward obedience generously, drew the leading artists of the age. Italy's creative center shifted from Florence to Rome. The two centuries from the end of the fifteenth to the end of the seventeenth were to see Rome enriched with one mighty project after another. Thus it was that the dynamic, autocratic Pope Julius II summoned Michelangelo to Rome in 1503, and commanded him to design for him a tomb which would be grander than that of any other pope.

Casa Buonarotti, Florence. Photo Alinari-Art Reference Bureau

Battle between men and lapiths, an unfinished relief in stone by Michelangelo, created when he was about 16. It owes its composition to Roman battle reliefs (see for example page 238), but has a fury all its own.

Michelangelo at Rome: Early Achievements

As a boy Michelangelo, through sheer talent, had won the luckiest place any budding artist could hope for when he was accepted into Lorenzo de Medici's household. There he could study drawing and sculpture; at the dinner table he could listen daily to the conversation of great and cultivated men. Lorenzo's interests were many. Among others he wanted to see the Italian language recognized for its beauty, as finer than Latin. In his house Dante and the other great Italian poets were read aloud, discussed, and lovingly memorized. Such experiences had their influence on the young Michelangelo; for the rest of his life he was to express his deepest private thoughts in sonnet form.

The death of Lorenzo in 1492 cut short this ideal pattern of living and threw Michelangelo on his own. But he was ready for the challenge. His feats as a sculptor drew ever wider and wider attention, eventually that of the pope himself. Michelangelo, at the age of 29, arrived in Rome at the pope's command. Sixty stormy years followed. He was constantly buffeted by the ever shifting whims of nine different popes, by the scheming attacks of jealous rivals, and even by the hideous misfortunes of war which swept over Rome and his native Florence. Two qualities seem to have carried him through such a life: his power as an artist which no one could equal, and his fierce personal integrity which sometimes led him to speak candidly and act independently when other men trembled to be themselves.[2]

Hardly had Michelangelo completed a magnificent plan for Pope Julius' tomb, and started carving statues for it, than the pope began to change his mind and objectives. He engaged the architect Bramante to replace the ancient 1200 year old basilica of St. Peter with a gigantic domed structure, to be the greatest church in the world. Bramante, being jealous of Michelangelo, planned to discredit him. He argued that to complete the tomb during the pope's lifetime would be a bad omen, and urged him instead to instruct Michelangelo, a sculptor, not a painter, to decorate with frescoes the ceiling of the Vatican's new chapel, built by order of Pope Sixtus IV, and therefore called the *Sistine* Chapel.

The pope innocently fell in with the scheme and not only compelled Michelangelo to paint the ceiling but hounded him constantly to hurry. Michelangelo for his part rose to the challenge, making designs for the decoration, and then insisted on executing them himself without trained assistants. It took over four years to design and complete the complex of paintings on a ceiling 115 feet long and 45 feet wide. How it would have looked with the *secco* work (or retouching) which Michelangelo intended we shall never know. The impetuous pope had the scaffolding removed too soon, so that he might celebrate Mass in the chapel on All Saints' Day, 1512. The ceiling was the marvel of all Rome. The young Rafael immediately altered his own painting style to try to equal it. Bramante was foiled. But the strain on Michelangelo of working overhead day after day affected his vision for months. When we realize that the whole fresco was created at arm's length distance, boxed in by scaffolding, but that it carries perfectly to viewers standing on the floor 60 feet below, the work seems a miracle.

The great fresco, surging with restless power, can be thought of as having for its central theme the opposition between creation and destruction. In the first five of the nine scenes which run the length of the ceiling, God himself creates the universe, then creates Adam, then Eve. In the sixth scene Adam and Eve destroy their opportunity to live forever in Eden. In the most important of the last three, the wickedness of mankind moves God to destroy with the Flood much of what he has created.

Around the sides, seated in attitudes of deep study, thought, or sudden inspiration, sit immense superhuman beings, both men and women. They are the Hebrew prophets and the pagan *sibyls* (or female prophets) through whom God, in other ages, revealed truth to mankind. In triangular spaces between these are ten scenes of variously posed men and women which Michelangelo chose to call the ancestors of Jesus. In the four corners of the

ceiling are scenes mostly of patriotic violence, taken from the Old Testament, in which the weak subdue the mighty: David slays Goliath; Judith saves Israel by slaying the invading Holophernes; Queen Esther condemns Haman, persecutor of her people, to a terrible death; and Moses sets up a brazen serpent among the Israelites. Filling spaces between all these scenes are over 100 minor human figures in a glorious variety of action and repose. Their presence constantly breaks up what would otherwise show as hard division lines between sections of the ceiling.

Above and below respectively: the Prophets Zachariah and Jonas, from the west and east ends, respectively, of the Sistine ceiling.

The more important figures increase, one after the other, in brooding massiveness and bold foreshortening from west to east. Compare, for instance, the bearded prophet Zachariah at one end with the spectacularly

foreshortened figure of Jonas at the other. We seem actually to be watching Michelangelo's own power as it grew while he worked.

Since the ceiling was to be viewed from any point on the floor below, Michelangelo was careful to play down perspective. Everywhere he avoided trying to show great depth, and gave not only each section, but each side of each section, its own vanishing point. These sections and divisions were determined by the ceiling's vaulted structure.

The Sistine Chapel ceiling, one of the world's wonders, was completed in 1512, when Michelangelo was 37. Soon afterward the fierce old Julius II died, and into his place stepped a new pope, Leo X, Lorenzo de Medici's worldly minded son. For the next 21 years, with only one short break, he and then Clement VII, another Pope belonging to the Medici family, dominated Rome and the Roman Catholic Church.

Northern Europe Revolts Against the Popes

It would have been hard to find two more unsuitable leaders to weather the terrible crisis through which the Church was about to pass. Actually the crisis was double. The popes brought on one of them by their worldly luxury and their cynical ways of raising money; they brought on the other by involving themselves (as they had for centuries past) in power politics.

Leo X set off the first crisis, by far the more world shaking of the two. Partly to raise funds to build the new St. Peter's basilica in Rome, and partly to help a German archbishop who was short of money, Leo declared a new sale of indulgences, or pardons for sin. But this time he permitted people to buy pardons for relatives already dead, thus releasing souls from punishment for sins committed while they had been alive. The traveling monks responsible for making the sales assured buyers that:

> As soon as the coin in the coffer rings,
> The soul from Purgatory springs.[3]

The sales were limited to an area of central Germany, the lands of the archbishop who needed help.[4]

The device of selling forgiveness had been tried too often on a hard-headed people whose religious beliefs were strong and sincere. When Martin Luther, a young German monk and professor of theology at the University of Wittenberg, the son of an iron miner, challenged the pope's power to forgive souls their sins, with or without paying for so doing, multitudes of Germans, from the most powerful princes to the most humble peasants, rose to his support.

Partly by a miracle of good luck and partly because of Luther's wide popular support, neither the pope nor the new Holy Roman Emperor, Charles V, dared burn him to death as a heretic. Instead, during an active life of about 30 years, Luther succeeded in literally creating a new form of Christianity, or rather, as he and his followers felt confident, a return to a form true to the teachings of Jesus.

One of the great ideas inspiring Luther's life and teachings was that Christianity is for all men equally, not for certain classes more than others. He declared that all men should be permitted to eat the holy bread and drink the holy wine which were prepared during the Mass—that this privilege should not be for priests alone. All people who attended Mass, he believed, were there to *share actively* in the church service, not merely to be present passively, as if something were being done *for* them. He therefore composed hymns, both words and music, for everyone to sing during the service, thus enabling them to become part of it. For centuries before this, church music had been in the hands of the clergy and trained choirs only.

Martin Luther, by his friend the German artist, Lucas Cranach.

Metropolitan Museum of Art, New York

Luther declared that every man has a divinely inspired conscience, which he can awaken by reading the Bible for himself. So that all men could read it, he therefore translated the Old and New Testaments into powerful, poetic German, not from the Latin, but from the Greek and Hebrew originals. This he could never have done unless the great scholars of the Italian Renaissance had mastered these languages and made them available to other learned Europeans.

Last of all, Luther believed that man, as a creation of God, is of himself utterly unable to save himself from punishment for his sins: that it is only God's all-powerful mercy that can save him. Man's only hope to be saved from eternal punishment, therefore, was his faith in God. The Catholic belief is that faith alone is not enough, but that men should also act as if they had this faith, by trying to do God's will.

Luther was a man of moderation. But the religious movement he started rolled on like a great stream descending a mountain, traveling with more fury in some places than others. In parts of Germany the horribly oppressed peasants, stirred by Luther's teachings about man's equality, rose and murdered their cruel feudal lords. In others, mobs broke into churches and smashed religious statues as "idols". On all such violence Luther turned with a fury of his own, especially directed at the violent peasants. He probably shares the blame for the brutal manner in which their revolt of the year 1525 was crushed. Be that as it may, when Luther died in 1546, he left the *Lutheran* form of Christianity a solidly permanent fact. It was the first *Protestant denomination,* so called because it *protested* the corruption and certain beliefs of the Roman Catholic Church.

Other great religious leaders arose to follow Luther's example. Ulrich Zwingli founded a Protestant Church in Switzerland; Jean Calvin, the austere, brilliant Frenchman, established another in France, thus dividing that nation between Catholics and Protestants. The kings of Denmark, Sweden, Norway, and last of all England formally broke with the pope and declared their countries to be Protestant. By 1560 most of northern Europe was lost to the pope. The *Protestant Reformation* was a reality.

It was a religious movement, but it pointed to the direction in which the people of Europe were heading politically. They were heading away from feudalism with its different levels of society, from high to low, and with its lands cut into many pieces, each controlled by a ruling family, which changed hands depending on who married whom. They were heading toward *nationalism,* where everyone, in his own right, is a citizen of a land with definite borders and controlled by a central government in which the citizens were eventually to have some share. The change from one to the other was gradual. It was not to become complete for centuries. But it was on its way.[5]

The Pope Suffers Humiliation in His Own City

The other catastrophe to befall the papacy was less lasting in its effects but more violent. It was caused by the other Medici pope, Clement VII, embroiling himself, just as other popes had before him, in international politics.

The Holy Roman Emperor Charles V, by various means and strokes of good fortune, had brought together into his empire or as allies a large part of continental Europe, including not only Germany and Austria, but Spain, Flanders, and the "Two Sicilies." The kingdom of France found itself almost surrounded. Francis I of the royal house of Valois was fighting for his kingdom's life against the ambition of Charles V of the house of Hapsburg to make all Europe his.

In a struggle of this scale the city-states of northern Italy, so brilliant yet so disunited by jealousy, were of lesser importance. The popes, with their religious prestige, wealth, and mercenary armies, counted for more. Clement VII allowed himself at one point to become an important ally of Francis I. In the wearisome war that dragged on from 1521 until 1552, the armies of France and the emperor fought up and down Italy, taking and retaking cities. At one point, the emperor's army happened to be near Rome just as the emperor ran out of funds to pay his mercenary troops. Like all such troops when unpaid, their discipline vanished, and they paid themselves by ruthlessly seizing and sacking the city. The pope, in the impregnable Castel Sant Angelo, could not be harmed, but the rest of the city was helpless.[6] This terrible event of the year 1527 exposed the papacy's political and military weakness just as the Protestant revolt had exposed its spiritual corruption. It was also a source of profound embarrassment to the conservative Emperor Charles V, one of whose ideals was the dual supremacy of emperor and pope. Still, as we shall presently see, Clement VII managed to turn the catastrophe to the permanent advantage of his own family.

Michelangelo's Later Achievements

While Rome was being sacked, Michelangelo was fortunately out of the city. He was back in his native Florence, carrying out the pope's orders to create a library for the Medici family's great collection of books, and a glorious tomb for some of the pope's Medici relatives. This library and tomb were almost the last buildings of great distinction to be built in Florence for 400 years, and they were built only because the pope financed them. Florence had ceased, at least temporarily, to be an outstanding center of financial power.

These two buildings mark a turning point in Italian architecture. In both of them Michelangelo dared to break the traditions laid down by Vitruvius. He used columns and other structural devices *decoratively* as no other architect would have dared. This was not an advance in the *structure* of the buildings, but in their *visual drama*. In so doing he pointed the way to a new, more inventive age in architecture (Mannerism and Baroque).

Michelangelo never finished the sculptures for the Medici tomb. The calamities of war broke in upon his world. When at last something like peace

Photo Societa Scala

was restored, Pope Clement VII, perhaps shaken by the troubles through which the Church was passing, called Michelangelo back to Rome, there to go to work again in the Sistine Chapel on a great fresco of Christ on Judgment Day.

Michelangelo's Last Judgment, *Sistine Chapel, created 1536–1541.*

For years Michelangelo had been thinking about such a fresco, to fill the wall surface of over 2000 square feet above the Sistine Chapel's altar. Even so, he spent eight years completing it. Pope Clement VII soon died, to be followed by Paul III, a wise old man grimly determined to reform the vices that had brought his Roman Catholic Church to defeat and disgrace. He summoned a great Church council, meeting at Trent in the neutral territory of Switzerland, to study questions of reform. Sternly he set his face against both simony and the sale of indulgences. Henceforth, cardinals, bishops, and priests were to be chosen for their personal worth alone. Sinners might hope to reach Heaven by paying only one price: sincere repentance. The pope's annual income shrank by two-thirds. But he still found ways to pay Michelangelo, whom he had long admired from a distance. "I have been longing for this opportunity for 30 years, and shall I not have it now I am Pope?" he said. So it was that the great painting was at last finished in 1541.

It smote the beholders like thunder. All who saw it were overwhelmed, some with pious awe, some with wonder at the mass of figures (each a masterpiece in itself, yet all related), still others with prudish horror to see so many naked bodies in a church. This last group had their way for a time, when a later pope ordered Michelangelo's giants to be overpainted with pretty garments in various shades of pink and blue. Still later another, wiser pope ordered this nonsense removed. The fresco has therefore suffered much. But what a wonder it still is!

There in the high center stands Christ, an expression in human form of power, of mastery over the forces of the universe, somehow prophetic, one can imagine, of the mastery which man has since achieved over physical matter. Directly beneath him a Heaven-shaking blast of Judgment Day trumpets sets a multitude of souls in motion as if by magnetic attraction and repulsion. From far below Christ's right hand (the viewer's left) awakening souls rise from their graves to find union with him. On his left other terror stricken souls find themselves drawn downward toward an underworld of everlasting night. True to his time, Michelangelo blended classical learning with Christian belief. He pictured Hell as did the pagan Greeks, separated from Earth by the River Styx, which all souls must cross in a boat piloted by brutal old Charon.

Michelangelo still had 23 years to live. He at last had time to return to work on the tomb of Pope Julius II, finishing it, 40 years after Julius first ordered it, in much reduced form, but still satisfactory to the dead pope's powerful relatives. A colossal statue of Moses, once intended to be a minor ornament, became the tomb's crowning glory.

Opposite page, top: plan (simplified) of St. Peter's as actually completed. The nave has been lengthened to fit Baroque tastes. The relationship between the present basilica and the older one dating from the fourth century, which it replaced, is also shown. Directly below are (left) Bramante's proposed plan, and (right) Michelangelo's, which replaced Bramante's. Bottom: front elevation of St. Peter's as it is today, with a facade added in the seventeenth century, and Bernini's colonnade (described page 453).

The final major task of Michelangelo's life, reluctantly undertaken, was to oversee the continued building of the new St. Peter's basilica, which had suffered much both from lack of building funds and from the supervision of several tinkering architects. Michelangelo went back to what was best in Bramante's original plan, improved it where this seemed necessary, and became the champion for continuing it. He made a careful model of the church which still exists, put all his failing energy into pushing the work forward, and lived to see much of the central part completed, up to the dome. At last, in 1564, when close to 90, the wonderful, razor-tongued old man passed from this life. His body was taken back to his native Florence.

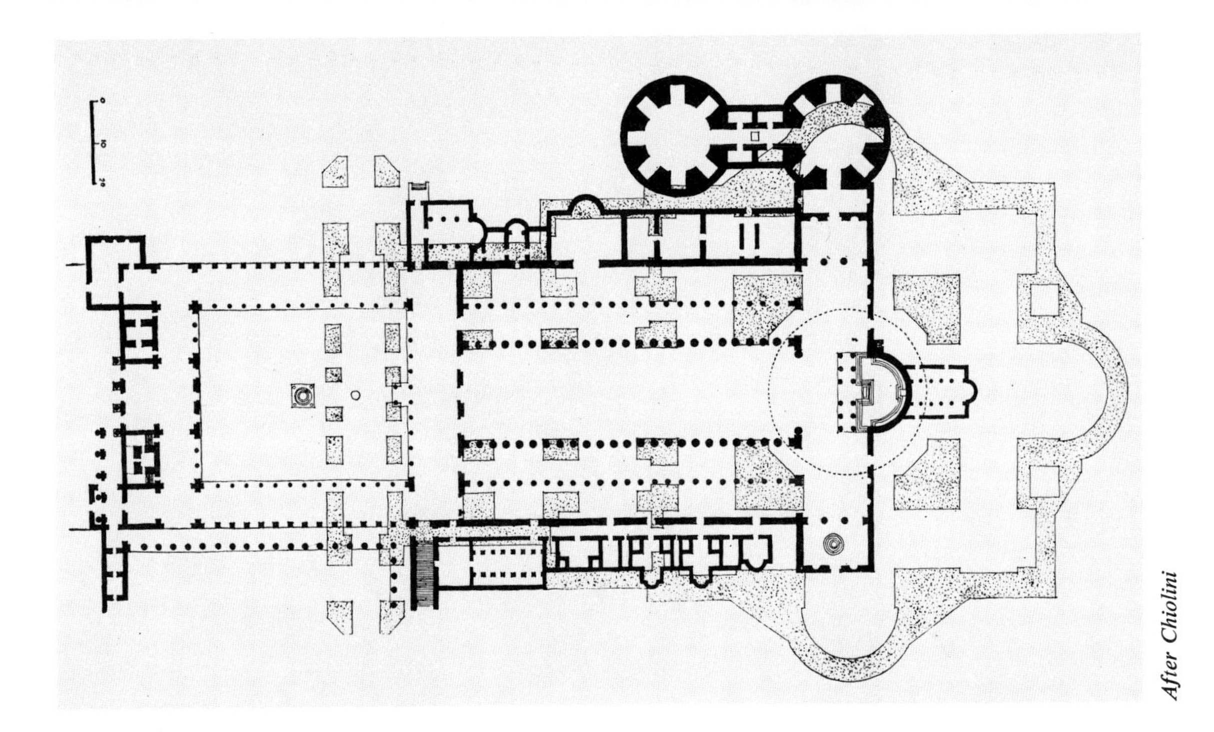

After Chiolini

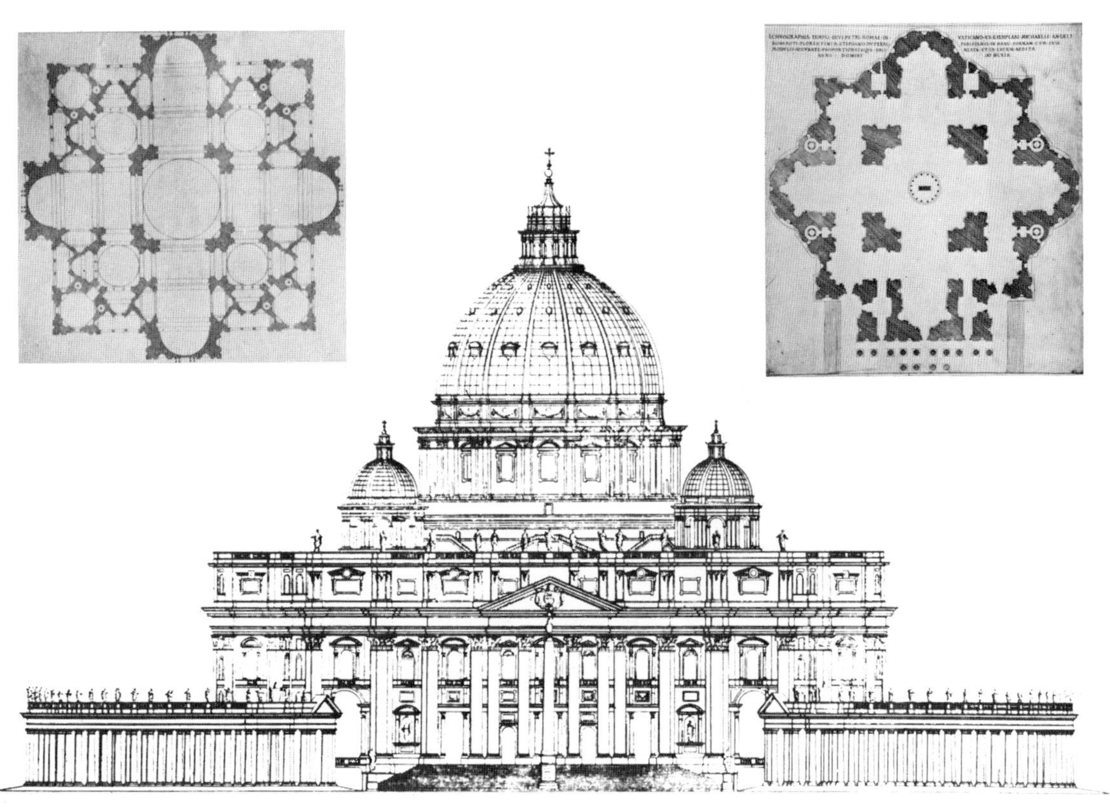

"Let no one marvel," wrote his dear friend Vasari, "that Michelangelo loved solitude, for he was devoted to art, which demands man to itself. And because those who study must avoid society, the minds of those who study art are constantly preoccupied, and those who consider this to be eccentricity are wrong, . . . genius demands thought, solitude, and comfort, and a steadfast mind."

Photo Societa Scala

Descent from the Cross, *by Jacopo Pontormo, painted 1528 for the Chapel of the Capponi family in the Church of Sta. Felicita, Florence. It is one of the great early landmarks of the Mannerist style. The young painters of the early sixteenth century were inspired by the fearless manner in which Michelangelo compelled the human figure to express emotion in his Sistine Chapel frescoes, and by his equally fearless adaptation of architecture to create desired powerful effects. They drove painting along the same path, altering human proportions, resorting to bizarre color schemes, and breaking old rules of symmetrical composition, to achieve new, jolting, often sensual results. Religious themes sometimes became little more than an excuse for experiments, of which the artists' worldly, sophisticated patrons urbanely approved.*

The Afternoon of Florentine Glory

The sacking of Rome by undisciplined mercenary troops in 1527 was a cause for profound embarrassment to the Emperor Charles V, who held as an ideal the joint universal authority of the emperor and the pope. By way of compensating Pope Clement VII, son of Lorenzo de Medici, for the humiliation caused him, Charles agreed to make not only Florence but the whole surrounding province of Tuscany a duchy belonging to the Medici family.

Metropolitan Museum of Art, New York (Rogers Fund, 1956)

Late Mannerist painting. The Vision of St. John the Divine, *by Dominikos Theotokopoulos, called El Greco, 1610–1614, 88×76 in. "And they cried with a loud voice, saying, How long, O Lord, holy and true, dost thou not judge and avenge our blood on them that dwell on the earth? And white robes were given unto every one of them." (Revelation 6:9–10.) From its birthplace in Florence the Mannerist style spread its influence outward, touching, among others, the Venetian master Tintoretto (see page 456). He in turn influenced a young Greek from Crete, who studied briefly in Venice before going on to Spain, where he spent the rest of his life. In El Greco's paintings we behold the triumphant freedom of a great artist's imagination, dominating and transforming visual images so that they become integral parts of original, often unconventional compositions, whose function is to convey intense religious experience. We also sense in them an artist's sensual delight in physical forms and in the feel and manipulation of paint.*

The free city of Florence stubbornly resisted the combined armies of pope and emperor, Michelangelo himself being in charge of some of the defenses. But surrender inevitably followed, and Alessandro de Medici was declared Duke of Tuscany in 1531. He was the first of eight Medici dukes to rule Florence. Thus, from the time that Cosimo de Medici became a leader in Florentine civic affairs in 1434, until the death of the last Medici duke in 1737, the family were almost continually the rulers of Florence for three centuries.

The Medici dukes proved to be conscientious men who effectively organized the resources of both city and province. Their rule left its physical mark on the city chiefly in the form of two buildings, the great ducal residence called the Pitti Palace, with its facade of rough stone, and the Uffizi, or administrative offices of the duchy. But the dukes never found the money to complete the city's cathedral, whose towers and west front stood unfinished until 1868.

Under the patronage of the dukes and their court, Florence continued for some decades to influence the world of the arts, even though in a rather precious manner, befitting the tastes of the leisured aristocrats who had become her rulers. The influence took chiefly three forms: the formation of the Mannerist school of painting, the establishment of the first learned academic societies, and the birth of opera.

Photo Alinari-Art Reference Bureau, Inc.

Galileo, Father of Modern Physics

In the very year that Michelangelo died, a child was born who was to carry forward Leonardo's pioneering in science, just as Michelangelo had in art. Galileo Galilei early proved himself a typical, many-sided Renaissance man, gifted as poet, artist, and scientist. He chose science. When he was 28 he became professor of mathematics at the University of Padua, a city near Venice, and under Venetian control.

Communication throughout Europe was constantly improving, partly because travel was more common, but chiefly because printing had made book publication easier. Thus the works of two astronomers, one a Pole and the other a Dane, were available to Galileo in Italy. Nicholas Copernicus had advanced the theory that the Sun, not the Earth, is the center of the universe, and that the Earth is merely one of six planets spinning around it. Tycho Brahe, royal astronomer to the king of Denmark, had spent years accurately recording the motions of planets and stars. These records seemed to support Copernicus' theory. But all such observations were still carried on as they had been ages ago in Egypt and Babylon: with the naked eye. Galileo was to take the next step. In his own words,

> In Venice, where I happened to be at the time, news came that a Hollander had presented to Count Maurice a glass by means of which distant things might be seen as perfectly as if they were quite close. That was all. Upon hearing this news, I returned to Padua, where I then resided, and set myself to think about the problem. The first night after my return, I solved it, and the following day I constructed the instrument and sent word of this to the same friends in Venice with whom I had been discussing the subject the previous day. Immediately afterward, I applied myself to the construction of another and better one, which I took to Venice six days later. There it was seen with great admiration by nearly all the principal gentlemen of that republic for more than a month on end, to my considerable fatigue. Finally . . . I presented it to the ruler [or *doge*, of Venice] in a full meeting of the Council. How greatly it was esteemed by him . . . is shown by ducal letters . . . reappointing and confirming me for life to my professorship at the University of Padua at double my former salary.[7]

By combining two glass lenses, one convex and one concave, Galileo had made a telescope which could magnify objects 30 times. With it he soon discovered that moons (not one but four) revolve about the planet Jupiter, like a little solar system. This added support to Copernicus' theory.

But Europe was far from ready to greet these discoveries with joy. Medieval thinking was still ever present. A mighty picture of the world, based on Church doctrine, had been slowly built up by the skillful use of logic. This picture was what men *were instructed to believe* was the truth, not what they could see with their merely mortal eyes. If a man disbelieved in it openly, he was in danger of torture or death. The professor of philosophy at the University of Padua refused to pollute his vision by even looking through Galileo's telescope. The Roman Catholic Church, shocked by the Reformation into rigid defensiveness, declared that Copernicus' theory that the Earth moved violated Christian belief. Galileo, after one hard experience, avoided directly colliding with the all-powerful Church. Instead he did what he could *to advance scientific thinking* (rather than his own specific ideas about the universe), knowing that as such thinking became more common the rigid old beliefs would collapse.

Galileo therefore did what was a rare thing in those days. He conducted scientific experiments, carefully choosing subjects which to the Church seemed harmless, such as the motion of falling objects, rolling spheres, and

Entrance to the Laurentian Library, Florence, designed by Michelangelo, 1524–1526, to house Lorenzo's collection of books. This is a sculptor's bold approach to architecture. The double columns, set in recesses, have no function as supports; neither do the curving forms beneath them. The framed windows are blind. The curves in the steps are needless. All are there to create a powerful and original work of art, through which one moves when entering the library. Such original work in architecture was to be carried forward after Michelangelo's death, first in the Mannerist and then in the Baroque period.

projectiles. The simple facts which he thus uncovered he used as a basis for logical thinking, just as the fathers of the Church had built logically on Church doctrine. But the difference was, of course, that Galileo based his reasoning on what he could see and measure with his own two eyes, and on what others could therefore see and measure with theirs, if they chose.

Galileo as a scientist was completely modern. In Denmark Tycho Brahe's successor, John Kepler, was discovering laws governing astronomy, not for their own sake, but in pursuit of the age-old idea that the heavenly bodies, as they move, make harmonious supermusic. Kepler was trying to discover the secret laws of harmony on which he believed God had founded the universe. This was not true of Galileo. His brilliant use of experiment, logic, and mathematics was simply aimed at understanding the universe as it appears to us. Beyond that he was always ready to say, "I do not know."

Galileo's experiments with everyday objects such as falling weights and rolling balls revealed some basic laws governing all motion. He found, first, that *all bodies, whether heavy or light, speed up at a constant rate as they fall* (unless air resistance interferes). He found, next, that *all bodies keep a constant state of rest or motion until some other force changes that motion.* Thus a ball on a level surface gradually slows down, not because it "runs out of steam," but because friction slowly retards it. His next conclusion combined these discoveries. *If falling bodies speed up, instead of moving at a constant speed, this must be because the Earth acts on them with an attracting force.* This force he called *gravity.*

Although he carried on no known researches in human anatomy, Galileo's writings suggest that he was part of a developing trend in his age, in his opinions as to how the human body is constructed. As inventors kept improving different simple machines, the idea kept naturally occurring to many men: might not the human body, although vastly more complex than anything so far invented, be a machine too? This idea, first raised as a question, was to become more convincing as time passed.

In spite of much physical illness all his life, Galileo lived until 1642 and the ripe age of 78. He was Europe's first great *inductive* scientist; his influence on future generations was to be profound.

Bernini, Michelangelo's Successor

After Michelangelo died in 1564, sixty years passed before another man of towering artistic genius appeared in Rome. Giovanni Lorenzo Bernini, a young sculptor born in Naples of a Florentine father, while still a youth showed the spectacular promise which could attract the attention of the great Pope Urban VIII. Before he was 30 he had been placed in charge of completing St. Peter's basilica. For most of his long life (1598–1680) he was an inexhaustible source of wonders in sculpture, architecture, and painting, with excursions into the writing and production of drama.

In 100 years Italian ideas about what was beautiful and interesting in art had changed. A new age had arrived, with distinct characteristics of its own, which today we designate by the name *Baroque.*[8] For all the seventeenth cen-

Alinari-Art Reference Bureau, Inc.

Alinari-Art Reference Bureau, Inc.

tury, and far into the eighteenth, Baroque styles in art, architecture, landscape design, and interior decoration ruled all Europe. But its center of origin was Rome, where the popes were making a superhuman effort to reaffirm by every means possible the supreme authority of the Roman Catholic Church. It was the age of counterattack on the Protestant Reformation, in other words, the *Counter-Reformation*. Bernini and a host of other artists working to serve this cause made use of at least three fundamental changes in art which Michelangelo had already launched.

Above left: David *as conceived by Michelangelo, and, right, by Bernini. Both men were in their mid-twenties when they created these statues, but they were inspired by the tastes of two different periods, 125 years apart. Michelangelo's David, though intensely alive, is full of balance and almost godlike poise; detail is at a minimum. Bernini's deliberately avoids the vertical pose, is charged with motion and counter-motion, displays violent passion, and is loaded with stage props, such as the discarded armor.*

The Baroque Style

Asymmetrical Composition

One quality of Michelangelo's painting and sculpture which was especially useful to later artists was *their effect on the viewer of power and dynamic motion. The works of the great Renaissance artists who came before him generally show an interest, not so much in power and motion, as in repose and balance*. They loved stable, solid bilaterally symmetrical composition. They carefully measured out the refined proportions into which they divided the picture plane. They placed the vanishing point of a picture's perspective at or near its center. Within these limits they often showed a great deal of motion, but they controlled it with these design devices. Michelangelo too used now one, now another, of these stabilizing devices. When he did we can feel the forces in the painting being held in a kind of uneasy suspension. See if you do not feel this when you look at the *Last Judgment*.

Photo courtesy E. Kidder-Smith, New York

Baroque exploitation of illusion at its height: the barrel vault of the Church of Jesus (Il Gesu), Rome. This, the mother church of the militant order of Jesuits, the Society of Jesus, was erected beginning in 1568. Perhaps in keeping with the ideas of Alberti, it was built with an austerely plain white ceiling. Over a century later this severe whiteness was transformed into the restlessly ornate spectacle shown here. The vault is "pierced" on the left by an apparent heavenward plunge into deep space, balanced on the right, in typical Baroque style, by the mass of near-hovering figures. Through the device of trompe l'oeil *painting, the heavenly drama (or melodrama) is made to float down past its frame into the church itself. The rest of the vault is*

But Michelangelo also created another form of composition in which he turned away from the calm balance of bilateral symmetry. *He created an asymmetrical* (that is, *unsymmetrical*) *composition with two sides, one in conflict or contrast with the other*. The men who came after him seized on this device and explored it to the limits of their vision. They discovered that the contrast could be of many kinds. But of these perhaps their favorite was that between *near and far*. One-half or more of the painting would be in the foreground, the balance leading off to some remote vista; the painting's vanishing point would be shifted dramatically to this side. To link the two halves, the painter would often portray action of some kind in the foreground but direct its drive toward the deep distance. Thus he would make his painting *dynamic*, that is, *conveying a feeling of motion rather than repose*. Baroque painters in the service of the popes used such techniques to convey an image of the Church itself as dynamic. It was a style of art admirably suited to the taste of an age in which people were everywhere aroused by the conflict between Catholics and Protestants, by the drama of new power, and by travel into distant parts of the newly discovered Earth.

Massiveness, Richness, and Interplay of Light and Shade

Still another way in which Michelangelo pointed the way to a new era was his daring in breaking away from Vitruvius' rigid rules of architectural design. He combined columns and other structural units in new ways to create fresh, and again *powerful*, effects. In the period which followed him, one architect after another pushed his daring experiments to bolder and bolder extremes. Always their interest was to convey power and to give a sense of greater and greater richness. Power they conveyed by making the building look massive, its columns not only imposing, heavy, and gigantically tall, as in the days of the Roman empire, but also grouped sometimes in twos. Richness they conveyed through a wealth of sumptuous decoration, and by making an ever greater interplay of light and shadow on the building surface. This latter they sometimes achieved by making the building front actually curve in and out. These effects were never assembled haphazardly, but carefully organized to create one united, overwhelming effect, like an artistic cannon aimed at the innocent viewer's head.

Virtuosity in Figure Drawing

A third aspect of Michelangelo's art which especially fascinated men who came after was his mastery of massively muscled, active human beings in every imaginable position, which he could freely create without reference to posing models. This kind of mastery required several skills: an intimate knowledge of anatomy, both skeletal and muscular; and a command of drawing, attained only by years of practice. It also required a knowledge of perspective, to show the human figure accurately foreshortened. All this knowledge became a part of every Baroque artist's education. Many other men were thus able to approach Michelangelo's *technical* mastery, but often without his sensitive artistic judgment.

Theatricality

But men of the Baroque period had other tastes and interests which Michelangelo may have ignored, perhaps scorned. Of these the strongest was expressed by the rising popularity of drama, and its place of exhibition, the theatre. The concept of a play, tragedy or comedy, with a skillfully constructed plot mounting to a thrilling climax, admirably fitted those times. For Europe was rushing like a comet toward the climax of her power, challenged by new opportunities for adventure and enriched by new resources beyond her previous dreams. Thus inspired, great playwrights appeared in Europe in the next two centuries, men like Lope de Vega in Spain, Shakespeare and Ben Jonson in England, Moliere, Corneille and Racine in France.

Along with the composing of plays went the designing of theatrical costumes, scenery, stages on which to act, and theaters to hold actors and audiences. *One of the most important parts of stage design is the creating of effects, whose whole aim is to move the viewer by creating an illusion, often by trick devices.* Baroque artists began to employ some of these devices as developed in the theater to intensify the impact of their work on the viewer.

endlessly encrusted with stucco ornament and figures. The work took thirteen years to complete (1672–1685) and was executed, apparently under the direction of Bernini, by two of his pupils, the painter Giovanni Battista Gauli and the sculptor Antonio Raggi.

The Exploitation of Distance

Photo Enit, Rome

Fireworks at Venice, honoring the Feast of the Holy Redeemer, a performance harking back to the Baroque era.

Another Baroque innovation was a change in building design and emphasis. Bramante and Michelangelo had been true sons of the Renaissance, for they had wholeheartedly believed in Alberti's concept of what a church should be: domed and radially symmetrical. Another great Italian Renaissance architect, Andrea Palladio, had conveyed the same idea when he designed dwelling places for noblemen. But Baroque architects, moved by the demands of their employers and patrons for buildings displaying an impressive show of power, played up the frontal aspect of the building as seen by those approaching it from a distance. When they designed palaces and churches they did everything they could to make the facades awe-inspiring from a long way off. And once the visitor was inside the building, architects next sought to heighten his feeling of awe by making him walk a long way to reach the point where the center of power lay. Thus, when designing churches they returned to the practice of lengthening the nave and prolonging the worshiper's journey toward the altar. In palaces they compelled the visitor to walk long corridors, or climb imposing flights of stairs, or both, to reach the audience chamber or throne room where sat the ruling prince.

Waterpower and Firepower as Artists' Materials

Still another favorite delight of the Baroque period was the creative display of water in fountains and of exploding gunpowder in fireworks. The fireworks, of course, were temporary affairs, over in a night, when some king was crowned, some victory won, or some saint's day celebrated. (To this day the tradition continues: fireworks are set off at Christmas in Florence, at the feast of the Holy Redeemer in Venice, at Corpus Christi in Seville, on Independence Day all over the USA, and so on.) Fountains are more permanent; many Baroque fountains still exist, among them the astonishing inventions of Bernini at Rome.

Bowl of fruit and flowers, a still life *by the Spanish painter Francisco de Zurbarán (1598–1664). Artists of the seventeenth century were the first in Europe to paint such studies of objects to be enjoyed for their color, texture, and arrangement.*

Courtesy Classics Department, University of California, Berkeley

Bernini's approach to St. Peter's, as seen from the roof of the basilica.

Bernini, Prince of Baroque Architects and Sculptors

In the work of Bernini we see all these new concepts masterfully handled. His most spectacular achievement, which no visitor to Rome today can miss, was the design of the approach to St. Peter's. True to the taste of his age, Bernini exerted every available atom of inspired ingenuity and knowledge to make this approach overwhelmingly imposing. The visitor who approaches the church on foot (as almost everyone once had to) must trudge a seemingly endless distance. First, he must cross a great elliptical plaza, enriched by a central obelisk and two splashing fountains, and guarded on either side by forests of gigantic columns standing four deep. Next he enters a broad avenue, flanked by more columns, before him an unimpeded view of the gigantic church. Thus he slowly approaches the center of Catholic Christendom, personally overawed by a display of majesty and power.

But to Bernini distance alone was not enough. The columns gradually diminish in size the nearer they stand to St. Peter's. Thus the visitor's eyes are deceived into thinking the distance greater and the already immense church still more immense than they really are.

Bernini's sculpture was the marvel of his age. To us it is a continual violation of the *integrity of materials*. By this we mean *a respect for the structure, native texture, and grain of the stuff with which we are working*. For Bernini's pride and delight seemed to be to make marble look like everything it was not. By various technical tricks of stoneworking he made its surface resemble velvet, silk, feathers, and even clouds! He tortured it sometimes into lace and sometimes into tree foliage, depending on what he happened to be creating. But to the people of his own time this was a heroic triumph over matter. Here was a man who could make stone become anything he willed! A god among artists! And when it came to expressing power, his sculptures could be fairly explosive. It is not surprising to learn that Bernini, among other achievements, wrote drama.

Alinari-Art Reference Bureau, Inc.

Above: Fountain of the Four Rivers, one of many created by Bernini for the city of Rome. The four chief figures encircling the fountain personify four of the world's great waterways, a dramatic example of Baroque global thinking. Right: colossal bronze canopy which enshrines the high altar of St. Peter's directly under the center of the dome. The designing of this canopy (or baldacchino*) was the first major project which Bernini received. He was 26 at the time, and it took him eight years to complete it. Pope Urban VIII obtained the metal for it (and for a battery of cannon to protect the Castel Sant Angelo) by ordering the removal of the bronze supporting beams from the portico of the Pantheon. They were replaced with beams of wood. During the seventeenth century the ruins of Rome were repeatedly mined for Baroque building materials.*

Vatican photo

Venetian Painting: Three Glorious Centuries

Venice, Italy's wealthiest and longest lasting commercial city, mirrored her power by her greatness in art for a longer time than any other Italian city. Florence ceased to be an important creative center by 1600. Rome was such a center when individual popes so willed it, and lost her significance as an originator of new ideas after the death of Bernini. But Venice continued to be a center of artistic invention down to the last quarter of the eighteenth century.

Venice was especially remarkable for her great painters. Giovanni Bellini (1430–1516), Giorgione (1476–1510), Titian (1477–1576), Tintoretto (1518–1594), Veronese (1528–1588), Giovanni Battista Tiepolo (1696–1770), Francesco Guardi (1712–1793)—these are perhaps the most renowned among many. With the exception of Giorgione and Guardi, whose work was of a modest size and for private enjoyment, these men had astonishing inventive power on a large scale. Tintoretto, for example, created and completed a painting 75 feet long and 30 feet high (entitled *Paradise*), containing hundreds of figures, in one week!

Less well known is their inventiveness in developing new painting media. These were discovered and perfected between about 1460 and 1540, during the historical period in which Venice was replacing Constantinople, after its seizure by the Turks, as the greatest Christian city facing the Mediterranean. It was the Venetian painting media which enabled her artists to work with a richness, depth, and speed which the world had never before known. It was these media, also, which freed them from the rigid requirements for step-by-step preparation demanded by both fresco painting and by van Eyck's careful technique.

When the training of artists was taken over by *academies* (see page 478) in the late seventeenth and early eighteenth centuries, and ceased to be a matter of apprenticeship under a master, the great painting workshops gradually disappeared, and with them the painting secrets, passed on from master to apprentice from generation to generation, disappeared also. With the loss of the techniques the quality and lasting power of painting suffered. Not until new ways of seeing the world inspired a new period of invention in painting media (see Project 58) has this dark age begun to end.

The Venetians wanted to use van Eyck's precious, jewel-like technique on great wall surfaces. They wanted to keep the richness of van Eyck's colors and the depth of his shadows, so much more intense than in fresco or watercolor. But they wanted those colors to have a dull rather than a shiny surface, for a shiny wall destroys the visibility of the painting on it. They also wanted to free themselves from van Eyck's labored, painstaking way of working, area by area, on a wet oil surface (see Project 45), and of having to wait until this was dry before coming back to rework it.

The Venetians made essentially two discoveries: first, that by cooking linseed oil with a compound of lead a new compound was formed which is not only faster drying than pure oil, but is a much finer and richer medium for paints; second, that by combining a little beeswax with this medium it could be made to dry dull (or matt). Everyone with a strong interest in art should have the opportunity to try these media for himself. In Project 48, therefore, there is given a reconstruction of what is believed to have been the Venetian technique as perfected in the sixteenth century (or rather two of its probably many versions, each artist having his own), somewhat simplified to fit modern conditions. We must remember that the artists of the period ground their own colors; today this is generally done commercially.

Photo courtesy Scuola di San Rocco and Sr. Terisio Pignatti, Venice

The Nativity, *by the Venetian painter Tintoretto (1518–1594), one of a series he painted for the Scuola di San Rocco, Venice. The painting is an example of Tintoretto's ability to improvise human figures in action. In this he was inspired by the example of Michelangelo, as were a host of other sixteenth and seventeenth century artists.*

The Thirty Years' War

Two etchings by the French graphic artist Jacques Callot, 1633, when the Thirty Years' War was at its height. For a description of etching *see page 473.*

Achenbach Collection, San Francisco

In the course of Bernini's creative lifetime at Rome, northern Europe was undergoing fresh convulsions. We have seen how, in the preceding century (the sixteenth), two struggles had shaken the continent: the Protestants had striven for religious freedom in a world controlled by Catholics, and the kingdom of France had fought to keep independent from the encircling Holy Roman Empire. Early in the seventeenth century these two struggles became merged into a sinister single one. The Thirty Years' War, raging from 1618 to 1648, was at first a "holy" war of Catholics against Protestants within the empire, but later embroiled other nations, especially France and her ally Sweden. When the war at last ground to an exhausted halt, Protestants had won certain permanent rights in large parts of Europe, and France had defeated the armies of the empire. But the price of these victories was staggering. Great stretches of Germany over which armies had fought back and forth were reduced to desolate wasteland. Their farming population had shrunk by nearly one-half, and city population by one-third. It was as tragic as the Black Death had been two centuries earlier.

The Netherlands Becomes a Nation

A refreshing by-product of this dismal war was the breaking away of the Netherlands from the iron rule of Spain. For 80 years the tough, stubborn Dutch had resisted the submission which Spanish kings had demanded, basing their demands on that marriage, already in the dim past, of Philip the Good to Isobel of Portugal (see page 393). In the course of the struggle the seven northernmost Dutch provinces united to form the modern world's first *republic*, and declared themselves Protestant, thus becoming anti-Spanish in every way possible.[9] By 1639 the Dutch Republic was a reality which even Spain had to recognize. But southern Flanders, which is today Belgium, continued Catholic and dominated by the Spanish until the rising power of France snatched it from Spain and for a time made it her own.

The Rise of French, Dutch, and English Power

The center of Europe's financial power now shifted away from the countries which had first explored the New World and had shortsightedly stripped it, wherever they could, of its precious metals. Spain and Portugal had built colonial empires in Central and South America, and the Portuguese had built a prosperous trade with India, the East Indies, China, and parts of Africa. But other European nations had proved stronger in war. The English had defeated the great Spanish Armada in 1588. Fifty years later, in 1639, the Dutch had proved their independence by defeating a Spanish fleet at nearly the same place in the English Channel. Meanwhile, in one historic land battle after another, brilliantly generaled French armies had proved superior to supposedly invincible Spaniards.

These three nations, France, the Netherlands, and England, were now to build great new empires in other parts of the world by taking colonies and trade from Portugal and Spain. They then began to amass wealth through trade and colony building, practices less spectacular, but more rewarding, than the fierce search for gold.

The great French, Dutch, and English trading and colonizing enterprises, with arms stretching halfway round the globe, demanded a vast outlay of capital to pay for ships, crews, weapons, and the equipment of traders and colonists. Never before had such sums been needed for investment. They were far beyond the capacity of any single financier to meet. Neither the Medici nor the Fugger banks at their height could have met this demand for money. The Dutch, English, and French governments, to meet this emergency, permitted the formation of companies to trade in and otherwise exploit certain defined areas overseas. The existence of the company and its purposes and areas of operation were defined in a *charter* granted by the ruling sovereign or government. Thus came into being the English East India Company in 1660, to be followed by similar companies in the Netherlands and France.

To raise funds, the companies then sold *shares in the company* to as many people as would buy, with the understanding that profits made by the company would later be distributed as *dividends* among the shareholders. The value of each share was fixed. In England this was at first £100. Thus the men of that time developed a new, broader method of finance, bringing to a single enterprise the capital of thousands of individual investors.

Part of the company's profits came from importing finished goods, chiefly textiles of cotton and silk, from countries such as India and China. But an even larger part came from the import of bulk materials: rice, cocoa, tea, coffee, sugar, pepper, tobacco, dark blue indigo dye, and mahogany timber. These materials were sometimes bought in foreign markets. But more and more, colonists from Europe grew them for the companies on their own overseas plantations (or, in the case of mahogany, lumbered it in Central American jungles). These plantations demanded a large unskilled or semi-skilled labor force. Wherever they could, colonists hired or compelled natives to supply this labor. But where natives were rebellious, or nearly extinct from European diseases to which they had low immunity, colonists judged it prudent to import laborers of their own. Thus did seventeenth and eighteenth century Europe commit its single most shameful act: the purchase of black tribesmen captured in central Africa for mass transport as slaves to plantations, chiefly in the New World. The countries to start the practice, Portugal and Spain, were those in closest contact with the Muslim world, where slavery was common. But this can hardly be called an excuse. The English and the Dutch, who made large profits from the trade for over a century, could not claim such an excuse at all. The cancer bred by this brutal example of man's inhumanity to man still gnaws at the vitals of the world. In several Muslim countries slavery still exists. In others, many people refuse to let its memory die.

Foundations of Modern Capitalism: Joint Stock Company, Stock Market, Central Bank

The new method of raising capital by selling shares, which was invented to meet the great problem of financing overseas companies, soon proved useful to meet problems at home. Companies with more modest purposes, such as digging a mine or building a mill, began to sell or *issue* shares to whoever would buy, with a promise of dividends when the enterprise showed a profit. The time came when a man wished to invest in a company which had already raised its capital and had stopped issuing shares. What was he to do? He could try to find another man who wished to dispose of shares he already held. If two such men found each other, bargaining would follow. How much were the shares to cost? Their original price? More? Less? If other men also were eager to buy these particular shares, the demand would make their value go up. But if the man already holding the shares wanted to get rid of them and had trouble finding a buyer, he might have to lower the selling price to get them off his hands.

As the number of kinds of shares, and the number of men holding them, increased, it became natural for investors to frequent certain spots where they could keep track of news about the shares they held: whether or not they were popular and in demand, what new shares were being issued, who wanted to buy, who to sell, and so on. Thus came into being market places for the sole purpose of buying and selling shares in enterprises. Such an *exchange market*, with a building of its own, was founded in Amsterdam in 1613. Others later appeared in Brussels, Paris, and London.

At nearly the same time (1609) the city of Amsterdam brought a new orderliness and security to its business life by founding the *Bank of Amsterdam*, where foreign coins were exchanged, the quality of coinage was controlled, and all large bills of exchange had to be cleared. The next important step in European banking practice was to be made in London in 1694 with the founding of the *Bank of England.* This great institution not only controlled the minting of coins, but it also began cautiously to issue paper money and to lend to merchants at interest. For the first time outside of China (see page 347) a country could use a central bank to control one aspect of its prosperity by regulating the amount of money in circulation. If prices were too high, the bank could tighten the money supply by withdrawing some from circulation, and by making money harder to borrow (raising interest rates). In a time of low prices it could do the reverse.

The Old Stock Exchange, Amsterdam, *by Job Berckheyder, painted 1668 or after, when the Exchange was already over 50 years old.*

Museum Boymans - van Beuningen, Rotterdam

Frans Hals Museum, Haarlem

Gallery of the Hague

Above: Banquet of the Officers of the St. George Militia Company, *nearly 12 feet long, painted by Frans Hals in 1616. This veterans' organization was one of many whose members met annually to refresh their memories of past victories over the Spaniards. It was the practice to raise money for such group portraits by subscription. Each member who subscribed was anxious to be well represented. The artist had the delicate task of slighting nobody. Left:* The Young Bull, *by Paulus Potter, painted in 1645, when the artist was 22. This is a life-size study on a canvas nearly 10 feet wide, made at a time when the Dutch were leading the world in animal husbandry.*

New Farming Methods: Special Crops for Cattle

Although the Netherlands and Flanders had become divided as to religion, they were united by location, race, and language. Perhaps more important still, they were alike economically, for throughout the flat, rich farmland of both countries stood a series of merchant cities, supported by such solid industries as shipbuilding, woolen and linen weaving, herring salting, and cheese making. In spite of the constant troubles and damages of war in the late sixteenth and seventeenth centuries, these cities managed even to advance the prosperity which had distinguished them during the medieval and Renaissance periods. And it was here that Europeans made one more step forward in conquering the problem of an adequate food supply.

For centuries the diet of most Europeans had been long on starches (carbohydrates) supplied by grains. It had been short on proteins, though beans had proved a moderate protein supply. Only the privileged classes, about one-tenth of the whole population, could afford the luxury of a regular meat diet, often obtained through the sport of hunting.

The best source of protein foods is cattle, which provide meat and milk. Milk spoils rapidly unless converted into butter, which will last a year when salted, or cheese, which will last much longer. European cattle, as a source of meat and milk, were often few in number and poor in quality because of their poor and limited food supply. They were put to graze on land lying fallow or on land unfit for crop raising. If too many cattle were pastured, they would graze the land off too soon and starve to death over the winter. If they were put to graze on land where grain could be raised, they cut down the farmer's profits. This cycle could be broken only when many customers could afford to pay higher prices for protein-rich foods than they could for bread. The farmer could then afford to raise cattle rather than grain.

This was just what began to happen in Flanders and the Netherlands. The merchant towns made wonderful markets for meat and cheese, so wonderful that neighboring farmers *began to raise special crops, to feed, not humans directly, but cattle which would in turn feed humans.* These special crops were chiefly cabbages, turnips, and carrots, which store well over the winter, thus ensuring cattle a rich diet all year round. Dairymen could now afford to build stables to house their cattle all winter. In response to both treatments, cattle became heavier, and their milk yield greater and richer.

In the early seventeenth century, therefore, the daily diet of many northwestern Europeans took a great stride forward. This forward stride is mirrored in the paintings of the period. The men and women looking out at us are larger and fuller bodied than in the times of van Eyck. And while van Eyck's paintings are full of exquisitely wrought objects on a small scale, those of the seventeenth century are often heavy with a spirit of generous abundance.

Two Great Northern Baroque Painters

As long-time holders of wealth, the people of Flanders and the Netherlands had richly developed tastes and the means to gratify them. Antwerp, the center of Catholic Flanders, was a city of sophisticated ways. The great city of Amsterdam, a sort of northern Venice, and the center of the Protestant Netherlands, early became a publishing center, where presses turned out the first pocket-sized editions of the great Roman and Greek writers. The music of the region had long been showing the way to the rest of Europe, for it was here that one composer after another had developed that beautiful interweaving of melodies into a harmonious whole known as *counterpoint*, or contrapuntal composition. Competent painters in this area could make a good living, for the prosperous farmers and merchants liked to decorate the walls of their comfortable homes with pictures of the things that meant most to

National Gallery, Vienna

National Gallery, Washington, Mellon Collection

Two great northern Baroque painters as they saw themselves. Left: Peter Paul Rubens (1577–1640), self-portrait at age 60. Right: Rembrandt van Ryjn (1606–1669), self-portrait at age 53.

them: ships at sea, broad stretches of good farmland under different kinds of weather, richly heaped up food, and portraits of themselves. These were the solid, material tastes of a people devoted to business, but eager for the enjoyment of life, with all their senses. In their society, wealth was more widely distributed and enjoyed than in bourgeois fifteenth century Florence. And as the Dutch Republic won its independence and began to build a colonial empire, the volume of this wealth increased. So did the demand for paintings.

Of the host of Dutch and Flemish painters working to satisfy this demand, two stand out, each seeming to sum up in his work and his personal life the character of a different region. One was the son of an aristocrat, a devout Catholic, whose life from beginning to end was a kind of triumphal progress. His palatial studio, visited constantly by admiring noblemen, was at Antwerp, the Flemish center of wealth. The other man was the son of a simple miller, an earnest Protestant, whose stormy life carried him to the heights of wealth and fame, then into abject poverty, in the Dutch center of wealth, Amsterdam.

In these ways they differed. Their likeness were equally strong; both possessed integrity, seemingly boundless creative energy, and that elusive quality we call genius. The name of the first was Rubens, of the second Rembrandt.

Los Angeles County Museum, Hearst Foundation Fund

One of Rubens' swift sketches for a larger painting: Hercules taming the Nemean Lion. *12×14 inches. This is an example of the painting techniques described on the opposite page.*

Rubens

Peter Paul Rubens must have shown promise as an artist while still a child. His family launched him on the best education Antwerp could give, including a long apprenticeship under the finest local painters. These men were still working in the painstaking manner developed by Jan van Eyck, almost 200 years earlier (see page 393).

In the year 1600, when Rubens was 23 and his schooling and apprenticeship were complete, he decided to travel to Italy, as his father had before him, to see the marvels of painting there. He stayed eight years. When he came back to Antwerp, he had absorbed the best that Italy had to give an artist. At Rome he had studied Michelangelo's gigantic achievements, and had seen painters, sculptors, and architects developing the new dynamic Baroque style. In Venice he had seen the work of Titian and other great painters, and learned the latest advances in preparing and applying oil paints.

For the rest of his life, with few interruptions, Rubens settled down to concentrated production at home. From his studio came a seemingly endless parade of paintings, ordered by the highest nobility of Europe, sometimes for their own palaces and castles, sometimes for Catholic churches. Having discovered brilliant improvements of his own in the oil painting methods he had learned in Venice, he gave Baroque painting a freedom, richness, and power which made him the supreme painter of the period, just as Bernini was to be its supreme sculptor and architect. On rare occasions when he tore himself away from his beloved work, it was to act as an ambassador to England for the King of Spain. It was Rubens who was responsible for bringing peace between the two countries, thus taking England out of the Thirty Years' War. Rarely has the world seen in one man this particular combination of great talents.

Though some find their fleshy, detail-laden richness oppressive, Rubens' paintings are first of all intended for enjoyment. He had a quality like Bernini; he was a *virtuoso*, a man who could do anything with his material, creating warm velvet, cold steel, soft satin, a lion's hide, a baby's cheek, a ripe peach, a rock, all with accuracy, delight, and ease. Such power, in an age long before cameras, was a continual source of wonder and pleasure to others. In his handling of paint, Rubens seems to have followed certain basic ideas, to be discovered only by looking for them.

Baroque Painting

Solid Lights Versus Liquid Shadows

Rubens, first of all, had learned from others and further developed for himself a powerful way of handling light and shadow. Light usually reveals something solid, since a solid body is required to reflect the light back to our eyes. But shadows, wherever they fall, act like stains; they simply make solid objects harder to see. Rubens therefore *painted light objects with solid, opaque paint, paint with body to it, chiefly white lead (or entirely white lead where required). Shadows he created with paints diluted to semitransparent stains, through which one could see objects, but less distinctly.* The paints which he diluted to form these stains were either black or a mixture of black and brown (commonly called *bistre*).

He painted on a surface which had first been colored a soft grey. On this he could draw easily with white chalk instead of sooty charcoal. But the chief reason for using the grey background was that he could work in both directions from it, toward solid white and toward fluid dark, with equal ease.[10]

Warm Versus Cool

Next, Rubens paid attention to the power or contrast between the *temperatures of colors. Artists refer to colors in the red-orange-yellow group as hot or warm*, depending on how intense they are. *They call those in the green-blue-violet group cold or cool* for the same reason. Most of the colors in nature are subdued, that is, warm or cool, rather than hot or cold, and *the difference becomes noticeable and more enjoyable when they appear together in contrast.*

Thus a subdued brown (bistre) will look warm when placed beside grey. By the same contrast the grey will look cool. Even two different kinds of grey, one with a faint touch of red in it, or orange, the other without, will look different in warmth and coolness. You can try this out for yourself. *You will notice that they have to be together before you feel the warm-cool difference.*

An example of the Baroque use of a limited palette. Portrait studies by Anthony Van Dyck, Rubens' most distinguished pupil.

Royal Museum, Brussels

Rubens knew this principle and applied it logically. Not only did he make the backgrounds of his paintings grey, midway between light and dark, but *he also made that grey slightly brownish so that it would be neutral, or midway between contrasting hots and colds or warms and cools of color.* When he put a wash of ordinary black-and-white grey on such a background, it immediately looked cool, even bluish. A brown with a slight touch of orange in it, when placed on the background, immediately stood out as warm. Rubens would often work out a study for a whole painting, starting from a neutral background, with nothing but three paints (white, black, and

Alte Pinakothek, Munich

Alte Pinakothek, Munich

Two examples of Rubens' marvelous variety. Above: a furious lion hunt. Top: infant children with a garland of fruit. Both are typical examples of Baroque composition, in which the action starts at one side (here the right) and moves to the other, at the same time leading the eye of the viewer into the distance. Within this directional movement there is a brilliant interplay of forces. It is doubtful if the great Baroque painters, with their concern for spontaneity and drama, relied on

rich brown), and turpentine with which to dilute them. By blending these in various ways and placing contrasts side by side, he would produce a whole picture full of warms and cools, making the observer feel that it was much more richly colored than it really was.

Why did he do this? And why would any painter want to do it? Partly because *it simplified the problems of relating warms and cools while he was working them out*, and partly because our eyes respond with real pleasure (often without knowing why) to warm-cool differences skillfully used, but enjoy much less a painting overloaded with intense, gaudy colors all "shouting" at us at once.

Rubens had other reasons as well. In his own day the most easily obtainable kind of red, with a slightly orange tinge, was a mineral, an oxide of iron.

But it was not intense. It could be made to *look* intense only by surrounding it with subdued colors, such as browns and greys. Blue, on the other hand, was costly. It was made by grinding to powder a semiprecious stone, *lapis lazuli*, imported from Turkey (like its sister stone, *turquoise*, whose name is the French word for Turkish). But even if an artist could afford to use it (and Rubens could), there were other drawbacks. The wonderful painting media of the period had just one serious flaw: they tended to make this costly blue look slightly greenish. And when this blue was mixed with white it tended to look ash-grey. So even Rubens used it sparingly, much of the time not at all. By placing grey next to areas of red-orange, he could make the grey appear to be soft blue. This was a common practice of the period, and the illustration on page 464 is an example. (This optical effect, known as *simultaneous contrast of colors*, is examined more fully on page 535.)

Rubens Perfects the Materials

Last of all, there was Rubens' method of grinding and applying paint. He seems to have made his own discoveries, based on what he had learned in Venice. In his age no shops sold ready-filled paint tubes. Artists bought the different ingredients and carefully combined them in their studios. They bought bristles and brass wire and made their own brushes on whittled wooden handles. Every artist knew his materials intimately, having learned all about them during his apprenticeship. New techniques were looked on with suspicion, and for this reason some painters warned Rubens that his pictures would spoil as they aged. Luckily time has proved these prophets of gloom wrong.

Those of us today who wish to try Rubens' painting material must go through a good deal of labor. Not until we have done so will each of us find out whether it has something of personal value in added beauty of color, in ease of application, or in richness of paint texture. Those who wish to experiment will find help in Projects 48 through 50.

Rubens did not apply his paints to walls, as the great Italians often did. The wall surfaces of north European churches were greatly reduced by the large windows needed in those regions, and the walls of northern houses and palaces were often hung with tapestries. Instead he worked on wood panels, sometimes of great size, and on the newly discovered painting surface, *tightly stretched canvas*, carefully coated to make it nonabsorbent, which the great Italien painters in Venice had led the world in using.

Rubens' three techniques together—his use of solid whites and liquid darks, his interplay of warm against cool starting from a neutral background, and the oil painting media which he and his apprentices prepared in his studio—gave him a marvelous tool for creating paintings. The flow from brain through hand to painting surface was direct and easy. Gone were the days of making first a careful line drawing, then giving it light and shade, and then laying in colors. Rubens drew with his brush, spreading light and shadow in masses as broad as his brush was wide. Behind this, of course, lay a long intensive training in line drawing, which had made his hand sure. Like other thoroughly apprenticed painters of his age, he was a complete master of his tools; when he drew he seldom had to struggle with changes.

geometrical design-schemes, such as those in use during the Middle Ages and the Renaissance.

Gemäldegalerie, Staatliche Museen, Berlin

Private collection

Rembrandt

The simple, devout parents of Rembrandt van Ryjn (fon Rhine) must have recognized that their sixth son in a family of nine had a brilliant future. For they sacrificed to send him to the Latin school at Leyden, so that "he might in the fullness of time be able to serve his native city and the Republic with his knowledge."[11] The sentence still rings with the serious devotion the Dutch felt for their country, newly liberated from Spain by blood, tears, and toil. But the father soon recognized that he had made a mistake; his son's kind of brilliance lay not in language but art. So when Rembrandt was 13 he was apprenticed to a painter in Leyden, worked under him for three years, then moved to the greatest Dutch city of all, Amsterdam, spent six months, and came home determined to study independently. After six years of this self-education and some local fame, he felt ready to compete in the "big city." At 24 he went back to Amsterdam to build a career.

Opposite page: St. John the Baptist Preaching, *by Rembrandt, of which the central portion was painted in 1637, when the artist was twenty-nine. Years later, about 1650, Rembrandt enlarged the painting on all four sides, introducing many new figures. His swift sketch for the original composition is reproduced above. Even in its enlarged version the painting was never completed. But Rembrandt seems to have attempted to encompass the whole of humanity, in its endless variety of character and response, in the crowd surrounding the Baptist.*

A few city records, and Rembrandt's own paintings, drawings, and etchings, are about all we have from which to reconstruct the next 40 years of his life. We gather that he soon won fame. With fame came wealth, which he did not know how to keep. He married a rich and beautiful wife, who, after bearing him two sons, fell ill and died young. Her relatives sued Rembrandt for the return of her property. For the rest of his life he seems to have lived in uneasy poverty, sometimes in the Amsterdam slums. There is a dramatic contrast between the gorgeous paintings of his first period, and the sober ones of his second. Unlike the prudent Rubens, who died leaving a large fortune, Rembrandt seems never to have been able to focus his attention on money. But when we look at a Rembrandt painting it is hard to imagine his having been able to chat easily, as did Rubens, while painting. The whole intense man seems to have gone into every stroke of the brush.

The subjects of Rembrandt's paintings are many, but certain themes keep recurring. One is self-portraiture. He painted himself over 40 times, from youth to old age, in various costumes, postures, and moods. In them all, the same sensitively inquiring expression in his brown eyes seems to keep saying, "Who am I?" We gain the impression that Rembrandt was a man deeply thoughtful, introspective, and like the great Socrates of a former age bent on self-knowledge.

Another theme, expressed in many more paintings, is the constant exploration of religious subjects. These paintings were far removed in spirit from Rubens' elegant, eloquent display pieces for Catholic churches. The stern Protestant Dutch were against such "idols." They had stripped their Gothic churches of ornament and whitewashed the interior walls. Thus each worshiper might without distraction commune directly with his God, through prayer, singing hymns, reading scripture, and hearing four-hour sermons.

Rembrandt's religious paintings are personal comments on the Bible, the result of reading and rereading it (in a powerful Dutch translation), and of feeling and personally reliving what he read. His Bible characters belong, in bodily features, manners, and clothing, to Rembrandt's own time and place. He sometimes seems to have used as models the Jews of the Amsterdam Ghetto, especially after he lost his wealth. To show that the events occurred in the Holy Land, he frequently clothed them as he must have seen travelers from that far land dressed: in Turkish turbans and robes! It does not matter. The power of a great artist, and the brooding of a deep mind and tender heart, transform each painting into a completely moving statement of "this is how it was." Paintings such as these would be bought, supposedly, by pious customers for their homes. But many hardly look as if painted for sale. They look more like personal meditations, made for oneself. In this respect they grow progressively stronger from Rembrandt's youth to age.

Rembrandt painted many portraits (those good sources of income) with the same sensitive, penetrating vision with which he painted himself or characters from the Bible.

But we must look past the fascinating subject matter to perceive another of the secrets of Rembrandt's greatness: *his power to create a strong composition less with figures than with the light and shadow falling upon them.* The farther north one travels in Europe (or anywhere else on Earth), the more indirectly the sunlight falls, and the more softly golden it therefore becomes. From the pale sharp brilliance of Athens to the golden light of Florence and Venice is a long step; but from Florence and Venice to Amsterdam with its warm, honey colored light and deep shadows is greater still. Rembrandt's lights and shadows are so rich that we can practically feel the air slowly moving through his pictures.

Mounted drummers, drawing by Rembrandt in mixed media (pen, chalk, watercolor, a little oil color). Perhaps drawn from memory after viewing a parade.

To achieve these effects he seems to have had full command of Rubens' methods of preparing oils, using solid lights and fluid darks, and playing

British Museum

National Gallery, London

Gemäldegalerie, Berlin-Dahlem

Above left: Saskia, Rembrandt's wife, as the goddess Flora. 4 ft high, 1635. Above right: old man seated, perhaps intended to represent the patriarch Jacob. 20 in. high, after 1650. Rembrandt's style changed with the years, ornate wealth of detail giving place to subdued simplicity, with an increasing respect for texture of the paint. Below: small drawing in leadpoint of a child being taught to walk.

warm against cool tones. But there are differences. Rembrandt made his light areas, where sunlight falls full on people and objects, much more heavy with solid paint, enjoying the material as if it were a good meal. And his shadows are less cool, so that the whole painting tends to be warm, as if created on a genial summer afternoon, usually indoors, where light falls from just one source among somber, sleeping shadows. Blue he rarely used. He created with few colors but, even more than Rubens, gave the impression of many by skillful contrast.

British Museum

One of Rembrandt's many portraits of his father. Etched 1635.

Etching as a Technique: Rembrandt as an Etcher

Early in his career Rembrandt practiced another mode of artistic expression, especially suited to wide distribution at modest prices. This was *etching*. To make an etching, one coats a copper plate with wax, makes a scratch-drawing in the wax with a needle, and then bathes the surface with acid. Where scratches in the wax will admit it, the acid eats into the metal, more or less deeply, depending on how long the etcher lets the bath last. When the acid is washed off and the wax removed, the plate is ready for printing just like an engraved plate. Ink is rubbed into the hollows but wiped off everywhere else. Moistened paper is pressed on the plate so hard that it picks up the ink, and the etching is complete. *Dry-point* etching can also be made simply by scratching directly on the copper plate with a steel needle. The needle raises a slight furrow, called a *bur*, which catches the ink and gives the lines in a dry-point etching a quality of their own.

Rembrandt's etchings, which in his lifetime may often have sold for pennies, today are among the most costly in the world, just as are his paintings. For etching is a sternly demanding medium. One must be a thoroughly experienced draughtsman, and in drawing Rembrandt was one of the world's supreme masters. These drawings of his, often dashed off with a quill pen dipped in sepia ink, have an astonishingly personal quality, like strong handwriting. The racing speed with which he transferred to paper an idea as it took form in his imagination can excite us today, across space and time.

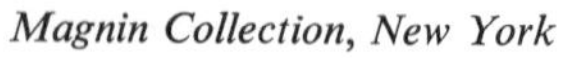
Magnin Collection, New York

Statens Museum for Kunst, Copenhagen

The Dutch Republic's Time of Greatness

Above left: The Geographer, *by Jan Vermeer (1632–1675). In the sixteenth and seventeenth centuries the whole planet Earth became available for mapping, and in this field the Netherlands led the world. Above right: the French philosopher and mathematician Rene Descartes, as sketched by Frans Hals, in about 1649, in preparation for a formal portrait. About 6 inches high.*

Rembrandt was only one of a host of Dutch painters working in the mid-seventeenth century. Among them were some remarkable men—the powerful, impetuous Frans Hals of Haarlem and the gloriously detached Jan Vermeer of Delft, to mention two. All these men seem to have mastered Rubens' techniques, and to have modified them in different ways to suit their personal tastes. It was a great period. But the marvel was that the painters were only a part of it. The little Dutch Republic was achieving wonders on all fronts: founding colonies overseas, holding her own as a sea power on the world's oceans, and defending her borders against the brilliantly generaled armies of a larger, more powerful, and more ambitious country, the kingdom of France. Within those borders the wise Dutch policy of tolerating the religious and political views of others was repaying them richly. The Netherlands had become the home of intellectual giants whose quiet discoveries were to help shape the future thought of Europe.

René Descartes, a Frenchman who did his best work in Holland, made the first great advance in mathematics since the Hellenistic Greeks when he developed analytic geometry and the technique of precisely locating objects through the use of rectangular coordinates. There now existed for the first time a link between algebra and Euclid's geometry.[12] Christian Huygens, a

Dutch physicist, advanced Galileo's studies of motion. Other Dutch scientists of the same period were advancing biology, medicine, and microscope technique.

In the field of philosophy, two foreigners, working on Dutch soil, towered above all others in early seventeenth century Europe. One was, again, the Catholic Frenchman, René Descartes; the other was a Portuguese Jew, Benedict Spinoza. Both men were sharing in a new age in which the scientist's role was becoming greater and greater. How was an intelligent scientist to study the human body as a marvelously constructed machine on weekdays, and on Sundays go to church for the good of his eternal soul? How could a soul and a machine be connected? Descartes made a naïve attempt at a solution by suggesting that body and soul were united through a small organ imbedded in the brain, the pineal gland (now known to secrete certain hormones). Spinoza went much further. He realized that the problem was vastly greater, that it involved the entire universe. If the planets move around the sun as if they were parts of a machine, and if perhaps the same laws govern the stars also, where in this vast machine is there room for God? And if men and women are small machines living in a vast one, do they have souls? If so, how are their souls connected with their bodies, and with God himself? Spinoza's answers to these questions were developed in theorems founded on axioms and definitions, just like Euclid's geometry. It was an amazing piece of architecture whose stones were words and ideas, held together by the strong cement of logic.

There is no separation, Spinoza declared, between the universe of living creatures, planets, and stars, on the one hand, and God, on the other. God *is* the universe. All solid things, whether grain of sand or drop of water, plant or animal or man, planet or star, are parts of his body; all people's minds are fragments of his mind. Men's intellects are imperfect because they are limited fragments of God's limitless one. And of God's nature we know almost nothing. As Spinoza put it, "God possesses infinite aspects of which we know but two: thought and extension." And, "the more we know about particular things the more we know about God." To Spinoza, scientific research was a form of worship.

Greatness Precedes Decline

The tremendous burst of achievement on all fronts, by one of Europe's smallest nations, could not last. Through this period of greatness the little country almost unbelievably was also racked at onetime by civil war. By 1700 the country's drive had exhausted her resources. She lost her command of the sea and, therefore, large parts of her overseas empire. This change was paralleled by a steep decline in all cultural fields, including painting. The masters seem to have ceased taking on apprentices, perhaps because young men were turning to other fields. The magic secrets of Baroque painting were lost, only to be tentatively rediscovered in our own century by painstaking research. And not until our own century did the Dutch regain importance in science and art. Meanwhile the centers of high achievement passed, for a time, elsewhere.

The Rising Power of France

Louis XIV, surrounded by runners and aides, including his chaplain, gives the order to storm the beseiged city of Dunkerque, part of a tapestry designed by Charles le Brun and woven at the Gobelin factories outside of Paris. It is also an example of Baroque asymmetral composition: a near group on one side displaying a dynamic thrust into deep space on the other.

In the year 1643, Louis XIII, king of France, died. "I am Louis XIV! I am Louis XIV!" shouted his little son, then aged five. Louis XIV he was to remain for 72 long years, dominating the destiny of western Europe's largest, richest country. It was also the most powerful. For Louis XIII, or rather his iron-willed chief minister, Cardinal Richelieu, had carried forward the task begun by Phillip Augustus 500 years earlier, of making France a united nation. Louis XIV, when he came of age, was to complete the task. Although he was a small man, only five feet five inches, he was in all respects a ruler. Just as Bernini was *the* Baroque sculptor and architect, and Rubens *the* Baroque painter, so Louis XIV was *the* Baroque monarch, who made himself a center of radiant power, the Sun King as he was called, governing France as if the land were an extension of his own body. "L'état c'est moi!" he cried. The kingdom, it is I!

Rubens never saw Louis XIV; he died when the future king was two. But Bernini did, and carved a living portrait of him in marble. In 1665, the king, then 27 years old, invited the great architect to present plans for the completion of the royal palace of the Louvre, then being erected at Paris. Bernini presented four different plans, none of which was to prove satisfactory. At least one reason for this failure seems to have been Bernini's unawareness of the difference between the strong southern sunlight of Rome and the more subdued light of northern France. The French royal architects surmised that the palace interior, as he had designed it, would be dark in places. A commission of three Frenchmen, one of whom had just translated Palladio's work on architecture, took over the Louvre's completion.

At the same time Louis was erecting another vast palace some miles outside the city, at Versailles (VairSIGH). Its immense scale and the formal gardens, terraces, fountains, and pools which radiate from it are, in their extravagant display of power, typically Baroque. This display was calculated. By his personal example, Louis XIV believed that he was leading France forward into a new age of glory, in politics, war, literature, and the arts, including that of refined living. The astonishing mixture of shrewdness and folly in his beliefs and policies propelled the nation along a terrible double path to glory and ruin. The people of the time were caught up in living a fateful drama which, in its turn, inspired great dramatists, as few ages can. Corneille and Racine wrote tragedies; Moliere wrote bitter, satirical comedies. A courtier of the period wrote concerning the life at Versaille, "Its pleasures are visible but false; its sorrows hidden but real."

The great palace had another purpose. Louis required the powerful nobles, who had lived on their estates as nearly independent rulers, to spend their lives close to his person at court. There a life of continual display and

Work going forward on completion of the Louvre, 1672. Engraving by Sebastien le Clerc. The inscription, in French and Latin, reads: "Picture of the machines which have served to raise the two great stones which cover the front of the chief entrance to the Louvre."

amusement sapped the rugged strength which had made them dangerous. They became merely courtiers, forgetting the differences which had marked them as from one or another part of the land, speaking instead with a Parisian accent, and dressing, conversing, and living after the example of the king.

For Louis was trying to create a modern nonfeudal state, with a strong central government, an organized civil service, and a realistic fiscal system. The economy of the land, and especially trade and manufacture, came under as close regulation as the world has ever seen. Louis chose a remarkable man, Jean-Baptiste Colbert, as his Minister of Finance. Colbert, the son of a solid, bourgeois merchant, was ambitious to make the kingdom of France show a profit, just like any good business enterprise. This meant that more money should be coming into the country than was going out. And what would attract money? The sale of goods, as many as possible. Colbert, in other words, aimed to achieve a *favorable balance of trade*. He did it by setting standards, not only for the price of everything bought and sold, but for the high quality of everything manufactured. He also discouraged the import of foreign goods by charging high tariffs. It was an endlessly detailed task, but Colbert succeeded in creating the desired profit.

To what avail? Louis' realism was sadly one-sided. He had only one idea of what a king's aims should be: personal and national glory. Faster than Colbert built up wealth, Louis wasted it in wars against neighboring kingdoms. For not only did he have two of Europe's greatest generals, the Viscount of Turenne and the Prince of Condé, but he had as well its most brilliant engineer of fortifications, Vaubin, and its greatest innovator of army discipline and equipment, Louvois. Through them he brought to France some triumphs, and along with them the alarmed distrust of France's neighbors, who at last united to give her some crushing defeats, on land and sea. When Louis died, and his coffin was borne in state through the Paris streets, many in the crowds shouted curses. He left behind him a debt, staggering for those days, of three billion French *livres*, or six hundred million dollars.

Mercantilism, the pattern of closely regulated business, manufacture, and import duties in order to show a favorable trade balance, was copied by other European nations and became the familiar economic policy of the eighteenth century. It was a strictly self-centered, mutually defeating policy. For how could *every* nation show a favorable trade balance, attracting more money than it exported?

Under Louis was founded an *Academy of Painting and Sculpture*. The Academy was an assembly, a sort of club of the most eminent artists of France, at first selected by the king and after that self-perpetuating. But the honor had a certain mixture of bondage. For the Academy was intended as part of a system aimed literally at the production and maintenance of artists according to certain specifications. By law, nobody in France might display art publicly unless he was an *Academician* (or Academy member) and even then only once every two years, at great exhibitions, or *Salons*, held at Paris. The Academy became the final judges of French taste in art, almost but not quite. For more powerful than what pleased them was what pleased the king.

The Academy was permitted to decide what should be taught in the *Ecole Academique*, or state-supported art school, a coldly severe place to which students were admitted by examination, there to spend years drawing from plaster casts of antique sculpture before being admitted to the drawing of living models. The writings of Leonardo da Vinci on the training of art students, already over 150 years old, were resurrected by the French and consulted as a guide. Color was discouraged. The fact that Greek and Roman sculpture had once been alive with color was not realized, since time had eroded it away! The French were in pursuit of high, pure standards in art, and seemed to confuse purity with whiteness. But the policy of running an art school in this manner was copied widely, and even today still lingers on in some places. It has given to the term *academic art* a justly unfavorable meaning, namely, *art inspired more by teaching and tradition than by one's own awareness*.

The cream of the graduates of the Ecole Academique were awarded prizes. The *Prix de Rome* entitled them to five years' study in Italy. Artists were then considered ready to return to France and to devote their lives to the painting of great scenes taken from Greco-Roman history, the Bible, or some other lofty source, to be exhibited in Salons and perhaps bought by the government.

But this icy system could not suppress French imagination, wit, sensuality, and love of exquisite color. Private buyers abounded who wanted portraits, or who hungered to be charmed or amused by pictures, not merely awe-stricken. And then, of course, artists could show what they wished in their own studios or in shops.

The Hand Kiss, *a drawing in black and white chalk, by Jean Honoré Fragonard (1732–1806), a popular painter during the reign of Louis XV and XVI. Fragonard was an Academician and winner of the Prix de Rome, who later turned to painting informal and popular subjects.*

The Academy of Painting and Sculpture was in its turn only one of a group of academies devoted to literature, music, architecture, the dance, and the sciences. The prestige of membership was great, and so, therefore, was their influence in establishing goals toward which the talent and intellect of France aspired. In careful distinction to these lofty pursuits or *arts*, the king authorized the setting of other equally high standards for the *crafts*, and the training of craft apprentices. Under these standards, French furniture, tapestries, metalwork, goldsmith work, textiles, etc., became remarkable for soundness and elegance.

But the great drawback to any kind of daring creation was that the intellectual atmosphere of France was not free. In 1685 Louis XIV declared the country strictly Catholic. Many able, intelligent Frenchmen who happened to be Protestants fled abroad. Besides this the king, and through him the nobility, could make any man he wished disappear without a trace into life imprisonment. The risk of causing displeasure to the ruling class hung over every man who had a boldly original thought or idea.

Policies like these continued under the Sun King's less forceful son, Louis XV, who went on wasting his country's resources on *prestige* wars with France's neighbors, while the French colonies overseas and the navy, needed to protect her overseas trade, suffered from neglect. The brilliance and heroism of individual French colonizers and admirals of this period was remarkable. Repeatedly they lost to the sober British for lack of support from home. At the same time, the French nobility, by now thoroughly accustomed to a life at court, had grown estranged from the peasantry on their distant estates, looking on them solely as a source from which to squeeze revenue to support lives of elegance and pleasure. Under this treatment the French peasantry suffered intensely. France was a sick nation, ripe for revolution. "Après moi le déluge," muttered Louis XV on his deathbed. "After me the deluge."

Portrait bust of Voltaire dated 1778, when he was an old man, by Jean-Antoine Houdon, the greatest French portrait sculptor of the eighteenth century.

National Gallery of Art, Washington, D.C., Chester Dale Collection

Against this state of affairs one brilliant, heroic, impudent Frenchman, Voltaire, spent a lifetime of outraged, witty protest. Twice imprisoned, twice exiled, he never ceased writing what he fiercely pleased, at one moment demanding religious freedom, at another popularizing the latest scientific discovery, and at another defending some sufferer from injustice. To him more than to any other single man seems to belong the credit for the violent changes which were to rock France shortly after his death in 1778.

The greatest intellectual advances of the late seventeenth and early eighteenth centuries, therefore, occurred chiefly (though not entirely) outside of France. Music developed most freely in Germany, Austria, and Italy.[13] England, where personal rights were by this time respected as fully as they had been in the Netherlands for a century, led in science, mathematics, and philosophy. Robert Boyle laid the foundations of modern chemistry. Isaac Newton, picking up the threads of advancement in physics where Galileo and Kepler had left them, developed for the first time in man's history a theory of motion and force which applied to every object in the universe, whether grain of sand, apple, boulder, moon, planet, or star. He recognized Galileo's force of gravity, and extended its application. All bodies attract each other, he declared. The attraction one body exerts on another increases with the body's size and density. The attraction decreases the farther apart the bodies happen to be. The moon would travel in a straight line through space if it were not for the pull which the Earth exerts upon it. This is just enough to keep the moon's path constantly curving, but not enough to pull the two spheres together. The moon, a much smaller body, also exerts a lesser pull on the Earth. Pebbles and sand grains do not cling together (as if magnetized) because the pull of gravity between them is too minute.

Newton and the remarkable European philosopher Leibniz seem each to have made independently the same new discoveries in mathematics. Using analytical geometry as Descartes had created it, they developed a new method of dealing precisely with motion and change. This invention, at first called the "theory of fluctions," has since been renamed *integral and differential calculus.*

The English philosophers, a soberly critical group, particularly the Scotchman David Hume, analyzed the human thinking process to show how difficult it is to arrive at real knowledge, and how easy it is to make grandiose statements about man, the universe, and God, statements with no actual basis in the kind of human experience which we can share. Galileo's scientific method had indeed come a long way in changing the intellectual climate of thinking Europe.

The Struggle for Colonies

It was in the nature of things that the three ambitious, expanding, colonizing nations which faced the Atlantic should have come into conflict. Of the three, the Netherlands as the smallest, with the least command of natural resources at home, was the first to be forced into a secondary place, though she managed to retain a far-spread empire in the islands of the East Indies, which she had taken from Portugal. The French and the English then entered into a world-wide struggle for colonial mastery of rich prizes such as North America and India. From this struggle England emerged victorious, creating a colonial empire on which "the sun never set." She compelled the Netherlands to surrender the colonies they had planted on the southern tip of the African continent. John Barrow, representing the British government, toured the region in 1797 (see Chapter 1).

"Europe supported by Africa & America," an engraving by William Blake, 1792, as illustration for a book of travels.

The colonies which Europeans were carving out for themselves by ruthlessly fighting and crowding back "primitive" peoples in different parts of the world were largely unfit places for artists. The struggle for survival and conquest neither allowed men time for quiet creation nor encouraged most people to buy luxuries, such as works of art. And if the colonists had any interest in the art of the "savages" they were attacking, it must have been mere passing curiosity.

In a distinct group were the artists who accompanied explorers and who carried back to Europe their pictured impressions of the New World, its animals, plants, and human inhabitants. What is generally most striking about their work is that they saw the native Americans through eyes trained in the Baroque tradition, and drew them in poses full of classical elegance, in a manner totally alien to the natives' natural stance. Seldom has the adage that "we see what we know" been more clearly illustrated.

A.W. Mellon Collection, Washington, D.C.

Esther Fiske Hammond Collection, Brookline, Massachusetts

Redwood Library, Newport, Rhode Island

Left: Benjamin West (1738–1820), self-portrait at 33. Center: John Singleton Copley (1738–1815), self-portrait at 38. Right: Gilbert Stuart (1755–1828), self-portrait at 23.

America's First Distinguished Painters

But as time passed, conditions in some colonies became better for artists, or at least for portrait painters. There is also in some men such a thing as talent and will-power so strong that nothing will hold them back. In the British North American colonies at least three such men appeared, close to the middle of the eighteenth century, whose destiny made them not merely artists, but artists of international influence. Two of these men were born in the same year, 1738. One, Benjamin West, the son of a barrel maker and innkeeper, started life near Philadelphia in a community of Quakers. The other, John Singleton Copley, was an orphan whose widowed mother sold tobacco in a little shop on the Boston waterfront. The third and youngest, Gilbert Stuart, a carpenter's son, was born in 1755 near Providence, Rhode Island, in a snuff mill built by his father.

By the time West was 22, a self-taught genius of splendidly tranquil disposition (which he doubtless owed to Quaker self-discipline), he had earned enough money painting portraits of Philadelphia merchants to sail off to Italy, never to return to his native America. Even in the colonies, where not one example of Italian art could yet be found, everyone believed the legend that Italy was the world's art center. West's power and reputation grew like a slow-moving sky rocket. When he traveled from Italy to England and decided to settle in London, he became the close friend of King George III (or as close as anyone could approach eighteenth century royalty). He was a founder, in 1768, of the British Royal Academy, the sober, late-blooming counterpart of the magnificent French Academy established by Louis XIV over a century earlier. It is hard to believe that the British Academy, which was to have so profound an influence for good or ill on Britain's painters, should have been launched by a young American back-woodsman, and that for years he should have been the Academy's respected president. But such was the case.

As a painter Benjamin West was versatile and ambitious, given to creating on canvas great scenes which challenged his powers of composition and imagination—scenes from the Bible and the history of his own time. As a *man* he was endlessly encouraging to younger artists, especially from the colonies, who were beginning to follow his example by journeying to Europe to complete their artistic education.

Of these one of the first, and surely the greatest, was Copley, a sensitive, withdrawn young man, who had suffered cruelly from poverty in his child-hood. By sheer drive, ability, and toil, Copley first taught himself to paint and then won himself a small fortune as Boston's outstanding portrait painter. Working alone, with next to no European examples before him, he developed a style of his own, strong, austere, cleanly defined, and dominated by cool colors.

In 1766 he mustered the courage to send one of his paintings overseas to London, hoping it might be thought fit to include in the annual exhibition of the Society of Artists (the forerunner of the Royal Academy). The paint-ing, *Boy with Squirrel*, was the first painting to go from the colonies to Eng-land. It was a startling sensation to British artists, even to Benjamin West. Though they criticized it for the very qualities we admire today, they still respected it, and elected Copley to their society, the first overseas American to be so honored.

Ten years later, Copley, still feeling inferior to European artists, left his prosperous practice in Boston and his wife and four children just as the American Revolution was catching fire, determined to improve himself professionally. He was never to return. Helped by West, he settled in London, made over his strong natural style to fit richer European tastes, and in a few years earned enough money to bring his family to England. In later life he believed that he had harmed himself as an artist. When public taste began to turn to other painters, he died a grief stricken man. But his son, John Singleton Copley, Jr., was to rise to social and political glory. He became a peer with the title of Lord Lyndhurst, and served as Britain's Chancellor of the Exchequer (equivalent to Secretary of the Treasury).

Gilbert Stuart, the youngest of the three, grew up poverty stricken and wildly excitable. His patience and his hands, which habitually trembled, allowed him to learn, somehow, to paint human heads and shoulders, and little else. But what power he had in that narrow field! Eyewitness accounts still exist of his pausing before each brush stroke to get control of his hand before making the decisive dab that did precisely what he wanted. He too

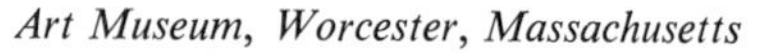
Art Museum, Worcester, Massachusetts

Private collection

Right: Boy with Squirrel, *John Singleton Copley's portrait of his half-brother, the first painting made on American soil to win professional recognition in Europe. It won Copley membership in Britain's Society of Artists in 1766. Above:* Mrs. Perez Morton, *by Gilbert Stuart, 1802.*

somehow made his way overseas (in 1775, when he was 20) to England. In the course of time, like an iron filing drawn to a magnet, he too joined the group in London whom Benjamin West befriended. Instantly popular because of his dashing charm, highly gifted as a portraitist, and always deeply in debt, Stuart spent a mad 17 years in England and Ireland, then in 1792, perhaps to escape his creditors, returned to America, which was by that time the proudly independent United States.

Almost at once he became the new nation's unchallenged leader among artists. In the course of the next 36 years he painted practically everyone of importance at least once, General Washington times without number. But we have now crossed an invisible bridge of time into a new age, which we shall consider in the next chapter.

Eighteenth Century England Before the Great Revolutions

Let us try to reconstruct the European world prior to about 1750, and since England was soon to be the pioneer of change, let us focus our reconstruction there. Perhaps the most striking difference between that far-off world and ours was the smaller population. Imperial Rome in the time of Trajan had

Marriage a la Mode, I, *by William Hogarth, the first in a series of six scenes painted in 1745 tracing the disastrous course of an eighteenth-century marriage. In this first scene a noble lord is arranging the betrothal of his son to the daughter of a rich tradesman. In return the tradesman is arranging to pay off the nobleman's debts incurred by his over-ambitious attempt to build a palatial mansion, visible out the window. The lord, suffering from gout, sits proudly pointing to his family tree which springs from William the Conqueror. The young couple, bored, weak and over-indulged, sit completely indifferent to each other, while the man who in later scenes turns out to be the villain of the story whispers honeyed words in the girl's ear.*

held at least a million people. In about 1700, London, already the largest city in Europe, was only half as large. Even so, one out of every ten Englishmen lived there.

Early eighteenth-century London can be looked upon as a galaxy of focal points. Of these the most spectacular was the royal palace at Whitehall, where their royal highnesses the king and queen, surrounded by a complex retinue of lords and ladies in waiting, counselors, secretaries, servants on various levels, and guardsmen, held court amid great ceremony and ruled the worlds of politics and fashion. Hardly less spectacular as a center of ceremony but already greater in power were the Houses of Parliament, the House of Lords and the increasingly powerful House of Commons, still in the firm grip of the landed gentry. For land and the products of farming were still the chief source of England's wealth and Englishmen's power. Lesser focal points were the town houses of England's noble lords, each a minor palace, each with its own complex retinue of retainers and servants, to which their lordships came from their country estates, riding in great coaches, whenever Parliament, the king, or the social season summoned them.

Filling up much of the rest of London were thousands of minutely small focal points, the close-knit families of London's tradesmen, merchants and artisans: cloth merchants, wine merchants, tea merchants, butchers, greengrocers, tailors, shoe and bootmakers, wigmakers, swordsmiths, goldsmiths, furniture makers, printers, engravers, an endless array of callings. The master of each household, his wife, their children, their surprisingly large number of servants (perhaps three or four), and often two or three apprentices, lived,

Collection Mr. and Mrs. Paul Mellon, Washington, D.C.

View of London and the Thames on Lord Mayor's Day, by Antonio Canaletto, 37×50 in., about 1746. The Lord Mayor's barge, attended by barges of the city's chief guilds, is on its way to Westminster where the Mayor will be sworn in according to ancient custom. A complex landscape such as this was perhaps created with the aid of a camera obscura, *or precursor of the box camera. It was a black tent with a small hole at the top and a table within. By mirror and lens the outside scene was projected onto the table, where the artist could then draw outlines of objects simply by tracing. All that remained was to make reproduction of the scene automatic. This last step was to be taken in 1826, when Joseph Niepce invented the chemically sensitive photographic plate.*

worked, and sold finished goods, all under one roof, in a manner reminding us of the Middle Ages.

Among these minute focal points were the houses of artists, painters whose livelihood came from portraits, landscapes, and magnificent scenes inspired by ancient history, paintings destined to hang in ornate gilt frames in drawing rooms belonging to persons of wealth. To these men (just as to the fashionable public who supported them) the giants of the late Italian Renaissance, Raphael, Michelangelo, Titian and others, were still the ideal. Alone among them William Hogarth (1697–1764) stands out for his shrewdly daring originality. Apprenticed first to a silversmith, he later mastered engraving, drawing and painting by sheer dogged determination. He then set about painting the tumultuous, many-sided life of London as he saw it. Recognizing the popularity of the London theatre, he captured the same popularity for his paintings by producing them in series, as scenes in a dramatic story. Thus came into being *Industry and Idleness* (the contrasting stories of two London apprentices) *Marriage a la Mode*, *A Harlot's Progress*, and others. Recognizing also that the costliness of paintings limited their saleability, he reached out to a wider market by reproducing his paintings as engravings. His success was tremendous; he died bearing the title of Sergeant Painter to the King.

Of the four or five million Englishmen and women who lived outside London, only about one fourth lived in towns at all. The rest lived in little farming villages, each usually containing five hundred people or less, dotted over England's green countryside and connected by a network of winding, badly rutted roads. But if the connecting links between village and village were wretched by our standards, the connections between persons in each village had a vitality and permanence which make our own look fragile or vague. In each village not only was the population so small that everyone knew everyone else; ancient customs of cooperation bound them actively together. Every farmer tilled one or more narrow strips of land, but everyone shared the right to graze his cows on the village common. Plowing and harvesting were community undertakings, especially harvesting, when everyone, man, woman or child, farmer or not, turned out week after week, late summer and fall, to help garner the various crops. The lord or other land-owning gentleman who lived in the neighborhood, who owned the many strips of farmland, and whose family had often been a fixture for generations, administered the law. The parish church, often centuries old, was a central meeting place once a week and its repair was a matter of common concern.

Then each village was largely self-sufficient. Bread, beer and cheese, candles and "washing balls" (soap) were home made. Thread was spun, dyed, and woven at home, from wool sheared from local sheep. Local blacksmiths hammered out the tools, local tanners and cobblers made the boots and shoes, local joiners and masons built the houses to which local thatchers added the roofs. In an earlier period men were still known by their callings rather than by surnames, but by the eighteenth century the name of the calling had *become* the surname. The endless lists of Smiths in modern telephone directories hints at the ancient universal demand for iron workers in eighteenth-century England and earlier.

The fact that everything in each village was hand made gave men and women an opportunity which we do not have, that of practicing various folk arts. If most of these were rather folk crafts, where the potters and smiths and builders, the tailors and cobblers and embroiderers, turned out the same traditional forms all their lives with only timid variations, each man or woman still had the satisfaction of having made things well, things whose looks and durability had been tested and approved by lifelong neighbors.

In the farming villages of England there were strong ties of still another kind, dramatizing the villagers' work as farmers, the importance to them of the passing seasons, and their connection through these with their own remote past. These ties were supplied by the village festivals and forms of recreation, which stretched back into England's neolithic age. Christmas, Easter, St. John the Baptist's Day, and Michaelmas were Christianized replacements of pagan festivals as old as Stonehenge celebrating the four great solar events of each year (the shortest and longest days, and the equinoxes). These in turn marked divisions of the year vitally important to farmers and animal breeders. Some country dances, and the use of mistletoe and holly at Christmas, were vestiges of the religious practices of England's long-vanished farmer-hunters and perhaps of their priests, the druids. Fairy tales, an already disappearing art form, handed down for countless generations by word of mouth, were the remnants of pre-Christian beliefs in the spirits, friendly or hostile, who dwelt in England's fields and forests. And occasionally one could find some old woman who secretly brewed herbal cures for ailments, sold love potions, or for a small price offered to rescue cattle from the evil eye. These were the last ghostly remains of England's shamans.

Such was life in the early eighteenth century, rich in ties between man and man, between man and the work of his hands, and between man and his remote past. But before the century was to end, forces of a new kind were to start eroding or shattering those ties one by one. Human life was to take new and difficult directions, never again to find its way back.

Photo Hirmer Verlag, Munich

Late Baroque ornateness at its height: the Bavarian Pilgrimage Church "Die Wies," constructed 1745–1754 from plans by the German architect Dominikus Zimmermann.

Eighteenth Century Europe: The Shift in Taste

In 1700 the Baroque era was in full swing. Wherever men had wealth and exerted power they gave themselves a magnificently florid setting, heavy with gilded sculpture and rich-hued drapery. Not buildings alone, but the furniture within them, and the coaches and ships in which men of rank traveled, were ponderously ornate. The music to which they listened had the glorious, complex richness and power of Bach, Handel, Vivaldi, and Gabrieli. Then, in the mid-century, began a swing in the opposite direction. Let us consider two possible causes for this.

The aristocrats of Europe, who cherished the tradition of "glory" or personal display, were waning in power, as wealth based on ownership of land gradually decreased in importance and wealth from commerce began to replace it. This slow change had been going forward in Europe for centuries. It was not yet violent enough to cause a revolution in society, only a revolution in taste, as the sober, common sense approach to life of the merchant began to make itself felt in contrast to the spendthrift vanity of a declining nobility.

Bibliotheque Nationale, Paris

Neoclassical severity at its height. Design for a tomb for Sir Isaac Newton, by the French architect Etienne-Louis Boullée, 1784.

Another force at work was the slow discovery that the coolly logical methods of the mechanic, the engineer, and the pure scientist were proving to be a key to man's gradual mastery of the forces of nature. Confidence in this discovery was slow and hesitant, but it was on its way.

Just after 1750 people's taste began gradually to turn away from Baroque richness, toward the simple and austere in art and architecture. The chief spokesman for the change was a German, Johann Joachim Winckelmann (1717–1768), who is regarded as the leading founder of *Neoclassicism.* In 1755 he published a work, *On the Imitation of Greek Works of Art*, in which he held up as ideals the "noble simplicity and calm grandeur" of the Hellenic world, as it was then known. A great stimulus to the enthusiasm for a return to classic simplicity was given by the rediscovery of the ruins of Hellenistic Pompeii and Herculaneum (or, perhaps more accurately, the interest in classicism stimulated the rediscovery). In 1764 Winckelmann published Europe's first serious history of art, in which he extolled Greek art above Roman. A trend was launched which was to continue well into the next century.

But this groping toward ancient Greek ideals did not include a revival of Greek standards of proportion; rather the reverse. In England, one of Europe's two leading centers of advance in science, the experimental approach was beginning to invade fields of taste. By the end of the century the English artist John Constable was declaring that painting was an experimental science, like physics. It may not be surprising, therefore, to find English writers on architecture stating that the proportions of a building cannot be predetermined mathematically, but must be planned entirely on the basis of how they look to the human eye. They attacked even the simple ratios of proportion initiated by Alberti and publicized by Palladio. Architecture was to enter on an age of what can be called empirical design, in which proportions were determined by the personal sense-perceptions of the architect.

Courtesy the Consulate of India, San Francisco

India's most famous structure, the Taj Mahal, at Agra, on the bank of the Jumna River, northern India. It was erected between 1631 and 1653 at the command of the Mohammedan ruler Shah Jehan. The Shah intended that this pure white marble structure should have an exact duplicate, in black marble, on the Jumna's opposite bank. But one of his sons deposed him before the extravagant dream could be realized.

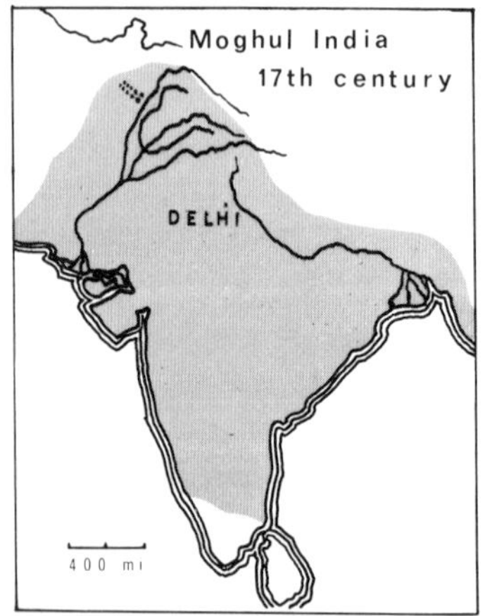

India's Moghul Empire

At the beginning of the sixteenth century India was a land divided. In the north, across the great Indus-Ganges plain, spread an empire ruled by Mohammedan Turks. The south was under the rule of native kings who were Hindus. Then, in 1524, an invader came down the Khyber Pass and smote a blow which was to change the course of history.

This invader was a Mohammedan ruler of mixed Turkish and Mongol ancestry, Zahir-ud-din Muhammed, called Babur (BahBUHR), or the Tiger. Starting out from his small kingdom in what is today Afghanistan with only 12,000 men, he entered India's northern plain intent on fulfilling his ambition of making India his. When armies ten times larger than his came against him, he defeated them decisively. The secret of his success was partly superior tactical sense and partly artillery, which he introduced into India. When he died six years later he had made a strip of land right across north India his, and had founded a dynasty of maharajas known as the Moghuls (apparently a corruption of the word Mongol).

Babur's grandson, Muhammed Akbar, was a man with a rare combination of talents and perceptions. In military affairs he was outstanding; before his death in 1605 he had united all India, from the Himalayas to her southern tip, a domain slightly larger than Asoka's of the fourth century B.C. (see page 244). Once the land was conquered, he set up an efficient, honest civil administration, in which justice was evenly dispensed and the tax burden reduced.

Akbar was remarkable in another way; in religion he was completely tolerant, respecting Mohammedans and Hindus alike. He invited Jesuit missionaries to his palace to participate in debates on the relative merits of various religions. Satisfied with none, he proposed one of his own, which died with him. His patronage of the arts and literature was generous. His library contained 24,000 volumes, whose contents were read to him; for Akbar as a boy had imperiously refused to learn to read or write.

Akbar's grandson, Shah Jehan, was an oppressive ruler who returned to the policy of persecuting all but Mohammedans, desecrating Hindu temples, expelling Christian missionaries, and grinding down the people with excessive taxes for his gratification and glory. The most famous monument to his reign is the Taj Mahal, the tomb he erected for himself and his favorite wife. To complete it, 22,000 men toiled 22 years. The mingling influences of East and West helped determine its design. The great pointed arches are Persian in origin; much of the marble work was carried out by specially imported Italians.

Shah Jehan's last years were embittered by the spectacle of his four sons warring for the right to succeed him. The course of the Moghul empire from this time on was downward. Ever weaker maharajas ruled with an ever feebler grip. Into this power vacuum the French and English moved in the eighteenth century, and fought for the right to exploit the nearly helpless prize. The winner was England.

Louvre, Paris

East meets West in seventeenth century Amsterdam. Shah Jehan with a Falcon, on Horseback, *as copied from a Moghul miniature in about 1655, by Rembrandt, on Japanese paper! Rembrandt made several free copies of Indian miniatures, which were just beginning to reach the Netherlands in the course of his lifetime.*

Precious objects created for Chinese emperors of the Ch'ing dynasty. Far right and lower left: a mountain landscape, carved from a single piece of lapis lazuli. Both faces are shown. On the right face a poem by one of the emperors has been incised, and the incisions filled with gold; 9×13 inches. Upper left and lower right: a porcelain vase, 30 inches high. As one turns the vase, the scene on it slowly changes, but the opposite faces are in complete contrast.

The audience hall (or T'ai-ho-tien) of the Chinese emperors, in the great palace compound of the Forbidden City, Peking. Red columns support roofs of yellow tile, all approached by bridges, walks and stairways of white marble.

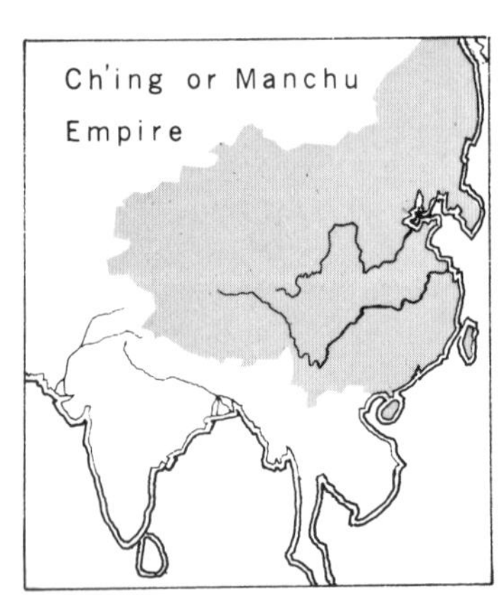

China's Ch'ing Dynasty

The great Ming dynasty followed the typical pattern of weakening as time advanced, and was finally racked by civil war. The internal conflict laid the country open to one more sweeping invasion from the north. In 1644 the Manchus came through the Great Wall, defeated the rebel government which had just overthrown the last Ming emperor, and, by seizing the reins of power at Peking, made the vast realm theirs. The new Ch'ing dynasty thus established was therefore a foreign one. It was to remain in power until the Revolution of 1912 dethroned its last member. The Ch'ing dynasty wisely preserved all Chinese institutions, imposing only one convention, namely that all men shave the forehead and wear their hair in a pigtail, as a sign of submission. This practice also continued until 1912, among Chinese everywhere in the world.

It was during the later Ming and Ch'ing dynasties that China stagnated as an international power. In the early sixteenth century she perhaps led the world in civilization. By the eighteenth, still sure of herself, she was being left behind by aggressive European advances in technology and exploration. In the nineteenth, her resulting comparative weakness was to be tragically revealed.

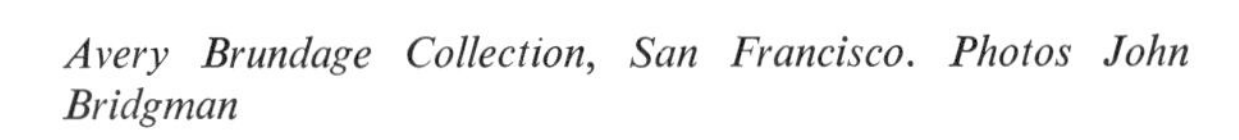

Avery Brundage Collection, San Francisco. Photos John Bridgman

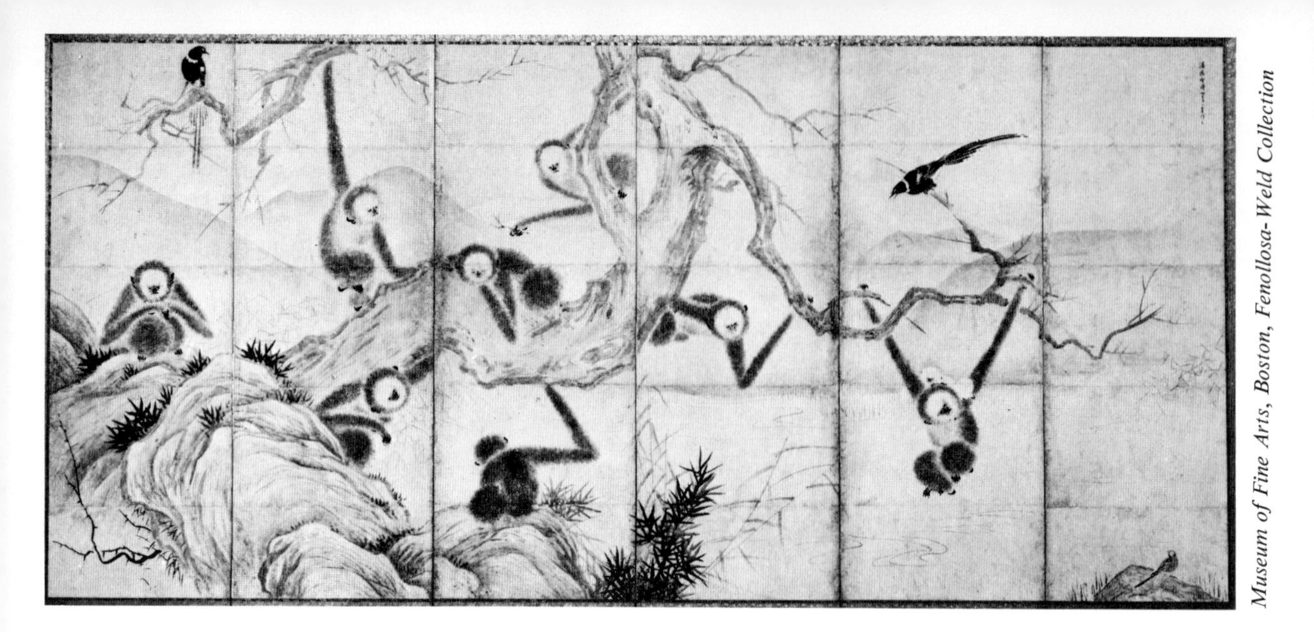

Museum of Fine Arts, Boston, Fenollosa-Weld Collection

The portable screen or movable partition, a useful piece of Japanese household furniture, was commonly adorned with exquisite painting, which increased in magnificence with the passing centuries. Above: the famous monkey screen, by the Japanese master draughtsman Sesshiu. Thirteenth century. Far right: another famous screen, waves breaking on rocks, by Korin, a Japanese master of a later period. Eighteenth century.

Japan's Flowering in Isolation

Of the great centers of power in the Orient, Japan alone maintained her independence from invaders and European influence. She united the whole chain of islands into an empire under a single ruler. She repeatedly enriched herself by contact with the cultures of China and, to some extent, India. Out of these enrichments she forged a civilization of her own, remarkable for its blend of refinement and strength.

The strongest political characteristic of Japan has been the tendency to a double center of government. The emperor, or *Tenno*, a divine person descended from the sun goddess Amaterasu, was the universal object of reverence, remote from ordinary contact with his subjects. The *shogun* was the administrative officer who dealt with political realities, and sometimes kept the emperor a virtual prisoner. Perhaps because of the strung-out nature of the country, Japan tended to remain feudal. The land was governed locally by a number of lords, or *Daimyo*, each with his Japanese version of a moated castle, and surrounded with warrior retainers, or *samurai*.

A remarkable quality of Japan's civilization has been the logical clarity with which its institutions, customs, and techniques have been conceived. In this respect the Japanese are comparable to the French. It is perhaps significant that each nation has been the creator of a unique variety of swordplay, each in its own way as brilliant and subtle as it is deadly. The fundamental difference has been that in Japan swordsmanship was treated with far greater seriousness. The skill of the samurai was part of a total way of life, involving mental and spiritual discipline. The making and mounting of Japanese sword blades was no mere craft; it was an art.

Especially striking has been the Japanese interpretation of Buddhism. This world religion reached Japan in several forms of which two are outstanding by their contrast. One looks upon the Buddha as a comforting savior, in whom mankind needs merely to believe in order to win eternal peace in Nirvana. This form is known as Amida, or "Pure Land" Buddhism. The other attempts to look on the Buddha as what he was: a man who had

Museum of Fine Arts, Boston, Fenollosa-Weld Collection

obtained insight into the nature of reality through self-discipline and deep meditation, or *dhyana*. It is the aim of those who follow this form of Buddhism to capture the Buddha's fundamental method and win an insight into reality for themselves. This courageous and direct practice the Japanese call Zen (from Zenna, a Japanese version of dhyana). Essentially, Zen is an experience of mental self-discipline and the sharpening of one's powers of concentration —under seasoned masters and lasting on the average ten years—whose aim is the experience of insight. What that experience is, the masters of Zen point out, cannot be conveyed in words. To talk about it is to miss it. It is not to be confused with trances or self-hypnosis. Nor can it be achieved passively through comfortable shortcuts. The highly focused intelligence which the practice of Zen develops has been put to various practical uses by the Japanese, for example, in swordplay, archery, calligraphy, and painting.

In the seventeenth century the Japanese, after tentatively tolerating European missionaries and merchants for some time, became suspicious of their motives and, except for a single Dutch post at Nagasaki, expelled them all. For over two centuries the land was to remain in splendid isolation.

In the seventeenth century Japanese craftsmen began to pay special attention to the Chinese technique of reproducing paintings by block printing. Japan's steadily growing merchant class bought such prints in large numbers for personal enjoyment. In response to the demand, artists designed increasingly dramatic pictures, and the craftsmen steadily refined their techniques. This scene of a storm off the Japan coast was created by the painter Gakutei, in the late eighteenth century.

Courtesy Charles Tuttle, Rutland, Vermont, and Tokyo

NOTES

[1] From the *Life of Leonardo*, A. Gaddiano, about 1540. Quoted from *Leonardo da Vinci* (Phaidon, 1944), p. 16.

[2] For example, when Pope Julius ordered Michelangelo to enrich the Sistine Chapel ceiling by using gold and bright colors, he answered, "Holy Father, in those days they did not wear gold; they never became very rich, but were holy men who despised wealth." Pope or no pope, Michelangelo kept the coloring of the ceiling subdued. His words could also have been a veiled thrust at Julius, who was far from other-wordly.

[3] Only souls whose sins were mild enough to deserve temporary punishment in Purgatory could be released. Not even the popes of the Medici family dared risk selling forgiveness for sins which had earned eternal punishment in Hell.

[4] The archbishop's problem was that he had just bought a second archbishopric (Magdeburg and Lüneburg) to add to his own (Augsburg) and had not enough money to pay the pope for it.

[5] The pace at which different parts of Europe moved toward becoming true nations was faster in some places than others. France had begun to be something like a nation under Philip Augustus in the thirteenth century (see page 340). At the opposite extreme, "Germany," even in Luther's time, was a mixed patchwork of over 300 areas held by feudal lords, bishops, archbishops, and merchant towns, some swearing loyalty to the Holy Roman Emperor, others to the pope.

[6] An eyewitness description of the capture of Rome can be found in *The Life of Benvenuto Cellini Written by Himself*, Vol. I, Chapters xxxiv–xxxviii.

[7] From Galileo's treatise, *The Assayer*, published 1626. In *The Controversy on the Comets of 1618*, Drake and O'Malley (University of Pennsylvania Press, 1960).

[8] The word *Baroque* seems to have originated with the name of Federigo Barocci (1528–1612), a north Italian, whose paintings at Rome influenced other artists. Between the Renaissance and Baroque periods art historians recognize another, called the period of *Mannerism*. See the illustrations, pages 444 to 446.

[9] The political design of the Dutch Republic is described in No. XX of *The Federalist Papers*, by Alexander Hamilton, James Madison, and John Jay.

[10] The common practice today of starting with a white canvas keeps the painter's eyes continually dazzled. The instant he covers the last inch of canvas, all the values in the painting change.

[11] From *Account of the City of Leyden*, J. Orlers, 1641; published when Rembrandt was 35.

[12] Another Frenchman of genius, Pascal, who stayed in his native land, was the first to reduce the laws of chance and probability to mathematical form. He was, that is, the father of statistics, a necessity to modern science.

[13] François Couperin, one of a family of great Parisian musicians and composers, is sometimes called "the French Bach." No one ever refers to Bach as "the German Couperin."

BOOKS ABOUT THE SIXTEENTH, SEVENTEENTH, AND EIGHTEENTH CENTURIES

EUROPE

GENERAL

The Story of Civilization, W. and A. Durant (Simon & Schuster, New York). VI: *The Reformation;* VII: *The Age of Reason Begins, 1558–1648;* VIII: *The Age of Louis XIV;* IX: *The Age of Voltaire.*
The Age of the Reformation, R. H. Bainton (Van Nostrand paperback, No. 13).
Nationalism, Its Meaning & History, H. Kohn (Van Nostrand paperback, No. 8).

TURKEY

The Seljuks in Asia Minor (Praeger paperback, 1957).
Turkey of the Ottomans, L. M. J. Garnett.
The Fall of Constantinople, S. Runciman (Cambridge University Press, 1965).
Tamerlaine the Earthshaker, H. Lamb (Garden City Pub. Co., 1928).
Suleiman the Magnificent, Sultan of the East, H. Lamb (Garden City Pub. Co., 1951).
Oriental Carpets, K. Erdman (Universe Books, New York, 1962).
Living Architecture: Ottoman, U. Vogt-Goknil (Grosset and Dunlop, New York, 1966).
Great Sea Battles, O. Warner (Macmillan, New York, 1963). Lepanto to Leyte Gulf.

EXPLORATION AND ITS CONSEQUENCES

Travel and Discovery in the Renaissance, 1420–1620, B. Penrose (Atheneum paperback 10, New York, 1962).
Christopher Colombus: Four Voyages to the New World (Corinth paperback, New York, 1961).
The African Slave Trade: Pre-Colonial History, 1450–1850, B. Davidson (Atlantic-Little Brown paperback, Boston, 1965).

REFORMATION ENGLAND

Henry VIII: a Study of Power in Action, J. Bowle (Little Brown, Boston, 1965).
The Pageant of Elizabethan England, E. Burton (Scribner paperback).
Palaces & Progresses of Elizabeth I, I. Dunlop (J. Cape, London, 1962). Fascinating look at everyday life of a sixteenth century monarch; illustrated.
Painting in Britain, 1530–1790, E. K. Waterhouse (Pelican History of Art Series, 1962).
The Armada, G. Mattingly (Houghton Mifflin paperback Sentry 17, 1959).
William Shakespeare, a biography by A. L. Rowse (Book of the Month Club).
Life and Society in the Age of Jonson, Knight.
Ben Jonson's plays (Yale University Press) (paperbacks).
Inigo Jones, C. S. Ramsay (Scribners, New York, 1924).
Commonwealth and Protectorate; the English Civil War and its Aftermath, I. Roots (Schocken, New York, 1967).
Sir Isaac Newton: A Biography, L. T. Moore (Dover paperback).

ITALY, SIXTEENTH CENTURY

The Late Renaissance and Mannerism, L. Murray (Praeger paperback, p. 219, 1967).
Italian Mannerism, J. Briganti (Van Nostrand, New York); 100 illustrations in color.

Mannerism, the European Style of the 16th Century, F. Wurtenberger (Holt, Reinhart & Winston, New York, 1962). Another lavishly illustrated book.
Michelangelo, L. Goldscheider (Phaidon, 4th ed.).
Michelangelo, A. Bertram (Dutton Vista paperback); well illustrated.
Complete Poems and Selected Letters of Michelangelo, C. Gilbert, ed. (Random House, 1963).
Vesalius (University of California Press, 1964).
The Autobiography of Benvenuto Cellini, 2 Vols. (Brentano's, New York, 1906). Abridged edition (Washington Square Press, W590).
Later Italian Painting, 1500–1900, F. M. Godfrey (Tiranti, London, paperback).
Casting a Torso in Bronze by the Cire Perdue Process, E. J. Parlanti (Tiranti, London, 1953). Valuable aid to understanding process described by Cellini; 40 pages.
Titian, E. Ripley (Lippincott).

BAROQUE AND ROCOCO EUROPE

The Age of the Baroque, 1610–1660: The Rise of Modern Europe, J. C. Friedrich (Harper TB3004, 1952).
Baroque Art in Rome, L. van Matt and V. Mariani (Universe Books, New York).
Art & Architecture in Italy, 1600–1750, R. Wittkower (Pelican History of Art, 1958).
Bernini, H. Howard (Pelican paperback, 1965).
Gian Lorenzo Bernini, Sculptor, R. Wittkower (Phaidon, 1966).
17th Century Painting, R. Cogniat (Compass Books 9, 1964).
18th Century Painting, W. Photiades (Compass Books 10, 1963).
Baroque and Rococo Art, G. Bazin (Praeger paperback, 1964).
The Creation of the Rococo, F. Kimball (Norton paperback, N268, 1943).
Tiepolo, V. Crivellato (Norton).

DUTCH PAINTING

Dutch Painting of the 17th Century, E. Meijer (McGraw-Hill, New York).
Dutch Painting, S. Slive (Abrams paperback).
Dutch Painting, P. Mitchell (Golden Press).
Rubens, a Biography, E. Ripley (Walck).
Rembrandt, Life and Work, revised ed., J. Rosenberg (Phaidon).
Rembrandt as a Draughtsman, O. Benesch (Phaidon).
Drawings of Rembrandt, introduction by S. Slive. 2 Vols. (Dover, New York).
Rembrandt and the Gospel (Meridian paperback).
Rembrandt Etchings, H. S. L. Wright (Boston Book).
Individual Artists; Inexpensive Editions
El Greco; Rembrandt; Michelangelo; Rubens (Abrams Pocket Library).
Breughel; Giorgione; Caravaggio; Michelangelo Paintings; Michelangelo Sculptures; Vermeer (Hawthorne Books, New York, All the Paintings of . . . Series).
Canaletto; Vermeer; Bosch; El Greco; Frans Hals; Titian (Barnes & Noble Art Series).
Breughel (Premier Art Library).
El Greco; Breughel (Skira); small volume series.
Velasquez; Rembrandt Self-Portraits (Tudor ABC Series).

DRAWINGS

Flemish and Dutch Drawings; German Drawings, 16th Century to Expressionism; French Drawings, 15th Century to Gericault; Spanish Drawings (Sherwood Publishers, New York, Drawings of the Masters).

FILMS

Velasquez, color, sound, 15 minutes (International Film Bureau, Inc.).
Rembrandt, Poet of Light, B & W, sound, 13 minutes (International Film Bureau, Inc.). The use of black and white is intentional, to bring out Rembrandt's use of light.

ASIA

CHINA, INDIA

Chinese Household Furniture, G. N. Kates (Dover paperback); 123 illustrations. Styles prior to western influence.
The Moghul Empire, Its Rise and Legacy, M. Prawdin (revised edition 1961, MacMillan paperback 92542).
Moghul India: Paintings & Precious Objects (Distributed for Asia House by Abrams, New York).
Indian Painting, P. S. Rawson (Universe Books, New York, 1961). Gandhara to nineteenth century.

JAPAN

Japan, a History in Art, B. Smith (Simon & Schuster, New York, 1964).
Masterpieces of Japanese Screen Painting, J. C. Covell (Crown, New York, 1962).
Sesshiu's Long Scroll, a Zen Landscape Scroll (Tuttle, Rutland Vt. & Tokyo).
Japanese Porcelain, S. Jenyns (Praeger, New York, 1965).
The Ceramic Art of Japan, H. Muensterberg (Tuttle).
The Folk Arts of Japan, H. Muensterberg (Tuttle).
Masters of the Japanese Print, from Moronobu to Utamaro, A. Gatles (Abrams, New York, 1964).
The Floating World, J. A. Michener (Random House, New York, 1954). Japanese prints.
Modern Japanese Prints, an Art Reborn, O. Statler (Tuttle, 1956–61).
Inexpensive Editions

Persian Art; Early India Art; Tong-ko and Westernmost China; Chinese Painting XI–XIV Centuries; Japanese Religious Art; Yamato-e School of Painting; Chinese Ink Painting; Japanese Picture Scrolls; Chinese Style Landscape Art; Golden Screen Paintings of Japan; Ukiyo-e (woodcuts); *Handcrafts; Japanese Ceramics;* and the following Japanese artists:

Sotatsu; Korin; Utamaro; Hokusai; Hiroshige; Shataku; Sesshiu; Taigu; Okyo (Crown, New York, Art of the East Series).

Japanese Religious Art 21; *Hand Scrolls* 22; *From Sesshiu to Ukiyo-e* (woodcuts) 23; Color Prints (Tudor ABC Series).

If any artist of the late eighteenth century can be called a prophet, who somehow sensed what vast changes lay ahead for the world of the coming century, it was the Spaniard Jose Goya (1746–1828)[1]*. Right: we see his imagination at play, perhaps foreseeing the population explosion which since Goya's time has threatened to make man a gigantic problem to himself and all life on Earth, or perhaps sensing the rising power of Europe's masses, just beginning to break the bonds of autocratic rule by one revolution after another. Below: in another imaginative work, Goya foresees man's conquest of the air. An etching from the series called* The Proverbs.

Prado, Madrid

Metropolitan Museum of Art, New York. Dick Fund

10 1776 TO THE PRESENT

Preview

The year 1776 was in several ways a fateful one. In that year a group of thirteen colonies in America revolted against the mother country's effort to regulate their trade by the policies of mercantilism. Seven years later they were an independent nation. Six years after that they had adopted the world's most enlightened constitution, setting a pattern for other nations to follow for over a century.

In the same year a quiet, astute Scotchman, Adam Smith, after ten years of labor, published the modern world's first and perhaps greatest work on political economy, *An Inquiry into the Nature and Causes of the Wealth of Nations*, a book which still works its influence on men's minds. That year also came midway between the series of inventions by which another Scotchman, James Watt, converted the clumsy, inefficient steam engine as it then existed into a practical, versatile power source, far outstripping the three sources which men already commanded: muscle, water, and wind. In the same year the western world's first iron-chain suspension bridge[2] was built, in Wales, thus ushering in a new structural principle, *tension*, to balance the age-old one of compression. And in the neighborhood of that year the French scientist Lavoisier demonstrated the existence of oxygen as a gas, laying a course from which both chemistry and physics were to take new directions.

In the year 1776, then, or close to it, men took some particularly adventurous steps *in political organization, economic thought, engineering, and pure science*—four fields of action which have changed the world at a rate hitherto undreamed of.

The short span of time from 1776 to the present has been explosive with the release of forces totally new to this planet, and new to all who inhabit it, whether man, animal, bird, fish, insect, or plant. Of all Earth's creatures we humans have been and are the source of this release. Steam generated by burning wood, then by coal, and finally by oil; hydro-electric power; the internal combustion engine; new chemical explosives; new fuels for jet and interplanetary propulsion; atomic power generated by fission and fusion these are the new power tools we have shaped for ourselves. Just as astonishing has been our gathering of knowledge. It has been estimated that, between the year 0 A.D. and about 1776, the store of human knowledge doubled; that by 1900 it had doubled again; by 1950 once again; and by 1965 still again. But with each advance in power and knowledge we have created problems: How to apply this power with restraint and judgment? How to dispose of its lethal by-products and wastes? How to use knowledge with wisdom?

Our knowledge has enabled us to control disease and the death rate, especially that of children, and to improve diet and living conditions in

Courtesy Henry Francis du Pont Winterthur Museum, U.S.A.

Benjamin West's unfinished-portrait of the American peace commissioners who came to London on their way to Paris for the signing of the treaty concluding the American Revolution, 1783. Left to right: John Jay, John Adams, Benjamin Franklin, Temple Franklin, Henry Laurens.

certain still limited areas of the Earth. But the opportunity to enjoy life, and enjoy it longer, has had the startling effect of making man himself into something like a blind physical force which has swelled into a population explosion, threatening to overrun Earth's surface, pollute its waters, and befoul its air. Knowingly or not, man has created the situation. Man must solve the problems. In this chapter we shall sketch some of the vast changes of the past two centuries or less, and their influence on the arts, causing some to change beyond recognition and others to be born.

The American Revolution

The American Revolution was a many-sided event. It was the first break between New World and Old, wherein the New declared that its destiny was its own. Struggles for power and between loyalties were involved, but so was something else. *The Revolution was in part guided by abstract principles and beliefs as to the nature of man and of government.* Theory, that is, helped to shape action. In the previous 75 years, European philosophers, notably John Locke in England and Charles de Montesquieu in France, had developed these principles on paper. It remained for well-read and practical statesmen in the colonies to bring them to flesh-and-blood life. The concept that *all men are equal, not as to their abilities, which obviously vary, but as to their rights to life, liberty, justice, and the pursuit of happiness,* is to us a commonplace. But in the eighteenth century it boldly defied the still accepted belief that men's rights depended on the class in which "it had pleased God" to place them. The concept of society as a pyramid, composed of human layers, in which privileges increased as one approached the top, took centuries to die.[3] In fact it is not yet dead.

For some comments on the music of this general period see Appendix A pages 608–13.

The French Revolution

Hardly had this new theory of man guided one nation to birth than it became a motive force in the violent rebirth of another. The French Revolution erupted under conditions vastly more hostile than the American one, and was therefore bloodier. (Louis XVI was beheaded; his son, the Dauphin, or Crown Prince, died in prison.) Not only did the revolutionaries have to shatter the rigid shell of an existing system, the kingdom and arrogant nobility of France, but they did so surrounded by other kingdoms whose rulers, in terror for their own power, instantly cooperated in attempting to crush the revolt.

To meet this threat from outside their borders, the French created a *citizen army*, larger and more formidable than anything a king of the same period could produce. A king's army fought merely for pay; a citizen army, stirred by a new force, patriotism or national pride, fought for something less tangible but more compelling. A king's army was only as large as his revenues would allow; a citizen army could mobilize a nation's total resources into the building of a war machine. For the first time, conscription, the draft, made every adult male a potential soldier.

At first the citizen army was defensive, and successfully repelled invaders from French soil. Then, under the stern hand of that statesman and military genius, Napoleon, it went on the offensive, hurling itself against one neighboring kingdom after another. Spain, Austria, the various German and Italian States, Flanders, and Holland fell. Everywhere the victorious French spread republican doctrines. Of these, the visual symbol which everybody (whether or not he could read) could understand was the "tree of liberty," which the conquerors set up in the public squares of towns wherever they went. Two time-honored rulers fell from power, their titles abolished forever: the Holy Roman Emperor and the Doge of Venice.

Napoleon began to reveal a new, disquieting side of his ambitions. When the tide of French enthusiasm for his victories was running full, he made his brothers and other relatives kings of the conquered lands ringing France, and over them placed himself as emperor. In this strangely contradictory way, the new theories of the rights of man and the new form of constitutional government were scattered all over Europe like seeds. Long after Napoleon was dead, and the various Bonaparte brothers had lost their temporary seats on those thrones, to be replaced by more reactionary monarchs, the "radical" ideas remained, taking root everywhere in men's minds and eventually sprouting to action in the wave of revolutions which were to sweep across Europe in 1848.

The French empire at the height of Napoleon's power, 1810–1812. Dark grey: France proper. Dark and medium grey: French empire. Light grey: "Greater Empire" or kingdoms subject to Napoleon.

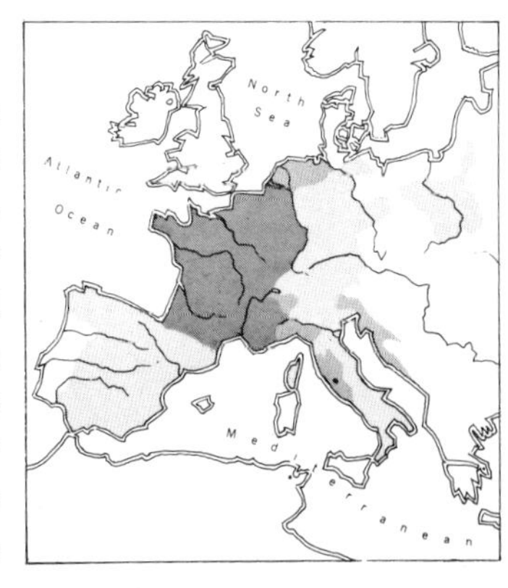

Louvre, Paris

Left: propaganda painting for the French Revolution: The Death of Marat *(Maráh), by Jacques-Louis David. Marat was a debauched tyrant, stabbed to death in his bath by the heroic fiancée of a young man he was determined to see guillotined. David made Marat into a pathetically tragic figure, a public benefactor cruelly struck down. Below: self-portrait of Jacques-Louis David (in grey coat with red collar and cuffs), at the height of his career.*

Louvre, Paris

The Artists' Role in the French Revolution

In all this chain of events, from the years before the French Revolution through its crisis known as the Reign of Terror and on into its hardening into a dictatorship under Napoleon, artists were intensely active. At times some particular painting even acted as a rallying point for public feeling, intensifying that feeling and giving it direction. Most French artists were enthusiastic supporters of the Revolution, recognizing it as a liberator of human beings from a rigid and corrupt society. This support had its tragic side, for artists risked destroying their own chief source of support, the aristocrats who had freely employed them, and the kingdom which had at times subsidized them.

The deepest desire of most of the artists, however, seems to have been to share in creating a new, freer, and more moral society. They even attacked the old structure of artistic prestige by abolishing the Academy of Painting and Sculpture and by throwing open the great annual Salons to all competitors. From 1789, the year the Revolution erupted, to 1795, the number of paintings admitted to the Salon rose from 350 to over 3000. They replaced the old Academy with an organization called the *Popular and Republican Society of the Arts* which would admit practically anyone whose patriotism was unquestioned! The École Académique became, and remains to this day, the École des Beaux Arts (School of Fine Arts).

The National Convention, the elected body which was governing France at this time, paid some attention, but not enough, to the part artists were playing in the cause, and to the sacrifices they were making. The Convention voted public funds for the recognition of artistic achievement, only a fraction of which was distributed. As a group the artists of France suffered severely from want at this time.

Jacques-Louis David and Napoleon

The most distinguished, politically active, and materially successful painter of the French Revolution was Jacques-Louis David (Dah-VEED) (1748–1825). Always impetuous, and with a childhood jaw injury which made speech difficult, his power as a draftsman was enough to start him on the ladder to success through the École Académique in Paris (see page 479). He competed for the Prix de Rome, nearly starved himself to death in grief at not winning it, returned to the attack, won the precious prize, and spent

David's painting of Napoleon's coronation ceremony. David chose the moment at which Napoleon placed a crown on the head of his wife, Josephine. This explains Napoleon's comment on the painting, quoted on page 506.

Louvre, Paris

his five years in Rome. Returning to Paris just before the Revolution, he exhibited three severely Neoclassical paintings, all based on historical or legendary events drawn from Greco-Roman history, and all involving a theme of personal sacrifice for the sake of honor or the public good. Their spirit was welcomed by a people preparing to risk ruin in order to remake their nation. David's fame was immediate, and with fame came power and political distinction. He became a *Jacobin*, or member of the most radical faction of the Revolution; briefly became President of the Convention; led in the abolition of the Academy of Painting and Drawing (École Académique); and supported Robespierre, the architect of the hideous Reign of Terror in which French aristocrats and intellectuals were guillotined by the thousand. His political paintings of this brief, intense period mirror the crisis of the just reborn French nation. Another side of his activity, highly spectacular at the time but now lost, was his work of directing great national festivals whose aim was to give the people of France a new sense of unity. David was called "Pageant Master of the Republic."

When Robespierre at last mercifully fell from power, he in turn was guillotined and his supporters imprisoned. For months David lay in jail, daily expecting death. When at last he was freed, thanks to his wife's efforts, he was a changed, subdued man. And when one day the young Napoleon walked into his studio and allowed him to start his portrait (never to be finished), David seems to have found an idol, a "strong man" to whom he could look for security. So complete was his submission that he was soon to modify even his painting style, obedient to Napoleon's views on art (finely developed through years spent in military school!). Napoleon rewarded him by commanding him to paint the scene of his coronation as emperor. But he replaced David's magnificent public festivals, in which the people shared, with military parades, which the people were allowed merely to watch.

When the huge canvas, 33 feet long and 21 feet high, was finished, Napoleon, surrounded by generals and courtiers, paid an official visit to David's studio to view it. After staring long in silence, he at last said, "It is well done, David, very well. You have divined my thoughts; you have represented me as the embodiment of French chivalry!" After further praise he went so far as to lift his hat and to say in a ringing voice, "David, I salute you!" With the correct blend of emotion and restraint, David replied, "Sire, I receive your salutation in the name of all artists . . ."

The coronation painting was only one example of Napoleon's financing of art as an official expression of the French state. Not only did he commission other artists to paint other lesser events of his reign, but he also changed the official organization of artists back again into a strictly professional, government-supported group (the Académie des Beaux Arts) with complete control over selection of paintings for the Salons. The Académie in turn became a division of the *Institute de France*, whose members represented the best of French creators in several fields, including music. Like many other systems that he launched (in law, education, etc.), this one continued after his downfall.[4] It is to David's credit that when Napoleon was overthrown, and a king was once more planted on the French throne, he chose exile rather than submission. He died ten years later in Brussels in 1825.

Alfred Wiggin Collection, Boston Public Library

Captured French naval officers being entertained by British sailors, a familiar incident common in the Napoleonic wars. The drawing, by Thomas Rowlandson, presents the British viewpoint.

Napoleon's Dogged Enemies

There were two European powers that Napoleon could not conquer. To the west, across the English Channel, was Britain, supreme now on the seas thanks to the misguided policies of Louis XIV and XV, who had both neglected to build up French colonial and naval strength. Far to the east lay the empire of the Czars, still a backward land, though vaster in sheer size than all Europe together. Both powers were hostile to France, fearful alike of the "dangerous" new ideas about human rights and of Napoleon's seemingly boundless ambitions. Napoleon for his part probably feared his two enemies. Overconfident of his capacity to defeat them, he hungered to remove them as threats.

Against the British, Napoleon at first used his favorite weapon of direct attack. But an armed invasion attempt across the channel was a disaster, and the British navy, in the battles of Nile and Trafalgar, twice defeated the French. Napoleon then resorted to economic warfare, hoping slowly to ruin England by blockading her trade with the European continent.

Against Russia, Napoleon believed he could move more directly. In the summer of 1812 he led a magnificent army across Europe, straight into the heart of the Russian empire, and by late autumn had seized Moscow itself. The Russians, setting their capital ablaze, fought him with fire and starvation. In the dead of winter, Napoleon was forced to retreat. With a worn fragment of his army he returned to Paris, compelled to recognize his attack on Russia as an utter failure and his blockade of English trading ships ineffective. He was never the same again. In less than two years, and after two decisive defeats at Leipzig and then Waterloo, he was the prisoner of the British, fated to spend the rest of his life on a lonely island in mid-Atlantic. With relief the crowned heads of Europe tried to set back the clock by restoring kings to the French throne, only to see them swept away in later revolutions, in 1830, and again in the critical year of 1848. The hands of the clock would not even stand still, for the force moving them was the hunger of men for the dignity of freedom.

Metropolitan Museum of Art, New York. Gift of Mrs. Francis Ormond

Above: etching by Goya, self-portrait at age 50. Below: Unhappy Mother *from Goya's* The Disasters of War, *published in 1810.*

Goya

In the whole of Europe there was, it seems, just one artist who was willing to see the horrors of Napoleon's wars through the eyes of the helpless ordinary people who had to endure them. This was Goya. Like many another artist, his parents were extremely poor. But unlike the others he seems never to have lost a complete identity with the people from whom he sprang. For though Goya became the favorite painter of Spanish royalty and nobility, he had an astonishing gift for painting them as if at scornful arm's length, and without mercy for revealing them as they were.

By contrast he was perhaps the first European artist to show the poor and the suffering as if from within. When a French army under one of Napoleon's generals invaded Spain, Goya produced a series of etchings, called *The Disasters of War*, which revealed unflinchingly that aspect of warfare which was commonly soon forgotten because no one troubled to record it. He was the first artist to dare to speak (in pictures) for the exploited bottom stratum of Europe's society, the peasants and laborers on whose backs the whole aristocratic superstructure rested.[5]

Achenbach Collection, San Francisco

Louvre, Paris

Above: Liberty Leading the People, *by Eugene Delacroix (1798–1863) captures the spirit of the French Revolution of 1830, in which the people of Paris rose to topple Louis XVIII from his throne, on which he had been placed after Napoleon's overthrow. This is one of the few historical paintings ever executed in which a symbolic figure is successfully made part of a realistic setting. It won admission to the Paris Salon of 1831 because of its patriotic theme. But other artists of the period resented its lack of cold, supposedly classical restraint, after the manner of David and other winners of the Prix de Rome. Delacroix was the first important French painter to refuse even to compete for that prize, and who never set foot in Italy. With him Paris came into its own as Europe's art center. Below, left: European revolutions, 1820–1830. Below, right: Delacroix (de-la-CRWAH) as he saw himself at 31. A personal acquaintance said of him, "Delacroix is of a violent and fiery temper, but full of self-control, and a perfect man of the world."*

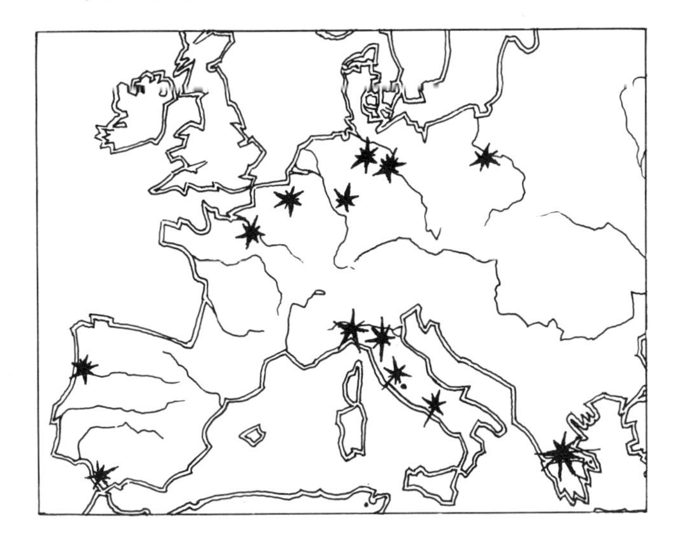

Louvre, Paris

Earl Fitzwilliam Collection, Wentworth Woodhouse, England

The practice of painting portraits of racehorses began in England in the early eighteenth century. This beautiful example of combined dynamic rhythm and disguised bilaterally symmetrical composition, Frieze of Brood Mares and Foals, *was painted by George Stubbs in 1762.*

England's Production Revolution

Even before these convulsive changes, touched off by the American Revolution, had begun to reshape life in continental Europe, another revolution, much more quiet but just as potent, was under way in England, with fateful consequences for England's farmers and craftsmen. Men of an aggressive practical bent began to increase that part of the country's productive capacity which they happened to control. One man after another moved to better his own personal condition, usually, it seems, without any particular awareness of the effect of his action on others. One of the results was to remake England into the productive center of the world, an achievement which depended in part on England's financial practices, the best in Europe.

As England's production revolution and its sister revolution in technology have spread to other lands, these in their turn have equaled or surpassed England. Advantages for certain limited areas of the world have been great: lives transformed in certain ways by more goods, a host of inventions, better health, advanced education. Along with these benefits for some, the consequences of these revolutions have been the spread of certain forms of human blight, indicating that the forces man has released to form the industrialized state are still far from under his control. When the world's population and its food supply have been brought everywhere into humane balance, when unemployment ceases to be a mounting curse, when industrial wastes have been checked from their befoulment of water and air, when war has been recognized by all men everywhere as a form of suicidal insanity, and when ways have been found to restore creative wholeness to the life of every man, woman and child, then and only then will the industrialized state have become man's servant. Technical knowledge sufficient to achieve these goals seems already available; what is needed is an act of the human will, directed to the problems of men on earth with the same intensity now being focused on interplanetary exploration.

Let us attempt a simplified sketch of the production revolution as it began in England.

Agriculture

Inspired in part by the increasing demand for English wool, and in part by farming developments in the Netherlands, English noblemen and other landowners began to break up the ancient cooperative pattern which had made their estates human communities. Each peasant had had his own strip of planting area, but all had cooperated in plowing and harvesting. And certain areas were open to all as grazing areas for animals. The hundreds, perhaps thousands, of people on each estate were thus bound together by mutual needs and by shared labor and land. But this social structure, inherited from the Middle Ages, though strong in human ties, was weak in production. The many small planting strips wasted land. Common grazing lands could easily be overloaded with cattle or worn out. The whole system resisted change, and especially the increased demand for wool. The landholders found a simple solution: they dispossessed their peasants.

In the eighteenth century some landowners began to throw together the many little strips of land, formerly held by their tenants, into broad fields, and enclosed them with walls, fences, or hedges. Here they could plow, plant crops, or graze sheep according to a single plan which each landowner, or his farm overseer, could change at will. By experiment they discovered new patterns of crop rotation surpassing any already known. And the peasants? Some were rehired as farm laborers and some as workmen to improve roads (needed to move greater loads of farm produce to market). Some drifted to towns in search of work; some migrated to the New World; some died of want. But the change went forward. Large landholders, using the new, more profitable methods, began to force small ones out of business and then bought up their land. By 1870 about 2000 men held 18 million acres, half of England's farmland.

At the same time other men were transforming England's domestic animals by selective breeding. Between 1710 and 1795, in one English market for example, the average weight of beef cattle rose from 370 to 800 pounds, and of sheep from 28 pounds to 80! On many estates, owners took pride in their magnificent specialized horses, selectively reared for racing, coaching, or hauling heavy loads.

Two systems of agriculture superimposed. The rows of hedges or enclosures radiating from the village of Padbury, Buckinghamshire, England, were determined by surveyors in 1796. Beneath them the late afternoon sun reveals the original pattern of strips which prior to that had existed since the Middle Ages.

Photo courtesy of J. K. S. St. Joseph

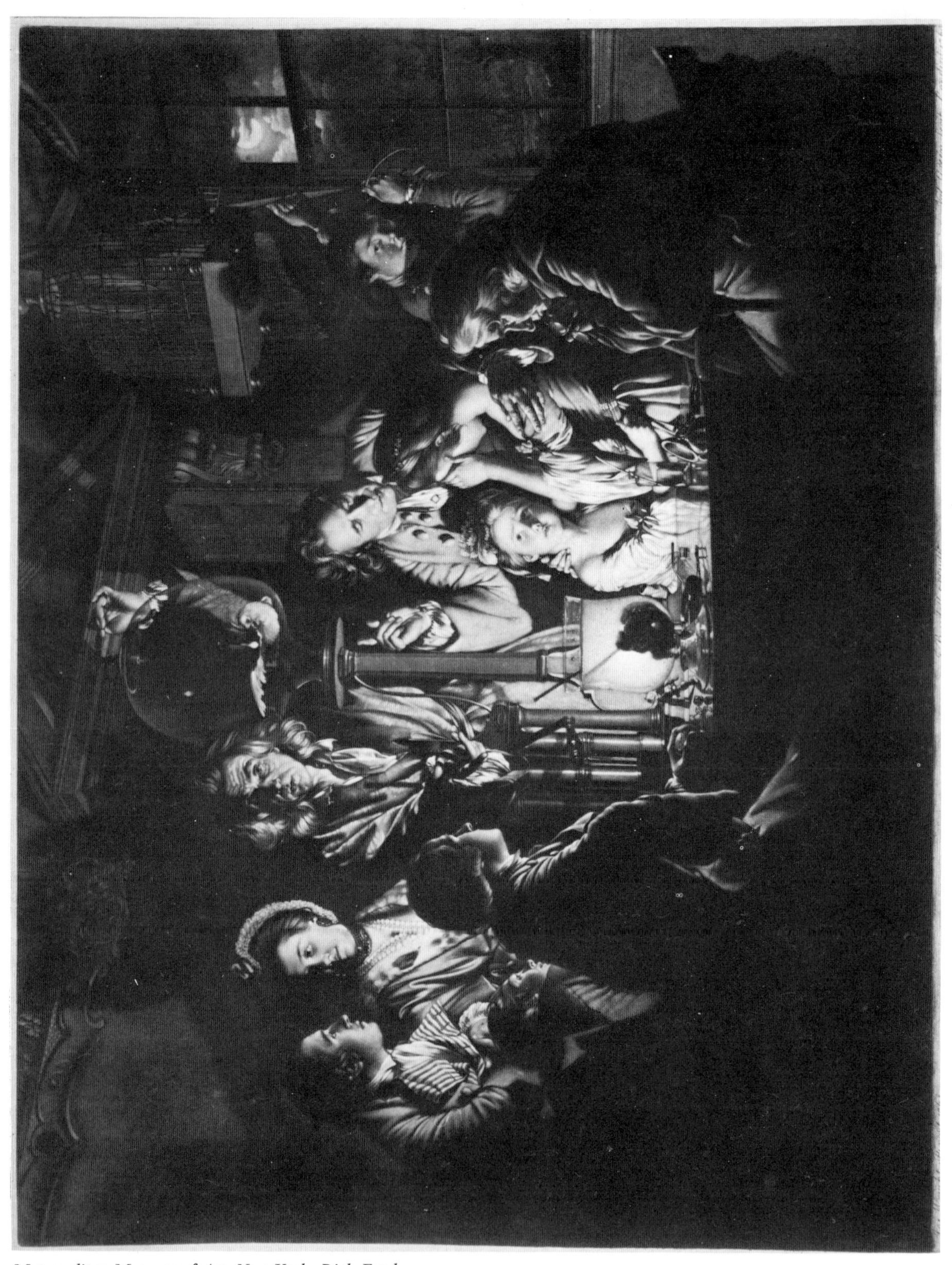

Metropolitan Museum of Art, New York. Dick Fund

Industry

Still other Englishmen were transforming the production of finished goods. The spinning, weaving, and dying of woolen thread, and the shaping of cloth into garments, had for ages been largely household occupations, like baking bread. But inventors of mechanical thread spinners, then looms, and finally sewing machines changed all this. Speed and volume of production pushed aside the old hand-crafts at about the time the landowners were uprooting the English peasantry from the land, breaking the patterns of living which had made those hand-crafts possible. The new machines required more power than a single man or woman could generate. At first horses supplied this, then flowing water, and then that new device the steam engine. The spinning and weaving machines therefore had to be grouped in factories, near these sources of power.

Wood, of which all the first machines were built, proved inadequate to the stresses of steam power and had to be replaced by iron. To withstand this new wear and tear on machinery, on the engines which turned their wheels, and on the boilers which generated their steam pressure, iron in its turn had to be tough, not brittle. Inventors discovered improved methods for iron smelting, and then for making and shaping steel. Charcoal, that destroyer of forests, which had once been the only fuel for making iron, proved inadequate to the new demands. Foundry owners replaced it with coal and then coke (coal heat treated to remove the sulfur which could make iron and steel unworkable). In 150 years, between 1700 and 1850, British steel production leaped from 12 thousand tons a year to over 2 million (nearly 17,000%!).

Next, the *parts* of machines had to fit with a precision never before needed. Other inventors therefore developed *machine tools*—drill presses and metal lathes in which a cutting edge could be firmly held and adjusted to bite into metal to an exact depth.

Transportation

Thus came into being *a complex of machine industries:* coal mines, iron mines, steel foundries, toolmakers, enginemakers, machinemakers, and finally the products of those machines for distribution and sale to the people. This complex, which had begun to invade England's meadows and woods with grimy, brick walled factories amid forests of chimneys, depended for success on one more element. Men had to find ways to haul loads of hitherto undreamed weight (coal, iron ore, iron and steel bars, machines, finished goods), and to do the job cheaply and fast. The new power source, the steam engine, was presently put to work propelling locomotives and steamships. Of the two, the steamship offered the hardest problems, solved only with the invention of fuel-saving engines and the screw propeller. Locomotives demanded level roadbeds of crushed rock supporting rails of iron. And since the vibrations of the new trains tended to jar masonry loose, iron became the preferred material for railway bridges. When both steamship and locomotive had been made effective, the last working part in England's new production complex was complete and in place.

Opposite page: science becomes popular in England. An Experiment with the Air Pump, *by Joseph Wright of Derby (1739–1797), depicts an early demonstration of the necessity of oxygen to life.*

Library of Congress

William Blake

Title page of William Blake's poem America, *1795, whose text and illustrations he engraved.*

The artist who seems to have been most profoundly aware of his times and their fateful effect on human beings was in his own lifetime almost completely unrecognized, and died as he had spent his hard-working life, a poor man. William Blake (1757–1826) was blessed with astonishing gifts. Born on the outskirts of London, son of a simple tradesman (a hosier or stocking maker), he was a poet with such a powerful imagination that it could at times transform his vision of the world. When only six he is said to have come running home one beautiful day, wide-eyed with wonder, to say that he had seen a tree in which angels were sitting. His mother, sensing his sincerity, restrained the boy's father from punishing him for lying.

As a man Blake was as remarkable an artist as he was a poet. But perhaps his greatest power, to which poetry and art played supporting roles, was his ability to look deeply into the causes of human conduct, individual and collective, to discover the sources of human sorrow arising from that conduct, and to transform his discoveries into the vivid imagery of dramatic poetry, profusely illustrated with his own drawings.

Blake's life spanned a period of upheaval. His boyhood years were the happiest he was to know. England was at peace, and the beauty of her fields and woods, spreading out close to Blake's neighborhood, inspired him as an earthly paradise to which as a man he was to look back with longing. When he was fifteen his father apprenticed him to an engraver, launching him in the trade he was to follow all his life. Three years later Blake's world of peace was shattered by the American Revolution. That the Revolution became a war was chiefly the work of King George III and his reactionary Parliament. For an important segment of public opinion, especially centered in the merchants and tradesmen of London and Bristol, was sympathetic to the American colonies and their determination to become a republic. The war was extremely unpopular. As it progressed so did desertions from the British army, and so did violence in the streets of London, climaxed by a week-long riot in 1780 (the Gordon riots) in which burning and looting were at length suppressed only by the use of the king's troops. Blake, his sympathies all with the cause of freedom, watched the whole sequence of events. Some years later he was to dramatize the Revolution in one of his long poems, entitled *America.* The chief characters of this epic are heroes and superhuman beings symbolizing both sides of the conflict. The destructive forces which the war released upon the colonies are shown as flying back across the Atlantic to bring havoc upon England.

When the French Revolution broke out in 1789, Blake's sympathies were again with the revolutionaries. Again he watched the leaders of his own country mobilize against the cause of popular freedom abroad and the voice of dissent at home: Englishmen accused of holding "republican" ideas were subject to intimidation as subversives. Blake watched the rise of Napoleon, and when Napoleon changed from champion of the French Republic to Emperor and would-be conqueror of Europe, Blake concluded, probably correctly, that this change was at least in part an over-response to attempted repression (the "Crusade against France") exerted from outside by Europe's ruling monarchs.

At the same time forces were at work in Blake's private life. When he was twenty-five he married a beautiful and sympathetic girl who for the next forty years was to prove an ideal wife, except perhaps in one respect. Brought up in a strictly Puritan family, she seems to have taken years to accept her husband's belief in the innate goodness of human instincts, thereby causing a division at whose seriousness we can only guess. Then his tremendous gifts as poet and painter were constantly frustrated by lack of recognition and the demands of his trade. When even his trade failed him at times because of lack of employment, and he and his wife were reduced to near starvation, his cup of sorrow overflowed.

Through all these trials Blake's creative genius somehow managed to find expression in a series of astonishing drawings and in his epic poems, the

British Museum

"Prophetic Books," some of which he printed page by page in his own engraving shop. In his lifetime these works were largely ignored. Those men who were aware of his existence inclined to regard him as a remarkable lunatic. Decades after his death, when his work began to receive wider attention, Blake was considered to have been something of a mystic who dwelt apart in his own private world of visions, and who drew from it the inspiration for his poetry and art. Only in recent years has a study of Blake's work from various viewpoints revealed the intensity of his interest in the world of his time, and the profundity of his interpretation of man as the creator of that world.

While scientists and inventors were following Newton's footsteps in giving a quantitative and rational interpretation to the universe, while landowners were logically pursuing a policy of efficiency by turning tenant farmers off their lands, and while factory owners were driving thousands to work in "dark, satanic mills," Blake was raising a question. *What happens to man when he allows cold reason and logic* (which Blake personalized as a superbeing called Urizen) *to rule supreme above all other faculties as the guide to his creative drives?* Blake's response was one that an artist is best suited to give: *when this is allowed to happen, the whole psychic structure of man is dislocated and he becomes less than human.* Blake respected human reason; few could use it more subtly than he. But he recognized it as properly a tool of man, or, in his symbolism, as a ministering servant rather than a ruler. To Blake, *man's normal ruling principle is his center of sensitive awareness.* Though Blake firmly rejected all forms of conventional religion, he applied to this principle symbolic names such as the Lamb of God and the Messiah. He distinguished it from imagination, which he regarded as still another of several servants of man.

Blake's dramatization of the various kinds of internal suffering which befall psychically dislocated man, and the resulting tragedies set in motion in his world, have been recognized as remarkably modern. Parallels have been found between his concepts and those of C. G. Jung, one of the fathers of psychoanalysis. And while many social, political and economic theorists, three of whom we shall presently read about, were soon to advance various theories directed at curing society's ills, none was to look as deeply as did Blake into man himself for the causes.

> The Angel that presided o'er my birth
> Said, "Little creature, form'd of Joy & Mirth,
> Go love without the help of any Thing on Earth."
>
> *From Blake's manuscripts, about 1810*

Turner, Master of Landscape

One artist who seems to have perceived these great changes and expressed one aspect of them on canvas was Joseph Mallord William Turner (1775 to 1851), a barber's son whose talent won him admission to the art school of the Royal Academy in London while he was still a boy. There are stories that Benjamin West encouraged him in his early years. When he was 21, after an unhappy love affair, Turner became something of a "loner," and

Opposite page: "The Lamb of God has rent the Veil of Mystery," *an illustration by William Blake for Night VIII of his unpublished epic dream-poem* Vala, or the Four Zoas. *For its probable significance see this page.*

poured his energy for the next half century into landscape painting. He would disappear on endless walking tours, studying the countryside throughout the British Isles and Western Europe. Of these journeys the sole records are his sketchbooks, full of jotted drawings and watercolors. In the long course of his life as an artist he developed a style of great power, revealing immense distances, cliffs, valleys, mountains, and rivers flooded with light, and the sea in all moods from sunny and calm to stormy. Unlike Goya, to whom a painting without human beings seems to have been meaningless, Turner's sweeping views of the world are lonely and rarely contain people, unless they are massed into crowds and thus become one of the forces of nature. For it was in terms of such forces that he seemed, finally, to see the world. His great later paintings sometimes rock and swirl with them, and ordinary solid things are merely suggested, dissolving away into insignificance before them. The new power of steam, which many an elegant painter shunned as no subject for an artist, caught Turner's imagination just as much as did wind and light.

National Gallery, London

Self-portrait of J. M. W. Turner as a young man, at 27.

Through the sales of his paintings, and of the many engravings made from them, Turner became a rich man. He died intending to leave much of his fortune in a fund for the support of his fellow artists, but his will was so vaguely, even illiterately written, that his wishes could not be carried out. His pictures and drawings, numbering thousands, were left to Britain's National Gallery; £20,000 went to the Royal Academy. The rest went to his relatives, whom, with the exception of his beloved old father, he had always shunned.

England's Production Revolution Continued: Applications at Home and Abroad

The men whose will and ingenuity had created England's great production complex were quick to find many ways to use it. Among the first of these was the extension of factory methods of spinning and weaving from wool to cotton. For a century and more the East India Company had been buying cotton fabrics ready-woven in India for transport to Britain. Instead merchants now began to buy Indian raw cotton and to ship it home for spinning and weaving on English power spinners and power looms. Of the finished goods some were actually reshipped to India for sale there. British manufacturers and merchants prospered; the economy of India suffered. Soon planters in the southern United States found they could make a profit by raising cotton instead of tobacco and selling cotton bales to the British.

Manufacturers next applied the machine process to entirely new materials —the production of tableware and crockery, furniture and wallpaper, boots and shoes, to mention a few. When Napoleon was preparing for the ill-starred invasion of Russia, his quartermasters found themselves buying army boots made in Britain which had been smuggled onto the continent past the French blockade.

And when Napoleon had at last been defeated and exiled, enterprising men in France and other European nations began to copy British methods. At first they imported British machinery, then developed their own machine

National Gallery, London. Reproduced by courtesy of the Trustees

Rain, Steam, and Speed, *by J. M. W. Turner, 1844, when the artist was 70. Turner here shows an early express train crossing one of the world's first iron bridges, on route to London. Physical details blur and dissolve as if to allow the forces at work to become visible.*

and tool making potential. The young United States, unhampered by tradition and with vast resources of land and raw materials, began to develop her own industrial complexes of heavy industry (just as in Europe), where sources of coal and iron were close together, and her lighter industries near sources of water power and of fuel for steam power.

Markets

The power to produce new volumes of goods, and to transport them quickly and cheaply, is useless unless one can sell them at a profit. Buyers must be found, and in large numbers. Buyers for British goods came from several sources. There was, first of all, Britain herself. As her food supply grew more abundant, and as factories provided a living for hosts of people in a limited area, England could and did support more people than ever before. A land which in 1700 could support less than six million was by 1850 supporting eighteen million. These new multitudes were, of course, buyers of the very clothes and home furnishings they were helping to produce.

Next, there was the nearby continent of Europe. Here, in spite of the devastating wars which England managed partially to avoid, a population increase was also on the way, but the production revolution, already begun in England, was there somewhat delayed. The demand for English goods in continental Europe was therefore strong enough at first to attract those goods right through a naval blockade.

Bibliotheque Nationale, Paris

A French chocolate mill of the early nineteenth century (1819), powered by steam and with frame supported by cast-iron Corinthian columns. In the nineteenth century a number of daring experimenters in structural engineering (see opposite page) began to use iron as building material on an unheard of scale. With the coming of cast and wrought iron, the standards of architectural design and taste, painstakingly developed over the centuries to apply to stone as a building material, suddenly became obsolete. Designers at first reacted by reproducing classical architectural forms in iron. They then began to strike out on their own, searching for new forms suited to the new material.

Then there were England's new colonies. India as a market for British goods has already been mentioned. The once great Moghul empire, afflicted with weak rulers, had become a helpless prize over which the British and French fought in the eighteenth century. England won, and step by step made the whole subcontinent hers, from Ceylon to the Himalayas. At the same time, British pioneers in Australia and New Zealand (which the British had claimed in 1786) and Canada (taken from France in 1756) created a constant demand for goods from the homeland, especially before these colonies had developed their own industries.

And then there was that other huge Oriental empire, China. By bitter experience with the Portuguese, the Chinese emperors had learned to keep a tight rein on merchants from Europe, limiting them to certain ports and barring them from the interior. The Chinese attitude toward Europeans in the seventeenth and eighteenth centuries is expressed by a famous letter from the emperor Chien Lung to King George III of England in response to the king's request for a trading agreement:

> I set no value on objects strange and ingenious, and have no use for your country's manufactures . . . I have expounded my views in detail and have commanded your tribute envoys to leave in peace on their homeward journeys. It behooves you, O King, to respect my sentiments and to display even greater devotion and loyalty in the future.

But the British were fast outstripping the Orient technically, in creating "objects strange and ingenious," including weapons. It was a knowledge of their new power, perhaps, which made the British of the nineteenth century ruthlessly aggressive, especially toward countries which had fallen behind in the production revolution. In 1838 and 1856 the British declared wars on the Chinese, forcing them to open their realm to British trade,[6] travelers, and missionaries. China, her weakness revealed, suffered partial and humiliating dismemberment as other European nations, following the British example, tore away ports and provinces from the great land mass for their own.

For the countries of western Europe, especially France, the newly united Germany, and the just created kingdom of Belgium, were catching up industrially with the British.[7] Each country's industrial complex was like a monster demanding to be fed more raw materials than its own country could produce, and requiring the disposal of its products by sale in markets overseas. The conquerors of the nineteenth century were hungry, not for gold, but (1) for sources of raw material which they could turn into finished goods at home, and (2) for markets where they could sell those finished goods abroad. With Britain, these conquering nations therefore entered into a drive to seize those parts of the Earth's surface which were still "unclaimed," that is, held by peoples unprepared to defend themselves against the most modern nineteenth century weaponry. Africa, south of the Sahara, the last continent to be fully colonized, became a prize divided between England, France, Belgium, and Germany. In 1897, for example, a British force striking inward from the central African coast conquered the ancient kingdom of Benin, burning and looting its capital (see page 64).

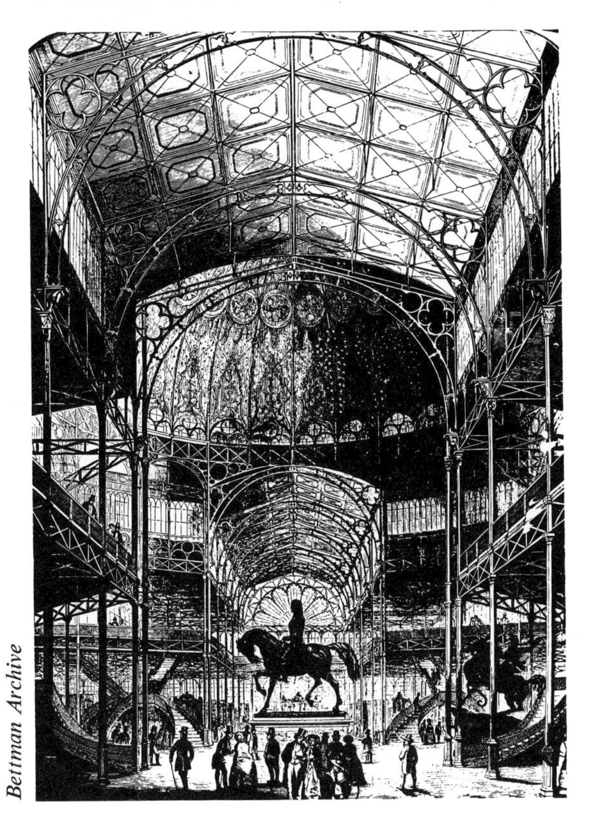

Bettman Archive

Left: the Crystal Palace, New York City, erected 1853, for an Exhibition of the Industry of All Nations. Its construction of cast iron and glass, and its name, were inspired by the Crystal Palace erected near London two years earlier for a similar exhibition. The building was an octagon, with a groundfloor area of 111,000 square feet. This picture shows the dome, which rose 170 feet above the building's center. Below: the Great Eastern, the world's first giant ocean liner, an English vessel. Its double hull of riveted wrought iron was designed in 1860 by Isambard Kingdom Brunel. He also designed the railway bridge glimpsed in Turner's painting, page 517.

Bettman Archive

Right: the Eiffel Tower, named after its engineer-designer, and erected as part of the Paris Exhibition of 1889, was for 40 years the world's tallest structure (984 feet). Its design is determined by structural requirements, and its particular kind of beauty emerges from the meeting of those requirements. The flexibility of the material (wrought iron) and the reduction of wind resistance due to the open structure were matters of deep interest at the time.

Courtesy French Embassy, New York

The young United States, moved to similar aggressive policies by her own commercial needs, compelled the hitherto tightly closed empire of Japan in 1859 to open her doors to American trade and travel. Japan's adaptive response to this experience was unique in the Oriental world. In the next 45 years she westernized and industrialized herself to such a point that she could fight a successful war with a great western power, Imperial Russia. Less than 30 years after that (1932) she was raiding the wreck of the Chinese empire more boldly and successfully than any European country had.

Last of all, there were the new independent nations of Central and South America, which had begun to stage American-style revolutions[8] against the kingdoms of Portugal and Spain. To these new revolutionary governments the British were sympathetic, not so much from a love of liberty as because the new nations were as a rule easier to trade with when independent than when they were Spanish and Portuguese colonies. True to the theory of mercantilism, these kingdoms had tried to control their colonies' trade to their own advantage.

In agriculture North America soon began to lead the world. American inventors created labor-saving farming machinery—first harvesters, then various kinds of mechanical plows, harrows, and planters. The enormous scale of the new farmlands that opened on the mid-western prairies, as pioneers and Federal troops supplied by railroads drove the Plains Indians off their hunting grounds and destroyed the trampling herds of buffalo, made such equipment a necessity. Soon the United States was outproducing Britain in grain, and shipping it there for sale at lower prices than the British themselves could demand. The British, having taught the world how to farm, found themselves resorting to perishable crops which they could still raise at a profit. For grain (and later, meat) they began to rely on foreign imports to support their ever swelling population.

England herself, now leading the world in manufacturing, could afford to abandon the rigid trade barriers of mercantilism and adopt a generous attitude of *free trade*, welcoming all foreign imports without discrimination. The writings of Adam Smith were working their gradual influence on British thinking. He had shown that *the wealth of a nation does not depend on how much money it has, so much as on how rapidly money and goods are changing hands, both within the nation and between each nation and its neighbors. In this interchange the flow of money and goods should be about equal in both directions. This*, he maintained, *could be achieved by free competition among the world's manufacturers and merchants, rather than by government controls. The secret of wealth, therefore, was in the encouragement of that free interchange, rather than in its interruption by artificial barriers.*

Smith, in his quiet, measured way, attacked the trade restrictions of the mercantile system as self-defeating. He also pointed out the harmful effects of the old guild system, which prevented workmen from moving easily from one trade to another, or even from one neighborhood to another, in response to changing demand. *A nation's economy is strong*, he said, *if it is adaptable. This adaptability springs from free competition, where individual men, having seen that a new demand for labor or goods exists, can act swiftly to meet it.*

The Artist as Journalist: Honoré Daumier

As Europe's population grew, especially in the cities, so did the popular demand for newspapers. In the course of time this demand led to the invention of machine devices for setting type (by linotype), reproducing pictures (by photogravure), and printing (by rotary presses powered by steam and then electricity). These advances began to occur after 1880. Prior to that time the weekly and then daily preparation of newsprint was a matter of hand labor. Illustrators, for instance, drew on the smooth, white painted surface of wooden blocks, and wood engravers then slowly converted these blocks into woodcuts before printing could begin.

After 1800 the reproduction of illustrations was speeded by the invention of *lithography*. It was found that if the illustrator drew with an oily pencil or crayon directly on a certain kind of limestone found in Bavaria, and the stone was then dampened with water so that it repelled oily printers' ink everywhere except where the surface was already oily from the crayon, exact prints of the drawing could be made from the surface of the stone.[9] One of the first artists to experiment with lithography was Goya, toward the end of his life.

The most remarkable and prolific lithographic artist the world has yet seen was the Frenchman Honoré Daumier. The span of his quiet, hard working life, from 1808 to 1878, spent almost entirely in Paris, enabled him to witness a period of bewildering change—growth, triumph, defeat, and recovery. Napoleon fell from power when Daumier was seven. The revolutions of 1830 and 1848, which at last put an end to kingly rule in France, occurred during his youth and early middle age. Later he was to watch the French government once more call itself an empire under Napoleon's grandson, Napoleon III, go down to defeat in the Franco-Prussian War of 1870, crush a revolution of the Parisian proletariat against the bourgeoisie, and at last become permanently a republic.

Street Players, *detail of an ink and wash drawing by Honoré Daumier, about 1860. For other examples of Daumier's work see pages 524, 530, 556.*

Collection Mme. Esnault-Pelterie

During all those years Daumier made a living as a newspaper illustrator. No one knows where he learned his astonishing mastery of drawing or his insight into human frailty. It was the combination of these two powers which made his thousands of drawings of all sides of Parisian life immensely popular. He captured on paper a whole generation in the life of a great city. We see in his lithographs no pretenses about how people or things *should* look, no theories about beauty, but a direct response of compassion, scorn, indignation, amusement, delight, disgust, or wonder at what the Parisian world spread before his eyes. But though his response may have been direct, his drawing never was; he worked entirely from memory.

Daumier's lithographs were his public side, made for an audience. Privately, in his great, bare studio in the attic above his house in Paris, he worked to please only himself. Hundreds of his drawings still exist, in which his pencil seems to have moved with a fury wilder than Rembrandt's to capture his own variety of truth. As a painter he was a constant explorer; his paintings look as if always in process, as if completing them was not his aim, but the greater understanding of form, or the capturing of a moment of action or feeling. And then there are his sculptures, made as if to help him seize on

Private Collection, Switzerland

Print Collectors, *an informal study in oils by Honoré Daumier. Only white and two colors, brown and blue (perhaps burnt siena and ultramarine), seem to have been used. By mixing these Daumier was able to create a wide range of warms and cools, an equal mixture of brown and blue making a near black. With these simple materials Daumier makes two men come alive, standing in vividly contrasting poses, bathed in strong light and deep shadow.*

a man's character all over and from all sides before pinning him down with a murderous caricature.

Human Consequences of the Production Revolution

Adam Smith's attack on the rigid policies of mercantilism and the old craft guilds took a long time to influence men's thinking, and by the time his ideas were accepted they were already partially out of date. Adam Smith had recognized that there was a conflict between employers and employees, or masters and laborers as he called them, employers wanting to force wages down, and employees to raise them. He also recognized that in this conflict the employers had the advantage. He could not foresee that this clash of interests was a mere warning breeze, the forerunner of a hurricane.

For the whole structure of society in western Europe was violently shifting.

By the two revolutions, in politics and production, merchants and manufacturers who together composed the class of bourgeoisie had seized control of governments and converted them from kingdoms into republics.[10] They had dispossessed kings and nobility of their power, reducing these aristocrats to mere ornaments of society. But these same bourgeoisie had dispossessed another level of society also. These were the peasants who had lost their strips of land, and the millions of hand-craft workers whose simple spinning wheels, looms, and other tools had been made obsolete by machines. *A large part of Europe's population had lost control of the tools of production, and had nothing left to sell but the labor of their hands.* They formed a whole class of society which has been called the *proletariat.*

The greatest opportunity for the proletariat to sell their labor was to be found in the new and growing complexes of mine and factory. Here men, women, and children were at first willing to go to work for the most pathetically small wages, for twelve or more hours a day, seven days a week, merely to keep alive. Every night they went home to wretched houses, cheaply built and without plumbing, to spend a few hours of exhausted sleep before going out to another grinding day. From this terrible life men could see scant hope of escape, or even of relief, except perhaps by occasionally getting drunk on poisonously bad liquor.

Many of the mine and factory owners were, for their part, completely callous to the plight of their employees. They were making a profit from both the sale of factory products and the rent from the cheap housing which they owned. If a man, woman, or child walked off the job, became ill, died, or was killed by machinery, there was always someone desperately waiting, ready to fight starvation by taking his place. Such was life in the great new factory towns, of which Birmingham and Manchester in England were typical, where production by machine went forward amid human suffering, degradation, and epidemic disease.

The proletariat were at first helpless in fighting their terrible plight. They had no voice in government and no representatives in Parliament. For in the eighteenth and early nineteenth centuries only persons of means (and not all of *them*) were entitled to vote. When laborers merely gathered peacefully to discuss their troubles, the meetings were sometimes scattered by charging, sabre-swinging cavalry, with a senseless toll of dead and wounded. The laborers would then in turn vent their rage by wrecking machinery and setting factories ablaze. This often happened when the factories were temporarily closed after overproducing.

In Britain the force which gradually broke and changed such conditions was that of conscience. Beginning in 1832, a few strong-willed reformers goaded Parliament into passing laws which controlled working conditions in factories. Next, step by step voting privileges were extended to more and more British adults, until (as late as 1929) the franchise was complete.

As the production revolution spread to continental Europe, human society plodded through the same painful steps: a proletarian class was forced into existence, its members were shamefully exploited, suffered from lack of representation in government, and after much delay and destructive violence were at last somewhat relieved by social legislation and the right to vote.

The machine age reveals some fallacies in existing standards of beauty. *The aristocracy of Europe had used and enjoyed art for many purposes, of which one was to display their power through the amount of human handwork required to produce their clothes, house furnishings, houses, gardens, and carriages. Any man who could wear a coat heavily embroidered and enriched with lace, or sit at his ease in a room whose walls were elegantly paneled and carved, announced thereby that he could command the labor of many craftsmen. At the same time aristocrats prided themselves on standards of restrained good taste, as part of their superiority to the rest of society. This often (though not always) kept their display from becoming "vulgar." When machinery replaced human labor, the new bourgeoisie, who were making money as factory owners or managers, recognized that they could buy cheaply an imitation of handwork and in this respect look like aristocrats overnight. They at first lacked the aristocrats' long background of educated good taste, and were willing to spend money on anything that was full of "detail." Many of these, to an aristocrat, would have been hideous.*

Bettman Archive

The Birth of Socialism

But the long period of suffering, before the proletariat of Europe found relief from cruel exploitation and from voicelessness in government, stirred men in England, France, and Germany to think about the terrible conditions they saw in the new industrial towns. What were the causes and what was the cure for this sickness of society? Their solutions were various, often conflicting. But they tended to agree that a healthy society was possible, free from these evils, and that to produce it *society*, rather than individual men, must control the new powers of production which factory owners were handling irresponsibly. Thus, in the early nineteenth century, when the misery of Europe's laboring classes was at its bitterest, came into being a wide variety of political theories usually grouped together under the name of *socialism*. Their aim was a constructive reorganization of society. But they were widely divided over how this was to be done.

Of the originators of these theories the first was the Count de St. Simon (1760–1825), a brilliant French aristocrat who fought in the American Revolution but remained aloof from the French one, being at the time engrossed in study. His noble aim was to gain an insight into the total trend of history, so that he might formulate basic ideas as to what direction civilization should take next. He saw the period from the Middle Ages to the nineteenth century as one of dissolution, the breakup of Christian religious unity into sects and the breakup of Europe's political unity into nations (to Asia he paid scant heed). Searching for new principles which would generate a new Europe, he found them in the forces of industry, finance, and science. To direct and focus these forces, he proposed the complete planning of production, both within nations and between them internationally. The planning was to be in the hands of outstandingly able men in industry and banking, who were to be advised by scientists and artists. The motive power of society was to be man's released creative power, taking visible form in production, whether of manufactured goods, scientific discoveries, or works of art. Everyone was to be paid according to the amount and quality of his production. One of his aims was to help "the largest and poorest class," the proletariat, whom he called *industrials*, a term he also applied to factory owners. He saw the industrials as united against a common enemy, the *inactives*, all those who lived as parasites off the labor of others. Among these inactives he included all military men; the future world, in St. Simon's plan, was to be at peace. St. Simon was remarkable as a prophet of planned economies, which some European nations have only lately begun to adopt with success.

Bettman Archive

Claude Henri de St. Simon. After an engraving by Perrot.

Approaching the problem of a dislocated society from a different angle, from the bottom upward instead of the top down, was the Welshman Robert Owen (1771–1858). He put his faith not in magnificent schemes for over-all planning, but in voluntary cooperation among workingmen, and between workmen and their employers. By his own example as a mill owner he showed that manufacturers could serve their own ends by actively improving the welfare and education of working people. Thus they increased the workmen's purchasing power, creating a greater market for the manufacturers' goods, and spurring the prosperity of the whole society. Owen was

Bettman Archive

Robert Owen, Welsh industrialist and philanthropist. Detail from a painting by W. H. Brooke, 1834.

deeply concerned over society's power to shape men's characters for good or ill. When employers were slow or obstinate in seeing his point, he turned to the organizing of labor unions and the formation of workmen's cooperatives, by which they could better their own lot. But he was against strikes and violence, a lifelong believer in the power of reason and persuasion. The farmers' and consumers' cooperatives which exist today in various countries including the United States can trace their origins, indirectly, to Robert Owen.

The Fabian Variety

On a basis of ideas and experiments such as these, the British have developed their own practical kind of socialism, which they have viewed as taking form through legal channels, as a continuation of reforms already under way. It has evolved slowly, in response to England's changing social and economic problems as these have become urgent. It has been flexible rather than planned. (British labor unions were declared lawful in 1824; the reform of Parliament began in 1832.) The British socialists advocated the inclusion of the proletariat in government by extending to them the right to vote, while at the same time improving their education so that their votes would be intelligent. Thus a socialist state, if it came at all, would do so because an informed public desired it. The British socialists advocated, also, the education of the bourgeoisie into the wise use of their power. This power, they further believed, should be limited. They believed that the productive forces which had repeatedly gotten out of hand could be controlled, and that certain key industries, notably railways, coal mining, and steel production, should therefore be under government management—a public responsibility instead of a private enterprise.

The movement included among its early advocates men keenly aware of the value of art and beauty in human living. Of these, one of the earliest was John Ruskin, a great English authority on Italian Renaissance art. Another was the many-sided genius William Morris, poet, business man, and one of the originators of the modern concept of interior design. He not only created patterns (inspired by plant forms) for wallpapers, textiles, and carpets, but saw the production through to completion in his own small factories. He attempted to break down the barrier between artists and craftsmen which the French and British Academies had created. These men, of only moderate influence themselves, paved the way for more influential people, including Sidney and Beatrice Webb and George Bernard Shaw, who guided the founding of *Fabian Socialism*, so named in respectful memory of the Roman general Quintus Fabius Maximus, who 2000 years earlier had helped overcome Hannibal by wearing him down through delaying tactics. Fabian Socialism has played an important part in shaping the present Labor Government of Britain.

Opposite page: working drawing for Columbine and Bluebell *chintz design, by William Morris. The design reached the production stage by 1876.*

Columbine
The property of Morris Company
26 Queen's Square
Bloomsbury
London W.C.

The Refugees, a bronze relief by Honoré Daumier. It perhaps conveys the sorrows of people involved in the unsuccessful proletarian revolt in Paris, 1848. About 15 by 30 in.

National Gallery of Art, Washington, D.C. Rosenwald Collection

The Marxist Variety

But while the political atmosphere of Britain made a gradually developing form of socialism practical as a cure for the social ills of the early nineteenth century, no such atmosphere prevailed in Germany and eastern Europe. Here for centuries emperors of feudal realms had held sway. Germany was beginning to take shape as a nation under an autocratic ruler, Frederick William IV of Prussia, whose aim was to preserve an outmoded landed aristocracy. He was hostile to republican government,[11] high finance, industry, and labor unions, as challenges to his authority. Within this oppressed state the proletariat, at the bottom of the heap of oppression, were in the most wretched plight of all.

German political thinkers responded to this clock-stopping tyranny with a wide range of beliefs and theories. In Switzerland, Paris, Brussels, or London, out of reach of the Prussian police who pounced on any German voicing suggestions of even mild reform, these exiles waged intense controversies among themselves as to which of their plans for political, economic, or intellectual action was preferable, not only for the good of Germany but of all Europe. Out of this controversy one man emerged, by virtue of his depth of knowledge, powerful logic, and sheer intolerance of opposition, to affect the future course of history.

Karl Marx (1818–1883), strong-willed son of a mild-mannered German lawyer, grew up with an intense interest in the world of culture and the intellect. Something sensitive in his nature seems to have made him exceptionally aware that a large section of his fellow men were deprived by poverty, overwork, and want of education from access to his own advantages. This awareness seems to have been the driving force which was to propel Marx through a life of intellectual toil and tumult, physical exile, and at times bitter privation.

Mastering the tools of German philosophy as a technique of thinking, and entering a long study of recent European history, he set himself the practical problem of understanding why the French Revolution, which had promised so much for the transformation of Europe, had sunk back into approval of a dictatorship under Napoleon, and had then relapsed into a return to kingly rule. He came to the conclusion that the failure sprang from men's lack of understanding of the forces actually involved. In a search for this understanding he developed a number of theories which have affected human thinking ever since. They can be accepted, qualified, or denied, but hardly ignored.

One of these is the economic determination of human thought. It is pointless, Marx maintained, to appeal to men to adopt policies which conflict with the sources of their economic security. Appeals to the bourgeoisie to yield concessions to the proletariat, or to the proletariat to cooperate with the bourgeoisie, he called futile. St. Simon had failed to interest French working men; Robert Owen had failed to convert the British wealthy class. He maintained that the bourgeoisie had usurped the power of the old landed aristocracy and at the same time had reduced Europe's lower classes to a proletariat who had nothing to sell but the toil of their hands. These two classes, the only important ones left, had become by this act alienated, with no hope of cooperation. The only hope for progress lay in their conflict. From such a conflict the proletariat, because they had "nothing to lose but their chains" and because of their steadily mounting numbers, were fated eventually to emerge the victors. Once the victory had been won, alienation would end, class distinctions disappear, and a new age of man would dawn in which the need for government would largely vanish. Because of his analysis of the causes of social and economic dislocation, Marx, and his loyal friend Frederick Engels, called his variety of socialism *scientific*, in contrast to those of St. Simon, Owen, and others, which he called *utopian* (or never-never land).

In 1847 an organization called the Communist League, meeting in London to escape the Prussian police, invited Karl Marx to prepare a statement of policy and action. The League was composed of German workingmen, but its goals were international. Marx, living in Brussels at the time, prepared with Engels' collaboration a powerfully worded statement which has since become famous, the *Communist Manifesto*. Its opening sentence was "The history of all hitherto existing society is the history of class struggles;" its closing one, "Working men of all countries, unite!" At the time Marx was 29.

The *Manifesto* seems to have been spread to various workingmen's organizations in a continental Europe already poised for revolts, and it probably shared in moving some of them. Two months after its publication there broke out in Paris the Revolution of April 1848, which overthrew a French king for the third and last time. The Parisian proletariat, contrary to the spirit publicized in Delacroix' painting of 1830, tried unsuccessfully to turn it into a revolt against the bourgeoisie also.

European revolutions, 1848.

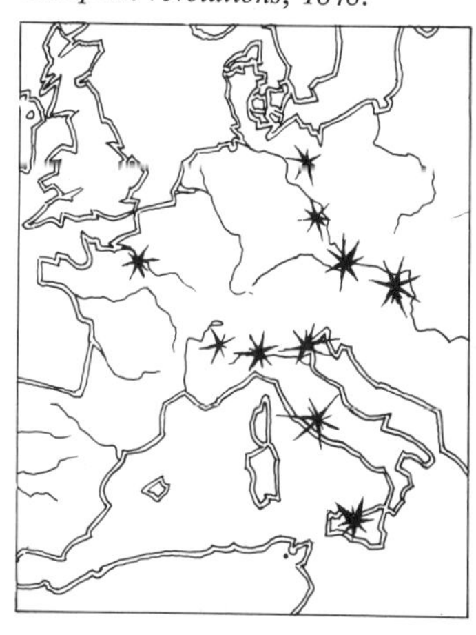

As time went on Marx and Engels, watching the course of world events and ever widening their studies, came to depart from their earlier views. In 1872 Marx stated that the working classes in the United States, England, and the Netherlands were successfully winning their goals by using their voting rights. In 1891, after Marx's death, Engels said the same thing of France. In later editions of the *Manifesto* Engels attached a footnote to the first sentence. Research, he stated, had revealed that in "primitive," that is, tribal societies, class struggle did not exist.

Lenin's Communist Party

But in eastern Europe the problems were different. Although by 1880 Germany led the world in its programs of state insurance for workmen, recognition of labor unions, and other social legislation, the German government's purpose was partly cynical—to keep socialist revolutionaries quiet and to keep power in the hands of the emperor, aristocracy, and manufacturers. The Austrian empire was still largely unindustrialized. And the vast Russian empire, which extended by this time across Siberia to the Pacific, was a hopelessly conflicting chaos of ancient institutions, corruption, inefficiency, and progress, with the fastest growing population in Europe. It was an inviting country, therefore, for a Russian, V. I. Lenin, to revive the demand for revolution, even though he was determined to make it more than merely Russian. In 1902 he founded a political party composed of hardened revolutionists, prepared to use any means to gain political control anywhere, in the name of the proletariat. He regarded the democratic process with contempt. Socialist groups more moderate than his he looked on as his prey, and showed his associates techniques for joining them in seeming friendliness, only to take them over or destroy them from within.

Their first chance to seize power successfully happened to come in Russia in 1917, when the huge Russian empire fell to pieces under the strain of World War I. Under Lenin's leadership, his minority party (called *Bolsheviki*, or "majority") forcefully seized political control of Russia. Lenin and his associates then launched the gigantic task of completely making over the geographically largest nation in the world into a completely socialized state, in which just one class, the proletariat, was recognized. As a blueprint they used the theoretical writings of Karl Marx, as summed up in his major work, *Capital.*

The contrast between the ideals and the methods of the new government was more extreme than anything in Napoleon's empire. After Lenin's death in 1924, controlling power rested in the hands of a complete and coldly treacherous dictator, Joseph Stalin, and remained there until his death in 1953. But in 50 years the well-being and average education of the Russian people have advanced centuries from somewhere in the Dark Ages. This improved well-being seems in its turn to be having certain long-range effects. Both the social structure and form of government show signs of gradually changing and evolving, but not in the direction Marx predicted over a century ago. His pure, classless, and truly communistic society seems more unreal than ever. Marx was more utopian than he had imagined.

Cosmos Explorers, *detail from a painting by the Soviet Russian artist A. A. Deinekin, 1961.*

The Arts Today in the USSR

The Soviet Russian government has followed the policy of generously supporting artists if, in return, they use their talents as social tools. A painting, piece of sculpture, musical composition, poem, novel, play, or movie receives praise from the government's official critics when it is judged suitable to arouse the enthusiasm of the Russian people in the correct direction, that is, the strengthening and advancement of the completely socialized state. Content comes first. Russian painting, for example, is often what we would call commercial illustration, but executed in a conservative style aimed at reaching millions of people with backward or unformed tastes. Anything like experiment or exploration of the abstract and subjective possibilities of painting have usually been punished by the government with public rebuke. If at such a time the artist fails to make a public confession of error his support is cut off. And since the government controls all jobs, he must then choose what the government hands him.[12]

The Soviet government is hostile not only to any form of experiment in art which is without "social content," or which fails to be readily understandable by the whole population, but it is also sensitive to any art product which carries a criticism of the existing system. In 1958 the Russian novelist Boris Pasternack was awarded the Swedish Nobel Prize in International Literature. The Soviet government forbade him to accept it, as part of the discipline meted out to him for publishing the novel, *Dr. Zhivago*, a partially unfavorable picture of Soviet society. The book has been banned in the Soviet Union, but has had a wide circulation elsewhere.

The Gymnasts' Squad, *by D. Zhilinsky, 1966. The painting suggests that the Soviet government's rigid standards of art criticism may be relaxing slightly. Until recently a composition such as this one, with its strong emphasis on visual pattern, would probably have been condemned as "formalist."*

The thirteenth and most recent Symphony by Dmitri Shostakovich, a choral and orchestral setting for five poems by the young Russian poet Yevgheny Yevtoshenko, was permitted a performance in 1962. The Soviet government then ordered a revision of the first movement (on the poem *Babi Yar*). Revisions were dutifully made and the work performed again the following year. The government, still apparently dissatisfied, has so far blocked further performances simply by doig nothing.

A tape recording of the revised work affords a remarkably dramatic listening experience, even though the listener may not understand one word of Russian, and even though the music sounds as if it had been composed perhaps a half-century ago. Shostakovich, born in 1906, has spent his life composing under the eye (or ear) of the official Soviet critics.

Even if we bear in mind that in Soviet Russia the motion picture, like other art forms, is aimed at conveying socialist propaganda, we must still recognize the magnificent achievements of the Soviet movie director Sergei Eisenstein, who died in 1948. *The Battleship Potemkin*, a silent film, is one of the world's classics whose sequences have been studied by makers of movies everywhere, and probably will be for years to come. Another remarkable silent film of his, even though in our view historically distorted, is *Ten Days that Shook the World* (original title, *October*). Of his great sound pictures, one, *Alexander Nevsky*, has a special orchestral accompaniment by the composer Prokofieff.

The Advance of the Physical Sciences

Outstripping the revolutionary changes in politics, social thought, and production which we have so far sketched in this chapter were others in pure and applied science. A brilliant application of scientific knowledge occurred during the French Revolution. In 1791 the National Convention assigned to a committee of *savants*[13] the reform of the nation's outworn and inconvenient methods of measuring distance, weight, and volume. The resulting *metric system*, because of its simplicity and logical clarity, has won acceptance far beyond the borders of France, especially among research scientists.

At the same time other men were studying forces hitherto unknown or undefined. The Englishman Michael Faraday spent most of his life experimenting with magnetism and electricity, laying foundations for the release of electrical energy. Other men—Joule in England, Ampère in France, and Ohm in Germany, for example—carried forward the study of electricity until they had clearly defined the new force and found ways to measure it. The English mathematician James Clark Maxwell then summarized their combined knowledge in mathematical formulas and equations, expressed in the language of Newton's calculus, and known as the *laws of electricity and magnetism*. Fifty years later the Italian scientist and engineer Marconi applied these laws to the invention of wireless telegraphy, and the American Lee de Forest pushed on to the invention of radio and television. The world's men of science and engineering were gradually, quietly, drawing together into a sort of informal community, whose shared knowledge was speeding discovery ever faster.

Experimenting in another direction, scientists were coming to the conclusion that the structure of matter, just as the Greek philosophers had once surmised, is *atomic*. The atomic theory was first clearly stated in modern times by James Dalton, an Englishman, close to 1800. Seventy-five years later a Russian scientist Mendelëeff arranged the chemical elements then known in a *periodic table*, in groups of eight ascending in atomic weight, whose chemical behavior kept repeating those of the eight just below. Where gaps in the table occurred, Mendelëeff predicted that elements would be discovered to fill them, predictions soon to be fulfilled. This grouping of the chemical elements was later discovered to be based on their atomic structure, and this structure in its turn was discovered to be built of electrical energy. The first nation to put the new chemical knowledge to work industrially on a large scale was the newly united German empire.

Science and the Artists of Nineteenth Century Paris

The matter-of-fact study of nature, and the relentless use of nature's forces to speed production, were beginning to transform people's everyday lives as never before. Thoughtful men in many walks of life were moved to ask the question, "What else matters?" Auguste Comte, the leading philosopher of the early nineteenth century, was declaring that the scientific method, applied to whatever men could see, hear, and touch, was the only worthwhile form of human activity. Paris (where he lived) was becoming the intellectual and cultural center of Europe. It was there that artists began to flock, not Rome. And it was at Paris that some artists began to ask, why not follow Comte's advice? Why not approach even painting scientifically? The most forward looking among them, the ones we still remember today, began to experiment along these lines. They began to exclude imagination from their work, to focus on scenes they could see, away from the artificial surroundings of their studios, and to use in their painting scientific discoveries concerning light, color, and human vision. Sir Isaac Newton had already analyzed the color spectrum in 1661. In 1839, a Frenchman, Michel Eugène Chevreul, published the first known book attempting a scientific analysis of color contrasts.[14] (This is a good place to try Project 54.) Since that time the analysis and organization of color has been repeatedly studied for different purposes.

These painter-experimenters, known first as *Realists* and then as *Impressionists*, soon found themselves in a completely new position for artists. They found everybody against them: the juries of the Paris Salons, the influential art critics who wrote for the newspapers, and the angry public. And at the very same time, science, which had beguiled them into this unpopular situation, was dealing them another cruel blow. It was robbing them of their bread-and-butter money.

The advance in chemical knowledge had opened the way indirectly for a new technical breakthrough, the invention of the *photographic plate*, exposed to light under controlled conditions, in a camera equipped with lenses and an adjustable opening. The *camera obscura* (see the illustration, page 486) had been the camera's forerunner in principle, lacking the photographic plate only. The world's first photograph seems to have been made in

National Gallery of Art, Washington, D.C., Chester Dale Collection

Opposite page: Of all the French Impressionists the most remarkable was Claude Monet (1840–1926). Cézanne once described him as "nothing but an eye, but what an eye!" In his many studies of the facade of Rouen Cathedral, of which one is shown here, the structure of the great building dissolves into glorious color, each time different depending on the time of day and the weather (1892–1894).

1826 by a Frenchman named Niepce. It took eight hours to expose. Another Frenchman, Daguerre, immediately advanced the process, and Fox Talbot, an Englishman, carried it still further by inventing the *photographic negative* from which he then made positive prints. Photographers began to do in minutes or less what would have taken an artist months, namely to create the likeness of a whole group of people, complete with a wealth of facial variety, detail of clothing, and background scenery. The invention was immediately in demand, chiefly for taking portrait photographs. The rising class of bourgeoisie had found a cheap substitute for costly painted portraits, once within the reach of the privileged classes only. There were artists of the time who believed, and publicly stated, that photography was a completely satisfying substitute for everything the artist strove to do. For such men there was just one path open, to become photographers themselves.

Photography was, in a way, a final solution to the problem which Brunelleschi had been the first to attack 400 years earlier when he made a precise study of the Baptistry at Florence from a fixed point of view. It is easy to say that Brunelleschi's little painting, or at least the way he went about making it, was the only accurate one, the only "true" one possible.

But artists who understood their profession were quick to see where photography belonged. The great Eugene Delacroix eagerly joined one of the first photographic societies, declaring photography to be a valuable aid to the artist, but no more. The true aim of the artist, he recognized is not to *copy*, but to *compose*.

The lives of artists, nevertheless, were deeply affected, not only from the loss of portrait commissions, but for deeper reasons. As new social and industrial forces kept constantly changing their world, and as new scientific knowledge kept changing their vision of it, they found themselves continually inspired to create new ways of painting which embodied these changes. They found themselves perceiving more keenly, and changing their ideas about painting more rapidly, than the general public. Instead of appealing to public taste, they found themselves somewhere out in front of it, a group of lonely experimenters with less popular support than ever before in history. Miraculously this hard challenge has not apparently decreased either the number or the creative power of artists. Instead it has stimulated them over the past century to a marvelous burst of experiment and invention.

Paul Cézanne

Perhaps the supreme nineteenth century example of this life of experiment, in terms not only of achievement but of the sacrifices it required, was Paul Cézanne (1839–1906). To summarize his life in a sentence, Cézanne was the son of a wealthy banker, was therefore free to devote all his life to painting, and died honored as a great leader of progress in art. What the summary leaves out is a tormenting undercurrent of frustration and suffering. Cézanne endured nearly a lifetime of rejection, either cool or angry, by the accepted art circles of Paris, his paintings constantly refused by the juries of the Paris Salons, and his style savagely attacked or ridiculed by leading

Museum of Modern Art, New York. With permission of Mr. André Meyer

Cézanne's snow scene. He painted it in 1880, after staying with some friends on their estate near Paris. Heavy snow was an unusual experience to Cézanne, most of whose best work was done under the stronger light and warmer sun of the region around Aix in southern France.

art critics. His closest friends sympathized with him as "never having matured." All this he endured while living on an allowance barely enough for one, but supporting, somehow, a wife and child. For Cézanne's father could never accept his son's determination to paint. Not until the old man died did Paul begin to enjoy financial security; he was then nearly 50. And not until 1904, two years before Cézanne died, did the Paris Salon willingly accept his paintings, and leading critics praise them.

This lifetime of bitter trials left its mark on Cézanne's health and emotions. Once, in his last years, when a young man expressed admiration for his painting, Cézanne snarled, "Don't make fun of me young man, see!" then sensing his mistake said tearfully, "Ah, what wrong that mob has done me! So it is the (landscape of) Sainte-Victoire of course that you so much liked. Well I never! You really like that canvas? Tomorrow you shall have it . . ."[15]

He suffered, finally, from diabetes, but kept constantly at work, writing to his son such sentences as, ". . . only oil painting can keep me going. The search must go on. It is nature I have to render . . . but there I go again, always saying the same thing." Within a week of his death he was still painting.

Just what advances did Cézanne make? He expressed his own beliefs and aims in a tentative, open-ended way. He distrusted freezing them into rules which might get between him and his perpetual search for truth. He sensed that this search is endless for the artist in one way just as it is for the scientist in another.

And there is a certain scientific quality to Cézanne's mature work. It is focused on things he could study directly: landscapes, motionless people, or arrangements of fruit and furniture—still lifes—all of which he had to have right before him as he worked. These excited him intensely as subjects for paintings, but his excitement stopped there. Any person who posed for him became of equal importance with a mountain or an apple, expected to stay

Courtesy M. Jacques Daber, Paris

The photograph from which Cézanne worked in creating the composition shown in the previous illustration. Note the removal of useless detail, the close following of the photograph where it can help the composition, and the departure from it where the composition required.

motionless indefinitely, for Cézanne was an extremely slow, as well as deeply thoughtful, painter. His work betrays no trace of human involvement. The contrast with the work of men like Delacroix and Daumier is startling. Yet his purpose was not self-centered. He once remarked that "The painter should consecrate himself entirely to the study of nature and try to produce paintings which will teach (others)."

But Cézanne was not *copying* nature. He was doing something much more remarkable: transforming it. The object before him to be painted he called his *motif*, his starting point. Cézanne sensed that since the universe in which we live is a single, vast, consistent structure held together by the operation of physical laws (such as gravity), slavishly to copy any part of this universe is just to imitate a fragment, something incomplete. By contrast, a work of art must be in its own way complete. *Every time an artist produces a painting, sculpture, poem, drama, symphony, or building, he creates a little universe.* This is what it is to create, as distinct from merely making or assembling things, or copying them.

Cézanne devoted his life to the problem of translating fragments of the great physical universe into a series of little universes on canvas. His greatness rests, perhaps, on his magic power to do this and remain true to both at once, to maintain, as it were, a state of tension between them. He recognized that just as the great universe holds together and moves because it operates true to certain physical laws, so a painting is held together as a visual experience by certain laws of its own. Unlike the laws of science, which are discovered, the source of the laws of painting is *the artist himself*. As he grows and changes, they too tend to change.

Not all the laws which govern Cézanne's paintings were original with him. He was keenly aware of this, and of himself as part of a great tradition, to which his own additions were, he believed, modest. He once remarked that his ambition was to create "something solid, like the art in the museums."

Cézanne's Painting

Picture Plane Versus Illusion of Nature

Cézanne, like most other painters of any importance up to his time, recognized that a painting is two things at once. It is a flat colored surface, or *picture plane*, a self-sufficient work of art in its own right. It is also a study of some aspect of nature, conveying an illusion of depth.[16] By constantly recognizing these two facts as he worked, Cézanne created a state of tension between the two, but *he gave first place to the small universe of the picture plane. Its laws, its consistency, and its beauty had to come first.* This was one of his great achievements, and it was this that the men of his time could not accept. They expected to see this aspect, the composition, concealed behind the illusion, instead of dominating it.

Total Interdependence of Parts

If a painting is to be truly self-sufficient as a work of art, all its parts must be interdependent. Everything in it must contribute to unity; no needless

Portrait of Madame Cézanne, *by her husband, Paul Cézanne. Her figure fills the space from bottom to top of the canvas like a piece of powerful architectural sculpture. Her slight leftward lean is balanced by the armchair's rightward bulge. The distance backward from her knees to her hands is shortened in order to unite in a single strong design the lower and upper sections of the painting. The color modulations are everywhere rich, to be enjoyed both in themselves and as part of the total painting.*

Museum of Fine Arts, Boston. Bequest of Robert Treat Paine II

National Gallery of Art, Washington, D.C. Gift of Eugene and Agnes Meyers, 1959

Still Life with Apples and Peaches, *by Paul Cézanne, 1895. The table, bowl, and pitcher are all tipped and distorted in one direction, to balance the strong directional drive of the drapery in the other.*

parts must distract the viewer. This aspect of his work Cézanne conveyed in conversation by bringing the fingers of his two hands together until they interlocked. "I advance all of my canvas at one time together," he said; and, "drawing and color are not separate. During the process of painting, one draws." By some miracle of concentration he kept the whole picture plane developing at once, refusing to let himself get sidetracked. For this reason Cézanne's uncompleted paintings are often compositions as exciting as those he considered finished. Even the size and direction of each brush stroke contributes to the unified structure of the whole!

For this reason Cézanne carefully selected from his *motif* just those elements he needed to create a complex but unified composition. He also moved them as the structure of the slowly emerging composition demanded. One can almost watch Cézanne himself making such selections and changes by studying one of the rare paintings he made from a photograph (a snow scene, too cold to study directly, pages 538-39). Cézanne had seen the actual spot in the winter of 1880. To give consistency to the whole composition, he sometimes tipped up the immediate foreground, so that it became more in harmony with the vertical objects farther back, and so that it led the viewer's eyes strongly upward to them from the bottom edge of the canvas.

Altered Perspective

Since the picture plane comes first, Cézanne avoided, and abhorred, what he called "holes in the canvas," that is, plunges into illusions of far perspective, which invited the viewer's vision into deep space. Leonardo seems to have followed the same principle when he placed a large tree firmly over the vanishing point in his *Adoration of the Kings*. Cézanne brought distant objects forward and made them loom large as important parts of the total composition, instead of allowing them to shrink away into insignificance as they would in a photograph. Thus he avoided destroying the painting as a strong piece of design, as would have happened if its lower part were full of large, strongly colored forms, and its upper part full of ever fainter and smaller ones.

When he did this he made use of an important fact of vision: *people do not always feel depth in a painting because the laws of perspective are rigidly followed there, but simply because objects are shown as overlapping, one behind the other.* By making the objects in his paintings overlap in correct sequence, he could create the moderate depth he desired, and could at the same time alter the sizes of objects to satisfy the demands of the composition.

Lost and Found Contours

Since all parts of a work of art must be interdependent and connected, Cézanne was careful to avoid cutting any single part of the painting completely off from the remainder, by means of an unbroken contour line. At some point he usually permitted each object's sharp outline to become indistinct, even to merge with its surroundings. He did this subtly. One has often to search for the place where a building, a tree, or an apple dissolves, as it were. The total result, strangely enough, is refreshingly natural.

Geometric Forms

Cézanne once wrote to a friend, "One must first of all study geometric forms: the cone, the cube, the cylinder, the sphere. When one knows how to render these things in their form and their planes, one ought to know how to paint." Looking at his paintings, we do not discover these forms boldly exposed. Instead they must have influenced his thinking less directly, while he worked. The effect is especially noticeable in his fruit. Somehow, without being untrue to the rich color of apples, Cézanne has first of all made them beautiful spheres. And we suddenly realize what strength and elegance Cézanne gave them by thinking *sphere* when creating them. If we look further, we realize that Cézanne must constantly have used the same device, of thinking of one suitable geometric shape after another while painting, to lend strength to the form of different objects throughout his compositions.

Tension and Dynamism

One of the great differences between the vast physical universe and Cézanne's small painted ones was, obviously, that the latter are motionless. The great Baroque painters, who filled their canvases with the dramatic thrusts and counterthrusts of figures in *apparent* motion, were unsuited to Cézanne's style of studying motionless nature. How could he give such painting vitality? If it cannot exist on the canvas, perhaps it can be stirred in the viewer.

He solved the problem by tipping and distorting forms. When a supposedly stable object leans slightly from the vertical, or slopes from the horizontal, a reaction is automatically set off in the viewer—he wants to straighten it before it falls. Something deep in all our pasts is thus roused, going back to the time when we were trying to keep our balance when learning to walk. When the tipping is done subtly, we can be stirred in this way without understanding why. Cézanne sometimes exploited this and other devices to make his seemingly static paintings arouse currents and countercurrents of corrective impulses in viewers. He balanced these forces as carefully one against another as if he were an engineer balancing weights, thrusts or stresses. *His mode of design, also, is generally asymmetrical.* Thus he made his paintings *dynamic;* he put *tensions* into them, which is another way of saying that they have a dynamic effect by arousing tensions in us. Some of Cézanne's critics, blind to the kind of aesthetic pleasure to which he was inviting them, have declared that his vision was defective. The device was not new with Cézanne, however. See Botticelli's *Adoration of the Kings*, p. 389.

Color Modulation

It is impossible to find in a later Cézanne painting any large surface colored solidly with a single hue. Such a blockish use of color he hated. Each inch of his paintings constantly changes in small color patches which form gradations and contrasts. The viewer can enjoy these intensely by slowly passing his gaze over them. In terms of color a Cézanne painting is therefore astonishingly alive, an endlessly rewarding field for exploration and discovery. The over-all effect is a richness which often makes his work stand out more compellingly than others in a gallery. To give this richness a quality of freshness, Cézanne carefully practiced an informal brush stroke. No matter how endlessly he labored to create certain effects (slowly piling up an inch or more of paint on the canvas) the final result creates the illusion of a sketch!

But Cézanne's greatest pride was his use of *color as a means of modeling forms.* As we have already seen, the artists of earlier times had made the shaded side of objects dark with washes or discolorations of black or bistre. Instead, Cézanne used *cool* colors, violets and dull purples, for shadows, and *warmer colors* in a rising gradation for parts of the object in the light, sometimes passing back to pale cool for the most strongly lighted parts. For objects whose color in the light is cold (such as pale blue), he sometimes reversed the sequence and made the shadows warmer than the light parts, but still leaning toward a subdued purple. The total effect is not merely to make the color rich; it also appeals to us as true. We begin to realize that shadows are colors, not merely dark patches.

Cézanne was not the first to discover the color of shadows. A series of other French artists, the *impressionists*, of whom Cézanne was for a time a member, had explored this. Cézanne's innovation was to use color to build up shapes, as a way of giving them solidity (he is commonly referred to as a *post-impressionist*).

Collection of the late Samuel Courtauld, London

The Bridge at Courbevoie, *a painting by Georges Seurat, 1885–1886.*

Georges Seurat

Another artist remarkable for his objectivity was Georges Seurat (1859–1891), who perhaps came as close as any nineteenth-century artist could to achieving a scientific approach to his painting. He worked out the proportions of his canvases and the compositions he created on them with mathematical precision, relying heavily on mean-and-extreme proportion. Thus he revived a device which had apparently lain abandoned by painters for centuries. Avoiding the tensions and dynamic tipping employed by Cézanne, he resorted to carefully placed vertical and horizontal forms, the result being a fascinating quality of repose.

In the use of color he was equally fastidious. He had studied the color theories of M. E. Chevreul and others, and from these he had developed a method of applying pure colors to the canvas in intermingled dots. If the viewer stood at a sufficient distance, the dots seemed to blend somewhat, to form still other colors of a sparkling freshness. This method Seurat called *Divisionism.* With reluctance he prepared a written summary of his methods a year before his death at the age of thirty-one.

Vincent van Gogh and Paul Gauguin

While Cézanne and Seurat were living out their lives of detached study, two other artists were convulsed with their separate agonies of involvement with the dehumanizing forces at work in European society. Vincent van Gogh

(1853–1890), son of a Dutch clergyman, shocked his convention-bound family by trying to become a missionary to a colony of coal miners. Failing to pass the necessary examinations in preaching, he turned at length to painting, and for the next ten years lived the intense life of an artist, supported by his understanding brother Theo, an art dealer in Paris.

Van Gogh's first paintings, made in the Netherlands, show little awareness of color. His great concern seems to have been to reveal helpless human misery. When his brother encouraged him to travel, van Gogh went first to Paris, where he discovered Impressionist and Divisionist painting, then moved on to southern France, where the intense light and color of the landscape were a revelation to him. He became absorbed in the problem of capturing this color on canvas. As a daring user of color he developed great power, but his strength in drawing was also great; his canvases are alive with forms vividly revealed through the vigorous sympathy of his compulsive brush strokes. Despairing of surmounting his periods of intense melancholy, he committed suicide at the age of thirty seven. He seems never to have lost the missionary drive. His paintings and drawings reveal an uncomplicated directness perhaps aimed at bringing delight to simple people who live by toil.

Paul Gauguin (1848–1903) was at first a successful Parisian stockbroker, whose latent talent as an artist drove him in his mid-thirties to break with his wife and children and to devote his life to painting. Deeply dissatisfied with the world of Paris, he sought to return to a simpler, purer kind of society. First he retired to the peasant world of Britanny, where he did

Woodcutter, *a drawing by Vincent van Gogh, 1885, while he was still in the Netherlands.*

Stedelijk Museum, Amsterdam

Museum of Modern Art, New York. Abby Aldrich Rockefeller Fund

Japanese influence on Parisian art. Color lithographed screen by Pierre Bonnard, 53 in. high, 1897. The flat dramatic shapes were probably inspired by Japanese prints, which were becoming available in Paris at that time (see example page 495). At about the same time Claude Debussy was composing his Images *for piano, one of which was inspired by his impression of the motionless fish on a Japanese screen.*

some of his most original work. Still dissatisfied, he moved to southern France where for a time he and van Gogh lived and worked together. But the personalities of the two men had a mutually destructive effect. Presently Gauguin fled to Tahiti, a French island possession on the opposite side of the planet. He spent most of the remainder of his life in Polynesia, painting, struggling with ill health, and coming into repeated conflict with the island authorities on behalf of the natives.

Gauguin's greatest strength as a painter was his use of flat colors arranged in daringly original shapes. His work had a wide effect not only in France but throughout Europe, especially Germany. His greatest successor was Henri Matisse (1869–1954), one of the giants of twentieth century art. Contemporary poster and advertising design with its imaginative use of arresting two-dimensional pattern and strong color owes its existence in part to the example of these men.

Art Nouveau

As the nineteenth century drew to a close, men involved in the arts, in Europe and England, were deeply concerned over the now recurrent problem of a new art suited to the times. They, like others before them, were aware of the dislocation in men's creative and productive lives which the machine age had shared in producing. Their solutions were various: some wanted to reject and abandon machine production and to restore the world of the handcraftsman. Others saw the impossibility of this and aspired instead to transform machine production into a source of beauty. But how? Out of the ferment of their deeply concerned discussion, chiefly carried on through publications in various countries, there emerged a short-lived but richly fruitful movement whose style, or styles, affected all sides of the arts, architecture, painting, sculpture, and the minor arts of design in wood, metals and glass, bookbinding and illustration. The name which this international movement finally acquired was *art nouveau.* Its essence seems to have been to give to the form of every created object an organic unity. This organic form was often inspired by plant or animal forms but at its best was by no means a copy of them. Rather each designer seemed to bring into existence a new organism with every object he created. One strong inspiring influence in the movement came from Oriental art, especially Japanese prints, whose dynamic sinuousness and exquisite design sense were just winning appreciation.

It has been said that the movement did not last because of its reliance on handcrafting and its consequent costliness. Perhaps also the creation of forms having an organic unity were in such violent contradiction to the disjointedness and dislocation evident in human living around 1900 that they could not win serious permanent acceptance. The art forms which did express this disjointedness were soon to attract universal attention.

Art Nouveau in its many aspects is now being rediscovered and appreciated after having lain for decades in neglect. Those seeing examples of it for the first time have the advantage of a fresh eye. It also may well appeal to those seeking a new unity in human living.

Doorway in Art Nouveau *style, Paris, about 1900. Organic forms vitalize both the stonework and the metal grill.*

Fratelli Fabbri Editori, Milan

Cézanne as Father of Cubism

In Cézanne's last paintings we can see color modulation leading him step by step into an ever greater concern with analyzing forms. This was logical; if one is going to show a form turning toward the light by a gradation of colors, one must think a great deal about where the correct point lies at which to move from one color to the next. One is really dividing the surface into a series of planes, each at a slightly different angle, and therefore deserving a slightly different color. In Cézanne's final paintings we can almost watch his mind at work breaking forms down into a series of plane surfaces. It was this aspect of his work which was to stimulate the next great Parisian advance in art, *cubism*.

Below: head study by Pablo Picasso, 1907. Collection Mr. and Mrs. Georges Seligmann, New York. Bottom: Bakoto cemetery guardian, from central Africa. Lowie Museum, University of California, Berkeley. Picasso saw Bakoto sculpture for the first time in 1907, and it contributed to his experiments with severe geometric forms which finally reached fulfillment in cubism.

Pablo Picasso: Early Stage

In 1900 the young Spanish artist Pablo Picasso, then 19, came from Barcelona, the art center of Spain, to Paris, that of Europe. He came with the quiet intention of exploring everything that painters had already achieved, and of discovering and digesting their constructive secrets, so that out of them he might distill his own mode of expression. This was the dream of a giant. But Picasso was equal to it, destined for 60 years to lead, charm, amaze, and outrage first Paris, then Europe, and finally the world, with his inexhaustible power to transform anything he touched into something magically alive as art. He has worked with many materials, and in many styles, some utterly unlike and conflicting. For there are many Picassos, or rather many sides to one man who still has always remained himself. He has been in turn capable of deep emotional involvement in human suffering, complete detachment in the uncompromising advance of painting, and ironic opportunism when turning out something calculated to shock a rich art patron into buying. The marvel is that he has been all these things, and more, without violating the integrity of that mysterious being underneath, Pablo Picasso.

Les Demoiselles d'Avignon

The paintings and drawings of the young Picasso reveal two strong directions: one is a probing exploration of various styles, a constant process of testing, accepting, rejecting, and re-creating to suit his own vision; the other is an intense and sensitive awareness of other human beings, their joys, pleasures and sorrows. A pastel done by Picasso at 21, a young couple in a Barcelona cafe, shown in Prologue Illustration VII, reveals this awareness. These two forces in his nature seem to have merged to produce a painting which shook the Parisian art world to its foundations in 1907. By this time Picasso had studied Cézanne's later paintings in which forms are broken down into planes, an approach which Picasso had already been exploring in his own landscapes. He had also discovered the harshly geometrical simplifications of African sculpture. In developing *Les Demoiselles d'Avignon* he drew on both these sources as modes of expression.

From its beginning, Picasso's intent seems to have been a strongly moralizing one, based, perhaps, on a remembered experience in a Barcelona

Museum of Modern Art, New York, acquired through the Lillie P. Bliss Bequest

The Avignon Street Girls (Les Demoiselles d'Avignon), *Picasso's masterpiece of 1906–1907. Thirty years were to pass before such another outcry was to burst from him* *(see page 562).*

brothel. The first studies, which still survive, show a two-sided composition in which a figure holding a skull, possibly a clergyman, is preaching to a group of naked women. But as his exploration of the subject deepened he kept simplifying and strengthening it, removing the descriptive or story-telling aspect and making the figures and the composition speak together instead. The result is an astounding outcry in which sympathy and revulsion mingle. The leaping composition, conveying the impression of a fire out of control, is achieved through the violent distortion, flattening, and geometrization not only of the five figures but of the drapery and furniture surrounding them. The women's eyes are unaligned, suggesting that the distortion is internal also. Of the five women, three are in various stages of dehumanization, as revealed by Picasso's use of forms borrowed from African masks. The remaining two fix the viewer with an agonized hypnotic stare. "Behold this world's human wreckage!" they seem to cry.

Collection Mr. and Mrs. Ralph Colin, New York

Collection Mr. and Mrs. Joseph Pulitzer, Jr., St. Louis

Above: the Rower, *by Picasso, 1910. An example of analytical cubist painting. Below:* Woman's head, *by Picasso, 1909. Analytical cubist sculpture. Right:* Harlequin, *by Picasso, 1918. An example of Synthetic Cubism, in which the forms discovered during the analytical period are used creatively and imaginatively.*

Collection Museum of Modern Art, New York

Cubism: Analytical and Synthetic

After this gigantic achievement Picasso withdrew into a detached absorption with the further dissection and geometrizing of forms. In this absorption other artists of the period joined him, especially Georges Braque. The result was the movement known as cubism. The paintings which these men produced at first played down or omitted color. All we see in them is a sort of diagram, usually in an extremely shallow picture space, in which whatever the painter was looking at is literally destroyed, dissected, taken to pieces, and replaced by a geometric construction which is a record, not so much of the object (the *motif*), as of the painter's thinking about it. Picasso, looking back on his cubist experiments, once remarked, "We wanted to paint not what you *see* but what you *know* is there." No two cubists' interpretations of the same motif would ever be the same, since no two minds analyze in the same manner, or from the same viewpoint.

Having developed their techniques for analyzing forms, Picasso, Braque, and others then went on to use them in paintings alive with color and invention. They passed from a period of *analytical* to one of *synthetic* (that is, creative) cubism.

George F. Goodyear and the Buffalo Fine Arts Academy

Collection Museum of Modern Art, New York

Whitney Museum of American Art, New York

Left: Unique Form of Continuity in Motion, *by Umberto Boccioni, 1913. Top right:* Dog on Leash, *by Giacomo Balla, 1912. Example of the Italian futurist interpretation of motion. Above:* Nude Descending a Staircase, *1913, by Marcel Duchamp, who said of it that it was a study of movement, but avoiding the crude colors of the futurists and following instead the color of the cubists.*

Futurism, Italian Offshoot of Cubism

The cubist painters of Paris had focused their attention, as had Cézanne, on motionless objects. When Italian artists visiting Paris discovered cubist methods, the idea struck them of applying it to objects in motion. They were keenly interested in the fact that when we see a moving object our eyes pick up many impressions at lightning speed which our minds combine into a single image. This was one of the revelations of the then new art of motion pictures. The Italian *futurists*, as they called themselves, began to experiment with the analysis of these images and their parts. This short-lived offshoot of Cézanne's original form analysis was interrupted by the First World War.

While this sequence of developments in painting and sculpture was under way, a different one was taking shape which was to have a far greater and more lasting influence. To understand it let us look at the course which pure mathematicians had been taking in the 60 years previous.

The New Mathematics, as of 1840 and After

A revolutionary change in nineteenth century abstract thinking began in 1840 when a Russian mathematician, Nicholas Lobachevski, published a pamphlet innocently entitled *On the Theory of Parallels.* What would happen, Lobachevski inquired, if we were to change just one of the axioms on which Euclid's geometry was based? The axiom he chose to change was the one which assumes that through a point (call it *A*) in a plane just one line can be drawn which will be parallel to another line (call it *BC*) already on the plane. *Suppose,* wrote Lobachevski, *that we assume more than one line can be drawn through A, parallel to BC. What then?*

He answered his own question by creating from Euclid's axioms and this single new one an entirely new geometry, all perfectly logical. What was the difference between Lobachevski's geometry and Euclid's? *It was to be found in the kind of space in which each could exist.* Euclid's geometry seems true for the kind of space in which we live. But who knows whether somewhere in the universe there exists a twisted, distorted kind of space where Lobachevski's geometry fits experience?

Presently another mathematician, a German named Riemann, was taking the next logical step. *Let us,* he said, change the axiom about parallels again, and *assume that through external point A no line can be drawn parallel to BC!* He then proceeded to create a geometry based on *this* axiom. And he thus found himself defining still another, queerly distorted kind of space which —who knows?—might exist in the universe somewhere.

Thus mathematicians found that by making simple changes in Euclid's axioms they could create new geometries, each existing in its own non-Euclidean space, where straight lines refuse to behave as we see them doing daily. *These new spaces exist solely in the minds of men as ideas,* but they *are* ideas—in that sense they are real. The effect on mathematical thinking was profoundly stirring; mathematicians began to experiment with axioms: "Let us assume—What then logically follows?" Mathematics, in other words, became a completely, freely creative art. Its materials were logic, and abstract ideas developed by logical reasoning from axioms selected at will, but with no necessary connection with the world as we know it.

The effect on mathematical development was astonishing. Today it is estimated that twenty men, each spending a lifetime, could hardly master the whole field of mathematics as it now exists. Vast stretches of this field are purely creative, involving ideas which exist in the human mind alone, with no foreseeable application to any known situation or problem.

The Birth of Nonobjective Painting

Shortly after 1900 something similar began to happen in painting. The Russian painter Vassily Kandinsky (1866–1944) was at this time experimenting with landscapes containing intensely vivid color relationships. Not only was he using colors strong in themselves, but his concern was also how to place them side by side in such a way as to make them "sing," that is, thrill the viewer. What happened next (in 1905) he tells best himself:

Kunsthalle, Hamburg

Three stages in Kandinsky's development as a painter: Left: Arab Cemetery. *Below, left:* Painting with White Form, *No. 166, in his early, free, nonobjective style, 1913. Below, right:* Accompanied Contrast, *No. 613, in his later, hard-edged style, 1935.*

Guggenheim Museum, New York

Guggenheim Museum, New York

It was near dusk, I was re-entering my studio with my box of colors, after a study, still deep in my thoughts and in the memory of my finished work, when I suddenly saw on the wall a painting of an extraordinary beauty, blazing with an interior light. I paused spellbound, then approached this picture-puzzle, in which I saw nothing but forms and colors, and whose subject remained incomprehensible to me. Quickly I found the key to the puzzle: it was one of my own paintings which had been hung on the wall upside down.

I knew then clearly that subject matter was needless in my painting. A frightful abyss opened at my feet . . . *What should replace subject matter?*[17]

Kandinsky struggled several years before he successfully created a kind of painting completely without subject matter, each one a universe of its own. Cézanne's thread of tension between visible world and painting had at last been cut. Painting could now move where it chose.

Kandinsky does not seem to have been directly influenced by the pure mathematicians who had already done the same thing in their own field. Rather, the same general direction of thinking among Europeans which had produced the mathematicians also produced him. What influenced him directly during his experimental period was the thought that if music could delight people through combining musical notes without imitating the *sounds* of nature, surely painters could do the same with colors and forms which never imitated nature's sights. His efforts were interrupted by the First World War, and by the Russian Revolution which shortly followed. Kandinsky offered his services to the new Russian government, found his freedom to create threatened, and chose to spend the rest of his life in exile. For the next quarter of a century he devoted himself to creating paintings in the style called *nonobjective*, that is, self-sufficient and referring to no outside object.

Kandinsky's influence mounted like a slow but compelling tide. Artist after artist began to experiment, each with creating painted worlds of his own. Sculptors presently began to experiment nonobjectively in three dimensions. The movement came into its own after the Second World War, spreading to many nations, notably the United States and Japan. For the first time artists seemed to be developing an international style, whose forms could speak to anyone who loved color and form, regardless of his local surroundings. But in the later stages of this style, when the United States became its most expressive and progressive center, other influences were also active, which we must go back and trace.

The New Psychology: The Muses are Hunted to Their Hiding Place

In 1900 the writings of the Viennese physician Sigmund Freud (1856–1939), the father of psychoanalysis, began to bring before the general public the results of his researches. Freud was a lucid writer, capable of making his points with drama and wit, and so he was widely read. His concepts of the human being as a thinking and feeling structure were complex, many-sided, and highly organized. Only one side of it concerns us here. This was Freud's description, or "discovery," of the unconscious (or *subconscious*) mind.

In his work with patients Freud had become interested in slips of the tongue and dreams. He found these seeming trifles sometimes gave valuable clues to things which patients with emotional problems were trying to conceal from themselves by "putting them out of their minds." Freud would lead his patients to face whatever they were shunning. Once they had faced it they could often return to thinking and feeling normally.

The success of his technique led Freud to recognize that *there is a part of the human mind to which thoughts can be moved, out of consciousness.* It also seemed clear that *from this unconscious region there is a natural flow of ideas into the conscious mind*, for a forceful reversal of the flow seems to produce psychological dislocation and blockage. Freud spoke of the unconscious mind as the anteroom, or waiting room, outside the conscious mind.

Freud was a physician, concerned entirely with the mentally ill. But if we look at his findings as applying to people in health, we find that he may have explained an experience common to creative people, among them artists. This is the astonishing one of having an idea for a work of art or a solution to a problem emerge into consciousness complete, or partially so. Men in different ages have explained in it different ways. Some, like Homer, believed that a goddess, a Muse, had "inspired" them, that is, filled them with the completed idea. Others have looked on their created work as having a life of its own, which "told" them how to proceed. Freud suggested that the source of inspiration, of suddenly emerging creative ideas, was man himself, and that it lay miraculously in his own unconscious self. The mystery of creation, still unsolved and perhaps unsolvable, was at least moved to a more logical place.

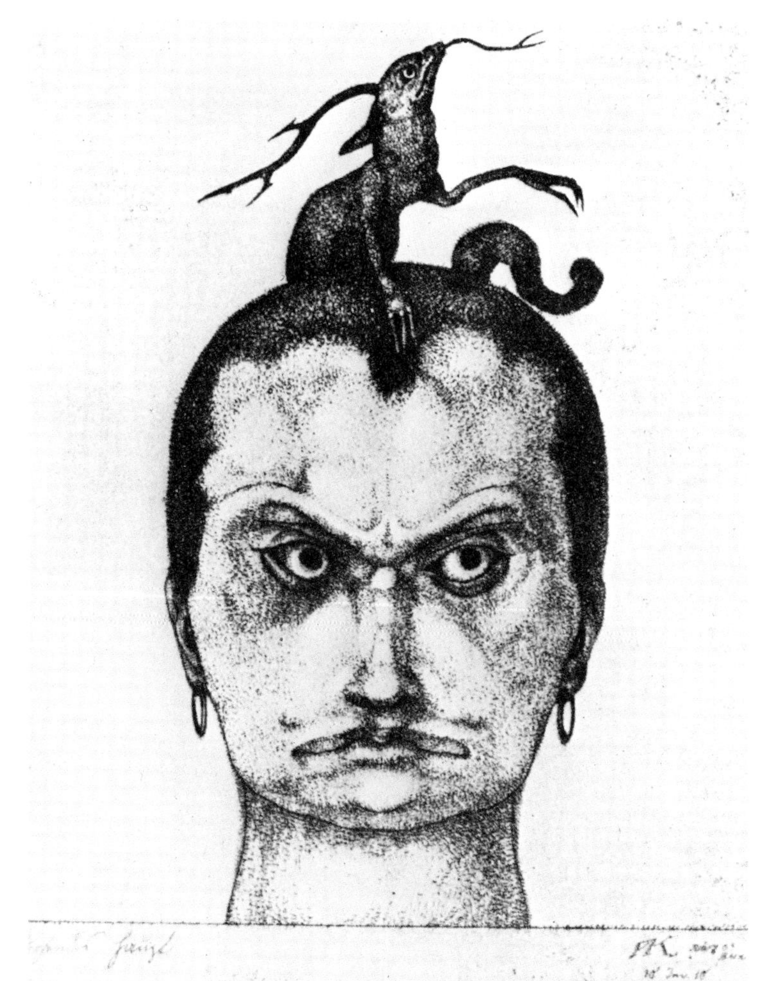

Threatening Head, *etching by Paul Klee, 1905.* *For more on Klee see page 560.*

The New Biology: Darwin's Concept of Evolution

But perhaps the profoundest change worked on the minds of nineteenth century man by scientific thinking was the discovery that *we seem to be living in a world slowly changing and evolving according to physical laws.* From the most ancient times men had imagined that the universe was the work of some super-being, who had shaped it, started it, was watching over it to see that it performed either without change or in great recurring cycles (see pages 103, 183 84, 327), and some day, when he so willed, might perhaps destroy it. Working from statements in the Old Testament, an eighteenth century English bishop had even painstakingly attempted to prove that the world had been created in the year 4004 B.C. But while he was earnestly thus occupied, a French astronomer, Pierre Simon Laplace, was making the first attempt to show that the stars and planets gradually take form, as intensely hot bodies, by mutual attraction among the myriad particles of nebulae by the familiar force of gravity.[19] Shortly after that the Englishman Sir Charles Lyell published the *Principles of Geology*, showing that the Earth had reached its present state through change involving a gradual cooling process, over billions of years.

Then, in 1859, Charles Darwin published his *Origin of Species*, soon followed by *The Descent of Man*. The two books changed the course of men's thinking more deeply, perhaps, than any others of the century. In them Darwin, who had spent five years of his youth with an exploring party in the Pacific for the British Navy, presented detailed evidence to support certain conclusions. These were that the plants and animals of the Earth, including man, far from being created, were the result of slow development, or *evolution*, from simple, primitive life forms to complex, highly organized ones.

To many people such ideas seemed to attack the very foundations of the universe and religion. But after their shock and anger had somewhat subsided, many could see that LaPlace, Lyell, and Darwin had done more than explain plausibly how the universe, the Earth, and all its creatures including man had come to be. They had also helped create a new concept, that of *developing change in nature*. Men began to apply it in other ways, for instance to human society. Why continue to look at history as a long treadmill series of wars and reigns of kings? Why not see it as a slow development of culture, emerging from primitive brutality and ignorance upward into the light of an ever higher civilization toward a goal of enlightened peace? Looking at the most agreeable side of nineteenth century life, they believed the goal might be near.

But was it? There was another side to Darwin's theory of evolution that also seemed to ring true. This was his grim view of how the evolution of organisms occurs. Each generation of creatures, he pointed out, overproduces offspring. Some have to be eliminated. How? By being crowded out of existence by those fittest for survival. These are the ones who find or fight their way to what food there is, before it is gone. Evolution, in other words, proceeds by *natural selection*, by competition to the death among a great variety of creatures, from which only a few survive.

The European Balance, *by Honoré Daumier. He sensed how precarious the balance was as early as 1866, when he drew this cartoon for a Paris newspaper.*

Museum of Fine Arts, Boston, W. G. R. Allen Estate

A Political Parallel to Darwinism. The First World War

Such was the bitter lesson that Darwin taught the world. A look beneath the flashy surface of late nineteenth century life seemed to bear him out. Competition was mounting at a savage rate, and who was winning? The most aggressive, the best armed, the most efficient, the *fittest*. Which countries were wealthiest, most powerful, most influential? Those which had created the best production complexes at the expense even of their own proletariat; those with the biggest and best armies and navies; those which most ruthlessly carved out colonial empires by overcoming peoples less well armed; those competing most successfully with other nations for international trade. In private life, which men lived most magnificently, with a wealth which made their word law? Those who had known best how to ruin their business competitors, their fellow bourgeoisie, in advancing their own fortunes.

Though hindsight now makes the outcome seem obvious, it was hard at the time to foresee or at least to face it. As competition mounted, a political device which European nations had long employed to maintain an uneasy peace was turning into dynamite. This device was the balance of power, a series of alliances which divided Europe into two armed camps, each deterred from fighting the other by the size of the opponent. Since no effective form of international law existed, such a makeshift device seemed the only one workable. As the destructiveness of weapons kept mounting, any advance made by one nation had to be nervously matched by others. The presence of general conscription in one nation led to conscription in all. The tension kept being screwed tighter and tighter by the German empire, hungry for

Entry of Christ into Brussels in 1889, *by the Belgian artist James Ensor; dimensions 8½ × 14 ft. Ensor's* motif *was the annual Brussels carnival, ushering in the season of Lent. The wearing of bizarre masks was part of the celebration. Ensor developed the scene into a scathing expose of the contrast between the religion which Europe professed and the debasing materialism it practiced. For example, Belgium was at this time developing its new colony of the African Congo by building railroads and opening mines, at a cost to the native African population which has been estimated in millions of lives.*

Casino Communal, Knokke-le-Zoute, Belgium

military and commercial supremacy, compelling other European nations to groan under a mounting military burden, and nudging Britain into allying herself with a rising non-European power, Japan. The United States at this time traditionally avoided such alliances.

Four times in the early twentieth century, diplomacy barely averted war. Not so the fifth time, in August 1914. The triggering event was the murder of just two persons! But once launched, the war roared on like a forest fire for four years, involving most of the world, even the United States. Twenty million men were killed or wounded; countless civilians suffered starvation or epidemic disease; untold wealth was destroyed. Through the smoke of the struggle a certain deep trend in human events emerged. The world's last empires disappeared to be replaced by popular governments of differing kinds; the German, Austro-Hungarian, Russian, Turkish, and British empires all suffered different fates, ranging from dismemberment (Turkish, Austro-Hungarian, German), through violently revolutionary change (Russian), to orderly conversion into a commonwealth (British). The first of all to go, the Chinese empire, had become a republic three years before the war had started (1912), but with too weak a central government to stay united. The last to undergo change was the British empire (1931).

Killed in Action, *a drawing by Kaethe Kollwitz, 1921. Frau Kollwitz (1867–1945) wife of a physician practicing in a working people's suburb of Berlin, was an artist whose depth of human sympathy found constant expression in her work.*

The Baltimore Museum of Art. Gift of Mr. and Mrs. Albert Lion

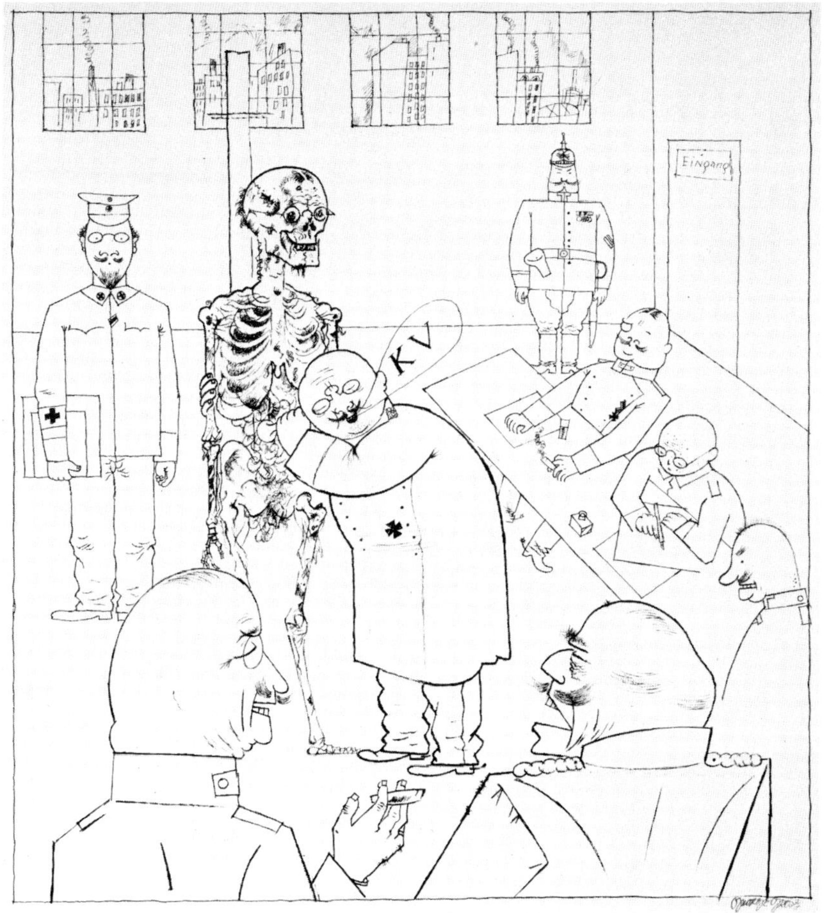

Collection Museum of Modern Art, New York. A. Conger Goodyear Fund

Fit for Active Service, *a drawing by Georg Grosz toward the close of World War I, a commentary on the German army's desperate effort to fill its ranks (KV is the German equivalent of OK). For another of Grosz' scathing political cartoons, drawn in a later period, see page 563.*

Dadaism, Child of Suffering

The senselessness of the whole struggle inspired an intense but short-lived movement in the arts, chiefly among young men who felt themselves betrayed by the society which had spawned the war. Some were French, one or two German, and their leader, Tristan Tzara, a Romanian. Taking form in neutral Switzerland in 1916, then moving to Paris after the war, the group assailed all kinds of civilized conduct as senseless. They produced works of "anti-literature" from disjointed nonsense phrases, "anti-music" from random noise, and "anti-art" from forms drawn, painted, or glued together at random, as their form of rejecting existing cultural standards. Since the movement had nothing constructive to offer to replace what it ridiculed, its life was short. The world was hungry to rebuild. But the *Dada* movement, as it called itself, was a bitter commentary on a tragic age. The art movement to rise from its ashes was surrealism.

Over forty years later a movement called neo-Dada became part of a much larger and long lasting period of expression, in which a revolt against art forms and social forms was and is only a part. Combined with revolt is a respect for the uninhibited act springing direct and uncensored from the unconscious world of an individual or of an entire group or crowd. The *happening* is perhaps the most spectacular form (or anti-form) which this many-sided mode of expression has so far taken. The results can sometimes be partially captured with movie camera and tape recorder. But it is the event itself which is considered important, not its preservation.

Paul Klee

Freud's definition of the unconscious mind has therefore had its effects on artists. One of the first to recognize and exploit it was the remarkable Swiss painter Paul Klee (KLAY). Klee (1879–1940) was by his own experience naturally endowed to appreciate Freud's theory. As a child, already constantly at work drawing and painting, he would sometimes find himself creating monsters so terrible that he would run to his mother for protection! Where could they have come from? What a relief to learn that their lair was merely his own unconscious self.

Klee came of a musical family and was himself musically educated. He too was fascinated by the abstract possibilities of art. He knew Kandinsky well, and did as much as any artist toward defining principles on which abstract art could develop.[18] His own work is a remarkable balance between a free use of whatever emerged into his consciousness and its reshaping according to principles of abstract design and color. And there is almost always present a touch of his delightfully sophisticated humor.

The Storm *by the Belgian surrealist Rene Magritte, 1933.*

Collection the late Kay Sage Tanguy, Woodbury, Connecticut

Collection of the artist

André Breton and Surrealism

A more serious and literal use of Freud's ideas took shape under André Breton, who began his career as a medical student in Switzerland. He was fascinated by Freud's opinion that the strange, seemingly unrelated images of our dreams, often merging one into another, are really "trying to tell us something," that they are united by some truth which we are concealing from ourselves. Breton originated a kind of literature and painting which has been called *surrealist*, or "above real," in which real images are thrown together as in a dream with a deeper, "surreal" meaning implied as lurking behind them. This meaning often completely escapes the reader or viewer, but the puzzling suggestion of its presence gives good surrealistic work its greatest, often hypnotic, charm. The movement was active between the two World Wars. Some of its members even created surrealist moving pictures: Luis Buñuel, Man Ray, and the short-lived French genius Jean Vigo.

Philosophy Illuminated by the Light of the Moon and the Setting Sun, *by the Spanish surrealist painter Salvador Dali, 1939. Dali gave a photographically accurate quality to his dream images, thus making the unreal seem startlingly real. This was perhaps the first purely imaginative use of photographic realism in painting since the invention of the sensitive plate.*

Collection Museum of Modern Art, New York. On extended loan from the artist

National Socialism Versus Protest Art

Guernica, *by Pablo Picasso, 1937, 11 ft × 25 ft 8 in.*

The greatest constructive effort to come from the First World War was the attempt to extend the principles of popular government from persons to nations, in order to create a world government through a *League of Nations*, international justice through a *World Court*, and cooperative international finance through a *World Bank*. But these efforts were ineffective. The member nations refused to provide a policing agency for their own disciplining. Mutual distrust was still too great. The United States, still hesitant about involving itself in world politics, refused even to join the League, although its own president, Woodrow Wilson, had led in creating it.

At the same time Darwin's theory that the most effective competitor, not the most humane, is the one to survive was being driven to its logical extreme. Three of the world's leading nations, all suffering from shortages of land and raw materials for their bulging populations, were totally reorganizing themselves into weapons designed to carve out what they wanted from the surface of the planet. In each country a ruling military and financial clique combined to achieve this. The people were totally mobilized for production and war, their sleeping will to fight aroused by holding up to their eyes imaginary enemies and the dreams of empire. Opposing political leaders were imprisoned or assassinated. The people of Japan were already disciplined to revere and obey their emperor; their docile fighting energies were turned against mainland China, but Japan's war lords saw this as only a step to a larger Pacific empire. The people of Italy were hypnotized into reducing the free African nation of Ethiopia (a fellow member with Italy of the League of Nations) into a colony. But Italy's dictator, Benito Mussolini, dreamed also of an Italian empire embracing the Mediterranean. The people of Germany were turned against a large minority group within their own borders, the Jews, who were imprisoned and massacred wholesale[20] on various cynically false excuses. By such means the dictator Adolf Hitler reduced the population pressure, helped solve the unemployment problem, and confiscated enough wealth to help finance his country's war machine. For he too had his dream: to conquer Europe as the German empire had failed to do, and to wreak revenge for its humiliation in the previous World War. With this aim he was preparing to overcome Germany's western neighbors by *total war*, that is, to soften them by corrupting their political leaders before moving on to destroy their armies, air forces, railroads, and civilian centers of war production. This kind of thorough organization, aimed at enabling one nation to prey on others, has been called *national socialism*.

The art and architecture produced under the three European dictatorships of this period (1920–1939), those of Hitler, Mussolini, and Stalin, were alike for their imposing dullness and vulgarity, although politically Stalin as a leader of the proletariat was hostile to Mussolini and Hitler, whose dictatorships were dominated by the bourgeoisie. By contrast, the rare examples of *protest art* which escaped destruction, and whose creators somehow escaped death, are as terribly alive as an open wound.

The greatest single example of protest art from this period is the work of Pablo Picasso, the Spaniard living in Paris. When his native land erupted into civil war in 1936, and different foreign dictatorships moved in to "help" each opposing faction,[21] he saw Spain torn by forces greater than herself, and the advanced techniques of modern warfare tested on her innocent civilians. His colossal painting *Guernica* is an outcry against the aerial bombing of a helpless Spanish town of that name.

A Writer, Is He? *drawn by Georg Grosz, 1936, prior to World War II, as a commentary on the Nazi Party's methods of gaining control by terror and torture.*

The Bauhaus in Germany, 1919 to 1933

Shortly after the close of the First World War, the German architect Walter Gropius was asked to reopen and direct an important art school in the city of Weimar. Gropius was aware of the concepts which had inspired Art Nouveau, and he profited from their strengths and shortcomings alike. He began by breaking down the distinction between fine arts and crafts, making sure that all students were instructed in each field by both an artist (or *form master*) and a craftsman in the artist's medium. Later, when adequately trained students had been graduated, some of them returned to combine both the art and the craft instructor in one teacher.

Gropius realized that the new age of mass production was putting new demands on artists, that the creation of beautiful mass-produced objects was possible, but that such designs required technical knowledge, by the designers, of manufacturing processes. He is responsible for the creation of *industrial design* as an independent creative activity. He gathered about him a group of brilliant teachers, of whom Paul Klee was one and Kandinsky another.

Later when the school was moved to Dessau, Gropius designed the buildings into which the school moved. When he returned to private practice after a few years, his place was taken by another remarkable architect, Ludwig Mies van der Rohe, who directed the Bauhaus until it was closed by order of Hitler in 1933. Gropius and van der Rohe both left Germany a few years later and came to the United States, Gropius to become Dean of the Harvard School of Architecture, and van der Rohe to become Director of Architecture at the Illinois Institute of Technology in Chicago. Both men have designed extensively in this country, to our great good fortune.

The German word *Bauhaus* means literally "build-house," or, more broadly, school of architecture. But the wise directors and faculty gave the word its widest possible application to all kinds of creation in visible form. *These men were among the first in our age to search for and clarify modern principles of design and to show that the lowliest craftsman becomes an artist, not by whether or not he changes his calling, but by whether or not he employs design principles in what he makes.* Pottery making, furniture making, weaving, and metalwork, were given a new dignity, and have since become respected courses in art schools. The men of the Bauhaus made a great stride forward from the dry, narrowing methods of the academies, the most important stride that has yet been made.

Transmission electron micrograph of the element tantalum. Magnification 200,000 times. The dark swirls are strains caused by atoms of the element carbon entering the tantalum crystal.

Photo R. E. Villagrana and G. Thomas. Courtesy Physica Status Solidi

The New Physics and Astronomy: Relativity Theory

While parts of the civilized world were, it seemed, eagerly preparing to wreck civilization as a whole, the world's pure scientists were pursuing their researches as if on another planet. Physicists were patiently examining the subatomic structure of matter and the behavior of radiant energy. Astronomers were exploring and charting immense stretches of the stellar universe. At both extremes of the scale, the minutely small and the unimaginably vast, they were running into evidence that matter and light are far from obedient to

Newton's laws of motion. These laws work well enough for the solar system, but that is only about seven billion miles across,[22] a mere pinpoint in the sun's parent galaxy, the great spiral of the Milky Way. And the Milky Way in its turn is only one of uncounted galaxies spread in all directions through space.

The work of creating a new theory which explained these discoveries, and which replaced Newton's picture of the universe with a more exact one, was the achievement of a gentle Swiss physicist, Albert Einstein, who published his theory in simple form as early as 1905, and followed it with a more thorough version several years later. In the course of finding a mathematical picture of the universe to fit recent discoveries, Einstein searched through the already completed work of creative mathematicians, and found just what he was looking for. Space, he found, does not exactly fit Euclid's picture of it; when one looks at it in terms of millions of light-years, Riemann's seems to fit it better; space is slightly bent! Furthermore, certain strange facts about the behavior of light can be explained only if we assume that time can stretch and shrink; that time and space are *related*, so that as time stretches space shrinks, and vice versa! Because of this strange space-time relationship, in which neither is fixed or absolute, Einstein grouped his ideas under the name of the *theory of relativity*. The theory not only accounted for the behavior of light energy traveling between stars, but it also agreed with discoveries made by the physicist Max Planck and others as to the behavior of energy within the atom.

Carl van der Voort Gallery, San Francisco

No. 165–168, *by Ernest Posey, 1968. Acrylics, ruling pen and other mechanical drawing tools, on canvas, about 6 by 3 ft. The original is aglow with prismatic colors against a dark ground.*

Einstein's theories were by their very nature out of popular reach; few people understood them exactly. But they had an astonishingly wide influence indirectly, and still do. Beyond the thoughts that time and space are not firm, rigid absolutes, and that space itself is perhaps curved, was another one, about the nature of "truth" itself. Euclid's geometry and Newton's laws had looked like eternal truths, until Einstein's replaced them, and made them obsolete. Would not Einstein's in turn be someday replaced? And would the replacements ever cease? Might they not, rather, go on forever, always seeming to get closer to the truth, but never seizing it?

These considerations were philosophical. The new vision of the universe, revealed by these researches and interpreted by Einstein, also had its profound influence on the arts. New concepts in painting, sculpture, literature, and music were to emerge, and to these we will shortly return.

The Second World War

The members of the League of Nations had refused to discipline themselves. Without an international policing device they were powerless to deal with the three dictatorships of Germany, Italy, and Japan, whose leaders held the democratic process in contempt. The democratic nations, especially France and England, at first tried to appease these dictatorships by granting them concessions. When Japan invaded Manchuria, Italy overran Ethiopia, and Germany claimed part of Czechoslovakia, no one raised a finger. But when Germany overran Poland, Italy invaded north Africa, and Japan struck at Hawaii, the Philippines, and Singapore, the rest of the world roused itself almost too late. To subdue the combined power of the three aggressors took six years. Casualties in the armed forces involved ran to thirty million, and there were inestimable losses in civilian life, health, and wealth. The world's physicists, who had been quiet recluses since the time of Galileo, suddenly assumed international importance as the keepers of the secrets of a terrible new source of power, atomic fission. The United States became a center for research into its possible use as a weapon. Thither the world's leading physicists were rushed, including some whom Hitler had driven from Germany because of their Jewish origins. By 1945 a workable explosive had been prepared and was promptly put to use. Two Japanese cities were destroyed, each by a single bomb, and with combined casualties of nearly a quarter of a million civilians.

Just as the First World War was followed by the fall of empires, so the second revealed a further shift in political power: the disappearance of Europe's overseas colonies as one after another seized or was granted independence. In this the leader was the subcontinent of India. Under the guidance of the remarkable Mohondas Ghandi, the East Indians patiently practiced non-violent resistance to British rule. They protested the ruin of their cotton industry (see page 518) by a mass return to the household hand-spinning of cotton thread. They defied the British monopoly of salt manufacture by pilgrimage to the sea in hundreds of thousands, to make salt in violation of the British law forbidding it. With a resolute avoidance of bloodshed, Ghandi at the cost of his own life steered India to independence two years after the Second World War. Unfortunately a group of Muslim politicians, led by Sir Mohammed Ali Djinna, forced the formation of a separate Muslim state, East and West Pakistan. What might have been a single nation was dismembered. Thousands of Muslim and Hindu lives were lost during the violent population adjustments following this partition, and the stage was set for future tragedy.

But Mohondas Ghandi's heroic example of nonviolent opposition to oppression was to inspire other men far from India. In the United States the Reverend Martin Luther King, Jr. used the same peaceful means to oppose discrimination against his fellow black Americans. Beginning with a successful drive to integrate the bus service in his native city of Birmingham, Alabama, he eventually gave his life in the cause of freedom, just as Ghandi had.

In the twenty-five years following the close of the war, the Dutch East Indies became the nation of Indonesia, and the vast African continent began to bloom with independent republics. The sprawling fragments of China congealed into two nations, each under a dictator: a small one under Chiang Kai-Shek on the island of Taiwan, and a vast one, with the world's largest population, on the Chinese mainland, under the rigidly Marxist Communist rule of Mao Tse-tung.

The "lessons" perhaps partially learned from the Second World War have been painfully simple. They are that man and his rights everywhere deserve equal respect, and that cooperation rather than competition between nations is the key to human progress. Many had professed belief in them, but few had practiced them; and by persistently ignoring them, nations had brought civilization close to ruin. The United Nations and a host of other, lesser organizations for cooperation on vital international problems give hope for the future. The Unites States, emerging from its practice of shunning foreign entanglements and problems, has deeply involved itself in foreign aid. We have devised many programs, and contributed many billions of dollars, toward helping some nations recover from the war, and toward assisting others to develop modern economies and educational systems. Where these programs are effectively meeting the long-range needs of particular regions, rather than merely supporting or arming governments regardless of the social and economic results, they provide a major encouragement to the world's permanent prosperity and peace.

Painting in the United States, 1800 to 1913

While European artists of the nineteenth century had been deeply concerned with political, scientific, and philosophical considerations, those in the United States had been chiefly inspired by sheer wonder, first at the vast continent their fellow citizens were gradually penetrating, and later at the emergence of towns and cities from the wilderness. This remarkable quality of wonder touched America's leading artists for a century. Men like Thomas Cole, Thomas Moran, and Albert Bierstadt gloried in the virgin landscape. John James Audubon studied and dramatically recorded North American bird and animal life. George Catlin, working in a totally different style, was equally fascinated by the American Indian. The progress of American urban life in the new land was recorded by a series of artists from Caleb Bingham, before the Civil War, to John Sloan and his friends of the "Ash Can School" between 1890 and 1915, who delighted in every visual aspect of their beloved New York City.

Some of this group, led by Arthur B. Davies, realized that American art had been going its way in isolation, and decided to show the country what artists were doing in Europe by arranging an exhibition of painting and some sculpture from abroad as well as the United States. The resulting Armory Show of 1913 (so called from the place where it was held, the huge New York National Guard Armory) has ever since been regarded as a turning point in our artistic development. The American public, with a mixture of shock, amusement, and delight, discovered what the daring artist-experimentalists of Europe were achieving, but without much awareness of the theoretical problems their work attempted to solve. The star controversial piece of the show was the *Nude Descending a Staircase* in which the French painter Marcel Duchamp combined a cubist approach to form with a futurist study of motion. One New York journalist described it as "an explosion in a shingle factory."

The American Production Complex, 1789 to the Present

Other aspects of American life had been far less isolated, especially that of engineering, in which the United States was proving to be a center in its own right. Important American inventions began with Eli Whitney's cotton gin in 1793, continued through Robert Fulton's successful steamboat and submarine, and Samuel F. B. Morse's telegraph (1844), to a whole burst of discoveries close to 1900: Bell's telephone; Edison's electric light bulb,

Private collection

Left: Snowy Heron, *by the American naturalist and artist John James Audubon, about 1825. His dramatic and exquisitely detailed studies of the birds and animals of North America represent an almost superhuman accomplishment. Below:* Keokuk, chief of the Sauk and Fox tribes, on horseback, *by George Catlin, 1832. Opposite page: two examples of American nineteenth century landscape painting over half a century apart. Above:* Schroon Mountain, The Adirondacks, *by Thomas Cole, oil painting, 1834. Below:* The Adirondack Guide, *by Winslow Homer, watercolor, 1894.*

Smithsonian Institution, Washington, D.C.

Cleveland Museum of Art

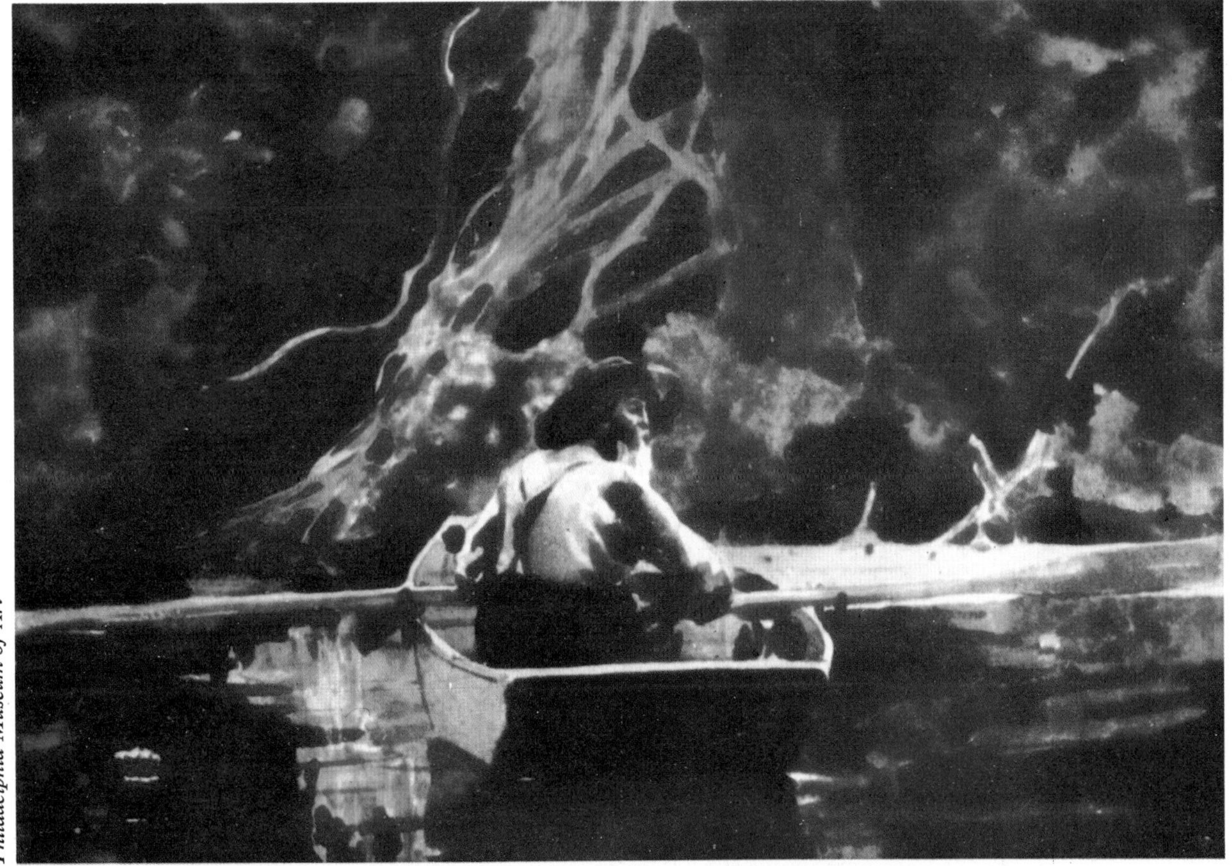

Philadelphia Museum of Art

Boatman's National Bank, St. Louis

University of Pennsylvania

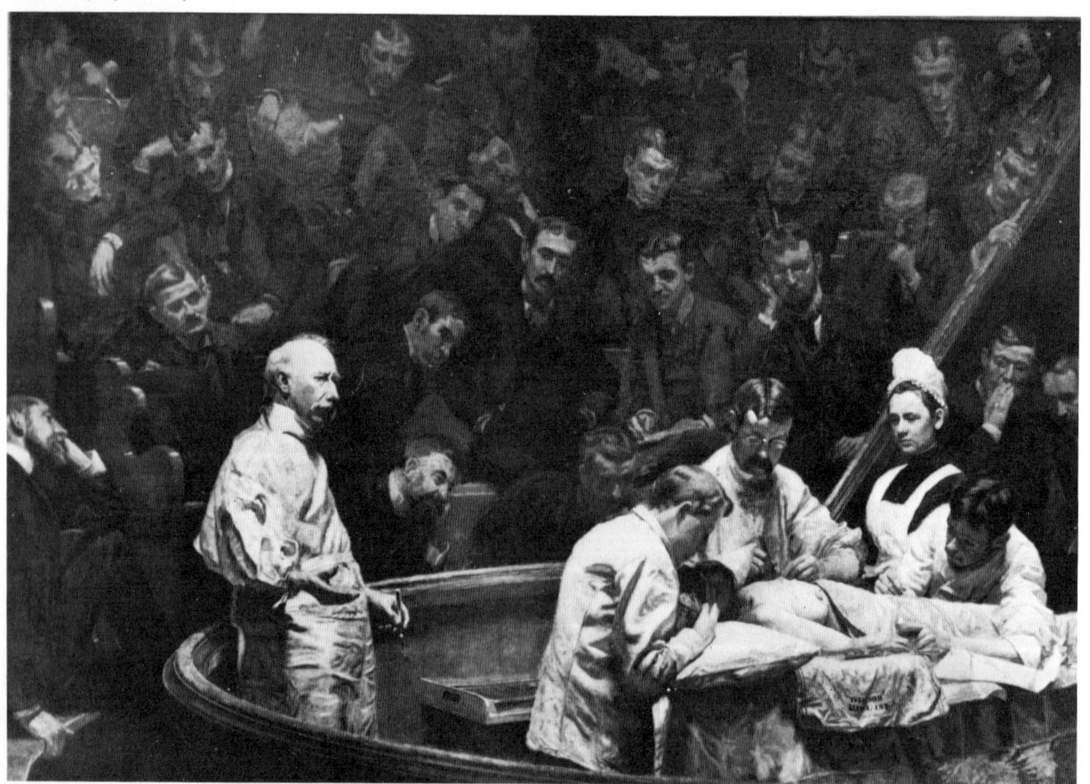

Whitney Museum of American Art, New York. Photo Geoffrey Clements

The growth of American town life, as interpreted by artists. Opposite page, above: Stump Speaking, *by Caleb Bingham, about 1854. Below:* The Agnew Clinic, *by Thomas Eakins, 1889. This page, right:* Hammerstein's Roof Garden, *by William Glackens, about 1901. Right below:* Six O'Clock, Winter, *by John Sloan, 1912.*

Phillips Collection, Washington, D.C.

phonograph, and motion picture camera; Armat's motion picture projector; and finally the mastery of flight by the Wright brothers. At the same time American industrial engineering was beginning to lead the world, just as its heavy industries had begun to outproduce other nations, including even Britain. Robert Taylor was speeding production through the use of time-and-motion studies, Henry Ford through development of the assembly line. In 1926 Robert A. Goddard ushered in the age of rocketry and interplanetary space travel by launching the world's first successful liquid-fuel rocket, at Auburn, Massachusetts, "the Kittyhawk of the space age."

In 50 years, American industry has repeatedly transformed itself by investing heavily in scientific research, and by changing both its products and its production methods as these researches indicated. Two fields of advance should particularly be mentioned: the development of *synthetic materials*, ranging from plexiglass to nylon, and the opening of the field of electronics. After radio and television, the most spectacular devices to emerge have been various types of *computers*, with electric memories capable not only of storing billions of facts but also of recalling, sorting, grouping, and regrouping them in seconds. Perhaps the most vital development of all, as a matter of human survival, seems to be the *constructive use of atomic energy* as a fuel. The world's fuel supplies will some day be exhausted. Long before they are, a substitute will probably have to be found for the internal combustion engine burning mineral fuels, if the atmosphere is to be saved from destructive pollution endangering life itself. Atomic fuel would perhaps be suitable for this purpose.

Below: The Poet Enflamed, *portrait of Leroi Jones, by Reginald Gammon, acrylic on canvas. Bottom: photograph of Reginald Gammon.*

Courtesy Ruder and Finn, New York

Accompanying these advances in industry and engineering, the United States currently leads the world in agricultural research and in the spread of its findings to farmers. This is significant, especially when we consider that, in the past, civilizations which have made strides and innovations in food production have tended also to make great cultural contributions.

The financing of the American production complex has been an increasingly enormous undertaking. Through trial and error, gained by hard experience, especially during the depression years of the 1930's, the country has developed a "mixed economy" in which free enterprise and government owned services operate together to keep business initiative in private hands and at the same time provide some degree of financial and health security for a large part of the population. We shall have cause for satisfaction at this achievement only when it is extended to all citizens. In this the wealthiest and most powerful nation in the world, poverty, disease, and unemployment in certain regions and among certain groups are still prevalent. The most disadvantaged group of all are the former possessors of the land, the American Indians.

A Tragedy from the Past Still Afflicts Us

The most serious long range problem with which the American people have found themselves wrestling, not once, but repeatedly during their history, has been the conflict between human ideals of equality among men and the presence in their midst of millions of human beings, held, first, in the bondage of slavery, and after that deprived of the complete enjoyment of citizenship. The framers of the American Constitution in 1789 perhaps

Photo courtesy Mrs. John Alexander-Sinclair, London

Left: Ambulance Call, *by Jacob Lawrence, about 1940. Below: photograph of Jacob Lawrence by the late Carl van Vechten.*

looked on slavery as a dying institution and therefore hardly mentioned it, although they made specific allowances for its existence. But by 1800 the demand for cotton, spurred by the production revolution in England and next in New England, and speeded by the invention of the cotton gin, began to change the crop pattern on southern plantations. To meet the new market, vast stretches of land were planted with cotton, and this in turn revived a demand for unskilled, distasteful labor which could be performed most cheaply, it was believed, by slaves.

The black African slaves of the United States have been by far the nation's largest minority group, one-eighth of the total population (4 million in 1860). Their ancestors had arrived in the Western Hemisphere in chains from many different parts of west Africa, each with its local language. To prevent uprisings their purchasers were usually careful to mix them; many slaves literally could not talk to each other until they had learned the white man's language, and this in a crude form. For they were at first taught just enough to enable them to understand orders. Basic African customs, especially those of the family, were shattered. Within a generation or two all links with their traditional past had been destroyed, except perhaps for certain basic patterns of rhythm and singing, which later were to serve as a starting point for the black American's major contribution to the arts in the United States: jazz music (see Appendix A). Their much larger contribution to the building of the nation has been an enormous quantity of unpaid and underpaid labor.

This complete cultural break with his past has made the plight of the black American unique among minority groups. Other such groups, when suffering discrimination, have been able to rely on their carefully preserved memories of a stirring tradition to which they could turn for moral support. Immigrants from Ireland, Germany, Italy, Jewish Europe, China and Japan have all had a culture and a language of their own to turn to while experiencing exclusion. The American Indians, pushed off onto their reservations, have managed to preserve traces of theirs. The black American not only was made to lose his traditions, but those who neither knew nor cared that it had existed used its absence to try to prove that he was inferior as a human being. The degradation systematically produced in him was assumed to be a part of his nature.

The stirring of the American conscience over this state of injustice has been fitful. In the mid-nineteenth century it was so violent as to help produce one of the world's major civil wars, followed by the complete outlawing of slavery, the addition to the Constitution of the fourteenth and fifteenth amendments, and the rewriting of antislavery laws in the southern states. But within five years of the close of the Civil War the northern states had begun to forget the black American's problems. Southerners, learning and forgetting nothing, found effective methods to regain their tyranny. A series of Supreme Court decisions of that period rendered the fourteenth and fifteenth amendments ineffective. In the north the growing labor unions, fearing overcompetition, began to exclude black Americans from membership and therefore from work. Real estate operators, fearing a lowering of values and a loss of profit, often excluded them from the purchase of homes in any but restricted areas. In these and a host of other ways the majority of black Americans have been cut off from a chance to earn a decent living or fully to enjoy what they did earn. At the same time, white Americans with full access to these opportunities have repeatedly instructed the black American to "earn respect by standing on his own two feet," just as they themselves were.

Caught in this endless round of frustration, black citizens have repeatedly hoped that their service to the country in various wars would win them something approaching acceptance. As members of the armed forces they have fought and labored, often under humiliating circumstances, to find themselves briefly treated like heroes, then expected to return uncomplainingly to their former life of left-over jobs (when available), left-over housing, under-education, segregated living, and in certain southern states disenfranchisement. In 1963, 200,000 black Americans, led by Bayard Rustin, Dr. Martin Luther King, and others, made one of the most dramatic and dignified appeals for justice in the nation's history by converging on Washington, holding a great mass meeting, and dispersing without a single unfavorable incident, all in one day. Thus did a host of Americans of African descent speak to the conscience of individual Americans everywhere.

Federal legislation of 1964–65, enforcing voting rights and striking down some forms of segregation, has served as the beginning of an answer to this great appeal. But much more is necessary before the long standing wreckage caused by unequal opportunity can be rebuilt. Herbert J. Gans, professor of sociology and education at Columbia University, testifying before the

Photo courtesy Mrs. John Alexander-Sinclair, London

President's Commission on Civil Disorders in December 1967, made twenty-one specific proposals aimed at improving the lot of *all* disadvantaged Americans. They included the following:

Gradual abandonment of welfare except for the aged and disabled; the system to be replaced by a negative income tax and allowance for dependents. A certain income would be established as basic. Those families earning more would pay a tax; those earning less would be paid by the government.

Establishment of job training programs on a massive scale.

Creation of job opportunities, also on a massive scale, both by government and by private initiative.

Passage and energetic enforcement of further antisegregation laws, including the elimination of residential segregation.

Discontinuance of those parts of urban renewal and the Model Cities Program which compel the wholesale relocation of residents.

Financing through the Federal government of an "education revolution" aimed at better education for slum and ghetto children.

The Commission's full report was published in the spring of 1968.

Left: Mother and Child, *by Elizabeth Catlett. Below: photograph of Miss Catlett by M. Yampolsky.*

The Brooklyn Museum

Incantation, *by Charles Sheeler, 1940. Sheeler was a leader in the development of this country's own school of precise hard-edged painting, years before the arrival of precisionist artists from Europe.*

Art in the United States Since 1930

After the Great Depression overwhelmed the country early in 1930, the government developed various creative countermeasures, one of which was the Works Progress Administration (WPA), designed to give employment to millions at a time when little or no work was otherwise to be found. It was at this time that the United States made its only large-scale public investment in its artists, prior to the Congressional act of 1965 in support of the arts. The art subsidiary of the WPA kept thousands of American artists working in their chosen field. Under the able direction of one man, Holger Cahill, they achieved certain important things: they revived the neglected practice of making American public buildings beautiful with painting and sculpture; they gave the nation an awareness of its own creative past by compiling the great *Index of American Design*, full of beautifully executed illustrations of American folk art; and they kept working and developing personally as artists. When the Second World War broke upon us in 1941, the government found already at hand a large professional staff ready to create posters, explanatory charts for weapon assembly, and an array of other needed material.

But the ominous approach of the war had already been shaping the course of American art in a different way. In the middle and late 1930's some of Europe's most remarkable artists began to arrive in this country as exiles. The first to come were Germans, driven from their native land by Hitler's hostility to intellectuals. Among these were two men who by their teaching and example have profoundly influenced art in this country for 25 years. Both are nonrealistic painters, but in style and personality poles apart. The late Hans Hoffman, dynamically expressive, conducted his own school in New York and Cape Cod. Joseph Albers, a meticulous precisionist, now retired as dean of the Yale Art School, has summarized his findings in a monumental work on color, *Interaction of Color*. Both men have approached their painting and their teaching with remarkable analytical and theoretical power. Hoffman took American artists by storm. It was largely to him that the school known as *abstract expressionism* owed its immense popularity for over a decade after the Second World War. Albers' influence has been quieter, more retiring, but its results appear to be perhaps as strong, if somewhat later blossoming, in the recent rediscovery of the school of hard-edge painting aimed at optical effects.

Composition in White, Black and Red, *by Piet Mondrian, 1936, four years before he left the Netherlands for the United States.*

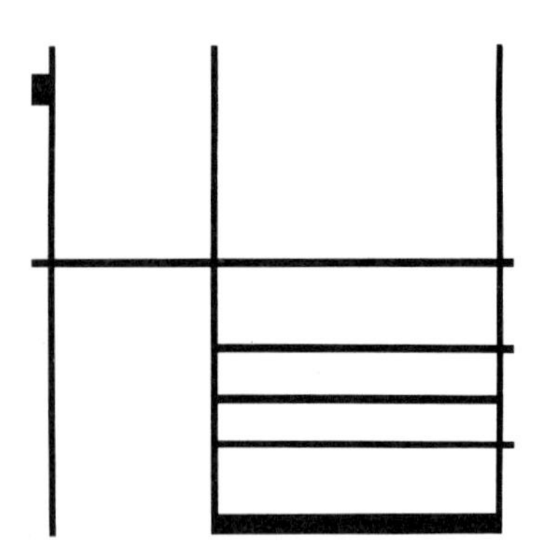

Collection the Museum of Modern Art, New York

By 1940, the year of the fall of France and the Battle of Britain, the trickle of European intellectuals taking refuge in the United States had become a torrent. The composers Igor Stravinsky, Arnold Schoenberg, and Bela Bartok, orchestra conductors such as Otto Klemperer, internationally famous architects such as Walter Gropius and Mies van der Rohe, the surrealist painters Ives Tanguy, Max Ernst, and Salvador Dali, and the English graphic artist Stanley William Hayter came in haste and remained to make this country their home. One of the most remarkable of these refugees was the Dutch precisionist Piet Mondrian, who spent four years in New York City before his death in 1945. Mondrian's influence on applied design of all kinds, from architecture to linoleum, has been great. He lived a life of almost monastic devotion to the development of aesthetic

Left: Homage to the Square, Legendary Pasture, *by Joseph Albers, one of a long series of paintings with identical format, whose sole aim has been the exploitation of color relations. Below:* Meadow Splendor, *by Hans Hoffman, 1959.*

Collection Mr. and Mrs. Edward L. Barnes, Mt. Kisco, N.Y. Photo Wendy Straus

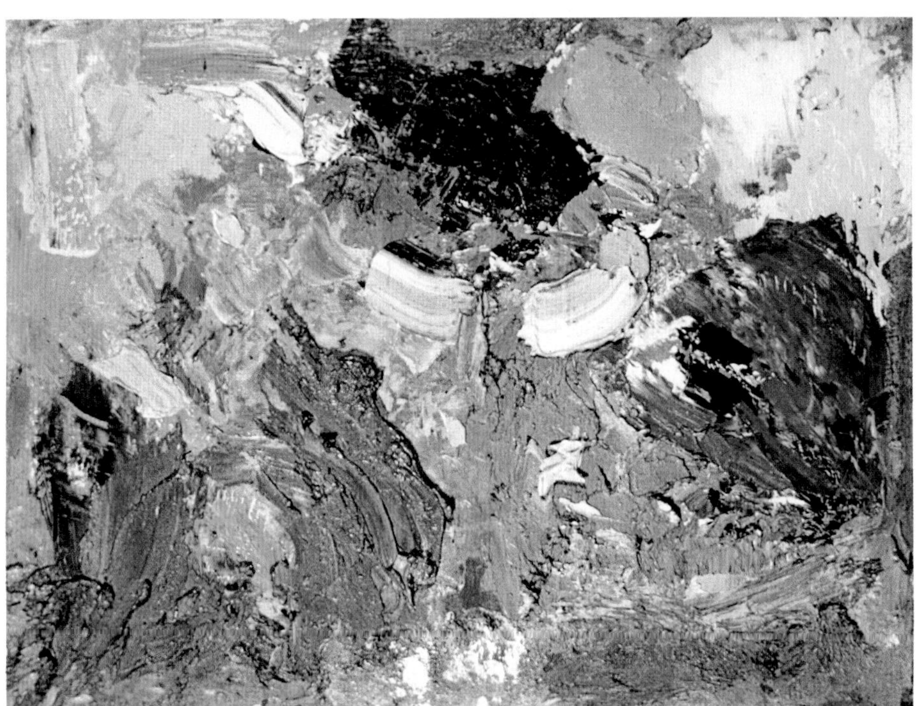

Milwaukee Art Center

purity in art. He reduced his forms of expression to a stark minimum of vertical and horizontal black lines, areas of primary colors, and off-white. Living in an apartment in which all surfaces (even his bed sheets) were pale grey, he developed his compositions on a wall by pasting up tapes and color areas, endlessly studying and moving them until a satisfying, almost hypnotic balance emerged which he could call a finished composition.

While America was being thus culturally enriched, millions of men were being exposed to a similar enrichment, even if under the hardest possible circumstances, by being transported to remote parts of the Earth in the armed forces. Especially remarkable were the results of rotating troops through Japan in the army of occupation and during the Korean War. The number of men whose eyes were opened to the distinctive qualities of Japanese living, including art, was enough to create a wave of interest in this country, and to influence our own tastes toward simplicity and an awareness of natural beauty. We have become increasingly responsive to the grain and texture of materials, especially wood, to inventive relationships between dwelling and garden, and to asymmetrical interior design. Japanese Buddhism of the Zen school has interested some, though few have wished to submit themselves to the years of practice in concentration on which that severe form of self-realization depends.

Abstract Expressionism

Through all this rush of events certain distinctively American varieties of painting have taken form. One, the clean-edged treatment of industrial and mechanical motives appeared after the First World War. Another, which appeared after 1945, may perhaps best be called relativistic painting. No single point in such a painting contains any element which invites the eye to pause and focus. It nowhere reaches a climax. Everything depends on relationships, and these seem, in some cases, to be as countless in number as the galaxies in the universe. At the same time there is a freshness in their execution which creates the impression, or illusion, that they have emerged straight from the unconscious mind of the painter. Of this type of painting Jackson Pollock, Willem de Kooning, and Franz Kline have been among the leaders, each in his individual way.

These artists can also be looked at as belonging to the larger school of *abstract expressionists* developing at the same time. The school, for all its immense variety, has had certain distinctive characteristics.

1. *Complete nonobjectivity:* each painting or sculpture is an absolute with no intended reference, direct or indirect, to "real" visual experience.

2. *No illusionistic space in paintings:* the picture plane is everything. A certain tension between advancing and receding forms is present, but this is achieved through advancing and receding colors and values. The sculptors, on the other hand, have often worked with the conscious intent of *shaping*, *bending*, and *distorting* space.

3. *Asymmetrical composition:* the tradition that became dominant in the Baroque period and continued through Cezanne became the accepted convention of this school also.

4. *Dominance of the materials:* the manner in which these are handled is displayed rather than concealed, whether it be oil paint, welded metal, or some other.

5. *Spontaneity:* although an abstract expressionist work of art may have developed slowly and painfully, the result, by convention, must look like an inspired sketch, paint being often flung around with a good deal of spatter, and the whole work giving an impression of open-endedness, as if the act of

creating it had been an important part of the completed work (hence the name *action painting*).

6. *Creation as part of personal evolution:* the artist's development, *through his succession of paintings*, has been sometimes obtruded as more important than the paintings themselves. This has led occasionally to the exhibition of paintings which were meaningless in themselves (much to the anger of some critics). But the basic idea, even when impaired by bad taste, is of great importance for every artist, or rather every human being, to grasp. This is that human life at its best can be a continuing growth process, and that the life of the artist is a remarkably sensitive means to realizing this growth. Darwin's concept of evolution is here applied, neither to the whole race, nor to one civilization, but to the human individual.

7. *An international style:* abstract expressionist painters have made their contributions from many points on the planet, speaking to each other, as it were, across great distances and sharing in international exhibitions. One of its most highly experimental centers has been Japan (the Gutai group in Osaka). In the best abstract expressionist art one can therefore see merging the *indirect* emotional influences stirred by civilization's major intellectual advances during the whole previous century: those in creative mathematics, relativistic physics, astronomical exploration, the Freudian concept of the unconscious, the Darwinian concept of evolution given an individual application, and the gradual drawing together of the whole human race.

But even a school based consciously or unconsciously on such an astonishing synthesis as this can be worked to death. Art students have been so thoroughly introduced to it that it has now deservedly been called academic. Large corporations and banks have shrewdly invested in abstract expressionist paintings and sculpture to grace their halls and directors' meeting rooms.

Whitney Museum of American Art, New York. Photo Geoffrey Clements

Mahoning, *by Franz Kline, oil, 80 × 100 in., 1956. For a number of years Kline developed each of his powerful abstract expressionist paintings entirely in black, white and occasional greys.*

Art Institute, Chicago

Albright-Knox Art Gallery, Buffalo, N.Y.

Whitney Museum of American Art, New York

Opposite page, above: Convergence, *by Jackson Pollock, 1952. Before his death in a motor accident in 1956, Pollock was perhaps the supreme example of the abstract expressionist painter. Discarding brushes and laying his canvases flat on the floor, he poured, splashed or dripped paint in a manner at once daringly free and constantly controlled by his feeling for rhythm and over-all composition. The result was a series of paintings which are an interplay of dynamic rhythms and textures. Opposite page, below:* Construction after the Enjoyment of a Mulberry Tree, *welded metal sculpture by Henry Bertoia. Left:* Thorn Blossom, *brazed metal sculpture, by Theodore Roszak, 1947. Below:* Excavation, *by Willem de Kooning, 1950. Born in Holland (1904), de Kooning came to this country at the age of twenty-two. In the late 1930's, he began to influence through his own work the art of his time. This influence has slowly mounted, so that today he is one of the country's most distinguished* avant garde *painters.*

Art Institute, Chicago

Richard Feigen Gallery, New York

Above: Print 5, *by Bridget Riley, 1965. Paint on plastic. Below:* Cinematic Painting, *by the German artist Wolfgang Ludwig, 1964. Oil on composition board, diameters, 2 ft. An illusionistic painting, whose two centers seem to pulsate.*

For the past few years artists have been striking out, therefore, in many new directions. Never before has their work been so many-sided in materials, content, and compositional structure. The clear-cut distinction between painting and sculpture, as well as between the "work of art" and the industrially created object, has tended to blur. The spray gun and industrial silk screening have invaded painting. Neon lighting has invaded sculpture.

The trend can perhaps be summarized as a many-sided exploration *away from* abstract expressionism. Where the style of abstract expressionists had been highly personal, artists (especially sculptors) next began to create forms so baldly impersonal that they could be and have been reproduced by others from the artist's specifications. Where abstract expressionists had created complex compositions depending for their power on an interplay of forms and colors, the new artists have produced forms of stark simplicity, to be accepted for their uncompromisingly self-sufficient selves. Where abstract expressionists had constantly aimed at spontaneity, some of their successors have applied abstract principles of optical illusion and color contrast in a meticulously studied manner. Where abstract expressionists were devoted to asymmetrical composition, more recent artists have resurrected other basic compositional schemes—decorative rhythms and patterns, bilateral and radial symmetry. And where abstract expressionists had been visually inner-directed, many later artists have taken delight in the opposite approach, dead-pan or satirical objectivity, sometimes seizing on the most garish aspects of the visual world for motifs. This astonishingly diverse, inventively rich period of reaction seems in its turn to be reaching its climax. What new directions will emerge next are yours to determine. For further current examples see pages 584, 585, 616.

Collection of the artist

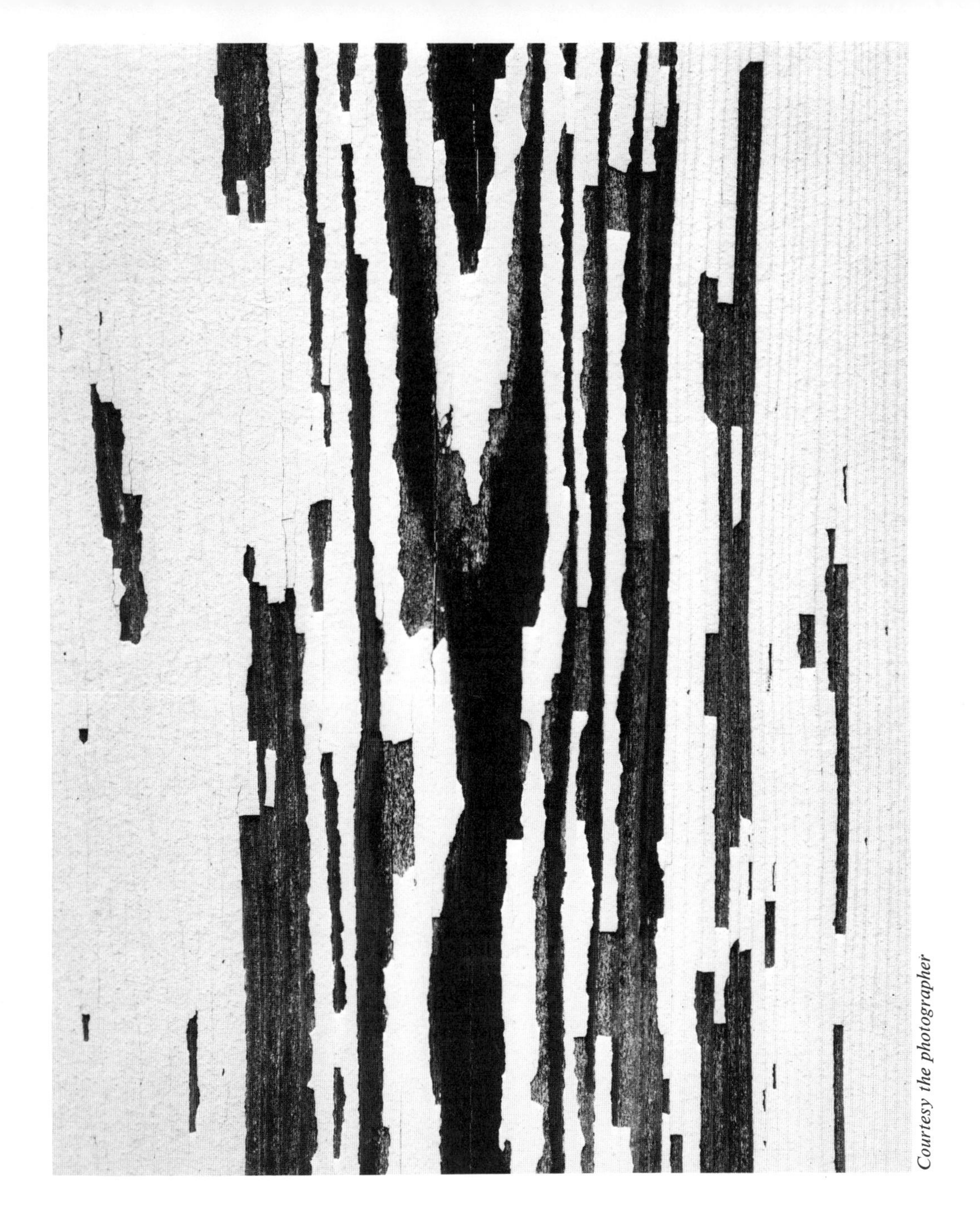

Courtesy the photographer

Wood and Whitewash, *photograph by Ansel Adams, 1960. Another photograph by Mr. Adams appears on page 50.*

Photography, Still and Motion, in the United States

With the beginning of the twentieth century the United States began to move into an important position in photography. The invention of the motion picture camera and projector were immediately exploited commercially to provide the nation with cheap mass entertainment. Between 1911 and 1920, motion picture production steadily grew as an industry, with its manufacturing center finally settling in southern California. Amid the enormous volume of unimportant and, today, uninteresting films turned out in those early years, a few stand out as the work of men who were successfully shaping a great new art with laws of its own. Because films were at this time still silent, they were limited for their effects entirely to visual images and

All Things Do Live in the Three, *by Richard Anuszkiewicz, 1963. Oil on canvas, about 22×36 in. A study in simultaneous contrast of colors.*

Museum of Modern Art, New York. By permission of the owners, Mr. and Mrs. Robert M. Benjamin

pantomime acting. Their achievements ranged from Mack Sennett's patterns of violent motion as developed in his one- and two-reel comedies, to the colossal conceptions of David W. Griffith, whose *Birth of a Nation* and *Intolerance*, running to 12 reels each, were landmarks in the creative making of films. Griffith's use of atmospheric effects to heighten suspense, his carefully chosen close-ups of faces and other details, and his masterly handling of crowds have had their lasting influence on other directors, Sergei Eisenstein among them.

During the First World War, while European film making was at a standstill, the American film industry seized the opportunity to move into the world's markets, at the price of cheapening its product. The industry remained a major one, so far as earnings were concerned, until the advent

Design for a plastic penny, by Robert Indiana. "The New Glory Penny is a polychromatic, decagonal one-cent piece proposed for 1963 and would be a welcome change from the familiar copper coins long in use."

Courtesy Stable Gallery, New York. Photo Eric Pollitzer

of television. Efforts by the motion picture companies to stage a comeback through wide-screen productions and other devices, have been only partially successful. A favorable result of the competition between movies and television has been the recent burst of low-budget motion pictures produced and acted by people with strong artistic convictions. In this, Americans have been inspired by the example of European producers, whose remarkably inventive and sensitive pictures have often been produced at amazingly low cost. For decades the ideas created in these European movies have been a source of cautiously watered-down imitation by American producers, when their own films have been at a productive high and a creative low.

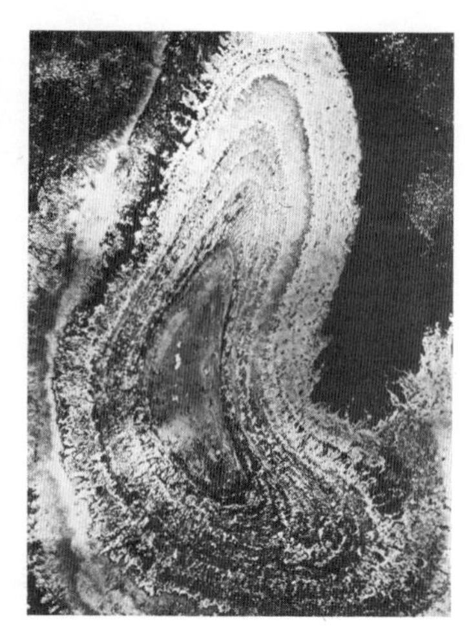

Untitled photograph by Carl Chiarenza.

Courtesy of the photographer

Since 1900 American *still photography* has been fathered by the lifetime example and personal stimulation of two remarkable men, Alfred Stieglitz and Edward Steichen, each working in his own way. They have in their turn inspired a series of brilliant successors: Edward Weston, Ansel Adams, Imogene Cunningham, Irving Penn, Richard Avedon, and Wayne Miller, to mention only some. The relationship between creative photographers on the one hand, and painters and sculptors on the other, has been one of mutual respect, mutual give-and-take. Photographers have looked appreciatively at paintings and sculpture, and painters and sculptors at photography. More important, however, has been the fact that these men are all artists who have sought to give expression to the culture of which they, and we, are a part. And all have shared in forming the style of this culture.

Nineteenth and Twentieth Century Architecture: Advances in Materials and Concepts

As already suggested, the past 150 years have seen the complete remaking of building construction and therefore of architectural design. This has been partly a matter of new materials and partly of new theoretical concepts applied to them. Let us look at these in order.

In 1670 the Frenchman Bernard Perrot developed a method for mass producing window glass. A century later, in England, the first successful process for making cement appeared, leading within 50 years to the development of *concrete*, in which correct proportions of sand and gravel are fused in cement. Over the same span of time the English were also experimenting with bridges and other structures of cast and wrought iron. Engineers and architects in France were soon experimenting with the new materials. The Eiffel Tower, erected in 1889, is the world's supreme example of wrought-iron construction. But five years previously, in 1884, *structural steel* was already beginning to take its place in the United States. Three materials, *concrete, steel, and sheet glass*, used in various combinations, began to determine the character of modern building before 1900. The cooperative use of concrete and steel to produce *reenforced concrete* and *prestressed concrete* is a much more recent advance. Still more recent has been the introduction of two new materials. *Sheet aluminum*, remarkable for lightness, moldability, and resistance to weathering, has come into use in a variety of ways, as sheathing and even for structural support. Last of all, the possibilities of *plastics* in building are now being explored, and point to the launching of still another revolution in building construction and design.

The United States pavilion at Expo 67, Montreal: Buckminster Fuller's geodesic dome. Although about 200 feet in diameter, this is only a small example of the scale on which such a dome can be constructed. It has been envisioned as enclosing an entire city in a gigantic bubble, within which temperature, humidity and other atmospheric properties could be controlled at will.

As a consequence new building heights have become possible, as well as new building spans (dwarfing the Pantheon), and a progressive reduction of the ratio between mass of building material and the space the material encloses. *Truss construction*, *cantilevered construction*, and the development of the *I-beam* as the most practical steel construction unit were all demonstrated before 1880. But before that date something else had occurred in a world the casual observer never sees, the world of abstract thinking. Methods had been perfected not only for pretesting the strengths of all materials, but also for calculating mathematically the stresses they would have to endure. Architecture had ceased to be a matter solely of trial-and-error experience and inspired guesswork.

The most revolutionary step in building construction made in this age is just beginning to find application. Since man first began to build, his structures have relied on a single form of stress, that of *compression*, the pull of gravity which has made piled-up materials stay in place. Early in the nineteenth century inventive builders began to experiment with the opposite form of stress, *tension*. The world's first iron suspension bridge was built in Wales in 1776. The first one of steel was built in the United States about a century later, in 1878. Meanwhile, between 1840 and 1846, the wire-spoked bicycle wheel, whose strength is entirely a product of tension, had been developed in England. It was not until 1950 that new strides in the use of tension in construction were made by the American designer-engineer Buckminster Fuller. The uses of his remarkable ideas still seem to be highly specialized.

Beginning in 1884 *steel frame construction* came increasingly into play. The American architect William Le Baron Jenney was the first to use it, in

Photo Lucile Dandelet

Marin County Civic Center, California. Although a multitude of buildings exist which Wright designed for private individuals and corporations, this is the sole example of his civic planning which achieved realization.

the twelve floor Home Insurance Building in Chicago, and to realize the new possibilities for large window spaces. For the steel frame now did all the work of support; walls had become mere fill-ins, and could become, if the designer wished, a single sheet of glass. Louis Sullivan followed Jenney's practices, and was the first architect to develop a new concept of architectural beauty which was harmonious with the structural advance. Sullivan's pupil, Frank Lloyd Wright, went on to become one of the greatest architects of the twentieth century, or perhaps of any century.[23]

Wright's life, which began in 1869, spread over a span of 90 richly productive years. When he died in 1960, he still seemed in his prime; in 37 different places buildings were going up, or about to go up, according to his designs! One of these, the only civic building he was ever permitted to see realized, is the Marin County Civic Center. Like every other Wright design, it is alive with invention, constantly tempered, it seems, by two questions which Wright must constantly have put to himself: *How will this building enrich the lives of the people who will use it?* and *How harmonious is this boldly adventurous structure with the world which made it possible—with the world of nature which supports and surrounds it and with the world of human history from which it has sprung, like a leaf from a tree?* With Wright's questions sounding in our ears, let us bring to a close this chapter, and this book.

EPILOGUE

We started this book by looking at the two faces of art, the familiar welcoming one and the strange, elusive one. We close, having looked at much more, at the many faces of man himself, as he has lived many lives in different times and places. In each time and each place we have looked on his face as an artist. And we have tried to look beyond that face to the inner man. How came he, at that particular place and time, to practice art? We have seen some of the causes which the world has offered, inviting, compelling, or grudgingly permitting him to practice it, and some of the many forms his practice has taken. But the direct answer to the question is still deceptively simple: he practiced art because he wanted to.

Is wanting enough? The things we want intensely usually have some connection with our need to live, to grow, even to survive. We realize now that the creative life nourishes the creator, feeds his intellectual and emotional growth just as food nourishes his body. The emergence of new, hitherto unseen images, unthought ideas, unheard sounds into our consciousness, their testing and organization by our conscious minds, their translation into physical form for all to see or hear or think, and their resulting reaction on the one who brought them into being—this cycle repeated again and again, each cycle conditioning the next—spells an open-ended life: personal evolution.

Is personal evolution enough? As communication binds the whole world together, living to one's self becomes impossible. Does the creative life have value outside itself? Let us go back to some unfinished business in the last chapter, to some questions left unanswered, seemingly far away from the present problem. There we briefly described how in the 1930's Germany, Japan, and Italy converted themselves into weapons for carving from other nations what they wanted, and how the Second World War was the outcome of their attempt to carve it. Their whole coldly focused effort seemed to be based on a sound scientific principle, namely, that the fittest survive. Why then did they fail?

The very science from which they overhastily drew the principle has also answered the question. *Complete fitness to meet certain conditions is invincible, until the conditions change. It then becomes worse than useless. For complete fitness is usually achieved at the cost of flexibility, sensitivity, and awareness that change is occurring.* The study of paleontology, of the creatures of the remote past, has twice revealed what seems to have been a massive destruction by the forces of nature of life forms whose efficiency to survive was unchallenged until their world altered, and their weapons or shells prevented them from altering with it. Each time it was the small, unarmed, adaptable organisms which were ready to change, to adjust to the new, who survived. Each time it was they who inherited the Earth.

The German Luftwaffe lost the Battle of Britain because its warplane designs had been frozen for mass production. The British, meanwhile, had been putting first emphasis on inventiveness, had created the marvelously sensitive device of radar, and when the war broke out were still developing their planes for speed and armament. The fate of France, Belgium, and Holland affords an even more glaring example of inadaptability. Like giant turtles they had settled down behind the protective shell of their fortifications, disdaining even to cooperate in uniting them. The German war machine had merely to strike at the points where one segment of national fortification met the next, and the line was punctured. By contrast the United States, entering the war late, was fortunately free to approach its war preparations inventively, and was actually aided by creative minds living here in exile, unwanted under dictatorships.

Where lies the point of these wartime examples for us as individuals, aspiring to live in a peaceful world? No nation is greater than the individuals who compose it. Therefore, if a nation is to rise above rigidity, so must its citizens. Whoever lives a life constantly receptive to experience, constantly open to the creative ideas which that experience generates in him, and ever ready to give those ideas tangible, critically analyzed form, helps lift and transform all society, not only by what he produces, but also by how he lives and by what he is.

You are the salt of the Earth. But if the salt lose its savor, wherewith will the world be salted?

NOTES

[1] His full name: Francisco José de Goya y Lucientes.

[2] No one now knows whether the idea was discovered independently, or whether some traveler brought it from China, where such bridges had been in use for centuries.

[3] To the British, whether in England or their colonies, revolution in the interest of political liberty and human rights was no new thing. In the seventeenth century, England led the world by twice refusing the rule of absolute (and Catholic) monarchs, whose philosophy of government resembled that of Louis XIV. British writers accompanied these actions by much controversy for and against the theory that kings have the right, given by God, to rule with unchecked power. The final British verdict was that they did not, that the law was greater than the kingly will.

[4] Napoleon gave France a new economic security by authorizing the *Bank of France*, in 1800, with powers resembling those of the Bank of England.

[5] It was not this "lowest" stratum of society, but the middle-class merchants, or bourgeoisie, who had been responsible for the French Revolution, and who had finally replaced kings and nobility as rulers of France. In 1793, when the French laboring classes, led by a man named Babeuf, tried to take over the Revolution from the middle classes (of whom David was a member), they were repulsed with an iron hand.

[6] Included among British exports to China was the narcotic opium, which the Chinese emperors wished to exclude as harmful to the people, and the British wished to sell at a profit regardless of its effects. The war of 1838 is often called the "Opium War."

7 Italy too became a single nation at this time, but advanced industrially more slowly, held back by a shortage of iron and coal resources.

8 Before she was 50 years old the United States found it necessary to protect these fledgling republics against European aggression by declaring them within her sphere of influence (Monroe Doctrine, 1823).

9 This is a simplified description of the lithographic process. The quarries of lithographic limestone are now practically exhausted, but a single stone can be used many times. Passable substitutes have been found.

10 Or, as in England, a republic with the outward trappings of a kingdom.

11 The German parliament, the Reichstag, a body duly elected by various German states which had made themselves over after the French Revolution, offered Frederick William IV the crown, as ruler of a newly formed Germany. He contemptuously refused to accept it from them, declaring that the right to wear it was already his from God. Within the next 30 years the German government under Emperor William I and his chancellor Count von Bismarck, without abandoning this attitude, successfully masked it under a number of shrewd reforms.

12 The Soviet censorship of the arts underwent a brief relaxation during the administration of Nikita Khrushchev.

13 *Savant*, the French word for man of knowledge. Science at this time was still considered a branch of philosophy. They did not separate for nearly a century.

14 *Concerning the Law of the Simultaneous Contrast of Colors*, by M. E. Chevreul. Chevreul was director of the great Gobelin Tapestry Works at Paris, founded under Louis XIV. He was also a distinguished chemist.

15 As reported by Joachim Gasquet in *Paul Cézanne* (Paris, 1926).

16 See the Illustrations, pages 379—81, 385, 404—5, for three Renaissance painters' approach to this double problem, by apparently using two geometrical devices, proportion and perspective, on the same surface.

17 *Regard sur le Passé*, by V. Kandinsky (Drouin, Paris, 1946), p. 20.

18 In his *Pedagogical Textbook*, notes on his lectures delivered at the *Bauhaus*, Weimar and Dessau, 1922 and after.

19 Laplace's theory was later shown to be in error, but was replaced by others involving interaction of the same forces. The latest and most satisfactory seems to be that of the Cambridge astrophysicist Fred Hoyle.

20 The total number killed has been estimated at six million.

21 The faction of General Francisco Franco was supported by Mussolini. The Spanish Republican government was "aided," that is, subverted, by Communists supported by Stalin, using Lenin's methods. Throughout the struggle the world's democratic powers remained neutral.

22 The diameter of the orbit of Pluto (discovered in 1930) around the Sun is roughly 7.3 billion miles, or a little over one light-hour.

23 The first half of this century has been an age of architectural giants. Ranking in importance with Wright have been the Swiss Le Corbusier (whose given name is Charles Edward Jeanneret) and the German L. Mies van der Rohe, among others.

BOOKS ABOUT THE NINETEENTH AND TWENTIETH CENTURIES

LATE EIGHTEENTH AND NINETEENTH CENTURIES

The World We Have Lost, P. Laslett (University paperback VP167, 1956).
The Age of Reason, L. J. Snyder (Van Nostrand paperback No. 6).
Essential Works of the Founding Fathers (Bantam, NM1011).
The Federalist Papers, by Adams, Hamilton & Jay (Dutton, Everyman's Library 519).
The Era of the French Revolution: Ten Years that Shook the World, L. Gershoy (Van Nostrand paperback No. 22).
The Great Mutiny, J. Dugan (Literary Guild of America, Garden City, New York, 1965). British counterpart to the American and French Revolutions.
Nelson and the Age of Fighting Sail, D. Warner and Adm. C. Nimitz (1963).
Napoleon and the Awakening of Europe, F. Markham (Collier paperback, 1965).
France, 1814–1919, the Rise of Liberal Democratic Society, J. B. Wolf.
British Constitutional History Since 1832, R. L. Schuyler and C. C. Weston (Van Nostrand paperback No. 18).
The Making of the English Working Class, F. P. Thompson (Random House paperback V322).
Revolution and Reaction, 1848–1852: A Mid-Century Watershed, G. Brunn (Van Nostrand paperback No. 31).
The Rise and Fall of Western Colonialism, S. C. Easton (Praeger paperback).

FILM

Jefferson the Architect, B & W, sound, 11 minutes, International Film Bureau, Inc.
The Ever Changing Sky, color, sound, 18 minutes, International Film Bureau, Inc. A film on the life and work of John Constable.

TWENTIETH CENTURY

The World of the Twentieth Century, L. J. Snyder (Van Nostrand paperback No. 4).
The Great Ascent: The Struggle for Economic Development in Our Time, R. L. Heilbroner (Harper and Rowe, New York, 1963).
American Capitalism: its Promise & Accomplishment, L. M. Hacker (Van Nostrand paperback No. 20).
The Pluralistic Economy, E. Ginzberg and others (McGraw-Hill, New York).
The Rich Nations & the Poor Nations, B. Ward (Norton paperback).
Dilemmas of Urban America, R. C. Weaver (Harvard University Press, 1965).
The Negro in the Making of America, B. Quarles (Macmillan paperback AS534, 1964).
The Negro Family in the United States, E. F. Frazier (revised & abridged edition, University of Chicago Press paperback, 1966).
The Nature of Prejudice, G. W. Allport (Doubleday Anchor paperback).
The Autobiography of Malcolm X (Grove Press, New York, paperback, 1964–65).
Poverty U.S.A., T. Gladwin (Little, Brown, Boston, 1967).

AFRICA, CHINA, INDIA, USSR

The Washing of the Spears, D. R. Morris (Simon & Schuster, New York, 1965). Zulu uprising.
Dingane, King of the Zulu, 1828–1840, P. Becker (Crowell, New York, 1965).
A History of Postwar Africa, J. Hatch (Praeger, New York, 1965).
Emergent Africa, Scipio (Houghton Mifflin, 1965).
Africa, from Independence to Tomorrow, D. Hapgood (Atheneum, 1965).
India, Pakistan and the West, P. Spear (Oxford paperback, 1967).

The Middle East and the West, B. Lewis (Harper paperback, New York, 1964).
China's Response to the West: a Documentary Survey 1839–1923, S. Teng and J. K. Fairbank (Athenaeum paperback No. 44).
Agricultural Practices & Principles in Communist China (US Joint Publications Research Service, New York, 1959).
Chinese Art in the 20th Century, M. Sullivan (University of California Press, 1959).
The Conquest of Violence: The Ghandian Philosophy of Conflict, revised ed., J. V. Bondurant (University of California Press paperback 115).
Democracy and Economic Change in India, G. Rosen (University of California Press CN147, 1967).
India as a Secular State, D. E. Smith (Princeton paperback 76, 1963).
Marxism, 100 years in the Life of a Doctrine, B. E. Wolf (Dial Press, New York, 1965).
Karl Marx, His Life and Environment, I. Berlin (Galaxy paperback, 1959).
Marx's Concept of Man, E. Fromm (paperback, F. Ungar Pub. Co., New York, 1962).
The Great Experiment: Russian Art, 1863–1922, C. Gray (Abrams, New York). A period of brilliant experiment in painting and sculpture, finally suppressed by Stalin.
Kruschev and the Arts, the Politics of Soviet Culture, 1962–1964, P. Johnson (MIT Press, 1965).

ART BY PERIODS AND MOVEMENTS

A Concise History of Modern Painting, H. Read (Praeger paperback, 1959).
A Concise History of Modern Sculpture, H. Read (Praeger paperback, 1964).
Three Hundred Years of American Painting, A. Elliott (Time, Incorporated, New York, 1957).
American Sculpture, A. T. Gardner (Metropolitan Museum of Art, New York).
The Story of the Armory Show, M. N. Brown (NY Graphic Society, 1963).
The Two Worlds of American Art: the Private and the Public, B. Ulanov (Macmillan, New York, 1965). Comprehensive survey since 1900.
William Morris as Designer, R. Watkinson (Reinhold, New York, 1967).
Art Nouveau, M. Amaya (Dutton paperback 23, 1966).
Fauvism, J.-E. Muller (Praeger, New York, 1967).
Cubism and Twentieth Century Art, R. Rosenblum (H. Abrams, New York, 1960).
The German Expressionists, a Generation in Revolt, R. S. Meyers (Praeger, New York, 1966).
Dada, H. Richter (McGraw-Hill paperback, 1965).
The History of Surrealist Painting, M. Jean (Grove Press, New York, 1960).
Concerning the Spiritual in Art and Painting in Particular, V. Kandinsky (Wittenborn paperback, 1959).
The Pedagogical Sketchbook, P. Klee (Praeger paperback, 1953).
Abstract Painting, Background and American Phase, T. B. Hess (Braziller, New York).
Pop Art, L. C. Lippard (Praeger, New York, 1966).
Assemblage, Environments & Happenings, A. Kaprow (H. Abrams, New York, 1966).
Optical Illusion in the Visual Arts, R. Carraher & J. Thurston (Reinhold, New York. 1966).
Directions in Kinetic Sculpture, P. Selz (University of California Printing Department, Berkeley, 1966).
Funk, P. Selz (University of California Art Museum, Berkeley, 1967).

Language of Vision, G. Kepes (Paul Theobald, 1944).
Sign, Image, Symbol, G. Kepes editor (Braziller, New York, 1966).
Module, Proportion, Symmetry, G. Kepes editor (Braziller, New York, 1966).

DRAWING, GRAPHIC TECHNIQUES

20th Century Drawings, Part I: 1900–1940; Part II: 1940 to the Present (Sherwood Publishers, Drawings of the Masters Series, New York).
Modern Prints & Drawings: a Guide to a Better Understanding of Modern Draughtsmanship, P. J. Sachs (Knopf, New York, 1954). Many good illustrations and a good explanatory text, including graphic techniques briefly stated.
The Technique of Lithography, P. Weaver (Reinhold, New York, 1965).
Creative Lithography & How to Do It, G. Arnold (Dover T1208, 1941).
Silk Screen Techniques, Biegeleisen and Cohn (Dover T433).
Master Draughtsman Series (Borden Pub. Co., Los Angeles).

PHOTOGRAPHY, STILL AND MOVING

The Photograph, A Social History, M. F. Braive (McGraw-Hill, New York, 1966).
The History of Photography from 1839 to the Present Day, B. Newhall (Museum of Modern Art, New York, 1964).
America and Alfred Stieglitz, a Collective Portrait, W. Frank, ed. (Lit Guild, New York, 1937).
Cinema Eye, Cinema Ear: Some Key Film Makers of the 60'*s*, J. R. Taylor (Hill & Wang, New York, 1964).
Film as Art, R. Arnheim (University of California Press paperback, 1957—58).
Film & Its Techniques, R. Spottiswoode (University of California Press, 1964).
Animation Art in the Commercial Film, E. L. Levitan (Reinhold, New York, 1960).

ARCHITECTURE AND CITY PLANNING

A History of Modern Architecture, J. Joedicke (Praeger, New York).
The Autobiography of an Idea, L. H. Sullivan (Dover, 1962). Sullivan's organic theory of architecture revolutionized architectural thinking.
Toward a New Architecture, Le Corbusier (Praeger, 1959).
Structures, P. L. Nervi, translated by G. and M. Salvadori (Dodge Corp., New York, 1956).
Aesthetics & Technology in Building, P. L. Nervi (Harvard University Press, 1965).
Saturday Review, August 29, September 19, October 10, 1964: three articles by Buckminster Fuller.
Twentieth Century Engineering (Museum of Modern Art, New York, 1964).
Curvilinear Forms in Architecture (Portland Cement Association, Chicago, 1964).
Cities, L. Halprin (Reinhold, New York, 1963).
Freeways, L. Halprin (Reinhold, New York, 1966).
Not So Rich As You Think, G. R. Stewart, illustrations by R. Osborne (Houghton Mifflin, Boston, 1968).
The Death and Life of Great American Cities, Jane Jacobs (Vintage paperback V-241).
Garden Cities of Tomorrow, E. Howard (MIT Press paperback).

FILMS

Town Planning, B & W, sound, 15 minutes, International Film Bureau, Inc.
Suburban Living—Six Solutions, B & W, sound, 59 minutes, International Film Bureau, Inc.
Brasilia, color, sound, 13 minutes, International Film Bureau, Inc.

APPENDIX A: SOME NOTES ON THE MUSIC OF DIFFERENT CULTURES, AND SPECIMEN RECORDINGS

Chapters 1 and 2

The music of other peoples, especially tribal societies, often sounds extremely strange when heard for the first time. We can perhaps bridge this gap of unfamiliarity between them and ourselves by listening with certain questions in mind. For example: Why is this particular music being performed? Is it to please the listener, to move him with fear, or perhaps to hypnotize him? Or is it to ease the feelings of a single person, singing or playing out his joy, love or sorrow like a solitary bird?

Again, is this a medicinal chant for the cure of sickness? Is it a war dance? Is it part of an initiation or religious ceremony? Is it part of a ceremony surrounding a chief or king? Or is it, as with the "talking drums" of central Africa, a form of communication? There are certain facts, also, which if borne in mind, will make such music more understandable.

Primitive melody is often extremely simple, involving perhaps two or three different notes, and often repeats itself endlessly. The notes are determined by the natural span of the singer's voice, not by such elaborate systems as an eight-note octave, to which our own ears are trained. Solo melody, whether sung or played, is often without regular rhythm or beat, pouring out, to repeat the simile used above, like a bird's song. But the song, unlike that of a bird, is a song with words.

Primitive rhythm, on the other hand, can be extremely complex, and a real challenge to appreciate. It also involves forms of pleasure other than listening, namely the thrill which rhythmic action gives to the whole body. The performers, in other words, are often the ones enjoying the music by living it, the audience being incidental.

It is interesting to notice how tribal societies combine melody and rhythm. Group singing, for instance, is usually full of rhythm, since rhythm is needed to keep the singers together. But solo singing, when accompanied by rhythm, sometimes goes along independent of it, as if the two were unconnected, or only loosely so.

REFERENCES

Primitive Song, by C. M. Bowra (World paperback, 1962).
Our Musical Heritage, by C. Sachs (Prentice-Hall, N.Y., 1948).

RECORDINGS

Numbers indicate Folkways recordings, unless otherwise designated; italic numbers indicate stereo recordings, otherwise monaural.

Chapter 1

Australian tribal music (4439).
Music of the Kung Bushmen (4487).
Eskimo, Alaska and Hudson's Bay (4444).
Pigmies of the Ituri Forest, central Africa (4457, 4483).

Chapter 2

American Indian: Dances (6510); Flathead (4445); Great Lakes (4003); Sioux and Navajo (4401); Southwest Indians (4420, 8850); Healing Songs of the American Indians (FE4251); Hopi Katchina Songs (FE4994).
Africa: Bantu (6912, 10″); Baoule of Ivory Coast (4476); Bulu of Cameroons (4451); Cameroons (4372); Congo, west (4427); Dahomey prince's festival (Counterpoint/Esoteric 537); Equatorial Africa (4402); Topoke of Congo (4477); Watusi of Ruanda (4428); Wolo of Senegal (4462); Yoruba drums, Nigeria (4441).
Polynesia: Hawaiian chant, hula and Kiona music (8750); Maori songs, New Zealand (4433); Tahiti (Criterion 201, 1600, 1700, 1800 and 1900).
Melanesia: New Guinea (International 25013).
Mexico: Indian music (4413, 8851); Mexatec Indian Mushroom Ceremony (8975); Tarascan music (8867); Yaqui dances (6957, 10″).
Peru: Music of Peru (4415, 4456).

Chapters 3, 4, and 5

As men developed a life based on agriculture and later created far-reaching systems of government, they also invented systems for accurately measuring distance, time, weight, and value. We easily overlook the fact that they have also found how to measure sound. Each of the great agrarian cultures developed its own system of sound-measurement, grouping notes into *scales*, most commonly containing either five or seven notes. For all of these the starting point seems to have been the human voice. The voices of men, and the higher ones of women and children, are roughly what we today would call an *octave* apart. The range of ordinary conversation covers what we would call a *fourth* (three whole-steps and one half-step of our modern scale). This perhaps explains why the notes most commonly found in the scales which different cultures have developed tend to be 1) an octave apart and 2) a fourth apart. Otherwise the world's various scales tend to vary widely. The people of each culture have become used to their own, regard it as standard, and find the scales of other cultures strange or unpleasant. In our own culture we think of a scale as ascending, from low notes to high notes. But in other cultures the scale often descends, especially when the scale is for the human voice rather than for instruments.

As men's consciousness of music increased, their wonder at it seems to have mounted. This wonder was of two kinds—at the power of music over human emotions and at the physical laws which govern sound. The Egyptians, for example, seem to have discovered that two strings of equal tautness could sound an octave apart if one was half the other's length (ratio 1 to 2); that they would sound a fourth apart if the length ratio was 3 to 4; and a *fifth*, or four-and-a-half whole notes, apart if the length ratio was 2 to 3. The Chinese made similar discoveries with whistles made from bamboo pipes whose relative lengths, like the Egyptians' strings, were carefully measured. Music, thus governed by law, and in turn governing human feelings, was regarded with profound religious respect as one of the great forces of the universe. In different cultures this respect took different forms, often showing a strong trace of magic. Chants, when sung to the correct *melody* and at the correct pitch, were believed to have power over sickness, the forces of nature, and the gods themselves. The Egyptians seem to have believed that music could strengthen *Maat*, or harmony between gods and men, in the human heart. The men of Mesopotamia, with their materialistic outlook, were perhaps more concerned with changing the will of the gods than their own natures. The words of their sacred chants, to be sung by choirs of priests in temples, still survive on clay tablets. Remains of Mesopotamian musical instruments have been discovered.

How the music of Egypt and Mesopotamia sounded we can only guess. But in India the hymns of the Rig-Veda (see p. 191) are probably still being sung to the ancient three-note melodies which have been as sacred as the hymns themselves for the past 3,000 years. But this is only one small facet of Indian music. By the second century A.D. a seven-note scale had been developed, and by the ninth century Indian music had taken the general shape which still identifies it to this day. It is of a profoundly meditative character, intended for a solo performer whose role is to improvise with voice or instrument on one or another of India's age-old collection of *ragas* or short melodies accompanied by a *tala* or complex-rhythmed drumbeat. Indian music is never frozen into a musical score, as ours is, simply because no two performances are expected to be the same. Because of its intimate nature and its emphasis on the solo performer, Indian music has no concern for large orchestras.

RECORDINGS

Music of India, Morning and Evening Ragas; Angel.
Kalpana Variations: Instrumental and Dance Music of India; Nonesuch H72022.
Folk Music of India (Folkways FE4409).
Music of Indonesia (Folkways FE4406), FE4537.

In ancient China the emperor performed yearly ceremonies and sacrifices on which the survival of the state and the success of the farming season were believed to depend (see p. 254). These ceremonies, which included singing and instrumental music, were aimed at bringing harmony between heaven and earth. It was believed that this harmony could be achieved only when music was sung and played in the correct pitch. The pitch was believed to be different for each month of the year, and each pitch was the starting-point for a five-note scale judged suitable for the ceremonies of that month. The complete range of these pitches and their scales formed a series of 24 notes, which the Chinese made permanent on a set of 24 chimes, each chime a slender slab of jade. Early in its history China had developed over 200 different musical instruments—wind, string, and percussion. Orchestras and choirs at the court of the emperor required performers in hundreds. The great Chinese sage Confucius (pp. 257–59) was a lifelong music lover who established music as a respected part of Chinese life. In one of his maxims he states: "The noble-minded man's music is mild and delicate, keeps a uniform mood, enlivens and moves. Such a man does not harbor pain or mourn in his heart. Violent and foolhardy movements are foreign to him."

RECORDINGS

Music of China:
Classic Chinese (FW6812, 10″).
Traditional Chinese Opera.
The Ruse of the Empty City; FW8882.
Beating the Emperor's Robe; FW8883.
Poems of T'ang and Sung Dynasties (Peking Dialect); FLW9921.
Music of Japan
Japanese Buddhist Ritual; FE4449.
Gagaku, Imperial Court Music; Lyrichord *LLST7126*.
Japanese Koto Music with Shamisen and Shakuhashi; Lyrichord *LLST7131*.

To return to the west, Greek music had its origins in both Egypt and Mesopotamia. Greek musical instruments had names which were Mesopotamian in origin. The basic instruments were the pipe or *aulos* and the stringed instrument or *kythara*, from whose name the word guitar is a descendant. These remained in use for centuries, although, as musical composition became more complex, the aulos was given more finger holes and the kythara more strings. See the illustration on p. 221.

Greek musical theory, by contrast, was developed by Pythagoras (p. 181), who is believed to have spent years of study in Egypt. He started with what were probably Egyptian discoveries that strings under equal tension but with differing ratios of length produce notes with predictable distances apart (ratio 1 to 2, an octave apart; ratio 3 to 4, a fourth apart, such as C and F; ratio 2 to 3, a fifth apart, such as C and G). From this beginning he went on to develop precise definitions for the other notes in the *modes*, or different sequences of notes covering an octave, on which the Greeks had been basing their music. Of these the one which was to remain basic throughout the history of Greek music was called the Dorian mode. In present day notation it would look like this:

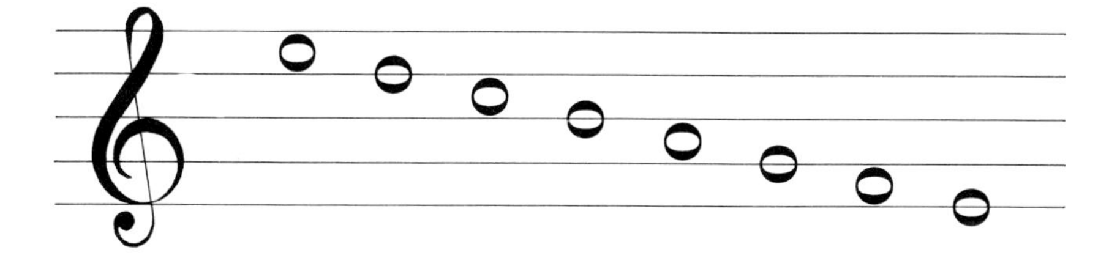

After Pythagoras other great Greek musical theorists, notably Aristoxenos in the fourth century B.C. and Ptolemy of Alexandria in the second, brought that theory to comprehensive perfection. It was a perfection suited to the Greek use of music rather than to ours. For to the Greeks music was a supporter of singing and dancing and was therefore shaped by and held down to the requirements of human speech and bodily action. The Greeks seem to have ignored purely instrumental performances as we know them.

Greek speech moved in a manner different from ours. We stress certain syllables by saying them louder, and our voices move high or low at will when pronouncing them. The Greeks, instead, did not stress a syllable by making it noisier; they simply lingered on its vowel longer. Furthermore, their vowels, when written, were marked to show whether the speaker's voice should go up (/), go down (\), or go up-and-down (⌒) on the marked syllable (the markings were of course determined by customs going back to times before writing had been invented). In other words, Greek speech was already musical. Greek poetry arranged the long and short syllables in patterns. Greek song-music merely brought out more dramatically the up-and-down voice pattern and the long-or-short syllable pattern that were already there.

The Romans accepted Greek musical theory and practice, finding this easy because of the basic likenesses between the Latin and Greek languages. The Romans' one contribution, if such it can be called, seems to have been the conversion of music on certain occasions into a "spectator sport," depending entirely on sounds created by instruments. Thus for the first time instruments which could create sounds louder and more space-filling than the human voice (the hydraulic pipe-organ, bronze trumpets, and stringed instruments "as big as chariots") were brought into combined action at Roman circuses as part of the entertainment provided for a passive thrill-loving audience described on p. 233.

To the Romans, as to the Greeks, music was first of all melody. The only attention to what we would call harmony was the sounding together of notes an octave apart (as when men and boys sang together), or a fourth or a fifth apart. Hydraulic organs were built with banks of pipes automatically playing these combinations together. A pair of notes a third apart, such as

C and E, though popular today, was in classical times thought to produce a discord, at least by musical theorists.

RECORDINGS

Greek Music:
History of Music in Sound, vol. 1.
2000 Years of Music, 1.
Modern Greek Heroic Oral Poetry; Folkways FE4468.

Chapter 6

The great upheavals in the Mediterranean world during the fourth and fifth centuries A.D., that is to say, the barbarian invasions of the Western Roman Empire, the influence of the Near East on the Byzantine Empire, and the replacement of pagan religions by Christianity, are all reflected in the music that emerged during and after these upheavals. The most fundamental changes affecting music were in speech, as people of foreign background brought their own modes of speaking into the two Empires, diluting and transforming those of Greeks and Romans. The inflection of speech in predictable up-and-down patterns faded out, as did the long and short sounding of vowels. Stressing by loudness and softness of voice came in instead. And such, fundamentally, the speech of Europeans has remained ever since.

These characteristics of speech were strong among the people of Syria, who we have seen (p. 275) influenced the style of Christian art in the Byzantine Empire. They seem to have played a similar role in the development of Christian music. It is perhaps to them that we owe the *hymn*, a devotional poem with a strong rhythm, divided into short stanzas, each to be sung to the same tune. To a Greek of the Hellenic or Hellenistic worlds such an arrangement would have been impossible; the words in each stanza would have set their own melody. The basic musical change might be described as this, that melody was freed from the arbitrary ups and downs of speech. Speech now followed wherever melody determined it should go, rather than the other way round. Rhythm at the same time became a matter of loud-soft sound rather than long-short. But at the same time the basic theories developed by the Greeks were respected, and whether or not they were rightly understood they were the ideal by which musical theory of the ensuing centuries was guided. The various *modes* or chains of successive notes adopted by the Roman Church for use in worship were to bear Greek names.

Just as the fathers of the Church, both east and west, accepted only one interpretation of Christian teaching, calling all others heresy (p. 269), so they also established a limited group of sacred melodies and modes for singing church music. The churches of the Byzantine Empire had such a group, most of which has been lost. The churches governed from Rome also had theirs, established in the fifth and sixth centuries, which we know today as Ambrosian and Gregorian Chant. Thus while music was beginning to escape being bound to speech patterns, in another way it was being bound by the dictates of religion.

RECORDINGS

Jewish Music: History of Music in Sound, vol. 1, 2000 Years of Music.
Byzantine Music: History of Music in Sound, vol. 2, Philips World Series 1302; Music Guild M44.
Ambrosian Chant: History of Music in Sound, vol. 2, Vox DL343.
Gregorian Chant: History of Music in Sound, vol. 2, Christmas Mass, London 5217. Easter Mass, London 5222, and ARC3001.
Non-religious music: History of Music in Sound, vol. 2, 2000 Years of music.

Arabian music originated in the southern tip of the Arabian peninsula, known as Arabia Felix, which was the fountainhead of other aspects of Arabian culture, including Arabic writing (p. 288). Like the music of the Greeks, it was a support for sung poetry and dance (but of a character culturally independent of Greek influence). When the teachings of Mohammed united the Arab world in the militant religion of Islam, and the words of the Koran became the authority governing all forms of conduct, there was at first extensive debate on the propriety of music. Objections were eventually overcome, and as the Arabians spread their conquests and grew in power, their centers of government at Damascus and then Baghdad became also centers of wealth supporting, poets and musicians. The glory of their combined creation and performance are now known only indirectly through the written descriptions of listeners. This musical period reached its climax at the same time as did the Muslim Empire in the East, in the mid-ninth century.

The great Muslim cities were also centers of scholarly research. The same men who were translating Euclid's geometry (p. 294) were translating works on Greek musical theory. Inspired by these, Muslim philosopher-musicians began to compose their own theoretical works. During the ninth to thirteenth centuries the city of Cordova in Moorish Spain became an outstanidng center of theoretical musical study. It was from there that knowledge of Greek theory spread into medieval Europe through translations from the Arabic. From Moorish Spain also came Medieval Europe's favorite stringed instrument for accompanying the solo voice, the *lute*. Its origin was a Moorish instrument shaped like a mandolin called *al oudh* (literally, the wood), which originated in Persia.

RECORDINGS

Arabic and Druse Music, including accompaniment on the oudh; FE4480.
Music of Saudi Arabia; FE4421.
Algerian Berber Music; FE4341.
Music of Morocco; FE4339.
Folk and Traditional Music of Turkey; FE4404.

Chapter 7

The next centuries reveal the slow faltering process by which generations of composers gradually broke music ever freer from bondage, first to human speech and later to the rigid rules of the Church. Beginning in the sixth century the Benedictine monasteries of France were havens within which monks with a bent for composing began, in the ninth century, to experiment and gradually develop new musical ideas, always, of course, for purposes of worship. Their first efforts were crude. They tried to combine sacred melodies by singing two at once. The fact that the two melodies sometimes had different words indicated that the composers' attention dared to be less on word meaning than on the sounds created. From such simple beginnings, generation after generation of churchmen gradually achieved the next great leap forward in musical composition, the skillful weaving together of several melodies both traditional and new, in one beautiful prolonged texture, known as *polyphony*.

Beginning in the tenth and eleventh centuries the Benedictine monasteries made another cultural contribution to the age. They conducted schools to which great feudal lords, often illiterate themselves, sent their sons. At some of these schools, especially at the Monastery of St. Martial at Limoges in central France, the monks gave the young noblemen a thorough education in music. When the youths returned to their castles they put this education to their own uses. Vying to excel each other in ingenious, sophisticated originality, they composed complexly rhymed songs, chiefly to their lady loves. They called themselves *finders* (of new poems and melodies), that is, (in Southern French) *troubadours* and (in Northern French) *trouvères*. Since they were literate, they put their songs, both words and music, into writing, so that hundreds still exist today.

These two developments in French music, the experiment with polyphony within the stern requirements of the Church, and the free invention of melodies and verse forms by young aristocrats, came together in the twelfth and thirteenth centuries at Paris, the intellectual center of France and medieval Europe. There a succession of great composers, Leoninus, Perotinus, Pierre de la Croix, all men of the Church, brought medieval polyphony to a glorious flowering. At the same time gothic church architecture, the University of Paris, and the political union of large parts of France under Phillip Augustus were taking form. It was a great age (see pp. 325–38).

A favorite musical composition of this period was the *motet*. It consisted of three or more voices each singing a different melody, often with different words, but so combined as to form a united flowing stream of musical sound. Of these melodies the most important one was often a traditional Gregorian chant, with words from the scriptures in Latin. The other melodies supported this one, and were sometimes invented by the composer, sometimes even borrowed from troubadour music. When all were woven together they sometimes created discords. The composers of the period gradually built up a system of rules determining among other things where and when such discords could be permitted. The composers also found that in order to keep the different voices sounding together a strict pattern of rhythm was needed. Here religious symbolism played a part in patterning music just as it did in determining the proportions of architecture. For the rhythm, made of three beats regularly repeated, was called "perfect" not because it was especially pleasing to men's ears but because the number three symbolized the Holy Trinity—Father, Son, and Holy Spirit.

Throughout the fourteenth century the school of Parisian music was recognized to be the greatest in Europe. The Pope himself turned to Paris for directors of music at St. Peter's. Perhaps the greatest in the succession of brilliant Parisian composers of this period was Guillaume de Machault (about 1300–1377), a priest and man of affairs respected in the fields of both music and diplomacy by the most powerful rulers of France. He is credited with having composed the first setting for the Mass by a single composer which aimed at musical consistency throughout.

RECORDINGS

Chant, ninth to thirteenth century: Music from the Monastery of St. Gall (Anthology of Swiss Music on Records, vol. 1); CT64-1.
Troubadour and trouvére music: Music of the Middle Ages, vol. 1.
Twelfth century, *The Play of Daniel:* Decca DL9402.
Leonin and Perotin: Music of the Middle Ages, vols. 2, 7; Music at Notre Dame, 1200–1375; Bach Guild 622.
Pierre de la Croix: no listed recordings.
Thirteenth century motet: French Music of the Gothic Era; Bach Guild 656.
Fourteenth century: Guillaume de Machaut, mass and non-religious compositions; ARC3032.

Chapter 8

The glory of France as the cultural center of western Europe was tragically eclipsed by the invasions of English kings who believed large parts of France to be theirs by feudal right. These invasions came to a climax in the battle of Agincourt (1415) which shattered for a time the fighting power of French chivalry. A regent of the king of England established his court at Paris, and this had one musical advantage. The leading musician among the courtiers, John Dunstable (about 1370–1453), exerted a valuable influence on European music which might have been impossible if he had remained in England. But for the next forty years French energy was expended on the heavy task of slowly winning back the land from foreigners.

During this period centers of musical supremacy rose elsewhere. In the fourteenth and fifteenth centuries the Italian city states were involved in the great intellectual, scholarly and artistic revolution known as the Renaissance. The ears of Italians seem to have been chiefly fascinated by the sound of words; they were the first men of modern Europe to arrive at a sophisticated standard of language (in their case Tuscan). Rather it was in northern Europe, on the domain of the powerful dukes of Burgundy, where artists such as the brothers van Eyck were appreciated, that great musicians also were appreciated and encouraged. Flemish music, as developed by composers such as Guillaume Dufay (about 1400–1474) and Jean de Ockeghem (about

The Soldier, *by the Spanish painter Rafael Canogar, 1966. Oil on canvas, 80×67 in.*

Courtesy the artist.

Frightened Boy with Dog, *woodcut by the print maker and sculptor Leonard Baskin.*

Museum of Fine Arts, Boston. Gift of Peter Wick

1430–1495), became the inspiration of the rest of Europe. All across western Europe noblemen were beginning the practice of hiring choirs for their private chapels and for entertainment, each chapel under the direction of an able, often distinguished, composer. In search for the best they could find, the nobility usually turned to the domain of Burgundy, so that musicians from there, chiefly Flemish and Dutch, were in great demand. At Florence, Lorenzo de Medici, the Magnificent, employed a Flemish composer, Heinrich Isaak, to oversee the music of his princely household. As might be expected in an age of humanism, during a Renaissance both southern and northern, music in the fifteenth century was becoming more human, more concerned with giving delight to the human ear than in adhering to religious symbolism, churchly tradition, and arbitrary rules. It was in the Renaissance period that the custom of four-part singing (soprano, alto, tenor, bass) became established. Motets were freed from their rigid medieval tempos to become more free flowing. A delightful form of song, the *madrigal*, came into existence, and the favorite instrument for accompanying singers was the lute. Harmony, or the enriching of melody by a succession of beautiful chords instead of by entwining one melody with others, began to absorb the attention of composers.

The greatest composer of the period lived at its climax. Josquin Després (about 1450–1521), another Flemish composer, was summoned to Rome by Pope Sixtus IV to direct the new choir he had founded, called to this day the Sistine Choir. Josquin was therefore composing music for the Vatican while Rafael was creating the *School of Athens* and the *Disputa*, and while Michelangelo was at work on the Sistine Chapel ceiling. Because of his magnificent mastery of all the important musical techniques then known, and his power to convert them into sublime music, Josquin Després is sometimes called the Michelangelo of music. From one end of Europe to the other men sang and performed his works. Martin Luther said of him, "Other masters do as the notes will, but Josquin makes them do as he wills."

RECORDINGS

John Dunstable: Music of the Middle Ages, vol. 8.
Music of the Burgundian Court, 1430–1500; Bach Guild 634.
Guillaume Dufay: Mass, "*Se la face*"*;* Bach Guild 653 or *70653*. Mass, "*L'Homme Armé*"*;* Lyrichord 150 or *7150*.
Jean de Ockeghem and others: ARC3052.
Music of the Court of Lorenzo the Magnificent; Decca 9403 or *79413*.
Josquin Després: Mass, "Pange Lingua"; Decca 9410 and ARC*73159*. Mass, "Hercules Dux Ferrariae" and motets; Music Guild 134 or *S134*.
Lute Music from the Royal Courts of Europe; Victor *LSC2924*.

Chapter 9

In the late sixteenth century there began a mighty wave of innovation and experiment which revolutionized European music for the next 300 years.

The center of this revolution was Italy, and its first inklings were to be observed in the city of Florence. There a group of aristocrats, poets and scholars became absorbed in the problem of creating drama with a musical setting in a style inspired by Greek tragedy. Basing their views on passages from Plato, they determined to put music back into the role of supporting and clarifying a singer's words rather than concealing it with complex polyphony. Active in this group of learned gentlemen was Vincenzo Galilei, father of Galileo the physicist. Their first attempts at combining dramatic poetry with music were performed before limited audiences and led later to the public performance of the first Italian opera, *Euridice*, in 1600. The occasion was a royal one, the wedding of Henry IV of France to the daughter of the Duke of Tuscany, Maria de Medici.

The new dramatic use of music proved to be the delight of Italian aristocrats. Presently noble families, even the Pope himself, were not only supporting the composers of opera but building opera houses for the pleasure of themselves and their chosen guests. In 1637, at Venice, was opened the first opera house charging admission. Opera thus became available to a different level of society and at the same time became dependent on popular taste. It was not long before opera, which was at first devoted to lofty tragedy, had developed also another kind, broad and witty comedy (*opera buffa*). By 1700 Venice alone had 16 opera houses.

The growth of opera was only one side of Italy's amazing musical innovation. While music was in one way being made once more the servant of the human voice, in another it was being freed from voice limitations more than ever. The seventeenth century marks the development of musical instruments which can be thought of as replacing the human voice, giving performers a greater freedom of range. At Cremona the instrument makers Amati, Stradivari and Guarneri gave the violin, viola and violoncello the form they have kept ever since. The harpsichord with its range of four octaves and tonal enrichment of two keyboards freed a single performer to play complex chords at will. And that queen of instruments, the organ, acquired greater richness and variety than ever before, thanks to the patient ingenuity of organ builders.

Newly opened possibilities such as these stimulated great advances in harmony and a constant experiment with new forms of musical composition, from which sonatas, trios, quartets, concertos and symphonies were to be developed in the next century. The first giant of the new musical age was Claudio Monteverdi (1567–1643), who combined in his greatest works three new concepts: the importance of the singing voice, experiments with harmony, and the dramatic use of instruments. He spent the latter part of his life in Venice, and made that city a center of operatic music just as Tintoretto and others (p. 456) had already made it a center for painting. Shortly before Monteverdi's arrival Giovanni Gabrieli (1558–1613) was directing music at St. Mark's cathedral, composing music for choirs of trumpets whose harmonious blasts rang out over the city from the bell tower. At Rome Girolamo Frescobaldi (1583–1644), the greatest organist of his day, was performing to audiences of thousands at St. Peter's, filling the immense spaces of the newly completed cathedral with waves of sound.

RECORDINGS

Monteverdi: opera, L'Incoronazione di Poppea; 4 records, Cambridge 901 and *7901*.
Gabrieli: Canzoni for Brass choirs; 3 records, Westminster 1008 and *S1008*.
Frescobaldi: organ music; Vox PL 8780 (1954). With others, Cambridge *2513*.
Monteverdi and Orlando di Lasso (1532–1594): madrigals; Crossroads 22160023 and *22160024*.
Giovanni da Palestrina (1525–1594): Mass of Pope Marcellus and motets; Arc *73182*.
Historic organs of Europe, played by E. Power Biggs:
Spain; Columbia *MS7109*.
Switzerland (includes Europe's oldest surviving organ, built 1390); *MS6855*.
14 Different European Organs, qualities compared through a single piece of music (Bach's toccata in D minor); ML 5032.
Arcangelo Corelli (1653–1713), perfecter of style for the solo violin: 12 Sonatas for Violin and Continuo; 3 records, Everest 6163 and *3163*.
Composers for Harpsichord:
Francois Couperin (1668–1733): Bach Guild 619.
Domenico Scarlatti (1685–1757): any of 13 Westminster records (Valenti performing).

In France music was taking a different direction, thanks to the taste of royalty and aristocrats. A traditional custom of the king of France and the members of his court, of performing formal dances before the public on certain occasions, as climax to a ceremonial display involving other dances and choral singing, inspired the composing of royal dance music, music for voices, choreography, and the design of elaborate costumes. From these magnificent performances, staged at the court of Louis XIV, two art forms developed—*ballet* and a French version of opera. But it was a young Italian, Jean Baptiste de Lully (1632–1687) (brought to France at fourteen and remaining there the rest of his life), who took these musical materials and gave them mature operatic form.

RECORDINGS

Jean Baptiste de Lully: Operatic Arias; Lyrichord 16; Ballet, *Les Amants Magnifiques; Triomphe de l'Amour;* Baroque 1839 or *2839*.
Jean Phillipe Rameau (1683–1764): Ballet, *Les Indes Galantes;* Vox 1070 or *501070* (on reverse is Lully's ballet suite for Molière's *Bourgeois Gentilhomme*).
Francois Couperin (1668–1733): *L'Apotheose de Lully;* Baroque 1814 or *2814*.

The great achievements and innovations of the Italians stirred a wave of musical creation and performance which swept Europe. North Europeans who participated in this creation usually did so after spending a formative period in Italy. Georg Friedrich Handel (1685–1759) and Christoph Willibald Gluck (1714–1787) both began their musical careers in this way. Handel spent his most fruitful later years in England creating magnificent oratorios, each with an original form of its own. Gluck composed in Vienna and Paris, where he slowly achieved a new concept of opera in which singing, instrumental music, and action were more organically united than ever before.

RECORDINGS

Handel: opera, *Semele;* 3 records, Oiseau Lyre 5098–5100; oratio, *Hercules;* 3 records, Victor *LSC6181.*
Gluck: opera, *Orfeo ed Eurydice;* 3 records, Victor *LSC6169;* opera overture, *Iphigénie in Aulide;* Angel 36175 or *S36175.*

By contrast the greatest musical genius of the age, Johann Sebastian Bach (1685–1750), knew Italian music only indirectly through musical scores. Instead he drew his greatest inspiration from the traditional polyphonic music of northern Europe. He breathed a new life into a musical form which had been thought to be outmoded and dying. But Bach could use the resources of Italian music when he chose. He heightened the dramatic intensity of sacred music by composing it in an operatic style, even though this at first shocked conservative members of German Lutheran congregations.

In the course of this musical revolution the age-old preference for combinations of notes in fifths and fourths disappeared. Human tastes in sound changed, and what in one age seemed pleasing became in another irritating and jarring. Instead, combinations of notes in thirds (for instance C to E) became the popular basis for building chords. The basic sounds from which music was constructed also became stabilized in the form of two kinds of scale, *major* and *minor*, each made of seven notes before reaching a repetition (that is, reaching a note with half the vibration rate of the starting note). From a third scale, the *chromatic*, made of twelve notes, each a half step apart, a composer could make either a major or a minor scale starting from any note he chose, that is, starting from any *key* on a harpsichord or organ. Thus we find Bach, who was active in establishing these standards, publishing collections of his own keyboard music composed from major and minor scales respectively, starting each in turn on a different key of the instrument. And his great Chromatic Fantasia and Fugue displays the rich possibilities of the keyboard without such limitations.

RECORDINGS

Johann Sebastian Bach: Organ Favorites (Biggs); Columbia *MS6261.* St Matthew Passion (Klemperer); 5 records, Angel 3599 or *S3599.* St Matthew Passion (Woelde); 4 records, Everyman *SRV269–272.* Well Tempered Keyboard (Landowska); any of 6 records, Victor LM6801. Chromatic Fantasia and Fugue (Landowska); Angel COLH-71. Chromatic Fantasia and Fugue (Valenti); Lyrichord 47 or Columbia *MS6516.*

Chapter 10

In the closing half of the eighteenth century there emerged a new development in musical taste parallel to the austere classical revival launched by Winckelmann (p. 489). The new spirit demanded music logically clear in form, readily followed by the listener, and contrived with elegance and wit. Complex polyphonic music, after its revival by Johann Sebastian Bach, again sank into disfavor, and simple melodies enriched by *homophony* or a succession of chords, became the music of the day. Four different sons of Bach, each an outstanding composer in his own right, had a share in shaping the musical forms which the new music was to take. Of these forms the basic one was the *sonata*, and its important derivatives are the symphony of four movements, the concerto of three movements, and the string quartet. Two towering musical geniuses, Franz Joseph Haydn (1732–1809) and Wolfgang Amadeus Mozart (1756–1791), later brought these forms to perfection for different groupings of instruments. Haydn, who spent much of his long life as court musician to a Hungarian prince, was free to develop his musical ideas in security. Mozart spent the opposite kind of a life, never sure where his money was coming from next and dying at age 35. Besides composing some of the world's most exquisite instrumental music, his achievement in opera has been likened to that of Shakespeare in spoken drama. The center of this musical development was northern Europe, with Vienna the focal point.

RECORDINGS

The Sons of Bach: Folkways 3341.
Haydn (suggestions for sampling): Symphonies 88 and 92; Westminster 14616. Quartets, Opus 20 No. 4, and Opus 76 No. 2; Concert Disc 1228 or *228*.
Mozart: Piano Concertos No. 24 in C minor, and No. 27 in Bb; Westminster 18267. Quintet in G minor; Westminster 9036 and Deutsche Gramaphone *138057*. Symphonies 25 and 41; Vox 11820. Opera, *Don Giovanni;* 4 records, Deutsche Gramaphone 139260–63.

Through all the revolutions and fluctuations in musical taste, men continued to fit music ever more closely to the needs of human expression. The next two steps in this progress were made, first by a series of instrument builders who created the piano, and second by the life work of one composer, Beethoven. The keyboard instrument of the Baroque period, the noble harpsichord, had two serious limitations: it was unresponsive to the subtleties of human touch, and it lacked carrying power. When contrasted with the wonderful loud-soft range of the violin, its own loud-soft range was revealed to be mechanical. And when it was moved out of aristocratic drawing rooms into large concert halls (supported by ticket sales), its voice sounded thin. The piano remedied both these deficiencies. Its technical perfection required a century. Haydn and Mozart knew the piano in its early form. Mozart composed for it extensively.

Ludwig van Beethoven (1770–1826) made the sonata and its derivatives such powerful vehicles of human expression that he nearly exhausted their possibilities. With the exception of the work of Johannes Brahms (1833 to 1897), the musical literature of the nineteenth century is crowded with lesser (even if lengthier) attempts. Beethoven brought one period to a close and heralded the next. In spirit a revolutionary, he believed in every man's right to personal freedom. The spectacle of Napoleon leading the French Revolution in the cause of liberty inspired him to compose his great third symphony, the Eroica. But when Napoleon assumed the role of dictator, Beethoven tore up the dedication page bearing his name.

RECORDINGS

Beethoven: Symphony No. 3, Opus 55, in Eb (Walter); Columbia MS*6036* (von Matacic); Parliament 129 or *S129*. Piano Sonatas Opus 109 in E and Opus 111 in C; London 9315 or *6276*.

Brahms: Piano Music; Angel 35027–8. Symphony No. 4 in E; Victor *LSC2297*.

Great musical achievement had to lie next in new directions. Hector Berlioz (1803–1869) never learned to perform well on any instrument. Yet he is acclaimed as the father of modern orchestration. He was as well a brilliant writer who composed the librettos of his own operas. A sort of musical Napoleon, he possessed an imagination of gigantic scope lit by fires of volcanic passion. Yet his logical organizing judgment was always in command. He grouped orchestras, bands, and choirs for the performance at Paris of his great *Mass for the Dead* as other composers might have grouped individual players. His whole interest was in *programme music*, whose aim is to tell a dramatic story rather than to develop abstract musical ideas.

Richard Wagner (1813–1883) possessed a similar largeness of vision. His goal in life was to combine music, poetic drama, and the visual art of stagecraft in a great artistic super-synthesis. To achieve this goal he abandoned the conventional pattern of opera and created his own, keeping the action in constant flow, uninterrupted by display pieces to show off individual performers or groups (arias, duets, and ballets). Throughout the performance he kept orchestral music also in constant flow, sensitively bringing out each step in the action and supporting each character. These and other innovations created powerful enemies everywhere. But he was also winning friends, who succeeded in raising money for a Wagner theatre at Bayreuth in Bavaria. Just as Germany was attaining political identity as a nation for the first time in history, Wagner was producing gigantic musical dramas based on the German heroic past, both pagan and Christian, vividly reminding the new nation of its heritage.

RECORDINGS

Berlioz: *Romeo and Juliet;* 2 records, *LDS6098. Symphonie Fantastique* and *Lelio; 2-CBS32B10010.*

Wagner: Opera, *Tristan and Isolde;* 5 records, Angel 3588. If you really want

to listen to Wagner, try the Ring Cycle; 19 records! Angel RING.
Giuseppe Verdi (1813–1901): Opera, *Falstaff;* 3 records, M3L-350 or *M3L-750*.

At the opposite end of the scale of musical creation, composers were writing gem-like settings for poetry, usually short poetry, the solo human voice being accompanied by the piano only. In the most sensitive of these songs (*lieder* in German) the melody changed to fit each verse. Hugo Wolf (1860–1903) wrote nearly 300 such lieder. Among these were musical settings for the sonnets of Michelangelo.

RECORDINGS

Wolf: *Goethe-Lieder;* Angel 35474.

In France the impressionist movement in painting (p. 535) found a parallel in the music of Claude Debussy (1862–1918), whose innovations in orchestral sound opened the doorway to some of the great musical changes of the twentieth century. Debussy broke completely with conventional forms of musical composition. He broke with the rules of harmony governing which chords should follow other chords. He even broke away from the concepts of major and minor, and based his music on scales originating in the Orient, in the Middle Ages, or with himself. His whole aim was to create glorious illusions or sound-experiences from a succession of chords of which his own exquisitely original taste was the sole judge. His choice of which instruments of the orchestra should produce these sounds was also completely original and daring. His subjects, rather than overpowering and heroic, were delicately elusive, as indicated by the titles he chose: *Clouds*, *The Sea*, *The Submerged Cathedral*, *Gardens in the Rain*, *Festivals*. His first great success, *The Afternoon of a Faun* (1894), was an orchestral prelude to a work by the poet Mallarmé. The climax of his achievement was his musical setting for the dream-tragedy *Pelléas and Mélisande* (words by Maurice Maeterlinck), in which Debussy achieved a closer union between music, words and action than even Wagner had managed. World War I was a terrible experience for him, and he died a few months before its close, while German long-range artillery was still bombarding Paris. His own personal victory was complete. He had freed French music from the tyranny of the German musical tradition then dominating Europe.

Toward the close of Debussy's career he was to see the rise of a young Russian composer, an experimentalist like himself but of a different temperament. Igor Stravinsky's *Rite of Spring* for orchestra was first performed at Paris in 1913, when Stravinsky was thirty one. Its intense primitive rhythms and jarring dissonances created a musical shock much like that on artists created by Picasso's *Demoiselles d'Avignon* six years earlier. Stravinsky could easily have exploited this sensation in later compositions. Instead he turned to austerely restrained forms of music, ever following his own private sense of direction which has guided him ever since.

RECORDINGS

Debussy: *La Mer, Prélude a l'Après-Midi d'un Faun, Jeux;* CBS*32110056. Pelléas et Mélisande;* 3 records, London 4379 or *1379*, Angel 3561 or *S3561*.
Stravinsky: *Sacre du Printemps* (1913); Columbia ML5719 or *MS6319*. Ballet, *Apollo* (1928); Columbia *MS6803*. Various compositions (1952 to 1967); Columbia ML6454 or *MS7054*.

Following Debussy, daring experiments with existing harmonies, scales, and musical instruments gradually became increasingly popular in Europe and eventually in the United States. But there was one man who needed no example to stimulate him to such experiments, and whose taste at the same time was excellent enough to make the results superior. He was Charles Ives (1874–1954), a New England insurance man of all things[1], who composed music as an avocation and in isolation. But as early as 1906 Ives was already musically ahead of his time. Both music and innovation came naturally to him, for his father, a bandleader in Danbury, Connecticut, had also been an inventor of band instruments. The titles Ives gave his music implied a loving involvement with local New England and its heritage. But the music itself, far from being provincial, is daring, complex, sensitive, and shot through at times with an irresistible sense of humor. His second piano Sonata has been called (by Lawrence Gilman) the greatest single piece of music so far composed by an American. Ives entitled it *Concord, Massachusetts, 1840—1860*.

Another remarkable American composer whose style originated at home was George Antheil (1901–59). He spent most of his creative life in Paris, where he convinced Igor Stravinsky (see below) that original music was being written in the United States independent of contemporary European influence. His *Airplane Sonata* (1922) was an attempt to capture music he had heard pouring from radios in an extraordinary dream. In 1923–24 he composed his *Ballet Mecanique*, in "his dissonant, ultra-modernistic, mechanistic" style. A moving picture accompaniment was made by Fernand Léger, in which a similarity between moving machinery and repeated human gestures is suggested.

RECORDINGS

Ives: Variations on *America*, for organ (1891), composed when Ives was 17; Nonesuch *71200*. Symphony, *Holidays* (1904–1913); Composers Recordings, Inc., 190 or *S190*. *The Unanswered Question* (1908) and other orchestral pieces; Vanguard *C10013*.
Antheil: *Ballet Mecanique*; revised edition of 1953; Urania Records.

A further stride in musical innovation was to free sound from the limitations of traditional instruments. A pioneer in this form of creation was Edgar Varèse (1885–1965), born in Paris, who came to this country in 1916, where he lived the rest of his life. That life was completely absorbed in trying out

[1] Another New England insurance man with a remarkable avocational gift was the poet Wallace Stevens.

every source of sound he could find or invent, including sound produced electronically, always with the aim of combining his discoveries into new music. The titles he gave his work convey their strange tonal quality: *Hyperprism*, *Ionisation*, *Density 21.5*, *Poème Electronique*, etc.

Experiments with electronic sound have since been carried forward brilliantly by Pierre Boulez (born 1925) in France, and by Karlheinz Stockhausen (born 1928) in Germany, among others.

RECORDINGS

Varèse: Works (1924–1958); Columbia ML5478 or *MS6146*.
Boulez: *Marteau Sans Maitre;* Harmonia Mundi 30682 or *530682*.
Stockhausen: *Momenta;* Nonesuch *71157*.

Another direction of musical experiment was the opposite of Debussy's practice of ignoring established rules of composition. Arnold Schoenberg (1874–1951), a Viennese, decided by about 1920 that he had exhausted the possibilities of conventional composing. He set about making a new set of rules, based on a succession of twelve notes (a *tone row*) without a conventional tone center and on chords created from combinations of fourths instead of thirds. Alban Berg (1885–1935), Schoenberg's pupil, created music much more appealing to the ear. And Anton von Webern (1883–1945), accidentally shot at the close of World War II, composed fascinatingly epigrammatic music of great brevity in this style. Beginning in 1948 the American Milton Babbitt pushed the application of Schoenberg's concepts to their logical extreme. No one yet knows whether Schoenberg's tone-row based music will some day be popularly enjoyed.

RECORDINGS

Schoenberg: Pierrot Lunaire (1912); Everest 6171 or *3171*. Variations for orchestra (1928) and other works; Columbia *M2S767*. String trio (1946) and other works; Columbia M2L294 or *M2S694*.
Berg and Webern: 5 movements for string quartet (Webern) and Lyric (Berg); Victor *LSC2531*.
Babbitt: Composition for 4 instruments (1948) and for viola and piano (1950); Composers Recordings, Inc. 138.

The fact that this may happen, and that it has already happened in the past to other composers, when music that sounded shockingly revolutionary to one generation sounded merely pleasant to the next, has raised some questions about what artistic taste is really made of. At one extreme is the belief that every human being contains a divine ability to recognize the beautiful and the ugly, just as his conscience is supposed to know good from evil. At the opposite extreme is the belief that we like what we get used to and dislike only the unfamiliar. Where lies the truth of the matter?

A great deal of contemporary musical composition has been based on the second of these two views. The haphazard and the accidental have been deliberately brought into ensemble performances, so that instruments would sound together in no predictable manner. Non-musical sounds have been taped and purposely mixed to create unexpected experiences for the ears, musical happenings. The fact that people have focused their attention on such experiences as *audiences* may have had at least the valuable effect of bringing them to listen to and perhaps for the first time appreciate the tumultuous sounds of the ordinary world with which they are surrounded. This is a point made by John Cage (born 1912), the outstanding deviser of this kind of experience.

RECORDING

Cage: *Aria with Fontana Mix* (Berio's *Circles* on reverse); Time *8003.*

But people certainly know what they like, sometimes even when they hear it for the first time. Jazz, starting in the miserable honkytonks of New Orleans, kept spreading, first to Chicago, then across the nation, then abroad, as irresistible dance music. At the same time it developed and evolved, attracting motionless audiences fascinated by a combination of players who gave each other opportunities to improvise without destroying continuity. Blues, which seemed to be a permanent side of jazz, now begins to vanish like a cloud as black Americans recognize in it the expression of a hopeless and defeated past generation. Suddenly, a decade ago, from an unexpected corner of the planet (provincial England), four young men appeared with a new, freshly satirical song to sing to a new beat. Instantly the younger generation loved them, everywhere. From the seed they planted sprang up the New Sound, created by a host of groups with wonderful insane names, its rich, deafening dissonances and its rhythms, driving more relentlessy than Beethoven's Destiny, often drowning the magic words of the vocalist. Where does such great enthusiasm come from? Surely from something deeper than rat-in-maze conditioning. The tree from the seed the Beatles planted still grows, and who knows what flowers and fruit it will produce next, or where?

Meanwhile the endless experiment with sound, its sources, combinations, and organization, goes forward. From the ever growing multitude of results here are a few scattered examples:

Elliott Carter (born 1908): Quartet No. 1; Columbia ML5104.
Witold Lutoslawsky (born 1913): *Trois Poèmes;* MUZA XL0237.
György Ligeti (born 1923): *Atmosphères;* Columbia *MS6733.*
Salvatore Martirano (born 1927): *Underworld;* Heliodor 25047 or *S25047.*
Toru Takemitsu (born 1930): *November Steps* (1967); Victor LM7051 or *LSC7051.*
Krzysztof Penderecki (born 1933): *Threnody;* Victor 1239 or *S1239.*
Mario Davidovsky (born 1934): *3 Synchromisms;* Composers Recordings, Inc. 204 or *S204.*
Jean-Claude Eloy (born 1938): Equivalences; Everest SDBR6170 or *3170.*

APPENDIX B: VITRUVIUS' STATEMENT CONCERNING HUMAN PROPORTION AND ITS INTERPRETATION BY LEONARDO

Vitruvius' Statement, from The Ten Books of Architecture, beginning of Chapter I, Book III

"Without symmetry and proportion there can be no principles in the design of any temple; that is, if there is no precise relation between its members, as in the case of a well shaped man."

"For the human body is so designed by nature that the face, from the chin to the top of the forehead and the lowest roots of the hair, is a tenth part of the whole height; the open hand from the wrist to the tip of the middle finger is just the same; the head from the chin to the crown is an eighth, and with the neck and shoulder from the top of the breast to the lowest roots of the hair is a sixth; from the middle of the breast to the summit of the crown is a fourth. If we take the height of the face itself, the distance from the bottom of the chin to the under side of the nostrils is one third of it; the nose from the under side of the nostrils to a line between the eyebrows is the same; from there to the lowest roots of the hair is also a third, comprising the forehead. The length of the foot is one sixth of the height of the body; of the forearm, one fourth; and the breadth of the breast is also one fourth. The other members, too, have their own symmetrical proportions, and it was by employing them that the famous painters and sculptors of antiquity attained to great and endless renown."

Leonardo's Restatement of Vitruvius, With the Illustration Shown Here

The architect Vitruvius states in his work on architecture that the measurements of a man are arranged by Nature thus:—that is that four fingers make one palm, and four palms make one foot, six palms make one cubit, four cubits make once a man's height, and four cubits make a pace, and twenty four palms make a man's height, and these measurements are in his buildings.

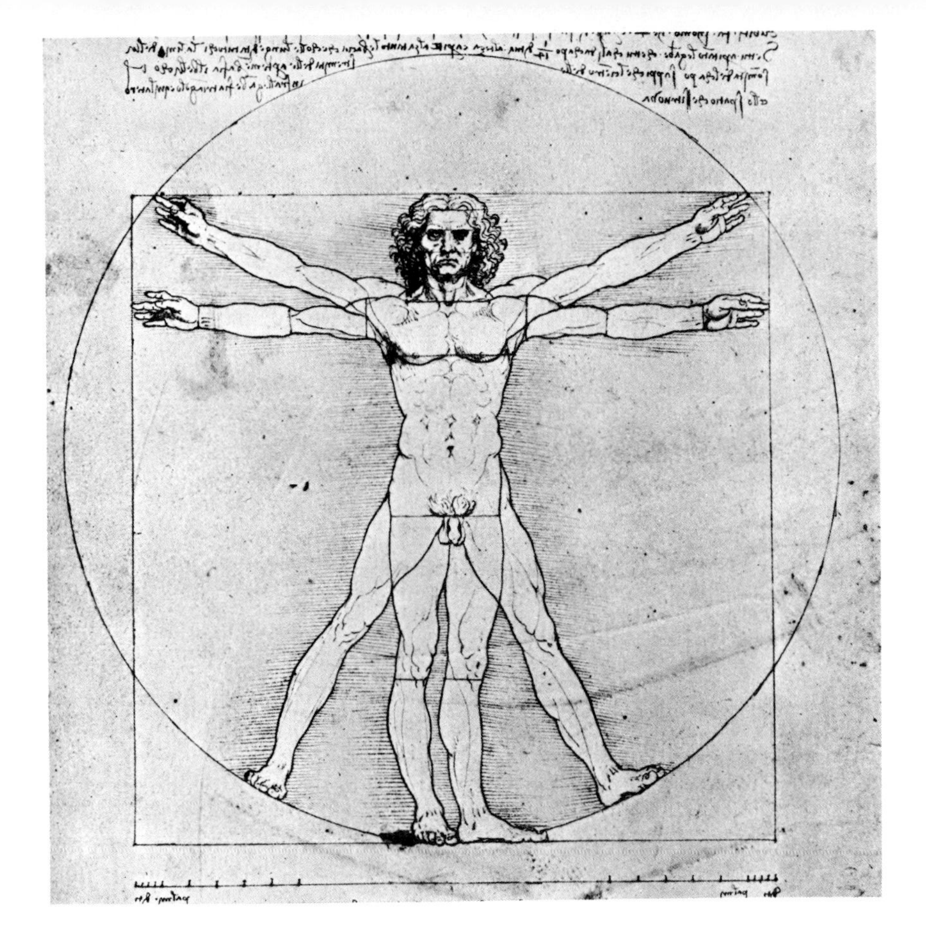

If you set your legs so far apart as to take a fourteenth part from your height, and you open and raise your arms until you touch the line of the crown of the head with your middle fingers, you must know that the centre of the circle formed by the extremities of the outstretched limbs will be the navel, and the space between the legs will form an equilateral triangle.

The span of a man's outstretched arms is equal to his height.

From the beginning of the hair to the end of the bottom of the chin is the tenth part of a man's height; from the bottom of the chin to the crown of the head is the eighth of the man's height; from the top of the breast to the crown of the head is the sixth of the man; from the top of the breast to where the hair commences is the seventh part of the whole man; from the nipples to the crown of the head is a fourth part of the man. The maximum width of the shoulders is in itself the fourth part of a man; from the elbow to the tip of the middle finger is the fifth part; from this elbow to the end of the shoulder is the eighth part. The complete hand will be the tenth part. The penis begins at the centre of the man. The foot is the seventh part of the man. From the sole of the foot to just below the knee is the fourth part of the man. From below the knee to where the penis begins is the fourth part of the man.

The parts that find themselves between the chin and the nose and between the places where the hair and the eyebrows start each of itself compares with that of the ear, and is a third of the face.

Venice Academy R 343

Untitled, *by William Martin, San Francisco, 1971. Oil on canvas, diameter 24 in. Martin is a leader in a current trend in painting aptly called metaphysical realism.*

INDEXES

Name Index

Subject Index